We greatly appreciate your assistance.

Publisher	John Wait
Editor-in-Chief	John Kane
Cisco Representative	Anthony Wolfenden
Cisco Press Program Manager	Jeff Brady
Production Manager	Patrick Kanouse
Development Editor	Andrew Cupp
Senior Project Editor	San Dee Phillips
Copy Editor	Interactive Composition Corporation
Technical Editors	Eric Osborne
	Alex Raj
	Andy Schutz
	Raymond Zhang
Editorial Assistant	Tammi Barnett
Book and Cover Designer	Louisa Adair
Composition	Interactive Composition Corporation
Indexer	JBIndexing Inc.

CISCO SYSTEMS

Corporate Headquarters
Cisco Systems, Inc.
170 West Tasman Drive
San Jose, CA 95134-1706
USA
www.cisco.com
Tel: 408 526-4000
 800 553-NETS (6387)
Fax: 408 526-4100

European Headquarters
Cisco Systems International BV
Haarlerbergpark
Haarlerbergweg 13-19
1101 CH Amsterdam
The Netherlands
www-europe.cisco.com
Tel: 31 0 20 357 1000
Fax: 31 0 20 357 1100

Americas Headquarters
Cisco Systems, Inc.
170 West Tasman Drive
San Jose, CA 95134-1706
USA
www.cisco.com
Tel: 408 526-7660
Fax: 408 527-0883

Asia Pacific Headquarters
Cisco Systems, Inc.
Capital Tower
168 Robinson Road
#22-01 to #29-01
Singapore 068912
www.cisco.com
Tel: +65 6317 7777
Fax: +65 6317 7799

Cisco Systems has more than 200 offices in the following countries and regions. Addresses, phone numbers, and fax numbers are listed on the
Cisco.com Web site at www.cisco.com/go/offices.

Argentina • Australia • Austria • Belgium • Brazil • Bulgaria • Canada • Chile • China PRC • Colombia • Costa Rica • Croatia • Czech Republic
Denmark • Dubai, UAE • Finland • France • Germany • Greece • Hong Kong SAR • Hungary • India • Indonesia • Ireland • Israel • Italy
Japan • Korea • Luxembourg • Malaysia • Mexico • The Netherlands • New Zealand • Norway • Peru • Philippines • Poland • Portugal
Puerto Rico • Romania • Russia • Saudi Arabia • Scotland • Singapore • Slovakia • Slovenia • South Africa • Spain • Sweden
Switzerland • Taiwan • Thailand • Turkey • Ukraine • United Kingdom • United States • Venezuela • Vietnam • Zimbabwe

About the Authors

Lancy Lobo, CCIE No. 4690 (Routing ans Switching, Service Provider), is a network consulting engineer in the Cisco Systems Advanced Services group, supporting the Cisco strategic service provider and enterprise customers. He has more than 10 years experience with data communication technologies and protocols. He has supported the Cisco strategic service provider customers to design and implement large-scale routed networks. He holds a bachelor's degree in electronics and telecommunication engineering from Bombay University and a dual MBA degree in project management and information technology from Jones International University, Denver. He plans to earn his Ph.D. in business organization and management at Capella University.

Umesh Lakshman is a technical project systems engineer with the Service Provider Field Labs at Cisco. He supports Cisco sales teams by demonstrating and testing advanced technologies such as MPLS to SP customers in a presale environment. Umesh has condusted several trainings for customers on MPLS, MPLS VPNs, and QoS implementations in MPLS networks. Umesh has a bachelor's degree in electrical and electronics engineering from Madras University and a master's degree in electrical and computer engineering from Wichita State University in Kansas.

About the Technical Reviewers

Andy Schutz, CCIE No. 11554, has been with Cisco for more than four years acting as a technical marketing engineer (TME) in a number of different groups. Andy was one of the original TMEs on the Cisco 10000 ESR platform after beginning as a TME for the Cisco IP DSLAMs. Andy has also served as the lead TME for broadband aggregation and related technologies for Cisco. Andy obtained his CCIE in the service provider track with a DSL focus shortly after coming to Cisco. Prior to Cisco, Andy worked at a CLEC providing DSL service and at Sprint. Andy enjoys spending time with his family and looks forward to the day when the Green Bay Packers bring home yet another Lombardi Trophy.

Raymond Zhang is a senior network architect for INFONET responsible for global IP backbone infrastructure, routing architecture planning, and its evolutions. His current main areas of interest are large-scale backbone routing, traffic engineering, performance and traffic statistical analysis, MPLS-related technologies, multi-service QoS, IPv6, and multicast. Raymond is an active member of IETF and has contributed to several drafts in the areas of MPLS TE, inter-AS traffic engineering, and others. He has a master of engineering from the City University of New York (CUNY).

Alex Raj is a software architect at Cisco Systems, with a primary focus on MPLS technologies. During the last nine years at Cisco, and previously at Cabletron Systems, he has been involved in developing several software architectures, as well as in design and implementation in the areas of ATM, MPLS, cell-mode MPLS, and High Availability. He also worked on the MPLS deployment phases in planning for many large-scale WAN service provider networks. He has filed several patents in the area of LAN switching, MPLS, multicast, and FRR and coauthored a few IETF drafts in the area of High Availability and ATM MPLS signaling interworking.

MPLS Configuration on Cisco IOS Software

Lancy Lobo, CCIE No. 4690

Umesh Lakshman

Cisco Press

800 East 96th Street
Indianapolis, Indiana 46240 USA

MPLS Configuration on Cisco IOS Software

Lancy Lobo, CCIE No. 4690

Umesh Lakshman

Copyright © 2006 Cisco Systems, Inc.

Published by:
Cisco Press
800 East 96th Street
Indianapolis, IN 46240 USA

Printed in the United States of America 1 2 3 4 5 6 7 8 9 0

First Printing April 2010

Library of Congress Cataloging-in-Publication Number: 2004102839

ISBN: 1-58705-199-0

Trademark Acknowledgments

All terms mentioned in this book that are known to be trademarks or service marks have been appropriately capitalized. Cisco Press or Cisco Systems, Inc. cannot attest to the accuracy of this information. Use of a term in this book should not be regarded as affecting the validity of any trademark or service mark.

Warning and Disclaimer

This book is designed to provide information about configuring MPLS, MPLS VPN, MPLS traffic engineering, MPLS QoS, Layer 2 VPN, and VPLS on Cisco IOS software. Every effort has been made to make this book as complete and as accurate as possible, but no warranty or fitness is implied.

The information is provided on an "as is" basis. The authors, Cisco Press, and Cisco Systems, Inc. shall have neither liability nor responsibility to any person or entity with respect to any loss or damages arising from the information contained in this book or from the use of the discs or programs that may accompany it.

The opinions expressed in this book belong to the authors and are not necessarily those of Cisco Systems, Inc.

Corporate and Government Sales

Cisco Press offers excellent discounts on this book when ordered in quantity for bulk purchases or special sales.

For more information please contact: **U.S. Corporate and Government Sales**   1-800-382-3419
corpsales@pearsontechgroup.com

For sales outside the U.S. please contact: **International Sales**   international@pearsoned.com

Feedback Information

At Cisco Press, our goal is to create in-depth technical books of the highest quality and value. Each book is crafted with care and precision, undergoing rigorous development that involves the unique expertise of members from the professional technical community.

Readers' feedback is a natural continuation of this process. If you have any comments regarding how we could improve the quality of this book, or otherwise alter it to better suit your needs, you can contact us through e-mail at feedback@ciscopress.com. Please include the book title and ISBN in your message.

Dedications

I would like to dedicate my work in this book to my late father, Mr. D.V. Raja Lakshman. Without his blessings and guidance, I wouldn't be here today. Thanks, Dad!
—Umesh

This book is dedicated to my wife, Natasha, and my daughter, Elena, for their sacrifices, love, patience, and support, without which this book would not have been possible.

To my mother and father, Celine and Lawrence Lobo, and my brother, Loy, for all the years of love, support, and prayers.

To my in-laws, Stany and Jessie Almeida, whose support and prayers have made this undertaking possible.
—Lancy

Acknowledgments

From Umesh Lakshman:

Thanks to the Almighty God for his blessings and watching over me and helping me complete this undertaking successfully.

I would like to express my gratitude to my co-author, Mr. Lancy Lobo, for giving me the opportunity to help him in this endeavor. Thanks to the entire Cisco Press team whose guidance and diligence has enhanced this book. Thanks to Andrew Cupp for making sure the book content was delivered on time. Thanks to Raina Han for putting up with unforeseen delays during the initial writing phase and for coordinating the writing process. Special thanks to John Kane and Jim Schachterle for valuable guidance through the entire writing process.

Thanks to my manager of more than three years, Mr. Russell Tarpey, for enabling and supporting this undertaking, and for his constant encouragement.

I would like to recognize the technical reviewers, Eric Osborne, Alex Raj, Andy Schultz, and Raymond Zhang for their advice and attention to detail.

Thanks to the GSR VPLS team, namely Javed Asghar, Muhammad Waris Sagheer, and Leigh Hunt, for helping us with content and software to demonstrate VPLS on the GSR.

Thanks to John Klemm, Chad Frisby, and Yinglam Cheung from IXIA for helping us with equipment and guidance for Chapter 15. Thanks to Mike Haugh from Spirent Communications for his guidance with the Smartbits chassis and application. Thanks to Ryan Crawford from Agilent Technologies for supporting us with the N2X configuration. I would also like to thank my family in India for their support during the development of this book.

From Lancy Lobo:

I thank Lord Jesus for giving me this opportunity to write this book, for his blessings, and for being there for me always.

I would like to thank my manager, Andrew Houck, for supporting me in this book venture. I thank all the folks at Cisco Press, especially John Kane, Andrew Cupp, Raina Han, and Jim Schachterle, for their understanding and patience whenever we were late in submitting our chapters. I would like to thank all the technical reviewers for their suggestions and insights into several topics. I thank all the external vendor representatives from IXIA, Spirent, and Agilent for their support during this venture.

Finally, I would like to thank my co-author, Umesh Lakshman, for his efforts and his ability to concentrate and work on this book despite several personal crises that occurred during the writing of this book. This book wouldn't have been possible without his energy and enthusiasm.

This Book Is Safari Enabled

The Safari® Enabled icon on the cover of your favorite technology book means the book is available through Safari Bookshelf. When you buy this book, you get free access to the online edition for 45 days.

Safari Bookshelf is an electronic reference library that lets you easily search thousands of technical books, find code samples, download chapters, and access technical information whenever and wherever you need it.

To gain 45-day Safari Enabled access to this book:

- Go to http://www.ciscopress.com/safarienabled
- Enter the ISBN of this book (shown on the back cover, above the bar code)
- Log in or Sign up (site membership is required to register your book)
- Enter the coupon code DLM1-RTPL-CYLQ-3HLX-XLRQ

If you have difficulty registering on Safari Bookshelf or accessing the online edition, please e-mail customer-service@safaribooksonline.com.

Contents at a Glance

Table of Contents

Chapter 9   MPLS Traffic Engineering   375

Chapter 10   Implementing VPNs with Layer 2 Tunneling Protocol Version 3   419

Icons Used in This Book

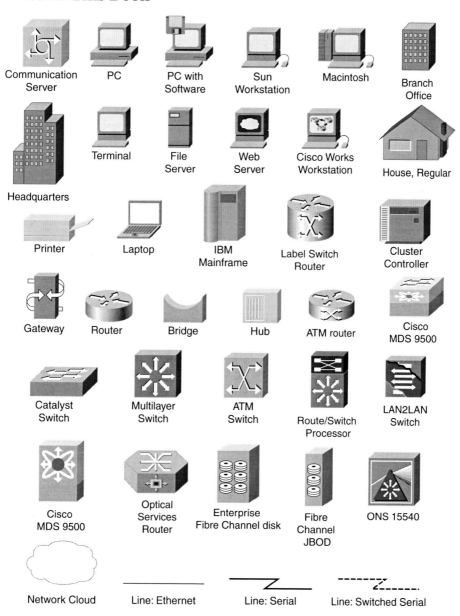

Communication Server

PC

PC with Software

Sun Workstation

Macintosh

Branch Office

Headquarters

Terminal

File Server

Web Server

Cisco Works Workstation

House, Regular

Printer

Laptop

IBM Mainframe

Label Switch Router

Cluster Controller

Gateway

Router

Bridge

Hub

ATM router

Cisco MDS 9500

Catalyst Switch

Multilayer Switch

ATM Switch

Route/Switch Processor

LAN2LAN Switch

Cisco MDS 9500

Optical Services Router

Enterprise Fibre Channel disk

Fibre Channel JBOD

ONS 15540

Network Cloud

Line: Ethernet

Line: Serial

Line: Switched Serial

Command Syntax Conventions

The conventions used to present command syntax in this book are the same conventions used in the IOS Command Reference. The Command Reference describes these conventions as follows:

- **Boldface** indicates commands and keywords that are entered literally as shown.
- *Italics* indicate arguments for which you supply actual values.
- Vertical bars (|) separate alternative, mutually exclusive elements.
- Square brackets [ ] indicate optional elements.
- Braces { } indicate a required choice.
- Braces within brackets [{ }] indicate a required choice within an optional element.

Foreword

Not too long ago, I had the opportunity to take a video crew into the streets of New York City to prepare a fun opening video segment for a meeting that I was hosting. I began to interview a number of unsuspecting New Yorkers as they walked by on a variety of topics that popped into my head. As luck would have it, MPLS was one of the topics that I focused on in my quest to get some interesting video content. The question I was asking repeatedly was, "What does MPLS stand for?" The myriad responses I got were quite diverse from "My People Love Song" from an Irish tourist to "Major Pain in My Legs" from a typical New Yorker. All in all, no one could tell me anything about MPLS. The audience met my expectations and clearly provided some comic relief on the meeting agenda.

Subsequent to filming my video montage in New York City, I have assumed responsibility for the service provider segment globally for Cisco Systems. I think if I took the same approach of taking a camera crew out to ask this audience what MPLS stands for, not only would they be able to provide me with the correct answer but also would tell me why MPLS is so important to them. If you are reading this foreword, I'm assuming that Multiprotocol Label Switching is or might be important to you, or you simply have too much time on your hands.

The importance of MPLS can be traced to the fact that the demand from consumers for new and innovative services requires today's service providers to look at more efficient ways to deliver voice, video, and data. These demands create several challenges for an industry that can no longer simply build larger or separate pipes/networks to meet their business needs. The need for a competitive advantage has required service providers to start thinking about building next-generation systems that converge networks and services, as well as applications. The convergence is being driven by the need for them to reduce cost. For many, the next level of network convergence requires the migration of legacy infrastructures and services based on Time Division Multiplexing (TDM), Frame Relay, and Asynchronous Transfer Mode (ATM) technologies onto a more flexible, efficient IP/MPLS packet infrastructure. Cisco has worked with a number of service providers globally on the convergence of these networks and the preliminary data demonstrates savings in the billions of dollars over a three to five year period. In addition to reducing their operational expenses, service providers globally are looking to grow their revenue streams by offering new and innovative services. All these new services are being offered over IP infrastructures. Today, IP/MPLS is the key driver for building next-generation networks that maximize cost and offer the foundation to build new services.

Cisco provides a comprehensive strategy for building next-generation networks with IOS MPLS. The Cisco MPLS capabilities combine the intelligence and scalability of routing with the reliability and manageability of traditional carrier networks. As a result, service providers can deliver highly scalable, differentiated, end-to-end IP and VPN services with simplified configuration, management, and provisioning. Touted as the "DNA of tomorrow's telecom" by independent telecommunications market research firm Heavy Reading, Cisco IOS offers cutting edge technology that enables service providers to deliver innovative services for new revenue growth while reducing network costs.

Case in point, Equant, a member of the France Telecom group, required a converged network platform built on a private backbone that could be easily managed, scalable, economical, and flexible to meet diverse requirements of its large global customers. The Cisco MPLS VPN solution matched Equant's vision of a multiservice, international communications platform. Equant's IP VPN service is now available in more than 140 countries worldwide, serving 1300 multinational customers with over 27,000 connections.

Cisco is committed to leadership in next-generation networking by continuing to deliver innovative MPLS features and functionality to enable its customers to build powerful intelligent networks. I highly recommend *MPLS Configuration on Cisco IOS Software* as required reading for those in search of practical guidance of the technology and nuances of configuring MPLS for next-generation networks for voice, video, data, and application service offerings across a wide variety of deployment scenarios. Regardless, I can guarantee you will be prepared for an interview in my next video.

Carlos Dominguez
SVP, Worldwide Service Provider Operations
Cisco Systems, Inc.

Introduction

MPLS technology first emerged within the networking industry for IP core networks primarily as a mechanism to provide VPN services and traffic engineering capabilities. MPLS is now being extended toward the Metro-Ethernet/optical and access-network segments to extend the benefits realized in the core and provide a true end-to-end architecture for the delivery of packet data services.

The goal of this book is to familiarize readers with MPLS technologies and their configurations. The book provides a practical hands-on approach to MPLS-related technologies.

Who Should Read This Book?

The book is intended to cover basic and advanced MPLS concepts and configuration. The book does not just emphasize MPLS but also extends to applications and deployments associated with MPLS such as MPLS traffic engineering, Layer 2 VPN, and VPLS. This book can be used by anyone who wants to understand MPLS and its operation. This book can also be used by network engineers who configure and manage an MPLS-based network as well as for those engineers preparing for the CCIE Service Provider lab exam.

Overall, the book's intent is to tremendously increase your awareness of the finer aspects associated with configuring MPLS and implementing it in various scenarios.

How This Book Is Organized

This book is meant to be read cover-to-cover for those who are new to MPLS; however, for intermediate to advanced users of MPLS, it allows you to move between chapters and sections of chapters to cover only the material that you need for additional information or for areas you are working with specifically.

The following is a summary of the chapter contents:

- **Chapter 1, "MPLS Overview"**—Provides an introduction to MPLS theory and basic operation with coverage of what is a label and its function in MPLS. In addition, it covers the concepts of data plane and control plane and their operation in a cell-mode and frame-mode MPLS domain.

- **Chapter 2, "Basic MPLS Configuration"**—Discusses configuration steps to configure cell-mode and frame-mode MPLS.

- **Chapter 3, "Basic MPLS VPN Overview and Configuration"**—Covers fundamentals of MPLS VPN operation including multiprotocol BGP operation, VPN version 4 route exchange, and basic MPLS VPN configuration in the provider network.

- **Chapter 4, "PE-CE Routing Protocol—Static and RIP"**—Discusses implementing MPLS VPN using static and RIP PE-CE routing.

- **Chapter 5, "PE-CE Routing Protocol—OSPF and EIGRP"**—Discusses implementing MPLS VPNs using OSPF and EIGRP PE-CE routing protocols along with OSPF sham-link operation and configuration.

- **Chapter 6, "Implementing BGP in MPLS VPNs"**—Covers concepts related to BGP PE-CE routing, configuring and implementing route-reflectors, as well as confederations in MPLS VPN networks. Theory and operation of BGP PE-CE for MPLS VPN hub-and-spoke implementations are also covered.

- **Chapter 7, "Inter-Provider VPNs"**—Introduces inter-provider VPNs and discusses analyzing various options that can be used to provision inter-provider MPLS VPNs.

- **Chapter 8, "Carrier Supporting Carriers"**—Discusses the concepts related to Carrier Supporting Carriers models. This chapter also discusses various CSC models such as customer carrier *not* running MPLS, customer carrier running MPLS, customer carrier providing MPLS VPN service, and benefits related to implementing CSC.

- **Chapter 9, "MPLS Traffic Engineering"**—Covers Traffic Engineering basics, constraint-based routing and operation in MPLS TE, and configuring MPLS traffic engineering, as well as the mapping of customer MPLS VPN traffic to different TE tunnels. In addition, advanced features such as fast reroute link protection are also covered.

- **Chapter 10, "Implementing VPNs with Layer 2 Tunneling Protocol Version 3"**—Covers concepts and configurations related to implementing Layer 2 VPNs over non-MPLS enabled provider networks using L2TPv3. In addition, the configuration to implement Layer 3 VPNs over L2TPv3-based provider architecture is also covered.

- **Chapter 11, "Any Transport over MPLS (AToM)"**—Examines various modes of transporting Layer 2 protocols over MPLS. This chapter covers configuration of L2 VPN for like-to-like and any-to-any L2 technologies.

- **Chapter 12, "Virtual Private LAN Service (VPLS)"**—Covers VPLS components and operation, VPLS configuration and verification, and VPLS topologies.

- **Chapter 13, "Implementing Quality of Service in MPLS Networks"**—Covers the basics of MPLS QoS, and configuring and implementing Uniform and Short pipe mode operation.

- **Chapter 14, "MPLS Features and Case Studies"**—Examines various MPLS features such as route target rewrite, Multi-VRF CE, VRF selection based on source IP address and policy-based routing, NAT and HSRP integration to MPLS VPN, Layer 2 VPN pseudowire switching and redundancy, class-based tunnel selection, and implementation of Layer 3 hierarchical VPNs over Layer 2 VPN infrastructure. In addition, the theory and configuration for implementing VPLS on a GSR as well as BGP Site-of-Origin are also covered.

In addition, you can find a bonus Chapter 15, "Testing MPLS" online at http://www.ciscopress.com/title/1587051990.

CHAPTER 1

MPLS Overview

Multiprotocol Label Switching (MPLS) has evolved from being a buzzword in the networking industry to a widely deployed technology in service provider (SP) networks. In recent years, MPLS has also been adopted by the enterprise and federal market segments. MPLS is a contemporary solution to address a multitude of problems faced by present-day networks: speed, scalability, quality of service (QoS) management, and traffic engineering. Service providers are realizing larger revenues by the implementation of service models based on the flexibility and value adds provided by MPLS solutions. MPLS also provides an elegant solution to satisfy the bandwidth management and service requirements for next-generation IP–based backbone networks.

This chapter introduces you to the following basic MPLS concepts:

- Unicast IP forwarding in traditional IP networks
- Architectural blocks of MPLS
- MPLS terminology
- CEF, FIB, LFIB, and LIB
- MPLS label assignment
- MPLS LDP session establishment
- MPLS label distribution and retention
- Penultimate hop popping
- Frame-mode MPLS operation and loop prevention
- Cell-mode MPLS operation, VC-merge, cell interleaving, and loop prevention

Unicast IP Forwarding in Traditional IP Networks

In traditional IP networks, routing protocols are used to distribute Layer 3 routing information. Figure 1-1 depicts a traditional IP network where network layer reachability information (NLRI) for network 172.16.10.0/24 is propagated using an IP routing protocol. Regardless of the routing protocol, packet forwarding is based on the destination address alone. Therefore, when a packet is received by the router, it determines the next-hop address using the packet's destination IP address along with the information from its own forwarding/routing table. This process of determining the next hop is repeated at each hop (router) from the source to the destination except in the case of policy-based routing where a certain outbound policy might affect packet forwarding.

Figure 1-1 *Traditional IP Forwarding Operation*

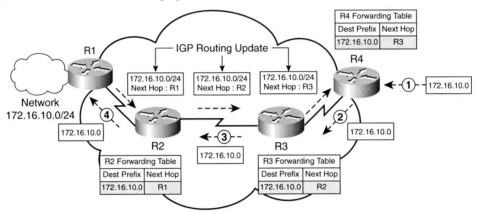

As shown in Figure 1-1, in the data forwarding path, the following process takes place:

1 R4 receives a data packet destined for 172.16.10.0 network.

2 R4 performs route lookup for 172.16.10.0 network in the forwarding table, and the packet is forwarded to the next-hop Router R3.

3 R3 receives the data packet with destination 172.16.10.0, performs a route lookup for 172.16.10.0 network, and forwards the packet to next-hop Router R2.

4 R2 receives the data packet with destination 172.16.10.0, performs a route lookup for 172.16.10.0 network, and forwards the packet to next-hop Router R1.

Because R1 is directly connected to network 172.16.10.0, the router forwards the packet on to the appropriate connected interface.

Overview of MPLS Forwarding

In MPLS enabled networks, packets are forwarded based on labels. These labels might correspond to IP destination addresses or to other parameters, such as QoS classes and source address. Labels are generated per router (and in some cases, per interface on a router) and bear local significance to the router generating them. Routers assign labels to define paths called Label Switched Paths (LSP) between endpoints. Because of this, only the routers on the edge of the MPLS network perform a routing lookup.

Figure 1-2 illustrates the same network as depicted in Figure 1-1 with MPLS forwarding where route table lookups are performed only by MPLS edge border routers, R1 and R4. The routers in MPLS network R1, R2, and R3 propagate updates for 172.16.10.0/24 network via an IGP routing protocol just like in traditional IP networks, assuming no filters or summarizations are not configured. This leads to the creation of an IP forwarding table. Also, because the links connecting the routers are MPLS enabled, they assign local labels for destination 172.16.10.0 and propagate them upstream to their directly connected peers using a label distribution protocol; for example, R1 assigns a local label L1 and propagates it to the upstream neighbor R2. R2 and R3 similarly assign labels and propagate the same to upstream neighbors R3 and R4, respectively. Consequently, as illustrated in Figure 1-2, the routers now maintain a label forwarding table to enable labeled packet forwarding in addition to the IP routing table. The concept of upstream and downstream is explained in greater detail in the section "MPLS Terminology."

Figure 1-2   *Forwarding in the MPLS Domain*

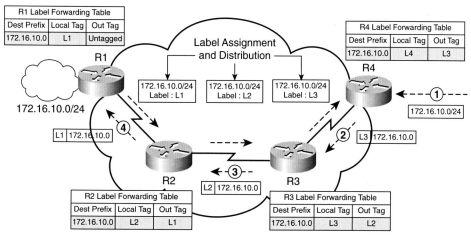

As shown in Figure 1-2, the following process takes place in the data forwarding path from R4 to R1:

1 R4 receives a data packet for network 172.16.10.0 and identifies that the path to the destination is MPLS enabled. Therefore, R4 forwards the packet to next-hop Router R3 after applying a label L3 (from downstream Router R3) on the packet and forwards the labeled packet to R3.

2 R3 receives the labeled packet with label L3 and swaps the label L3 with L2 and forwards the packet to R2.

3 R2 receives the labeled packet with label L2 and swaps the label L2 with L1 and forwards the packet to R1.

4 R1 is the border router between the IP and MPLS domains; therefore, R1 removes the labels on the data packet and forwards the IP packet to destination network 172.16.10.0.

Architectural Blocks of MPLS

MPLS functionality on Cisco devices is divided into two main architectural blocks:

- **Control plane**—Performs functions related to identifying reachability to destination prefixes. Therefore, the control plane contains all the Layer 3 routing information, as well as the processes within, to exchange reachability information for a specific Layer 3 prefix. Common examples of control plane functions are routing protocol information exchange like in OSPF and BGP. Hence, IP routing information exchange is a control plane function. In addition, all protocol functions that are responsible for the exchange of labels between neighboring routers function in the control plane as in label distribution protocols (explained in detail in section "LDP Session Establishment").

- **Data plane**—Performs the functions relating to forwarding data packets. These packets can be either Layer 3 IP packets or labeled IP packets. The information in the data plane, such as label values, are derived from the control plane. Information exchange between neighboring routers creates mappings of IP destination prefixes to labels in the control plane, which is used to forward data plane labeled packets.

Figure 1-3 depicts the control plane and data plane functions.

Figure 1-3   *Control Plane and Data Plane on a Router*

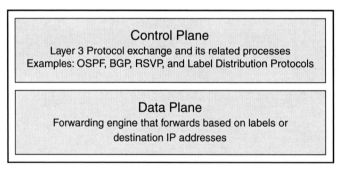

MPLS Terminology

This section provides an overview of the common MPLS-related terminology used for the rest of this book:

- **Forwarding Equivalence Class (FEC)**—As noted in RFC 3031(MPLS architecture), this group of packets are forwarded in the same manner (over the same path with the same forwarding treatment).

- **MPLS Label Switch Router (LSR)**—Performs the function of label switching; the LSR receives a labeled packet and swaps the label with an outgoing label and forwards the new labeled packet from the appropriate interface. The LSR, depending on its location in the MPLS domain, can either perform label disposition (removal, also called *pop*), label imposition (addition, also called *push*) or label swapping (replacing the top label in a label stack with a new outgoing label value). The LSR, depending on its location in the MPLS domain, might also perform label stack imposition or disposition. The concept of a label stack is explained later in this section. During label swapping, the LSR replaces only the top label in the label stack; the other labels in the label stack are left untouched during label swapping and forwarding operation at the LSR.

- **MPLS Edge-Label Switch Router (E-LSR)**—An LSR at the border of an MPLS domain. The ingress Edge LSR performs the functions of label imposition (push) and forwarding of a packet to destination through the MPLS-enabled domain. The egress Edge LSR performs the functions of label disposition or removal (pop) and forwarding an IP packet to the destination. Note that the imposition and disposition processes on an Edge LSR might involve label stacks versus only labels.

Figure 1-4 depicts the network in Figure 1-2 with all routers identified as LSRs or Edge LSRs based on their location and operation in the MPLS domain.

Figure 1-4 *LSR and Edge LSR*

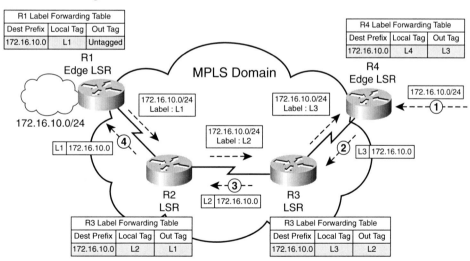

- **MPLS Label Switched Path (LSP)**—The path from source to destination for a data packet through an MPLS-enabled network. LSPs are unidirectional in nature. The LSP is usually derived from IGP routing information but can diverge from the IGP's preferred path to the destination (as in MPLS traffic engineering, which is discussed in Chapter 9, "MPLS Traffic Engineering"). In Figure 1-4, the LSP for network 172.16.10.0/24 from R4 is R4-R3-R2-R1.

- **Upstream and downstream**—The concept of *downstream* and *upstream* are pivotal in understanding the operation of label distribution (control plane) and data forwarding in an MPLS domain. Both *downstream* and *upstream* are defined with reference to the destination network: prefix or FEC. Data intended for a particular destination network always flows *downstream*. Updates (routing protocol or label distribution, LDP/TDP) pertaining to a specific prefix are always propagated *upstream*. This is depicted in Figure 1-5 where downstream with reference to the destination prefix 172.16.20.0/24 is in the path R1-R2-R3, and downstream with reference to 172.16.10.0/24 is the path R3-R2-R1. Therefore, in Figure 1-5, R2 is downstream to R1 for destination 172.16.20.0/24, and R1 is downstream to R2 for destination 172.16.10.0/24.

Figure 1-5 *Upstream and Downstream*

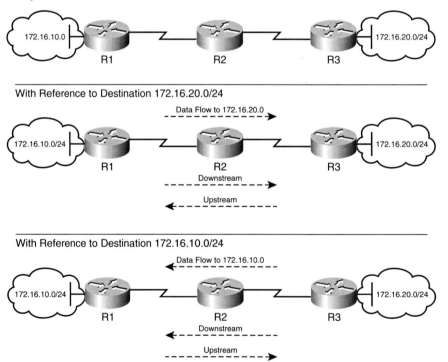

- **MPLS labels and label stacks**—An MPLS label is a 20-bit number that is assigned to a destination prefix on a router that defines the properties of the prefix as well as forwarding mechanisms that will be performed for a packet destined for the prefix.

The format of an MPLS label is shown in Figure 1-6.

Figure 1-6 *MPLS Label*

An MPLS label consists of the following parts:

- 20-bit label value

- 3-bit experimental field

- 1-bit bottom-of-stack indicator

- 8-bit Time-to-Live field

The 20-bit label value is a number assigned by the router that identifies the prefix in question. Labels can be assigned either per interface or per chassis. The 3-bit experimental field defines the QoS assigned to the FEC in question that has been assigned a label. For example, the 3 experimental bits can map to the 7 IP precedence values to map the IP QoS assigned to packets as they traverse an MPLS domain.

A *label stack* is an ordered set of labels where each label has a specific function. If the router (Edge LSR) imposes more than one label on a single IP packet, it leads to what is called a label stack, where multiple labels are imposed on a single IP packet. Therefore, the *bottom-of-stack indicator* identifies if the label that has been encountered is the bottom label of the label stack.

The TTL field performs the same function as an IP TTL, where the packet is discarded when the TTL of the packet is 0, which prevents looping of unwanted packets in the network. Whenever a labeled packet traverses an LSR, the label TTL value is decremented by 1.

The label is inserted between the Frame Header and the Layer 3 Header in the packet. Figure 1-7 depicts the label imposition between the Layer 2 and Layer 3 headers in an IP packet.

Figure 1-7 *MPLS Label Imposition*

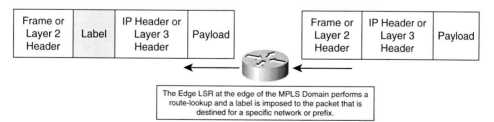

If the value of the S bit (bottom-of-stack indicator) in the label is 0, the router understands that a *label stack* implementation is in use. As previously mentioned, an LSR swaps only the top label in a label stack. An egress Edge LSR, however, continues label disposition in the label stack until it finds that the value of the S bit is set to 1, which denotes a bottom of the label stack. After the router encounters the bottom of the stack, it performs a route lookup depending on the information in the IP Layer 3 Header and appropriately forwards the packet toward the destination. In the case of an ingress Edge LSR, the Edge LSR might impose (push) more than one label to implement a label stack where each label in the label stack has a specific function.

Label stacks are implemented when offering MPLS-based services such as MPLS VPN or MPLS traffic engineering. In MPLS VPN (see Chapter 3, "Basic MPLS VPN Overview and Configuration"), the second label in the label stack identifies the VPN. In traffic engineering (see Chapter 9), the top label identifies the endpoint of the TE tunnel, and the second label identifies the destination. In Layer 2, VPN implementations over MPLS, such as AToM (see Chapter 11, "Any Transport over MPLS [AToM]") and VPLS (see Chapter 12, "Virtual Private LAN Service [VPLS]), the top label identifies the Tunnel Header or endpoint, and the second label identifies the VC. All generic iterations of the label stack implementation are shown in Figure 1-8.

Figure 1-8   *MPLS Label Stack*

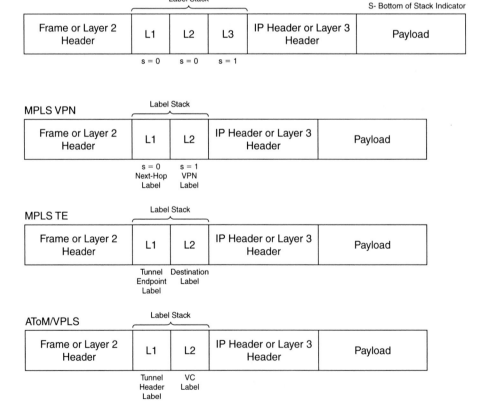

MPLS Control and Data Plane Components

Cisco Express Forwarding (CEF) is the foundation on which MPLS and its services operate on a Cisco router. Therefore, CEF is a prerequisite to implement MPLS on all Cisco platforms except traditional ATM switches that support only data plane functionality. CEF is a proprietary switching mechanism used on Cisco routers that enhances the simplicity and the IPv4 forwarding performance of a router manifold.

CEF avoids the overhead of cache rewrites in the IP Core environment by using a Forwarding Information Base (FIB) for the destination switching decision, which mirrors the entire contents of the IP routing table. There is a one-to-one mapping between FIB table and routing table entries.

When CEF is used on a router, the router maintains, at a minimum, an FIB, which contains a mapping of destination networks in the routing table to appropriate next-hop adjacencies. *Adjacencies* are network nodes that can reach one another with a single hop across the link layer. This *FIB resides in the data plane*, which is the forwarding engine for packets processed by the router.

In addition to the FIB, two other structures on the router are maintained, which are the Label Information Base (LIB) and Label Forwarding Information Base (LFIB). The distribution protocol in use between adjacent MPLS neighbors is responsible for the creation of entries in the LIB and LFIB.

The *LIB functions in the control plane* and is used by the label distribution protocol where IP destination prefixes in the routing table are mapped to next-hop labels that are received from downstream neighbors, as well as local labels generated by the label distribution protocol.

The *LFIB resides in the data plane* and contains a local label to next-hop label mapping along with the outgoing interface, which is used to forward labeled packets.

Information about reachability to destination networks from routing protocols is used to populate the Routing Information Base (RIB) or the routing table. The routing table, in turn, provides information for the FIB. The LIB is populated using information from the label distribution protocol and from the LIB along with information from the FIB that is used to populate the LFIB.

Figure 1-9 shows the interoperation of the various tables maintained on a router.

Figure 1-9 *MPLS Control and Data Plane Components*

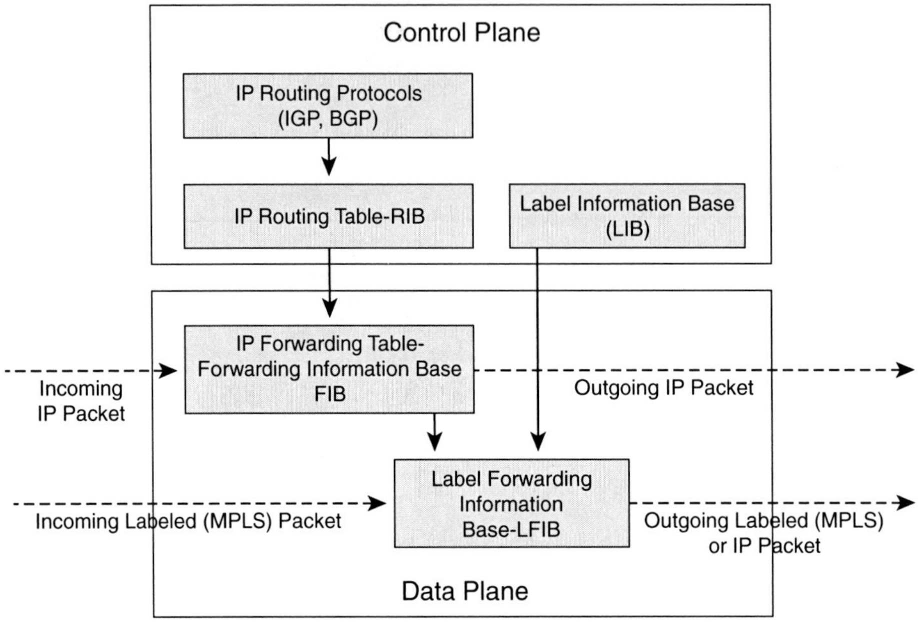

MPLS Operation

The implementation of MPLS for data forwarding involves the following four steps:

1 MPLS label assignment (per LSR)

2 MPLS LDP or TDP session establishment (between LSRs/ELSRs)

3 MPLS label distribution (using a label distribution protocol)

4 MPLS label retention

MPLS operation typically involves adjacent LSR's forming an LDP session, assigning local labels to destination prefixes and exchanging these labels over established LDP sessions. Upon completion of label exchange between adjacent LSRs, the control and data structures of MPLS, namely FIB, LIB, and LFIB, are populated, and the router is ready to forward data plane information based on label values.

MPLS Label Assignment

A label is assigned to IP networks reachable by a router and then imposed on data packets forwarded to those IP networks. IP routing protocols advertise reachability to destination networks. The same process needs to be implemented for routers or devices that are part of the MPLS domain to learn about the labels assigned to destination networks by neighboring routers. The label distribution protocol (LDP or TDP) assigns and exchanges labels between adjacent LSRs in an MPLS domain following session establishment. As previously mentioned, labels can be assigned either globally (per router) or per interface on a router.

LDP Session Establishment

Following label assignment on a router, these labels are distributed among directly connected LSRs if the interfaces between them are enabled for MPLS forwarding. This is done either by using LDP or tag distribution protocol (TDP). TDP is deprecated and, by default, LDP is the label distribution protocol. The command **mpls label protocol** {**ldp** | **tdp**} is configured only if LDP is not the default label distribution protocol or if you are reverting from LDP to TDP. The command can be configured in global and interface configuration mode. The interface configuration command will, however, override the global configuration.

TDP and LDP function the same way but are not interoperable. It is important to note that when Cisco routers are in use, the default protocol that is running on an MPLS-enabled interface is dependent on the version of IOS running on the device; care must be taken when configuring Cisco routers in a multivendor environment. TDP uses TCP port 711 and LDP uses TCP port 646. A router might use both TDP and LDP on the same interface to enable dynamic formation of LDP or TDP peers depending on the protocol running on the interface of the peering MPLS neighbor. LDP is defined in RFC 3036 and is implemented predominantly between adjacent peers (adjacencies as defined by the IGP). In some cases, LDP sessions can also be configured between nonadjacent peers, where it is called a directed LDP session, which is covered in more detail in Chapters 11 and 12.

There are four categories of LDP messages:

- **Discovery messages**—Announce and sustain an LSR's presence in the network
- **Session messages**—Establish, upkeep, and tear down sessions between LSRs
- **Advertisement messages**—Advertise label mappings to FECs
- **Notification messages**—Signal errors

Figure 1-10 *LDP Session Establishment*

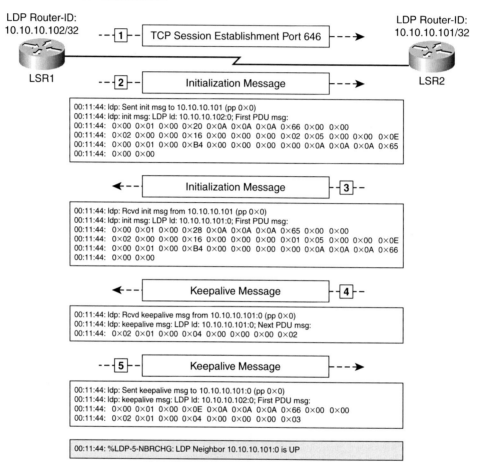

All LDP messages follow the type, length, value (TLV) format. LDP uses TCP port 646, and the LSR with the higher LDP router ID opens a connection to port 646 of another LSR:

1 LDP sessions are initiated when an LSR sends periodic hellos (using UDP multicast on 224.0.0.2) on interfaces enabled for MPLS forwarding. If another LSR is connected to that interface (and the interface enabled for MPLS), the directly connected LSR attempts to establish a session with the source of the LDP hello messages. The LSR with the higher LDP router ID is the active LSR. The active LSR attempts to open a TCP connection with the passive LSR (LSR with a lower router ID) on TCP port 646 (LDP).

2 The active LSR then sends an *initialization* message to the passive LSR, which contains information such as the session keepalive time, label distribution method, max PDU length, and receiver's LDP ID, and if loop detection is enabled.

3 The passive LDP LSR responds with an initialization message if the parameters are acceptable. If parameters are not acceptable, the passive LDP LSR sends an *error notification message*.

4 Passive LSR sends keepalive message to the active LSR after sending an initialization message.

5 The active LSR sends keepalive to the passive LDP LSR, and the LDP session comes up. At this juncture, label-FEC mappings can be exchanged between the LSRs.

MPLS Label Distribution with LDP

In an MPLS domain running LDP, a label is assigned to a destination prefix found in the FIB, and it is distributed to upstream neighbors in the MPLS domain after session establishment. The labels that are of local significance on the router are exchanged with adjacent LSRs during label distribution. Label binding of a specific prefix to a local label and a next-hop label (received from downstream LSR) is then stored in the LFIB and LIB structures. The label distribution methods used in MPLS are as follows:

- **Downstream on demand**—This mode of label distribution allows an LSR to explicitly request from its downstream next-hop router a label mapping to a particular destination prefix and is thus known as *downstream on demand* label distribution.

- **Unsolicited downstream**—This mode of label distribution allows an LSR to distribute bindings to upstream LSRs that have not explicitly requested them and is referred to as *unsolicited downstream* label distribution.

Figure 1-11 depicts the two modes of label distribution between R1 (Edge LSR) and R2 (LSR). In the downstream-on-demand distribution process, LSR R2 requests a label for the destination 172.16.10.0. R1 replies with a label mapping of label 17 for 172.16.10.0. In the unsolicited downstream distribution process, R1 does not wait for a request for a label mapping for prefix 172.16.10.0 but sends the label mapping information to the upstream LSR R2.

Figure 1-11   *Unsolicited Downstream Versus Downstream on Demand*

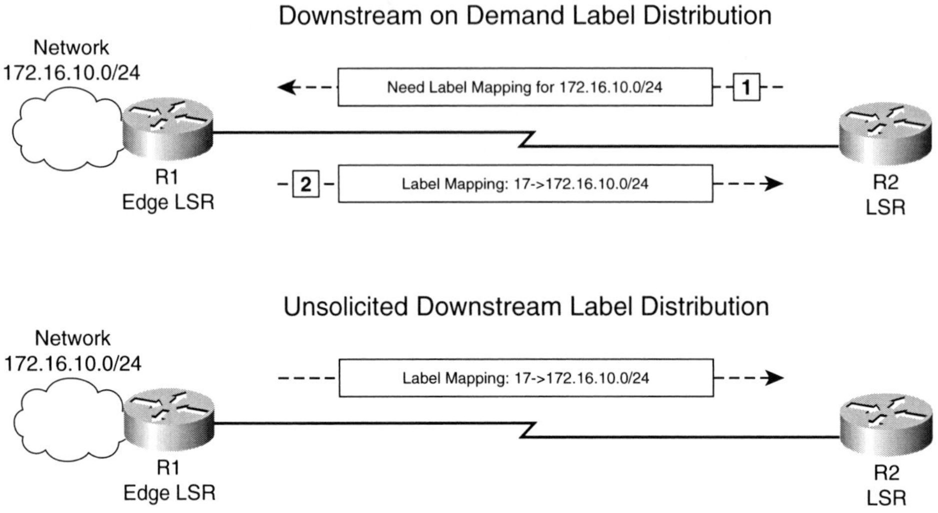

Downstream on Demand Label Distribution

Network
172.16.10.0/24

Need Label Mapping for 172.16.10.0/24 — 1

R1
Edge LSR

2 — Label Mapping: 17->172.16.10.0/24

R2
LSR

Unsolicited Downstream Label Distribution

Network
172.16.10.0/24

Label Mapping: 17->172.16.10.0/24

R1
Edge LSR

R2
LSR

MPLS Label Retention

If an LSR supports *liberal label retention mode*, it maintains the bindings between a label and a destination prefix, which are received from downstream LSRs that might not be the next hop for that destination. If an LSR supports *conservative label retention mode*, it discards bindings received from downstream LSRs that are not next-hop routers for a destination prefix. Therefore, with liberal retention mode, an LSR can almost immediately start forwarding labeled packets after IGP convergence, where the numbers of labels maintained for a particular destination are large, thus consuming memory. With conservative label retention, the labels maintained are labels from the confirmed LDP or TDP next-hop neighbors, thus consuming minimal memory.

Special Outgoing Label Types

LSRs perform the operation of label swapping, imposition, or disposition depending on their location in the MPLS domain. In certain cases, the incoming label maps to special outgoing labels that define the operation to be performed at the upstream LSR or router. These labels are propagated by the downstream LSR during label distribution to the upstream LSR. The following outlines the types of outgoing labels that can be associated with a packet:

- **Untagged**—The incoming MPLS packet is converted to an IP packet and forwarded to the destination (MPLS to IP Domain transition). This is used in the implementation of MPLS VPN (discussed in Chapter 3).

- **Implicit-null or POP label**—This label is assigned when the top label of the incoming MPLS packet is removed and the resulting MPLS or IP packet is forwarded to the next-hop downstream router. The value for this label is 3 (20 bit label field). This label is used in MPLS networks that implement penultimate hop popping discussed in the next section.

- **Explicit-null Label**—This label is assigned to preserve the EXP value of the top label of an incoming packet. The top label is swapped with a label value of 0 (20 bit label field) and forwarded as an MPLS packet to the next-hop downstream router. This label is used in the implementation of QoS with MPLS.

- **Aggregate**—In this label, the incoming MPLS packet is converted to an IP packet (by removing all labels if label stack is found on incoming packet), and an FIB (CEF) lookup is performed to identify the outgoing interface to destination (used in MPLS VPN implementations, which is discussed in Chapter 3).

Figure 1-12 illustrates the usage of these label types.

Figure 1-12 *Special Label Types*

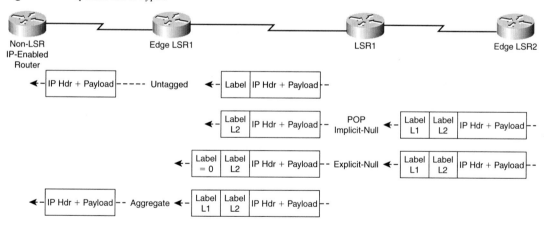

Penultimate Hop Popping

Penultimate hop popping is performed in MPLS-based networks where the router upstream to the Edge LSR removes the top label in the label stack and forwards only the resulting packet (either labeled IP or IP packet) for a particular FEC. This process is signaled by the downstream Edge LSR during label distribution with LDP. The downstream Edge LSR distributes an *implicit-null (POP)* label to the upstream router, which signals it to pop the top label in the label stack and forward the resulting labeled or IP packet. When the packet is received by the Edge LSR, no lookup is performed in the LIB if the incoming packet is an IP packet. Therefore, penultimate hop popping saves a single lookup on edge routers. The operation of penultimate hop popping is depicted in Figure 1-13.

Figure 1-13 *Penultimate Hop Popping*

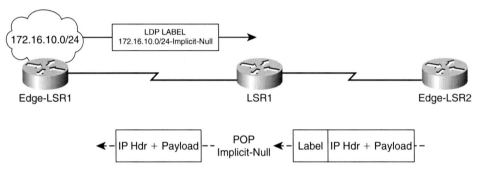

As illustrated in Figure 1-13, the downstream Edge LSR1 distributes an implicit-null label mapping for network 172.16.10.0/24 to its upstream LSR1. Upon receiving a labeled packet, LSR1 pops the top label and sends the resulting IP packet to the Edge-LSR1.

Frame-Mode MPLS

In frame-mode MPLS, routers running MPLS exchange pure IP packets (penultimate hop popping) as well as labeled IP packets with one another in an MPLS domain. In an MPLS domain, label switching is done by parsing the frame header and then performing label imposition (push), label disposition (pop), or label swapping depending on the LSR's location in the network. Data link layer connectivity in a frame-mode MPLS domain is established using serial HDLC/PPP, Ethernet, or ATM. ATM brings us to another aspect of Layer 2 connectivity where cells are used to transport IP packets. Note that although there might be ATM links in the MPLS domain, it is possible to run regular IP point-to-point links (routed PVCs). In such cases, it is still considered frame-mode MPLS and not cell-mode MPLS, although the Layer 2 protocol is ATM.

Frame-Mode MPLS Operation

Figure 1-14 shows how label allocation and distribution take place in frame-mode MPLS. The figure depicts two Edge LSRs, R1 and R4, connected via two LSRs, R2 and R3. After IGP convergence and LDP neighbor establishment, the LSRs assign a local label for 172.16.10.0/24 and propagate this label upstream, as depicted in Figure 1-14. Therefore, the control and data structures, namely FIB, LFIB, and LIB, are populated with the appropriate values, as illustrated in Figure 1-14.

Figure 1-14 *Frame-Mode MPLS Label Assignment and Distribution*

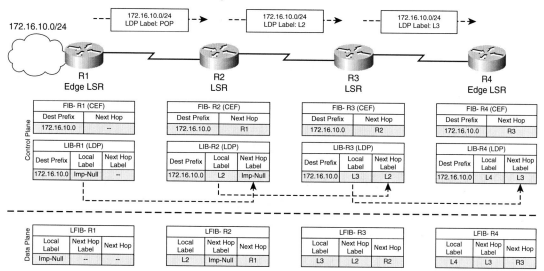

As portrayed in Figure 1-14, Edge LSR R1 assigns an *implicit-null* local label and propagates the same upstream to LSR R2. LSRs R2 and R3 assign local labels L2 and L3, respectively, for destination network 172.16.10.0 and propagate them upstream. The label allocation can either be unsolicited downstream or downstream on demand label allocation; the only difference being that in downstream on demand label allocation, the upstream LSR requests a label for the destination network.

After label allocation and distribution, the FIB, LIB, and LFIB structures are as depicted in Figure 1-14 with reference to destination prefix 172.16.10.0.

Forwarding a data packet destined for 172.16.10.0 via the MPLS domain is depicted in Figure 1-15, where the Edge LSR R4 imposes a label L3 (next-hop label as learned from downstream LSR) and forwards the labeled packet to the downstream LSR R3. R3 performs a label swap of ingress label L3 for egress label L2. On R2, the ingress label of L2 maps to an *implicit-null* label. Therefore, LSR R2 removes the top label (L2) and forwards the resultant IP packet to Edge LSR R1, as shown in Figure 1-15.

Routers receiving a frame can identify the type of payload by the use of the protocol/type field in the frame header. For example, in the case of Ethernet, the 13th and 14th octets of an Ethernet or IEEE 802.3 packet (after the preamble) consist of the "Ethernet Type" or "IEEE 802.3 Length" field. A value of 0x0800 in these octets identifies an IP packet as the Layer 2 frame payload. A value of 0x8847 identifies an MPLS unicast payload in the Layer 2 frame. Thus, the router identifies the frame received on an interface as either containing an IP packet or a labeled IP packet.

Figure 1-15 *Frame-Mode MPLS Forwarding*

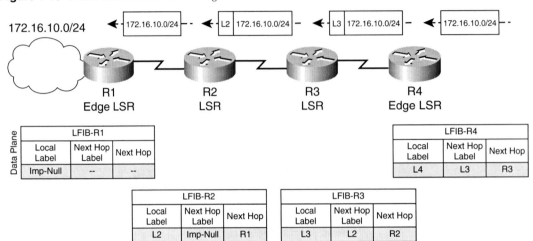

Loop Prevention in Frame-Mode MPLS

The label distribution protocols, namely LDP and TDP, predominantly rely on loop prevention mechanisms provided by the IGP implemented in the MPLS domain. However, to avoid infinite looping of packets in the MPLS domain, the TTL field in the label header is used. The functionality of the TTL field in the label header is the same as the TTL field in the IP Header. The TTL value is an integer from 0–255 that is decremented by one every time the packet transits a router (IP TTL) or an LSR (Label TTL).

When the TTL value of an IP packet becomes zero, the router discards the IP packet, and an ICMP message stating that the "TTL expired in transit" is sent to the source IP address of the IP packet. This mechanism prevents an IP packet from being routed continuously in case of a routing loop. The same procedure is employed with the label TTL value.

When an IP packet enters a label switched domain, Cisco routers functioning as Edge LSRs copy the IP TTL value from the IP packet header onto the TTL value of the label. When the labeled packet encounters an LSR, the label TTL is decremented by 1. This process continues until the labeled packet is converted back into an IP packet at the egress Edge LSR in the MPLS domain, where the label TTL is copied back onto the IP TTL in the IP header. This process is called *IP to label TTL propagation*.

TTL propagation can be disabled in the MPLS domain. When TTL propagation is disabled, the IP TTL is not copied into the label TTL field, but instead, a value of 255 is written into the label TTL field. IP to label TTL propagation is enabled by default on Cisco routers. Configuration of the **no mpls ip propagate-ttl [forwarded | local]** command on an Edge LSR (privilege mode) can be used to disable IP to label TTL value propagation for either *forwarded* traffic or *locally generated* traffic as depicted by the **forwarded** and **local** options of the command. The **no** version of the command places a TTL value of 255 in the label TTL value.

When propagation is enabled, the command allows a **traceroute** to show all the hops in the path, including LSRs in the MPLS domain. For example, when traffic is generated by a network in the IP domain not locally connected (like Ethernet LAN or local loopback) to an Edge LSR, the **forwarded** option disables the IP to MPLS label TTL value propagation. Therefore, when a customer performs a **traceroute** via the provider network, the MPLS domain is transparent to the customer. This is the most common application of this command.

However, if the traffic was to be generated locally by a loopback interface on the Edge LSR, the IP TTL to label TTL value propagation will occur. Therefore, the provider can still perform any troubleshooting if required using **traceroute** commands. If no options are configured, the TTL propagation is disabled for both locally generated traffic and forwarded traffic. This hides the structure of the MPLS network from a **traceroute** command.

Figure 1-16 provides an example of the **no MPLS IP propagate-ttl forwarded** command when configured on Edge LSRs in a network. The following steps occur on the routers in Figure 1-16 when a traceroute is performed from Router A to Router B via the MPLS domain:

1 Router A sends a traceroute packet with destination of 172.16.20.1 with an IP TTL value of 1. When this packet is received by Router R1 (Edge LSR), the TTL value is decremented to 0 and an ICMP TTL exceeded message is sent back to the source.

2 Router A sends a traceroute packet with destination of 172.16.20.1 with an IP TTL value of 2. Router R1 receives this packet and decrements the IP TTL value to 1. Because IP TTL to label TTL propagation is disabled for forwarded traffic, the IP TTL is not copied onto the label TTL. The packet is label switched from R1 with label TTL value of 255. Routers R2 and R3 forward the packet toward the destination but decrement only the label TTL and not IP TTL. At Router R4, the packet's IP TTL value is now decremented to 0, and an ICMP TTL Exceeded message is sent back to the source.

3 Router A sends a traceroute packet with destination of 172.16.20.1 and IP TTL of 3. Router R1 receives the packet and decrements IP TTL to 2 and label switches the packet with label TTL of 255 to R2. R2 and R3 decrement the label TTL values and, at router R4, the packet's IP TTL is now decremented to 1. Router R4 forwards the packet to Router B where the IP TTL is decremented to 0 and an ICMP TTL Exceeded message is sent back to the source.

Figure 1-16 *IP to Label TTL Propagation*

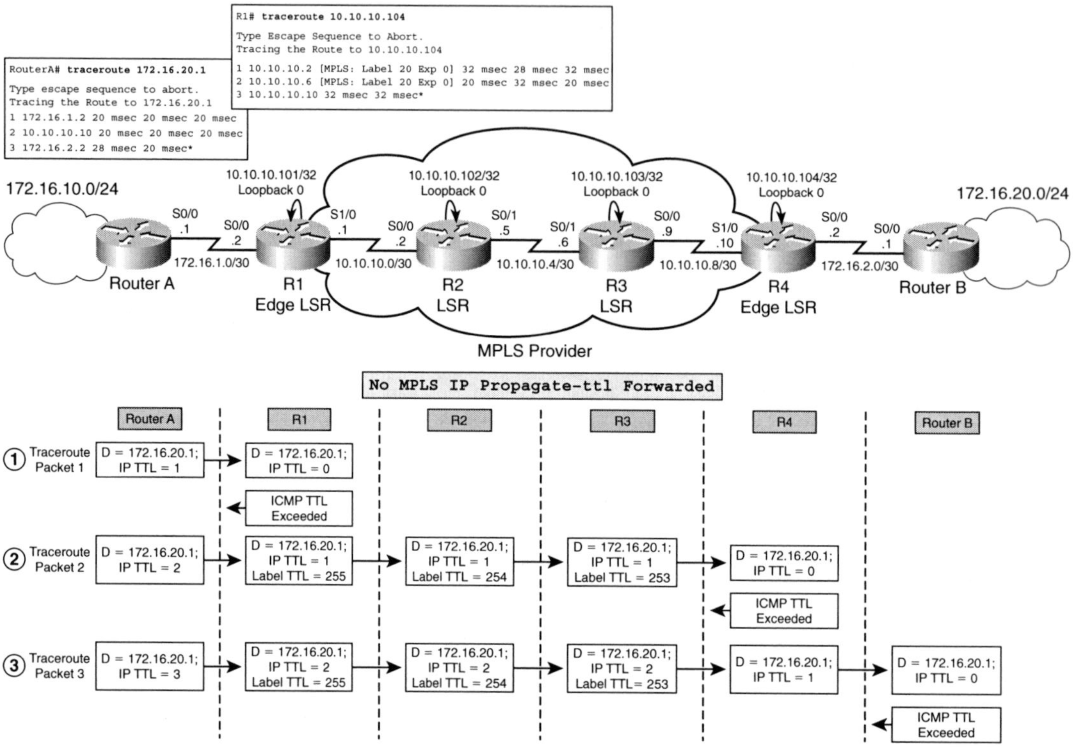

As depicted in Figure 1-16, the traceroute from R1 (Edge LSR) to R4's loopback interface shows all hops in the provider network because IP TTL to label TTL mapping is not disabled for *local* networks.

Cell-Mode MPLS

When using ATM connectivity between devices, MPLS applies to cells, not frames. Cells are used to transport data plane information. When ATM labels are used in an MPLS core, the operating mode of MPLS is called cell-mode MPLS. As previously mentioned, peering between LSRs via routed ATM PVCs can also be implemented but is considered a frame-mode implementation.

In cell-mode MPLS, the LSRs in the core of the MPLS network are ATM switches that forward data based on the ATM header. If the ATM LSR functions as a pure ATM switch (data plane), an external control plane component also called the label switch controller (LSC) is required for propagation of control plane information. In some cases, however, the ATM LSR is capable of propagating control plane information as well as forwarding data plane information and thus does not require an external control plane component.

When the ATM LSR has an external LSC component for control plane information exchange, the ATM switch in the ATM LSR performs only data plane forwarding. To enable MPLS in the ATM domain, the VPI/VCI field in the ATM header is used as the label. Therefore, a label is inserted between the ATM header and IP header, and the VPI/VCI field of the ATM header forwards the cells. This mechanism allows for data plane forwarding of labeled packets. Control plane packets, such as protocol information exchange in routing protocols and label distribution protocols, are exchanged between edge ATM LSRs and the control plane component of the ATM LSR over a control virtual circuit (control VC).

In cell-mode MPLS, the label used in the MPLS domain is the same format as the regular MPLS label, as shown earlier in Figure 1-6. To ensure that cells are forwarded using MPLS, the VPI/VCI values forward the labeled cells. This label is inserted between the ATM header and the IP header in the cells that are forwarded to the ATM LSR, as shown in Figure 1-17.

Figure 1-17 *Cell-Mode MPLS Label Imposition*

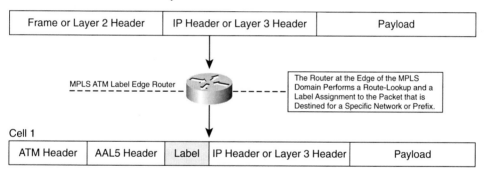

Figure 1-18 shows a cell-mode MPLS network with an ingress edge ATM LSR, a core ATM LSR, and an egress edge ATM LSR. The interfaces of the LSRs in the MPLS domain that carry pure cells are called *Label Switching controlled-ATM interfaces (LC-ATM)* as the VPI/VCI pairs for the virtual circuits are used by the protocol for distribution and exchange of labels in the ATM domain. *ATM-LSR* is an ATM switch that runs MPLS on the control plane and performs MPLS forwarding between LC-ATM interfaces on the data plane by means of traditional ATM cell switching. In the integrated ATM LSR implementation, the LC-ATM interfaces carry both the data plane packets as well as the control plane packets (on VC 0/32). If an ATM switch is connected to an external LSC together functioning as the ATM LSR, the Edge ATM LSRs form a control plane adjacency with the LSC, and the LSC identifies the data plane forwarding (ingress labels to egress label mappings) on the LSC-ATM interfaces of the ATM switch in the ATM LSR.

As portrayed in Figure 1-18, a control plane adjacency is required between adjoining ATM switches or LSRs in the ATM domain for IGP and label distribution protocol packet exchange. To ensure appropriate forwarding of IP routing information through an ATM switch, all the ATM LSRs and ATM Edge LSRs form an IP adjacency by creating an in-band VC that is used only for control information. The *VPI/VCI* used for this control VC is 0/32 (default) and needs to be configured on all ATM switches and ATM Edge LSRs in the MPLS ATM domain. Therefore, the MPLS control VC is configured by default on all switches to be with VC 0/32 and uses the aal5snap encapsulation as defined in RFC 2684. The control VC can be changed from the default value of 0/32 on an ATM LSR; however, for proper information exchange and adjacency formation between two ATM LSRs, the control VC must be configured as the same.

Figure 1-18 *Cell-Mode MPLS Domain*

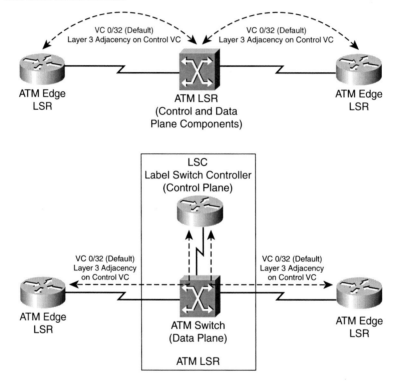

Cell-Mode MPLS Operation

To enable MPLS in the ATM domain, the top label in the label stack that is inserted between the ATM header and IP header is encoded as the VPI/VCI of the virtual circuit in use. The mechanism allows for the proper forwarding of data plane packets; control plane packets are exchanged on a *control VC* between directly connected ATM LSRs.

Figure 1-19 shows an ATM network with A1 and A2 being the ATM LSRs, and R1 and R2 are edge ATM LSRs. Network 172.16.10.0/24 is directly connected to R1.

The process of label allocation and distribution is the same as frame-mode MPLS in cell-mode MPLS operation. The downstream ATM Edge LSR R1 allocates a local label for network 172.16.10.0 and propagates the same upstream. This process is repeated on the

ATM LSRs A1 and A2. The only difference between cell-mode and frame-mode MPLS are that no penultimate hop popping occurs at the penultimate hop ATM LSR, and the labels assigned are the VPI/VCI values copied from the ATM header. In addition to the previously mentioned differences, cell-mode MPLS uses an interface level label space versus frame mode that can either use an interface level or router level label space.

Assuming that the VPI assigned to all virtual circuits (and thus the label VPI values) on R1, R2, A1, and A2 is 1, and L1, L2, L3, and L4 are the respective VCIs associated with R1, A1, A2, and R2, the FIB, LIB, and LFIB values on the ATM LSRs and the Edge ATM LSRs are as depicted in Figure 1-19.

Figure 1-19 *Label Allocation and Distribution: Cell-Mode MPLS*

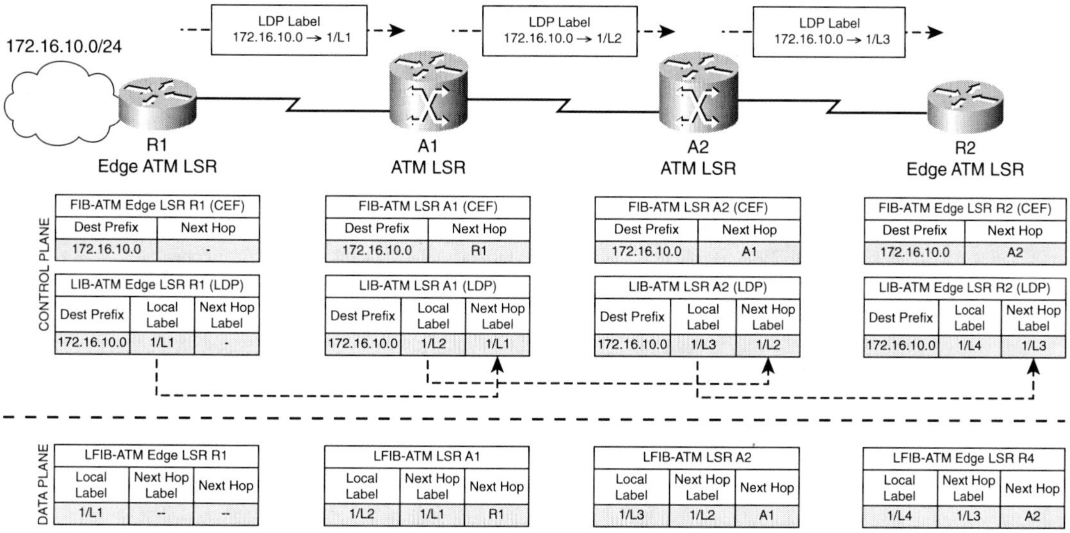

Data plane operation in the cell-mode MPLS network is as follows:

1 When a data packet destined for network 172.16.10.0/24 is received on R2, it imposes an outgoing label of 1/L3 and forwards the same to downstream ATM LSR A2.

2 LSR A2 does an LFIB lookup and replaces the top label of 1/L3 with next-hop label of 1/L2 and forwards the cells to ATM LSR A1.

3 LSR A1 also performs an LFIB lookup and replaces the top label with next-hop label of 1/L1 and forwards the cells to ATM Edge LSR R1. Note that unlike frame-mode MPLS, the penultimate hop LSR does not pop the top label prior to forwarding to the Edge LSR in a cell-mode MPLS implementation. Therefore, upon receiving the cells, Edge ATM LSR pops the label and performs a lookup to identify the path to the destination network 172.16.10.0/24, which is directly connected.

The data plane forwarding operation in cell-mode MPLS is depicted in Figure 1-20.

Figure 1-20 *Data Plane Operation: Cell-Mode MPLS*

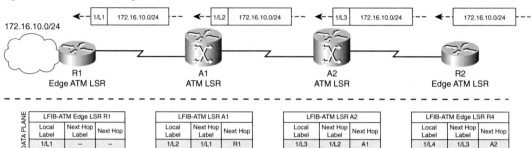

Loop Detection in Cell-Mode MPLS

In cell-mode MPLS, the ATM header does not posses a TTL field such as in the IP header or in a label when implementing frame-mode MPLS to enable loop detection by the use of TTL values in the header. The label distribution protocol used in the control plane for label allocation and distribution relies on the Layer 3 protocols to primarily perform the functions of loop detection.

LDP contains two mechanisms to enable loop detection in cell-mode MPLS. As previously mentioned, LDP sends messages in the form of TLVs. Two such TLVs are used in cell-mode MPLS to enable loop detection in cell-mode MPLS. This is also often called loop detection using path vectors (RFC 3035). Figure 1-21 depicts the LDP message format with the LDP PDU header consisting of the *version*, *PDU length,* and *LDP identifier* fields, as well as the LDP message. As shown in Figure 1-21, the LDP message type consists of the *U bit*, *F bit*, *message type*, *length*, and *value*.

Figure 1-21 *LDP PDU and Message Format*

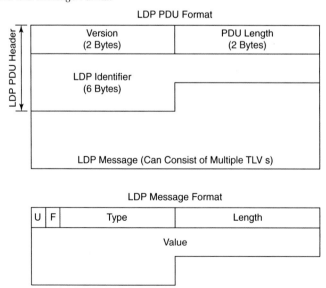

The *U bit* or the *unknown TLV bit* if set (=1) is ignored and the rest of the message is processed. If the U bit is unset (=0), the message is ignored, and a notification (error report) is sent to the source.

The *F bit* or *forward unknown TLV bit* is applicable only when the U bit is set (=1) and the LDP message containing the unknown TLV is to be forwarded. If the message with the U-bit set is received and the F bit is set, the message is forwarded.

Type identifies how the *value* field is to be interpreted. In the cell-mode MPLS implementation, the type field can identify a hop-count or a path vector for loop detection.

Length identifies the length of the *value* field in octets.

Value is an octet string defining the value for the *type* field.

In cell-mode MPLS loop detection, the first TLV that is used is called the hop count TLV, which is propagated during label distribution along with the specific destination prefix. The hop count TLV format and implementation is depicted in Figure 1-22.

Figure 1-22 *Hop Count TLV Implementation in Cell-Mode MPLS*

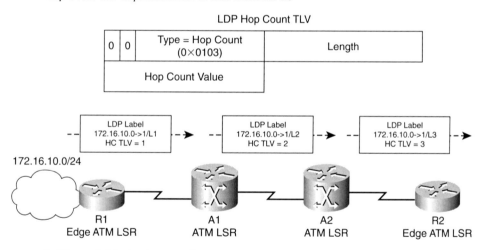

In Figure 1-22, the format of the hop count TLV and its implementation are depicted. The hop count TLV is an optional message during LSP setup between LSRs. The function of the hop count TLV is to calculate the number of LSR hops along an LSP during setup. In the network in Figure 1-22, Router R1 advertises the local label to reach the destination prefix 172.16.1.0 with a hop count TLV of 1. Upon receiving this label, the ATM LSR A1 advertises its local label L2 to upstream LSR A2 after incrementing the hop count TLV value to 2. This process is repeated in LSR A2 whereby the LSR advertises its local label to upstream edge ATM LSR R2 with a hop count TLV value of 3. Therefore, Edge ATM LSR R2 now knows that the number of hops to reach network 172.16.1.0/24 is 3.

The second loop detection mechanism employed in cell-mode MPLS is with the use of the path vector TLV. For readers familiar with BGP, the path vector TLV is similar to the use of

AS path processing in BGP where the update is rejected if an AS in the AS-Path attribute is the same as the receiver's AS number. The path vector TLV is used to prevent LDP request message loops in the cell-mode domain. The path vector TLV contains a list of router IDs of routers that the update or the request has traversed. So, if you receive an update or a request with your own router ID in the path vector TLV, the request, of course, is ignored. Figure 1-23 depicts the path vector TLV message format and its operation.

Figure 1-23 *Path Vector TLV Message Format and Operation*

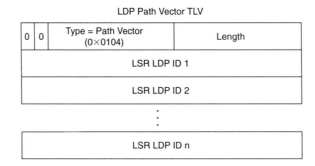

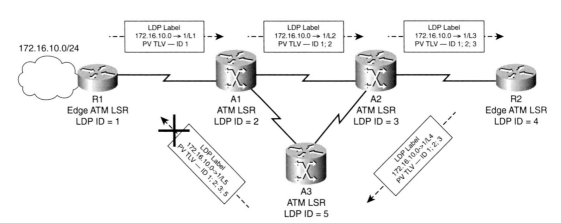

In Figure 1-23, the LSR LDP IDs are simplified to be 1, 2, 3, 4, and 5 for R1, A1, A2, R2, and A5. The Edge ATM LSR R1 places its LSR LDP ID (ID=1) in the path vector TLV value and forwards the advertisement upstream to ATM LSR A1 during the LDP message exchange for FEC 172.16.10.0/24. A1 appends its LSR LDP ID (ID=2) in the path vector TLV value field and forwards the same upstream to A2. (Forwarding of label mapping to A3 is not depicted for simplicity.) A2 appends its LDP ID (ID=3) to the path vector TLV message and forwards the same to LSR A3 and Edge ATM LSR R2. When A3 places its LDP ID in the path vector TLV and sends a label mapping for the FEC 172.16.10.0/24 back to A1, A1 detects its own LDP ID in the path vector TLV and thus rejects this update/label mapping for the FEC, thus avoiding loops. In cell-mode MPLS, no TTL is implemented to prevent indefinite routing loops, but the hop count TLV sets the maximum number of hops, and the path vector TLV is implemented to prevent actual loops in LDP.

ATM VC-Merge

In cell-mode MPLS, a single label is maintained per destination for each upstream LSR requesting the information. This leads to an increase in the number of labels that are maintained in the core ATM LSRs when a large number of Edge ATM LSRs are connected to the same ATM LSR. Certain optimization techniques can be employed that can reduce the number of labels that need to be maintained on a per LSR basis.

Virtual circuit merge (VC-merge) is the most common methodology employed in cell-mode MPLS that enables a fewer number of labels to be maintained per LSR. In VC-merge, an LSR maintains labels per destination and uses the same outgoing label for the same destination from different upstream LSRs. Figure 1-24 depicts the network in Figure 1-19 with an additional Edge ATM LSR R3 connected to ATM LSR A2. Without VC-merge enabled, A2 allocates two separate labels for the destination 172.16.1.0/24 and propagates them upstream to Edge ATM LSRs R2 and R3. R2 receives a next-hop label of 1/L3 and R3 receives a next-hop label of 1/L5 for the same destination.

Figure 1-24 *Cell-Mode MPLS Without VC-Merge*

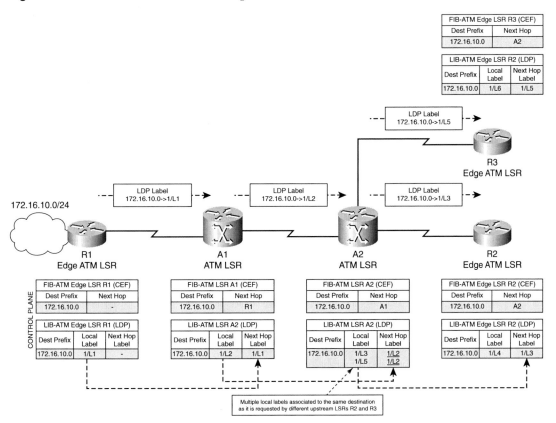

However, with VC-merge enabled, Edge ATM LSRs R2 and R3 both receive the same label of 1/L3 as the next-hop label mapping to destination 172.16.1.0, which provides label space savings on the ATM LSRs, as shown in Figure 1-25.

Figure 1-25 *Cell-Mode MPLS with VC-Merge*

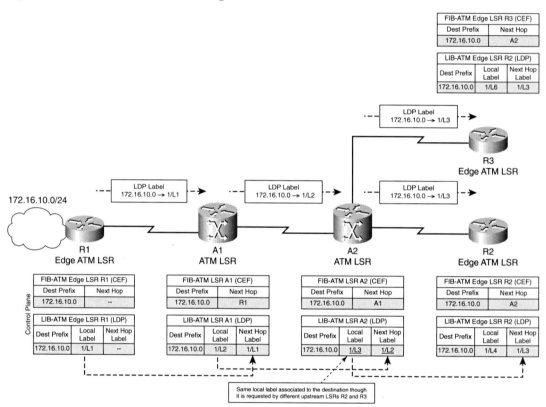

Cell Interleave with VC-Merge Implementation

After implementation of VC-merge on the ATM switches in the core, an issue arises: cell interleaving. With VC-merge, the same VC label is used for multiple upstream neighbors to send traffic to the same destination. If multiple upstream neighbors send traffic simultaneously to the same destination, the ATM LSR cannot guarantee that traffic from the two sources to the same destination will not be interleaved in transit as they use the same VC to the downstream neighbor toward destination.

Because the VC values are the same for all the cells, although the traffic is from two different sources, the downstream LSRs are incapable of identifying the correct source of the traffic. As shown in Figure 1-26, the ATM LSR A2 connected to multiple Edge LSRs R2 and

R3 (as depicted in Figure 1-25) need to send a request for labels mapping to the same destination downstream and need to maintain multiple labels for each Edge LSR connected to the switch for each destination prefix.

Figure 1-26 *Cell Interleave with VC-Merge*

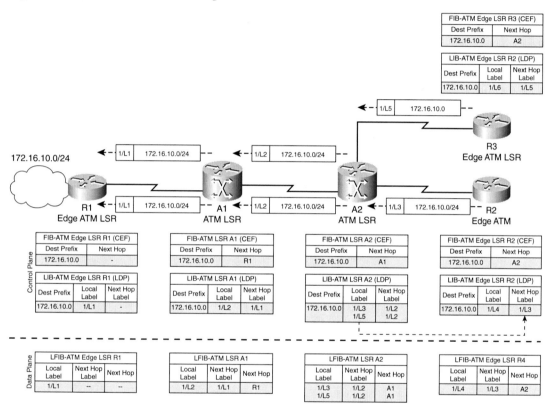

In some cases, the ATM switch is capable of buffering cells from a single source to a particular destination when traffic from another source to the same destination is transmitted downstream. The ATM switches buffer packets until they receive a cell with the end of frame bit set. The cells in the buffer are transmitted only if no traffic using the same VC to the destination is currently in transit from the ATM switch. Therefore, in this case, VC-merge is fully functional but introduces delays in transit as multiple sources are unable to send traffic to the same destination.

In the absence of buffering capabilities, the ATM LSR needs to have VC-merge disabled to avoid cell interleaving and associated issues.

CHAPTER 2

Basic MPLS Configuration

In the first chapter, you were introduced to the MPLS forwarding model in which labels are used to forward packets for a certain destination network. You were also provided details on frame- and cell-mode MPLS operation.

In this chapter, the following topics are covered:

- Frame-mode MPLS configuration and verification
  - Basic frame-mode MPLS configuration and verification
  - Frame-mode MPLS over RFC 2684 (obsoletes RFC 1483) routed PVC
- Cell-mode MPLS over ATM configuration and verification
  - Basic cell-mode MPLS configuration and verification
  - Configuring cell-mode MPLS with and without virtual circuit merge (VC-merge)
  - MPLS over VP tunnels configuration and verification
  - Configuring MPLS over ATM using BPX ATM switch and 7200 as label switch controller (LSC)

Frame-Mode MPLS Configuration and Verification

In frame mode, MPLS uses a 32-bit label that is inserted between the Layer 2 and Layer 3 headers. Layer 2 encapsulations like HDLC, PPP, Frame Relay, and Ethernet are frame-based except for ATM, which can operate either in frame mode or cell mode.

Basic Frame-Mode MPLS Overview, Configuration, and Verification

Figure 2-1 shows a frame-based MPLS provider network providing MPLS services to sites belonging to *Customer A*. The frame-based provider's network consists of routers R1, R2, R3, and R4. R1 and R4 function as Edge Label Switch Routers (LSRs) while R2 and R3 serve as LSRs.

Figure 2-1 *Frame-Mode MPLS Provider Network*

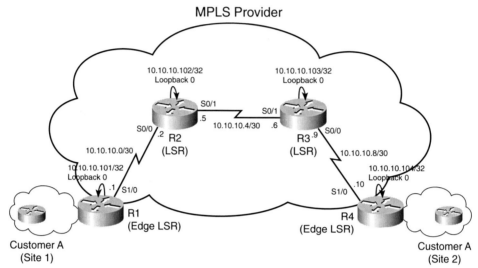

Figure 2-2 illustrates the configuration flowchart to implement frame-mode MPLS on the provider network shown in Figure 2-1. The configuration flowchart assumes that IP addresses are preconfigured where required.

Figure 2-2 *Frame-Mode MPLS Configuration Flowchart*

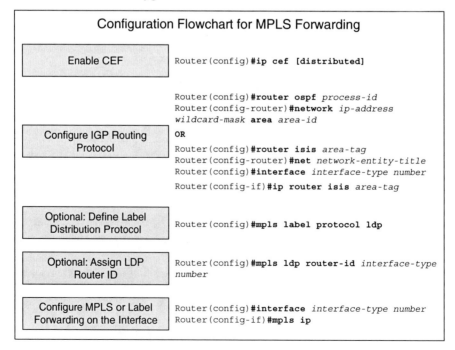

Basic Frame-Mode MPLS Configuration Steps

The steps to configure frame-mode MPLS are based on the configuration flowchart outlined in Figure 2-2. Ensure that IP addresses are configured prior to following these steps:

Step 1   **Enable CEF**—CEF is an essential component for label switching and is responsible for imposition and disposition of labels in an MPLS network. Configure CEF globally on routers R1, R2, R3, and R4 by issuing the **ip cef [distributed]** command. Ensure that CEF is not disabled on the interface. If disabled, enable CEF on the interface by issuing **ip route-cache cef** in interface mode. Use the **distributed** keyword in the global configuration mode for Cisco platform capable of distributed CEF switching. Example 2-1 highlights the configuration to enable CEF on R2. Similarly enable CEF on R1, R3, and R4.

Example 2-1   *Enable CEF*

```
R2(config)#ip cef distributed
R2(config)#do show running-config interface s0/0 | include cef
 no ip route-cache cef
R2(config)#interface s0/0
R2(config-if)#ip route-cache cef
```

Step 2   **Configure IGP routing protocol**—Configure the IGP routing protocol; in this case, OSPF. Enable the interfaces on R1, R2, R3, and R4 that are part of the provider network in OSPF using **network** *ip-address wild-card-mask* **area** *area-id* command under the OSPF routing process. Example 2-2 highlights the OSPF configuration on R2. Similarly configure OSPF on R1, R3, and R4.

Example 2-2   *Configure IGP Routing Protocol on R2*

```
R2(config)#router ospf 100
R2(config)#network 10.10.10.0 0.0.0.255 area 0
```

Enabling the label distribution protocol is an optional step. TDP is deprecated, and by default, LDP is the label distribution protocol. The command **mpls label protocol {ldp | tdp}** is configured only if LDP is not the default label distribution protocol or if you are reverting from LDP to TDP protocol or vice versa. The command can be configured in the global as well as in the interface configuration mode. The interface configuration command will, however, override the global configuration.

Step 3   **Assign LDP router ID**—LDP uses the highest IP address on a loopback interface as the LDP router ID. If there is no loopback address defined, the highest IP address on the router becomes the LDP router ID. To force an interface to be an LDP router ID, **mpls ldp router-id** *interface-type* *number* command can be used. The loopback interface address is recommended because it always remains up. Configure the loopback 0 interface on the R2 router to be the LDP router ID as shown in Example 2-3. Repeat the configuration on R1, R3, and R4, assigning the local loopback interface as LDP router-id.

Example 2-3 *Assign LDP Router ID*

```
R2(config)#mpls ldp router-id loopback 0
```

Step 4 **Enable IPv4 MPLS or label forwarding on the interface**—Example 2-4 demonstrates the step to enable MPLS forwarding on the interface.

Example 2-4 *Enable MPLS Forwarding*

```
R2(config)#interface serial 0/0
R2(config-if)#mpls ip
R2(config)#interface serial 0/1
R2(config-if)#mpls ip
```

Verification of Basic Frame-Mode MPLS Operation

The steps to verify the frame-mode MPLS operation are as follows. All verification steps were performed on Router R2. Outputs of the commands have been truncated for brevity, and only pertinent lines are depicted:

Step 1 Example 2-5 verifies whether CEF is globally enabled or disabled on the router by issuing the **show ip cef** command. As shown in Example 2-5, CEF is disabled on R2. Example 2-5 shows if CEF is enabled on the router interfaces.

Example 2-5 *CEF Verification*

```
R2#show ip cef
%CEF not running
Prefix                 Next Hop              Interface
R2#show cef interface serial 0/0
Serial0/0 is up (if_number 5)
(Output truncated)
  IP CEF switching enabled
  IP CEF Fast switching turbo vector
(Output Truncated)
R2#show cef interface serial 0/1
Serial0/1 is up (if_number 6)
(Output Truncated)
  IP CEF switching enabled
  IP CEF Fast switching turbo vector
```

Step 2 Verify MPLS forwarding is enabled on the interfaces by issuing the **show mpls interfaces** command. Example 2-6 shows that MPLS is enabled on the serial interfaces. The IP column depicts Yes if IP label switching is enabled on the interface. The Tunnel column is Yes if LSP tunnel labeling (discussed later in Chapter 9, "MPLS Traffic Engineering") is enabled on the interface, and the Operational column is Yes if packets are labeled on the interface.

Example 2-6 *MPLS Forwarding Verification*

```
R2#show mpls interfaces
Interface            IP           Tunnel   Operational
Serial0/0            Yes (ldp)    No       Yes
Serial0/1            Yes (ldp)    No       Yes
```

Step 3 Verify the status of the Label Distribution Protocol (LDP) discovery process by issuing **show mpls ldp discovery**. This command displays neighbor discovery information for LDP and shows the interfaces over which the LDP discovery process is running. Example 2-7 shows that R2 has discovered two LDP neighbors, 10.10.10.101 (R1) and 10.10.10.103 (R3). The xmit/recv field indicates that the interface is transmitting and receiving LDP discovery Hello packets.

Example 2-7 *LDP Discovery Verification*

```
R2#show mpls ldp discovery
  Local LDP Identifier:
    10.10.10.102:0
    Discovery Sources:
    Interfaces:
        Serial0/0 (ldp): xmit/recv
            LDP Id: 10.10.10.101:0
        Serial0/1 (ldp): xmit/recv
            LDP Id: 10.10.10.103:0
```

Step 4 Issue **show mpls ldp neighbor** to verify the status of the LDP neighbor sessions. Example 2-8 shows that the LDP session between R2 and R1 (10.10.10.101), as well as between R2 and R3 (10.10.10.103), is operational. Downstream indicates that the downstream method of label distribution is being used for this LDP session in which the LSR advertises all of its locally assigned (incoming) labels to its LDP peer (subject to any configured access list restrictions).

Example 2-8 *LDP Neighbor Verification*

```
R2#show mpls ldp neighbor
    Peer LDP Ident: 10.10.10.101:0; Local LDP Ident 10.10.10.102:0
        TCP connection: 10.10.10.101.646 - 10.10.10.102.11012
        State: Oper; PIEs sent/rcvd: 26611/26601; Downstream
        Up time: 2w2d
        LDP discovery sources:
          Serial0/0, Src IP addr: 10.10.10.1
```

continues

Example 2-8 *LDP Neighbor Verification (Continued)*

```
        Addresses bound to peer LDP Ident:
          10.10.10.101    10.10.10.1
    Peer LDP Ident: 10.10.10.103:0; Local LDP Ident 10.10.10.102:0
        TCP connection: 10.10.10.103.11002 - 10.10.10.102.646
        State: Oper; Msgs sent/rcvd: 2374/2374; Downstream
        Up time: 1d10h
        LDP discovery sources:
          Serial0/1, Src IP addr: 10.10.10.6
        Addresses bound to peer LDP Ident:
          10.10.10.6      10.10.10.103    10.10.10.9
```

Control and Data Plane Forwarding in Basic Frame-Mode MPLS

Figure 2-3 shows the control and data plane forwarding operation in frame-mode MPLS.

Figure 2-3 *Frame-Mode MPLS Control and Data Plane Operation*

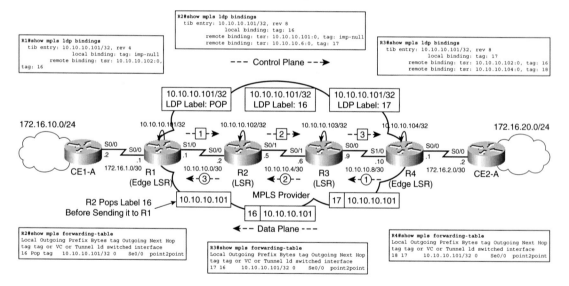

Control Plane Operation in Basic Frame-Mode MPLS

Figure 2-3 shows the control plane operation for prefix 10.10.10.101/32 from R1 to R4. The following steps are performed in the label propagation process for prefix 10.10.10.101/32:

Step 1   Example 2-9 shows that R1 sends an implicit null or the POP label to R2. A value of 3 represents the implicit-null label. R1 propagates the implicit-null label to its penultimate Router R2, which performs the POP function in the data forwarding from R4 to 10.10.10.101/32. If R1 propagates an explicit-null label, the upstream LSR R2 does not POP the label but assigns a label value of 0 and sends a labeled packet to R2.

Example 2-9 *MPLS Label Bindings on R1*

```
R1#show mpls ldp bindings
<output truncated>
  tib entry: 10.10.10.101/32, rev 4
        local binding:  tag: imp-null
        remote binding: tsr: 10.10.10.102:0, tag: 16
```

Step 2 Example 2-10 shows R2 assigning an LSP label 16 to 10.10.10.101/32. This label value is propagated to R3. This label value is imposed by R3 in the data forwarding path (for example, a packet originating from R4 to prefix 10.10.10.101/32 on R1).

Example 2-10 *Label Allocation and Distribution Verification on R2*

```
R2#show mpls forwarding-table
Local  Outgoing    Prefix          Bytes tag  Outgoing   Next Hop
tag    tag or VC   or Tunnel Id    switched   interface
16     Pop tag     10.10.10.101/32 0          Se0/0      point2point
17     Pop tag     10.10.10.8/30   0          Se1/0      point2point
18     Pop tag     10.10.10.103/32 0          Se1/0      point2point
19     19          10.10.10.104/32 0          Se1/0      point2point
```

Step 3 Example 2-11 shows that on R3, prefix 10.10.10.101/32 has been assigned a local label of 17 and an outgoing label of 16. The outgoing label is received from the Router R2. The local label of 17 has been propagated during label distribution to Router R4. Label 17 is used by R4 in the data forwarding path for data destined to prefix 10.10.10.101/32 located on R1 from R4.

Example 2-11 *Label Allocation and Distribution Verification on R3*

```
R3#show mpls forwarding-table
Local  Outgoing    Prefix          Bytes tag  Outgoing   Next Hop
tag    tag or VC   or Tunnel Id    switched   interface
16     Pop tag     10.10.10.0/30   0          Se0/0      point2point
17     16          10.10.10.101/32 0          Se0/0      point2point
18     Pop tag     10.10.10.102/32 0          Se0/0      point2point
19     Pop tag     10.10.10.104/32 0          Se1/0      point2point
```

Data Forwarding Operation in Basic Frame-Mode MPLS

The following steps are performed in the data forwarding path from R4 to prefix 10.10.10.101/32:

1 As shown in Figure 2-3, R4 imposes label 17 on the data packet originating from R4 destined to 10.10.10.101/32.

2 R3 does an LFIB lookup and swaps label 17 for 16 and forwards that data packet to R2.

3 R2 receives the data packet from R3, does a penultimate hop pop function, removes label 16, and forwards the data packet to R1.

Final Device Configurations for Basic Frame-Mode MPLS

The pertinent configurations for the devices in the frame-mode MPLS domain are shown in Examples 2-12 through Example 2-15.

Example 2-12 *R1 Configuration*

```
hostname R1
!
ip cef
!
mpls ldp router-id Loopback0
!
interface Loopback0
 ip address 10.10.10.101 255.255.255.255
!
interface Serial1/0
 description Connection to R2
 ip address 10.10.10.1 255.255.255.252
 mpls ip
!
router ospf 100
 network 10.10.10.0 0.0.0.255 area 0
```

Example 2-13 *R2 Configuration*

```
hostname R2
!
ip cef
!
mpls ldp router-id Loopback0
!
interface Loopback0
 ip address 10.10.10.102 255.255.255.255
!
interface Serial0/0
 description Connection to R1
 ip address 10.10.10.2 255.255.255.252
mpls label protocol ldp
mpls ip
!
interface Serial0/1
 description Connection to R3
 ip address 10.10.10.5 255.255.255.252
mpls label protocol ldp
mpls ip
!
router ospf 100
   network 10.10.10.0 0.0.0.255 area 0
```

Example 2-14 *R3 Configuration*

```
hostname R3
!
ip cef
!
mpls label protocol ldp
!
interface Loopback0
 ip address 10.10.10.103 255.255.255.255
!
interface Serial0/0
 description connection to R4
 ip address 10.10.10.9 255.255.255.252
 mpls ip
!
interface Serial0/1
 description connection to R2
 ip address 10.10.10.6 255.255.255.252
mpls ip
!
router ospf 100
 network 10.10.10.0 0.0.0.255 area 0
```

Example 2-15 *R4 Configuration*

```
hostname R4
!
ip cef
!
mpls label protocol ldp
!
interface Loopback0
 ip address 10.10.10.104 255.255.255.255
!
interface Serial1/0
 Description connection to R3
 ip address 10.10.10.10 255.255.255.252
 mpls ip
!
router ospf 100
network 10.10.10.0 0.0.0.255 area 0
```

Frame-Mode MPLS over RFC 2684 Routed PVC

Frame-mode MPLS can be implemented over RFC 2684 (previously RFC 1483) routed
PVCs. When using PVCs, RFC 2684 specifies the following methods of encapsulation to
carry traffic over ATM AAL5:

- **VC multiplexing**—A virtual circuit-based multiplexing method in which each VC
  carries one protocol. The user, therefore, defines one PVC per protocol.

- **LLC/SNAP encapsulation**—This method multiplexes multiple protocols over a
  single ATM virtual circuit.

Figure 2-4 shows the network topology for RFC 2684 routed.

Figure 2-4 *Topology: Frame-Mode MPLS Over RFC 2684 Routed PVCs*

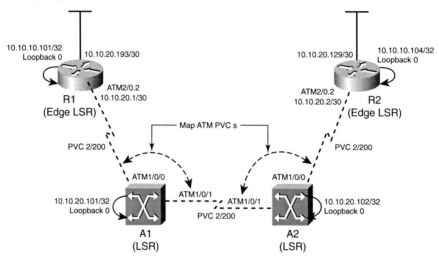

Figure 2-5 illustrates the flowchart to configure frame-mode MPLS on the provider network devices shown in Figure 2-4. The configuration flowchart assumes that IP addresses are pre-configured where needed.

Figure 2-5 *Frame-Mode MPLS Configuration Flowchart*

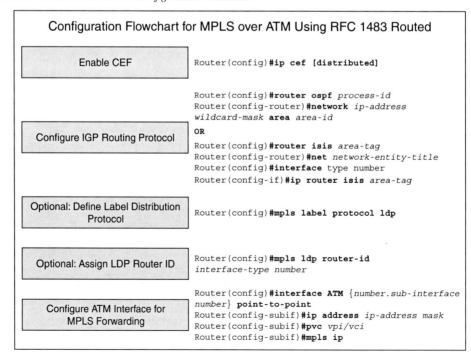

Figure 2-6 shows the flowchart for configuring the ATM PVC route on the LS1010 ATM switch.

Figure 2-6 *Configuration Flowchart for LS1010 ATM Switch*

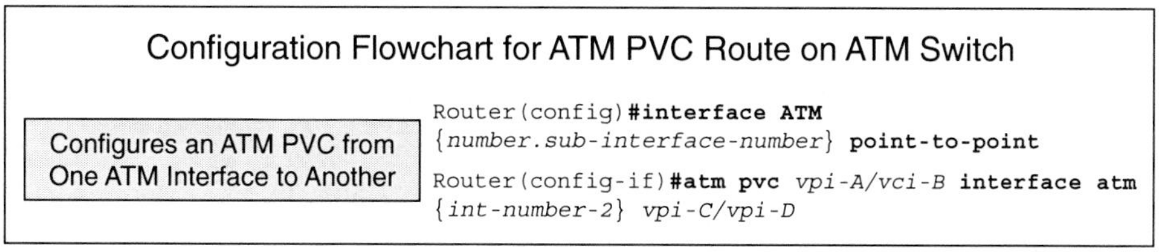

```
┌─────────────────────────────────────────────────────────────────────┐
│           Configuration Flowchart for ATM PVC Route on ATM Switch     │
│                                                                       │
│                              Router(config)#interface ATM             │
│  ┌──────────────────────────┐{number.sub-interface-number} point-to-point
│  │ Configures an ATM PVC from│                                         │
│  │ One ATM Interface to Another│ Router(config-if)#atm pvc vpi-A/vci-B interface atm
│  └──────────────────────────┘{int-number-2} vpi-C/vpi-D               │
└─────────────────────────────────────────────────────────────────────┘
```

Configuration Steps for Frame-Mode MPLS Over RFC 2684 Routed PVC

The steps to configure RFC 2684 bridged encapsulation over MPLS on R1 and R2 are as follows. Ensure that IP addresses are preconfigured on R1 and R2, as illustrated in Figure 2-4:

Step 1   Follow the steps shown in the "Basic Frame-Mode MPLS Configuration Steps" section. These steps are the same for frame-mode MPLS over RFC 2684 routed PVC. Follow those steps to configure frame-mode MPLS on R1 and R2:

Step 1—Enable CEF

Step 2—Enable IGP routing protocol

Step 3—Assign LDP router ID

Step 2   **Enable IPv4 MPLS or label forwarding on the interface**—Configure the ATM PVCs 2/200 on each of the appropriate subinterfaces on R1 and R2. The encapsulation used on the PVC is ATM aal5snap. Example 2-16 highlights the steps to configure ATM PVC.

Example 2-16 *Configure PVCs on R1 and R2*

```
R1(config)#interface ATM2/0.2 point-to-point
R1(config-subif)# pvc 2/200
R1(config-if-atm-vc)#  encapsulation aal5snap
R1(config-if-atm-vc)#  mpls ip
R2(config)#interface ATM2/0.2 point-to-point
R2(config-subif)#pvc 2/200
R2(config-if-atm-vc)#encapsulation aal5snap
R2(config-if-atm-vc)#  mpls ip
```

Configuration of the LS1010 ATM Switch

Configure the core ATM switches A1 and A2 to perform VC mapping from one interface to another. The PVC is a permanent logical connection that you must configure manually, from source to destination, through the ATM network. After it is configured, the ATM

network maintains the connection at all times. The configuration of an ingress PVC/
interface mapped to an egress PVC/interface needs to be performed only on one of the
ingress or egress interfaces. Therefore, on ATM switch A1, the configuration is performed
on interface ATM1/0/1 mapping PVC 2/200 to interface ATM1/0/0 PVC 2/200. The same
process is repeated on ATM switch A2, shown in Example 2-17.

Example 2-17 *Configure PVC Mapping on A1 and A2*

```
A1(config-if)#interface ATM1/0/1
A1(config-if)# description Connection to A2
A1(config-if)# atm pvc 2 200  interface  ATM1/0/0 2 200
```
```
A2(config-if)#interface ATM1/0/1
A2(config-if)# description connection to A1
A2(config-if)# atm pvc 2 200  interface  ATM1/0/0 2 200
```

Verification Steps for Frame-Mode MPLS Over RFC 2684 Routed PVC

The steps to verify frame-mode MPLS over RFC 2684 (previously RFC 1483) routed PVC
are as follows:

Step 1 Verify the operation of MPLS over RFC 2684 by performing a view of the
MPLS forwarding information base (LFIB), as shown in Example 2-18.

Example 2-18 *Verification of LFIB*

```
R1#show mpls forwarding-table
Local  Outgoing    Prefix          Bytes tag  Outgoing   Next Hop
tag    tag or VC   or Tunnel Id    switched   interface
36     Pop tag     10.10.10.104/32  0          AT2/0.2    point2point
37     Pop tag     10.10.20.128/30  0          AT2/0.2    point2point
R1#
```
```
R2#show mpls forwarding-table
Local  Outgoing    Prefix          Bytes tag  Outgoing   Next Hop
tag    tag or VC   or Tunnel Id    switched   interface
16     Pop tag     10.10.10.101/32  0          AT2/0.2    point2point
18     Pop tag     10.10.20.192/30  0          AT2/0.2    point2point
```

Step 2 As shown in Example 2-19, verify connectivity by issuing pings.

Example 2-19 *Verify Connectivity*

```
R1#ping 10.10.10.104
Type escape sequence to abort.
Sending 5, 100-byte ICMP Echos to 10.10.10.101, timeout is 2 seconds:
!!!!!
Success rate is 100 percent (5/5), round-trip min/avg/max = 1/1/4 ms
R4#
```
```
R2#ping 10.10.10.101
Type escape sequence to abort.
Sending 5, 100-byte ICMP Echos to 10.10.10.101, timeout is 2 seconds:
!!!!!
Success rate is 100 percent (5/5), round-trip min/avg/max = 1/1/4 ms
R4#
```

Final Device Configuration for Frame-Mode MPLS Over RFC 2684 Routed PVC

The final device configuration for R1, A1, A2, and R2 is shown in Example 2-20 through Example 2-23.

Example 2-20 *Configuration of R1*

```
hostname R1
!
ip cef
!
interface Loopback0
 ip address 10.10.10.101 255.255.255.255
!
interface Ethernet0
 ip address 10.10.20.193 255.255.255.252
!
interface ATM2/0
 no ip address
!
interface ATM2/0.2 point-to-point
 description connection to A1
 ip address 10.10.20.1 255.255.255.252
 mpls ip
 pvc 2/200
  encapsulation aal5snap
 !
router ospf 100
 network 10.10.0.0 0.0.0.255 area 0
```

Example 2-21 *A1 Configuration*

```
hostname A1
!
interface ATM1/0/0
 description connection to R1
!
interface ATM1/0/1
 description connection to A2
atm pvc 2 200  interface  ATM1/0/0 2 200
 !
```

Example 2-22 *A2 Configuration*

```
hostname A2
!
interface ATM1/0/0
 description connection to R2
 !
```

continues

Example 2-22 *A2 Configuration (Continued)*

```
interface ATM1/0/1
 description connection to A1
atm pvc 2 200  interface  ATM1/0/0 2 200
 !
```

Example 2-23 *R2 Configuration*

```
hostname R2
!
ip cef
!
interface Loopback0
 ip address 10.10.10.104 255.255.255.255
!
interface Ethernet0
 ip address 10.10.20.129 255.255.255.252
!
interface ATM2/0
!
interface ATM2/0.2 point-to-point
 description connection to A2
 ip address 10.10.20.2 255.255.255.252
mpls ip
 pvc 2/200
  encapsulation aal5snap
!
router ospf 100
 log-adjacency-changes
 network 10.10.0.0 0.0.255.255 area 0
```

Cell-Mode MPLS over ATM Overview, Configuration, and Verification

This section introduces you to cell-mode MPLS over ATM configuration. In MPLS over ATM networks, routers are connected to ATM-based provider networks consisting of ATM switches that forward data based on virtual circuits (VCs) provisioned on the ATM switches. Cell-mode MPLS uses the virtual path identifier/virtual channel identifier (VPI/VCI) fields in the ATM header as the label value.

ATM VCs exist locally (on a link between two adjacent ATM switches or two CPEs) and have two identifiers: VPI and VCI. These two identifiers are often referred to as a VPI/VCI pair. VPI and VCI numbers are part of ATM cell headers, and they are, therefore, carried in each ATM cell. Because there are two identifiers, you can have two different types of

ATM connections: virtual path and virtual channel. This hierarchy allows aggregation of the number of virtual channels into a single pipe (virtual path) between sites that need a large number of VCs.

The ATM switch is responsible for switching ATM cells on both the VC and VP. When the ATM switch is configured to switch cells on a VC, it has to look at both VPI and VCI fields of the cell in order to make a switching decision. Switching is done based on a table containing (port, VPI, VCI) tuplets for the input and output side of the VC. On Cisco IOS ATM switches, you can see this table with the **show atm vc** command. You can also configure the ATM switch to switch cells based only on the port and VPI number; this is called VP switching. For VP switching, the ATM switch uses a table consisting of (port, VPI) pairs for input and output. You can see this table on Cisco IOS ATM switches with the **show atm vp** command. When VP switching, the ATM switch uses only the VPI field of each ATM cell to make a switching decision, which reduces processing time. The same holds true for cell header rewrites. In VC switching, both VPI and VCI fields of the cell header are rewritten and possibly changed. However, in VP switching, only VPI fields can be changed, and the VCI field remains the same end-to-end.

Basic Cell-Mode MPLS Configuration and Verification

Figure 2-7 shows a basic cell-mode MPLS network in which R1 and R2 perform the ATM Edge LSR function while LS1010 ATM switches A1 and A2 serve as the ATM LSR.

Figure 2-7 *Cell-Mode MPLS Network*

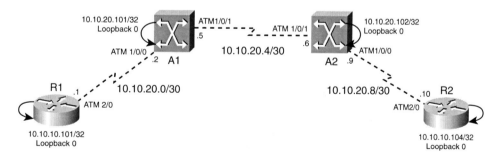

Basic Cell-Mode MPLS Configuration Flowchart for Edge LSRs

Figure 2-8 shows the configuration flowchart to set up basic cell-mode configuration on the Edge LSR R1 and R2.

Figure 2-8   *Basic Cell-Mode MPLS Configuration Flowchart for Edge ATM LSR*

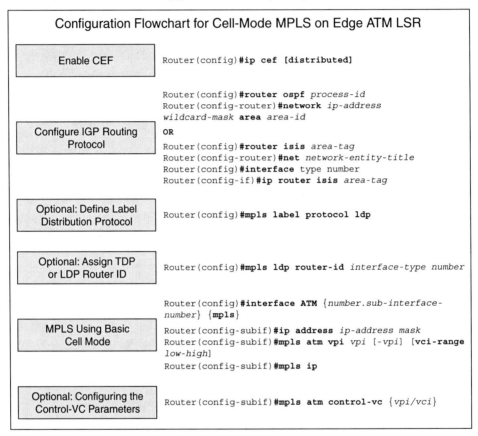

Basic Cell-Mode MPLS Configuration Flowchart for LSRs

Figure 2-9 shows the configuration flowchart for LSR A1 and A2.

Basic Cell-Mode MPLS Configuration Steps

The configurations for basic cell-mode MPLS are based on the configuration flowcharts outlined in Figure 2-8 and Figure 2-9. The functions of the Edge ATM LSRs are performed by routers R1 and R2, and the ATM switches A1 and A2 function as ATM LSRs in the cell-mode MPLS domain.

Figure 2-9 *Basic Cell-Mode MPLS Configuration Flowchart for ATM LSR*

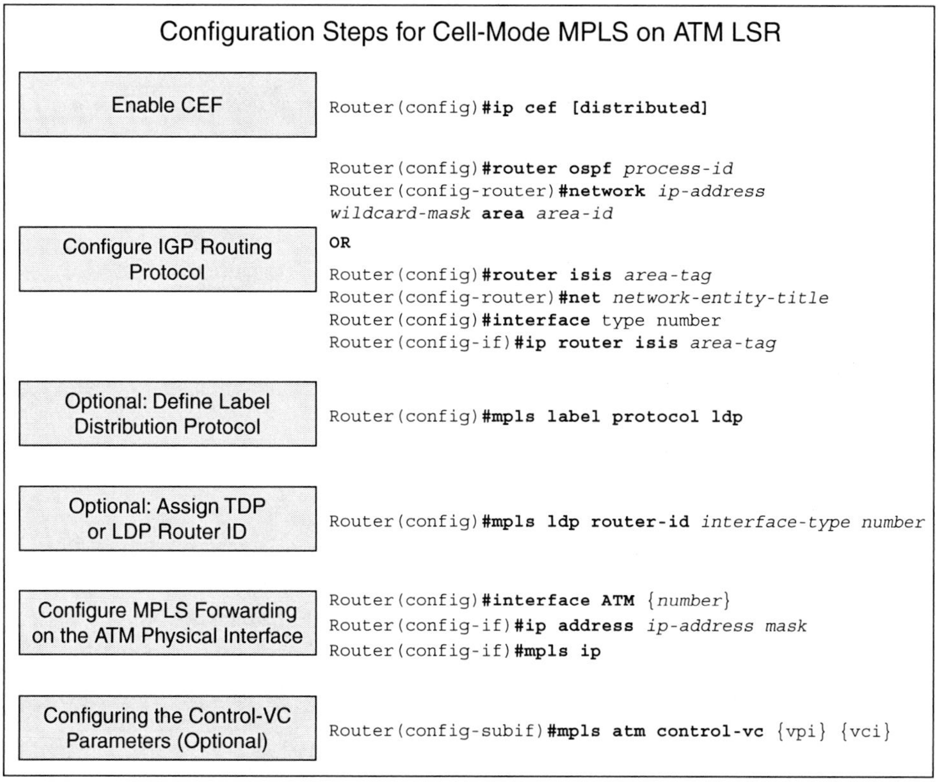

```
              Configuration Steps for Cell-Mode MPLS on ATM LSR

    ┌─────────────────────────┐
    │       Enable CEF        │    Router(config)#ip cef [distributed]
    └─────────────────────────┘

                                   Router(config)#router ospf process-id
                                   Router(config-router)#network ip-address
                                   wildcard-mask area area-id
    ┌─────────────────────────┐    OR
    │ Configure IGP Routing   │
    │       Protocol          │    Router(config)#router isis area-tag
    └─────────────────────────┘    Router(config-router)#net network-entity-title
                                   Router(config)#interface type number
                                   Router(config-if)#ip router isis area-tag

    ┌─────────────────────────┐
    │ Optional: Define Label  │    Router(config)#mpls label protocol ldp
    │ Distribution Protocol   │
    └─────────────────────────┘

    ┌─────────────────────────┐
    │  Optional: Assign TDP   │    Router(config)#mpls ldp router-id interface-type number
    │    or LDP Router ID     │
    └─────────────────────────┘

    ┌─────────────────────────┐    Router(config)#interface ATM {number}
    │ Configure MPLS Forwarding│   Router(config-if)#ip address ip-address mask
    │ on the ATM Physical Interface│ Router(config-if)#mpls ip
    └─────────────────────────┘

    ┌─────────────────────────┐
    │ Configuring the Control-VC│  Router(config-subif)#mpls atm control-vc {vpi} {vci}
    │  Parameters (Optional)  │
    └─────────────────────────┘
```

Configuration Steps for Edge ATM LSR

This section outlines the steps in the configuration of the Edge ATM LSR R1 for ATM or cell-mode MPLS. Ensure that loopback and interface IP addresses are preconfigured before following the steps:

Step 1   **Enable CEF**—As shown in Example 2-24, enable CEF globally. Repeat the same steps on R2.

Example 2-24 *Enable CEF*

```
R1(config)#ip cef
```

Step 2   **Configure the IGP routing protocol**—As shown in Example 2-25, configure OSPF as the IGP routing protocol. Repeat the steps on R2.

Example 2-25 *Configure IGP for IP Reachability*

```
R1(config)#router ospf 100
R1(config-router)#network 10.10.0.0 0.0.0.255 area 0
```

Step 3   **Configure MPLS forwarding on the interface**—Create an MPLS sub-interface on the ATM link to the connected ATM switch. Enable MPLS forwarding on the ATM subinterface. Example 2-26 demonstrates this step.

Example 2-26 *Enable MPLS Forwarding*

```
R1(config)#interface atm2/0.1 mpls
R1(config-subif)#description Connection to A1
R1(config-subif)#ip address 10.10.20.1 255.255.255.252
R1(config-subif)#mpls ip
R2(config)#interface atm2/0.1 mpls
R2(config-subif)#description Connection to A2
R2(config-subif)#ip address 10.10.20.10 255.255.255.252
R2(config-subif)#mpls ip
```

Configuration Steps for ATM LSR

This section demonstrates the steps to configure ATM switches A1 and A2. It is assumed that CEF is enabled on the switches and IP addresses are configured on the appropriate interfaces.

Step 1   **Configure OSPF as the IGP routing protocol**—Example 2-27 summarizes the step to configure OSPF on A1. Repeat the step on A2.

Example 2-27 *Configure IGP for IP Connectivity*

```
A1(config)#router ospf 100
A1(config-router)#network 10.10.0.0 0.0.255.255 area 0
```

Step 2   **Enable MPLS forwarding on the interface**—Enable MPLS forwarding on the ATM physical interfaces, as shown in Example 2-28.

Example 2-28 *Enable MPLS Forwarding*

```
A1(config)#interface atm1/0/0
A1(config-if)#mpls ip
A1(config)#interface atm 1/0/1
A1(config-if)#mpls ip
```

Note that no configuration has been made on the MPLS ATM sub-interfaces on the Edge ATM LSRs or LSRs with regards to the control-vc using the **mpls atm control-vc** command. This implies that all the control plane information is propagated and exchanged using the default control VC VPI/VCI values of 0/32. However, the user can change the control-vc associated on an interface in a cell-mode MPLS network. Changes made to the VPI/VCI values associated to the control-vc on an LSR interface must also be made on the connected LSR's interface to enable proper exchange of control plane information.

Verification of Basic Cell-Mode MPLS Configuration

The following steps outline the verification process for cell-mode MPLS operation. All verifications outlined were performed on Edge ATM LSR R1 and ATM LSR A1:

Step 1 Verify CEF is enabled on the router interfaces on Edge LSR R1, as shown in Example 2-29.

Example 2-29 *Verify CEF Is Enabled on the Interfaces*

```
R1#show cef interface atm2/0
ATM2/0 is up (if_number 12)
<truncated>
 IP CEF switching enabled
 IP Feature Fast switching turbo vector
IP Feature CEF switching turbo vector
```

Step 2 As shown in Example 2-30, verify that MPLS forwarding is enabled on the appropriate interfaces on R1 and A1.

Example 2-30 *Verify MPLS Forwarding*

```
R1#show mpls interfaces
Interface            IP     Tunnel   Operational
ATM2/0.1             Yes    No       Yes          (ATM tagging)
A1#show mpls   interfaces
Interface            IP     Tunnel   Operational
ATM1/0/0             Yes    No       Yes          (ATM tagging)
ATM1/0/1             Yes    No       Yes          (ATM tagging)
```

Step 3 Verify the status of the LDP discovery process by issuing **show mpls ldp discovery**. This command displays neighbor discovery information for LDP and shows the interfaces over which the LDP discovery process is running. Example 2-31 shows neighbor discovery information and interfaces where LDP is running on R1 and A1. The xmit/recv field indicates that the interface is transmitting and receiving LDP discovery Hello packets.

Example 2-31 *Verify MPLS LDP Discovery*

```
R1#show mpls ldp discovery
Local LDP Identifier:
    10.10.10.101:0
LDP Discovery Sources:
    Interfaces:
        ATM2/0.1: xmit/recv
            LDP Id: 10.10.20.101:1; IP addr: 10.10.20.2
            LDP Id: 10.10.20.102:2; IP addr: 10.10.20.6
A1#show mpls ldp discovery
Local LDP Identifier:
    10.10.20.101:0
LDP Discovery Sources:
    Interfaces:
        ATM1/0/0: xmit/recv
            LDP Id: 10.10.10.101:1; IP addr: 10.10.20.1
        ATM1/0/1: xmit/recv
```

Step 4 Issue **show mpls ldp neighbor** to verify the status of LDP neighbor
sessions. Example 2-32 shows that the LDP session between R1
and A1 is operational. Downstream on demand on R1 indicates the
downstream on demand method of label distribution is used for the LDP
session between R1 and A1 in which the LSR (R1) advertises its locally
assigned (incoming) labels to its LDP peer, A1, only when A1 requests
them.

Example 2-32 *LDP Distribution Protocol Neighbor Verification*

```
R1#show mpls ldp neighbor
Peer LDP Ident: 10.10.20.101:1; Local LDP Ident 10.10.10.101:1
        TCP connection: 10.10.20.2.38767 - 10.10.20.1.646
        State: Oper; PIEs sent/rcvd: 371/366; ; Downstream on demand
        Up time: 05:04:40
        LDP discovery sources:
          ATM2/0.1
A1#show mpls ldp neighbor
Peer LDP Ident: 10.10.20.102:2; Local LDP Ident 10.10.20.101:2
        TCP connection: 10.10.20.6.11002 - 10.10.20.5.646
        State: Oper; PIEs sent/rcvd: 28096/28083; ; Downstream on demand
        Up time: 2w3d
        LDP discovery sources:
          ATM1/0/1
Peer LDP Ident: 10.10.10.101:1; Local LDP Ident 10.10.20.101:1
        TCP connection: 10.10.20.1.646 - 10.10.20.2.38767
        State: Oper; PIEs sent/rcvd: 365/369; ; Downstream on demand
        Up time: 05:03:28
        LDP discovery sources:
          ATM1/0/0
```

Step 5 Verify OSPF routing table on R4, as shown in Example 2-33.

Example 2-33 *Verify OSPF Routing*

```
R1#show ip route ospf

       10.0.0.0/8 is variably subnetted, 7 subnets, 2 masks
O        10.10.20.4/30 [110/2] via 10.10.20.2, 05:51:42, ATM2/0.1
O        10.10.20.8/30 [110/3] via 10.10.20.2, 05:51:42, ATM2/0.1
O        10.10.10.104/32 [110/4] via 10.10.20.2, 05:51:42, ATM2/0.1
O        10.10.20.101/32 [110/2] via 10.10.20.2, 05:51:42, ATM2/0.1
O        10.10.20.102/32 [110/3] via 10.10.20.2, 05:51:42, ATM2/0.1
```

Step 6   Issue **ping** to 10.10.10.104 from R1 to ensure reachability, as displayed
in Example 2-34.

Example 2-34 *Verify Reachability*

```
R1#ping 10.10.10.104
Type escape sequence to abort.
Sending 5, 100-byte ICMP Echos to 10.10.10.104, timeout is 2 seconds:
!!!!!
Success rate is 100 percent (5/5), round-trip min/avg/max = 1/2/4 ms
```

Control and Data Forwarding Operation in Basic Cell-Mode MPLS Configuration

Figure 2-10 shows the control and data plane forwarding operation in cell-mode MPLS.

Figure 2-10 *Control and Data Plane Operation in Cell-Mode MPLS*

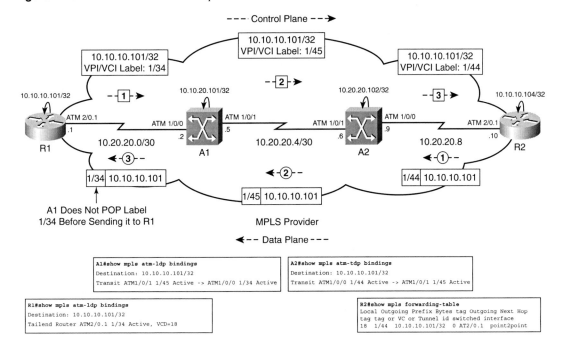

Control Plane Operation in Basic Cell-Mode MPLS Configuration

The control plane operation shows the label propagation for prefix 10.10.10.101/32 from R1 to R4. The following steps are performed in the label propagation process for prefix 10.10.10.101/32:

Step 1   Edge ATM LSR R4 requests a label for the 10.10.10.101/32 prefix using the LDP label mapping request from its downstream neighbor, ATM LSR A2. A2 requests a label for the 10.10.10.101/32 prefix using the LDP label mapping request from its downstream neighbor, ATM LSR A1. A1 in turn requests a label for the 10.10.10.101/32 prefix using the LDP label mapping request from its downstream neighbor, Edge ATM LSR R1. Edge ATM LSR R1 allocates a label to 10.10.10.101/32, which corresponds to its inbound VPI/VCI value 1/34, modifies the entry in the LFIB corresponding to 10.10.10.101/32, and sends it to A1 using an LDP reply. Example 2-35 shows the output of **show mpls atm-ldp bindings**.

Example 2-35 *Label Allocation and Distribution Verification on R1*

```
R1#show mpls forwarding-table
Local  Outgoing     Prefix          Bytes tag  Outgoing   Next Hop
tag    tag or VC    or Tunnel Id    switched   interface
18     1/35         10.10.10.104/32  0          AT2/0.1    point2point
25     1/37         10.10.20.8/30    0          AT2/0.1    point2point
26     1/36         10.10.20.4/30    0          AT2/0.1    point2point
27     1/38         10.10.20.101/32  0          AT2/0.1    point2point
28     1/39         10.10.20.102/32  0          AT2/0.1    point2point
R1#show mpls atm-ldp bindings
 Destination: 10.10.10.104/32
    Headend Router ATM2/0.1 (3 hops) 1/35  Active, VCD=19
 Destination: 10.10.20.4/30
    Headend Router ATM2/0.1 (1 hop) 1/36  Active, VCD=13
 Destination: 10.10.20.8/30
    Headend Router ATM2/0.1 (2 hops) 1/37  Active, VCD=15
 Destination: 10.10.20.101/32
    Headend Router ATM2/0.1 (1 hop) 1/38  Active, VCD=14
 Destination: 10.10.20.102/32
    Headend Router ATM2/0.1 (2 hops) 1/39  Active, VCD=16
 Destination: 10.10.10.101/32
    Tailend Router ATM2/0.1 1/34 Active, VCD=18
```

Step 2   A1 uses the VPI/VCI 1/34 received from R1 as its outbound VPI/VCI value, allocates a free VC that is mapped to the local inbound VPI/VCI 1/45, and modifies the LFIB entry for 10.10.10.101/32. A1 then sends VPI/VCI value 1/45 to A2 via an LDP reply. Example 2-36 shows the output of **show mpls atm-ldp bindings**. ATM LSR A1 prefix 10.10.10.104/32 has been assigned a local tag of 1/35 and an outgoing tag of 1/43. The outgoing tag is received from the downstream ATM LSR A2. During label distribution, the local tag of 1/35 has been propagated upstream to Router R1, which functions as the outgoing tag for the specific prefix 10.10.10.104/32 on R1.

Example 2-36 *Label Allocation and Distribution Verification on A1*

```
A1#show mpls atm-ldp bindings
 Destination: 10.10.20.101/32
    Tailend Switch ATM1/0/1 1/42 Active -> Terminating Active
    Tailend Switch ATM1/0/0 1/38 Active -> Terminating Active
 Destination: 10.10.20.0/30
    Tailend Switch ATM1/0/1 1/43 Active -> Terminating Active
 Destination: 10.10.10.104/32
    Transit ATM1/0/0 1/35 Active -> ATM1/0/1 1/43 Active
 Destination: 10.10.20.4/30
    Tailend Switch ATM1/0/0 1/36 Active -> Terminating Active
 Destination: 10.10.20.8/30
    Transit ATM1/0/0 1/37 Active -> ATM1/0/1 1/44 Active
 Destination: 10.10.20.102/32
    Transit ATM1/0/0 1/39 Active -> ATM1/0/1 1/45 Active
 Destination: 10.10.10.101/32
    Transit ATM1/0/1 1/45 Active -> ATM1/0/0 1/34 Active
```

Step 3   A2 uses the VPI/VCI 1/45 received from A1 as its outbound VPI/VCI value, allocates a free VC that is mapped to the local inbound VPI/VCI 1/44, and modifies the LFIB entry for 10.10.10.101/32. A2 then sends VPI/VCI value 1/44 to R2 via an LDP reply. Example 2-37 shows the output of **show mpls atm-ldp bindings**. As shown in Example 2-37, ATM LSR A2 prefix 10.10.10.104/32 has been assigned a local tag of 1/43 and an outgoing tag of 1/35. The outgoing tag is received from the downstream Router R4. The local tag of 1/43 is propagated upstream to ATM LSR A1 and functions as the next-hop tag or outgoing tag for prefix 10.10.10.104/32 on ATM LSR A1.

Example 2-37 *Label Allocation and Distribution Verification on A2*

```
A2#show mpls atm-ldp bindings
 Destination: 10.10.20.4/30
    Tailend Switch ATM1/0/0 1/33 Active -> Terminating Active
 Destination: 10.10.20.101/32
    Transit ATM1/0/0 1/34 Active -> ATM1/0/1 1/42 Active
 Destination: 10.10.20.102/32
    Tailend Switch ATM1/0/0 1/35 Active -> Terminating Active
    Tailend Switch ATM1/0/1 1/45 Active -> Terminating Active
 Destination: 10.10.20.0/30
    Transit ATM1/0/0 1/36 Active -> ATM1/0/1 1/43 Active
 Destination: 10.10.10.104/32
    Transit ATM1/0/1 1/43 Active -> ATM1/0/0 1/35 Active
 Destination: 10.10.20.8/30
    Tailend Switch ATM1/0/1 1/44 Active -> Terminating Active
 Destination: 10.10.10.101/32
    Transit ATM1/0/0 1/44 Active -> ATM1/0/1 1/45 Active
```

Step 4 Edge ATM LSR R2 uses VPI/VCI value 1/44 received from A2 as its outbound VPI/VCI value and modifies the entry in the LFIB. Example 2-38 shows the output of **show mpls atm-ldp bindings**. As shown in Example 2-38 on Edge ATM LSR R2, the mpls atm-ldp bindings show the local tag of 1/35 assigned to prefix 10.10.10.104/32. This local tag is propagated upstream to ATM LSR A2 and functions as the next-hop tag or outgoing tag for prefix 10.10.10.104/32 on A2.

Example 2-38 *Label Allocation and Distribution Verification on R2*

```
R2#show mpls forwarding-table
Local  Outgoing    Prefix          Bytes tag  Outgoing   Next Hop
tag    tag or VC   or Tunnel Id    switched   interface
16     1/36        10.10.20.0/30   0          AT2/0.1    point2point
17     1/33        10.10.20.4/30   0          AT2/0.1    point2point
18     1/44        10.10.10.101/32 0          AT2/0.1    point2point
19     1/34        10.10.20.101/32 0          AT2/0.1    point2point
20     1/35        10.10.20.102/32 0          AT2/0.1    point2point
R2#show mpls atm-ldp bindings
 Destination: 10.10.20.0/30
     Headend Router ATM2/0.1 (2 hops) 1/36  Active, VCD=16
 Destination: 10.10.20.4/30
     Headend Router ATM2/0.1 (1 hop) 1/33  Active, VCD=13
 Destination: 10.10.20.101/32
     Headend Router ATM2/0.1 (2 hops) 1/34  Active, VCD=15
 Destination: 10.10.20.102/32
     Headend Router ATM2/0.1 (1 hop) 1/35  Active, VCD=14
 Destination: 10.10.10.101/32
     Headend Router ATM2/0.1 (3 hops) 1/44  Active, VCD=18
 Destination: 10.10.10.104/32
     Tailend Router ATM2/0.1 1/35 Active, VCD=14
```

Data Forwarding Operation in Basic Cell-Mode MPLS Configuration

The following steps are performed in the data forwarding path from R4 to prefix 10.10.10.101/32:

Step 1 R4 imposes label 1/44 on the AAL5 cell originating from R4 and destined to 10.10.10.101/32.

Step 2 A2 does an LFIB lookup and swaps label 1/44 with 1/45 and forwards that AAL5 cell to A1.

Step 3 A1 receives the data packet from A2, does an LFIB lookup, swaps label 1/45 with 1/34, and forwards that AAL5 cell to R1. Penultimate hop popping is not supported on ATM devices because the label is part of the ATM cell payload and cannot be removed by ATM switching hardware. Therefore, A1, which is an ATM device, does not perform any penultimate hop popping function.

Final Device Configurations for Basic Cell-Mode MPLS

Example 2-39 through Example 2-42 outline the pertinent configurations for all the devices in the cell-mode MPLS domain.

Example 2-39 *R1 Configuration*

```
hostname R1
!
ip cef
!
interface Loopback0
 ip address 10.10.10.101 255.255.255.255
!
interface ATM2/0
!
interface ATM2/0.1 mpls
 description Connection to A1
 ip address 10.10.20.1 255.255.255.252
 mpls ip
!
router ospf 100
 log-adjacency-changes
 network 10.10.0.0 0.0.255.255 area 0
```

Example 2-40 *A1 Configuration*

```
hostname A1
!
interface ATM1/0/0
description Connection to R1
 ip address 10.10.20.2 255.255.255.252
mpls ip
!
interface ATM1/0/1
 description Connection to A2
 ip address 10.10.20.5 255.255.255.252
mpls ip
!
router ospf 100
 network 10.10.0.0 0.0.255.255 area 0
```

Example 2-41 *A2 Configuration*

```
hostname A2
!
interface ATM1/0/0
 description connection to R2
 ip address 10.10.20.9 255.255.255.252
mpls ip
!
```

continues

Example 2-41 *A2 Configuration (Continued)*

```
interface ATM1/0/1
 description connection to A1
 ip address 10.10.20.6 255.255.255.252
mpls ip
!
router ospf 100
 network 10.10.0.0 0.0.255.255 area 0
 !
```

Example 2-42 *R2 Configuration*

```
hostname R2
!
ip cef
!
interface Loopback0
 ip address 10.10.10.104 255.255.255.255
!
interface ATM2/0
!
interface ATM2/0.1 mpls
 description connection to A2
 ip address 10.10.20.10 255.255.255.252
 mpls ip
!
router ospf 100
 log-adjacency-changes
 network 10.10.0.0 0.0.255.255 area 0
```

Configuring Cell-Mode MPLS with VC-Merge

The VC-merge feature in cell-mode MPLS allows an ATM LSR to aggregate multiple incoming flows with the same destination address into a single outgoing flow. Therefore, when two Edge LSRs are sending packets to the same destination, the ingress label mapping to the two Edge LSRs are mapped to a single outgoing label. The number of VCs required for label switching is greatly reduced as the ATM switch maintains just one outgoing VC label for each destination prefix. VC-merge reduces the label space that needs to be maintained by sharing labels for flows toward the same FEC or prefix.

Figure 2-11 shows a cell-mode MPLS network. This is the same as the network shown in Figure 2-10 except the new Router R3 is added, which is connected to A1. Edge LSRs R1 and R3 share the same label space for the same destination prefixes on Edge ATM LSR R2.

Figure 2-11 *Cell-Mode MPLS Topology for VC-Merge*

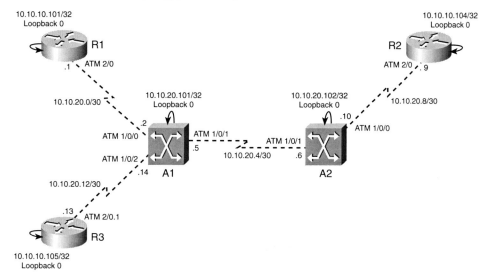

Configuration Flowchart for Cell-Mode MPLS with VC-Merge

The configuration flowchart for Edge ATM LSR for cell-mode MPLS with VC-merge remains the same as what was shown for basic cell-mode MPLS (refer to Figure 2-8). The only difference in the basic cell-mode MPLS configuration block and cell-mode MPLS with VC-merge for ATM LSR is the inclusion of the command shown in Example 2-43.

Example 2-43 *Enabling ATM VC-Merge*

```
A1(config)#mpls ldp atm vc-merge
```

Depending upon the hardware, the ATM VC-merge capability is enabled by default; otherwise, this feature is disabled. Please check Cisco Documentation at cisco.com.

Configuration Steps for Cell-Mode MPLS with VC-Merge on Edge ATM LSR

The configuration steps for cell-mode MPLS with VC-merge on Edge ATM LSR are the same as what was shown earlier in section "Configuration Steps for Edge ATM LSR."

Configuration Steps for Cell-Mode MPLS with VC-Merge on ATM LSR

The configuration steps for cell-mode MPLS with VC-merge on ATM LSR are the same as those shown in the section "Configuration Steps for ATM LSR," except that A1 is enabled with the VC-merge command **mpls ldp atm vc-merge**.

Final Configuration for Devices in Cell-Mode MPLS with VC-Merge

The configurations for R1, R2, and A2 remain the same as what was shown in the section "Final Device Configurations for Basic Cell-Mode MPLS." The configurations for R3 and A1 are shown in Example 2-44 and Example 2-45. Note that the configuration for A1 does not depict the **mpls ldp atm vc-merge** command, which implies that the ATM LSR A1 supports VC-merge functionality by default.

Example 2-44 *R3 Configuration (Truncated)*

```
hostname R3
!
ip cef
!
interface Loopback0
 ip address 10.10.10.105 255.255.255.255
!
interface ATM2/0
!
interface ATM2/0.1 mpls
 description connection to A1
 ip address 10.10.20.13 255.255.255.252
 mpls ip
!
router ospf 100
network 10.10.0.0 0.0.255.255 area 0
```

Example 2-45 *A1 Configuration (Truncated)*

```
hostname A1
!
interface Loopback0
 ip address 10.10.20.101 255.255.255.255
!
interface ATM1/0/0
 description Connection to R1
 ip address 10.10.20.2 255.255.255.252
mpls ip
!
interface ATM1/0/1
 description Connection to A2
 ip address 10.10.20.5 255.255.255.252
 mpls ip
!
interface ATM1/0/2
 description connection to R5
 ip address 10.10.20.14 255.255.255.252
mpls ip
!
router ospf 100
 network 10.10.0.0 0.0.255.255 area 0
```

Verification Steps for Cell-Mode MPLS with VC-Merge on ATM LSR

The following steps outline the verification procedure for cell-mode MPLS over ATM implementation with VC-merge on the ATM LSRs:

Step 1   Verify if ATM VC-merge is enabled on the ATM LSR by issuing the **show mpls atm-ldp capability** command on the ATM LSR. The output of this command is shown in Example 2-46.

Example 2-46 *ATM VC-Merge Capability*

```
A1#show mpls atm-ldp capability

              VPI          VCI           Alloc   Odd/Even VC-Merge
ATM1/0/0      Range        Range         Scheme  Scheme   IN   OUT
   Negotiated [1 - 1]      [33 - 16383]  UNIDIR            -    -
   Local      [1 - 1]      [33 - 16383]  UNIDIR            EN   EN
   Peer       [1 - 1]      [33 - 65530]  UNIDIR            -    -

              VPI          VCI           Alloc   Odd/Even VC-Merge
ATM1/0/1      Range        Range         Scheme  Scheme   IN   OUT
   Negotiated [1 - 1]      [33 - 16383]  UNIDIR            -    -
   Local      [1 - 1]      [33 - 16383]  UNIDIR            EN   EN
   Peer       [1 - 1]      [33 - 16383]  UNIDIR            -    -
```

Step 2   When VC-merge is implemented on A1, destinations reachable by R1 and R3 via A1 are provided the same next-hop labels. When a lookup of the label bindings for prefixes on ATM LSR A1 is performed, the same outgoing label is used for two different incoming labels from two different flows that map to the same destination prefix. This is shown in Example 2-47. The ATM LSR A1 maps two incoming labels, 1/35 and 1/34, from Edge ATM LSRs R1 and R5, respectively, to the same outgoing label 1/43 for the destination prefix 10.10.10.104/32 located on R1.

Example 2-47 *A1 VC-Merge Verification*

```
A1#show mpls atm-ldp bindings 10.10.10.104 255.255.255.255
Destination: 10.10.10.104/32
    Transit ATM1/0/0 1/35 Active -> ATM1/0/1 1/43 Active
    Transit ATM1/0/2 1/34 Active -> ATM1/0/1 1/43 Active
```

Configuring MPLS Over ATM Without VC-Merge

In MPLS over ATM without VC-merge, each path (with the same ingress router and same Forwarding Equivalent Class [FEC]) consumes one label VC on each interface along the path. This results in unnecessary exhaustion of the already scarce label space.

The network topology remains the same as what was shown in the section "Configuring Cell-Mode MPLS with VC-Merge." All configurations remain the same except, as shown in Figure 2-11, where VC-merge is disabled on A1. Example 2-48 highlights the configuration to disable VC-merge.

Example 2-48 *Disabling VC-Merge on A1*

```
A1(config)#no mpls ldp atm vc-merge
```

Verify MPLS Over ATM Without VC-Merge

As shown in Example 2-49, when VC-merge is disabled on ATM LSR A1, flows to the same destination are assigned different outgoing VC labels. **show mpls atm-ldp bindings** on A1 shows two different outgoing labels, 1/33 and 1/36, are assigned to the data flows from R3 and R1, respectively, to destination prefix 10.10.10.104/32. Because VC-merge is not used, one VC is allocated per route as determined by the prefix in the routing table.

Example 2-49 *A1: Disabled VC-Merge Verification*

```
A1#show mpls atm-ldp bindings 10.10.10.104 255.255.255.255
Destination: 10.10.10.104/32
    Transit ATM1/0/2 1/34 Active -> ATM1/0/1 1/33 Active
    Transit ATM1/0/0 1/33 Active -> ATM1/0/1 1/36 Active
```

MPLS Over VP Tunnels Configuration and Verification

A VP tunnel is a method of linking two private ATM networks across a public network that does not support SVCs. The VP tunnel provides a permanent path through the public network. VP tunnels are multiplexing/demultiplexing multiple VCs from multiple interfaces, or from the same interface, to the VP tunnel interface. When multiplexing, it changes the VPI field of VCs that goes through the VP to the same as the VPI number on the VPs. VCI numbers, though, can be arbitrary. However, for specific VCs, the VCI numbers on both VP tunnel interfaces (originating and terminating) need to be the same. In this section, you configure VP tunnels on the ATM switches to carry label information for MPLS over ATM VP tunnels. Figure 2-12 shows an MPLS network using VP tunnels.

Figure 2-12 *MPLS Over VP Tunnels Topology*

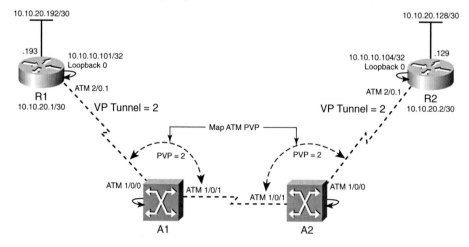

Configuration Flowchart for MPLS over VP Tunnels on Edge ATM LSR

The basic configuration flowchart for MPLS over VP tunnel is the same as what was shown in the section "Basic Cell-Mode MPLS Configuration and Verification" (refer to Figure 2-8).

Configuration Flowchart for Creating an ATM PVP on ATM Switch

The configuration flowchart for creating an ATM PVP is shown in Figure 2-13.

Figure 2-13 *Configuration Flowchart for MPLS Over VP Tunnel on ATM LSR*

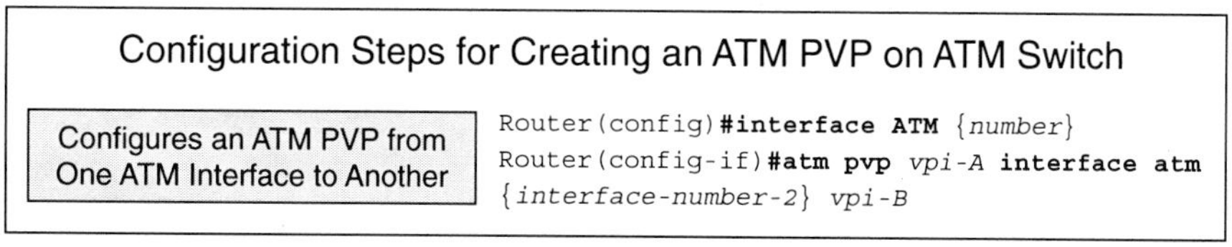

Configuration Steps for Creating an ATM PVP on ATM Switch

Configures an ATM PVP from One ATM Interface to Another	`Router(config)#interface ATM {number}`
	`Router(config-if)#atm pvp vpi-A interface atm`
	`{interface-number-2} vpi-B`

Configuration Steps for MPLS over VP Tunnels

Ensure necessary IP addresses are configured prior to following these steps. The steps to configure MPLS over VP tunnels are as follows:

Step 1 A VP connection is like a bundle of VCs, transporting all cells with a common VPI, rather than a specific VPI and VCI. A PVP is a permanent VP (like PVC). Example 2-50 shows how to configure the internal cross-connect (within the switch router) PVP on switch A1 between interface 1/0/0, VPI = 2 and interface 1/0/1, VPI = 2, and switch A2 between interface 1/0/0, VPI = 2 and interface 1/0/1, VPI = 2.

Example 2-50 *Configure VP Tunnels on ATM Switches*

```
A1(config)#interface ATM1/0/1
A1(config-if)# description Connection to A2
A1(config-if)# no ip address
A1(config-if)# atm pvp 2 interface  ATM1/0/0 2
A2(config)#interface ATM1/0/1
A2(config-if)# description connection to A1
A2(config-if)# no ip address
A2(config-if)# atm pvp 2 interface  ATM1/0/0 2
```

Step 2 Configure the VP tunnel using **mpls atm vp-tunnel** *vpi* **vc-range** {*start-of-vci-range-end-of-vci-range*} under the MPLS ATM subinterface. Enable MPLS on the created subinterface, as shown in Example 2-51.

Example 2-51 *Configure VP Tunnel on ATM MPLS Subinterface*

```
R1(config)#interface ATM2/0.1 mpls
R1(config-subif)# description Connection to A1
R1(config-subif)# ip address 10.10.20.1 255.255.255.252
R1(config-subif)# mpls atm vp-tunnel 2 vci-range 33-65535
R1(config-subif)#mpls ip

R2(config)#interface ATM2/0.1 mpls
R2(config-subif)# description connection to A2
R2(config-subif)# ip address 10.10.20.2 255.255.255.252
R2(config-subif)# mpls atm vp-tunnel 2 vci-range 33-65535
R2(config-subif)#mpls ip
```

Step 3   Configure IGP for IP connectivity across the VP tunnel on R1 and R2, as shown in Example 2-52.

Example 2-52 *Configure IGP*

```
R1(config)#router ospf 100
R1(config-router)# network 10.10.0.0 0.0.255.255 area 0
```

Verification Steps for MPLS over VP Tunnels

The steps to verify MPLS over VP tunnels are as follows:

Step 1   Verify operation of PVP on the ATM switches, as shown in Example 2-53.

Example 2-53 *Verify PVP Status*

```
A1#show atm vp
Interface    VPI    Type   X-Interface    X-VPI      Status
ATM1/0/0     2      PVP    ATM1/0/1       2          UP
ATM1/0/1     2      PVP    ATM1/0/0       2          UP

A2#show atm vp
Interface    VPI    Type   X-Interface    X-VPI      Status
ATM1/0/0     2      PVP    ATM1/0/1       2          UP
ATM1/0/1     2      PVP    ATM1/0/0       2          UP
```

Step 2   Verify OSPF routes on R1 by issuing **show ip route ospf**. Example 2-54 shows the networks received on R1 from R2.

Example 2-54 *Verify OSPF Routes*

```
R1#show ip route ospf
      10.0.0.0/8 is variably subnetted, 7 subnets, 2 masks
O        10.10.20.2/32 [110/1] via 10.10.20.2, 00:12:25, ATM2/0.1
O        10.10.10.104/32 [110/2] via 10.10.20.2, 00:12:25, ATM2/0.1
O        10.10.20.128/30 [110/11] via 10.10.20.2, 00:12:25, ATM2/0.1
```

Step 3   Verify connectivity across the VP tunnel using the **ping** command, as shown in Example 2-55.

Example 2-55 *Verify Connectivity Using Ping*

```
R1#ping ip 10.10.20.129 source 10.10.20.193
Type escape sequence to abort.
Sending 5, 100-byte ICMP Echos to 10.10.20.129, timeout is 2 seconds:
Packet sent with a source address of 10.10.20.193
!!!!!
Success rate is 100 percent (5/5), round-trip min/avg/max = 1/1/4 ms
```

Final Device Configurations for MPLS over VP Tunnels

The final device configuration for R1, A1, A2, and R2 is shown in Example 2-56 through Example 2-59.

Example 2-56 *R1 Configuration*

```
hostname R1
!
ip cef
!
interface Loopback0
 ip address 10.10.10.101 255.255.255.255
!
interface Ethernet0
ip address 10.10.20.193 255.255.255.252
!
interface ATM2/0
!
interface ATM2/0.1 mpls
 description Connection to A1
 ip address 10.10.20.1 255.255.255.252
 mpls ip
 mpls atm vp-tunnel 2 vci-range 33-65535
!
router ospf 100

  network 10.10.0.0 0.0.255.255 area 0
```

Example 2-57 *A1 Configuration*

```
hostname A1
!
interface ATM1/0/0
description Connection to R1

!
interface ATM1/0/1
 description Connection to A2
atm pvp 2  interface  ATM1/0/0 2
!
```

Example 2-58 *A2 Configuration*

```
hostname A2
!
interface ATM1/0/0
 description connection to R2
!
interface ATM1/0/1
 description connection to A1
 atm pvp 2  interface  ATM1/0/0 2
!
```

Example 2-59 *R2 Configuration*

```
hostname R2
!
ip cef
!
interface Loopback0
 ip address 10.10.10.104 255.255.255.255
!
interface Ethernet0
 ip address 10.10.20.129 255.255.255.252
!
interface ATM2/0
!
interface ATM2/0.1 mpls
 description connection to A2
 ip address 10.10.20.10 255.255.255.252
 mpls ip
 mpls atm vp-tunnel 2 vci-range 33-65535
!
router ospf 100
network 10.10.0.0 0.0.255.255 area 0
```

Implementing Cell-Mode MPLS with BPX8600 and 7200 as Label Switch Controller

Cell-mode MPLS can also be implemented by separating the control and data plane functions of an ATM LSR. The control plane function is performed by a device called the LSC or label switch controller, and the data plane function can be performed by an ATM switch such as the BPX8600 Series ATM switches. In the BPX with LSC design, the LSC is connected to the BPX ATM switch by trunks that can carry PVCs, SVCs, or MPLS Label VCs (LVCs). The control software is physically located in the LSC that is connected to the ATM switch by a physical connection also called the virtual switch interface (VSI) control link. The VSI control link could be an STM-1 link connected to a single port of a broadband switching module (BXM) linecard on the BPX8600. This is shown in Figure 2-14.

Figure 2-14 *BPX with LSC as LSR*

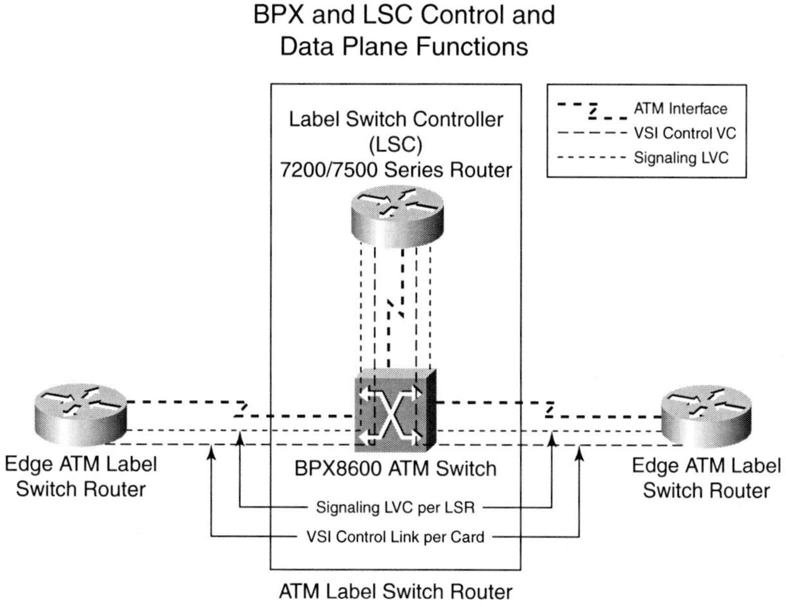

In Figure 2-14, the functions control plane is implemented using a BPX+LSC. The figure outlines a connection from each of the Edge ATM LSRs to the LSC connected to the BPX switch using LVCs. These signaling LVCs are maintained per LSR that the BPX+LSC is connected to. In addition, VSI control links are maintained per card on the BPX.

From a data plane perspective, data label VCs bypass the LSC and are switched using the BPX ports. Therefore, in the data plane, the traffic via the ATM label switch router traverses only the BPX ATM switch and not the LSC.

The signaling label VCs are on VPI/VCI values of 0/32 by default and will be cross-connected to a different VCI on the switch control link between the BPX and LSC. One key thing to note is that the LSC functions as the *VSI master* and the BPX functions as the *VSI slave*.

Configuring BPX+LSC as ATM LSR

This section deals with the configuration of a BPX+LSC as an ATM LSR to implement cell-mode MPLS. The topology used to implement this configuration is shown in Figure 2-15.

Figure 2-15 *BPX and LSC as ATM LSR: Topology*

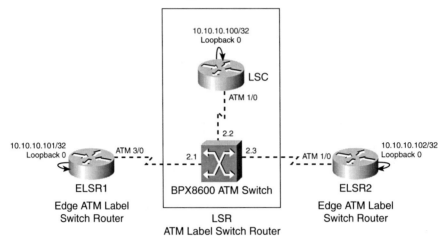

Figure 2-15 shows the physical connections for this section in which two Edge ATM LSRs are connected to a BPX 8600 switch. The LSC (7200 router) is also connected on the same switch. The numbers 2.1, 2.2, and 2.3 in Figure 2-15 pertain to *slot.port* on the BPX 8600 switch. The only IP addresses shown in this figure are those of the loopbacks on the LSR and ELSRs. Figure 2-16 shows the Edge ATM LSRs connected to the LSC in the control plane using the VSI control VCs as well as the signaling LVCs that originate from an *mpls* subinterface on the Edge ATM LSR and terminate on an *XtagATM* interface on the LSC. The XtagATM interface controls the trunks on the BPX that are connected to other LSRs.

Figure 2-16 *BPX and LSC as ATM LSR: Control Plane*

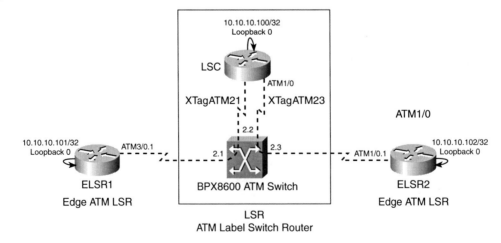

Configuring the BPX

The steps to configure the BPX are as follows:

Step 1   Verify the cards on the BPX by issuing **dspcds** command. As shown in
Example 2-60, the BXM-155 card connects and configures the trunks on
the BPX as well as the appropriate resources on the ports.

Example 2-60 *Viewing Cards on BPX*

```
bpxa             TRM   cisco:1          BPX 8620  9.2.30    Oct. 8 2004  15:18 MST

    FrontCard    BackCard                    FrontCard    BackCard
    Type   Rev  Type   Rev  Status          Type   Rev  Type  Rev   Status
 1  BME-622 KMB  SM-2   BD   Standby      9  Empty
 2  BXM-155 FJL  MM-8   BB   Active      10  Empty
 3  BXM-T3  FJL  TE3-12BA    Active      11  Empty
 4  BXM-622 FML  SM-2   BD   Standby     12  Empty
 5  BXM-155 FAL  SM-4   BB   Standby     13  Empty
 6  BXM-622 FPH  SM-2   BE   Standby     14  Empty
 7  BCC-4   HDM  LM-2   AC   Active      15  ASM   ACC  LMASM AC    Active
 8  Empty reserved for Card

Last Command: dspcds
Next Command:
```

Step 2   Enable the trunks on the ports 2.1, 2.2, and 2.3. This is as shown in
Example 2-60. Example 2-61 shows only the command to be used in the
"next command" section to enable the three trunks connecting to the two
Edge ATM LSRs as well as the LSC.

Example 2-61 *Configuring Trunks on the BPX (Commands)*

```
Next Command: uptrk 2.1
Next Command: uptrk 2.2
Next Command: uptrk 2.3
```

When the trunks are configured, view the trunk configuration using the
dsptrks command, as shown in Example 2-62.

Example 2-62 *Viewing Trunk Configuration*

```
bpxa             TRM   cisco:1          BPX 8620  9.2.30    Oct. 8 2004  15:26 MST

TRK       Type      Current Line Alarm Status          Other End
 2.1      OC3       Clear - OK                          -
 2.2      OC3       Clear - OK                          -
 2.3      OC3       Clear - OK                          -

Last Command: dsptrks
Next Command:
```

Step 3 Configuration of resources applied to the trunks already configured is performed using the **cnfrsrc** command on the BPX, as shown in Example 2-63.

Example 2-63 *Configuring Resources*

```
bpxa            TRM     cisco:1          BPX 8620   9.2.30     Oct. 8 2004   15:29 MST
Port/Trunk : 2.1
Maximum PVC LCNS:                  256        Maximum PVC Bandwidth:247207
                                              (Statistical Reserve: 1000)
Partition 1
Partition State :                  Enabled
Minimum VSI LCNS:                  600
Maximum VSI LCNS:                  1500
Start VSI VPI:                     240
End VSI VPI :                      255
Minimum VSI Bandwidth :            105000  Maximum VSI Bandwidth :            105000
VSI ILMI Config         :          0
VSI Topo Dsc            :          0        VSI Ses Ctrlr Id      :            255

Last Command: cnfrsrc 2.1 256 247207 y 1 e 600 1500 240 255 105000 105000
```

The command in Example 2-63 can be explained as "configure resources for trunk 2.1 where the maximum PVC LCNs are 256, the maximum PVC bandwidth is 247207; editing of VSI information is enabled, Partition ID is 1 and is enabled; the maximum VSI LCNs are 600 and the maximum VSI LCNs are 1500; the VSI VPI-range is configured to be between 240–255 and the minimum and maximum VSI bandwidths is 105000."

Repeat this command to configure resources for trunks 2.2 and 2.3. However, all trunks need to be part of the same partition (1). When completed, a **dsprsrc** issued for the appropriate trunk and partition IDs, as shown in Example 2-64, shows the resources allocated to the trunk.

Example 2-64 *Display Configured Resources*

```
bpxa            TRM     cisco:1          BPX 8620   9.2.30     Oct. 8 2004   15:37 MST
Port/Trunk : 2.2
Maximum PVC LCNS:                  256        Maximum PVC Bandwidth:247207
                                              (Statistical Reserve: 1000)
Partition 1
Partition State :                  Enabled
Minimum VSI LCNS:                  512
Maximum VSI LCNS:                  1500
Start VSI VPI:                     240
End VSI VPI :                      255
Minimum VSI Bandwidth :            105000  Maximum VSI Bandwidth :            105000
VSI ILMI Config         :          0
VSI Topo Dsc            :          0        VSI Ses Ctrlr Id      :            255

Last Command: dsprsrc 2.2 1
```

Step 4   MPLS labeled packets use the queues 10–14 on each port (one queue per class). To enable MPLS packet forwarding, configure the queues using the **cnfqbin** command. Example 2-65 shows the command to configure the qbin 10 on BPX trunk 2.2 as well as the output of the configuration.

Example 2-65 *Configuring Qbin's on BPX Ports for MPLS*

```
bpxa              TRM   cisco:1           BPX 8620  9.2.30     Oct. 8 2004  15:43 MST


Qbin Database 2.2 on BXM qbin 10          (Configured by User)
                                          (EPD Enabled on this qbin)


Qbin State:              Enabled
Discard Threshold:       65536 cells
EPD Threshold:           95%
High CLP Threshold:      100%
EFCI Threshold:          40%
Last Command: cnfqbin 2.2 10 e n 65536 95 100 40
```

Step 5   Finally, add an LSC shelf as a VSI master using the **addshelf** command. In Example 2-66, the first "1" after "VSI" is the VSI controller ID, which must be set the same on both the BPX 8650 and the LSC. The default controller ID on the LSC is "1." The second "1" after "VSI" is the partition ID that indicates this is a controller for partition 1. The "v" stands for a VSI controller.

Example 2-66 *Adding VSI Master Shelf*

```
bpxa              TRM   cisco:1           BPX 8620  9.2.30     Oct. 8 2004  15:48 MST
                        BPX 8620 Interface Shelf Information
Trunk    Name        Type      Part Id   Ctrl Id       Control_VC       Alarm
                                                       VPI   VCIRange
 2.2     VSI         VSI         1          1           0     40-54      OK

Last Command: addshelf 2.2 v 1 1 0 40
```

To verify, perform a **dsptrks**, and the trunk 2.2 appears with VSI on the other end column to show that a VSI master systems or device is connected on trunk 2.2, as shown in Example 2-67.

Example 2-67 *Verification of VSI*

```
a                 TRM   cisco:1           BPX 8620  9.2.30   Oct. 8 2004  15:51 MST

TRK       Type        Current Line Alarm Status          Other End
 2.1      OC3         Clear - OK                          -
 2.2      OC3         Clear - OK                          VSI(VSI)
 2.3      OC3         Clear - OK                          -
```

Configuration of the Label Switch Controller

Configuration of the LSC involves enabling the 7200/7500 series as a LSC for the BPX shelf and configuration of XTagATM interfaces to control the trunks on the BPX shelf:

Step 1 Configure the ATM interface connected to the BPX trunk 2.2 to be the VSI control link between the BPX and the 7200/7500. See Example 2-68.

Example 2-68 *Configure 7200/7500 Port as a LSC Port*

```
LSC(config)#interface ATM1/0
LSC(config-if)# no ip address
LSC(config-if)# tag-control-protocol vsi
```

Step 2 Configure the XTagATM interfaces as control links for the trunks 2.1 and 2.3 on the BPX using the **extended port** command on the LSC, as displayed in Example 2-69. Note that the numbering of the XTagATM interfaces maps to the actual trunk ports that they control on the BPX shelf. Therefore, XTagATM interface 21 controls BPX trunk 2.1, and XTagATM interface 23 controls BPX trunk 2.3.

Example 2-69 *Configure Control Links Using XTagATM Interfaces on LSC*

```
LSC(config)#interface ATM1/0
LSC(config-if)# no ip address
LSC(config-if)# tag-control-protocol vsi

LSC(config-if)#interface XTagATM21
LSC(config-if)# ip address 10.10.10.2 255.255.255.252
LSC(config-if)# extended-port ATM1/0 bpx 2.1
LSC(config-if)# mpls ip
LSC(config-if)#interface XTagATM23
LSC(config-if)# ip address 10.10.10.6 255.255.255.252
LSC(config-if)# extended-port ATM1/0 bpx 2.3
LSC(config-if)# mpls ip
```

Step 3 Configure OSPF as the IGP on the LSC, and include all interfaces for OSPF routing. See Example 2-70.

Example 2-70 *Configure IGP (OSPF) on LSC*

```
LSC(config)#router ospf 100
LSC(config-router)# log-adjacency-changes
LSC(config-router)# network 10.10.10.0 0.0.0.255 area 0
```

Step 4 Verify the operation of the VSI control interfaces using the **show controllers vsi status** command on the LSC. See Example 2-71.

Example 2-71 *Verify VSI Controller Status*

```
LSC#show controllers vsi status
Interface Name              IF Status   IFC State  Physical Descriptor
XTagATM21                        up        ACTIVE   0.2.1.0
switch control port             n/a        ACTIVE   0.2.2.0
XTagATM23                        up        ACTIVE   0.2.3.0
```

Configuration of Edge ATM LSRs

The configuration of the Edge ATM LSRs contains the same configuration as that of Edge ATM LSRs when implementing basic cell-mode MPLS, involving configuration of an MPLS subinterface under the ATM physical interface and other ATM-TDP parameters. OSPF is the IGP routing protocol. See Example 2-72.

Example 2-72 *Configuration of Edge ATM LSR*

```
ELSR1(config)#interface ATM3/0
ELSR1(config-if)# no ip address
ELSR1(config-if)#interface ATM3/0.1 mpls
ELSR1(config-subif)# ip address 10.10.10.1 255.255.255.252
ELSR1(config-subif)# mpls atm vpi 240-255
ELSR1(config-subif)# mpls ip
ELSR1(config)#router ospf 100
ELSR1(config-router)# router-id 10.10.10.101
ELSR1(config-router)# network 10.10.10.0 0.0.0.255 area 0
```
```
ELSR2(config)#interface ATM1/0
ELSR2(config-if)# no ip address
ELSR2(config-if)#interface ATM1/0.1 mpls
ELSR2(config-subif)# ip address 10.10.10.5 255.255.255.252
ELSR2(config-subif)# mpls atm vpi 240-255
ELSR2(config-subif)# mpls ip
ELSR2(config-subif)#router ospf 100
ELSR2(config-router)# network 10.10.10.0 0.0.0.255 area 0
```

The key command to be added in Example 2-72 is **mpls atm vpi**, which defines the VPI range to be used for the LVCs. This needs to match the configuration of the BPX, as shown in Example 2-64.

Verification of Cell-Mode MPLS with BPX+LSC Operation

Step 1   Verify TDP neighbor discovery and neighbor status on ELSR1, ELSR2, and LSC. Note that, because the LSC is only capable of ATM-TDP, the peering process appears as a TDP neighbor relationship and not a ATM-LDP neighbor relationship. See Example 2-73.

Example 2-73 *TDP Neighbor Verification*

```
ELSR1#show mpls ldp neighbor
    Peer TDP Ident: 10.10.10.100:1; Local TDP Ident 10.10.10.101:1
        TCP connection: 10.10.10.2.11375 - 10.10.10.1.711
        State: Oper; PIEs sent/rcvd: 813/809; Downstream on demand
        Up time: 11:39:02
        TDP discovery sources:
          ATM3/0.1, Src IP addr: 10.10.10.2
ELSR1#show mpls ldp discovery
  Local LDP Identifier:
    10.10.10.101:0
```

continues

Example 2-73 *TDP Neighbor Verification (Continued)*

```
            Discovery Sources:
            Interfaces:
                ATM3/0.1 (tdp): xmit/recv
                    TDP Id: 10.10.10.100:1; IP addr: 10.10.10.2
ELSR2#show mpls ldp neighbor
    Peer TDP Ident: 10.10.10.100:2; Local TDP Ident 10.10.10.102:1
        TCP connection: 10.10.10.6.11376 - 10.10.10.5.711
        State: Oper; PIEs sent/rcvd: 813/813; Downstream on demand
        Up time: 11:39:47
        TDP discovery sources:
            ATM1/0.1, Src IP addr: 10.10.10.6
ELSR2#show mpls ldp discovery
  Local LDP Identifier:
    10.10.10.102:0
    Discovery Sources:
    Interfaces:
        ATM1/0.1 (tdp): xmit/recv
            TDP Id: 10.10.10.100:2; IP addr: 10.10.10.6
LSC#show tag-switching tdp neighbor
Peer TDP Ident: 10.10.10.101:1; Local TDP Ident 10.10.10.100:1
        TCP connection: 10.10.10.1.711 - 10.10.10.2.11375
        State: Oper; PIEs sent/rcvd: 813/816; ; Downstream on demand
        Up time: 11:42:08
        TDP discovery sources:
            XTagATM21
Peer TDP Ident: 10.10.10.102:1; Local TDP Ident 10.10.10.100:2
        TCP connection: 10.10.10.5.711 - 10.10.10.6.11376
        State: Oper; PIEs sent/rcvd: 816/815; ; Downstream on demand
        Up time: 11:42:06
        TDP discovery sources:
            XTagATM23
LSC#show tag-switching tdp discovery
Local TDP Identifier:
    10.10.10.100:0
TDP Discovery Sources:
    Interfaces:
        XTagATM21: xmit/recv
            TDP Id: 10.10.10.101:1; IP addr: 10.10.10.1
        XTagATM23: xmit/recv
            TDP Id: 10.10.10.102:1; IP addr: 10.10.10.5
```

Step 2   Verify MPLS label exchange on the Edge LSRs, as shown in Example 2-74.

Example 2-74 *MPLS Label Mapping/Exchange Verification*

```
ELSR1#show mpls atm-ldp bindings
 Destination: 10.10.10.4/30
    Headend Router ATM3/0.1 (1 hop) 240/38  Active, VCD=21
 Destination: 10.10.10.100/32
    Headend Router ATM3/0.1 (1 hop) 240/40  Active, VCD=22
```

Example 2-74 *MPLS Label Mapping/Exchange Verification (Continued)*

```
Destination: 10.10.10.102/32
   Headend Router ATM3/0.1 (2 hops) 240/42  Active, VCD=23
Destination: 10.10.10.101/32
   Tailend Router ATM3/0.1 240/33 Active, VCD=19
   Tailend Router ATM3/0.1 240/35 Active, VCD=20
```
```
ELSR2#show mpls atm-ldp bindings
Destination: 10.10.10.0/30
   Headend Router ATM1/0.1 (1 hop) 240/38  Active, VCD=22
Destination: 10.10.10.100/32
   Headend Router ATM1/0.1 (1 hop) 240/40  Active, VCD=23
Destination: 10.10.10.101/32
   Headend Router ATM1/0.1 (2 hops) 240/42  Active, VCD=24
Destination: 10.10.10.102/32
   Tailend Router ATM1/0.1 240/33 Active, VCD=20
   Tailend Router ATM1/0.1 240/35 Active, VCD=21
```

Step 3   Verify IGP connectivity, as illustrated in Example 2-75.

Example 2-75 *Verification of IGP Connectivity*

```
ELSR1#show ip route ospf
     10.0.0.0/8 is variably subnetted, 6 subnets, 3 masks
O       10.10.10.4/30 [110/3] via 10.10.10.2, 12:14:50, ATM3/0.1
O       10.10.10.102/32 [110/4] via 10.10.10.2, 12:14:50, ATM3/0.1
O       10.10.10.100/32 [110/2] via 10.10.10.2, 12:14:50, ATM3/0.1
```
```
ELSR2#show ip route ospf
     10.0.0.0/8 is variably subnetted, 5 subnets, 2 masks
O       10.10.10.0/30 [110/3] via 10.10.10.6, 12:15:17, ATM1/0.1
O       10.10.10.100/32 [110/2] via 10.10.10.6, 12:15:17, ATM1/0.1
O       10.10.10.101/32 [110/4] via 10.10.10.6, 12:15:17, ATM1/0.1
```
```
LSC#show ip route ospf
     10.0.0.0/8 is variably subnetted, 5 subnets, 2 masks
O       10.10.10.102/32 [110/3] via 10.10.10.5, 12:15:37, XTagATM23
O       10.10.10.101/32 [110/3] via 10.10.10.1, 12:15:37, XTagATM21
```

Step 4   Confirm connectivity using ping between ELSRs, as shown in Example 2-76.

Example 2-76 *Verification of Reachability*

```
LSR1#ping 10.10.10.102

Type escape sequence to abort.
Sending 5, 100-byte ICMP Echos to 10.10.10.102, timeout is 2 seconds:
!!!!!
Success rate is 100 percent (5/5), round-trip min/avg/max = 1/2/4
```

Command Reference

Command	Description
Router(config)#**ip cef** [**distributed**]	Enables CEF operation. Use the **distributed** keyword for distributed switching platforms in which line cards maintain an identical copy of the FIB and adjacency tables. The line cards perform the forwarding function between port adapters, relieving the route processor of involvement in the switching operation.
Router(config-if)#**ip route-cache cef**	Enables CEF on the interface.
Router(config-if)#**mpls ip**	Enables MPLS forwarding on the interface.
Router(config)#**router ospf** *process-id* Router(config-router)#**network** *ip-address wild-card mask* **area** *area-id* Router(config-router)#**no auto-summary**	OSPF IGP configuration.
Router(config)#**router isis** *process-id* Router(config-router)#**net** *network-entity-title* Router(config)#**interface** *type number* Router(config-if)#**ip router isis** *process-id*	ISIS IGP configuration.
Router(config)#**mpls label protocol** {**ldp** | **tdp**} Router(config-if)#**mpls label protocol** {**ldp** | **tdp**}	Enables the preferred label distribution protocol as either TDP or LDP on the chassis or per interface.
Router(config)#**no mpls ip propagate-ttl** [**forwarded** | **local**]	Disables IP to label TTL mapping when a packet enters an MPLS-enabled domain.
Router(config)#**mpls ldp router-id** {*interface* | *ip-address*} [**force**]	Configuring the IP address or a specific interface as the router ID for the label distribution protocol. Use the **force** keyword for the configuration to take effect on a router to override earlier router ID selection or configuration.
Router(config)#**mpls label range** *min-label-value max-label-value* [**static** *min-label-value max-label-value*]	Defining label range.
Router(config-if)#**mpls mtu** *bytes*	Defining the MPLS MTU per interface.
Router(config)#**interface atm** *number.sub-interface-number* **mpls**	Configuring a tag-switching subinterface on an Edge ATM LSR for cell-mode MPLS label forwarding.

Command	Description
Router(config-subif)# **mpls atm control-vc** *vpi-value vci-value*	Configuring the control-vc parameters for protocol information exchange (control plane). Default value for control-vc is VPI/VCI of 0/32.
Router(config-subif)# **mpls atm vpi** *start-vpi-value* [*-vci-value*]	Configuring MPLS ATM VPI range (default: 1-1).
Router(config)#**mpls atm ldp vc-merge**	Enabling VC-merge on ATM LSR.
Router(config)#**tag-switching atm maxhops** *value*	Sets maximum hops for bindings from ATM cell-mode domain.
Router(config)#**mpls atm vp-tunnel** *vpi-value* [*vci-value-range*]	Identifies the subinterface as a VP tunnel with specified VPI values.

CHAPTER **3**

Basic MPLS VPN Overview and Configuration

MPLS technology is being widely adopted by service providers worldwide to implement VPNs to connect geographically separated customer sites. Chapters 1 and 2 introduce the basic concepts of MPLS and its operation, as well as configuring MPLS for data forwarding. This chapter builds on that foundation and shows how to use MPLS to provide VPN services to customers. This chapter also presents the terminology and operation of various devices in an MPLS network used to provide VPN services to customers.

The following topics will be covered in this chapter:

- Overlay and peer-to-peer VPN models
- Overview of MPLS VPN components and architecture
- VRFs, route distinguishers, and route targets
- MP-BGP operation and interaction
- Control plane and data plane operation in MPLS VPN
- Configuration of basic MPLS VPN

VPN Categories

VPNs were originally introduced to enable service providers to use common physical infrastructure to implement emulated point-to-point links between customer sites. A customer network implemented with any VPN technology would contain distinct regions under the customer's control called the *customer sites* connected to each other via the *service provider (SP)* network. In traditional router-based networks, different sites belonging to the same customer were connected to each other using dedicated point-to-point links. The cost of implementation depended on the number of customer sites to be connected with these dedicated links. A full mesh of connected sites would consequently imply an exponential increase in the cost associated.

Frame Relay and ATM were the first technologies widely adopted to implement VPNs. These networks consisted of various devices, belonging to either the customer or the service provider, that were components of the VPN solution. Generically, the VPN realm would consist of the following regions:

- **Customer network**—Consisted of the routers at the various customer sites. The routers connecting individual customers' sites to the service provider network were called *customer edge (CE)* routers.

- **Provider network**—Used by the service provider to offer dedicated point-to-point links over infrastructure owned by the service provider. Service provider devices to which the CE routers were directly attached were called *provider edge (PE)* routers. In addition, the service provider network might consist of devices used for forwarding data in the SP backbone called *provider (P)* routers.

Depending on the service provider's participation in customer routing, the VPN implementations can be classified broadly into one of the following:

- **Overlay model**
- **Peer-to-peer model**

When Frame Relay and ATM provided customers with emulated private networks, the provider did not participate in customer routing. The service provider was only responsible for providing the customer with transport of customer data using virtual point-to-point links. As a result, the service provider would only provide customers with virtual circuit connectivity at Layer 2; this implementation was referred to as the *Overlay model.* If the virtual circuit was permanent or available for use by the customer at all times, it was called a permanent virtual circuit (PVC). If the circuit was established by the provider on-demand, it was called a switched virtual circuit (SVC). The primary drawback of an Overlay model was the full mesh of virtual circuits between all customer sites for optimal connectivity (except in the case of hub and spoke or partial hub and spoke deployments). If the number of customer sites was N, N(N-1)/2 was the total number of circuits that would be necessary for optimal routing.

Overlay VPNs were initially implemented by the SP by providing either Layer 1 (physical layer) connectivity or a Layer 2 transport circuit between customer sites. In the Layer 1 implementation, the SP would provide physical layer connectivity between customer sites, and the customer was responsible for all other layers. In the Layer 2 implementation (depicted in Figure 3-1), the SP was responsible for transportation of Layer 2 frames (or cells) between customer sites, which was traditionally implemented using either Frame Relay or ATM switches as PE devices. Therefore, the service provider was not aware of customer routing or routes. Later, overlay VPNs were also implemented using VPN services over IP (Layer 3) with tunneling protocols like L2TP, GRE, and IPSec to interconnect customer sites. In all cases, the SP network was transparent to the customer, and the routing protocols were run directly between customer routers.

Figure 3-1 *Overlay and Peer-to-Peer Models*

Overlay Model

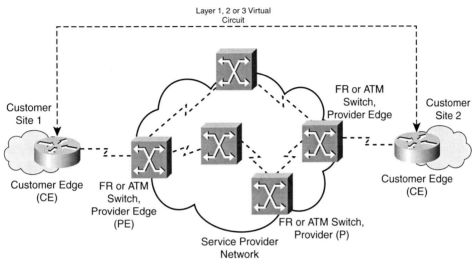

Peer-to-Peer Model

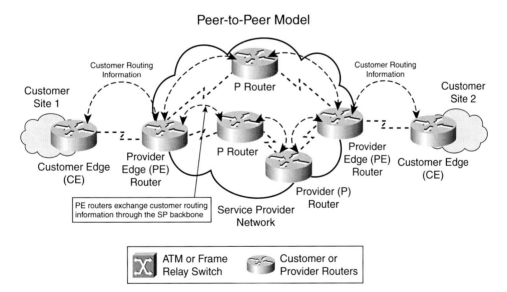

The *peer-to-peer model* was developed to overcome the drawbacks of the Overlay model and provide customers with optimal data transport via the SP backbone. Hence, the service provider would actively participate in customer routing. In the peer-to-peer model, routing information is exchanged between the customer routers and the service provider routers, and customer data is transported across the service provider's core, optimally. Customer routing information is carried between routers in the provider network (P and PE routers) and customer network (CE routers). The peer-to-peer model, consequently, does not require the creation of virtual circuits. As illustrated in Figure 3-1, the CE routers exchange routes with the connected PE routers in the SP domain. Customer routing information is propagated across the SP backbone between PE and P routers and identifies the optimal path from one customer site to another.

Separation of customer-specific routing information is achieved by implementing packet filters at the routers connecting to the customer network. Additionally, IP addressing for the customer is handled by the service provider. This process is also referred to as the shared PE peer-to-peer implementation. Figure 3-2 depicts the various implementations of the peer-to-peer model.

Figure 3-2 *Peer-to-Peer Model Implementations*

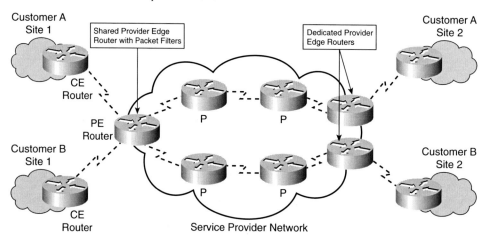

Controlled route distribution was another method of implementing the peer-to-peer model; routers in the core of the service provider's network contained network layer reachability information for all customers' networks. The PE routers (connecting customer network to provider network) in the provider network would contain only information pertaining to their connected customers. A *dedicated* PE router was required for each customer's site connecting to the provider network, and controlled route distribution would occur between P and PE routers in the SP backbone network. Only pertinent customer routes would be propagated to PE routers that were connected to sites belonging to a specific customer. BGP with communities was usually used in the SP backbone because it offered the most versatile route-filtering tools. This implementation is often referred to as the *dedicated PE peer-to-peer model*. This implementation, however, did not prove to be a viable operating business model due to the higher equipment costs that were incurred by the provider to maintain dedicated edge routers for customer sites connecting into the provider backbone. A need arose for deploying efficient VPN architectures that could implement a scalable peer-to-peer model.

MPLS VPN Architecture and Terminology

In the MPLS VPN architecture, the edge routers carry customer routing information, providing optimal routing for traffic belonging to the customer for inter-site traffic. The MPLS-based VPN model also accommodates customers using overlapping address spaces, unlike the traditional peer-to-peer model in which optimal routing of customer traffic required the provider to assign IP addresses to each of its customers (or the customer to implement NAT) to avoid overlapping address spaces. MPLS VPN is an implementation of the peer-to-peer model; the MPLS VPN backbone and customer sites exchange Layer 3 customer routing information, and data is forwarded between customer sites using the MPLS-enabled SP IP backbone.

The MPLS VPN domain, like the traditional VPN, consists of the customer network and the provider network. The MPLS VPN model is very similar to the dedicated PE router model in a peer-to-peer VPN implementation. However, instead of deploying a dedicated PE router per customer, customer traffic is isolated on the same PE router that provides connectivity into the service provider's network for multiple customers. The components of an MPLS VPN shown in Figure 3-3 are highlighted next.

Figure 3-3   *MPLS VPN Network Architecture*

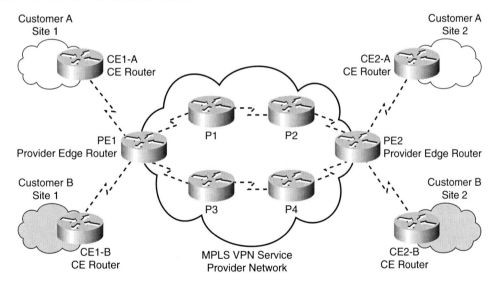

The main components of MPLS VPN architecture are

- **Customer network**, which is usually a customer-controlled domain consisting of devices or routers spanning multiple sites belonging to the customer. In Figure 3-3, the customer network for Customer A consists of the routers CE1-A and CE2-A along with devices in the Customer A sites 1 and 2.

- **CE routers**, which are routers in the customer network that interface with the service provider network. In Figure 3-3, the CE routers for Customer A are CE1-A and CE2-A, and the CE routers for Customer B are CE1-B and CE2-B.

- **Provider network**, which is the provider-controlled domain consisting of provider edge and provider core routers that connect sites belonging to the customer on a shared infrastructure. The provider network controls the traffic routing between sites belonging to a customer along with customer traffic isolation. In Figure 3-3, the provider network consists of the routers PE1, PE2, P1, P2, P3, and P4.

- **PE routers**, which are routers in the provider network that interface or connect to the customer edge routers in the customer network. PE1 and PE2 are the provider edge routers in the MPLS VPN domain for customers A and B in Figure 3-3.

- **P routers**, which are routers in the core of the provider network that interface with either other provider core routers or provider edge routers. Routers P1, P2, P3, and P4 are the provider routers in Figure 3-3.

MPLS VPN Routing Model

An MPLS VPN implementation is very similar to a dedicated router peer-to-peer model implementation. From a CE router's perspective, only IPv4 updates, as well as data, are forwarded to the PE router. The CE router does not need any specific configuration to enable it to be a part of a MPLS VPN domain. The only requirement on the CE router is a routing protocol (or a static/default route) that enables the router to exchange IPv4 routing information with the connected PE router.

In the MPLS VPN implementation, the PE router performs multiple functions. The PE router must first be capable of isolating customer traffic if more than one customer is connected to the PE router. Each customer, therefore, is assigned an independent routing table similar to a dedicated PE router in the initial peer-to-peer discussion. Routing across the SP backbone is performed using a routing process in the global routing table. P routers provide label switching between provider edge routers and are unaware of VPN routes. CE routers in the customer network are not aware of the P routers and, thus, the internal topology of the SP network is transparent to the customer. Figure 3-4 depicts the PE router's functionality.

The P routers are only responsible for label switching of packets. They do not carry VPN routes and do not participate in MPLS VPN routing. The PE routers exchange IPv4 routes with connected CE routers using individual routing protocol contexts. To enable scaling the network to large number of customer VPNs, multiprotocol BGP is configured between PE routers to carry customer routes.

Figure 3-4   *MPLS VPN Architecture*

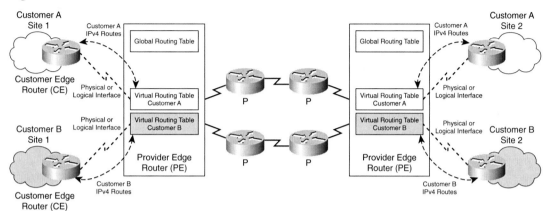

VRF: Virtual Routing and Forwarding Table

Customer isolation is achieved on the PE router by the use of virtual routing tables or instances, also called virtual routing and forwarding tables/instances (VRFs). In essence, it is similar to maintaining multiple dedicated routers for customers connecting into the provider network. The function of a VRF is similar to a global routing table, except that it contains all routes pertaining to a specific VPN versus the global routing table. The VRF also contains a VRF-specific CEF forwarding table analogous to the global CEF table and defines the connectivity requirements and protocols for each customer site on a single PE router. The VRF defines routing protocol contexts that are part of a specific VPN as well as the interfaces on the local PE router that are part of a specific VPN and, hence, use the VRF. The interface that is part of the VRF must support CEF switching. The number of interfaces that can be bound to a VRF is only limited by the number of interfaces on the router, and a single interface (logical or physical) can be associated with only one VRF.

The VRF contains an IP routing table analogous to the global IP routing table, a CEF table, list of interfaces that are part of the VRF, and a set of rules defining routing protocol exchange with attached CE routers (routing protocol contexts). In addition, the VRF also contains VPN identifiers as well as VPN membership information (RD and RT are covered in the next section). Figure 3-5 shows the function of a VRF on a PE router to implement customer routing isolation.

As shown in Figure 3-5, Cisco IOS supports a variety of routing protocols as well as individual routing processes (OSPF, EIGRP, etc.) per router. However, for some routing protocols, such as RIP and BGP, IOS supports only a single instance of the routing protocol. Therefore, to implement per VRF routing using these protocols that are completely isolated from other VRFs, which might use the same PE-CE routing protocols, the concept of routing context was developed.

Figure 3-5 *VRF Implementation on PE Router*

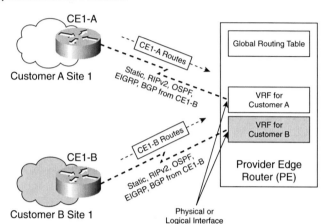

Routing contexts were designed to support isolated copies of the same VPN PE-CE routing protocols. These routing contexts can be implemented as either separated processes, as in the case of OSPF, or as multiple instances of the same routing protocol (in BGP, RIP, etc.). If multiple instances of the same routing protocol are in use, each instance has its own set of parameters.

Cisco IOS currently supports either RIPv2 (multiple contexts), EIGRP (multiple contexts), OSPFv2 (multiple processes), and BGPv4 (multiple contexts) as routing protocols that can be used per VRF to exchange customer routing information between CE and PE.

Note that the VRF interfaces can be either logical or physical, but each interface can be assigned to only one VRF.

Route Distinguisher, Route Targets, MP-BGP, and Address Families

In the MPLS VPN routing model, the PE router provides isolation between customers using VRFs. However, this information needs to be carried between PE routers to enable data transfer between customer sites via the MPLS VPN backbone. The PE router must be capable of implementing processes that enable overlapping address spaces in connected customer networks. The PE router must also learn these routes from attached customer networks and propagate this information using the shared provider backbone. This is done by the association of a route distinguisher (RD) per virtual routing table on a PE router.

A *RD* is a 64-bit unique identifier that is prepended to the 32-bit customer prefix or route learned from a CE router, which makes it a unique 96-bit address that can be transported between the PE routers in the MPLS domain. Thus, a unique RD is configured per VRF on the PE router. The resulting address, which is 96-bits total (32-bit customer prefix + 64-bit unique identifier or RD), is called a *VPN version 4 (VPNv4) address.*

VPNv4 addresses are exchanged between PE routers in the provider network in addition to IPv4 (32-bit) addresses. The format of an RD is shown in Figure 3-6. As shown in Figure 3-6, RD can be of two formats. If the provider does not have a BGP AS number, the IP address format can be used, and, if the provider does have an AS number, the AS number format can be used. Figure 3-6 also shows the same IP prefix, 172.16.10.0/24, received from two different customers, is made unique by prepending different RD values, 1:100:1 and 1:101, prior to propagating the addresses as VPNv4 addresses on the PE router.

Figure 3-6   *RD Operation in MPLS VPN*

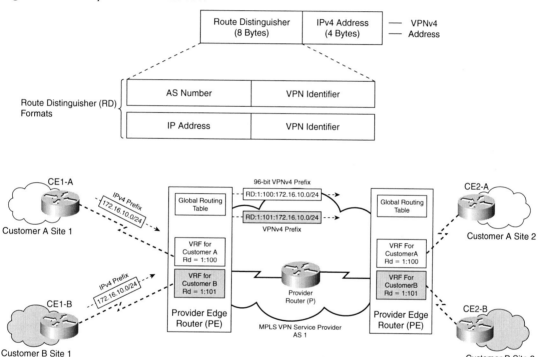

The protocol used for exchanging these VPNv4 routes between PE routers is *multiprotocol BGP* (MP-BGP). BGP capable of carrying VPNv4 (96-bit) prefixes in addition to other address families is called MP-BGP. The IGP requirement to implement iBGP (internal BGP) still holds in the case of an MPLS VPN implementation. Therefore, the PE router must run an IGP that provides NLRI information for iBGP if both PE routers are in the same AS. Cisco currently supports both OSPFv2 and ISIS in the MPLS provider network as the IGP. MP-BGP is also responsible for assignment of a VPN label. Packet forwarding in an MPLS VPN mandates that the router specified as the next hop in the incoming BGP update is the same router that assigns the VPN label. Scalability was a primary reason for the choice of BGP as the protocol to carry customer routing information. In addition, BGP enables the use of VPNv4 address in an MPLS VPN router environment that enables overlapping address ranges with multiple customers.

An MP-BGP session between PE routers in a single BGP AS is called an MP-iBGP session and follows rules as in the implementation of iBGP with regards to BGP attributes. If the VPN extends beyond a single AS, VPNv4 routes will be exchanged between AS at the AS boundaries using an MP-eBGP session.

Route targets (RTs) are additional identifiers used in the MPLS VPN domain in the deployment of MPLS VPN that identify the VPN membership of the routes learned from that particular site. RTs are implemented by the use of extended BGP communities in which the higher order 16 bits of the BGP extended community (64 total bits) are encoded with a value corresponding to the VPN membership of the specific site. When a VPN route learned from a CE router is injected into VPNv4 BGP, a list of VPN route target extended community attributes is associated with it. The *export route target* is used in identification of VPN membership and is associated to each VRF. This export route target is appended to a customer prefix when it is converted to a VPNv4 prefix by the PE router and propagated in MP-BGP updates. The *import route target* is associated with each VRF and identifies the VPNv4 routes to be imported into the VRF for the specific customer. The format of a RT is the same as an RD value. The interaction of RT and RD values in the MPLS VPN domain as the update is converted to an MP-BGP update is shown in Figure 3-7.

Figure 3-7 *RT and RD Operation in an MPLS VPN*

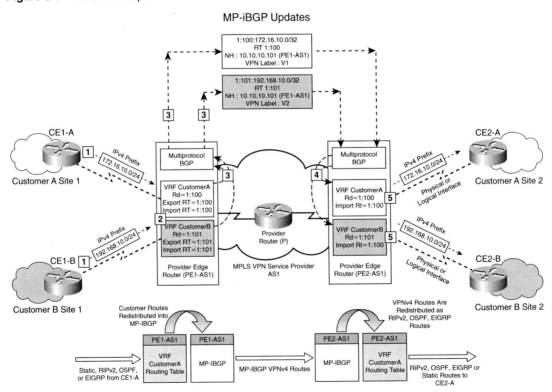

When implementing complex VPN topologies, such as extranet VPN, Internet access VPNs, network management VPN, and so on, using MPLS VPN technology, the RT plays a pivotal role. A single prefix can be associated to more than one export route target when propagated across the MPLS VPN network. The RT can, as a result, be associated to sites that might be a member of more than one VPN.

The following processes occur during route propagation in an MPLS VPN, as shown in Figure 3-7:

1 The prefix 172.16.10.0/24 is received from CE1-A, which is part of VRF CustomerA on PE1-AS1.

2 PE1 associated an RD value of 1:100 and an export RT value of 1:100 as configured in the VRF definition on the PE1-AS1 router.

3 Routes learned from connected CE routers CE1-A are redistributed into the MP-BGP process on PE1-AS1 where the prefix 172.16.10.0/24 is prepended with the RD value of 1:100 and appended with the route target extended community value (export RT) of 1:100 prior to sending the VPNv4 prefix as part of the MP-iBGP update between PE routers.

   The VPN label (*3 bytes*) is assigned for each prefix learned from the connected CE router's IGP process within a VRF by the PE router's MP-BGP process. MP-BGP running in the service provider MPLS domain thus carries the VPNv4 prefix (IPv4 prefix + prepended RD) in addition to the BGP route target extended community. Note that although the RT is a mandatory configuration in an MPLS VPN for all VRFs configured on a router, the RT values can be used to implement complex VPN topologies in which a single site can be a part of more than one VPN. In addition, RT values can also be used to perform selective route importing into a VRF when VPNv4 routes are learned in MP-iBGP updates. The VPN label is only understood by the egress PE (data plane) that is directly connected to the CE router advertising the prefix. Note that the next hops on PE routers must not be advertised in the BGP process but must be learned from the IGP for MPLS VPN implementation. The VPN label has been depicted by the entries V1 and V2 in Figure 3-7.

4 The MP-BGP update is received by the PE router PE2, and the route is stored in the appropriate VRF table for Customer A based on the VPN label.

5 The received MP-BGP routes are redistributed into the VRF PE-CE routing processes, and the route is propagated to CE2-A.

In addition, other BGP extended community attributes such as *site of origin (SoO)* can also be applied to the MP-iBGP update prior to propagation. The SoO attribute is used to identify the specific site from which the PE learns the route and is used in the identification and prevention of routing loops. The SoO extended community is a BGP extended community attribute used to identify routes that have originated from a site so that the re-advertisement of that prefix back to the source site can be prevented, thus preventing routing loops. The SoO extended community uniquely identifies the site from which a PE router has learned a route. SoO enables filtering of traffic based on the site from which it was originated. SoO filtering manages MPLS VPN traffic and prevents routing loops from occurring in complex and mixed network topologies in which the customer sites might possess connectivity across the MPLS VPN backbone as well as possess backdoor links between sites.

The implementation of a MPLS VPN in which all VPN sites belonging to a customer can speak to all other sites in the same customer domain is called a simple VPN implementation or *intranet VPN*. As mentioned earlier, RTs can be used to implement complex VPN topologies in which certain sites that are part of one customer's domain are also accessible by other customers' VPN sites. This implementation is called an *extranet VPN*. In addition, variants of extranet VPN, such as network management VPN as well as central services VPN and Internet access VPN, can also be deployed.

It is important to understand the concept of address families and their place in the operation of MP-BGP to enable the transport of VPNv4 routes with extended community attributes. Prior to RFC 2283, "Multiprotocol Extensions for BGP-4," BGP version 4 was capable of carrying routing information only pertaining to IPv4. RFC 2283 defines extensions to BGP-4 that enable BGP-4 to carry information for multiple network layer protocols. RFC 2283 states that to enable BGP-4 to support routing for multiple network layer protocols, the additions to BGP-4 must account for the ability of a particular network layer protocol to be associated with a next hop as well as the NLRI (network layer reachability information). The two new attributes that were added to BGP were Multiprotocol Reachable NLRI (MP_REACH_NLRI), and Multiprotocol Unreachable NLRI (MP_UNREACH_NLRI). MP_REACH_NLRI carries the set of reachable destinations together with the next-hop information to be used for forwarding to these destinations. MP_UNREACH_NLRI carries the set of unreachable destinations. Both of these attributes are optional and nontransitive. Therefore, a BGP speaker that does not support these multiprotocol capabilities will just ignore the information carried in these attributes and will not pass it to other BGP speakers.

An *address family* is a defined network layer protocol. An address family identifier (AFI) carries an identity of the network layer protocol associated with the network address in the multiprotocol attributes in BGP. (Address family identifiers for network layer protocols are defined in RFC 1700, "Assigned Numbers.")

The PE router, in essence, is an Edge LSR and performs all the functions of an Edge LSR. The PE router requires LDP for label assignment and distribution as well as forward labeled packets. In addition to the functions of an Edge LSR, the PE implements a routing protocol (or static routes) with connected CE routers per virtual routing table and requires MP-BGP to propagate prefixes learned from CE routers as VPNv4 prefixes in MP-iBGP updates to other PE routers along with the VPN label.

The P router's requirements are to run an IGP (either OSPF or ISIS) as well as have MPLS enabled to forward labeled packets (data plane) between PE routers. The IGP is used to provide, as well as propagate, NLRI to connected P and PE routers to implement an MP-iBGP session between PE routers (control plane). As explained in Chapters 1 and 2, LDP is run on the P router for label assignment and distribution.

MPLS VPN Control Plane Operation

The *control plane* in MPLS VPN implementation contains all the Layer 3 routing information and the processes within to exchange reachability information for a specific Layer 3 IP prefix in addition to label assignment and distribution using LDP (as explained in Chapter 1). The *data plane* performs the functions relating to the forwarding of both labeled as well as IP packets to the next hop toward a destination network. Figure 3-8 outlines the interactions of protocols in the control plane in an MPLS VPN implementation.

Figure 3-8 *Control Plane Interactions in MPLS VPN*

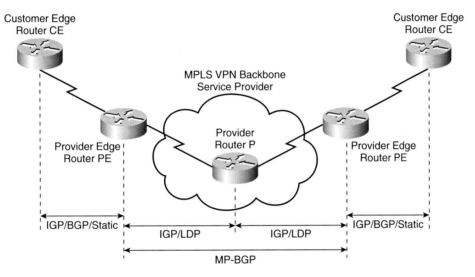

The CE routers are connected to the PE routers, and an IGP, BGP, or static route is required on the CE routers in conjunction with attached PE routers to gather and advertise NLRI information. In the MPLS VPN backbone consisting of P and PE routers, an IGP (usually either OSPF or ISIS) in addition to LDP is used between PE and P routers. LDP is used for allocation as well as distribution of labels in the MPLS domain. The IGP is used for NLRI information exchange as well as to map this NLRI into MP-BGP. MP-BGP sessions are maintained between PE routers in an MPLS VPN domain and exchange MP-BGP updates consisting of unique VPNv4 addresses in addition to BGP extended community attributes associated with specific VPNv4 addresses.

Packets from CE to PE are always propagated as IPv4 packets. Operation of the MPLS VPN control plane is shown in Figure 3-9. Figure 3-9 shows a simple VPN implementation with two sites belonging to Customer A connected to one another across a service provider's MPLS backbone.

Figure 3-9   *Control Plane Operation*

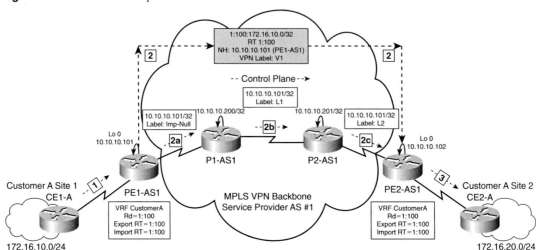

The following are the steps for control plane operation in MPLS VPN. The steps are outlined for prefixes advertised by the CEA-1 router and are shown in Figure 3-9:

Step 1   IPv4 update for network 172.16.10.0 is received by the egress PE router (data plane).

Step 2   PE1-AS1 accepts and transforms the IPv4 route, 172.16.10.0/24, to a VPNv4 route by assigning an RD 1:100, SoO, and RT 1:100 based on the VRF configuration on PE1-AS1. It then allocates a VPNv4 label V1 to the 172.16.10.0/24 update and rewrites the next-hop attribute to the PE1-AS1 loopback0 IP address 10.10.10.101. PE1-AS1 loopback 10.10.10.101 is reachable via IGP (OSPF) and LDP. Figure 3-9 shows the control plane operation and the label propagation for prefix 10.10.10.101/32 from PE1-AS1 to PE2-AS1 inside the provider network. This propagation takes place as soon as the MPLS VPN provider network is established and is always in place prior to any VPNv4 prefix being propagated across the MPLS VPN provider network. The following steps are performed in the label propagation process for prefix 10.10.10.101/32. This operation is shown for clarity:

(a)   2a: In Figure 3-8, Edge LSR PE2-AS1 requests a label for the 10.10.10.101/32 prefix using the LDP label mapping request from its downstream neighbor, LSR P2-AS1. P2-AS1 requests a label for the 10.10.10.101/32 prefix using the LDP label mapping request from its downstream neighbor LSR P1-AS1. P1-AS1, in turn, requests a label for the 10.10.10.101/32 prefix using the LDP label mapping request from its downstream neighbor, Edge LSR PE1-AS1. Edge LSR PE1-AS1 allocates a label of implicit-null (penultimate hop popping) to 10.10.10.101/32, modifies the entry in the LFIB corresponding to 10.10.10.101/32, and sends it to P1-AS1 using an LDP reply.

(b) 2b: P1-AS1 uses the implicit-null label received from PE1-AS1 as its outbound label value, allocates a label (L1) to prefix 10.10.10.101/32, and modifies the LFIB entry for 10.10.10.101/32. P1-AS1 then sends this label value to P2-AS1 via an LDP reply.

(c) 2c: P2-AS1 uses the label (L1) received from P1-AS1 as its outbound label value, allocates a label (L2) to prefix 10.10.10.101/32, and modifies the LFIB entry for 10.10.10.101/32. P2-AS1 then sends this label value to PE2-AS1 via an LDP reply.

Step 3 PE1-AS1 has the VRF configured to accept routes with RT 1:100 and therefore translates the VPNv4 update to IPv4 and inserts the route in VRF for Customer A. It then propagates this route to the CE2-A.

MPLS VPN Data Plane Operation

The prior section discussed update propagation along with the label assignment and distribution, both for MPLS packet forwarding as well as the VPN label. MPLS VPN data plane operation involves the usage of the label stack in which the top label in the label stack is the label assigned for the egress PE routers (data plane) next-hop address, and the second label in the label stack is the VPN label as assigned by the egress PE router connected to the CE router advertising the prefix. When using the label stack in an MPLS VPN implementation, the ingress/upstream PE router thus labels the incoming IP packet for a remote VPN destination with two labels.

The second label in the stack points toward an outgoing interface whenever the CE router is the next hop of the VPN route. The second label in the stack points to the VRF table for aggregate VPN routes, VPN routes pointing to null interface, and routes for directly connected VPN interfaces. This will be explained in more detail in the section "MPLS VPN Basic Configuration." P routers perform label switching on the LDP-assigned label toward the egress PE router. The egress PE router identifies the VPN label assigned with a VRF (that it has previously assigned) and either forwards the IP packet toward the CE router or performs another IP lookup in the VRF table to identify the next hop toward the destination.

Figure 3-10 depicts the various steps in the data plane forwarding of customer data from one customer site CE2-A to CE1-A connected using the SP's infrastructure.

Figure 3-10 *MPLS VPN Data Plane Operation*

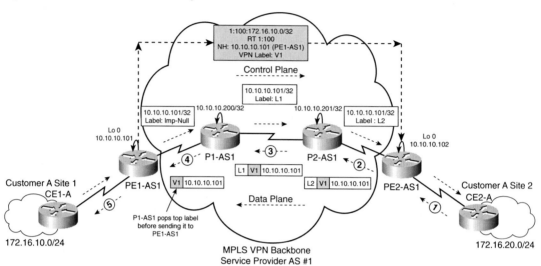

When data is forwarded to a specific prefix belonging to a VPN across the MPLS-enabled core, the top label in the label stack is the only one swapped as the packet traverses the backbone. The VPN label is kept intact and is removed only in the egress/downstream PE router. The resulting prefix is associated with an outgoing interface belonging to a specific VRF on the router depending on the value in the VPN label.

Here are the steps in the data plane forwarding shown in Figure 3-10:

Step 1 CE2-A originates a data packet with the source address of 172.16.20.1 and destination of 172.16.10.1.

Step 2 PE2-AS1 receives the data packet and appends the VPN label V1 and LDP label L2 and forwards the packet to P2-AS1.

Step 3 P2-AS1 receives the data packet destined to 172.16.10.1 and swaps LDP label L2 with L1.

Step 4 P1-AS1 receives the data packet destined to 172.16.10.1 and pops the top label because it receives an implicit-null label mapping for 10.10.10.101/32 from PE1-AS1. The resulting labeled packet (with VPN Label V1) is forwarded to PE1-AS1.

Step 5 PE1-AS1 pops the VPN label and forwards the data packet to CE1-A where the 172.16.10.0 network is located.

The key to understanding the operation of MPLS VPN is that the VPN label is never touched until it reaches the egress PE router toward the FEC. All the forwarding of traffic is done as explained in Chapter 1; the next-hop label mapping to the downstream PE router's loopback is used to forward the packet (in this case, labeled IP because of the presence of a VPN label) through the MPLS domain.

MPLS VPN Basic Configuration

This section outlines the generic configurations required on the routers in the service provider domain to implement MPLS VPN. The configurations of the PE and P routers will be covered in this section. The subsequent sections in this chapter delve into each of the configuration blocks on the PE and P routers alone. The configurations required to implement PE-CE routing sessions are discussed in Chapters 4 through 6, depending on the PE-CE protocol in use.

All configurations outlined in the following sections are performed in the network shown in Figure 3-11. For simplicity, only connected networks that are part of the VRF will be redistributed into the MP-BGP processes.

Figure 3-11 *Network Topology: MPLS VPN PE and P Configuration*

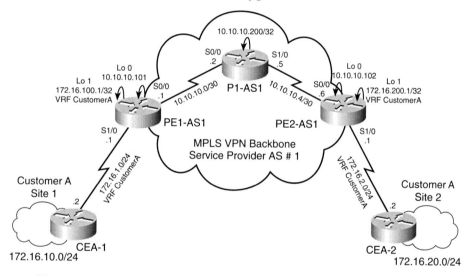

The topology in Figure 3-11 attempts to implement a simple intranet VPN between two sites belonging to Customer A, site 1 and site 2. The customer network consists of the CE routers CE1-A and CE2-A. In addition, two loopbacks (loopback 1) on PE1-AS1 and PE2-AS1 will be configured as part of the VRF *CustomerA* and be redistributed into the MP-BGP routing contexts.

Configuration of CE Routers

The configuration of route exchange between PE and CE routers involves the implementation of a routing protocol (or static/default routes) on the CE routers. No specific configuration other than the regular routing protocol configuration is required on the CE routers. On the PE router, VRF routing contexts (or address family contexts) are required for route exchange between the PE and CE. These routes are then mutually redistributed with the MP-BGP process per VRF. Configurations for the above based on protocol choice between PE and CE will be covered in Chapters 4 through 6.

Configuring MPLS Forwarding and VRF Definition on PE Routers

Configuring MPLS forwarding is the first step to provision the service provider's MPLS VPN backbone. This step ensures the service provider's readiness to provide MPLS-related services to prospective customers. At a minimum, the steps to configure MPLS forwarding on PE routers are

Step 1   Enable CEF.

Step 2   Configure IGP routing protocol on the PE router.

Step 3   Configure MPLS or label forwarding on the PE interfaces connected to P.

These steps have already been discussed in Chapters 1 and 2 and thus have not been shown.

In this section, we configure VRFs on the PE routers. Figure 3-12 shows the configuration steps on the PE routers to configure VRF definition.

Figure 3-12 *VRF Definition on PE Routers: Configuration Steps*

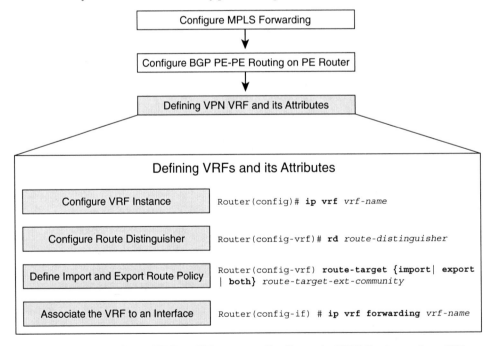

Step 1   **Configure VRF on PE router**—Configure the VRF **CustomerA** on PE1 and PE2-AS1 router. This results in the creation of a VRF routing table and a Cisco Express Forwarding (CEF) table for **CustomerA**. Example 3-1 shows **CustomerA** VRF being configured on PE1-AS1 router. Note the VRF name is case sensitive.

Example 3-1 *VRF Definition*

```
PE1-AS1(config)#ip vrf CustomerA
```

Note that creation or deletion of a VRF results in removal of the IP address from the interface. Example 3-2 illustrates the message that occurs on VRF deletion.

Example 3-2 *VRF Deletion*

```
PE1-AS1(config-vrf)#no ip vrf CustomerA
% IP addresses from all interfaces in VRF CustomerA have been removed
```

Step 2   **Configure the RD**—The RD creates routing and forwarding tables. The RD is added to the beginning of the customer's IPv4 prefixes to convert them into globally unique VPNv4 prefixes. Example 3-3 shows the configuration for defining the RD under the VRF.

Example 3-3 *Configuring VRF Parameters: RD*

```
PE1-AS1(config-vrf)#rd 1:100
```

The RD can be used in either of these formats:

— 16-bit AS number: Your 32-bit number (for example, 1:100)

— 32-bit IP address: Your 16-bit number (for example, 10.10.10.101:1)

RD for an existing VRF can be changed only after deletion of that VRF. Example 3-4 illustrates the concept.

Example 3-4 *Redefining VRF RD Value*

```
PE1-AS1(config)#ip vrf CustomerA
PE1-AS1(config-vrf)#rd 1:100
% Do "no ip vrf " before redefining the VRF
```

RD has to be unique for that particular VRF. No two VRFs on the same router can have similar RD. Trying to set the same RD on the VRF on the same router results in the message shown in Example 3-5.

Example 3-5 *RD Uniqueness*

```
PE1-AS1(config)#ip vrf CustomerA
PE1-AS1(config-vrf)#rd 1:100
% Cannot set RD, check if it's unique
```

Step 3   **Configure the import and export policy**—Configure the import and export policy for the MP-BGP extended communities. The policy is used for filtering routes for that particular RT. Example 3-6 provides the relevant configuration for defining import and export policy.

Example 3-6 *Configuring VRF Parameters: RT*

```
PE1-AS1(config-vrf)#route-target both 1:100
```

The **both** keyword in the previous command results in the configuration of import and export policy, and the configuration output is shown in Example 3-7.

Example 3-7 *RT Configuration Options*

```
PE1-AS1#sh run
Building configuration...
ip vrf CustomerA
 rd 1:100
 route-target export 1:100
 route-target import 1:100
```

Step 4   **Associate VRF with the interface**—Associate virtual routing/ forwarding instance (VRF) with an interface or subinterface in this CustomerA.

Associating the VRF to an interface results in removal of the IP address from that interface. This is only if VRF was associated to an interface that had the IP address already configured. This means that the IP address will have to be reconfigured after the VRF is associated with that interface. Example 3-8 shows the configuration for associating the VRF to an interface. Example 3-9 shows the removal of the IP address when **no ip vrf forwarding** *vrfname* is configured on the interface.

Example 3-8 *Associating VRF with Interface*

```
PE1-AS1(config)#interface serial4/0
PE1-AS1(config-if)#ip add 172.16.1.1 255.255.255.252
PE1-AS1(config-if)# ip vrf forwarding CustomerA
% Interface Serial4/0 IP address 172.16.1.1 removed due to enabling VRF CustomerA
PE1-AS1(config-if)#ip add 172.16.1.1 255.255.255.252
```

Example 3-9 *VRF Association to Interface IP Address*

```
PE1-AS1(config-if)#no ip vrf forwarding CustomerA
% Interface Serial4/0 IP address 172.16.1.1 removed due to disabling VRF CustomerA
```

Final VRF Configuration on PE1-AS1 Router

Example 3-10 shows the VRF configuration on the PE1-AS1 router.

Example 3-10 *VRF Configuration of PE1-AS1*

```
ip vrf CustomerA
 rd 1:100
 route-target export 1:100
 route-target import 1:100
!
interface Serial1/0
 description PE-CE link to CE1-A
 ip vrf forwarding CustomerA
 ip address 172.16.1.1 255.255.255.0
!
Interface Loopback1
 ip vrf forwarding CustomerA
 ip address 172.16.100.1 255.255.255.255
```

Verification of VRF Configuration on PE Routers

The **show ip vrf** command is used to verify if the correct VRF exists on the interface. Example 3-11 indicates that the correct VRF CustomerA is configured on the Serial1/0 interface on the PE1 router.

Example 3-11 show ip vrf *on PE1-AS1*

```
PE1-AS1#show ip vrf
  Name                         Default RD          Interfaces
  CustomerA                       1:100            Se1/0
                                                   Lo1
```

The **show ip vrf interfaces** command provides the listing of interfaces that are activated for a particular VRF. Example 3-12 shows that Serial1/0 is active for VRF VRF-Static.

Example 3-12 show ip vrf interfaces *on PE1-AS1*

```
PE1-AS1#show ip vrf interfaces
 Interface          IP-Address      VRF                        Protocol
 Serial1/0          172.16.1.1      CustomerA                  up
 Lo1                172.16.100.1    CustomerA                  up
```

Configuration of BGP PE-PE Routing on PE Routers

Configuring BGP PE-PE routing between the PE routers is the next step in an MPLS VPN deployment. The purpose of this step is to ensure that VPNv4 routes can be transported across the service provider backbone using MP-iBGP. The P router is transparent to this entire process and, therefore, does not carry any customer routes. Figure 3-13 illustrates the steps for configuring BGP PE-PE routing sessions between the PE routers.

Figure 3-13 *BGP PE-PE Routing Configuration Steps*

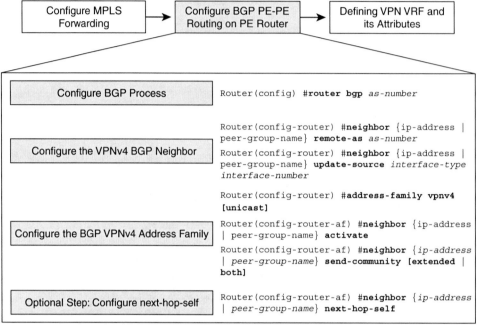

Step 1   **Configure BGP routing on PE routers**—Enable BGP routing and
         identify the AS on the PE1-AS1 and PE2-AS1 routers. Example 3-13
         highlights the configuration.

Example 3-13 *Configuring BGP Routing on PE Routers*

```
PE1-AS1(config)#router bgp 1
PE2-AS1(config)#router bgp 1
```

Step 2   **Configure the MP-iBGP neighbors**—Configure the remote MP-iBGP
         neighbor and use the loopback interface as the source of BGP messages
         and updates. Note that you have to use the **update-source** command only
         when the neighbor is peering to your loopback address. This is irrespective
         of whether it is an iBGP or eBGP neighbor. Example 3-14 shows the
         configuration for the PE1-AS1 and PE2-AS1 router.

Example 3-14 *Configuring MP-iBGP Neighbors*

```
PE1-AS1(config-router)#neighbor 10.10.10.102 remote-as 1
PE1-AS1(config-router)#neighbor 10.10.10.102 update-source loopback0
PE2-AS1(config-router)#neighbor 10.10.10.101 remote-as 1
PE2-AS1(config-router)#neighbor 10.10.10.101 update-source loopback0
```

Step 3 **Configure the VPNv4 address family**—Configure the address family for VPNv4 under the BGP configuration process. This step allows you to enter the VPNv4 address family to activate the VPNv4 neighbors. Activate the iBGP neighbor, which is essential for transporting VPNv4 prefixes across the service provider backbone. Using next-hop-self is optional and is primarily used when the service provider has an eBGP PE-CE routing with the customers, because internal BGP (iBGP) sessions preserve the next-hop attribute learned from eBGP peers, which is why it is important to have an internal route to the next hop. Otherwise, the BGP route is unreachable. To make sure you can reach the eBGP next hop, include the network that the next hop belongs to in the IGP or use the **next-hop-self neighbor** command to force the router to advertise itself, rather than the external peer, as the next hop.

In addition, configure the propagation of the extended communities with BGP routes so as to enable RT propagation, which identifies the VPNs that the routes have to be imported into. The configuration of the VPNv4 address family for PE1-AS1 and PE2-AS1 is shown in Example 3-15. Note that on some versions of IOS, adding the neighbor for VPNv4 route exchange using the **neighbor** *ip-address* **activate** command also automatically adds the **neighbor** *ip-address* **send-community extended** command. If the neighbor needs to be configured for both standard and extended community exchange, you will explicitly have to configure the **neighbor** *ip-address* **send-community both** command under the VPNv4 address family.

Example 3-15 *Configuring BGP VPNv4 Address Family*

```
PE1-AS1(config-router)#address-family vpnv4
PE1-AS1(config-router-af)# neighbor 10.10.10.102 activate
PE1-AS1(config-router-af)# neighbor 10.10.10.102 send-community extended

PE2-AS1(config-router)#address-family vpnv4
PE2-AS1(config-router-af)# neighbor 10.10.10.101 activate
PE2-AS1(config-router-af)# neighbor 10.10.10.101 send-community extended
```

Step 4 **Configure the IPv4 address family**—Configure the peer VRF IPv4 address family under the BGP configuration process. This step allows you to enter the IPv4 networks that will be converted to VPNv4 routes in MP-BGP updates. In Chapters 4, 5, and 6, the individual PE-CE routing protocol interaction configuration involving redistribution of PE-CE routing protocol contexts or instances will be configured in the IPv4 address family per VRF under the BGP process. For simplicity, redistribution of all connected networks is configured into the MP-BGP process. Example 3-16 shows the configuration on PE1-AS1 and PE2-AS1 routers.

Example 3-16 *Configuring BGP per VRF IPv4 Address Family (Routing Context)*

```
PE1-AS1(config-router)#address-family ipv4 vrf CustomerA
PE1-AS1(config-router-af)# redistribute connected
PE1-AS1(config-router-af)# exit-address-family
PE2-AS1(config-router)#address-family ipv4 vrf CustomerA
PE2-AS1(config-router-af)# redistribute connected
PE2-AS1(config-router-af)# exit-address-family
```

BGP PE-PE Routing Final Configuration on PE1-AS1 and PE2-AS1 Router

Example 3-17 shows the final BGP PE-PE routing configuration on the PE1-AS1 and PE2-AS1 router.

Example 3-17 *BGP PE-PE Configurations of PE1-AS1 and PE2-AS1 Routers*

```
!PE1-AS1 Router:
router bgp 1
 no synchronization
 neighbor 10.10.10.102 remote-as 1
 no auto-summary
 !
 address-family vpnv4
 neighbor 10.10.10.102 activate
 neighbor 10.10.10.102 send-community extended
 exit-address-family
 !
 address-family ipv4 vrf CustomerA
 redistribute connected
 no auto-summary
 no synchronization
 exit-address-family
!PE2-AS1 Router:
router bgp 1
 no synchronization
 bgp log-neighbor-changes
 neighbor 10.10.10.101 remote-as 1
 neighbor 10.10.10.101 update-source Loopback0
 no auto-summary
 !
 address-family vpnv4
 neighbor 10.10.10.101 activate
 neighbor 10.10.10.101 send-community extended
 exit-address-family
 !
 address-family ipv4 vrf CustomerA
 redistribute connected
 no auto-summary
 no synchronization
 exit-address-family
```

Verification and Monitoring of BGP PE-PE Routing on PE Routers

After configuring BGP PE-PE routing between the PE routers, you can verify that the MP-iBGP neighbors are operational by issuing any of the following commands:

- **show ip bgp vpnv4 * summary**
- **show IP bgp vpnv4 all**
- **show ip bgp summary**
- **show ip bgp neighbor** *ip-address*

Example 3-18 shows that the VPNv4 neighbor relationship is formed.

Example 3-18 *VPN Neighbor Relationship Verification*

```
PE1#show ip bgp vpnv4 all summary
BGP router identifier 10.10.10.101, local AS number 1
BGP table version is 7, main routing table version 7

Neighbor        V    AS MsgRcvd MsgSent   TblVer  InQ OutQ Up/Down   State/PfxRcd
10.10.10.102    4     1     202     200        7    0    0 00:00:39             0
```
```
PE2#show ip bgp vpnv4 all summary
BGP router identifier 10.10.10.102, local AS number 1
BGP table version is 1, main routing table version 1

Neighbor        V    AS MsgRcvd MsgSent   TblVer  InQ OutQ Up/Down   State/PfxRcd
10.10.10.101    4     1      11      11        1    0    0 00:07:16             0
```

Configuration of P Router

No special configurations need to be performed on the P routers P1-AS1 and P1-AS2 for MPLS VPN support. Because the P routers only participate in MPLS labeled packet forwarding, the only requirements are those of an LSR in an MPLS network, namely, IGP for NLRI exchange and LDP for label assignment and distribution. As always, CEF needs to be enabled on all interfaces configured for MPLS forwarding. Configuration of the P1-AS1 router is shown in Example 3-19.

Example 3-19 *P1-AS1 Configuration*

```
mpls ldp router-id loopback0
!
interface Serial0/0
  ip address 10.10.10.2 255.255.255.252
  mpls ip
```

continues

Example 3-19 *P1-AS1 Configuration (Continued)*

```
!
interface Serial1/0
  ip address 10.10.10.5 255.255.255.252
  mpls ip
!
Interface loopback0
  ip address 10.10.10.200 255.255.255.255
!
router ospf 1
network 10.0.0.0 0.255.255.255 area 0
!
```

Label Verification and Control and Data Plane Operation

After configuring devices in the network as per the previous steps, the verification of label
allocation and propagation can be performed on the PE and P routers using the commands
described in Figure 3-14.

Figure 3-14 *Label Allocation Verification and Control/Data Plane Operation*

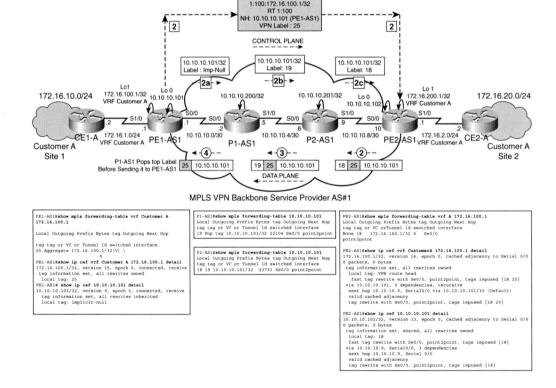

The control plane and data plane operation for network 172.16.100.1 as part of VRF
CustomerA is depicted in Figure 3-14. Note that the outgoing label mapped to prefix
172.16.100.1 on PE1-AS1 is aggregate and not untagged. For all networks that are directly
connected to the PE router (like loopbacks or interface IP networks) that are part of a VRF,
the outgoing label mapped in the LFIB is the aggregate label. If, however, the incoming
VPN packet is to be forwarded to a next-hop address (like that of a connected CE router),
the outgoing label mapping is untagged. Thus, aggregate and untagged labels that were
explained in Chapter 1 are encountered in MPLS VPN implementations.

Outbound Route Filters

When implementing large-scale MPLS VPN networks, sites belonging to different customers
might not be connected to all the PE routers in the MPLS VPN domain. The PE router in
the MPLS VPN network can, therefore, conserve resources by importing only VPNv4
routes that are to be imported into VRF instances configured on the PE router. To enable
such filtering of VPNv4 route information, the PE router must be capable of filtering MP-
iBGP updates so that information pertaining to these superfluous routes is not received. The
procedure for filtering routes based on the VRF configuration on the PE routers is called
automatic route filtering. Automatic route filtering is enabled by default on all Cisco routers
that are configured as PE routers. The exception is in the case of a PE router also performing
the functions of a route-reflector. The route-reflector must be capable of receiving routes
that might not be associated to any locally configured VRFs and reflect them to clients.
Therefore, on a PE router functioning as a route-reflector, the automatic route filtering
process is disabled to enable propagation of VPNv4 routes between route-reflector clients.

Automatic route filtering enables the PE router to reduce resource consumption by
rejecting information not pertaining to the VRFs configured on the router. Automatic
route filtering, however, does not avoid the superfluous routes from being received by the
PE routers.

Outbound route filtering (ORF) enables a PE router to advertise to its peers, outbound route
filters that peering PE routers can use while sending information to a PE router. The ORF
feature on PE routers works in conjunction with the route-refresh BGP capability. The route-
refresh BGP capability enables the PE router to request routing updates from its MP-iBGP
peers after undergoing a configuration change. In the event of an addition, deletion, or
modification of VRFs or their associated configurations on a PE router, the route-refresh
capability enables the PE router to update its routing tables. The route-refresh feature is
enabled by default on all Cisco routers configured for PE functionality. The ORF entries are
exchanged during session establishment between two PE routers through the use of the
BGP OPEN message as part of the route-refresh message. The format of a route-refresh
message is shown in Figure 3-15.

Figure 3-15 *Route-Refresh Message and Working of ORF*

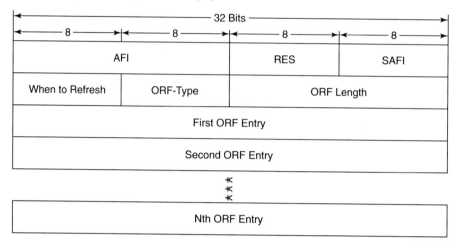

In large networks, the PE router might receive updates and then filter a list of unwanted routes based on its local inbound route filter. The ORF feature enables a PE router to push its inbound route filter to a remote peer and apply a filter from a remote peer as its outbound route filter. ORFs can be either prefix-based or extended-community based in VPNv4 route filtering. The prefix-based ORF allows a PE to export and/or receive the inbound route filter information with a peer based on the prefix associated with the route. In the extended-community based ORF, the PE can export/receive inbound route filter based on the extended community attributes associated with a VPNv4 route. Because the RT values are coded as part of the extended-community attributes in VPNv4 routes, the ORF feature can be used to advertise a subset of RTs for which the PE router can receive VPNv4 routing information. This process essentially reduces the burden of superfluous routing information being propagated in the MP-iBGP backbone as the peering PE router does not send VPNv4 routes pertaining to the subset of RTs configured as part of the ORF.

Figure 3-16 shows the operation and sample configuration for implementation of a prefix-based ORF. PE1-AS1 is configured with an inbound prefix-list that is propagated using the ORF capability configuration to PE2-AS1. PE2-AS1 will not accept this filter if the command **neighbor 10.10.10.1 capability orf prefix-list receive** is configured under the VPNv4 address-family. The verification of the ORF application on PE2-AS1 is also illustrated in Figure 3-16 with the output of the **show ip bgp neighbor** command. The output of this command depicts the ORF has been received with two entries. Note that because this ORF applies only to VPNv4 routes learned from PE2-AS1, this will not affect regular IPv4 route exchanges between PE1-AS1 and PE2-AS1.

Figure 3-16 *ORF Operation and Configuration*

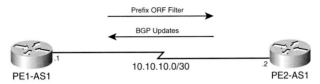

```
PE1-AS1 (config)# ip prefix-list PE1-AS1 seq 5 permit 192.168.1.0/24 le 32
PE1-AS1 (config)# ip prefix-list PE1-AS1 seq 10 den y 0.0.0.0/0 le 32

PE1-AS1 (config)# router bgp 1
PE1-AS1 (config-router)#    neighbor 10.10.10.2 remote-as 1
PE1-AS1 (config-router)#    address-family vpnv4
PE1-AS1 (config-router-af)#   neighbor 10.10.10.2 activate
PE1-AS1 (config-router-af)#   neighbor 10.10.10.2 send-community extended
PE1-AS1 (config-router-af)#   neighbor 10.10.10.2 capability orf prefix-list both
PE1-AS1 (config-router-af)#   neighbor 10.10.10.2 prefix-list PE1-AS1 in
PE1-AS1 (config-router-af)#   exit-address-family
```

```
PE2-AS1 (config)# router bgp 1
PE2-AS1 (config-router)#    neighbor 10.10.10.1 remote-as 1
PE2-AS1 (config-router)#    address-family vpnv4
PE2-AS1 (config-router-af)#   neighbor 10.10.10.1 activate
PE2-AS1 (config-router-af)#   neighbor 10.10.10.1 send-community extended
PE2-AS1 (config-router-af)#   neighbor 10.10.10.1 capability orf prefix-list
receive
PE2-AS1 (config-router-af)#   exit-address-family
```

```
PE2-AS1# show ip bgp neighbor 10.10.10.1

For address  family: VPNv4 Unicast
  BGP table version 1, neighbor version 1/0
Output queue size: 0
  Index 1, Offset 0, Mask 032
  Member of update-group 1
  AF-dependant capabilities:
         Outbound Route Filter (ORF) type (128) Prefix-list:
            Send-mode: received
            Receive-mode: advertised, received
  Outbound Route Filter (ORF): received (2 entries)
Prefix activity:                              ----        ----
  Prefixes Current:                             0           0
  Prefixes Total:                               0           0
  Implicit Withdraw:                            0           0
  Explicit Withdraw:                            0           0
  Used as bestpath:                            n/a          0
  Used as multipath:                           n/a          0

                                           Outbound     Inbound
Local Policy Denied Prefixes:              --------     -------
  Total:                                        0           0
Number of NLRIs in the update sent: max 0, min 0
```

Command Reference

Command	Description
Router(config)#**router bgp** *as-number*	Configures the BGP routing process.
Router(config-router)#**neighbor** {*ip-address*	*peer-group-name*} **remote-as** *as-number*	Specifies a remote BGP neighbor to establish a BGP session.
Router(config-router)#**neighbor** {*ip-address*	*ipv6-address*	peer-group-name} **update-source** *interface-type interface-number*	Allows the BGP sessions to use any operational interface for TCP connections. The loopback interface is used frequently.
Router(config-router)#**address-family vpnv4** [**unicast**]	Places the router in address family configuration mode, from which you can configure routing sessions that use VPN Version 4 address prefixes.

continues

Command	Description
Router(config-router-af)#**neighbor** {*ip-address* | *peer-group-name* | *ipv6-address*} **activate**	Enables the exchange of information with a BGP neighboring router.
Router(config)#**neighbor** {*ip-address* | *peer-group-name*} **next-hop-self**	Configures the router as the next hop for a BGP-speaking neighbor or peer group.
Router#**show ip bgp neighbors** [*neighbor-address*] [**received-routes** | **routes** | **advertised-routes** | {**paths** *regexp*} | **dampened-routes** | **received prefix-filter**]	Displays information about the TCP and BGP connections to neighbors.
Router#**show ip bgp summary**	Displays the status of all BGP connections.
Router(config)#**ip vrf** *vrf-name*	Configures a VPN routing/forwarding instance (VRF) routing table.
Router(config-vrf)#**rd** *route-distinguisher*	Creates routing and forwarding tables for a VPN VRF.
Router(config-vrf)#**route-target** {**import** | **export** | **both**} *route-target-ext-community*	Creates a route target extended community for a VPN VRF. *route-target-ext-community* adds the route target extended community attributes to the VRF's list of import, export, or both (import and export) route target extended communities.
Router(config-if)#**ip vrf forwarding** *vrf-name*	Associates a VRF with an interface or subinterface.
Router#**show ip vrf** [**brief** | **detail** | **interfaces** | **id**] [*vrf-name*] [*output-modifiers*]	Displays the set of defined VPN VRFs and associated interfaces.
Router(config-router-af)#**neighbor** *ip-address* **capability orf prefix-list** [**receive** | **send** | **both**] or Router(config-router)# **neighbor** *ip-address* **capability orf prefix-list** [**receive** | **send** | **both**]	Enables the ORF capability to be sent as part of BGP open message and route-refresh messages to configured neighbors.
Router(config-router-af)# **neighbor** *ip-address* **prefix-list** *prefix-list-name* [**in** | **out**] or Router(config-router)# **neighbor** *ip-address* **prefix-list** *prefix-list-name* [**in** | **out**]	Associates a prefix list to a configured BGP neighbor.

Command	Description
Router(config)# **ip prefix-list** *list-name* [**seq** *seq-value*] {**deny** *network/length* | **permit** *network/length*}[**ge** *ge-value*] [**le** *le-value*]	Creates a prefix list with configured entries in which len < ge-value < le-value <= 32.
Router#**show ip bgp vpnv4** {**all** | **rd** *route-distinguisher* | **vrf** *vrf-name*} [**rib-failure**] [*ip-prefix/length* [**longer-prefixes**] [*output-modifiers*]] [*network-address* [*mask*] [**longer-prefixes**] [*output-modifiers*]] [**cidr-only**] [**community**] [**community-list**] [**dampened-paths**] [**filter-list**] [**flap-statistics**] [**inconsistent-as**] [**neighbors**] [**paths** [*line*]] [**peer-group**] [**quote-regexp**] [**regexp**] [**summary**] [**labels**]	Displays VPN address information from the BGP table.

CHAPTER 4

PE-CE Routing Protocol— Static and RIP

Configuring MPLS VPNs is an integral function in service provider environments and enterprise networks. Preceding chapters provided you with basic concepts related to MPLS label distribution and propagation, and MPLS VPN concepts like route distinguisher, route targets, multiprotocol BGP, and label propagation in VPN networks.

This chapter introduces you to the following:

- Static PE-CE routing overview, configuration, and verification
- RIPv2 PE-CE routing overview, configuration, and verification
- RIPv1 PE-CE routing configuration and verification

Static PE-CE Routing Overview, Configuration, and Verification

Static PE to CE routing is one of the most common routing techniques used in MPLS VPN deployments. Static PE-CE routing is an optimal solution for sites either having a single PE-CE connection or limited number of subnets in the customer edge (CE) network or both. Static PE to CE routing also prevents the customer or the service provider from intentionally or accidentally flooding each other with false routing information. The service provider therefore retains control over customer routing. Static PE-CE routing might increase the provider's operational and administrative overheads to maintain static routes. This is because static PE-CE routing does not provide dynamic rerouting and therefore requires additional configuration for every new prefix on the PE routers and possibly on the CE router in the absence of a default route.

Static PE-CE routing involves the following:

On a CE router:

- Configuring static routes to specific remote CE networks in the same VPN

  or

- Configuring a static default route

On a PE router:

- Configuring a static VRF route to reach the connected CE router's networks. This static VRF route is redistributed in MP-iBGP and propagated as a VPNv4 prefix to the remote PE router.

The following are the advantages of using static PE-CE routing:

- Simple to implement
- Service provider retains control of customer routing
- Promotes a stable environment

The following are the disadvantages of using static PE-CE routing:

- No dynamic rerouting capability in failure scenarios
- Increase in administrative and operational overhead for service providers to maintain static routes

Configuration Flowchart to Implement Static PE-CE Routing

Figure 4-1 shows the configuration flowchart to implement static PE-CE routing on PE routers.

Figure 4-1 *Configuration Flowchart to Configure Static PE-CE Routing*

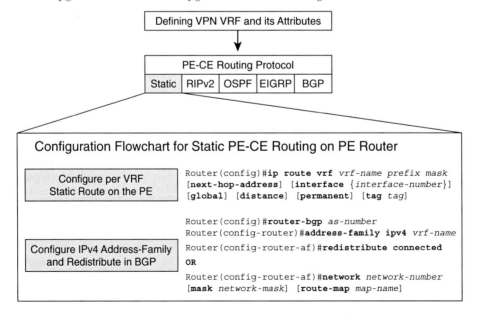

NOTE	Refer to Chapter 3, "Basic MPLS Overview and Configuration," for a configuration flowchart to define VRF and its attribute.

Configuring Static PE-CE Routing

The network topology in Figure 4-2 depicts an ATM-based MPLS VPN provider network providing MPLS VPN services to Customer A sites, Site 1 and Site 2. The MPLS provider network comprises PE1-AS1 and PE2-AS1 as PE routers. P1-AS1 and P2-AS1 are LS1010 switches and function as provider routers. The MPLS VPN provider network is running OSPF as the IGP routing protocol on PE1-AS1, P1-AS1, P2-AS1, and PE2-AS1. PE routers PE1-AS1 and PE2-AS1 are configured for MP-iBGP connectivity.

Figure 4-2 *Provider Network Implementing Static PE-CE Routing*

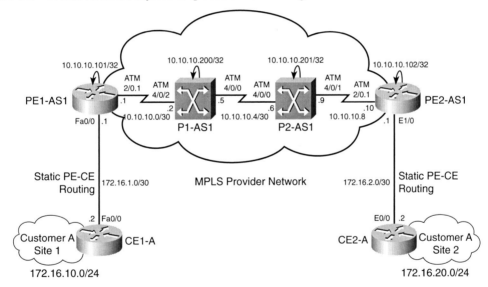

Customer A wants to have connectivity between the Site 1 network (172.16.10.0/24) and Site 2 network (172.16.20.0/24). Site 1 and Site 2 belong to the same VPN, VPN-A. Site 1 and Site 2 comprise CE routers CE1-A and CE2-A, which are connected to PE1-AS1 and PE2-AS1, respectively. A static default route is configured on CE1-A and CE2-A routers. The MPLS VPN provider network plans to deploy static PE-CE routing on PE routers PE1-AS1 and PE2-AS1.

Prior to configuring static PE-CE routing, ensure that IP addresses are preconfigured and VRFs defined on PE router. Example 4-1 provides the configuration related to defining VRF and its attributes on PE routers for static PE-CE routing.

Example 4-1 *Define VRF VRF-STATIC on PE Routers PE1-AS1 and PE2-AS1*

```
PE1-AS1(config)#ip vrf VRF-STATIC
PE1-AS1(config-vrf)# rd 1:100
PE1-AS1(config-vrf)#route-target both 1:100
PE1-AS1(config-vrf)#interface FastEthernet0/0
PE1-AS1(config-if)# ip vrf forwarding VRF-STATIC
PE1-AS1(config-if)# ip address 172.16.1.1 255.255.255.252
PE2-AS1(config)#ip vrf VRF-STATIC
PE2-AS1(config-vrf)# rd 1:100
PE2-AS1(config-vrf)# route-target both 1:100
PE2-AS1(config-vrf)#interface Ethernet1/0
PE2-AS1(config-if)# ip vrf forwarding VRF-STATIC
PE2-AS1(config-if)# ip address 172.16.2.1 255.255.255.252
```

The steps to configure static PE-CE routing are as follows:

Step 1 **Configure per VRF static route on PE routers**—Configure per VRF static route for VRF VRF-STATIC on the PE1-AS1 and PE2-AS1 router. This is shown in Example 4-2.

Example 4-2 *Configure per VRF Static Route on the PE Routers*

```
PE1-AS1(config)#ip route vrf VRF-Static 172.16.10.0 255.255.255.0 172.16.1.2
PE2-AS1(config)#ip route vrf VRF-Static 172.16.20.0 255.255.255.0 172.16.2.2
```

Step 2 **Configure IPv4 address-family and redistribute in BGP**—Create an IPv4 address family for VRF VRF-STATIC on the PE1-AS1 and PE2-AS1 router. Redistribute the per VRF static route configured in Step 1 into BGP on the PE1-AS1 and PE2-AS1 router. Also redistribute the connected interface in BGP on PE1-AS1 to ensure that the connected interface network is known to PE2-AS1 in order to reach the CE1-A network, 172.16.10.0. Instead of using the **redistribute connected** command, you can also use the BGP network command to advertise the connected interface. Example 4-3 demonstrates using the **redistribute connected** on PE1-AS1 and using BGP **network** command to advertise the connected interface on PE2-AS1.

Example 4-3 *Configure IPv4 Address Family and Redistribution in BGP*

```
PE1-AS1(config)#router bgp 1
PE1-AS1(config-router)#address-family ipv4 vrf VRF-STATIC
PE1-AS1(config-router-af)#redistribute static
PE1-AS1(config-router-af)#redistribute connected
PE2-AS1(config)#router bgp 1
PE2-AS1(config-router)#address-family ipv4 vrf VRF-STATIC
PE2-AS1(config-router-af)#redistribute static
PE2-AS1(config-router-af)#network 172.16.2.0 mask 255.255.255.252
```

Static PE-CE Routing—Final Device Configurations for CE Routers (CE1-A and CE2-A)

Example 4-4 shows CE router configurations for CE1-A and CE2-A.

Example 4-4 *CE1-A and CE2-A Router Configuration*

```
hostname CE1-A
!
interface Loopback0
 ip address 172.16.10.1 255.255.255.0
!
interface FastEthernet0/0
description connected to PE1-AS1
 ip address 172.16.1.2 255.255.255.252
!
ip route 0.0.0.0 0.0.0.0 172.16.1.1
```
```
hostname CE2-A
!
interface Loopback0
 ip address 172.16.20.1 255.255.255.0
!
interface Ethernet0/0
description connected to PE2-AS1
 ip address 172.16.2.2 255.255.255.255.252
!ip route 0.0.0.0 0.0.0.0 172.16.2.1
```

Static PE-CE Routing—Final Device Configuration for Provider Routers (P1-AS1 and P2-AS1)

Example 4-5 shows the configuration for LS1010 ATM switches performing the function of provider routers P1-AS1 and P2-AS1 in the MPLS VPN provider network.

Example 4-5 *P1-AS1 and P2-AS1 Router Configuration*

```
hostname P1-AS1
!
mpls label protocol ldp
mpls ldp router-id Loopback0
!
interface Loopback0
 ip address 10.10.10.200 255.255.255.255
!
interface ATM4/0/0
description connected to P2-AS1
ip address 10.10.10.5 255.255.255.252
mpls ip
!
interface ATM4/0/2
description connected to PE1-AS1
ip address 10.10.10.2 255.255.255.252
mpls ip
```

continues

Example 4-5 *P1-AS1 and P2-AS1 Router Configuration (Continued)*

```
!
router ospf 1
 network 10.0.0.0 0.255.255.255 area 0
hostname P2-AS1
!
mpls label protocol ldp
mpls ldp router-id Loopback0
!
interface Loopback0
 ip address 10.10.10.201 255.255.255.255
!
interface ATM4/0/0
description connected to P1-AS1
 ip address 10.10.10.6 255.255.255.252
 mpls ip
!
interface ATM4/0/1
description connected to PE2-AS1
 ip address 10.10.10.9 255.255.255.252
 mpls ip
!
router ospf 1
 network 10.0.0.0 0.255.255.255 area 0
```

Static PE-CE Routing—Final Device Configurations for PE Routers (PE1-AS1 and PE2-AS1)

Example 4-6 shows final configurations for PE1-AS1 and PE2-AS1 routers for static PE-CE routing.

Example 4-6 *PE1-AS1 and PE2-AS1 Router Configurations*

```
hostname PE1-AS1
!
ip cef
!
ip vrf VRF-STATIC
 rd 1:100
 route-target export 1:100
 route-target import 1:100
!
mpls label protocol ldp
mpls ldp router-id Loopback0
!
interface Loopback0
 ip address 10.10.10.101 255.255.255.255
!
interface FastEthernet0/0
 ip vrf forwarding VRF-STATIC
 ip address 172.16.1.1 255.255.255.252
```

Example 4-6 *PE1-AS1 and PE2-AS1 Router Configurations (Continued)*

```
!
interface ATM2/0
 no ip address
 no atm ilmi-keepalive
!
interface ATM2/0.1 mpls
 description Connection to P1-AS1
 ip address 10.10.10.1 255.255.255.252
mpls ip
!
router ospf 1
 network 10.0.0.0 0.255.255.255 area 0
!
router bgp 1
 no synchronization
 neighbor 10.10.10.102 remote-as 1
 neighbor 10.10.10.102 update-source Loopback0
 no auto-summary
 !
 address-family vpnv4
 neighbor 10.10.10.102 activate
 neighbor 10.10.10.102 send-community extended
 no auto-summary
 exit-address-family
 !
 address-family ipv4 vrf VRF-STATIC
 redistribute static
 redistribute connected
 no auto-summary
 no synchronization
 exit-address-family
!
ip classless
ip route vrf VRF-STATIC 172.16.10.0 255.255.255.0 172.16.1.2
hostname PE2-AS1
!
ip cef
!
ip vrf VRF-STATIC
 rd 1:100
 route-target export 1:100
 route-target import 1:100
!
mpls label protocol ldp
mpls ldp router-id Loopback0
!
interface Loopback0
 ip address 10.10.10.102 255.255.255.255
!
interface Ethernet1/0
```

continues

Example 4-6   *PE1-AS1 and PE2-AS1 Router Configurations (Continued)*

```
 description connected to CE2-A
 ip vrf forwarding VRF-STATIC
 ip address 172.16.2.1 255.255.255.252
!
interface ATM2/0
 no ip address
!
interface ATM2/0.1 mpls
 description connected to P2-AS1
 ip address 10.10.10.10 255.255.255.252
 mpls ip
!
router ospf 100
 network 10.10.0.0 0.0.255.255 area 0
!
router bgp 1
 no synchronization
 neighbor 10.10.10.101 remote-as 1
 neighbor 10.10.10.101 update-source Loopback0
 no auto-summary
 !
 address-family vpnv4
 neighbor 10.10.10.101 activate
 neighbor 10.10.10.101 send-community extended
 no auto-summary
 exit-address-family
 !
 address-family ipv4 vrf VRF-STATIC
 no auto-summary
 no synchronization
 redistribute static
 network 172.16.2.0 mask 255.255.255.252
 exit-address-family
!
ip classless
ip route vrf VRF-STATIC 172.16.20.0 255.255.255.0 172.16.2.2
```

Verification of Static PE-CE Routing

The steps to verify static PE-CE routing are as follows:

Step 1   **Verify BGP VPNv4 routing tables on PE1-AS1 and PE2-AS1**—
Check the BGP VPNv4 routing tables by issuing a **show ip bgp
vpnv4 vrf VRF-STATIC** on the PE routers. Example 4-7 shows that
PE1-AS1 and PE2-AS1 routers see routes for 172.16.20.0/24 (CE2-A)
and 172.16.10.0/24 (CE1-A) networks in their BGP table. Note that
172.16.2.0 is advertised with IGP as the origin because it was advertised

via network statement in BGP as compared to the 172.16.1.0/24 for which the origin code is incomplete because it was redistributed in BGP.

Example 4-7 *BGP VPNv4 Routing Table*

```
PE1-AS1#show ip bgp vpnv4 vrf VRF-STATIC
BGP table version is 67, local router ID is 10.10.10.101
Status codes: s suppressed, d damped, h history, * valid, > best, i - internal
Origin codes: i - IGP, e - EGP, ? - incomplete

   Network          Next Hop          Metric LocPrf Weight Path
Route Distinguisher: 1:100 (default for vrf VRF-STATIC)
*> 172.16.1.0/30    0.0.0.0                0            32768 ?
*>i172.16.2.0/30    10.10.10.102           0       100     0 i
*> 172.16.10.0/24   172.16.1.2             0            32768 ?
*>i172.16.20.0/24   10.10.10.102           0       100     0 ?
PE2-AS1#show ip bgp vpnv4 vrf VRF-STATIC
BGP table version is 61, local router ID is 10.10.10.102
Status codes: s suppressed, d damped, h history, * valid, > best, i - internal
Origin codes: i - IGP, e - EGP, ? - incomplete

   Network          Next Hop          Metric LocPrf Weight Path
Route Distinguisher: 1:100 (default for vrf VRF-STATIC)
*>i172.16.1.0/30    10.10.10.101           0       100     0 ?
*> 172.16.2.0/30    0.0.0.0                0            32768 i
*>i172.16.10.0/24   10.10.10.101           0       100     0 ?
*> 172.16.20.0/24   172.16.2.2             0            32768 ?
```

Step 2   **Verify VRF routing table on PE1-AS1 and PE2-AS1**—Check the VRF routing table to determine if routes are received from connected CE and remote CE routers belonging to the same VPN. Example 4-8 shows that PE1-AS1 has received 172.16.20.0/24 (CE2-A) and 172.16.2.0/24 routes from the PE2-AS1 router.

Example 4-8 *VRF-STATIC Routing Table on PE1-AS1 and PE2-AS1*

```
PE1-AS1#show ip route vrf VRF-STATIC
<output truncated for brevity>
     172.16.0.0/16 is variably subnetted, 4 subnets, 2 masks
B       172.16.20.0/24 [200/0] via 10.10.10.102, 00:02:12
S       172.16.10.0/24 [1/0] via 172.16.1.2
C       172.16.1.0/30 is directly connected, FastEthernet0/0
B       172.16.2.0/30 [200/0] via 10.10.10.102, 19:28:26
PE2-AS1#show ip route vrf VRF-STATIC
<output truncated for brevity>
     172.16.0.0/16 is variably subnetted, 4 subnets, 2 masks
S       172.16.20.0/24 [1/0] via 172.16.2.2
B       172.16.10.0/24 [200/0] via 10.10.10.101, 19:26:21
B       172.16.1.0/30 [200/0] via 10.10.10.101, 00:05:05
C       172.16.2.0/30 is directly connected, Ethernet1/0
```

Step 3 **Verify end-to-end connectivity using ping**—Verify end-to-end
connectivity between the CE1-A and CE2-A networks by issuing a ping
from CE1-A to network 172.16.20.0/24 on CE2-A and vice versa.
Example 4-9 shows that the ping has been successful.

Example 4-9 *Verify Reachability via Ping*

```
CE1-A#ping 172.16.20.1 source 172.16.10.1
Type escape sequence to abort.
Sending 5, 100-byte ICMP Echos to 172.16.20.1, timeout is 2 seconds:
Packet sent with a source address of 172.16.10.1
!!!!!
Success rate is 100 percent (5/5), round-trip min/avg/max = 1/2/4 ms
CE2-A#ping 172.16.10.1 source 172.16.20.1
Type escape sequence to abort.
Sending 5, 100-byte ICMP Echos to 172.16.10.1, timeout is 2 seconds:
Packet sent with a source address of 172.16.20.1
!!!!!
Success rate is 100 percent (5/5), round-trip min/avg/max = 1/2/4 ms
```

Static PE-CE Routing Command Reference

Table 4-1 shows the static PE-CE routing configuration command summary.

Table 4-1 *Static PE-CE Routing Command Reference*

Command	Purpose
Router(config)#**ip route vrf** *vrf-name prefix mask* [*next-hop-address*] [**interface** *interface-number*] [**global**] [*distance*] [**permanent**] [**tag** *tag*]	Establishes static routes for a VPN VRF.
Router(config)#**router bgp** *as-number*	Configures the BGP routing process.
Router(config-router)#**address-family ipv4** [**unicast**] **vrf** *vrf-name*	The **address-family** command puts the router in address family configuration submode. Within this submode, you can configure address family specific parameters for routing protocols, such as RIP and BGP, that can accommodate multiple Layer 3 address families.
Router(config-router-af)# **redistribute static**	Redistributes static routes.
Router(config-router-af)# **redistribute connected**	Redistributes connected interfaces in destination routing protocol.
Router(config-router-af)# **network** {*network-number* [**mask** *network-mask*] | *nsap-prefix*} [**route-map** *map-tag*]	Specifies the networks to be advertised by the BGP and multiprotocol BGP routing processes.

RIPv2 PE-CE Routing Overview, Configuration, and Verification

Static PE-CE routing can create administrative overheads for the service provider. Service providers, therefore, prefer to run dynamic PE-CE routing protocols for the following reasons:

- To avoid maintaining multiple static routes.
- Customer prefers to run a dynamic routing protocol.
- Customer has a dual-homed connection to the service provider.

In an RIPv2 PE-CE routing environment, an IPv4 routing context is configured for each VRF running RIP on the PE router. The RIP parameters are specified in the VRF routing context. Global RIP parameters, if entered in the RIP router configuration, are inherited by the RIP VRF routing context. These parameters can, however, be overwritten in the routing context.

Figure 4-3 shows a typical MPLS VPN network, where PE1-AS1 uses RIPv2 as the PE-CE routing protocol with CE1-A, and PE2-AS1 can run either RIPv2, OSPF, EIGRP, BGP, or static PE-CE routing protocol with CE2-A. PE1-AS1 receives RIPv2 routes from the CE1-A router. The received RIP routes are redistributed into MP-iBGP at the PE1-AS1 router and are transported across the backbone as VPNv4 routes to the PE2-AS1 router. These VPNv4 routes are redistributed back into RIPv2, OSPF, EIGRP, and BGP routes at the PE2-AS1 router and then propagated to the CE2-A router.

Figure 4-3 *MPLS VPN Network with RIPv2 PE-CE Routing*

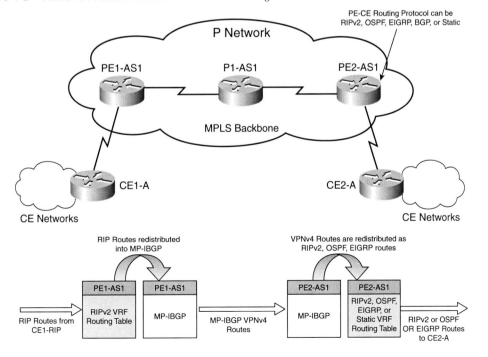

Configuration Flowchart to Implement RIPv2 PE-CE Routing

Figure 4-4 shows the configuration flowchart to implement RIPv2 PE-CE routing on a PE router.

Figure 4-4   *Configurations Steps for RIPv2 PE-CE Routing*

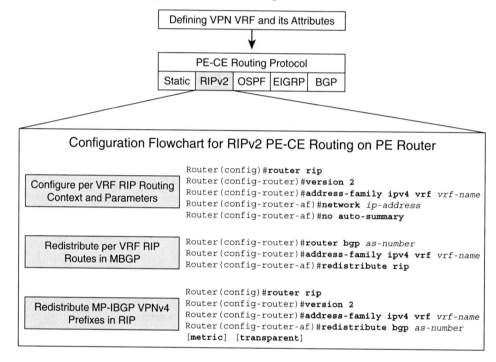

Configuring RIPv2 PE-CE Routing

The network topology in Figure 4-5 depicts an ATM-based MPLS VPN provider network providing MPLS VPN services to Customer A sites, Site 1 and Site 2. The MPLS provider network comprises PE1-AS1 and PE2-AS1 as PE routers. P1-AS1 and P2-AS1 are LS1010 switches and function as provider routers. The MPLS VPN provider network is running OSPF as the IGP routing protocol on PE1-AS1, P1-AS1, P2-AS1, and PE2-AS1. PE routers PE1-AS1 and PE2-AS1 are configured for MP-iBGP connectivity between them.

Customer A requires connectivity between the Site 1 network (172.16.10.0/24) and Site 2 network (172.16.20.0/24). Site 1 and Site 2 belong to the same VPN, VPN-A. Site 1 and Site 2 comprise CE routers CE1-A and CE2-A, respectively. CE1-A and CE2-A are connected to PE1-AS1 and PE2-AS1, respectively. CE1-A and CE2-A are already running RIPv2 routing protocol. RIPv2 PE-CE routing protocol on PE routers PE1-AS1 and PE2-AS1 is implemented as follows.

Figure 4-5 *MPLS VPN Provider Implementing RIPv2 PE-CE Routing*

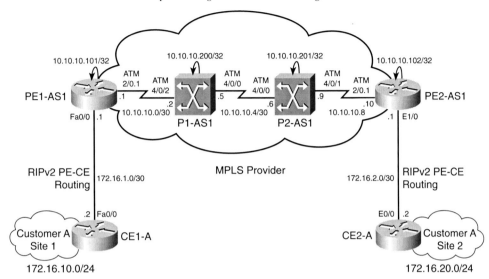

Prior to the configuration shown in Example 4-10, ensure that the provider network is provisioned to deliver MPLS VPN services to Customer A sites. Ensure that IP addresses are preconfigured and VRFs defined on PE router. Example 4-10 provides the configuration related to defining VRF and its attributes on PE routers for RIPv2 PE-CE routing.

Example 4-10 *Define VRF* **VRF-RIP** *on PE Routers PE1-AS1 and PE2-AS1*

```
PE1-AS1(config)#ip vrf VRF-RIP
PE1-AS1(config-vrf)# rd 1:100
PE1-AS1(config-vrf)#route-target both 1:100
PE1-AS1(config-vrf)#interface FastEthernet0/0
PE1-AS1(config-if)# ip vrf forwarding VRF-RIP
PE1-AS1(config-if)# ip address 172.16.1.1 255.255.255.252
PE2-AS1(config)#ip vrf VRF-RIP
PE2-AS1(config-vrf)# rd 1:100
PE2-AS1(config-vrf)# route-target both 1:100
PE2-AS1(config-vrf)#interface Ethernet1/0
PE2-AS1(config-if)# ip vrf forwarding VRF-RIP
PE2-AS1(config-if)# ip address 172.16.2.1 255.255.255.252
```

The steps to configure RIPv2 PE-CE routing on PE routers are as follows:

Step 1   **Configure per VRF RIP routing context and RIP parameters on PE routers**—Configure per VRF RIP routing context for VRF RIP under the RIP routing process on PE1-AS1 and PE2-AS1. Configure the per VRF RIP parameters under the address family. Example 4-11 shows this configuration step for PE1-AS1. Repeat the same steps for PE2-AS1.

Example 4-11 *Configure per VRF RIP Routing Context on PE Routers*

```
PE1-AS1(config)#router rip
PE1-AS1(config-router)# version 2
PE1-AS1(config-router)# address-family ipv4 vrf VRF-RIP
PE1-AS1(config-router-af)#network 172.16.0.0
PE1-AS1(config-router-af)# no auto-summary
PE1-AS1(config-router-af)# exit-address-family
```

Step 2   **Redistribute the per VRF RIP routes in BGP**—Example 4-12 shows
the step to redistribute the per VRF RIP routes into BGP on PE routers
PE1-AS1 and PE2-AS1. This configuration step is shown in
Example 4-12.

Example 4-12 *Redistribute RIPv2 Routes in BGP on PE Routers*

```
PE1-AS1(config)#router bgp 1
PE1-AS1(config-router)#address-family ipv4 vrf VRF-RIP
PE1-AS1(config-router-af)#redistribute rip
PE2-AS1(config)#router bgp 1
PE2-AS1(config-router)#address-family ipv4 vrf VRF-RIP
PE2-AS1(config-router-af)#redistribute rip
```

Step 3   **Redistribute MP-iBGP VPNv4 prefixes into RIP**—Redistribute the
MP-iBGP VPNv4 prefixes from remote PE1-AS1 into RIP per VRF
routing context on PE2-AS1 router. In RIP PE-CE routing, the RIP
metric is copied into the BGP multi-exit discriminator (MED) attribute.
This metric can be preserved across the CE network by configuring the
metric transparent option during redistribution from BGP into RIPv2,
and, by doing so, it is copied back from the BGP MED attribute into the
RIP version 2 metric. The configuration step is shown in Example 4-13.

Example 4-13 *Redistribute MP-IBGP Routes into RIP Routing Context on PE Routers*

```
PE1-AS1(config-router-af)#router rip
PE1-AS1(config-router)#address-family ipv4 vrf VRF-RIP
PE1-AS1(config-router-af)#redistribute bgp 1 metric transparent
PE2-AS1(config-router-af)#router rip
PE2-AS1(config-router)#address-family ipv4 vrf VRF-RIP
PE2-AS1(config-router-af)#redistribute bgp 1 metric transparent
```

RIPv2 PE-CE Routing—Customer Edge CE1-A and CE2-A Configuration

Example 4-14 shows the configuration on the CE1-A and CE2-A customer edge
routers.

Example 4-14 *CE1-A and CE2-A Router Configuration*

```
hostname CE1-A
!
interface Loopback0
 ip address 172.16.10.1 255.255.255.0
 !
interface FastEthernet0/0
description connected to PE1-AS1
ip address 172.16.1.2 255.255.255.252
 !
router rip
 version 2
 network 172.16.0.0
 no auto-summary
hostname CE2-A
!
interface Loopback0
 ip address 172.16.20.1 255.255.255.0
 !
interface Ethernet0/0
description connected to PE2-AS1
 ip address 172.16.2.2 255.255.255.252
 !
router rip
 version 2
 network 172.16.0.0
 no auto-summary
```

RIPv2 PE-CE Routing—Provider Edge PE1-AS1 and PE2-AS1 Configuration

Example 4-15 shows the final configuration on the CE1-RIP and CE2-RIP provider edge routers PE1-AS1 and PE2-AS1.

Example 4-15 *PE1-AS1 and PE2-AS1 Router Configuration*

```
hostname PE1-AS1
!
ip cef
!
ip vrf VRF-RIP
 rd 1:100
 route-target export 1:100
 route-target import 1:100
 !
mpls label protocol ldp
mpls tdp router-id Loopback0
 !
interface Loopback0
 ip address 10.10.10.101 255.255.255.255
 !
```

continues

Example 4-15 *PE1-AS1 and PE2-AS1 Router Configuration (Continued)*

```
interface FastEthernet0/0
description connected to CE1-A
 ip vrf forwarding VRF-RIP
 ip address 172.16.1.1 255.255.255.252
!
interface ATM2/0
 no ip address
 no atm ilmi-keepalive
!
interface ATM2/0.1 mpls
 description Connection to A1
 ip address 10.10.10.1 255.255.255.252
mpls ip
!
router ospf 1
 network 10.0.0.0 0.255.255.255 area 0
!
router rip
 version 2
 !
 address-family ipv4 vrf VRF-RIP
 version 2
 redistribute bgp 1 metric transparent
 network 172.16.0.0
 no auto-summary
 exit-address-family
!
router bgp 1
 no synchronization
 bgp log-neighbor-changes
 neighbor 10.10.10.102 remote-as 1
 neighbor 10.10.10.102 update-source Loopback0
 no auto-summary
 !
 address-family vpnv4
 neighbor 10.10.10.102 activate
 neighbor 10.10.10.102 send-community extended
 no auto-summary
 exit-address-family
 !
 address-family ipv4 vrf VRF-RIP
 redistribute rip
 no auto-summary
 no synchronization
 exit-address-family
```
```
hostname PE2-AS1
!
ip cef
!
ip vrf VRF-RIP
 rd 1:100
 route-target export 1:100
```

Example 4-15 *PE1-AS1 and PE2-AS1 Router Configuration (Continued)*

```
 route-target import 1:100
!
mpls label protocol ldp
mpls ldp router-id Loopback0
!
interface Loopback0
 ip address 10.10.10.102 255.255.255.255
!
interface Ethernet1/0
description connected to CE2-A
 ip vrf forwarding VRF-RIP
 ip address 172.16.2.1 255.255.255.252
!
interface ATM2/0
 no ip address
!
interface ATM2/0.1 mpls
 description connection to A2
 ip address 10.10.10.10 255.255.255.252
 mpls ip
!
router ospf 100
 network 10.10.0.0 0.0.255.255 area 0
!
router rip
 version 2
 !
 address-family ipv4 vrf VRF-RIP
 version 2
 redistribute bgp 1 metric transparent
 network 172.16.0.0
 no auto-summary
 exit-address-family
!
router bgp 1
 no synchronization
 neighbor 10.10.10.101 remote-as 1
 neighbor 10.10.10.101 update-source Loopback0
 no auto-summary
 !
 address-family vpnv4
 neighbor 10.10.10.101 activate
 neighbor 10.10.10.101 send-community extended
 no auto-summary
 exit-address-family
 !
 address-family ipv4 vrf VRF-RIP
 redistribute rip
 no auto-summary
 no synchronization
 exit-address-family
```

Verification of RIPv2 PE-CE Routing

The steps to verify RIPv2 PE-CE routing are as follows:

Step 1 **Verify BGP VPNv4 routing table on PE1-AS1 and PE2-AS1**—Check the BGP VPNv4 routing table to see if routes are received properly. Example 4-16 shows that PE1-AS1 receives 172.16.20.0/24. Repeat the same step on PE2-AS1.

Example 4-16 *Verify BGP VPNv4 Routing Table on PE Routers*

```
PE1-AS1#show ip bgp vpnv4 vrf VRF-RIP
BGP table version is 24, local router ID is 10.10.10.101
Status codes: s suppressed, d damped, h history, * valid, > best, i - internal
Origin codes: i - IGP, e - EGP, ? - incomplete

   Network          Next Hop          Metric LocPrf Weight Path
Route Distinguisher: 1:100 (default for vrf VRF-RIP)
*> 172.16.1.0/30    0.0.0.0                0         32768 ?
*>i172.16.2.0/30    10.10.10.102           0    100      0 ?
*> 172.16.10.0/24   172.16.1.2             1         32768 ?
*>i172.16.20.0/24   10.10.10.102           1    100      0 ?
```

Step 2 **Verify VRF routing table on PE1-AS1 and PE2-AS1**—Check the VRF routing table to see if routes advertised by local and remote CE routers are seen in the VRF routing table.

Example 4-17 shows that PE1-AS1 has received the 172.16.20.0 network from the PE2-AS1 and the 172.16.10.0/24 network from CE1-A.

Example 4-17 *Verify VRF Routing Table on PE Routers*

```
PE1-AS1#show ip route vrf VRF-RIP
<output truncated for brevity>
     172.16.0.0/16 is variably subnetted, 4 subnets, 2 masks
B       172.16.20.0/24 [200/1] via 10.10.10.102, 2d02h
R       172.16.10.0/24 [120/1] via 172.16.1.2, 00:00:06, FastEthernet0/0
C       172.16.1.0/30 is directly connected, FastEthernet0/0
B       172.16.2.0/30 [200/0] via 10.10.10.102, 2d02h
```

Step 3 **Verify end-to-end connectivity using ping**—Verify end-to-end connectivity between the CE1-A and CE2-A by issuing a ping from CE1-A to network 172.16.20.0/24 on CE2-A and vice versa. Example 4-18 shows that the ping has been successful.

Example 4-18 *Verify Reachability via Ping*

```
CE1-A#ping 172.16.20.1 source 172.16.10.1
Type escape sequence to abort.
Sending 5, 100-byte ICMP Echos to 172.16.20.1, timeout is 2 seconds:
Packet sent with a source address of 172.16.10.1
!!!!!
```

Example 4-18 *Verify Reachability via Ping (Continued)*

```
Success rate is 100 percent (5/5), round-trip min/avg/max = 1/2/4 ms
CE2-A#ping 172.16.10.1 source 172.16.20.1
Type escape sequence to abort.
Sending 5, 100-byte ICMP Echos to 172.16.10.1, timeout is 2 seconds:
Packet sent with a source address of 172.16.20.1
!!!!!
Success rate is 100 percent (5/5), round-trip min/avg/max = 1/2/4 ms
```

Control Plane Forwarding Operation

Figure 4-6 shows the path taken by the control packet originating from CE1-A to CE2-A.

Figure 4-6   *Control Plane Forwarding Between CE Routers*

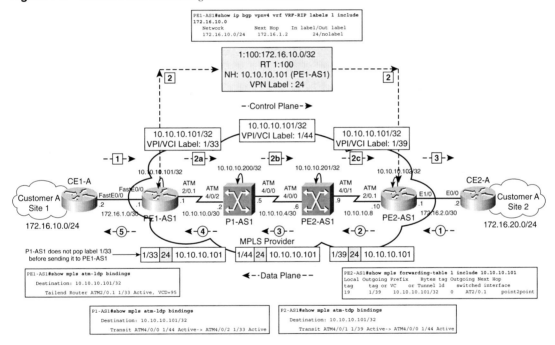

Step 1   CE1-RIP sends 172.16.10.0/24 as an IPv4 update to PE1-AS1:

```
PE1-AS1#show ip route vrf VRF-RIP | include 172.16.10.0
R       172.16.10.0/24 [120/1] via 172.16.1.2, 00:00:03, FastEthernet0/0
```

Step 2   Figure 4-6 shows that PE1-AS1 accepts and transforms the IPv4 route,
172.16.10.0/24, to a VPNv4 route by assigning an RD 1:100, SoO, and
RT 1:100 based on the VRF RIP configuration on PE1-AS1. It then
allocates a VPNv4 label 24 to 172.16.10.0/24 update and rewrites the
next-hop attribute to the PE1-AS1 loopback0 IP address **10.10.10.101**.

Now PE1-AS1, 10.10.10.101, *is reachable via IGP (OSPF) and LDP*. The following control plane operation shows the IGP label propagation for prefix 10.10.10.101/32 from PE1-AS1 to PE2-AS1 inside the provider network. This propagation takes place as soon as the MPLS VPN provider network is established and is always in place prior to any VPNv4 prefix being propagated across the MPLS VPN provider network. The following steps are performed in the label propagation process for prefix 10.10.10.101/32. This operation is shown for clarity:

— **Step 2A** In Figure 4-6, Edge ATM LSR PE2-AS1 requests a label for the 10.10.10.101/32 prefix using the LDP label mapping request from its downstream neighbor, ATM LSR P2-AS1. P2-AS1 requests a label for the 10.10.10.101/32 prefix using the LDP label mapping request from its downstream neighbor, ATM LSR P1-AS1. P1-AS1, in turn, requests a label for the 10.10.10.101/32 prefix using the LDP label mapping request from its downstream neighbor, Edge ATM LSR PE1-AS1. Edge ATM LSR PE1-AS1 allocates a label to 10.10.10.101/32, which corresponds to its inbound VPI/VCI value 1/33, modifies the entry in the LFIB corresponding to 10.10.10.101/32, and sends it to P1-AS1 using an LDP reply. Example 4-19 shows the output of **show mpls atm-ldp bindings** on PE1-AS1.

Example 4-19 *Label Allocation and Distribution Verification on PE1-AS1*

```
PE1-AS1#show mpls atm-ldp bindings
Destination: 10.10.10.101/32
   Tailend Router ATM2/0.1 1/33 Active, VCD=95
Destination: 10.10.10.4/30
   Headend Router ATM2/0.1 (1 hop) 1/33  Active, VCD=95
Destination: 10.10.10.8/30
   Headend Router ATM2/0.1 (2 hops) 1/34  Active, VCD=97
Destination: 10.10.10.102/32
   Headend Router ATM2/0.1 (3 hops) 1/35  Active, VCD=99
Destination: 10.10.10.200/32
   Headend Router ATM2/0.1 (1 hop) 1/36  Active, VCD=96
Destination: 10.10.10.201/32
   Headend Router ATM2/0.1 (2 hops) 1/37  Active, VCD=98
```

— **Step 2B** P1-AS1 uses the VPI/VCI, **1/33**, received from PE1-AS1 as its outbound VPI/VCI label value, allocates a free VC that is mapped to the local inbound VPI/VCI **1/44**, and modifies the LFIB entry for 10.10.10.101/32. P1-AS1 then sends VPI/VCI value **1/44** to P2-AS1 via an LDP reply, as shown in Figure 4-6. Example 4-20 shows the output of **show mpls atm-ldp bindings** on P1-AS1.

Example 4-20 *Label Allocation and Distribution Verification on P1-AS1*

```
P1-AS1#show mpls atm-ldp bindings
Destination: 10.10.10.200/32
    Tailend Switch ATM4/0/0 1/35 Active -> Terminating Active, VCD=70
    Tailend Switch ATM4/0/2 1/36 Active -> Terminating Active, VCD=74
Destination: 10.10.10.0/30
    Tailend Switch ATM4/0/0 1/33 Active -> ATM4/0/2 Terminating Active, VCD=69
Destination: 10.10.10.101/32
    Transit ATM4/0/0 1/44 Active -> ATM4/0/2 1/33 Active
Destination: 10.10.10.4/30
    Tailend Switch ATM4/0/2 1/33 Active -> ATM4/0/0 Terminating Active, VCD=73
Destination: 10.10.10.8/30
    Transit ATM4/0/2 1/34 Active -> ATM4/0/0 1/33 Active
Destination: 10.10.10.102/32
    Transit ATM4/0/2 1/35 Active -> ATM4/0/0 1/34 Active
Destination: 10.10.10.201/32
    Transit ATM4/0/2 1/37 Active -> ATM4/0/0 1/35 Active
```

— **Step 2C** P2-AS1 uses the VPI/VCI, **1/44**, received from P1-AS1 as its outbound VPI/VCI value, allocates a free VC that is mapped to the local inbound VPI/VCI **1/39**, and modifies the LFIB entry for 10.10.10.101/32. P2-AS1 then sends VPI/VCI value **1/39** to PE2-AS1 via an LDP reply. Example 4-21 shows the output of **show mpls atm-ldp bindings** on P2-AS1.

Example 4-21 *Label Allocation and Distribution Verification on P2-AS1*

```
P2-AS1#show mpls atm-ldp bindings
Destination: 10.10.10.0/30
    Transit ATM4/0/1 1/33 Active -> ATM4/0/0 1/33 Active
Destination: 10.10.10.4/30
    Tailend Switch ATM4/0/1 1/34 Active -> ATM4/0/0 Terminating Active, VCD=119
Destination: 10.10.10.200/32
    Transit ATM4/0/1 1/36 Active -> ATM4/0/0 1/35 Active
Destination: 10.10.10.201/32
    Tailend Switch ATM4/0/1 1/37 Active -> Terminating Active, VCD=120
    Tailend Switch ATM4/0/0 1/35 Active -> Terminating Active, VCD=126
Destination: 10.10.10.101/32
    Transit ATM4/0/1 1/39 Active -> ATM4/0/0 1/44 Active
Destination: 10.10.10.8/30
    Tailend Switch ATM4/0/0 1/33 Active -> ATM4/0/1 Terminating Active, VCD=125
Destination: 10.10.10.102/32
    Transit ATM4/0/0 1/34 Active -> ATM4/0/1 1/35 Active
```

Edge ATM LSR PE2-AS1 then uses VPI/VCI value 1/39, received from P2-AS1, as its outbound VPI/VCI value and modifies the entry in the LFIB. This is shown in Example 4-22.

Example 4-22 *Label Allocation and Distribution Verification on PE2-AS1*

```
PE2-AS1#show mpls forwarding-table
Local  Outgoing     Prefix            Bytes tag  Outgoing    Next Hop
tag    tag or VC    or Tunnel Id      switched   interface
16     1/34         10.10.10.4/30     0          AT2/0.1     point2point
18     1/33         10.10.10.0/30     0          AT2/0.1     point2point
19     1/39         10.10.10.101/32   0          AT2/0.1     point2point
22     1/36         10.10.10.200/32   0          AT2/0.1     point2point
23     1/37         10.10.10.201/32   0          AT2/0.1     point2point
25     Aggregate    172.16.2.0/30[V]  0
26     Untagged     172.16.20.0/24[V] 0          Et1/0       172.16.2.2
PE2-AS1#show mpls atm-ldp bindings
Destination: 10.10.10.0/30
   Headend Router ATM2/0.1 (2 hops) 1/33  Active, VCD=72
Destination: 10.10.10.4/30
   Headend Router ATM2/0.1 (1 hop) 1/34  Active, VCD=70
Destination: 10.10.10.200/32
   Headend Router ATM2/0.1 (2 hops) 1/36  Active, VCD=73
Destination: 10.10.10.201/32
   Headend Router ATM2/0.1 (1 hop) 1/37  Active, VCD=71
Destination: 10.10.10.101/32
   Headend Router ATM2/0.1 (3 hops) 1/39  Active, VCD=76
Destination: 10.10.10.102/32
   Tailend Router ATM2/0.1 1/35 Active, VCD=77
```

Step 3   PE1-AS1 has VRF RIP configured to accept routes with RT 1:100 and, therefore, translates the VPNv4 update to IPv4 and inserts the route in VRF RIP. It then propagates this route to the CE2-A.

Data Forwarding Operation

The data forwarding path originates from 172.16.20.1, which is the source address with the traffic destined to 172.16.10.1. Figure 4-6 traces the path of the data packet from the source to the destination:

Step 1   CE2-RIP originates a data packet with the source address of 172.16.20.1 and destination of 172.16.10.1.

Step 2   PE2-AS1 receives the data packet and appends the VPN label 24 and LDP label 1/39 and forwards the packet to P2-AS1. See Example 4-23.

Example 4-23 *Data Forwarding Verification on PE2-AS1*

```
PE2-AS1#show ip cef vrf VRF-RIP 172.16.10.0
172.16.10.0/24, version 17, epoch 0, cached adjacency to ATM2/0.1
0 packets, 0 bytes
  tag information set
    local tag: VPN-route-head
    fast tag rewrite with AT2/0.1, point2point, tags imposed: {1/39(vcd=76) 24}
```

Example 4-23 *Data Forwarding Verification on PE2-AS1 (Continued)*

```
        via 10.10.10.101, 0 dependencies, recursive
        next hop 10.10.10.9, ATM2/0.1 via 10.10.10.101/32
        valid cached adjacency
        tag rewrite with AT2/0.1, point2point, tags imposed: {1/39(vcd=76) 24}
```

Step 3   P2-AS1 receives the data packet destined to 172.16.10.1 and swaps LDP label 1/39 with 1/44. Example 4-24 shows the output of **show mpls atm-ldp bindings** *destination-prefix mask-length* on P2-AS1.

Example 4-24 *Data Plane Verification on P2-AS1*

```
P2-AS1#show mpls atm-ldp bindings 10.10.10.101 32
  Destination: 10.10.10.101/32
    Transit ATM4/0/1 1/39 Active -> ATM4/0/0 1/44 Active
```

Step 4   P1-AS1 receives the data packet destined to 172.16.10.1 and swaps LDP label 1/44 with 1/33. Example 4-25 shows the output of **show mpls atm-ldp bindings** *destination-prefix mask-length.* Penultimate hop popping is not supported on ATM LSRs because the label is part of the ATM cell payload and cannot be removed by ATM switching hardware. Therefore, P1-AS1, which is an ATM device, does not perform any penultimate hop popping function.

Example 4-25 *Data Plane Verification on P1-AS1*

```
P1-AS1#show mpls atm-ldp bindings 10.10.10.101 32
  Destination: 10.10.10.101/32
    Transit ATM4/0/0 1/44 Active -> ATM4/0/2 1/33 Active
```

Step 5   PE1-AS1 pops the label stack (both VPN label 24 and LDP label 1/33) and forwards the data packet to CE1-RIP where the 172.16.10.0 network is located.

RIPv1 PE-CE Routing Configuration and Verification

NOTE   RIPv1 is not recommended for MPLS VPN networks and is demonstrated here only for learning purposes.

The topology to demonstrate RIPv1 PE-CE routing is shown in Figure 4-7.

Figure 4-7 *Provider Implementing RIPv1 PE-CE Routing*

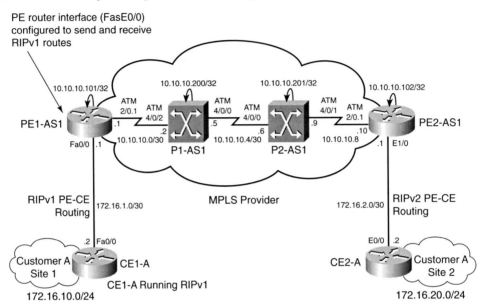

CE1-A is running RIPv1 routing protocol. Because CE1-A is sending RIPv1 routes, the interface on PE1-AS1 connected to CE1-A is configured to receive and send RIPv1 routes. IP addressing for the CE networks adheres to classful addressing. RIPv2 PE-CE routing configuration is still used on PE2-AS1 because the MP-iBGP session between PE routers transports only RIPv2 routes. Example 4-26 shows the necessary steps to configure PE1-AS1 interface connected to CE1-A to send and receive RIPv1 routes.

Example 4-26 *PE1-AS1 RIPv1 PE-CE Configuration*

```
PE1-AS1(config)#interface FastEthernet0/0
PE1-AS1(config-if)# ip vrf forwarding VRF-RIP
PE1-AS1(config-if)# ip address 172.16.1.1 255.255.255.0
PE1-AS1(config-if)#ip rip send version 1
PE1-AS1(config-if)#ip rip receive version 1
PE1-AS1#show ip protocols vrf VRF-RIP
Routing Protocol is "rip"
  Sending updates every 30 seconds, next due in 5 seconds
  Invalid after 180 seconds, hold down 180, flushed after 240
  Outgoing update filter list for all interfaces is not set
  Incoming update filter list for all interfaces is not set
  Redistributing: rip, bgp 1
  Default version control: send version 2, receive version 2
    Interface            Send  Recv  Triggered RIP  Key-chain
    FastEthernet0/0        1     1
  Maximum path: 4
  Routing for Networks:
    172.16.0.0
```

Example 4-26 *PE1-AS1 RIPv1 PE-CE Configuration (Continued)*

```
  Routing Information Sources:
    Gateway           Distance      Last Update
    172.16.1.2            120      00:00:14
  Distance: (default is 120)
```

RIPv1 PE-CE Routing—PE1-AS1 and CE1-A Final Configuration

Configuration for PE2-AS1, P1-AS1, P2-AS2, and CE2-A remains the same as what was shown in the "RIPv2 PE-CE Routing—Provider Edge PE1-AS1 and PE2-AS1 Configuration" section. Example 4-27 shows the PE1-AS1 and CE1-A final configuration.

Example 4-27 *CE1-A and PE1-AS1 Configuration—RIPv1 PE-CE*

```
hostname CE1-A
!
ip cef
!
interface Loopback0
 ip address 172.16.10.1 255.255.255.0
 !
interface FastEthernet0/0
 ip address 172.16.1.2 255.255.255.0
 !
router rip
 network 172.16.0.0
 no auto-summary
```
```
hostname PE1-AS1
!
ip cef
!
ip vrf VRF-RIP
 rd 1:100
 route-target export 1:100
 route-target import 1:100
 !
mpls ldp router-id Loopback0
 !
interface Loopback0
 ip address 10.10.10.101 255.255.255.255
 !
interface FastEthernet0/0
 ip vrf forwarding VRF-RIP
 ip address 172.16.1.1 255.255.255.0
 ip rip send version 1
 ip rip receive version 1
 !
interface ATM2/0
 no ip address
 no atm ilmi-keepalive
 !
interface ATM2/0.1 mpls
```

continues

Example 4-27 *CE1-A and PE1-AS1 Configuration—RIPv1 PE-CE (Continued)*

```
 description Connection to A1
 ip address 10.10.10.1 255.255.255.252
 mpls label protocol ldp
 tag-switching ip
!
router ospf 1
network 10.0.0.0 0.255.255.255 area 0
!
router rip
 version 2
 !
 address-family ipv4 vrf VRF-RIP
 version 2
 redistribute bgp 1 metric transparent
 network 172.16.0.0
 no auto-summary
 exit-address-family
!
router bgp 1
 no synchronization
 neighbor 10.10.10.102 remote-as 1
 neighbor 10.10.10.102 update-source Loopback0
 no auto-summary
 !
 address-family vpnv4
 neighbor 10.10.10.102 activate
 neighbor 10.10.10.102 send-community extended
 no auto-summary
 exit-address-family
 !
 address-family ipv4 vrf VRF-RIP
 redistribute rip
 no auto-summary
 no synchronization
 exit-address-family
```

Verification of RIPv1 PE-CE Routing

The steps to verify RIPv1 PE-CE routing are as follows:

Step 1 **Verify VRF routing table on PE1-AS1 and PE2-AS1**—Check the VRF routing table to see if routes to the CE networks are configured properly and remote routes from PE routers are received in the VRF.

Example 4-28 shows that PE1-AS1 has received routes from the PE2-AS1 router for the 172.16.20.0/24 network and has also received 172.16.10.0 network from CE1-A.

Example 4-28 *Verification of VRF Routes on PE1-AS1 and PE2-AS1*

```
PE1-AS1#show ip route vrf VRF-RIP
<output truncated for brevity>
      172.16.0.0/24 is subnetted, 4 subnets
B        172.16.20.0 [200/1] via 10.10.10.102, 00:08:53
R        172.16.10.0 [120/1] via 172.16.1.2, 00:00:04, FastEthernet0/0
C        172.16.1.0 is directly connected, FastEthernet0/0
B        172.16.2.0 [200/0] via 10.10.10.102, 00:06:07
PE2-AS1#show ip route vrf VRF-RIP
<output truncated for brevity>
      172.16.0.0/24 is subnetted, 4 subnets
R        172.16.20.0 [120/1] via 172.16.2.2, 00:00:12, Ethernet1/0
B        172.16.10.0 [200/1] via 10.10.10.101, 00:08:23
B        172.16.1.0 [200/0] via 10.10.10.101, 00:13:38
C        172.16.2.0 is directly connected, Ethernet1/0
```

Step 2   Verify RIP routes on CE routers CE1-A and CE2-A—Check the
BGP VPNv4 routing table to see if routes are received properly.
Example 4-29 shows that PE1-AS1 and PE2-AS1 routers see the
routes from 172.16.20.0/24 and 172.16.10.0/24 in their RIP routing
table.

Example 4-29 *Verify Routes on CE1-A and CE2-A*

```
CE2-A#show ip route
<output truncated for brevity>
      172.16.0.0/24 is subnetted, 4 subnets
C        172.16.20.0 is directly connected, Loopback0
R        172.16.10.0 [120/2] via 172.16.2.1, 00:00:04, Ethernet0/0
R        172.16.1.0 [120/1] via 172.16.2.1, 00:00:04, Ethernet0/0
C        172.16.2.0 is directly connected, Ethernet0/0
CE1-A#show ip route
<output truncated for brevity>
      172.16.0.0/24 is subnetted, 4 subnets
R        172.16.20.0 [120/2] via 172.16.1.1, 00:00:21, FastEthernet0/0
C        172.16.10.0 is directly connected, Loopback0
C        172.16.1.0 is directly connected, FastEthernet0/0
R        172.16.2.0 [120/1] via 172.16.1.1, 00:00:21, FastEthernet0/0
```

Step 3   Verify end-to-end connectivity using ping—Verify end-to-end
connectivity between the CE1-A and CE2-A by issuing a ping from
CE1-A to network 172.16.20.0/24 on CE2-A and vice versa. Example 4-30
shows that the ping has been successful.

Example 4-30 *Verify Reachability via Ping*

```
CE1-A#ping 172.16.20.1 source 172.16.10.1
Type escape sequence to abort.
Sending 5, 100-byte ICMP Echos to 172.16.20.1, timeout is 2 seconds:
Packet sent with a source address of 172.16.10.1
!!!!!
```

continues

Example 4-30 *Verify Reachability via Ping (Continued)*

```
Success rate is 100 percent (5/5), round-trip min/avg/max = 1/2/4 ms
CE2-A#ping 172.16.10.1 source 172.16.20.1
Type escape sequence to abort.
Sending 5, 100-byte ICMP Echos to 172.16.10.1, timeout is 2 seconds:
Packet sent with a source address of 172.16.20.1
!!!!!
Success rate is 100 percent (5/5), round-trip min/avg/max = 1/2/4 ms
```

RIP PE-CE Routing Command Reference

Table 4-2 provides the RIP PE-CE routing configuration command summary.

Table 4-2 *RIP PE-CE Routing Command Reference*

Command	Description
Router(config)#**router rip**	Configures the RIP routing process.
Router(config-router)#**version {1	2}**	Used to specify RIPv1 or RIPv2 routing protocol.
Router(config-router)#**address-family ipv4** **[unicast] vrf** *vrf-name*	The **address-family** command puts the router in address family configuration submode (prompt: (config-router-af)#). Within this submode, you can configure address family specific parameters for routing protocols, such as RIP and BGP, that can accommodate multiple Layer 3 address families.
Router(config-router-af)#**network** *ip-address*	Specifies a list of networks for RIP routing process. The command is used in router configuration mode. In an MPLS VPN environment, the command is configured in address-family mode.
Router(config-router-af)#**no auto-summary**	Disables the default behavior of automatic summarization of subnet routes into network-level routes. RIP Version 1 always uses automatic summarization. If you are using RIP Version 2, you can turn off automatic summarization by specifying the **no auto-summary** command. Disable automatic summarization if you must perform routing between disconnected subnets. When automatic summarization is off, subnets are advertised.

Table 4-2   *RIP PE-CE Routing Command Reference (Continued)*

Command	Description
Router(config-router-af)# **redistribute bgp** *as-number* [**metric**] [**transparent**]	Redistributes MP-BGP routes into RIP. The **transparent** option is used when the RIP metric needs to be preserved across the MPLS VPN network for RIP VPN sites.
Router(config)#**router bgp** *as-number*	Configures the BGP routing process.
Router(config-router-af)# **redistribute rip** [**metric**] *value*	Redistributes RIP routes into BGP IPv4 VRF routing context.
ip rip receive version [1] [2]	Specifies the RIP version to be received on an interface.
ip rip send version [1] [2]	Specifies the RIP version to be sent on an interface.

CHAPTER 5

PE-CE Routing Protocol— OSPF and EIGRP

Chapter 4, "PE-CE Routing Protocol—Static and RIP," provided you with an overview and steps to configure static and RIP PE-CE routing protocol in an MPLS VPN environment.

This chapter introduces you to OSPF and EIGRP PE-CE routing protocol concepts and includes the following:

- OSPF PE-CE routing protocol overview, configuration and verification
  - Traditional OSPF routing model
  - MPLS VPN or OSPF superbackbone concept
  - OSPF route-propagation using the MPLS VPN superbackbone
  - OSPF down bit and domain tag
  - Configuring and verification of OSPF PE-CE routing
  - OSPF sham-links
- EIGRP PE-CE routing protocol overview, configuration, and verification
  - EIGRP route propagation
  - Configuration flowchart for EIGRP PE-CE routing
  - Routing loops and suboptimal routing
  - BGP cost community feature
  - EIGRP site of origin (SoO) attribute

OSPF PE-CE Routing Protocol Overview, Configuration and Verification

Open Shortest Path First (OSPF) PE-CE routing protocol support was developed for service providers offering MPLS VPN services to customers who have deployed OSPF as their intra-site routing protocol and, hence, preferred usage of OSPF as the VPN inter-site routing protocol in an MPLS VPN environment. Forthcoming sections introduce you to the issues with implementing traditional OSPF routing models in MPLS VPN environments and the concept of the OSPF superbackbone to resolve them. In addition, the OSPF PE-CE routing configuration in an MPLS VPN environment and OSPF sham-links, used to resolve suboptimal routing caused by backdoor links between OSPF sites in MPLS VPN environments, are discussed.

Traditional OSPF Routing Model

The traditional OSPF domain is divided into backbone (Area 0) and non-backbone areas where non-backbone areas are connected to Area 0. Figure 5-1 shows Customer A implementing the traditional OSPF model in which non-backbone areas, Area 1 and Area 2 belonging to Site 1 and Site 2, respectively, are connected to the OSPF backbone area, Area 0.

Figure 5-1 *Traditional OSPF and MPLS VPN Routing Model*

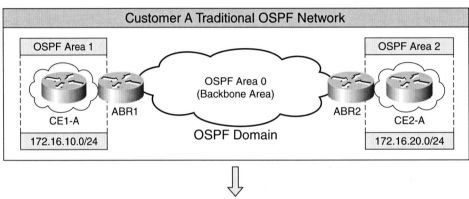

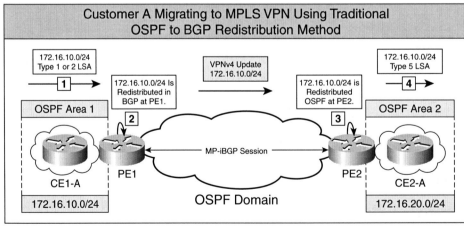

In an MPLS VPN environment, customer networks are connected to an MPLS VPN-enabled provider backbone. As shown in Figure 5-1, Customer A areas, Areas 1 and 2, are now connected to an MPLS VPN–enabled provider network. Area 1 and Area 2 have routers CE1-A and CE2-A running OSPF routing protocol. MP-iBGP is used between PE1 and PE2 to propagate routes between Site 1 (Area 1) and Site 2 (Area 2). Traditional OSPF-BGP redistribution is performed at PE routers, PE1 and PE2. Figure 5-1 depicts the following sequence that takes place in traditional OSPF-BGP redistribution:

1 Network 172.16.10.0/24 is advertised to the PE1 router by CE1-A as a Type 1 or Type 2 link-state advertisement (LSA).

2 Traditional OSPF-BGP route redistribution takes place where 172.16.10.0/24 is redistributed into BGP at PE1. This route is then propagated as a VPNv4 route to PE2.

3 At PE2, the BGP VPNv4 prefix 172.16.10.0/24 is redistributed in OSPF.

4 This redistributed route 172.16.10.0/24 is propagated as an external LSA Type 5 OSPF route.

Therefore, the OSPF route type, or LSA type, *is not preserved* when the OSPF route for 172.16.10.0 is redistributed into BGP when traditional OSPF routing rules are used in an MPLS VPN environment. Moreover, the following characteristics of OSPF external routes do not allow a smooth transition for a customer trying to migrate from traditional OSPF routing to the MPLS VPN routing model:

* Internal routes, regardless of their cost, are always preferred over external routes.

* External routes cannot be summarized.

* External routes are flooded throughout all OSPF areas.

* External routes could use a different metric type that is not comparable to OSPF cost.

* External LSA Type 5 routes are not inserted in stub areas or not-so-stubby areas (NSSA).

Another issue encountered in OSPF implementations with MPLS VPN is that the customer can have multiple sites in Area 0, as illustrated in Figure 5-2, and, therefore, deviate from the traditional OSPF hierarchy of single backbone Area 0 with all non-backbone areas connected to this Area 0.

Figure 5-2   *OSPF Hierarchy Issue*

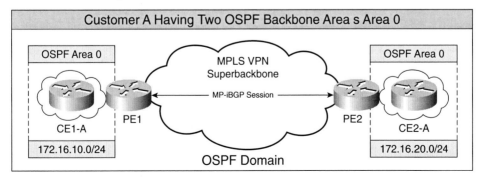

MPLS VPN or OSPF Superbackbone Concept

To circumvent the issues posed by the traditional OSPF routing model, the MPLS VPN architecture for OSPF PE-CE routing was expanded to allow transparent customer migration from traditional OSPF routing to the MPLS VPN routing model by introducing another backbone above the OSPF Area 0. This backbone is called the OSPF or MPLS VPN superbackbone.

As shown in Figure 5-3

- The non-backbone areas, Area 1 and Area 2, are directly connected to the MPLS VPN superbackbone that functions as an OSPF Area 0. Therefore, an actual Area 0 is not required as in the traditional OSPF domain. Area 0 is a requirement only when the PE router is connected to two different non-backbone areas belonging to the same OSPF domain on a PE router.

- The PE routers, PE1 and PE2, which connect OSPF areas in the customer domain to the superbackbone, appear as OSPF Area Border Routers (ABR) for the devices in the customer OSPF domains. CE routers CE1-A and CE2-A are not aware of any other OSPF areas beyond the MPLS VPN superbackbone because of its transparency.

- The MPLS VPN superbackbone is implemented using MP-iBGP between PE routers. OSPF information is carried across the MPLS VPN superbackbone using BGP extended communities. These extended communities are set and used by PE routers.

- There are no OSPF adjacencies or flooding in the MPLS VPN superbackbone for customer sites connected to the superbackbone, except when using OSPF sham-links.

Figure 5-3 *MPLS VPN or OSPF Superbackbone*

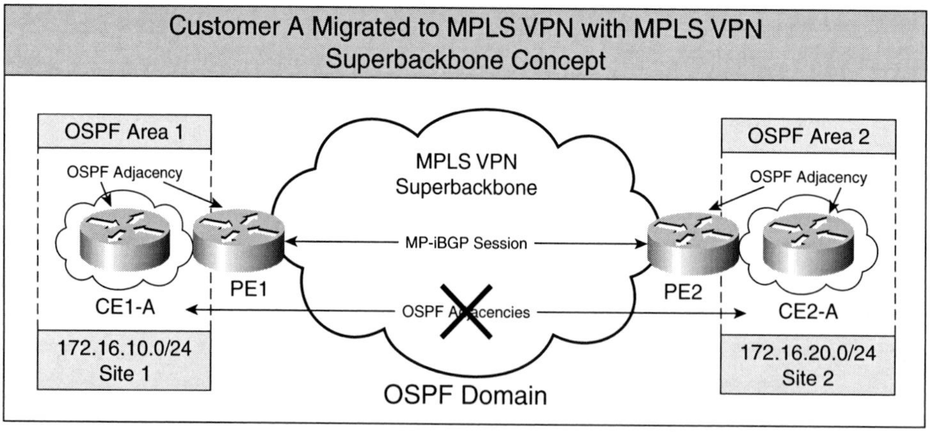

BGP Extended Communities for OSPF PE-CE Routing

In the MPLS VPN superbackbone, the following BGP extended attributes are carried:

- **OSPF Route Type**—Propagates OSPF route type information across the MP-iBGP backbone. Figure 5-4 shows the OSPF route type extended communities attribute.

Figure 5-5 depicts the OSPF route type detail for prefix 172.16.20.0, 192.168.99.0, and 192.168.199.0.

- **OSPF router ID**—Identifies the router ID of the PE in the relevant VRF instance of OSPF. This address is not part of the provider's address space and is unique in the OSPF network.

- **OSPF domain ID**—Identifies the domain of a specific OSPF prefix in the MPLS VPN backbone. By default, this value is equal to the value of the OSPF process ID and can be overwritten by the command **domain ID** *ip-address* under the OSPF process. If the domain ID of the route does not match the domain ID on the receiving PE, the route is translated to the external OSPF route (LSA Type 5) with metric-type E2, assuming the route was received in the VRF table. All routing between OSPF domains is via Type 5 LSAs.

Figure 5-4   *OSPF Route Type, Router ID, and Domain ID*

OSPF Route Type Community Attribute

Type = 0×0306 or 0×8000	OSPF Area Number	LSA Type	OSPF Options
◄── 2 Bytes ──►	◄──────── 4 Bytes ────────►	◄─ 1 Byte ─►	◄─ 1 Byte ─►

Type - It is encoded with a 2-byte type field, and its type is 0×0306. The type 0×8000 is also used to ensure backwards compatibility.

OSPF Area Number - 4 bytes, encoding a 32-bit area number. For external routes, the value is 0. A non-0 value identifies the route as being internal to the OSPF domain, and as being within the identified area. Area numbers are relative to a particular OSPF domain.

OSPF Route Type - 1 byte, encoded as follows:

Value	Route Type
1 or 2	For Intra-Area Routes (Type 1 or Type 2 LSA)
3	Summary Route or LSA Type 3
5	External Routes or Type 5 LSA. In this case, the area number Is 0.
7	NSSA Routes
129	For Sham Link Endpoint Addresses

OSPF Option - 1 byte field, it is used for external routes (Type 5 and 7 LSAs), if LSB of option = 1, route is of metric type E2.

OSPF Router ID

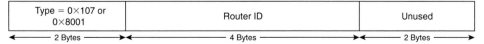

Type = 0×107 or 0×8001	Router ID	Unused
◄── 2 Bytes ──►	◄──────── 4 Bytes ────────►	◄── 2 Bytes ──►

OSPF Domain ID

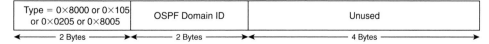

Type = 0×8000 or 0×105 or 0×0205 or 0×8005	OSPF Domain ID	Unused
◄── 2 Bytes ──►	◄── 2 Bytes ──►	◄──────── 4 Bytes ────────►

Figure 5-5 *OSPF Route Type, Router ID, and Domain ID Detail for 172.16.20.0, 192.168.99.0, and 192.168.199.0*

```
PE2-AS1#show ip bgp vpnv4 all 172.16.20.0
BGP routing table entry for 1:100:172.16.20.0/24, version 15
Paths: (1 available, best #1, table VRF-OSPF)
  Advertised to update-groups:
     1                                    OSPF Domain ID
  Local
    172.16.2.2 from 0.0.0.0 (10.10.10.102)
      Origin incomplete, metric 74, localpref 100, weight 32768, valid, sourced, best
      Extended Community: RT:1:100 OSPF DOMAIN ID:0x0005:0x0000006650200
        OSPF RT:0.0.0.2:2:0 OSPF ROUTER ID:172.16.102.1:512,
      mpls labels in/out 20/nolabel
```

Area 2   LSA Type 2   No Options   65 Is Equal to 101
                                            in Decimal. 101 Is
                                            the Process ID.

```
PE2-AS1#show ip bgp vpnv4 all 192.168.99.0
BGP routing table entry for 1:200:192.168.99.0/24, version 145
Paths: (1 available, best #1, table Cust_B)
  Advertised to update-groups:
     1
  Local
    192.168.2.2 from 0.0.0.0 (10.10.10.102)
      Origin incomplete, metric 84, localpref 100, weight 32768, valid,
sourced, best
      Extended Community: RT:1:200 OSPF DOMAIN ID:0x0005:0x000000CA0200
        OSPF RT:0.0.0.0:5:0 OSPF ROUTER ID:192.168.202.1:512,
      mpls labels in/out 28/nolabel
```

Area 0   LSA Type 5   No Options   CA Is Equal to 202
                                            in Decimal. 202 Is
Since the Option Field Is Not Set, 192.168.99.0   the Process ID.
Is a OSPF External Type 1 Route.

```
PE2-AS1#show ip bgp vpnv4 all 192.168.199.0
BGP routing table entry for 1:200:192.168.199.0/24, version 146
Paths: (1 available, best #1, table Cust_B)
  Advertised to update-groups:
     1
  Local
    192.168.2.2 from 0.0.0.0 (10.10.10.102)
      Origin incomplete, metric 20, localpref 100, weight 32768, valid,
sourced, best
      Extended Community: RT:1:200 OSPF DOMAIN ID:0x0005:0x000000CA0200
        OSPF RT:0.0.0.0:5:1 OSPF ROUTER ID:192.168.202.1:512,
      mpls labels in/out 27/nolabel
```

Area 0   LSA Type 5   Since the Option Field Is Set, 192.168.199.0
                        Is a OSPF External Type 2 Route.

OSPF Route-Propagation Using MPLS VPN Superbackbone Concept

OSPF route propagation in an MPLS VPN environment is not as traditional as the OSPF routing model and depends on the OSPF domain ID. By default, the OSPF domain ID is equal to the process ID configured on the PE router. The domain ID is set in the VPNv4 update when the OSPF route is redistributed into MP-iBGP.

OSPF Domain ID Is Same on All PE Routers

Figure 5-6 shows an MPLS network providing MPLS VPN services to Customer A. CE routers CE1-A and CE2-A at site networks 172.16.10.0/24 and 172.16.20.0/24 are in Area 1 and Area 2, respectively, while PE-CE links at both sites are in Area 0. OSPF process ID on both PE routers is 101. In addition, CE2-A functions as a traditional ASBR between the OSPF domain and external routing domains RIPv2 and EIGRP (AS101).

Figure 5-6 *Route Propagation When OSPF Domain (Process) ID Is Same*

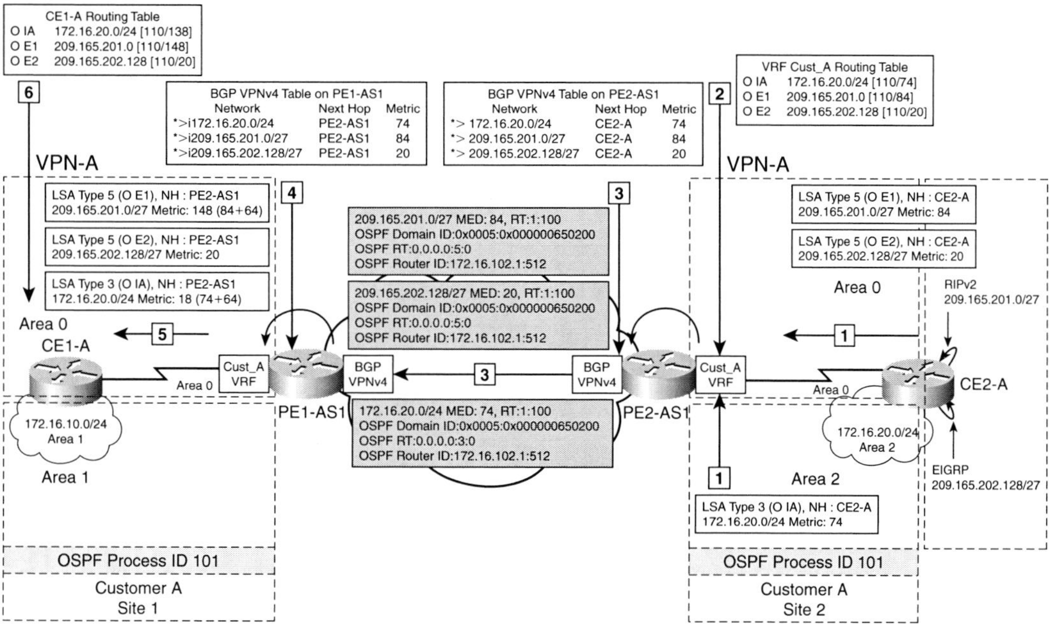

The following sequence takes place when CE2-A is sending 172.16.20.0/24, 209.165.127.0/27, and 209.165.202.128/27 to CE1-A:

1 CE2-A redistributes RIPv2 network 209.165.201.1 into OSPF and propagates it as an OSPF external Type 1 route (O E1) to PE2-AS1. EIGRP network 209.165.202.128/27 is redistributed at CE2-A and propagated as an OSPF external Type 2 (O E2) to PE2-AS1. CE2-A also sends 172.16.20.0/24 as an inter-area route (O IA) to PE2-AS1.

2 VRF Cust_A routing table on PE2-AS1 shows the received routes 172.16.20.0/24 as OSPF inter-area route with OSPF metric (cost) 74, 209.165.127.0/27 as an external Type 1 route with OSPF metric 84, and 209.165.202.128/27 route with OSPF metric 20.

3 As shown in Figure 5-6, the OSPF cost for 172.16.20.0/24, 209.165.127.0/27, and 209.165.202.128/27 is copied into extended BGP attributes as BGP MEDs when OSPF is redistributed into MP-BGP. The routes 172.16.20.0, 209.165.127.0, and 209.165.202.128/27 are then propagated to PE1-AS1 via MP-iBGP session.

4   PE1-AS1 receives the BGP VPNv4 routes 172.16.20.0/24, 209.165.127.0/27, and 209.165.202.128/27 from PE2-AS1 and inserts them in the BGP table. As illustrated in Figure 5-6, the OSPF metric for the routes are not altered and remain the same when propagated though the MP-BGP backbone.

5   The receiving PE router, PE1-AS1, redistributes the MP-BGP routes back into OSPF, verifies the domain ID, and if the domain ID of the route matches the domain ID on the receiving PE, PE1-AS1, it uses the original LSA type and the MED attribute to generate an inter-area summary (LSA Type 3) LSA. In Figure 5-6, the domain ID matches the domain ID on PE1-AS1, so PE1-AS1 reconstructs the original update and updates the metric based on the outgoing interfaces and propagates the 172.16.20.0/24 as an inter-area route to CE1-A. 209.165.127.0/24 and 209.165.202.128/27 are propagated as OSPF external Type 1 and Type 2 to CE1-A.

6   CE1-A receives the 172.16.20.0 as an inter-area route and 209.165.127.0 and 209.165.202.128/27 as OSPF external routes.

OSPF Domain ID Is Different on All PE Routers

As previously mentioned, OSPF domain ID by default is equal to the OSPF process ID configured on PE routers unless modified manually. If the process IDs are different on PE routers for sites belonging to same VPN, OSPF routes are seen as OSPF external routes (Type 5 OSPF LSA). As shown in Figure 5-7, when the PE1-AS1 router in OSPF Area 1 uses OSPF process ID 201 for Site 1 belonging to VPN VPN-A, and the PE2 router in OSPF Area 2 uses OSPF process ID 202 for Site 2 belonging to VPN VPN-A, external routes are seen at Site 1 for Site 2 networks and vice versa.

The following sequence of events takes place when CE2-A is sending 192.168.20.0, 192.168.99.0, and 192.168.199.0 to CE1-A:

1   CE2-B redistributes RIPv2 network 192.168.99.0 into OSPF and propagates it as an OSPF external Type 1 route (O E1) to PE2-AS1. EIGRP network 192.168.199.0/24 is redistributed and propagated as an OSPF external Type 2 (O E2) to PE2-AS1. CE2-B also sends 192.168.20.0/24 as an intra-area route (O) to PE2-AS1.

2   VRF Cust_B routing table on PE2-AS1 shows the received routes: 192.168.20.0 as an OSPF inter-area route with OSPF metric 74, 192.168.99.0/24 as an external Type 1 route with OSPF metric 84, and 192.168.199.0/24 is preserved as an external Type 2 route with OSPF metric 20.

3   The PE router, PE2-AS1, redistributes the OSPF routes 192.168.20.0, 192.168.99.0, and 192.168.199.0/27 into MP-BGP, copies the OSPF cost for those routes into the multi-exit discriminator (MED) attribute, and sets the BGP extended community route type (RT) to indicate the LSA type from which the route was derived, as well as the extended community attribute OSPF domain ID to indicate the process number of the source OSPF process. OSPF RTs carry information on the original area. The LSA type and the type for external routes are metric types.

4 PE1-AS1 receives the BGP VPNv4 routes 192.168.20.0, 192.168.99.0, and 192.168.199.0/27 with the same metric information from PE2-AS1. The information received is inserted in the BGP table. As shown in the figure, the OSPF metric for the routes are not altered and remain the same when propagated though the MP-BGP backbone.

5 PE2-AS1 checks the attributes received in the route, and, because the domain ID of the route does not match the domain ID on the receiving PE, the route is translated to the external Type 2 route (LSA Type 5) OSPF route. In this case, the domain ID matches the domain ID on PE1-AS1; therefore, PE1-AS1 will reconstruct the original update and update the metric based on the outgoing interfaces and propagate 192.168.20.0 as an inter-area route to CE1-B. 192.168.99.0 and 192.168.199.0/27 are propagated as OSPF external Type 1 and Type 2 to CE1-B.

6 CE1-B receives the 192.168.20.0 as an inter-area route and 192.168.99.0 and 192.168.199.0/24 as OSPF external routes.

Figure 5-7 *Route Propagation When OSPF Domain (Process) ID Is Different*

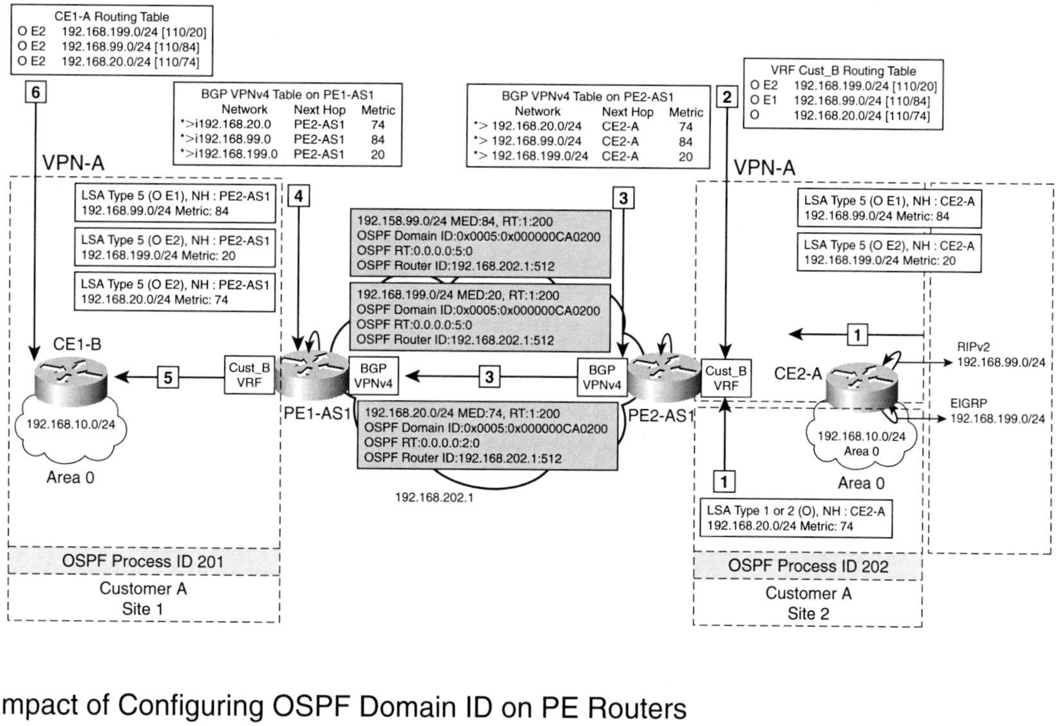

Impact of Configuring OSPF Domain ID on PE Routers

Manually configuring the OSPF domain ID changes the behavior of routes for Layer 3 VPNs connecting multiple OSPF domains. Configuring domain IDs helps control LSA translation (for Type 3 and Type 5 LSAs) between the OSPF domains and backdoor paths. The default domain ID is 0.0.0.0. Each VPN routing table on a PE router associated with an OSPF routing instance is configured with the same OSPF domain ID. Domain IDs are, hence, used to identify whether the routes originated from the OSPF domain or from external routing protocols. The OSPF domain ID helps identify which OSPF domain a route originated from, which allows classification of routes as Type 3 LSAs or Type 5 LSAs. In Figure 5-7, it is difficult to identify which routes received on CE1-A originated within OSPF or from external routing domains. As shown in Figure 5-8, by manually configuring the domain ID to be the same on PE1-AS1 and PE2-AS1, we can correctly identify which routes are external and which are internal.

Figure 5-8 *Route Propagation When OSPF Domain (Process) ID Is Manually Configured to Be the Same*

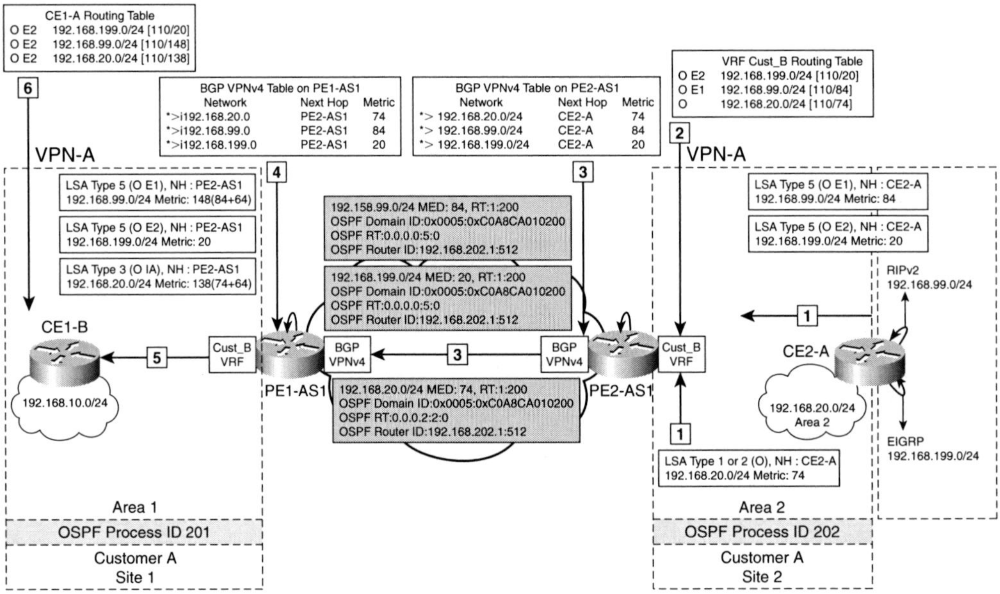

OSPF Down Bit and Domain Tag

Routing loops can occur in the MPLS VPN environment when customer edge routers are dual-homed to the service provider network. Figure 5-9 shows an MPLS VPN network implementing OSPF PE-CE routing for Customer A VPN-A sites, Site 1 and Site 2. Site 2 is in OSPF Area 2 and has multiple connections to the provider backbone.

As shown in Figure 5-9, the following sequence takes place, which can lead to a potential routing loop:

1 CE1-A sends a Type 1 router or Type 2 network LSA to the provider edge router, PE1.

2 PE1 router receives the intra-area OSPF route from CE1-A and redistributes it into MP-BGP.

3 The receiving PE router, PE2, redistributes the MP-BGP route into OSPF Area 2 as an inter-area summary route, LSA Type 3.

4 The summary route is propagated across the OSPF area and received by the other PE router, PE3, attached to the same area, Area 2.

5 PE3 selects the OSPF route, because the administrative distance of the OSPF route is better than the administrative distance of the MP-iBGP route. PE3, therefore, redistributes the route OSPF back into the MP-BGP process, potentially resulting in a routing loop.

Figure 5-9 *Route Propagation (OSPF Down Bit Not Set)*

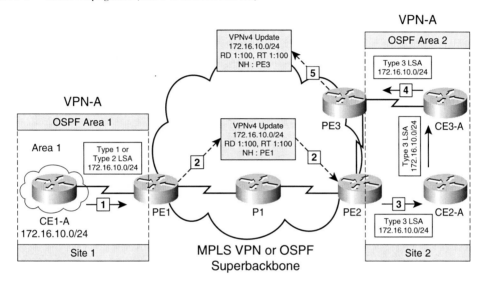

OSPF Down Bit

The routing loop shown in Figure 5-9 can be prevented by the use of the OSPF down bit, which is part of the options field in the OSPF header. The LSA header with the option field is shown in Figure 5-10.

Figure 5-10 *LSA Header and OSPF Down Bit*

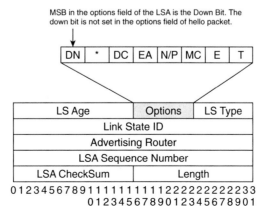

Figure 5-11 shows how the OSPF down bit is used to prevent the routing loop shown in Figure 5-10.

Figure 5-11 *Route Propagation When OSPF Down Bit Is Set*

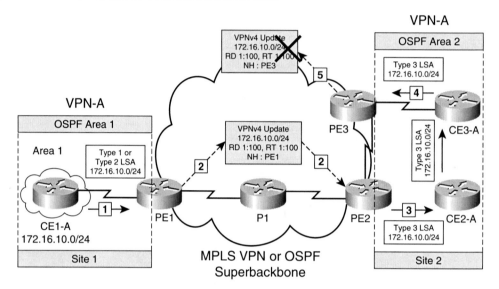

The following is the route propagation when the OSPF down bit is set:

1 CE1-A sends a Type 1 router or Type 2 network LSA to the provider edge router, PE1.

2 The PE1 router receives the intra-area OSPF route from CE1-A and redistributes it into MP-BGP.

3 The receiving PE router, PE2, redistributes the MP-BGP route into OSPF Area 2 as an inter-area summary route, LSA Type 3, with the OSPF down bit set.

4 The summary route with the down bit set is propagated across the OSPF area and received by PE3, which is attached to the same area, Area 2.

5 When the PE3 router receives the summary LSA with the down bit set, it does not redistribute the route back into MP-BGP.

OSPF Route Tag or VPN Route Tag

The down bit helps prevent routing loops between MP-BGP and OSPF, but not when external routes are announced, such as when redistribution between multiple OSPF domains or when external routes are injected in an area that is dual-homed to the provider network. The PE router redistributes an OSPF route from a different OSPF domain into an OSPF domain as an external route. The down bit is not set because LSA Type 5 does not support the down bit. The redistributed route is propagated across the OSPF domain.

A non-MPLS router can then redistribute the OSPF route into another OSPF domain. The OSPF route is propagated through the other OSPF domain, again without the down bit. A PE router receives the OSPF route. When the down bit is missing, the route is redistributed back into the MP-BGP backbone, resulting in a routing loop. This is shown in Figure 5-12 when external routes are propagated into the VPN sites.

Figure 5-12 *External Route Propagation in Dual-Homed CE*

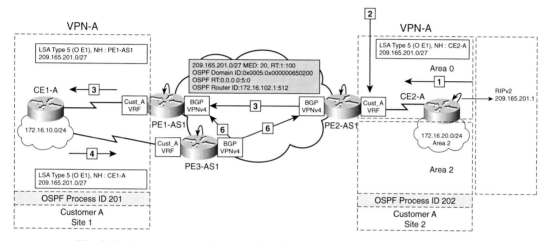

The following sequence of steps takes place:

1 CE2-A sends a Type 5 LSA for 209.165.201.0/27 to the provider edge router, PE2-AS1.

2 The PE2-AS1 router receives the external (O E1) OSPF route from CE2-A with the OSPF down bit set and then redistributes it into MP-BGP.

3 Assuming the receiving PE router is PE1-AS1, and, because it is redistributing to a different OSPF domain (201), PE1-AS1 clears the OSPF down bit and propagates the route to CE1-A as an external (O E1) route, LSA Type 5.

4 CE1-A receives the route without the OSPF down bit set and propagates the external route to PE3-AS1.

5 When the PE3-AS1 router receives the external route without the down bit set, it redistributes the route back into MP-BGP.

6 PE3-AS1, therefore, propagates the route to PE1-AS1 and PE2-AS1, which might cause a routing loop.

The routing loops introduced by route redistribution between OSPF domains can be solved with the help of the **tag** field, using standard BGP-OSPF redistribution rules. A non-OSPF route is redistributed as an external OSPF route by a PE router. By default, the tag field is set to the BGP-AS number. The redistributed route is propagated across the OSPF domain without the down bit but with the tag field set. When the route is redistributed into another OSPF domain, the tag field is propagated. Another PE router receives the external OSPF route and filters the route based on the tag field. The tag field matches the AS number so the route is not redistributed into MP-BGP.

Configuring and Verifying OSPF PE-CE Routing

The configuration flowchart for implementing OSPF PE-CE routing is shown in Figure 5-13.

Figure 5-13 *Configuration Flowchart for OSPF PE-CE Routing*

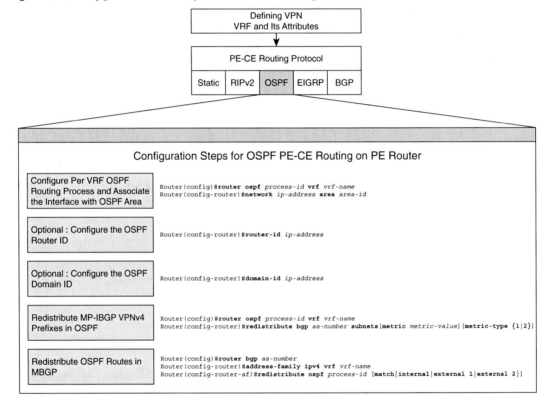

NOTE Cisco IOS versions prior to 12.3(4)T, 12.0(27)S, and 12.2(25)S have the limitation of 32 processes in which a separate OSPF process has to be created for each VRF so that the PE router can identify the OSPF routes belonging to the correct process. In an MPLS VPN environment, one process is used by MP-iBGP, one by an IGP routing protocol (OSPF, for example), one process for connected routes, and another for static routes. Therefore, out of 32, only 28 processes could be created for VRFs using OSPF PE-CE routing until the above mentioned versions.

Configuration Scenario 1—OSPF Process ID Is Same for Customer A and Different for Customer B VPNs

The objective of this setup is to understand how the OSPF process ID plays a part in deciding the type of route seen on customer edge routers running OSPF. Figure 5-14 shows MPLS VPN services being provided to Customer A and Customer B sites:

- **Customer A network**—Customer A has CE1-A and CE2-A located in the same VPN, VPN-A. They are part of the same OSPF domain. PE1-AS1 and PE2-AS1 have OSPF process ID 101 configured for VRF Cust_A on PE1-AS1 and PE2-AS1.

- **Customer B network**—Customer B has CE1-B and CE2-B located in the VPN, VPN-B. PE1-AS1 and PE2-AS1 have OSPF process IDs of 201 and 202 for Cust_B VRFs, respectively.

Figure 5-14 *MPLS VPN Network Implementing OSPF PE-CE Routing*

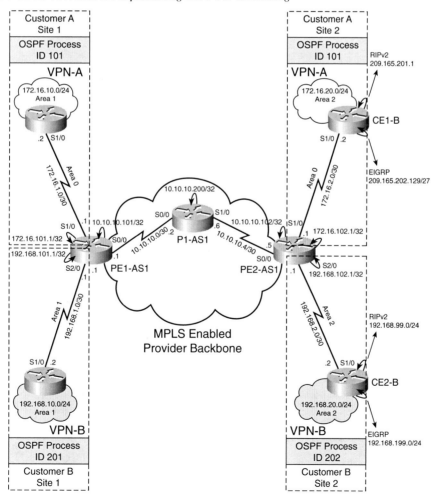

Before configuring, ensure that the provider network is provisioned to deliver MPLS VPN services to Customer A and B sites. Ensure that IP addresses are preconfigured and VRFs defined on PE routers. Example 5-1 provides the configuration for defining VRF and its attributes on PE routers for OSPF PE-CE routing for VRF Cust_A (Customer A).

Example 5-1 *Define VRF Cust_A on PE Routers PE1-AS1 and PE2-AS1*

```
PE1-AS1(config)#ip vrf Cust_A
PE1-AS1(config-vrf)# rd 1:100
PE1-AS1(config-vrf)# route-target both 1:100
PE1-AS1(config)#interface Serial1/0
PE1-AS1(config-if)# description connected to CE1-A
PE1-AS1(config-if)# ip vrf forwarding Cust_A
PE1-AS1(config-if)# ip address 172.16.1.1 255.255.255.252
PE2-AS1(config)#ip vrf Cust_A
PE2-AS1(config-vrf)# rd 1:100
PE2-AS1(config-vrf)# route-target both 1:100
PE2-AS1(config)#interface Serial1/0
PE2-AS1(config-if)# description connected to CE2-A
PE2-AS1(config-if)# ip vrf forwarding Cust_A
PE2-AS1(config-if)# ip address 172.16.2.1 255.255.255.252
```

The steps to configure OSPF PE-CE routing on the PE routers are

Step 1 **Enable per VRF OSPF Routing**—Enable per VRF OSPF routing for VRF Cust_A on PE routers PE1-AS1 and PE2-AS1 for Customer A and Cust_B on PE1-AS1 and PE2-AS1 for Customer B. Example 5-2 illustrates the configuration for enabling OSPF routing for the VRF Cust_A.

Example 5-2 *Enable per VRF OSPF Routing for Cust_A on PE1-AS1 and PE2-AS1*

```
PE1-AS1(config)#router ospf 101 vrf Cust_A
PE1-AS1(config-router)# router-id 172.16.101.1
PE1-AS1(config-router)# network 172.16.0.0 0.0.255.255 area 0
PE2-AS1(config)#router ospf 101 vrf Cust_A
PE2-AS1(config-router)# router-id 172.16.102.1
PE2-AS1(conig-router)# network 172.16.0.0 0.0.255.255 area 0
```

Step 2 **Redistribute OSPF Routes in BGP**—In this step, the OSPF routes received from the local CE routers is redistributed in MP-iBGP. It is necessary to include the **match** command option; otherwise, only OSPF internal routes will be redistributed in BGP. Example 5-3 shows the procedure to configure redistribution of OSPF routes in BGP.

Example 5-3 *Redistribute OSPF Routes in MP-BGP*

```
PE1-AS1(config)#router bgp 1
PE1-AS1(config-router)#address-family ipv4 vrf Cust_A
PE1-AS1(config-router-af)#redistribute ospf 101 vrf Cust_A match internal external
  1 external 2
PE2-AS1(config)#router bgp 1
```

Example 5-3 *Redistribute OSPF Routes in MP-BGP (Continued)*

```
PE2-AS1(config-router)#address-family ipv4 vrf Cust_A
PE2-AS1(config-router-af)#redistribute ospf 101 vrf Cust_A match internal
  external 1 external 2
```

Step 3 **Redistribute MP-IBGP in OSPF**—In this step, you redistribute the BGP VPNv4 routes into OSPF on PE routers, PE1-AS1 and PE2-AS1. Ensure that the **subnets** keyword is included when configuring redistribution; otherwise, Cisco IOS redistributes only the major networks and supernets. Example 5-4 shows the steps on PE1-AS1. Repeat the same steps on PE2-AS1.

Example 5-4 *Redistribute MP-IBGP in OSPF*

```
PE1-AS1(config)#router ospf 100 vrf Cust_A
PE1-AS1(config-router)# redistribute bgp 1 subnets
```
```
PE2-AS1(config)#router ospf 100 vrf Cust_A
PE2-AS1(config-router)# redistribute bgp 1 subnets
```

Final Configuration for Provider and Edge Routers

Example 5-5 shows the configuration for PE1-AS1, PE2-AS1, and P1-AS1.

Example 5-5 *PE1-AS1, PE2-AS1, and P1-AS1 Configuration*

```
hostname PE1-AS1
!
ip cef
!
ip vrf Cust_A
 rd 1:100
 route-target export 1:100
 route-target import 1:100
!
ip vrf Cust_B
 rd 1:200
 route-target export 1:200
 route-target import 1:200
!
interface Loopback0
 ip address 10.10.10.101 255.255.255.255
!
interface Loopback101
 description OSPF Router ID for VRF Cust_A
 ip vrf forwarding Cust_A
 ip address 172.16.101.1 255.255.255.255
!
interface Loopback201
 description OSPF Router ID for VRF Cust_B
 ip vrf forwarding Cust_B
 ip address 192.168.201.1 255.255.255.255
```

continues

Example 5-5 *PE1-AS1, PE2-AS1, and P1-AS1 Configuration (Continued)*

```
!
interface Serial0/0
 description connected to P1-AS1
 ip address 10.10.10.1 255.255.255.252
 mpls ip
!
interface Serial1/0
 description connected to CE1-A
 ip vrf forwarding Cust_A
 ip address 172.16.1.1 255.255.255.252
!
interface Serial2/0
 description connected to CE1-B
 ip vrf forwarding Cust_B
 ip address 192.168.1.1 255.255.255.252
!
router ospf 101 vrf Cust_A
 router-id 172.16.101.1
  redistribute bgp 1 subnets
 network 172.16.0.0 0.0.255.255 area 0
!
router ospf 201 vrf Cust_B
 router-id 192.168.201.1
 redistribute bgp 1 subnets
 network 192.168.0.0 0.0.255.255 area 1
!
router ospf 1
 router-id 10.10.10.101
 network 10.0.0.0 0.255.255.255 area 0
!
router bgp 1
 no synchronization
 neighbor 10.10.10.102 remote-as 1
 neighbor 10.10.10.102 update-source Loopback0
 no auto-summary
 !
 address-family vpnv4
 neighbor 10.10.10.102 activate
 neighbor 10.10.10.102 send-community extended
 exit-address-family
 !
 address-family ipv4 vrf Cust_B
 redistribute ospf 201 vrf Cust_B match internal external 1 external 2
 no auto-summary
 no synchronization
 exit-address-family
 !
 address-family ipv4 vrf Cust_A
 redistribute ospf 101 vrf Cust_A match internal external 1 external 2
 no auto-summary
```

Example 5-5   *PE1-AS1, PE2-AS1, and P1-AS1 Configuration (Continued)*

```
 no synchronization
 exit-address-family
hostname PE2-AS1
!
ip cef
!
ip vrf Cust_A
 rd 1:100
 route-target export 1:100
 route-target import 1:100
!
ip vrf Cust_B
 rd 1:200
 route-target export 1:200
 route-target import 1:200
!
interface Loopback0
 ip address 10.10.10.102 255.255.255.255
!
interface Loopback101
 description OSPF Router ID for VRF Cust_A
 ip vrf forwarding Cust_A
 ip address 172.16.102.1 255.255.255.255
!
interface Loopback202
 description OSPF Router ID for VRF Cust_B
 ip vrf forwarding Cust_B
 ip address 192.168.202.1 255.255.255.255
!
interface Serial0/0
 description connected to P1-AS1
 ip address 10.10.10.5 255.255.255.252
 mpls ip
!
interface Serial1/0
 description connected to CE2-A
 ip vrf forwarding Cust_A
 ip address 172.16.2.1 255.255.255.252
!
interface Serial2/0
 description connected to CE2-B
 ip vrf forwarding Cust_B
 ip address 192.168.2.1 255.255.255.252
!
router ospf 101 vrf Cust_A
 router-id 172.16.102.1
  redistribute bgp 1 subnets
 network 172.16.0.0 0.0.255.255 area 0
!
router ospf 202 vrf Cust_B
 router-id 192.168.202.1
```

continues

Example 5-5 *PE1-AS1, PE2-AS1, and P1-AS1 Configuration (Continued)*

```
 redistribute bgp 1 subnets
 network 192.168.0.0 0.0.255.255 area 2
!
router ospf 1
 router-id 10.10.10.102
 network 10.0.0.0 0.255.255.255 area 0!
router bgp 1
 no synchronization
 neighbor 10.10.10.101 remote-as 1
 neighbor 10.10.10.101 update-source Loopback0
 no auto-summary
 !
 address-family vpnv4
 neighbor 10.10.10.101 activate
 neighbor 10.10.10.101 send-community extended
 exit-address-family
 !
 address-family ipv4 vrf Cust_B
 redistribute ospf 202 vrf Cust_B match internal external 1 external 2
 no auto-summary
 no synchronization
 exit-address-family
 !
 address-family ipv4 vrf Cust_A
 redistribute ospf 101 vrf Cust_A match internal external 1 external 2
 no auto-summary
 no synchronization
 exit-address-family
```
```
hostname P1-AS1
!
interface Loopback0
 ip address 10.10.10.200 255.255.255.255
!
interface Serial0/0
 description connected to PE1-AS1
 ip address 10.10.10.2 255.255.255.252
 mpls ip
!
interface Serial1/0
 description connected to PE2-AS1
 ip address 10.10.10.6 255.255.255.252
 mpls ip
!
router ospf 1
 log-adjacency-changes
 network 10.0.0.0 0.255.255.255 area 0
```

Example 5-6 shows the configuration for CE1-A, CE2-A, CE1-B, and CE2-B.

Example 5-6 *CE1-A, CE2-A, CE1-B, and CE2-B Configuration*

```
hostname CE1-A
!
interface Ethernet0/0
 description VPN-A Site 1 network
 ip address 172.16.10.1 255.255.255.0
!
interface Serial1/0
 description connected to PE1-AS1
 ip address 172.16.1.2 255.255.255.252
!
router ospf 101
 network 172.16.1.0 0.0.0.255 area 0
 network 172.16.10.0 0.0.0.255 area 1
```
```
hostname CE2-A
!
interface Loopback0
description RIPv2 network
 ip address 209.165.201.1 255.255.255.224
!
interface Loopback1
description EIGRP network
 ip address 209.165.202.129 255.255.255.224
!
interface Ethernet0/0
 description VPN-A Site 2 network
 ip address 172.16.20.1 255.255.255.0
!
interface Serial1/0
 description connected to PE2-AS1
 ip address 172.16.2.2 255.255.255.252
!
router eigrp 1
 network 209.165.202.0
 no auto-summary
!
router ospf 101
 redistribute eigrp 1 subnets
 redistribute rip metric-type 1 subnets
 network 172.16.2.0 0.0.0.255 area 0
 network 172.16.20.0 0.0.0.255 area 2
 !
router rip
 version 2
 redistribute ospf 101 match internal external 1 external 2
 network 209.165.201.0
 no auto-summary
```
```
hostname CE1-B
!
interface Ethernet0/0
 description VPN-B Site1 network
```

continues

Example 5-6 *CE1-A, CE2-A, CE1-B, and CE2-B Configuration (Continued)*

```
 ip address 192.168.10.1 255.255.255.0
 !
 interface Serial1/0
  description connected to PE1-AS1
  ip address 192.168.1.2 255.255.255.252
 !
 router ospf 201
  network 192.168.1.0 0.0.0.255 area 1
  network 192.168.10.0 0.0.0.255 area 1
 hostname CE2-B
 !
 interface Loopback0
  ip address 192.168.99.1 255.255.255.0
 !
 interface Loopback1
  ip address 192.168.199.1 255.255.255.0
 !
 interface Ethernet0/0
  description VPN-B Site 2  network
  ip address 192.168.20.1 255.255.255.0
  !
 interface Serial1/0
  description connected to PE2-AS1
  ip address 192.168.2.2 255.255.255.252
  !
 router eigrp 1
  redistribute ospf 202 metric 1500 1 255 1 1500 match internal external 1 external 2
  network 192.168.199.0
  no auto-summary
 !
 router ospf 202
  redistribute eigrp 1 subnets
  redistribute rip metric-type 1 subnets
  network 192.168.2.0 0.0.0.255 area 2
  network 192.168.20.0 0.0.0.255 area 2
 !
 router rip
  version 2
  redistribute ospf 202 metric 1 match internal external 1 external 2
  network 192.168.99.0
  no auto-summary
```

Verify OSPF PE-CE Routing

The steps to verify OSPF PE-CE routing are as follows:

Step 1   Verify OSPF neighbor adjacency—This step ensures that there is
an OSPF neighbor relationship and adjacency is formed between the
provider edge (PE) router and customer edge (CE) router. Example 5-7
shows the output on the PE and CE router where the adjacency is formed,
indicated by the FULL state.

Example 5-7 show ip ospf neighbor *on PE1-AS1 and PE2-AS1*

```
PE1-AS1#show ip ospf neighbor
Neighbor ID     Pri   State       Dead Time   Address       Interface
10.10.10.200      0   FULL/  -     00:00:38    10.10.10.2    Serial0/0
192.168.10.1      0   FULL/  -     00:00:35    192.168.1.2   Serial2/0
172.16.10.1       0   FULL/  -     00:00:32    172.16.1.2    Serial1/0
PE2-AS1#show ip ospf neighbor
Neighbor ID     Pri   State       Dead Time   Address       Interface
10.10.10.200      0   FULL/  -     00:00:39    10.10.10.6    Serial0/0
192.168.20.1      0   FULL/  -     00:00:38    192.168.2.2   Serial2/0
172.16.20.1       0   FULL/  -     00:00:32    172.16.2.2    Serial1/0
```

Step 2 **Verify route propagation for Customer A**—These steps verify route propagation for 192.168.20.0, 192.168.99.0, and 192.168.199.0.

Example 5-8 shows the Cust_A VRF routing table where 172.16.10.0 is received as an intra-area OSPF route. 209.165.201.0/27 and 209.165.201.128/27 show up as OSPF external Type 1 and Type 2 routes, respectively.

Example 5-8 show ip route vrf Cust_A ospf 101 *on PE2-AS1*

```
PE2-AS1#show ip route vrf Cust_A ospf 101
      172.16.0.0/16 is variably subnetted, 6 subnets, 3 masks
O IA    172.16.20.0/24 [110/74] via 172.16.2.2, 01:14:00, Serial1/0
      209.165.201.0/27 is subnetted, 1 subnets
O E1    209.165.201.0 [110/84] via 172.16.2.2, 01:14:00, Serial1/0
      209.165.202.0/27 is subnetted, 1 subnets
O E2    209.165.202.128 [110/20] via 172.16.2.2, 01:14:00, Serial1/0
```

Cust_A OSPF routes are redistributed in MP-iBGP, and the OSPF metrics for 172.16.20.0, 209.165.127.0, and 209.165.202.128/27 are copied into extended BGP attributes as BGP MEDs. The routes 172.16.20.0/24, 209.165.201.0/27, and 209.165.202.128/27 are then propagated to PE1-AS1 via MP-iBGP session. Example 5-9 displays output of the **show ip bgp vpn vrf Cust_A** command on PE2-AS1. Example 5-10 displays output of the **show ip bgp vpnv4 all 172.16.20.0** command on PE2-AS1.

Example 5-9 show ip bgp vpn vrf Cust_A *on PE2-AS1*

```
PE2-AS1#show ip bgp vpn vrf Cust_A
   Network          Next Hop           Metric LocPrf Weight Path
Route Distinguisher: 1:100 (default for vrf Cust_A)
*> 172.16.20.0      172.16.2.2             74         32768 ?
*> 209.165.201.0    172.16.2.2             84         32768 ?
*> 209.165.202.128  172.16.2.2             20         32768 ?
```

Example 5-10 show ip bgp vpnv4 all **172.16.20.0** *on PE2-AS1*

```
PE2-AS1#show ip bgp vpnv4 all 172.16.20.0
BGP routing table entry for 1:100:172.16.20.0/24, version 138
Paths: (1 available, best #1, table Cust_A)
  Advertised to update-groups:
     1
  Local
    172.16.2.2 from 0.0.0.0 (10.10.10.102)
      Origin incomplete, metric 74, localpref 100, weight 32768, valid, sourced, best
      Extended Community: RT:1:100 OSPF DOMAIN ID:0x0005:0x000000650200
        OSPF RT:0.0.0.0:3:0 OSPF ROUTER ID:172.16.102.1:512,
      mpls labels in/out 34/nolabel
```

At PE1-AS1, the routes are received with metrics unchanged from their origination at PE2-AS1. PE1-AS1 redistributes the MP-BGP route back into OSPF, verifies the domain ID, and, if the domain ID of the route matches the domain ID on PE1-AS1, it uses the original LSA type and the MED attribute to generate an inter-area summary (LSA Type 3) LSA; otherwise, it generates an external route. In this case, the OSPF domain ID matches, and 172.16.20.0 is generated as an inter-area route to CE1-A, and the metric is modified to 138 (74 [original metric] + 64 [outgoing interface cost on PE1-AS1 to CE1-A, in this case, serial link = 64]). Example 5-11 displays output from the **show ip bgp vpnv4 vrf Cust_A** on PE1-AS1. Example 5-12 displays output from the **show ip route ospf** command on CE1-A.

Example 5-11 show ip bgp vpnv4 vrf Cust_A *on PE1-AS1*

```
PE1-AS1#show ip bgp vpnv4 vrf Cust_A
   Network          Next Hop          Metric LocPrf Weight Path
Route Distinguisher: 1:100 (default for vrf Cust_A)
*> 172.16.1.0/30    0.0.0.0                0          32768 ?
*>i172.16.2.0/30    10.10.10.102           0    100      0 ?
*> 172.16.10.0/24   172.16.1.2            74          32768 ?
*>i172.16.20.0/24   10.10.10.102          74    100      0 ?
*> 172.16.101.1/32  0.0.0.0                0          32768 ?
*>i172.16.102.1/32  10.10.10.102           0    100      0 ?
*>i209.165.201.0/27 10.10.10.102          84    100      0 ?
*>i209.165.202.128/27
                    10.10.10.102          20    100      0 ?
```

Example 5-12 show ip route ospf *on CE1-A*

```
CE1-A#show ip route ospf
     172.16.0.0/16 is variably subnetted, 6 subnets, 3 masks
O IA   172.16.20.0/24 [110/138] via 172.16.1.1, 01:15:26, Serial1/0
O IA    172.16.2.0/30 [110/65] via 172.16.1.1, 01:15:26, Serial1/0
O       172.16.101.1/32 [110/65] via 172.16.1.1, 01:16:13, Serial1/0
O IA    172.16.102.1/32 [110/65] via 172.16.1.1, 01:15:26, Serial1/0
```

Example 5-12 show ip route ospf *on CE1-A (Continued)*

```
      209.165.201.0/27 is subnetted, 1 subnets
O E1    209.165.201.0 [110/148] via 172.16.1.1, 01:15:21, Serial1/0
      209.165.202.0/27 is subnetted, 1 subnets
O E2    209.165.202.128 [110/20] via 172.16.1.1, 01:15:21, Serial1/0
```

Step 3   **Verify route propagation for Customer B**—These steps verify route
propagation for 192.168.20.0, 192.168.99.0, and 192.168.199.0.

Example 5-13 shows the Cust_B VRF routing table where 192.168.20.0
is received as an intra-area OSPF route. 192.168.99.0 and 192.168.199.0
are received as OSPF E1 and E2 routes, respectively.

Example 5-13 show ip route vrf Cust_B ospf 202 *on PE2-AS1*

```
PE2-AS1#show ip route vrf Cust_B ospf 202
O E2 192.168.199.0/24 [110/20] via 192.168.2.2, 00:39:02, Serial2/0
O E1 192.168.99.0/24 [110/84] via 192.168.2.2, 00:39:02, Serial2/0
O    192.168.20.0/24 [110/74] via 192.168.2.2, 00:39:02, Serial2/0
```

Cust_B OSPF routes are redistributed in MP-iBGP, and the OSPF
metrics for 192.168.20.0, 192.168.99.0, and 192.168.199.0 are copied
into extended BGP attributes as BGP MEDs. The routes are then
propagated to PE1-AS1 via MP-iBGP session. Example 5-14 displays
output from the **show ip bgp vpnv4 all | begin 192.168.20.0** command
on PE2-AS1. Example 5-15 displays output from the **show ip bgp vpnv4
all 192.168.99.0** command on PE2-AS1.

Example 5-14   show ip bgp vpnv4 all | begin 192.168.20.0 *on PE2-AS1*

```
PE2-AS1#show ip bgp vpnv4 all | begin 192.168.20.0
*> 192.168.20.0     192.168.2.2          74       32768 ?
*> 192.168.99.0     192.168.2.2          84       32768 ?
*> 192.168.199.0    192.168.2.2          20       32768 ?
```

Example 5-15   show ip bgp vpnv4 all 192.168.99.0 *on PE2-AS1*

```
PE2-AS1#show ip bgp vpnv4 all 192.168.99.0
BGP routing table entry for 1:200:192.168.99.0/24, version 145
Paths: (1 available, best #1, table Cust_B)
  Advertised to update-groups:
     1
  Local
    192.168.2.2 from 0.0.0.0 (10.10.10.102)
      Origin incomplete, metric 84, localpref 100, weight 32768, valid, sourced, best
        Extended Community: RT:1:200 OSPF DOMAIN ID:0x0005:0x000000CA0200
          OSPF RT:0.0.0.0:5:0 OSPF ROUTER ID:192.168.202.1:512,
        mpls labels in/out 28/nolabel
```

At PE1-AS1, the routes are received with metrics unchanged. PE1-AS1 redistributes the MP-BGP routes back into OSPF, verifies the domain ID, and, if the domain ID of the route matches the domain ID on PE1-AS1, it uses the original LSA type and the MED attribute to generate an inter-area summary (LSA Type 3) LSA; otherwise, it generates an external route. In this case, the OSPF domain ID does not match, so 192.168.20.0 is generated as an external route. Example 5-16 displays output from the **show ip bgp vpnv4 all | begin 192.168.20.0** command on PE1-AS1. Example 5-17 displays output from the **show ip route ospf** command on CE1-B.

Example 5-16 show ip bgp vpnv4 all **192.168.99.0** *on PE1-AS1*

```
PE1-AS1#show ip bgp vpnv4 all | begin 192.168.20.0
*>i192.168.20.0     10.10.10.102         74     100      0 ?
*>i192.168.99.0     10.10.10.102         84     100      0 ?
*>i192.168.199.0    10.10.10.102         20     100      0 ?
```

Example 5-17 show ip route ospf *on CE1-B*

```
CE1-B#show ip route ospf
O E2 192.168.199.0/24 [110/20] via 192.168.1.1, 00:48:46, Serial1/0
        192.168.201.0/32 is subnetted, 1 subnets
O          192.168.201.1 [110/65] via 192.168.1.1, 00:49:33, Serial1/0
O E2 192.168.99.0/24 [110/84] via 192.168.1.1, 00:48:46, Serial1/0
O E2 192.168.20.0/24 [110/74] via 192.168.1.1, 00:48:46, Serial1/0
        192.168.202.0/32 is subnetted, 1 subnets
O E2    192.168.202.1 [110/1] via 192.168.1.1, 00:48:46, Serial1/0
        192.168.2.0/30 is subnetted, 1 subnets
O E2    192.168.2.0 [110/1] via 192.168.1.1, 00:48:46, Serial1/0
```

Configuration Scenario 2—Using OSPF Domain ID Support for LSA Type 5/Type 3 Translation

Figure 5-15 shows an MPLS VPN network for Customer B in which CE1-B and CE2-B belong to the same VPN but have different process IDs. Configuring domain IDs helps control LSA translation (for Type 3 and Type 5 LSAs) between the OSPF domains and backdoor paths. Each VPN routing table in a PE router associated with an OSPF routing instance is configured with the same OSPF domain ID.

Configuration for this section remains the same as shown in configuration Scenario 1. Configuring **domain ID** *ip-address* under the OSPF routing process for VRF Cust_B is the only addition in this section. The configuration step is outlined here:

- **Configure OSPF domain ID**—Configure **domain ID** *ip-address* under the OSPF routing process for Cust_B. The domain ID has to be common for all PE routers for that VPN instance. Use loopback 202 on PE2 as the domain ID for Customer B. Example 5-18 shows how to configure the OSPF domain ID.

Figure 5-15 *MPLS VPN Network Using Domain ID Support*

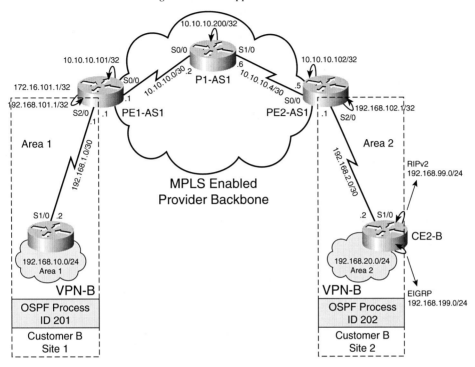

Example 5-18 *Configuring OSPF Domain ID*

```
PE1-AS1(config)#router ospf 201 vrf Cust_B
PE1-AS1(config-router)# domain ID 192.168.202.1
```
```
PE2-AS1(config)#router ospf 202 vrf Cust_B
PE2-AS1(config-router)# domain ID 192.168.202.1
```

Verify Route Propagation When Using OSPF Domain ID

Example 5-19 shows that when the OSPF domain ID is not configured, the CE1-B routing table shows all the routes being external.

Example 5-19 *Routing Table on CE1-B When OSPF Domain ID Is Not Configured*

```
CE1-B#show ip route ospf
O E2 192.168.199.0/24 [110/20] via 192.168.1.1, 00:00:08, Serial1/0
        192.168.201.0/32 is subnetted, 1 subnets
O          192.168.201.1 [110/65] via 192.168.1.1, 00:00:14, Serial1/0
O E2 192.168.99.0/24 [110/84] via 192.168.1.1, 00:00:08, Serial1/0
O E2 192.168.20.0/24 [110/74] via 192.168.1.1, 00:00:08, Serial1/0
        192.168.202.0/32 is subnetted, 1 subnets
O E2    192.168.202.1 [110/1] via 192.168.1.1, 00:00:14, Serial1/0
        192.168.2.0/30 is subnetted, 1 subnets
O E2    192.168.2.0 [110/1] via 192.168.1.1, 00:00:14, Serial1/0
```

Example 5-20 shows that when the OSPF domain ID is configured, the CE1-B routing table shows 192.168.20.0 as inter-area and 192.168.99.0 as external Type 1.

Example 5-20   *Routing Table on CE1-B When OSPF Domain ID Is Configured*

```
CE1-B#show ip route ospf
O E2 192.168.199.0/24 [110/20] via 192.168.1.1, 00:44:09, Serial1/0
        192.168.201.0/32 is subnetted, 1 subnets
O          192.168.201.1 [110/65] via 192.168.1.1, 00:45:15, Serial1/0
O E1 192.168.99.0/24 [110/148] via 192.168.1.1, 00:44:09, Serial1/0
O IA 192.168.20.0/24 [110/138] via 192.168.1.1, 00:44:14, Serial1/0
        192.168.202.0/32 is subnetted, 1 subnets
O E2     192.168.202.1 [110/1] via 192.168.1.1, 00:44:09, Serial1/0
        192.168.2.0/30 is subnetted, 1 subnets
O E2     192.168.2.0 [110/1] via 192.168.1.1, 00:44:09, Serial1/0
```

OSPF Sham-Links

Figure 5-16 shows an MPLS-enabled service provider network providing MPLS VPN services to Customer A sites belonging to the same VPN, VPN-A.

Figure 5-16   *MPLS VPN Network Using Backdoor Link*

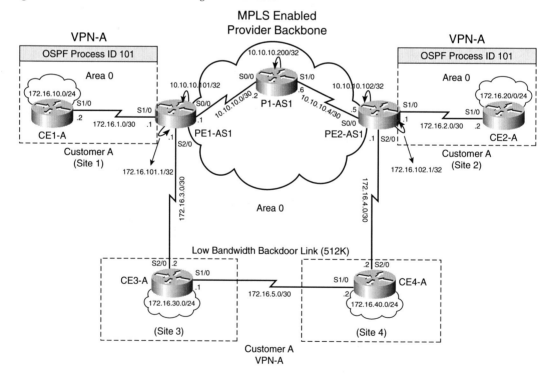

Customer A has four sites in VPN-A. All sites are in the OSPF area, Area 0. Site 3 and Site 4 in OSPF Area 0 are connected by a low bandwidth backdoor link (512 kbps). The backdoor link provides connectivity between Site 3 and Site 4 when the link to the provider backbone is down or disconnected. The sites are also connected to the high bandwidth BGP-based MPLS VPN backbone. This type of situation can result in suboptimal routing, as shown in Figure 5-17.

Figure 5-17 *Suboptimal Routing in MPLS VPN Network Using Backdoor Link*

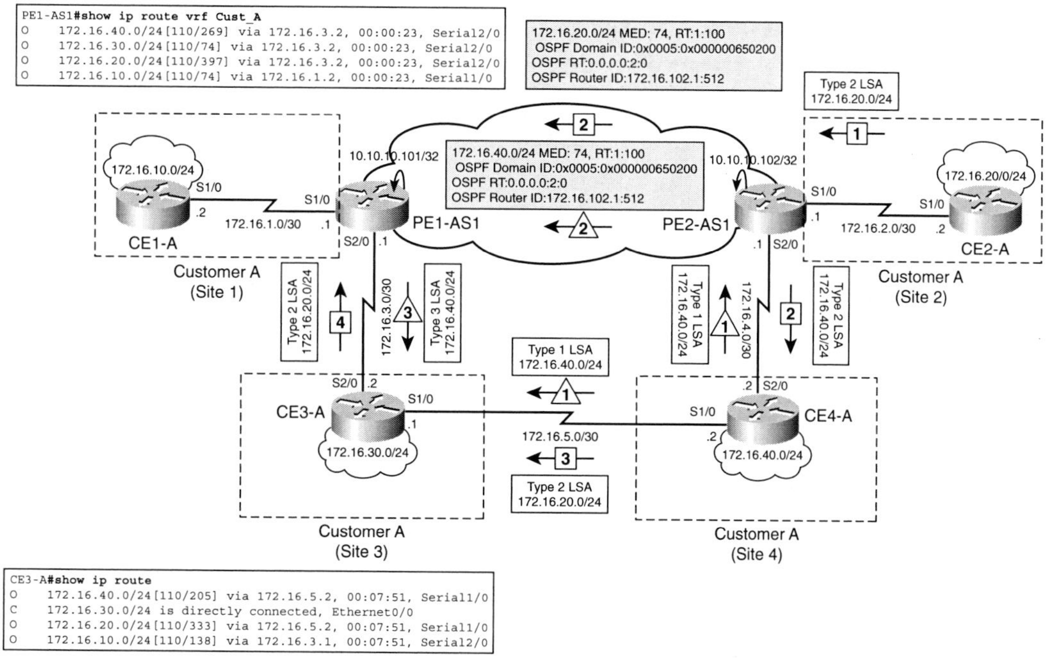

The following sequence takes place when 172.16.40.0/24 is propagated by CE4-A to CE3-A:

1 CE4-A sends a Type 1 LSA for 172.16.40.0/24 to the provider edge router, PE2-AS1 and CE3-A.

2 The PE2-AS1 router receives 172.16.40.0/24 as an intra-area route. It redistributes into MP-BGP.

3 PE1-AS1 redistributes 172.16.40.0/24 into OSPF and propagates 172.16.40.0/24 as an inter-area route to CE3-A.

4 CE3-A receives the 172.16.40.0/24 as an inter-area route from PE1-AS1 and as an intra-area route from CE4-A. In OSPF, intra-area routes are preferred over inter-area routes; therefore, CE3-A prefers the intra-area route from CE4-A and inserts it in the OSPF database.

This sequence of events also occurs with 172.16.20.0/24, which is propagated by CE2-A. Therefore, data packets originating from the 172.16.30.0 network (Site 3) to 172.16.40.0 (Site 4) will take the backdoor link. This also applies to traffic originating from 172.16.10.0 (Site 1) to 172.16.20.0 (Site 2) because any alternative routes from the MPLS VPN backbone would be inter-area routes, and intra-area routes are preferred. The traffic forwarding is, therefore, considered suboptimal because the backdoor link has low bandwidth and is intended for backup. Figure 5-18 shows the data forwarding path in an MPLS VPN network using a backdoor link (no sham links).

Figure 5-18 *Data Forwarding Path in MPLS VPN Network Using Backdoor Link*

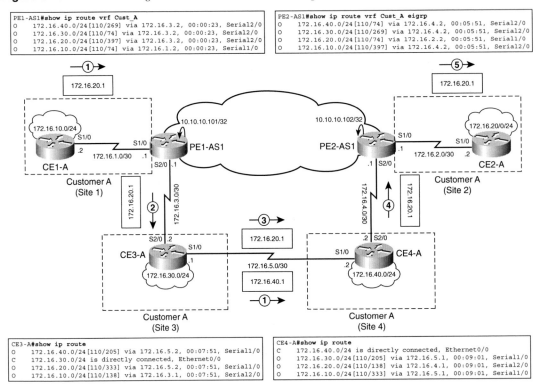

This situation can be avoided by using a sham-link. A sham-link is a logical link that belongs to the area (intra-area) but is carried by the BGP-based superbackbone. The two PE routers will be the endpoints of the sham-link. They will form an OSPF adjacency across it and flood intra-area LSAs via this link. The two sites that belong to Area 0 can have a sham-link between them and then receive intra-area OSPF routes via the backdoor link or the sham-link. When the sham-link is up, it is regarded as an unnumbered point-to-point OSPF link in the area belonging to the VPN sites. The sham-link is treated as a demand circuit (DC) by the OSPF in order to reduce the traffic flow over the sham-link. This implies that the regular LSA will flood over the sham-link but the periodic refresh traffic is avoided. Figure 5-19 shows a sham-link.

Figure 5-19 *Sham-Link*

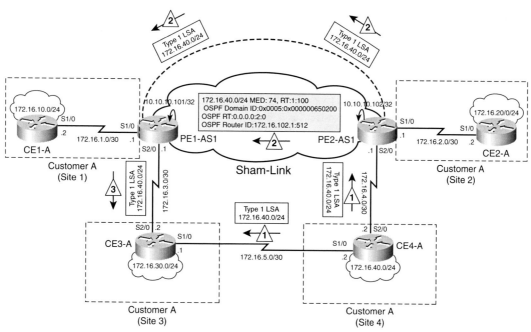

CE4-A sends 172.16.40.0/24 as LSA Type 1 to CE3-A, which then propagates the LSA to the PE1-AS1 router. The PE1-AS1 router has now received the OSPF-LSA Type 1 route from two directions from CE4-A via CE3-A and from PE2-AS1 via the OSPF sham-link. OSPF sham-link serves as an intra-area link between PE1-AS1 and PE2-AS1. The OSPF cost of the sham-link can be configured so that it will be lower than the cost of the backup link between CE3-A and CE4-A. The PE2-AS1 router therefore redistributes the OSPF route 172.16.40.0/24 into MP-BGP because the OSPF route was not received via a sham-link from PE1-AS1. The PE1-AS1 router also does not redistribute the route in MP-iBGP because the route was received from PE2-AS1 via the OSPF sham-link between PE1-AS1 and PE2-AS1. PE1-AS1 therefore installs the OSPF route received over the sham-link in its VRF routing table. The LSA for route 172.16.40.0/24 is then propagated into Site 3 to allow CE3-A to select the best path. Packets received from the Site 4 will, therefore, be routed across the MPLS VPN backbone and will use the high bandwidth link. Also, the CE3-A router at Site 3 selects the sham-link as the best path to reach 172.16.40.0/24. Therefore, the traffic between Site 3 and site 4 is optimally routed via the low cost sham-link between PE1-AS1 and PE2-AS1.

Configuration Flowchart for OSPF Sham-Links

Figure 5-20 shows the configuration flowchart to configure OSPF sham-links.

Figure 5-20 *Configuration Flowchart to Configure OSPF Sham-Links*

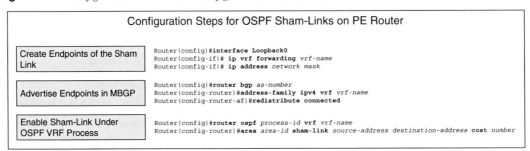

Configuration Scenario 3—OSPF Sham-Links

In this section, you use the MPLS VPN setup shown in Figure 5-17. Before configuring, ensure that the provider network is provisioned to deliver MPLS VPN services to Customer A sites. Ensure that IP addresses are preconfigured and VRFs are defined on PE routers.

To configure OSPF sham-links, follow these steps:

Step 1 **Create endpoints of the sham-link**—The first step is to create the endpoints of the sham-link by creating a loopback interface on each PE router and associating it to the VRF Cust_A of the VPN. This associates the sham-link in the VRF Cust_A for the VPN site. The address of the loopback interface should be an address in the VPN's address space, not the MPLS VPN service provider's address space because the sham-link is considered a link of the VPN customer and not the MPLS VPN service provider's. Example 5-21 shows this configuration on the PE1-AS1 and PE2-AS1.

Example 5-21 *Create Endpoints of the Sham-Link*

```
PE1-AS1(config)#interface Loopback101
PE1-AS1(config-if)# description sham-link Endpoint on PE1-AS1
PE1-AS1(config-if)# ip vrf forwarding Cust_A
PE1-AS1(config-if)# ip address 172.16.101.1 255.255.255.255
PE2-AS1(config)#interface Loopback101
PE2-AS1(config-if)# description sham-link Endpoint on PE2-AS1
PE2-AS1(config-if)# ip vrf forwarding Cust_A
PE2-AS1(config-if)# ip address 172.16.102.1 255.255.255.255
```

Step 2 **Redistribute the endpoints in MP-BGP**—Redistribute the sham-link endpoints created in Step 1 in BGP. This ensures that the PE routers have reachability to the endpoints. When the sham-link endpoint is created, it is necessary to ensure that each PE router has reachability to the endpoint. Such reachability information must be learned via BGP in each PE router, which can be done by redistributing the endpoint addresses to MP-BGP, as shown in Example 5-22.

NOTE   The endpoint address information should not be advertised via OSPF itself. The loopback interface should not be included in the OSPF 101 VRF process. It would cause a problem when a backdoor path exists between the two VPN sites. In such a scenario, the PE router that includes the endpoint address in the OSPF VRF process would exchange the endpoint address information via OSPF to the CE routers in LSA Type 1 or 2. The LSA would then propagate to the other side of PE router over the backdoor path. Although the other side of the PE would also receive the endpoint address information via MP-BGP, it will prefer the OSPF route rather than the BGP-learned route because of the administrative distance value. The sham-link will fail to be up because the endpoint address information is not learned via BGP. Example 5-22 shows how to redistribute the endpoints in MP-BGP.

Example 5-22 *Redistribute the Endpoints in MP-BGP*

```
PE1-AS1(config)#router bgp 1
PE1-AS1(config-router)#address-family ipv4 vrf Cust_A
PE1-AS1(config-router-af)# redistribute connected
PE2-AS1(config)#router bgp 1
PE2-AS1(config-router)#address-family ipv4 vrf Cust_A
PE2-AS1(config-router-af)# redistribute connected
```

Step 3   **Enable sham-link under OSPF VRF process**—Configure the sham-link under the OSPF process. Because the sham-link is considered an OSPF link within the area of the VPN sites, the area ID needs to be specified to match the VPN sites' area ID, and a cost value needs to be assigned to it. When there is a backdoor connection, the cost assigned can determine whether the traffic flows between the backdoor link and the sham-link. Example 5-23 shows the step on PE1-AS1. Repeat the same step on PE2-AS1.

Example 5-23 *Enable Sham-Link Under OSPF VRF Process*

```
PE1-AS1(config)#router ospf 101 vrf Cust_A
PE1-AS1(config-router)#area 0 sham-link 172.16.101.1 172.16.102.1 cost 1
PE2-AS1(config)#router ospf 101 vrf Cust_A
PE2-AS1(config-router)#area 0 sham-link 172.16.102.1 172.16.101.1 cost 1
```

Final Configuration for PE1-AS1 and PE2-AS1

Example 5-24 shows the configuration on PE1-AS1 and PE2-AS1.

Example 5-24 *Configuration on PE1-AS1 and PE2-AS1*

```
hostname PE1-AS1
!
ip cef
!
```

continues

Example 5-24 *Configuration on PE1-AS1 and PE2-AS1 (Continued)*

```
ip vrf Cust_A
 rd 1:100
 route-target export 1:100
 route-target import 1:100
!
interface Loopback0
 ip address 10.10.10.101 255.255.255.255
!
interface Loopback101
 description sham-link Endpoint on PE1-AS1
 ip vrf forwarding Cust_A
 ip address 172.16.101.1 255.255.255.255
!
interface Serial0/0
 description connected to P1-AS1
 ip address 10.10.10.1 255.255.255.252
 mpls ip
!
interface Serial1/0
 description connected to CE1-A
 ip vrf forwarding Cust_A
 ip address 172.16.1.1 255.255.255.252
!
interface Serial2/0
 description connected to CE1-B
 ip vrf forwarding Cust_A
 ip address 172.16.3.1 255.255.255.252
!
router ospf 101 vrf Cust_A
 router-id 172.16.101.1
 area 0 sham-link 172.16.101.1 172.16.102.1
 redistribute bgp 1 subnets
 network 172.16.1.0 0.0.0.255 area 0
 network 172.16.3.0 0.0.0.255 area 0
!
router ospf 1
 router-id 10.10.10.101
 network 10.0.0.0 0.255.255.255 area 0
!
router bgp 1
 no synchronization
 redistribute eigrp 101
 neighbor 10.10.10.102 remote-as 1
 neighbor 10.10.10.102 update-source Loopback0
 no auto-summary
 !
 address-family vpnv4
 neighbor 10.10.10.102 activate
 neighbor 10.10.10.102 send-community both
 exit-address-family
 !
 address-family ipv4 vrf Cust_A
```

Example 5-24 *Configuration on PE1-AS1 and PE2-AS1 (Continued)*

```
 redistribute connected
 redistribute ospf 101 vrf Cust_A match internal external 1 external 2
 no auto-summary
 no synchronization
 exit-address-family
hostname PE2-AS1
!
ip cef
!
ip vrf Cust_A
 rd 1:100
 route-target export 1:100
 route-target import 1:100
!
interface Loopback0
 ip address 10.10.10.102 255.255.255.255
!
interface Loopback101
 description sham-link Endpoint on PE2-AS1
 ip vrf forwarding Cust_A
 ip address 172.16.102.1 255.255.255.255
!
interface Serial0/0
 description connected to P1-AS1
 ip address 10.10.10.5 255.255.255.252
 mpls ip
!
interface Serial1/0
 description connected to CE2-A
 ip vrf forwarding Cust_A
 ip address 172.16.2.1 255.255.255.252
!
interface Serial2/0
 description connected to CE2-B
 ip vrf forwarding Cust_A
 ip address 172.16.4.1 255.255.255.252
!
router ospf 101 vrf Cust_A
 router-id 172.16.102.1
 area 0 sham-link 172.16.102.1 172.16.101.1
 redistribute bgp 1 subnets
 network 172.16.2.0 0.0.0.255 area 0
 network 172.16.4.0 0.0.0.255 area 0
!
router ospf 1
 router-id 10.10.10.102
 network 10.0.0.0 0.255.255.255 area 0
!
router bgp 1
 no synchronization
 neighbor 10.10.10.101 remote-as 1
```

continues

Example 5-24 *Configuration on PE1-AS1 and PE2-AS1 (Continued)*

```
 neighbor 10.10.10.101 update-source Loopback0
 no auto-summary
 !
 address-family vpnv4
 neighbor 10.10.10.101 activate
 neighbor 10.10.10.101 send-community both
 exit-address-family
 !
 address-family ipv4 vrf Cust_A
 redistribute connected
 redistribute ospf 101 vrf Cust_A match internal external 1 external 2
 no auto-summary
 no synchronization
 exit-address-family
```

Final Configuration for CE1-A, CE2-A, CE3-A, and CE4-A

Example 5-25 shows the configurations on CE1-A, CE2-A, CE3-A, and CE4-A.

Example 5-25 *Configurations on CE1-A, CE2-A, CE3-A, and CE4-A*

```
hostname CE1-A
!
interface Ethernet0/0
 description VPN-A Site 1 network
 ip address 172.16.10.1 255.255.255.0
!
interface Serial1/0
 description connected to PE1-AS1
 ip address 172.16.1.2 255.255.255.252
!
router ospf 101
 network 172.16.0.0 0.0.255.255 area 0
hostname CE2-A
!
interface Ethernet0/0
 ip address 172.16.20.1 255.255.255.0
!
interface Serial1/0
 description connected to PE2-AS1
 ip address 172.16.2.2 255.255.255.252
!
router ospf 101
 network 172.16.0.0 0.0.255.255 area 0
hostname CE3-A
!
interface Ethernet0/0
 ip address 172.16.30.1 255.255.255.0
!
interface Serial1/0
 bandwidth 512
 ip address 172.16.5.1 255.255.255.252
```

Example 5-25 *Configurations on CE1-A, CE2-A, CE3-A, and CE4-A (Continued)*

```
!
interface Serial2/0
 ip address 172.16.3.2 255.255.255.252
!
router ospf 101
 network 172.16.0.0 0.0.255.255 area 0
hostname CE4-A
!
interface Ethernet0/0
 ip address 172.16.40.1 255.255.255.0
!
interface Serial1/0
 bandwidth 512
 ip address 172.16.5.2 255.255.255.252
!
interface Serial2/0
ip address 172.16.4.2 255.255.255.252
!
router ospf 101
 network 172.16.0.0 0.0.255.255 area 0
```

Verify Sham-Link Operation

For route propagation without sham-link configuration, Example 5-26 shows that without sham-link 172.16.40.0, 172.16.20.0 is reachable via CE3-A.

Example 5-26 **show ip route vrf Cust_A** *on PE1-AS1*

```
PE1-AS1#show ip route vrf Cust_A
      172.16.0.0/16 is variably subnetted, 11 subnets, 3 masks
O        172.16.40.0/24 [110/269] via 172.16.3.2, 05:54:31, Serial2/0
O        172.16.30.0/24 [110/74] via 172.16.3.2, 05:54:31, Serial2/0
O        172.16.20.0/24 [110/397] via 172.16.3.2, 05:54:31, Serial2/0
O        172.16.10.0/24 [110/74] via 172.16.1.2, 05:54:31, Serial1/0
O        172.16.4.0/30 [110/323] via 172.16.3.2, 05:54:31, Serial2/0
O        172.16.5.0/30 [110/259] via 172.16.3.2, 05:54:31, Serial2/0
O        172.16.2.0/30 [110/387] via 172.16.3.2, 05:54:31, Serial2/0
```

Example 5-27 shows that without sham-link 172.16.30.0, 172.16.10.0 is reachable via CE4-A.

Example 5-27 **show ip route vrf Cust_A** *on PE2-AS1*

```
PE2-AS1#show ip route vrf Cust_A ospf 101
      172.16.0.0/16 is variably subnetted, 11 subnets, 3 masks
O        172.16.40.0/24 [110/74] via 172.16.4.2, 05:55:48, Serial2/0
O        172.16.30.0/24 [110/269] via 172.16.4.2, 05:55:48, Serial2/0
O        172.16.20.0/24 [110/74] via 172.16.2.2, 05:55:48, Serial1/0
O        172.16.10.0/24 [110/397] via 172.16.4.2, 05:55:48, Serial2/0
O        172.16.5.0/30 [110/259] via 172.16.4.2, 05:55:48, Serial2/0
O        172.16.1.0/30 [110/387] via 172.16.4.2, 05:55:48, Serial2/0
O        172.16.3.0/30 [110/323] via 172.16.4.2, 05:55:48, Serial2/0
```

Example 5-28 shows the routing tables on CE3-A and CE4-A without sham-link.

Example 5-28 *Routing Tables on CE3-A and CE4-A Without Sham-Link*

```
CE3-A#show ip route ospf
       172.16.0.0/16 is variably subnetted, 11 subnets, 3 masks
O        172.16.40.0/24 [110/205] via 172.16.5.2, 05:56:25, Serial1/0
O        172.16.20.0/24 [110/333] via 172.16.5.2, 05:56:25, Serial1/0
O        172.16.10.0/24 [110/138] via 172.16.3.1, 05:56:25, Serial2/0
O        172.16.4.0/30 [110/259] via 172.16.5.2, 05:56:25, Serial1/0
O        172.16.1.0/30 [110/128] via 172.16.3.1, 05:56:25, Serial2/0
O        172.16.2.0/30 [110/323] via 172.16.5.2, 05:56:25, Serial1/0
O E2     172.16.101.1/32 [110/1] via 172.16.5.2, 05:55:49, Serial1/0
O E2     172.16.102.1/32 [110/1] via 172.16.3.1, 05:55:50, Serial2/0
CE4-A#show ip route ospf
       172.16.0.0/16 is variably subnetted, 11 subnets, 3 masks
O        172.16.30.0/24 [110/205] via 172.16.5.1, 05:56:40, Serial1/0
O        172.16.20.0/24 [110/138] via 172.16.4.1, 05:56:40, Serial2/0
O        172.16.10.0/24 [110/333] via 172.16.5.1, 05:56:40, Serial1/0
O        172.16.1.0/30 [110/323] via 172.16.5.1, 05:56:40, Serial1/0
O        172.16.2.0/30 [110/128] via 172.16.4.1, 05:56:40, Serial2/0
O        172.16.3.0/30 [110/259] via 172.16.5.1, 05:56:40, Serial1/0
O E2     172.16.101.1/32 [110/1] via 172.16.4.1, 05:56:05, Serial2/0
O E2     172.16.102.1/32 [110/1] via 172.16.5.1, 05:56:06, Serial1/0
```

Example 5-29 shows the **traceroute** output when there is no sham-link.

Example 5-29 *Traceroutes Without Sham-Links*

```
CE3-A#traceroute 172.16.40.1
Type escape sequence to abort.
Tracing the route to 172.16.40.1
  1 172.16.5.2 20 msec 24 msec *
CE1-A#traceroute 172.16.20.1
Type escape sequence to abort.
Tracing the route to 172.16.20.1
  1 172.16.1.1 20 msec 24 msec 20 msec
  2 172.16.3.2 40 msec 40 msec 40 msec
  3 172.16.5.2 60 msec 60 msec 60 msec
  4 172.16.4.1 80 msec 80 msec 80 msec
  5 172.16.2.2 100 msec 100 msec *
CE1-A#traceroute 172.16.40.1
Type escape sequence to abort.
Tracing the route to 172.16.40.1
  1 172.16.1.1 20 msec 20 msec 20 msec
  2 172.16.3.2 48 msec 40 msec 40 msec
  3 172.16.5.2 60 msec 60 msec *
```

Example 5-30 shows that with the **OSPF** commands to verify sham links.

Example 5-30   *Sham-Links 172.16.40.0 and 172.16.20.0 Are Reachable via MP-iBGP Backbone*

```
PE1-AS1#show ip ospf sham-links
Sham Link OSPF_SL0 to address 172.16.102.1 is up
Area 0 source address 172.16.101.1
  Run as demand circuit
  DoNotAge LSA allowed. Cost of using 1 State POINT_TO_POINT,
  Timer intervals configured, Hello 10, Dead 40, Wait 40,
    Hello due in 00:00:03
    Adjacency State FULL (Hello suppressed)
    Index 3/3, retransmission queue length 0, number of retransmission 0
    First 0x0(0)/0x0(0) Next 0x0(0)/0x0(0)
    Last retransmission scan length is 0, maximum is 0
    Last retransmission scan time is 0 msec, maximum is 0 msec
PE1-AS1#show ip ospf neighbor

Neighbor ID      Pri   State        Dead Time   Address         Interface
10.10.10.200      0    FULL/ -      00:00:34    10.10.10.2      Serial0/0
172.16.102.1      0    FULL/ -          -       172.16.102.1    OSPF_SL0
172.16.30.1       0    FULL/ -      00:00:34    172.16.3.2      Serial2/0
172.16.10.1       0    FULL/ -      00:00:33    172.16.1.2      Serial1/0
```

Example 5-31 shows sham-links 172.16.40.0, 172.16.20.0, and 172.16.30.0 are reachable via MP-iBGP backbone.

Example 5-31   *Sham-Links 172.16.40.0, 172.16.20.0, and 172.16.30.0 Are Reachable via MP-iBGP Backbone*

```
PE1-AS1#show ip route vrf Cust_A ospf 101 172.16.40.0
O       172.16.40.0/24 [110/75] via 10.10.10.102, 00:19:23
PE1-AS1#show ip route vrf Cust_A ospf 101 172.16.20.0
O       172.16.20.0/24 [110/75] via 10.10.10.102, 00:19:23
PE2-AS1#show ip route vrf Cust_A ospf 101 172.16.30.0
O       172.16.30.0/24 [110/75] via 10.10.10.101, 00:19:58
```

Example 5-32 shows the routing table on CE3-A and CE4-A when the sham-link is configured depicting all routes now reachable via MP-BGP backbone.

Example 5-32   **show ip route ospf** *on CE3-A and CE4-A*

```
CE3-A#show ip route ospf
       172.16.0.0/16 is variably subnetted, 11 subnets, 3 masks
O         172.16.40.0/24 [110/139] via 172.16.3.1, 00:20:20, Serial2/0
O         172.16.20.0/24 [110/139] via 172.16.3.1, 00:20:20, Serial2/0
O         172.16.10.0/24 [110/138] via 172.16.3.1, 00:20:20, Serial2/0
O         172.16.4.0/30 [110/129] via 172.16.3.1, 00:20:20, Serial2/0
O         172.16.1.0/30 [110/128] via 172.16.3.1, 00:20:20, Serial2/0
O         172.16.2.0/30 [110/129] via 172.16.3.1, 00:20:20, Serial2/0
O E2    172.16.101.1/32 [110/1] via 172.16.3.1, 00:20:20, Serial2/0
O E2    172.16.102.1/32 [110/1] via 172.16.3.1, 00:20:20, Serial2/0
CE4-A#show ip route ospf
       172.16.0.0/16 is variably subnetted, 11 subnets, 3 masks
```

continues

Example 5-32 *show ip route ospf* on *CE3-A and CE4-A (Continued)*

```
O        172.16.30.0/24 [110/139] via 172.16.4.1, 00:20:39, Serial2/0
O        172.16.20.0/24 [110/138] via 172.16.4.1, 00:20:39, Serial2/0
O        172.16.10.0/24 [110/139] via 172.16.4.1, 00:20:39, Serial2/0
O        172.16.1.0/30 [110/129] via 172.16.4.1, 00:20:39, Serial2/0
O        172.16.2.0/30 [110/128] via 172.16.4.1, 00:20:39, Serial2/0
O        172.16.3.0/30 [110/129] via 172.16.4.1, 00:20:39, Serial2/0
O E2     172.16.101.1/32 [110/1] via 172.16.4.1, 00:20:39, Serial2/0
O E2     172.16.102.1/32 [110/1] via 172.16.4.1, 00:20:39, Serial2/0
```

OSPF PE-CE Routing Command Summary

Table 5-1 shows the relevant OSPF PE-CE routing commands used in this chapter.

Table 5-1 *OSPF PE-CE Routing Command Summary*

Command	Purpose
Router(config-router)#**area sham-link cost**	Configures a sham-link interface on a PE router in an MPLS VPN backbone; uses the **area sham-link cost** command in router configuration mode
Router#(config)#**router ospf** *process-id* **vrf** *vrf-name*	Configures the specified OSPF process for the VRF
Router#**show ip ospf sham-links**	Displays information about all sham-links configured for a PE router in the VPN backbone

EIGRP PE-CE Routing Protocol Overview, Configuration, and Verification

EIGRP PE-CE routing protocol is used by service providers for customers who use EIGRP as their IGP routing protocol and, hence, prefer to use EIGRP to exchange routing information between the customer sites across an MPLS VPN backbone. In an MPLS VPN environment, to achieve this, the original EIGRP metrics must be carried inside MP-BGP updates. This is achieved by using BGP extended community attributes to carry and preserve EIGRP metrics when crossing the MP-iBGP domain. These communities define the intrinsic characteristics associated with EIGRP, such as the AS number or EIGRP cost metric like bandwidth, delay, load, reliability, and MTU. As shown in Table 5-2, six extended BGP communities have been defined to carry the EIGRP routes across the MPLS backbone via MP-BGP.

Table 5-2   *BGP Extended Communities for EIGRP PE-CE Routing*

EIGRP Attribute	Type	Usage	Value
General	0x8800	EIGRP General Route Information	Route Flag and Tag
Metric	0x8801	EIGRP Route Metric Information and AS	AS and Delay
	0x8802	EIGRP Route Metric Information	Reliability, Next Hop, and Bandwidth
	0x8803	EIGRP Route Metric Information	Reserve, Load, and Maximum Transmission Unit (MTU)
	0x8804	EIGRP External Route Information	Remote AS and Remote ID
External	0x8805	EIGRP External Route Information	Remote Protocol and Remote Metric

Figure 5-21 gives the details on the extended BGP community attribute that are attached to sample routes 192.168.20.0 and 192.168.99.0.

Figure 5-21 *BGP Extended Communities Explained*

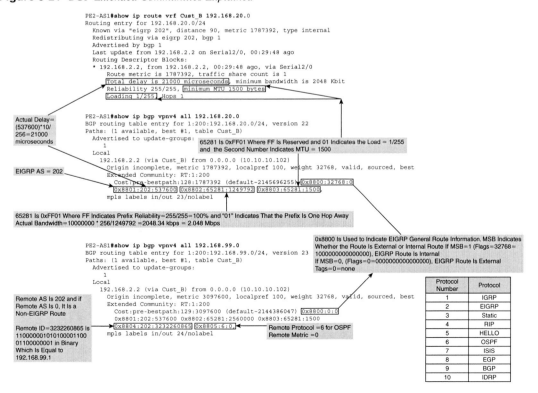

EIGRP Route Propagation

Route propagation in MPLS VPN networks using EIGRP PE-CE routing is based on EIGRP AS configured on the PE routers. In an MPLS VPN environment, EIGRP AS can be the same on all PE routers or different on all PE routers.

Route Propagation When EIGRP AS Is Same on All PE Routers

Figure 5-22 shows an MPLS VPN provider network providing MPLS VPN services to Customer A. PE1-AS1 and PE2-AS1 are configured for EIGRP AS 101.

Figure 5-22 *Route Propagation When EIGRP AS Is Same on PE Routers*

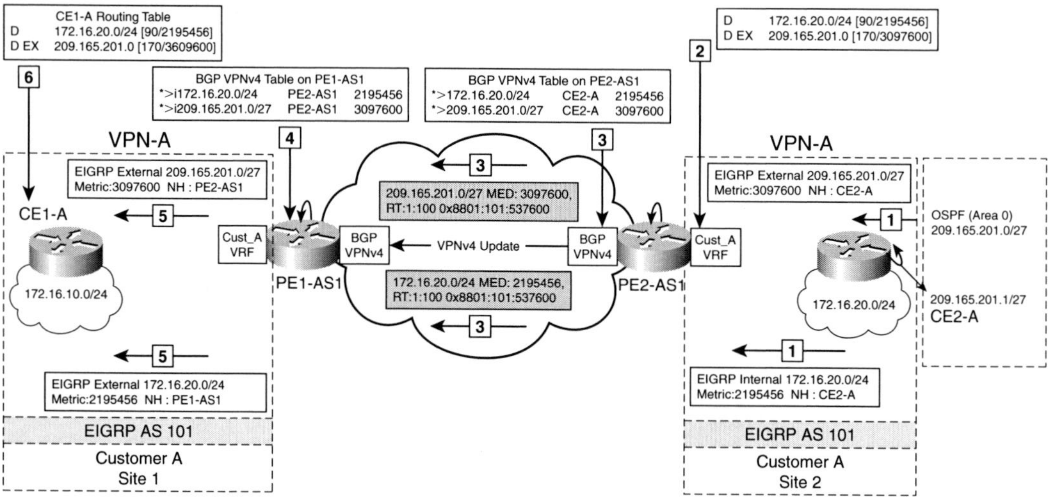

The following sequence takes place when CE2-A is sending 172.16.20.0 and 209.165.201.0 to CE1-A:

1 CE2-A redistributes OSPF network 209.165.127.0/27 as an EIGRP external route (D EX) and 172.16.20.0/24 as an internal route (D) to PE2-AS1.

2 Figure 5-22 shows that the VRF Cust_A routing table on PE2-AS1 receives 172.16.20.0/24 as internal route with EIGRP metric 2195456 and 209.165.127.0/27 as an external route with EIGRP metric 3097600.

3 The EIGRP metrics for 172.16.20.0 and 209.165.127.0 are copied into extended BGP attributes as BGP MEDs, and extended communities containing EIGRP information such as AS, MTU, route type, and so on are attached when EIGRP routes are redistributed into MP-BGP. The routes 172.16.20.0 and 209.165.127.0 are then propagated to PE1-AS1 via MP-iBGP session.

4 PE1-AS1 receives the BGP VPNv4 routes 172.16.20.0/24 and 209.165.127.0/27 from PE2-AS1. As shown in Figure 5-22, the EIGRP metric for the routes are not altered and remain the same when propagated though the MP-BGP backbone.

5 PE2-AS1 checks the attributes received in the route, and, if route type is *internal (if the MSB bit in the 0x8800 BGP extended community attribute is set)* and the source AS matches what is configured on the receiving PE router, the route is advertised as EIGRP internal route. If the route type is *external (MSB bit in 0x8800 is not set)*, the route is advertised to the CE as an external EIGRP route.

PE1-AS1, therefore, uses the extended community attribute information to reconstruct the original EIGRP routing update when redistributing from MP-BGP into EIGRP. This redistribution behavior takes place only if the PE2-AS1 EIGRP AS number is equal to the PE1-AS1, PE's EIGRP AS number. The PE routers act as EIGRP query boundaries. In this case, the route type for 172.16.20.0 is internal and source AS 101 matches on the receiving router PE1-AS1. Therefore, 172.16.20.0/24 is propagated as an EIGRP internal route to CE1-A. The route type for 209.165.127.0/27 is external and, therefore, is propagated to CE1-A as an external route.

6 As shown in the figure, CE1-A receives the 172.16.20.0 as an internal route and 209.165.127.0 as an external route.

Route Propagation When EIGRP AS Is Different on All PE Routers

If the two EIGRP AS numbers are different, the normal redistribution rules apply; that is, external EIGRP routes are created when the customer routes are redistributed into EIGRP from MP-BGP updates. Figure 5-23 shows an MPLS VPN provider network using different EIGRP AS on PE routers PE1-AS1 and PE2-AS1. Because the MPLS backbone is transparent to the CE routing protocol, no EIGRP adjacency is formed or EIGRP updates and queries sent across the PE routers.

Figure 5-23 *Route Propagation When EIGRP AS Is Different on PE Routers*

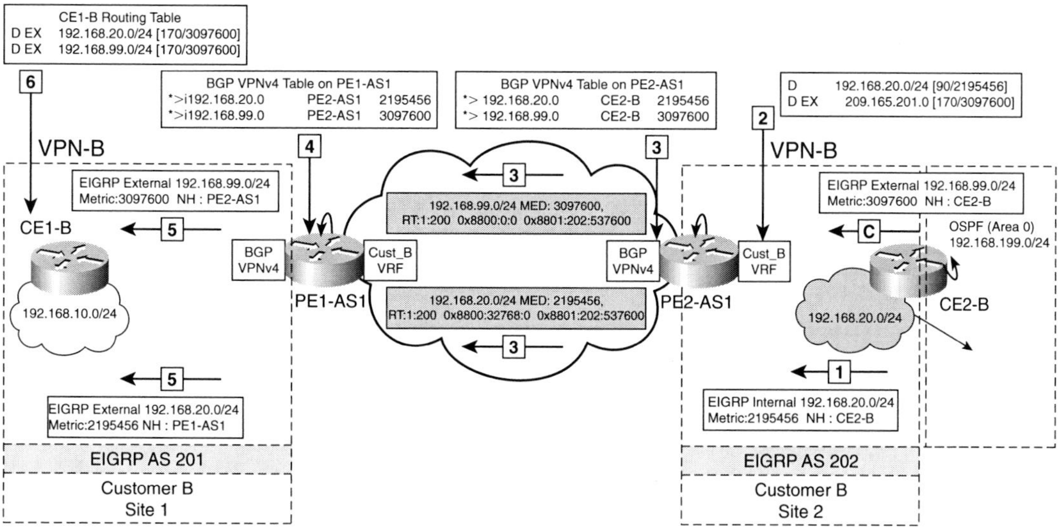

The sequence shown in 1 through 4 in the section "Route Propagation When EIGRP AS Is Same on All PE Routers" remains the same except for networks 192.168.99.0 and 192.168.20.0 and the metric:

1   PE2-AS1 checks the attributes received in the route, and, if the route type is **internal** and the source AS does not match or if the route type is **external**, the route is advertised to the CE as an external EIGRP route. The route will *not* use the extended community information because it did not originate from the same AS. Route type for 192.168.20.0 is internal and source AS, which is 202, does not match the configured AS on PE1-AS1 (201). Therefore, PE1-AS1 propagates that as an external route to CE1-A. The route type for 192.168.99.0 is external, and, therefore, both routes are propagated to CE1-A as external routes.

2   As illustrated in Figure 5-23, CE1-A receives 192.168.20.0/24 and 192.168.99.0/24 as external routes.

Configuration Flowchart for EIGRP PE-CE Routing

Figure 5-24 shows the configuration flowchart to configure EIGRP PE-CE routing.

Figure 5-24   *EIGRP PE-CE Routing Configuration Flowchart*

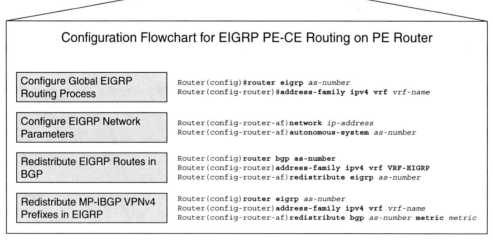

The following are key points to be noted from the configuration flowchart:

- Address family configuration mode is used to configure the EIGRP AS for a given VRF.

- To allow a single EIGRP process to be used, the EIGRP AS has to be configured within the EIGRP address family configuration mode.

Other EIGRP configuration steps are the same as with normal EIGRP configuration. The default metric should be specified for the redistribution of non-EIGRP routes.

Configuration Scenario 1: Basic EIGRP PE-CE Routing Configuration

The objective of this configuration scenario is to demonstrate EIGRP PE-CE configuration and EIGRP route propagation when PE routers belong to the same EIGRP AS for a VRF and when they are in different EIGRP AS for a VRF. Figure 5-25 shows an MPLS VPN service provider providing MPLS VPN services to Customer A and Customer B sites:

- **Customer A Network**—Customer A has CE1-A and CE2-A located in the same VPN, VPN-A. They are part of EIGRP AS 101. EIGRP AS 101 is configured for VRF Cust_A on PE1-AS1 and PE2-AS1.

- **Customer B Network**—Customer B has CE1-B and CE2-B located in the same VPN, VPN-B. CE1-B and CE2-B belong to different EIGRP AS, 201 and 202. PE1-AS1 and PE2-AS1 have EIGRP AS 201 and 202 configured for VRF Cust_B, respectively.

The steps to configure EIGRP PE-CE routing are as follows:

Step 1   **Enable the global EIGRP routing process**—Enable the global EIGRP routing process on PE routers, PE1-AS1 and PE2-AS1.

Step 2   **Define per VRF EIGRP routing context and parameters**—In this step, define

—   Per VRF EIGRP routing context for VRF Cust_A and Cust_B under the EIGRP routing process defined in Step 1. This number can be the same or different from the EIGRP AS number configured under the routing context.

—   Configure the networks that need to be enabled for EIGRP using the **network** command.

—   Ensure that **no auto-summary** is configured; otherwise, EIGRP summarizes networks at their classful boundaries. The command **no auto-summary** may be enabled by default depending on the version of IOS in use.

— To allow a single global EIGRP process to be used, the EIGRP
AS has to be configured within the EIGRP address family
configuration mode. This is accomplished by configuring
autonomous-system *as-number* in address-family mode. This
allows the same EIGRP AS number to be used in multiple VRFs.

Figure 5-25 *MPLS VPN Network Implementing EIGRP PE-CE Routing with Same and Different EIGRP
Autonomous Systems*

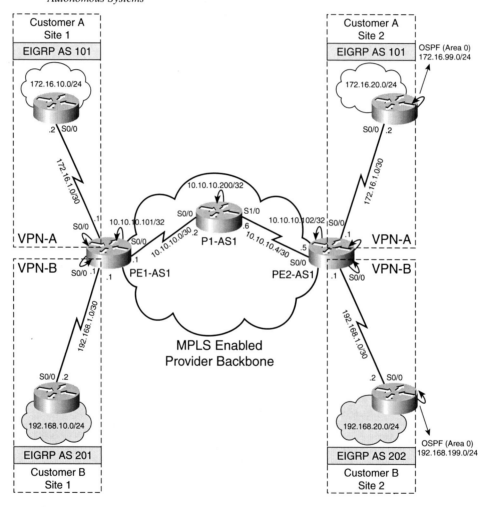

Steps 1 and 2 for VRF Cust_B are shown in Example 5-33.

Example 5-33 *Step 1: Enable EIGRP Routing Process and Step 2: Define VRF Routing Context*

```
PE1-AS1(config)#router eigrp 1
PE1-AS1(config-router)#address-family ipv4 vrf Cust_B
PE1-AS1(config-router-af)# network 172.16.0.0
PE1-AS1(config-router-af)# no auto-summary
PE1-AS1(config-router-af)# autonomous-system 201
PE1-AS1(config-router-af)# exit-address-family
```
```
PE2-AS1(config)#router eigrp 1
PE2-AS1(config-router)# address-family ipv4 vrf Cust_B
PE2-AS1(config-router-af)# network 172.16.0.0
PE2-AS1(config-router-af)# no auto-summary
PE2-AS1(config-router-af)# autonomous-system 202
PE2-AS1(config-router-af)# exit-address-family
```

Step 3 **Redistribute BGP VPNv4 routes in EIGRP**—In this step, you redistribute the BGP VPNv4 routes from the remote PE routers in EIGRP. Example 5-34 shows the configuration to redistribute BGP routes in EIGRP for PE1-AS1 for VRF Cust_A. Repeat the steps for Customer A VRF Cust_A on PE2-AS1 and Customer B VRF Cust_B on PE1-AS1 and PE2-AS1.

Example 5-34 *Redistribute BGP VPNv4 Routes in EIGRP*

```
PE1-AS1(config)#router eigrp 1
PE1-AS1(config-router)# address-family ipv4 vrf Cust_A
PE1-AS1(config-router-af)# redistribute bgp 1 metric 1000 100 255 1 1500
```

Step 4 **Redistribute EIGRP routes in BGP**—In this step, the EIGRP routes received from the local CE router are redistributed in BGP on the PE router. Example 5-35 shows the procedure to configure redistribution of EIGRP routes in BGP on PE1-AS1. Repeat the same steps on PE2-AS1 for VRF Cust_A. Similarly, redistribute EIGRP routes in BGP on PE1-AS1 and PE2-AS1 for VRF Cust_B. Use EIGRP AS 201 and 202 on PE1-AS1 and PE2-AS1 for VRF Cust_B.

Example 5-35 *Redistribute EIGRP Routes in BGP*

```
PE1-AS1(config)#router bgp 1
PE1-AS1(config-router)#address-family ipv4 vrf Cust_A
PE1-AS1(config-router-af)#redistribute eigrp 101
```
```
PE2-AS1(config)#router bgp 1
PE2-AS1(config-router)# address-family ipv4 vrf Cust_A
PE2-AS1(config-router-af)# redistribute eigrp 101
```

Final Configuration for PE Routers

Example 5-36 shows the final configuration for the PE routers.

Example 5-36 *Final Configuration for the PE Routers*

```
hostname PE1-AS1
!
ip cef
!
ip vrf Cust_A
 rd 1:100
 route-target export 1:100
 route-target import 1:100
!
ip vrf Cust_B
 rd 1:200
 route-target export 1:200
 route-target import 1:200
!
interface Loopback0
 ip address 10.10.10.101 255.255.255.255
!
interface Serial0/0
 description connected to P1-AS1
 ip address 10.10.10.1 255.255.255.252
 mpls ip
!
interface Serial1/0
 description connected to CE1-A
 ip vrf forwarding Cust_A
 ip address 172.16.1.1 255.255.255.252
!
interface Serial2/0
 description connected to CE1-B
 ip vrf forwarding Cust_B
 ip address 192.168.1.1 255.255.255.252
!
router eigrp 1
 auto-summary
 !
 address-family ipv4 vrf Cust_B
 redistribute bgp 1 metric 1000 100 255 1 1500
 network 192.168.1.0
 no auto-summary
 autonomous-system 201
 exit-address-family
 !
 address-family ipv4 vrf Cust_A
 redistribute bgp 1 metric 1000 100 255 1 1500
 network 172.16.0.0
 no auto-summary
 autonomous-system 101
 exit-address-family
 !
router ospf 1
 router-id 10.10.10.101
 network 10.0.0.0 0.255.255.255 area 0
```

Example 5-36 *Final Configuration for the PE Routers (Continued)*

```
!
router bgp 1
 no synchronization
 neighbor 10.10.10.102 remote-as 1
 neighbor 10.10.10.102 update-source Loopback0
 no auto-summary
 !
 address-family vpnv4
 neighbor 10.10.10.102 activate
 neighbor 10.10.10.102 send-community extended
 exit-address-family
 !
 address-family ipv4 vrf Cust_B
 redistribute eigrp 201
 no auto-summary
 no synchronization
 exit-address-family
 !
 address-family ipv4 vrf Cust_A
 redistribute eigrp 101
 no auto-summary
 no synchronization
 exit-address-family
hostname PE2-AS1
!
ip cef
!
ip vrf Cust_A
 rd 1:100
 route-target export 1:100
 route-target import 1:100
!
ip vrf Cust_B
 rd 1:200
 route-target export 1:200
 route-target import 1:200
!
interface Loopback0
 ip address 10.10.10.102 255.255.255.255
!
interface Serial0/0
 description connected to P1-AS1
 ip address 10.10.10.5 255.255.255.252
 mpls ip
!
interface Serial1/0
 description connected to CE2-A
 ip vrf forwarding Cust_A
 ip address 172.16.2.1 255.255.255.252
!
```

continues

Example 5-36 *Final Configuration for the PE Routers (Continued)*

```
interface Serial2/0
 description connected to CE2-B
 ip vrf forwarding Cust_B
 ip address 192.168.2.1 255.255.255.252
!
router eigrp 1
 auto-summary
 !
 address-family ipv4 vrf Cust_B
 redistribute bgp 1 metric 1000 100 255 1 1500
 network 192.168.2.0
 no auto-summary
 autonomous-system 202
 exit-address-family
 !
 address-family ipv4 vrf Cust_A
 redistribute bgp 1 metric 1000 100 255 1 1500
 network 172.16.0.0
 no auto-summary
 autonomous-system 101
 exit-address-family
!
router ospf 1
 router-id 10.10.10.102
 network 10.0.0.0 0.255.255.255 area 0
!
router bgp 1
 no synchronization
 neighbor 10.10.10.101 remote-as 1
 neighbor 10.10.10.101 update-source Loopback0
 no auto-summary
 !
 address-family vpnv4
 neighbor 10.10.10.101 activate
 neighbor 10.10.10.101 send-community extended
 exit-address-family
 !
 address-family ipv4 vrf Cust_B
 redistribute eigrp 202
 no auto-summary
 no synchronization
 exit-address-family
 !
 address-family ipv4 vrf Cust_A
 redistribute eigrp 101
 no auto-summary
 no synchronization
 exit-address-family
```

Final Configuration for CE Routers

Example 5-37 shows the final configurations for the CE routers for Customer A (CE1-A and CE2-A) and Customer B (CE1-B and CE2-B).

Example 5-37 *Final Configurations for CE1-A, CE2-A, CE1-B, and CE2-B*

```
hostname CE1-A
!
interface Ethernet0/0
 description VPN-A Site 1 network
 ip address 172.16.10.1 255.255.255.0
!
interface Serial1/0
 description connected to PE1-AS1
 ip address 172.16.1.2 255.255.255.252
!
router eigrp 101
 network 172.16.0.0
 no auto-summary
hostname CE2-A
!
interface Ethernet0/0
 description VPN-A Site 2 network
 ip address 172.16.20.1 255.255.255.0
!
interface Serial1/0
 description connected to PE2-AS1
 ip address 172.16.2.2 255.255.255.252
!
router eigrp 101
 network 172.16.0.0
 no auto-summary
hostname CE1-B
!
interface Ethernet0/0
 description VPN-B Site1 network
 ip address 192.168.10.1 255.255.255.0
!
interface Serial1/0
 description connected to PE1-AS1
 ip address 192.168.1.2 255.255.255.252
!
router eigrp 201
 network 192.168.1.0
 network 192.168.10.0
 no auto-summary
hostname CE2-B
!
interface Ethernet0/0
 description VPN-B Site2 network
 ip address 192.168.20.1 255.255.255.0
```

continues

Example 5-37   *Final Configurations for CE1-A, CE2-A, CE1-B, and CE2-B (Continued)*

```
!
interface Serial1/0
 description connected to PE2-AS1
 ip address 192.168.2.2 255.255.255.252
!
router eigrp 202
 network 192.168.2.0
 network 192.168.20.0
 no auto-summary
```

Verify Basic EIGRP PE-CE Routing

The steps to verify EIGRP PE-CE routing are as follows:

Step 1   **Verify EIGRP neighbor relationship**—Example 5-38 shows the output
on the PE1-AS1 and PE2-AS1.

Example 5-38   *Verify EIGRP Neighbor Relationship*

```
PE1-AS1#show ip eigrp vrf Cust_A neighbors
IP-EIGRP neighbors for process 101
H   Address          Interface       Hold Uptime    SRTT   RTO  Q  Seq Type
                                     (sec)          (ms)        Cnt Num
0   172.16.1.2              Se1/0    14  00:38:47   68     408  0  3
PE1-AS1#show ip eigrp vrf Cust_B neighbors
IP-EIGRP neighbors for process 201
H   Address          Interface       Hold Uptime    SRTT   RTO  Q  Seq Type
                                     (sec)          (ms)        Cnt Num
0   192.168.1.2      Se2/0           11  00:38:54   81     486  0  4
```

Step 2   **Verify EIGRP route propagation for Cust_B**—Use the following
sequence of steps to verify route propagation for Cust_B network
192.168.20.0 and 182.168.99.0.

Example 5-39 shows that PE2-AS1 receives 192.168.20.0 (metric
2195456) as an internal route.

Example 5-39   *Cust_B Routing Table on PE2-AS1*

```
PE2-AS1#show ip route vrf Cust_B eigrp
D EX 192.168.99.0/24 [170/3097600] via 192.168.2.2, 00:14:20, Serial2/0
D    192.168.20.0/24 [90/1787392] via 192.168.2.2, 00:14:20, Serial2/0
```

The EIGRP metric for 192.168.20.0 is copied into these attributes when
the EIGRP route is redistributed into MP-BGP, as shown in Example 5-40.
The command **show ip bgp vpnv4 all 192.168.20.0** shows the extended
BGP attributes that are attached to the route.

Example 5-40 *BGP VPNv4 Information for 192.168.20.0 on PE2-AS1*

```
PE2-AS1#show ip bgp vpnv4 vrf Cust_B 192.168.20.0
BGP routing table entry for 1:200:192.168.20.0/24, version 20
Paths: (1 available, best #1, table Cust_B)
  Advertised to update-groups:
     1
  Local
    192.168.2.2 (via Cust_B) from 0.0.0.0 (10.10.10.102)
    Origin incomplete, metric 1787392, localpref 100, weight 32768, valid, sourced,
      best
     Extended Community: RT:1:200
       Cost:pre-bestpath:128:1787392 (default-2145696255) 0x8800:32768:0
       0x8801:202:537600 0x8802:65281:1249792 0x8803:65281:1500,
      mpls labels in/out 23/nolabel
```

PE1-AS1 redistributing back from MP-BGP into EIGRP uses this information to reconstruct the original EIGRP routing update. Example 5-41 shows that the EIGRP metric for 192.168.20.0 is preserved when crossing an MP-BGP domain by using the BGP extended community attributes.

Example 5-41 *BGP VPNv4 Information for 192.168.20.0 on PE1-AS1*

```
PE1-AS1#show ip bgp vpnv4 vrf Cust_B 192.168.20.0
BGP routing table entry for 1:200:192.168.20.0/24, version 20
Paths: (1 available, best #1, table Cust_B)
  Not advertised to any peer
  Local
    10.10.10.102 (metric 97) from 10.10.10.102 (10.10.10.102)
     Origin incomplete, metric 1787392, localpref 100, valid, internal, best
     Extended Community: RT:1:200
       Cost:pre-bestpath:128:1787392 (default-2145696255) 0x8800:32768:0
       0x8801:202:537600 0x8802:65281:1249792 0x8803:65281:1500,
      mpls labels in/out nolabel/23
```

For Customer B, the two EIGRP AS numbers are different (201 on PE1-AS1 and 202 on PE2-AS1); therefore, normal redistribution rules apply. External EIGRP routes (D EX) are created when the 192.168.20.0 is redistributed into EIGRP from MP-BGP updates received on PE1-AS1 from PE2-AS1. Example 5-42 shows the EIGRP routing table on CE1-B.

Example 5-42 *EIGRP Routing Table on CE1-B*

```
CE1-B#show ip route eigrp
D EX 192.168.20.0/24 [170/3097600] via 192.168.1.1, 00:33:07, Serial1/0
       192.168.2.0/30 is subnetted, 1 subnets
D EX    192.168.2.0 [170/3097600] via 192.168.1.1, 00:39:28, Serial1/0
```

Step 3 **Verify EIGRP route propagation for Cust_A**—Use the following sequence of steps to verify route propagation for Cust_A network 172.16.20.0/24 and 209.165.201.0/27.

Example 5-43 shows that PE2-AS1 receives 172.16.20.0 (metric 1787392) as an internal route.

Example 5-43 *Cust_A VRF Routing on PE2-AS1*

```
PE2-AS1#show ip route vrf Cust_A eigrp
      172.16.0.0/16 is variably subnetted, 4 subnets, 2 masks
D        172.16.20.0/24 [90/1787392] via 172.16.2.2, 00:17:29, Serial1/0
      209.165.201.0/27 is subnetted, 1 subnets
D EX     209.165.201.0 [170/3097600] via 172.16.2.2, 00:17:29, Serial1/0
```

The EIGRP metric for 172.16.20.0 is copied into these attributes when the EIGRP route is redistributed into MP-BGP, as shown in Example 5-44. The command **show ip bgp vpnv4 all 172.16.20.0** shows the extended BGP attributes that are attached to the route.

Example 5-44 *BGP VPNv4 Information for 172.16.20.0 on PE2-AS1*

```
PE2-AS1#show ip bgp vpnv4 vrf Cust_A 172.16.20.0
BGP routing table entry for 1:100:172.16.20.0/24, version 15
Paths: (1 available, best #1, table Cust_A)
  Advertised to update-groups:
     1
  Local
    172.16.2.2 (via Cust_A) from 0.0.0.0 (10.10.10.102)
    Origin incomplete, metric 1787392, localpref 100, weight 32768, valid, sourced,
      best
    Extended Community: RT:1:100
      Cost:pre-bestpath:128:1787392 (default-2145696255) 0x8800:32768:0
      0x8801:101:537600 0x8802:65281:1249792 0x8803:65281:1500,
    mpls labels in/out 20/nolabel
```

PE1-AS1 redistributing back from MP-BGP into EIGRP uses this information to reconstruct the original EIGRP routing update. Example 5-45 shows that the EIGRP metric for 172.16.20.0 is preserved when crossing an MP-BGP domain by using the BGP extended community attributes.

Example 5-45 *BGP VPNv4 Information for 172.16.20.0 on PE1-AS1*

```
PE1-AS1#show ip bgp vpnv4 vrf Cust_A 172.16.20.0
BGP routing table entry for 1:100:172.16.20.0/24, version 15
Paths: (1 available, best #1, table Cust_A)
  Not advertised to any peer
  Local
    10.10.10.102 (metric 97) from 10.10.10.102 (10.10.10.102)
    Origin incomplete, metric 1787392, localpref 100, valid, internal, best
    Extended Community: RT:1:100
      Cost:pre-bestpath:128:1787392 (default-2145696255) 0x8800:32768:0
      0x8801:101:537600 0x8802:65281:1249792 0x8803:65281:1500,
    mpls labels in/out nolabel/20
```

Step 4   **Verify EIGRP routes on CE routers**—Example 5-46 shows that
CE1-A has received EIGRP internal routes for 172.16.20.0 because
ingress PE's PE2-AS1 EIGRP AS number 101 is equal to the egress PE's
PE1-AS1 EIGRP AS number.

Example 5-46   *EIGRP Routing Table on CE1-A*

```
CE1-A#show ip route eigrp
     172.16.0.0/16 is variably subnetted, 4 subnets, 2 masks
D       172.16.20.0/24 [90/2707456] via 172.16.1.1, 00:39:36, Serial1/0
D       172.16.2.0/30 [90/2681856] via 172.16.1.1, 00:39:36, Serial1/0
```

Step 5   **Verify connectivity between sites**—Verify connectivity between
Customer A sites. Example 5-47 shows the ping output.

Example 5-47   *Verify Connectivity Between Sites*

```
CE1-A#ping 172.16.20.1
Type escape sequence to abort.
Sending 5, 100-byte ICMP Echos to 172.16.20.1, timeout is 2 seconds:
!!!!!
Success rate is 100 percent (5/5), round-trip min/avg/max = 8/8/12 ms
CE1-B#ping 192.168.20.1
Type escape sequence to abort.
Sending 5, 100-byte ICMP Echos to 172.16.10.1, timeout is 2 seconds:
!!!!!
Success rate is 100 percent (5/5), round-trip min/avg/max = 8/8/12 ms
```

Routing Loops and Suboptimal Routing

Routing loop and suboptimal routing generally occur because of mutual redistribution
taking place between EIGRP PE-CE and MP-BGP in an MPLS VPN environment.

Routing Loops

Routing loops can occur in the following scenarios:

- A route received by a multihomed site from the backbone through one link can be
  forwarded back to the backbone via the other link.

- A route originated in a multihomed site and sent to the backbone through one link can
  come back through the other link.

Multihomed Site Reinjecting Routes into the Backbone

Figure 5-26 shows an MPLS VPN network for Customer A that has three sites, Site 1,
Site 2, and Site 3. Site 3 is multihomed. The figure also shows that EIGRP route
172.16.20.0/24 received by the multihomed site (Site 3) is again redistributed into the
backbone at PE1-AS1.

Figure 5-26 *Multi-Homed Site Reinjecting Routes into the Backbone*

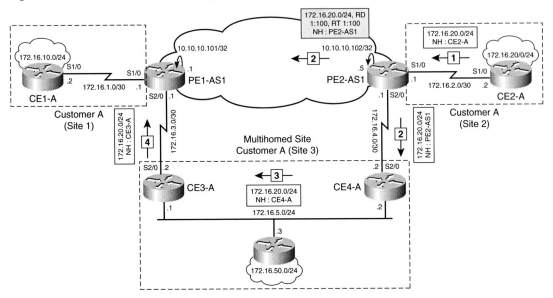

The following sequence takes place when reinjecting an EIGRP route into the backbone:

1 172.16.20.0/24 is advertised as EIGRP internal route to PE2-AS1.

2 PE2-AS1 propagates 172.16.20.0/24 to CE4-A via EIGRP and sends 172.16.20.0/24 via the MP-iBGP session to PE1-AS1.

3 CE4-A propagates 172.16.20.0/24 as an EIGRP internal route to CE3-A.

4 CE3-A propagates 172.16.20.0/24 as an EIGRP internal route to PE1-AS1.

PE1-AS1 has to make the decision of which route to choose:

- If the BGP update for 172.16.20.0/24 arrives first, it will be redistributed into EIGRP and sent to CE3-A. Because of the better composite metric, it will be preferred over the other EIGRP update because MPLS VPN does not add any delay or bandwidth limitation. This means that PE1-AS1 will never receive a second update and will, therefore, have only one possible path.

- If the EIGRP update arrives first, it will be redistributed into BGP and sent back to PE2-AS1. PE2-AS1 will still prefer the original EIGRP update, but PE1-AS1 will never select the BGP derived path because it always prefers locally originated routes.

Overall, in this network, even if the administrative distance for EIGRP and BGP are the same, the routing table prefers the route with the lowest administrative distance (EIGRP is 90 or 170; iBGP is 200) by default.

Backbone Reinjecting Routes into Multihomed Site

Figure 5-27 illustrates the other scenario in which the route 172.16.50.0/24 originating in the multihomed site might be advertised back through the link connected to the PE router.

Figure 5-27 *Backbone Reinjecting Routes into Multihomed Site*

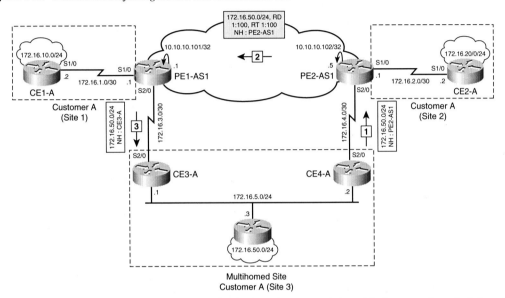

This type of behavior is not noticed when the network is stable because the administrative distance makes sure that both PE routers prefer the route learned via EIGRP.

Count to Infinity

Referring to Figure 5-27, when the network is stable, PE1-AS1 and/or PE2-AS1 have two available paths for 172.16.50.0/24: one learned via MP-iBGP and one directly via EIGRP. If 172.16.50.0/24 goes down for some reason, the following sequence takes place:

1 CE3-A and CE4-A routers send out query messages.

2 Assuming PE1-AS1 has two routes, one via EIGRP and the other via MP-iBGP, when PE1-AS1 receives a query message, it will respond with an alternate path that is still available via MP-iBGP.

3 CE3-A will get an alternate path to 172.16.50.0/24 via PE1-AS1.

4 PE1-AS1 will receive a withdrawal message from PE2-AS1.

5 PE1-AS1 will now have to withdraw the route that it has just advertised to CE3-A, which has propagated this information to CE4-A in the meantime, and CE4-A has already propagated it back to PE2-AS1.

6 The query message originated by the PE1-AS1 router is now trying to catch the previous advertisement of 172.16.50.0/24. By the time the query message reaches PE2-AS1,

PE2-AS1 has already advertised a new reachable update via MP-iBGP to PE1-AS1, which will again create an EIGRP update that will try to catch the previous query message.

7 This process of looping reachable/unreachable messages continues until the maximum number of hops is reached.

This type of behavior is referred to as "count to infinity."

Suboptimal Routing

Suboptimal routing often occurs because EIGRP (90 for internal and 170 for external routes) has a better administrative distance than iBGP (200). A routing table will always prefer an IGP-learned route because all IGPs have a better administrative distance (5 to 170) than internal BGP (200). As shown in Figure 5-27, PE1-AS1 receives two updates for 172.16.20.0/24: one via EIGRP from CE3-A and one via MP-iBGP from PE2. PE1-AS1 will use the EIGRP-learned route because it has a better administrative distance (90 or 170) than an internal BGP route (200). Therefore, as illustrated in Figure 5-28, data packets from CE1-A to CE2-A will be forwarded by PE1-AS1 to CE3-A, causing suboptimal routing.

Figure 5-28 *Suboptimal Routing*

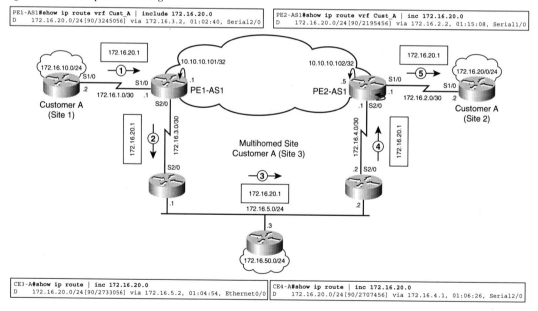

BGP Cost Community Feature and EIGRP Site of Origin

Routing loops and suboptimal routing can be avoided by using

- The BGP cost community feature, which can be used to force BGP to compare locally originated EIGRP routes and MP-iBGP routes based on the EIGRP metric

- The EIGRP site of origin (SoO) feature on PE and CE routers that can be used to prevent routing loops

BGP Cost Community Feature

The BGP cost community feature introduces a new BGP extended community attribute called the cost community. The cost community is a non-transitive extended community attribute that is passed to internal BGP and confederation peers but not external BGP peers. The cost community feature allows you to customize the local route preference and influence the best path selection process by assigning cost values to specific routes. The feature allows the PE router to compare routes coming from different protocols using different administrative distance values based on their metric. BGP routes carrying the BGP cost community attribute will use EIGRP administrative distance instead of iBGP administrative distance to enable this comparison without the need to statically modify the administrative distance of either protocol.

When routes are redistributed from EIGRP into MP-BGP, they will be tagged with the BGP cost community attribute that will carry the composite EIGRP metric in addition to individual EIGRP attributes. Figure 5-29 shows the cost community attribute.

Figure 5-29 *BGP Cost Community Attribute*

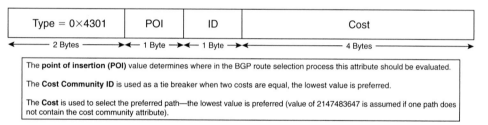

The point of insertion (POI) value makes sure that the BGP route selection uses the BGP cost community before evaluating whether the route is locally originated or not. This allows the comparison of iBGP routes with EIGRP routes. The BGP cost community will also be able to distinguish between internal and external EIGRP routes using the ID field: *internal routes will be encoded using ID 128, external routes will be encoded using ID 129.* The route selection process, when using BGP cost communities, prefers the lowest BGP Cost Community ID, which in turn behaves like a normal EIGRP route selection in which internal routes are preferred over external routes. Internal EIGRP routes have a lower BGP Cost Community ID than external EIGRP routes. The route selection will typically depend on the value in the BGP cost community's **Cost** field, which carries the composite EIGRP metric.

The pre-best path POI was introduced in the BGP cost community feature to support mixed EIGRP-based MPLS VPN network topologies that contain backdoor links. It was integrated in Cisco IOS Release 12.0(27)S, 12.3(8)T, and 12.2(25)S. This POI is applied automatically to EIGRP routes that are redistributed into BGP. The pre-best path POI carries the EIGRP route type and metric. This POI influences the best path calculation process by influencing BGP to consider this POI before any other comparison step. There is no configuration required for inducing POI. Figure 5-30 shows the BGP cost community operation.

Figure 5-30 *BGP Cost Community Operation*

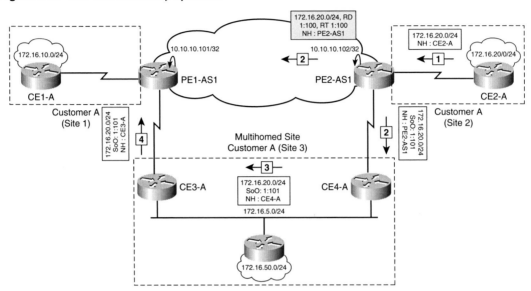

As shown in Figure 5-30, the following sequence takes place in which PE1-AS1 is able to select the best route based on the EIGRP metric and not based on administrative distance between EIGRP and iBGP:

1 CE2-A originates 172.16.20.0/24 to PE2-AS1.

2 PE2-AS1 forwards the route to CE4-A via EIGRP and to PE1-AS1 via MP-iBGP.

3 PE1-AS1 receives two updates for 172.16.20.0/24, one via EIGRP from CE3-A and one via MP-iBGP from PE2-AS1. PE1-AS1 will use the MP-iBGP learned route because it is now capable of comparing the EIGRP composite metric between the real EIGRP route (from CE3-A) and the MP-iBGP route (from PE2-AS1) that is using the BGP cost community attribute to carry the original EIGRP composite metric.

4 Packets from CE1-A to CE2-A will be forwarded by PE1-AS1 to PE2-AS1 because the routing table of VRF A contains the MP-iBGP route, which carried a lower composite EIGRP metric.

EIGRP SoO Attribute

To prevent routing loops, the EIGRP SoO attribute has been added to enable the tagging of internal and external EIGRP routes. This attribute is automatically exchanged between routing protocols (SoO-enabled EIGRP and MP-BGP) to prevent routing loops in multihomed environments where two-way redistribution is used. All CE routers must support this feature to enable the propagation of this attribute throughout the VPN, or at the minimum, the multihomed sites. The EIGRP SoO feature is used on PE and CE routers for the most effective loop prevention. Backdoor links are configured with EIGRP SoO for fastest convergence upon route loss.

Multihomed Sites and EIGRP SoO

Figure 5-31 illustrates how routes that are injected into a multihomed site get tagged with an EIGRP SoO value 1:101. The receiving PE router will check all updates against the SoO value configured on the interface through which the update was received. If the values are equal, the update will be rejected, preventing routing loops as well as ensuring optimal routing.

Figure 5-31 *Multihomed Site and EIGRP SoO*

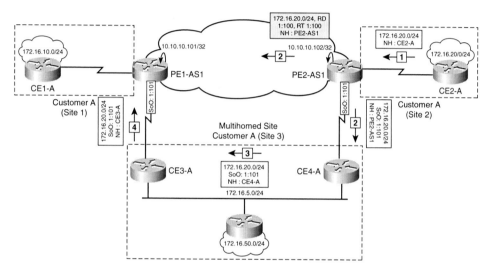

The following sequence takes place when 172.16.20.0/24 is propagated to CE1-A:

1. CE2-A originates a route 172.16.20.0/24.

2. PE2-AS1 forwards the route to CE4-A via EIGRP and to PE1-AS1 via MP-iBGP. The EIGRP route will be tagged with the new EIGRP attribute called SoO, here 1:101 to indicate that the route came from the MPLS backbone.

3. CE4-A forwards that 172.16.20.0/24 update to CE3-A.

4. PE1-AS1 receives two updates for 172.16.20.0/24, one via EIGRP from CE3-A and one via MP-iBGP from PE2-AS1. PE1-AS1 will use the BGP-learned route; the EIGRP route from CE3-A is filtered out because it contains the same SoO value as the interface through which the route was received.

Backdoor Link and EIGRP SoO

Figure 5-32 illustrates EIGRP SoO in sites, interconnected with a backdoor link.

The following sequence describes the process of route selection in this scenario:

1. CE2-A propagates 172.16.20.0/24 to PE2-AS1.

2. PE2-AS1 forwards 172.16.20.0/24, the route to CE4-A via EIGRP and to PE1-AS1 via MP-iBGP. The EIGRP route will be tagged with the EIGRP SoO value 1:20 to indicate that the route came from the MPLS backbone and was injected into Site 4 with 1:20.

3 PE1-AS1 receives two updates for 172.16.20.0, one via EIGRP from CE2 and one via MP-iBGP from PE2. Also note that the update, when traveling via the backdoor link, will carry EIGRP SoO value 1:20 when propagated to CE3-A, and CE3-A uses 1:10 to propagate this route to PE1-AS1.

4 PE1-AS1 receives two updates for 172.16.20.0/24, one via EIGRP from CE3-A with SoO 1:10, which it filters because it contains the same SoO value as the interface through which the route was received and only considers the one via MP-iBGP from PE2-AS1.

Figure 5-32 *Backdoor Link and EIGRP SoO*

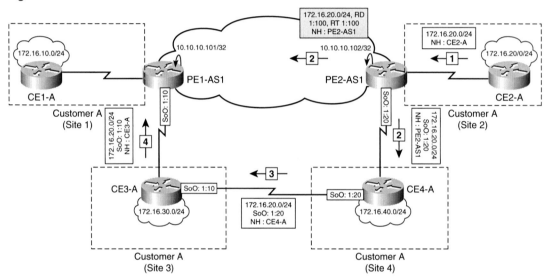

EIGRP SoO Configuration

Example 5-48 shows a sample EIGRP SoO configuration.

Example 5-48 *EIGRP SoO Configuration*

```
interface serial 2/0
ip vrf sitemap SOO-VPNA
!
route-map SOO-VPNA  permit 10
set extcommunity SoO 1:10
```

EIGRP PE-CE Configuration Scenario 2—BGP Cost Community Feature and EIGRP SoO in MPLS VPN Network with Backdoor Link

Figure 5-32 shows an MPLS VPN environment where Customer A has four sites. CE1-A, CE2-A, CE3-A, and CE4-A belong to Sites 1, 2, 3, and 4, respectively. All customer edge routers are running EIGRP as a PE-CE routing protocol and belong to AS 101. PE1-AS1 and PE2-AS1 are configured to run EIGRP PE-CE routing.

The objective of this setup is to demonstrate EIGRP PE-CE routing in an MPLS VPN environment when there is

- No BGP cost community or EIGRP SoO
- BGP cost community and EIGRP SoO involved

No BGP Cost Community or EIGRP SoO

Figure 5-33 shows the MPLS VPN network with routing table for Cust_A VRF on PE1-AS1 and PE2-AS1. This figure also shows the routing table for CE3-A and CE4-A. With no BGP cost community (CC) or EIGRP SoO, the data path

- For traffic originating from CE1-A (172.16.10.0) to CE2-A (172.16.20.0) is from CE1-A via CE3-A, CE4-A, and PE2-AS1 to destination network on CE2-A, and vice versa.
- For traffic originating from CE3-A (172.16.30.0) to CE4-A (172.16.40.0) is from CE3-A to CE4-A via the backdoor link and vice versa.
- For traffic originating from CE3-A (172.16.30.0) to CE2-A (172.16.20.0) is from CE3-A to CE4-A via the backdoor link, then to PE2-AS1, and then to destination network on CE2-A, and vice versa.
- For traffic originating from CE4-A (172.16.40.0) to CE1-A (172.16.10.0) is from CE4-A to CE3-A via the backdoor link, then to PE1-AS1, and then to the destination network on CE1-A, and vice versa.

Figure 5-33 *Suboptimal Routing Without BGP CC and EIGRP SoO*

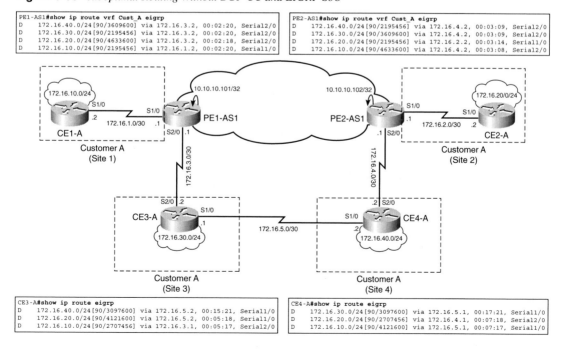

In other words, all these traffic paths are forwarded through the backdoor link connecting CE3-A and CE4-A. An example of the traceroute to 172.16.20.1 and 172.16.40.1 is shown in Example 5-49.

Example 5-49   *Traceroute to 172.16.20.1 and 172.16.40.1*

```
CE1-A#traceroute 172.16.20.1

Type escape sequence to abort.
Tracing the route to 172.16.20.1

  1 172.16.1.1 20 msec 20 msec 20 msec
  2 172.16.3.2 20 msec 20 msec 8 msec
  3 172.16.5.2 60 msec 40 msec 40 msec
  4 172.16.4.1 40 msec 48 msec 40 msec
  5 172.16.2.2 40 msec 40 msec *
CE1-A#traceroute 172.16.40.1

Type escape sequence to abort.
Tracing the route to 172.16.40.1

  1 172.16.1.1 20 msec 20 msec 32 msec
  2 172.16.3.2 20 msec 20 msec 20 msec
  3 172.16.5.2 40 msec 40 msec *
CE3-A#traceroute 172.16.40.1

Type escape sequence to abort.
Tracing the route to 172.16.40.1

  1 172.16.5.2 16 msec 20 msec *
CE3-A#traceroute 172.16.20.1

Type escape sequence to abort.
Tracing the route to 172.16.20.1

  1 172.16.5.2 20 msec 24 msec 20 msec
  2 172.16.4.1 20 msec 20 msec 20 msec
  3 172.16.2.2 28 msec 20 msec *
```

Using BGP CC or EIGRP SoO

There is no configuration required for BGP CC. Check Cisco.com for Cisco IOS using the BGP CC for EIGRP-based MPLS VPN networks with backdoor links. This scenario was performed using 12.0(31)S. EIGRP SoO is configured on PE1-AS1 and PE2-AS1 and on the backdoor links connecting CE3-A and CE4-A. Figure 5-34 shows routing with BGP CC and EIGRP SoO.

Figure 5-34 *Routing with BGP CC and EIGRP SoO*

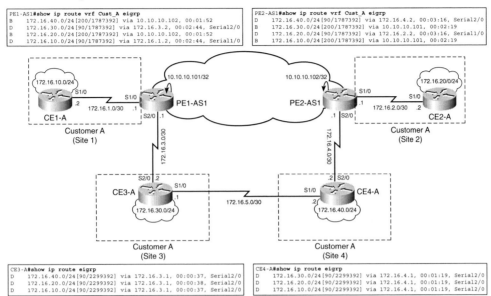

Final Configurations for Networks Using BGP CC and EIGRP SoO

The final configurations for networks using BGP CC and EIGRP SoO are shown in Example 5-50.

Example 5-50 *CE and PE Configuration for Network Using BGP CC and EIGRP SoO*

```
hostname CE1-A
!
interface Ethernet0/0
 description VPN-A Site 1 network
 ip address 172.16.10.1 255.255.255.0
!
interface Serial1/0
 description connected to PE1-AS1
 ip address 172.16.1.2 255.255.255.252
!
router eigrp 101
network 172.16.0.0
 no auto-summary
```
```
hostname CE2-A
!
interface Ethernet0/0
description VPN-A Site 2 network
 ip address 172.16.20.1 255.255.255.0
!
```

continues

Example 5-50 *CE and PE Configuration for Network Using BGP CC and EIGRP SoO (Continued)*

```
interface Serial1/0
 description connected to PE2-AS1
 ip address 172.16.2.2 255.255.255.252
!
router eigrp 101
network 172.16.0.0
 no auto-summary
```
```
hostname CE3-A
!
interface Ethernet0/0
 ip address 172.16.30.1 255.255.255.0
!
interface Serial1/0
 bandwidth 1000
 ip vrf sitemap SOO-VPNA
 ip address 172.16.5.1 255.255.255.252
!
interface Serial2/0
 ip address 172.16.3.2 255.255.255.252
!
router eigrp 101
network 172.16.0.0
 no auto-summary
!
route-map SOO-VPNA permit 10
 set extcommunity soo 1:10
```
```
hostname CE4-A
!
interface Ethernet0/0
 ip address 172.16.40.1 255.255.255.0
!
interface Serial1/0
 bandwidth 1000
 ip vrf sitemap SOO-VPNA
 ip address 172.16.5.2 255.255.255.252
!
interface Serial2/0
 ip address 172.16.4.2 255.255.255.252
!
router eigrp 101
 network 172.16.0.0
 no auto-summary
!
route-map SOO-VPNA permit 10
 set extcommunity soo 1:20
```
```
hostname PE1-AS1
!
ip cef
!
ip vrf Cust_A
```

Example 5-50   *CE and PE Configuration for Network Using BGP CC and EIGRP SoO (Continued)*

```
 rd 1:100
 route-target export 1:100
 route-target import 1:100
!
interface Loopback0
 ip address 10.10.10.101 255.255.255.255
!
interface Serial0/0
 description connected to P1-AS1
 ip address 10.10.10.1 255.255.255.252
 mpls ip
!
interface Serial1/0
 description connected to CE1-A
 ip vrf forwarding Cust_A
 ip address 172.16.1.1 255.255.255.252
!
interface Serial2/0
 description connected to CE3-A
 ip vrf forwarding Cust_A
 ip vrf sitemap SOO-VPNA
 ip address 172.16.3.1 255.255.255.252
!
router eigrp 1
 !
address-family ipv4 vrf Cust_A
 redistribute bgp 1 metric 1000 100 255 1 1500
 network 172.16.0.0
 no auto-summary
 autonomous-system 101
 exit-address-family
!
router ospf 1
 router-id 10.10.10.101
 network 10.0.0.0 0.255.255.255 area 0
!
router bgp 1
 no synchronization
 neighbor 10.10.10.102 remote-as 1
 neighbor 10.10.10.102 update-source Loopback0
 no auto-summary
 !
 address-family vpnv4
 neighbor 10.10.10.102 activate
 neighbor 10.10.10.102 send-community both
 exit-address-family
 !
 address-family ipv4 vrf Cust_A
 redistribute eigrp 101
 no auto-summary
 no synchronization
```

continues

Example 5-50 *CE and PE Configuration for Network Using BGP CC and EIGRP SoO (Continued)*

```
 exit-address-family
 !
route-map SOO-VPNA permit 10
 set extcommunity soo 1:10
hostname PE2-AS1
 !
ip cef
 !
ip vrf Cust_A
 rd 1:100
 route-target export 1:100
 route-target import 1:100
 !
interface Loopback0
 ip address 10.10.10.102 255.255.255.255
 !
interface Serial0/0
 description connected to P1-AS1
 ip address 10.10.10.5 255.255.255.252
 mpls ip
 !
interface Serial1/0
 description connected to CE2-A
 ip vrf forwarding Cust_A
 ip address 172.16.2.1 255.255.255.252
 !
interface Serial2/0
 description connected to CE4-A
 ip vrf forwarding Cust_A
 ip vrf sitemap SOO-VPNA
 ip address 172.16.4.1 255.255.255.252
 !
router eigrp 1
 !
address-family ipv4 vrf Cust_A
 redistribute bgp 1 metric 1000 100 255 1 1500
 network 172.16.0.0
 no auto-summary
 autonomous-system 101
 exit-address-family
 !
router ospf 1
 router-id 10.10.10.102
 network 10.0.0.0 0.255.255.255 area 0
 !
router bgp 1
 no synchronization
 neighbor 10.10.10.101 remote-as 1
 neighbor 10.10.10.101 update-source Loopback0
 no auto-summary
```

Example 5-50 *CE and PE Configuration for Network Using BGP CC and EIGRP SoO (Continued)*

```
 !
 address-family vpnv4
 neighbor 10.10.10.101 activate
 neighbor 10.10.10.101 send-community both
 exit-address-family
 !
 address-family ipv4 vrf Cust_A
 redistribute eigrp 101
 no auto-summary
 no synchronization
 exit-address-family
 !
route-map SOO-VPNA permit 10
 set extcommunity soo 1:20
```

Verify BGP CC and EIGRP SoO

The steps to verify BGP CC and EIGRP SoO are

Step 1   Example 5-51 shows traceroutes to 172.16.20.1 and 172.16.40.1.

Example 5-51 *Traceroute to 172.16.20.1 and 172.16.40.1*

```
CE1-A#traceroute 172.16.20.1

Type escape sequence to abort.
Tracing the route to 172.16.20.1

  1 172.16.1.1 20 msec 20 msec 44 msec
  2 10.10.10.2 60 msec 32 msec 20 msec
  3 172.16.2.1 32 msec 20 msec 40 msec
  4 172.16.2.2 48 msec 20 msec *
CE1-A#traceroute 172.16.40.1

Type escape sequence to abort.
Tracing the route to 172.16.40.1

  1 172.16.1.1 20 msec 20 msec 20 msec
  2 10.10.10.2 20 msec 20 msec 28 msec
  3 172.16.4.1 20 msec 32 msec 20 msec
  4 172.16.4.2 28 msec 28 msec *
CE3-A#traceroute 172.16.20.1

Type escape sequence to abort.
Tracing the route to 172.16.20.1

  1 172.16.3.1 20 msec 40 msec 20 msec
  2 10.10.10.2 28 msec 20 msec 20 msec
  3 172.16.2.1 20 msec 20 msec 20 msec
  4 172.16.2.2 20 msec 20 msec *
CE3-A#traceroute 172.16.40.1
```

continues

Example 5-51 *Traceroute to 172.16.20.1 and 172.16.40.1 (Continued)*

```
Type escape sequence to abort.
Tracing the route to 172.16.40.1

  1 172.16.3.1 20 msec 20 msec 20 msec
  2 10.10.10.2 20 msec 20 msec 20 msec
  3 172.16.4.1 20 msec 32 msec 20 msec
  4 172.16.4.2 20 msec 20 msec *
```

Step 2 Example 5-52 shows BGP extended community attributes associated
with 172.16.20.0 and 172.16.30.0.

Example 5-52 *BGP Extended Community Attributes Associated with 172.16.20.0 and 172.16.30.0*

```
PE1-AS1#show ip bgp vpnv4 all 172.16.20.0
BGP routing table entry for 1:100:172.16.20.0/24, version 21
Paths: (1 available, best #1, table Cust_A)
  Not advertised to any peer
  Local
    10.10.10.102 (metric 97) from 10.10.10.102 (10.10.10.102)
      Origin incomplete, metric 1787392, localpref 100, valid, internal, best
      Extended Community: RT:1:100
        Cost:pre-bestpath:128:1787392 (default-2145696255) 0x8800:32768:0
        0x8801:101:537600 0x8802:65281:1249792 0x8803:65281:1500,
      mpls labels in/out nolabel/25
```
```
PE1-AS1#show ip bgp vpnv4 all 172.16.40.0
BGP routing table entry for 1:100:172.16.40.0/24, version 23
Paths: (1 available, best #1, table Cust_A)
  Not advertised to any peer
  Local
    10.10.10.102 (metric 97) from 10.10.10.102 (10.10.10.102)
      Origin incomplete, metric 1787392, localpref 100, valid, internal, best
      Extended Community: SoO:1:20 RT:1:100
        Cost:pre-bestpath:128:1787392 (default-2145696255) 0x8800:32768:0
        0x8801:101:537600 0x8802:65281:1249792 0x8803:65281:1500,
      mpls labels in/out nolabel/27
```
```
PE2-AS1#show ip bgp vpnv4 all 172.16.30.0
BGP routing table entry for 1:100:172.16.30.0/24, version 22
Paths: (1 available, best #1, table Cust_A)
  Not advertised to any peer
  Local
    10.10.10.101 (metric 97) from 10.10.10.101 (10.10.10.101)
      Origin incomplete, metric 1787392, localpref 100, valid, internal, best
      Extended Community: SoO:1:10 RT:1:100
        Cost:pre-bestpath:128:1787392 (default-2145696255) 0x8800:32768:0
        0x8801:101:537600 0x8802:65281:1249792 0x8803:65281:1500,
      mpls labels in/out nolabel/26
```
```
PE2-AS1#show ip bgp vpnv4 all 172.16.10.0
BGP routing table entry for 1:100:172.16.10.0/24, version 20
Paths: (1 available, best #1, table Cust_A)
  Not advertised to any peer
  Local
```

Example 5-52   *BGP Extended Community Attributes Associated with 172.16.20.0 and 172.16.30.0 (Continued)*

```
10.10.10.101 (metric 97) from 10.10.10.101 (10.10.10.101)
  Origin incomplete, metric 1787392, localpref 100, valid, internal, best
  Extended Community: RT:1:100
    Cost:pre-bestpath:128:1787392 (default-2145696255) 0x8800:32768:0
    0x8801:101:537600 0x8802:65281:1249792 0x8803:65281:1500,
  mpls labels in/out nolabel/24
```

Step 3   Example 5-53 shows the routing table on CE3-A and CE4-A. The routing table
shows that the path to reach 172.16.40.0 and 172.16.30.0 is through MP-iBGP.

Example 5-53   *Routing Table on CE3-A and CE4-A*

```
CE3-A#show ip route eigrp
     172.16.0.0/16 is variably subnetted, 9 subnets, 2 masks
D       172.16.40.0/24 [90/2299392] via 172.16.3.1, 01:00:03, Serial2/0
D       172.16.20.0/24 [90/2299392] via 172.16.3.1, 01:00:03, Serial2/0
D       172.16.10.0/24 [90/2299392] via 172.16.3.1, 01:00:03, Serial2/0
D       172.16.4.0/30 [90/2273792] via 172.16.3.1, 01:00:03, Serial2/0
D       172.16.1.0/30 [90/2273792] via 172.16.3.1, 01:00:03, Serial2/0
D       172.16.2.0/30 [90/2273792] via 172.16.3.1, 01:00:03, Serial2/0
CE4-A#show ip route eigrp
     172.16.0.0/16 is variably subnetted, 9 subnets, 2 masks
D       172.16.30.0/24 [90/2299392] via 172.16.4.1, 01:00:44, Serial2/0
D       172.16.20.0/24 [90/2299392] via 172.16.4.1, 01:00:44, Serial2/0
D       172.16.10.0/24 [90/2299392] via 172.16.4.1, 01:00:44, Serial2/0
D       172.16.1.0/30 [90/2273792] via 172.16.4.1, 01:00:44, Serial2/0
D       172.16.2.0/30 [90/2273792] via 172.16.4.1, 01:00:44, Serial2/0
D       172.16.3.0/30 [90/2273792] via 172.16.4.1, 01:00:44, Serial2/0
```

EIGRP PE-CE Routing Command Summary

Table 5-3 shows the relevant EIGRP PE-CE routing commands used in this chapter.

Table 5-3   *EIGRP PE-CE Routing Command Summary*

Command	Description
Router(config-router-af)#**default-metric**	Sets metric for EIGRP
Router#(config-router-af)#**network** *ip-address*	Specifies a list of networks for the EIGRP routing process
Router#(config-router-af)#**autonomous-system** *as-number*	Configures an EIGRP routing process to run within a VPN routing and forwarding instance (VRF); uses the **autonomous-system** command in address family configuration mode
Router#**clear ip eigrp vrf neighbor**	Clears neighbor entries of the specified VRF from the RIB
Router#**show ip eigrp vrf neighbors**	Displays neighbors discovered by EIGRP that carry VRF information
Router#**show ip eigrp vrf topology**	Displays VRF entries in the EIGRP topology table
Router#**show ip eigrp vrf traffic**	Displays EIGRP VRF traffic statistics

CHAPTER 6

Implementing BGP in MPLS VPNs

BGP, though considered a complex routing protocol, is widely used for PE-CE routing in MPLS VPN networks. In prior chapters, you were introduced to various facets of configuring IGP PE-CE routing in MPLS VPN networks. This chapter explains BGP PE-CE routing and its configuration and utilization in an MPLS VPN environment.

The following BGP concepts are discussed:

- BGP PE-CE routing protocol overview, configuration, and verification
- BGP route-reflectors in an MPLS VPN environment
- BGP peer groups
- BGP confederations in an MPLS VPN environment

BGP PE-CE Routing Protocol Overview, Configuration, and Verification

BGP version 4 (BGP4) is the current de facto Internet standard for inter-domain (AS) exterior routing. In MPLS VPN networks, MP-BGP is used and plays a pivotal role in the transportation of VPNv4 prefixes across the service provider network. In traditional environments, customer networks prefer to use BGP in their networks and, therefore, use BGP as a PE-CE routing protocol when migrating from a non-MPLS based to an MPLS VPN based network. This helps the customer establish a consistent end-to-end routing policy. In an MPLS VPN network, BGP attributes for a VPN site are transparently transported across the service provider backbone to another site in the same VPN. Because there is a single routing protocol used across the VPN between service provider core and customer sites, the concept of redistribution does not apply.

BGP PE-CE peering in an MPLS VPN environment can be performed in two different ways:

- BGP PE-CE VPN sites implementing *unique* AS numbers
- BGP PE-CE VPN sites implementing *same* AS numbers

In the MPLS VPN network shown in Figure 6-1, an MPLS VPN service provider plans to provision BGP PE-CE routing protocol for two customers, Customers A and B. CE1-A and

CE2-A are CE devices belonging to Customer A located at Site 1 and Site 2, respectively. They are part of the same VPN, VPN-A. These CE devices are connected to provider edge devices PE1-AS1 and PE2-AS1 in the service provider network. CE1-A belongs to AS 65001 and CE2-A belongs to AS 65002. For Customer B network, CE1-A and CE2-A are the CE devices located at Site 1 and Site 2, respectively, and are part of the VPN, VPN-B. CE1-A and CE2-A belong to AS 65001 and are connected to PE1-AS1 and PE2-AS1, respectively.

Figure 6-1   *MPLS VPN Provider Provisioning BGP PE-CE Routing*

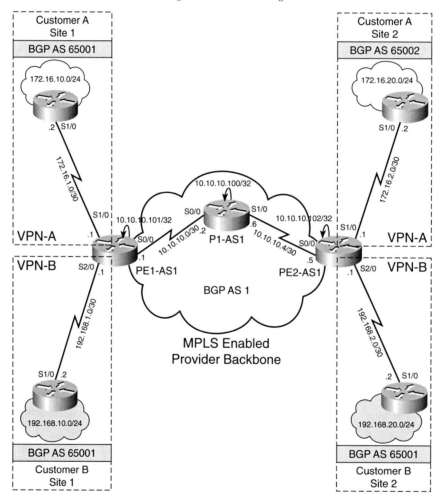

Implementing BGP PE-CE routing for the Customer A network is not an issue because the VPN sites use unique AS numbers. However, Customer B plans on using the same AS number on its sites. This causes an issue when migrating from a traditional non-MPLS based network topology, where the customer might use the same AS numbers at all his sites, to an MPLS VPN-based infrastructure due to the BGP loop prevention mechanism. The BGP loop prevention mechanism disallows customer sites having identical AS numbers to be linked by another AS number. In other words, if such a case occurs, routing updates from one site would be dropped when the other site receives them; therefore, connectivity cannot be established between the sites without additional configuration on the SP PE routers.

To explain this further, Figure 6-2 shows an MPLS VPN network provisioned for Customer B. As shown in Figure 6-2, BGP loop prevention mechanism on CE2-B finds 65001 in the AS-PATH; therefore, CE2-B rejects the 192.168.10.0/24 update from PE2-AS1 because it finds its own AS in the update.

Figure 6-2   *BGP Loop Prevention Mechanism*

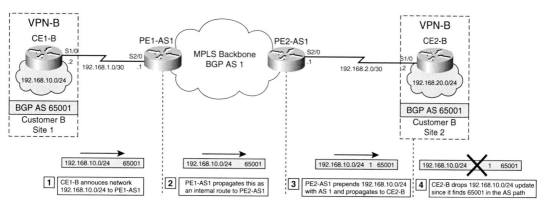

To circumvent the BGP loop prevention mechanism, the AS-PATH update procedure in BGP was modified. The current AS-PATH update procedure allows customer topologies to reuse AS numbers at the sites by using the *AS Override* functionality. The functionality is made active only when the first AS number in the AS-PATH is equal to the AS number of the receiving BGP router. As shown in Figure 6-2, the first AS number in the AS-PATH is 65001, which is the AS number of CE2-B, the receiving router.

Figure 6-3 shows the AS Override functionality when identical AS numbers are used at customer sites. The AS Override function causes all leading occurrences of the AS number of the receiving BGP router to be replaced with the AS number of the sending BGP router. As shown in Step 3 of Figure 6-3, when AS Override is used, AS 65001 in the AS-PATH is replaced with the AS number of the sending BGP router PE2-AS1, which is 1. Any other occurrences (further down the AS-PATH) of the receiving router's AS number are not replaced because they indicate a real routing information loop. In addition, an extra copy of the sending router's AS number is prepended to the AS-PATH (standard AS number prepending procedure that occurs on every eBGP update) to maintain proper AS hop count for proper BGP route selection. Step 3 in Figure 6-3 shows that PE2-AS1 prepends AS 1 to BGP update.

Figure 6-3 *AS Override Functionality*

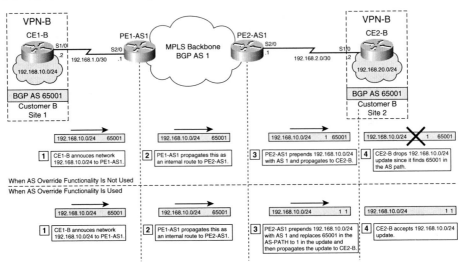

Configuration Flowchart to Implement BGP PE-CE Routing for VPN Sites with Unique and Same AS Numbers

Figure 6-4 shows the configuration flowchart to configure BGP PE-CE routing for VPN sites using unique and same BGP AS.

Figure 6-4 *Configuration Flowchart for BGP PE-CE VPN Sites Implementing Unique and Similar AS*

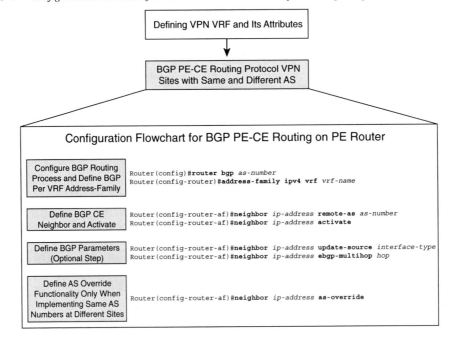

Implementing BGP PE-CE Routing for VPN Sites With Unique and Same AS Numbers

This configuration scenario demonstrates BGP PE-CE routing for VPN sites using same and different BGP AS numbers. You will use the topology shown in Figure 6-1, in which Customer A is using BGP AS 65001 and 65002 at Sites 1 and 2, respectively, and Customer B uses the same AS 65001 at both the sites. Before configuring, ensure that the provider network is provisioned to deliver MPLS VPN services to Customer A sites. It is also assumed that IP addresses are preconfigured and VRFs defined on PE routers. Example 6-1 provides the configuration steps defining VRF and its attributes on PE routers for BGP PE-CE routing.

Example 6-1 *Define VRF Cust_A and Cust_B on PE Routers PE1-AS1 and PE2-AS1*

```
PE1-AS1(config)#ip vrf Cust_A
PE1-AS1(config-vrf)# rd 1:100
PE1-AS1(config-vrf)# route-target both 1:100
PE1-AS1(config)#interface Serial1/0
PE1-AS1(config-if)# description connected to CE1-A
PE1-AS1(config-if)# ip vrf forwarding Cust_A
PE1-AS1(config-if)# ip address 172.16.1.1 255.255.255.252
PE1-AS1(config)#ip vrf Cust_B
PE1-AS1(config-vrf)# rd 1:200
PE1-AS1(config-vrf)# route-target both 1:200
PE1-AS1(config)#interface Serial2/0
PE1-AS1(config-if)# description connected to CE2-B
PE1-AS1(config-if)# ip vrf forwarding Cust_B
PE1-AS1(config-if)# ip address 192.168.1.1 255.255.255.252
```

The steps to configure BGP PE-CE routing on PE routers are as follows:

Step 1   **Configure per VRF BGP routing context on PE routers**—Configure per VRF BGP routing contexts for Cust_A and Cust_B under the BGP routing process on PE1-AS1 and PE2-AS1. Example 6-2 demonstrates the per VRF BGP configuration on PE1-AS1. Repeat the steps on PE2-AS1. Note that the address-family IPv4 VRF contexts are seen by default in a router's configuration when relevant configurations for forming MP-iBGP sessions are configured on PE routers. In that case, **address-family ipv4 vrf** *vrf-name* command under the BGP routing process is keyed in to enter a particular VRF's IPv4 address-family context so that further configurations can be performed (as shown in Step 2).

Example 6-2 *Configure per VRF BGP Routing Context on PE Routers*

```
PE1-AS1(config)#router bgp 1
PE1-AS1(config-router)#address-family ipv4 vrf Cust_A
PE1-AS1(config)#router bgp 1
PE1-AS1(config-router)#address-family ipv4 vrf Cust_B
```

Step 2 **Define and activate BGP CE neighbors**—In this step, under the BGP
VRF routing context created in Step 1, the remote BGP CE neighbors are
defined on the PE routers and activated. Example 6-3 shows the
configuration to define BGP CE neighbors on the PE routers.

Example 6-3 *Define and Activate BGP CE Neighbors*

```
PE1-AS1(config-router-af)#neighbor 172.16.1.2 remote-as 65001
PE1-AS1(config-router-af)#neighbor 172.16.1.2 activate
```
```
PE2-AS1(config-router-af)#neighbor 172.16.2.2 remote-as 65002
PE2-AS1(config-router-af)#neighbor 172.16.2.2 activate
```
```
PE1-AS1(config-router-af)#neighbor 192.168.1.2 remote-as 65001
PE1-AS1(config-router-af)#neighbor 192.168.1.2 as-override
PE1-AS1(config-router-af)#neighbor 192.168.1.2 activate
```
```
PE2-AS1(config-router-af)#neighbor 192.168.2.2 remote-as 65001
PE2-AS1(config-router-af)#neighbor 192.168.2.2 as-override
PE2-AS1(config-router-af)#neighbor 192.168.2.2 activate
```

CE Router Configuration

Example 6-4 shows the configuration on Routers CE CE1-A, CE2-A, CE1-B, and CE2-B.

Example 6-4 *CE1-A, CE2-A, CE1-B, and CE2-B Configuration*

```
hostname CE1-A
!
interface Ethernet0/0
description Customer A Site 1 network
 ip address 172.16.10.1 255.255.255.0
!
interface Serial1/0
description connected to PE1-AS1
 ip address 172.16.1.2 255.255.255.252
!
router bgp 65001
 no synchronization
network 172.16.10.0 mask 255.255.255.0
 neighbor 172.16.1.1 remote-as 1
 no auto-summary
```
```
hostname CE2-A
!
interface Ethernet0/0
description Customer A Site 2 network
 ip address 172.16.20.1 255.255.255.0
!
interface Serial1/0
description connected to PE2-AS1
ip address 172.16.2.2 255.255.255.252
 !
router bgp 65002
 no synchronization
network 172.16.20.0 mask 255.255.255.0
```

Example 6-4 *CE1-A, CE2-A, CE1-B, and CE2-B Configuration (Continued)*

```
 neighbor 172.16.2.1 remote-as 1
 no auto-summary
hostname CE1-B
!
interface Ethernet0/0
 description Customer B Site 1 network
 ip address 192.168.10.1 255.255.255.0
!
interface Serial1/0
description connected to PE1-AS1
 ip address 192.168.1.2 255.255.255.252
!
router bgp 65001
 no synchronization
 network 192.168.10.0
 neighbor 192.168.1.1 remote-as 1
 no auto-summary
hostname CE2-B
!
interface Ethernet0/0
 description Customer B Site 2 network
 ip address 192.168.20.1 255.255.255.0
!
interface Serial1/0
 description connected to PE2-AS1
 ip address 192.168.2.2 255.255.255.252
!
router bgp 65001
 no synchronization
 network 192.168.20.0
 neighbor 192.168.2.1 remote-as 1
 no auto-summary
```

Final Configuration for BGP PE-CE VPN Sites Implementing Unique and Same BGP AS Numbers

Example 6-5 shows the detailed and final configurations on the PE1-AS1, PE2-AS1, and P1-AS1 routers.

Example 6-5 *PE1-AS1, PE2-AS1, and P1-AS1 Final Configuration for BGP PE-CE VPN Sites Implementing Unique BGP AS*

```
hostname PE1-AS1
!
ip cef
!
ip vrf Cust_A
 rd 1:100
 route-target export 1:100
 route-target import 1:100
```

continues

Example 6-5 *PE1-AS1, PE2-AS1, and P1-AS1 Final Configuration for BGP PE-CE VPN Sites Implementing Unique BGP AS (Continued)*

```
!
ip vrf Cust_B
 rd 1:200
 route-target export 1:200
 route-target import 1:200
!
mpls ldp router-id Loopback0
!
interface Loopback0
 ip address 10.10.10.101 255.255.255.255
!
interface Serial0/0
 description connected to P1-AS1
 ip address 10.10.10.1 255.255.255.252
 mpls ip
 !
interface Serial1/0
 description connected to CE1-A
 ip vrf forwarding Cust_A
 ip address 172.16.1.1 255.255.255.252
 !
interface Serial2/0
 description connected to CE1-B
 ip vrf forwarding Cust_B
 ip address 192.168.1.1 255.255.255.252
 !
router ospf 1
 router-id 10.10.10.101
 network 10.0.0.0 0.255.255.255 area 0
!
router bgp 1
 no synchronization
 neighbor 10.10.10.102 remote-as 1
 neighbor 10.10.10.102 update-source Loopback0
 no auto-summary
 !
 address-family vpnv4
 neighbor 10.10.10.102 activate
 neighbor 10.10.10.102 send-community extended
 exit-address-family
 !
 address-family ipv4 vrf Cust_B
 neighbor 192.168.1.2 remote-as 65001
 neighbor 192.168.1.2 activate
 neighbor 192.168.1.2 as-override
 no auto-summary
 no synchronization
 exit-address-family
 !
 address-family ipv4 vrf Cust_A
 neighbor 172.16.1.2 remote-as 65001
```

Example 6-5 *PE1-AS1, PE2-AS1, and P1-AS1 Final Configuration for BGP PE-CE VPN Sites Implementing Unique BGP AS (Continued)*

```
 neighbor 172.16.1.2 activate
 no auto-summary
 no synchronization
 exit-address-family
hostname PE2-AS1
!
ip cef
!
ip vrf Cust_A
 rd 1:100
 route-target export 1:100
 route-target import 1:100
!
ip vrf Cust_B
 rd 1:200
 route-target export 1:200
 route-target import 1:200
!
mpls ldp router-id Loopback0
!
interface Loopback0
 ip address 10.10.10.102 255.255.255.255
!
interface Serial0/0
 description connected to P1-AS1
 ip address 10.10.10.5 255.255.255.252
 mpls ip
!
interface Serial1/0
 description connected to CE2-A
 ip vrf forwarding Cust_A
 ip address 172.16.2.1 255.255.255.252
!
interface Serial2/0
 description connected to CE2-B
 ip vrf forwarding Cust_B
 ip address 192.168.2.1 255.255.255.252
!
router ospf 1
 router-id 10.10.10.102
 network 10.0.0.0 0.255.255.255 area 0
!
router bgp 1
 no synchronization
 neighbor 10.10.10.101 remote-as 1
 neighbor 10.10.10.101 update-source Loopback0
 no auto-summary
 !
 address-family vpnv4
 neighbor 10.10.10.101 activate
```

continues

Example 6-5   *PE1-AS1, PE2-AS1, and P1-AS1 Final Configuration for BGP PE-CE VPN Sites Implementing Unique BGP AS (Continued)*

```
 neighbor 10.10.10.101 send-community extended
 exit-address-family
 !
 address-family ipv4 vrf Cust_B
 neighbor 192.168.2.2 remote-as 65001
 neighbor 192.168.2.2 activate
 neighbor 192.168.2.2 as-override
 no auto-summary
 no synchronization
 exit-address-family
 !
 address-family ipv4 vrf Cust_A
 neighbor 172.16.2.2 remote-as 65002
 neighbor 172.16.2.2 activate
 no auto-summary
 no synchronization
 exit-address-family
```
```
hostname P1-AS1
!
ip cef
!
interface Loopback0
 ip address 10.10.10.200 255.255.255.255
!
interface Serial0/0
description connected to PE1-AS1
 ip address 10.10.10.2 255.255.255.252
 mpls ip
!
interface Serial1/0
description connected to PE2-AS1
 ip address 10.10.10.6 255.255.255.252
 mpls ip
!
router ospf 1
 log-adjacency-changes
 network 10.0.0.0 0.255.255.255 area 0
```

Verifying BGP PE-CE Routing for VPN Sites Implementing Unique and Different BGP AS Numbers

The steps to verify BGP PE-CE routing for VPN sites implementing unique and different BGP AS numbers are

Step 1   **Verify BGP neighbor relationship on PE1-AS1 and PE2-AS1**—Verify the BGP neighbor relationship between PE-CE routers. Example 6-6 shows that the BGP neighbor relationship is *established* between PE1-AS1 and CE routers CE1-A and CE2-B. PE1-AS1 has received two prefixes from PE2-AS1 (10.10.10.102) and one from each CE router. The BGP neighbor relationship can also be verified by issuing **show ip bgp neighbor** *ip-address*.

Example 6-6   **show ip bgp vpnv4 all summary** *on PE Routers*

```
PE1-AS1#show ip bgp vpnv4 all summary
<output truncated for brevity>
Neighbor        V     AS MsgRcvd MsgSent   TblVer  InQ OutQ Up/Down  State/PfxRcd
10.10.10.102    4      1     11      11        9    0    0 00:06:30          2
172.16.1.2      4 65001     11      11        9    0    0 00:06:06          1
192.168.1.2     4 65001     11      11        9    0    0 00:06:05          1
```
```
PE2-AS1#show ip bgp vpnv4 all summary
<output truncated for brevity>
Neighbor        V     AS MsgRcvd MsgSent   TblVer  InQ OutQ Up/Down  State/PfxRcd
10.10.10.101    4      1     12      12        9    0    0 00:07:23          2
172.16.2.2      4 65002     12      12        9    0    0 00:07:30          1
192.168.2.2     4 65001     12      12        9    0    0 00:07:30          1
```

Step 2   **Verify VRF routing table on PE1-AS1 and PE2-AS1**—Check VRFs Cust_A and Cust_B routing table to see if CE networks are received by the connected PE routers. Example 6-7 outlines that PE1-AS1 has received CE2-A network (172.16.20.0/24) from the PE2-AS1 router and 172.16.10.0/24 from the connected CE router, CE1-A.

Example 6-7   *VRF Routing Table on PE Routers*

```
PE1-AS1#show ip route vrf Cust_A bgp
     172.16.0.0/16 is variably subnetted, 3 subnets, 2 masks
B       172.16.20.0/24 [200/0] via 10.10.10.102, 00:07:10
B       172.16.10.0/24 [20/0] via 172.16.1.2, 00:07:38
```
```
PE1-AS1#show ip route vrf Cust_B bgp
B    192.168.10.0/24 [20/0] via 192.168.1.2, 00:07:43
B    192.168.20.0/24 [200/0] via 10.10.10.102, 00:07:15
```
```
PE2-AS1#show ip route vrf Cust_A bgp
     172.16.0.0/16 is variably subnetted, 3 subnets, 2 masks
B       172.16.20.0/24 [20/0] via 172.16.2.2, 00:08:30
B       172.16.10.0/24 [200/0] via 10.10.10.101, 00:08:15
```
```
PE2-AS1#show ip route vrf Cust_B bgp
B    192.168.10.0/24 [200/0] via 10.10.10.101, 00:08:18
B    192.168.20.0/24 [20/0] via 192.168.2.2, 00:08:33
```

Step 3   **Verify BGP VPNv4 routing table on PE1-AS1 and PE2-AS1**—Check the BGP VPNv4 routing table to verify CE networks on the PE routers. Example 6-8 shows PE1-AS1 has 172.16.20.0/24 and 192.168.20.0/24 prefixes in the BGP table from the remote PE router, PE2-AS1, and 172.16.10.0 and 192.168.10.0 from the local CE routers, CE1-A and CE1-B. Similar output is also seen on PE2-AS1.

Example 6-8 *VPNv4 Routing Table on PE Routers*

```
PE1-AS1#show ip bgp vpnv4 all
BGP table version is 9, local router ID is 10.10.10.101
Status codes: s suppressed, d damped, h history, * valid, > best, i - internal,
              r RIB-failure, S Stale
Origin codes: i - IGP, e - EGP, ? - incomplete

   Network          Next Hop            Metric LocPrf Weight Path
Route Distinguisher: 1:100 (default for vrf Cust_A)
*> 172.16.10.0/24   172.16.1.2               0             0 65001 i
*>i172.16.20.0/24   10.10.10.102             0    100      0 65002 i
Route Distinguisher: 1:200 (default for vrf Cust_B)
*> 192.168.10.0     192.168.1.2              0             0 65001 i
*>i192.168.20.0     10.10.10.102             0    100      0 65001 i
```
```
PE2-AS1#show ip bgp vpnv4 all
BGP table version is 9, local router ID is 10.10.10.102
Status codes: s suppressed, d damped, h history, * valid, > best, i - internal,
              r RIB-failure, S Stale
Origin codes: i - IGP, e - EGP, ? - incomplete

   Network          Next Hop            Metric LocPrf Weight Path
Route Distinguisher: 1:100 (default for vrf Cust_A)
*>i172.16.10.0/24   10.10.10.101             0    100      0 65001 i
*> 172.16.20.0/24   172.16.2.2               0             0 65002 i
Route Distinguisher: 1:200 (default for vrf Cust_B)
*>i192.168.10.0     10.10.10.101             0    100      0 65001 i
*> 192.168.20.0     192.168.2.2              0             0 65001 i
```

Step 4 **Verify end-to-end connectivity via ping**—Verify end-to-end
connectivity between CE1-A and CE2-A by issuing a ping from CE1-A
to network 172.16.20.1/24 on CE2-A and vice versa. Example 6-9 shows
the result of the ping operation.

Example 6-9 *Verify End-to-End Connectivity on CE Routers*

```
CE1-A#ping 172.16.20.1 source 172.16.10.1
Type escape sequence to abort.
Sending 5, 100-byte ICMP Echos to 172.16.20.1, timeout is 2 seconds:
Packet sent with a source address of 172.16.10.1
!!!!!
Success rate is 100 percent (5/5), round-trip min/avg/max = 76/79/84 ms
```
```
CE1-B#ping 192.168.20.1 source 192.168.10.1

Type escape sequence to abort.
Sending 5, 100-byte ICMP Echos to 192.168.20.1, timeout is 2 seconds:
Packet sent with a source address of 192.168.10.1
!!!!!
Success rate is 100 percent (5/5), round-trip min/avg/max = 80/80/84 ms
```

Implementing Route-Reflectors in MPLS VPN Networks

BGP route-reflectors (RRs) are considered a scalability tool that allows network designers to steer away from BGP full mesh requirements. Classical iBGP split horizon rules mandate that updates received on eBGP sessions should be forwarded on all iBGP and eBGP sessions, but updates received on an iBGP session should be forwarded only on all eBGP sessions. This requires the BGP edge or boundary router (ASBR) to send updates to all other BGP-enabled routers in its own AS directly through individual iBGP sessions to each BGP router. RRs modify the iBGP split horizon rule and allow a specific router, under certain conditions, to forward all incoming iBGP updates to an outgoing iBGP session. This router is called a route-reflector.

Figure 6-5 shows a typical MPLS VPN-based network where, in the absence of RRs, whenever a new PE is introduced, each existing PE in the service provider network will require an additional BGP neighbor command associating it to the new PE. In BGP, updates received by a peer in an AS are not allowed to be forwarded to another peer within the same AS. Therefore, a BGP network must be fully meshed, with all peers adjacent to one another, as far as BGP routing updates are concerned. If the number of PEs becomes substantial enough to make this operation impractical (that is, adding neighbor commands in every PE), BGP RRs are recommended. RRs obviate the need to fully mesh the BGP peers and avoid the addition of neighbor commands to each PE. With RRs, the PEs would only require neighbors defined for each RR. Any updates, including VRF information, would be sent to the RR alone. The RRs are then responsible for propagating information received from PEs to all other PEs. Each time a new Edge LSR or PE is added, a neighbor statement pointing to the RR needs to be added on the new PE router, and on the RR, a neighbor statement pointing to the PE must be added.

RRs are also useful in the event of a route change in the customer network. Without RRs, the PE that locally terminates that portion of the customer network would have to update every PE peer participating in that VPN. RRs, therefore, help remove the burden of BGP updates from the PE.

RR Deployment Methods

In MPLS-based VPN networks, RRs can be deployed in several ways.

Option 1—Using PE Router as VPNv4 RR

In this option, the PE device is used as a RR. This type of setup is not recommended due to additional constraints of memory and CPU imposed on the PE router, which is handling both the functions of providing services to client edge routers as well as reflecting routes to several other PEs in the same MPLS domain. Figure 6-6 provides an illustration of PE routers, PE6-RR1 and PE7-RR2, which are being used as VPNv4 RRs.

Figure 6-5   *RRs*

Full Mesh MP-iBGP Sessions Between All PEs

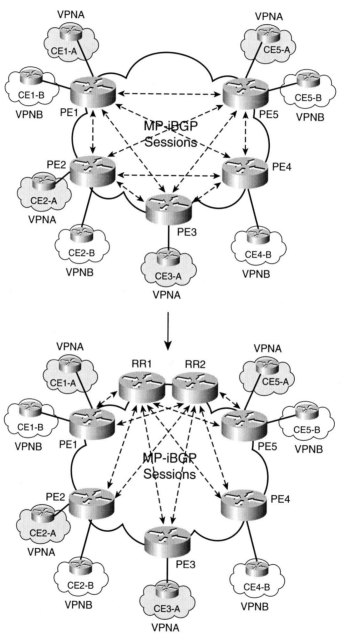

Each PE Has Only Two Sessions to the RRs

Figure 6-6   *PE Routers as RRs*

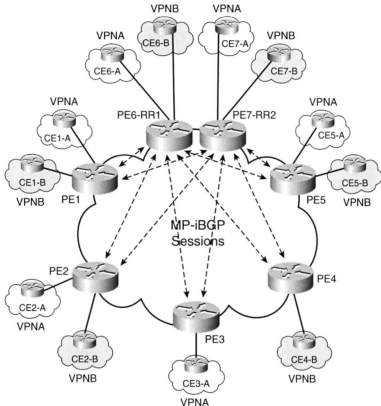

Each PE Has Only Two Sessions to the RRs

Option 2—Using P Router as IPv4 and VPNv4 RR

In this scenario, the provider (P) router is used both as an IPv4 and VPNv4 RR. The P router, in this case, handles not only the function of route reflection for IPv4 and VPNv4 routes, but also performs data forwarding operations for IPv4 traffic and VPNv4 traffic. Figure 6-7 shows a scenario in which the P routers, P1-RR1 and P2-RR2, are IPv4 RRs for the ISP's IPv4 network, which provides Internet services for Customer C and D. At the same time, those RRs serve as IPv4 and VPNv4 RR for the MPLS-enabled network, routing VPNv4 prefixes for VPNA and VPNB sites, as well as providing Internet services to those VPN sites. This scenario may not scale well in large MPLS VPN environments due to memory and CPU constraints imposed on the RR that not only provides IPv4 and VPNv4 routing services but also data forwarding functionality.

Figure 6-7 *P Routers as IPv4 and VPNv4 RRs*

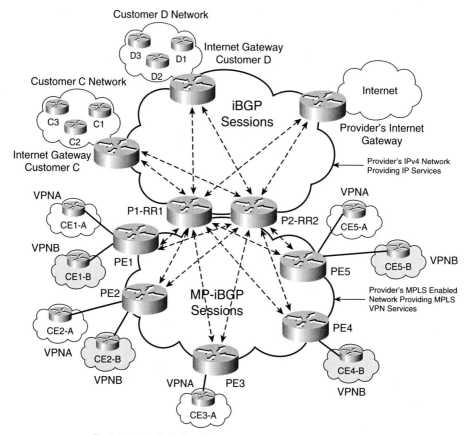

Each PE Has Only Two Sessions to the RRs. The RRs in This
Scenario Also Perform the Function of a P Router. The P Routers Provide the Path Not
Just for Control Plane Traffic But Also for Data Plane Traffic

Option 3—Using P Router as RR Only for VPNv4

In this scenario, the P router is used only as a VPNv4 RR. The P router will forward both control and data plane forwarding for VPN sites only.

Figure 6-8 shows the scenario in which RRs P1-RR1 and P2-RR2 are used for reflecting only VPNv4 routes and forwarding all data traffic between VPN client sites. This implementation can be used in large-scale MPLS VPN environments in which the provider network wants to isolate IPv4 functionality on the VPNv4 RR; however, this can increase the provider's cost to maintain a dedicated RR for IPv4 routing and a dedicated RR for VPNv4 routes.

Figure 6-8   *P Router Reflecting Only VPNv4 Routes*

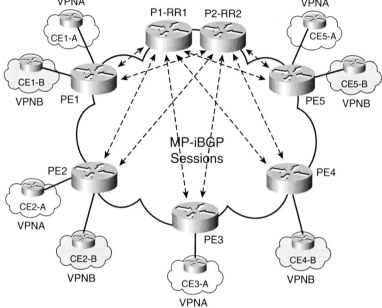

Each PE Has Only Two Sessions to the RRs

Option 4—Dedicated Router as RR for IPv4 and VPNv4

In this scenario, an additional router performs the function of reflecting IPv4 and VPNv4 routes. The router does not perform any data forwarding functions.

Figure 6-9 highlights the scenario in which P1-RR1 and P2-RR2 perform the function of reflecting VPNv4 and IPv4 routes and not that of data forwarding. This also increases the provider's operational costs because the provider has to dedicate routers as RRs for IPv4 and VPNv4 prefixes as well as ensure their PE routers have physical connectivity with each other for data forwarding functionality or are connected to a dedicated P router, which will perform data forwarding functionality.

Option 5—Dedicated Router as RR for Only VPNv4

In this approach, the RR performs the task of reflecting only VPNv4 routes and not that of data forwarding. This approach also requires a dedicated router that can handle this functionality.

Figure 6-9 *Dedicated IPv4 and VPNv4 RR for Control Plane Functionality*

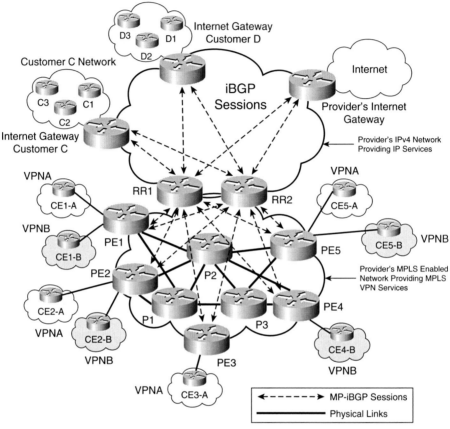

The RRs in This Scenario Perform Control Plane Forwarding for Both IPv4
and VPNv4 Routes. The RRs Do Not Perform Data Forwarding Function.

Figure 6-10 shows an MPLS environment adopting this approach. RR1 and RR2 reflect
only VPNv4 routes and perform no data forwarding function. Using this approach,
considerable savings in CPU and performance improvements can be realized but at the cost
of additional routers providing provider router functionality and increased cost in providing
physical connectivity between PE to P routers.

Option 6—Partitioned RRs

This scenario is used primarily in large-scale environments in which using the dedicated
VPNv4 RR does not scale to the demands of a large provider carrying a large number of
VPNv4 prefixes.

In this approach, as shown in Figure 6-11, RR1 reflects VPNv4 routes only for VPNA, and
RR2 reflects VPNv4 routes only for VPNB. There are no mandatory requirements that the

RR in this approach should not perform the data forwarding function. However, the decision to forward data traffic or not should be made after evaluating future network growth. The drawback would be the additional cost of maintaining separate routers for performing P router functionality and the cost of connectivity between PE and P routers. The complexity of the network could increase with the use of partitioned RRs.

Figure 6-10 *Dedicated VPNv4 RR for Control Plane Functionality*

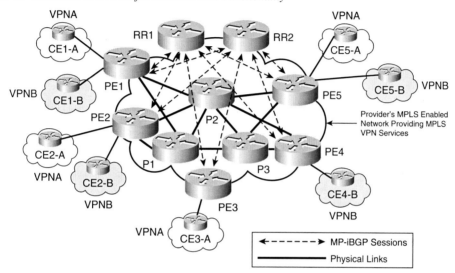

RR1 and RR2 Reflect Only VPNv4 Routes for VPNA and VPNB.
The RRs Do Not Perform Any Data Forwarding Functions.

Figure 6-11 *Route Partitioning Using RRs*

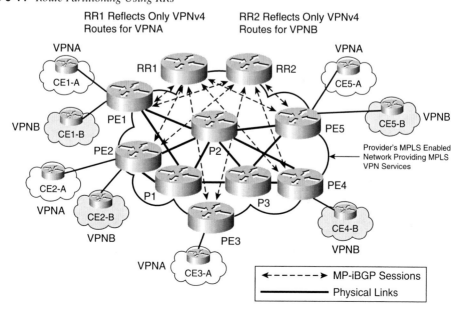

Configuring P Router as RR Only for VPNv4 Prefixes (Option 3)

The objective of this configuration scenario is to demonstrate the RR configuration when the P router serves as an RR and performs both the control plane and data forwarding functionality for VPNv4 prefixes only (option 3). To implement this configuration, the network topology shown in Figure 6-1 is used except that P1-AS1-RR (for this configuration, the scenario hostname for P1-AS1 in Figure 6-1 is P1-AS1-RR) is configured as a RR peering with PE routers PE1-AS1 and PE2-AS1. PE routers will be configured to peer with the RRs only.

Configuration Flowchart for P Router as RR for Only VPNv4 Prefixes

The configuration flowchart for implementing this scenario is shown in Figure 6-12.

Figure 6-12 *Configuration Flowchart to Implement RR*

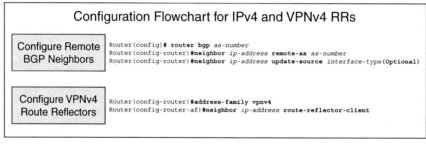

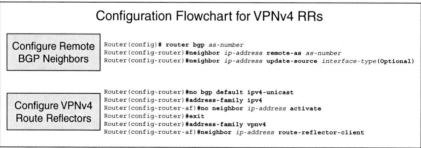

Configuration Step for PE Routers PE1-AS1 and PE2-AS1

To configure BGP peering on the PE routers PE1-AS1 and PE2-AS1 with the RR P1-AS1-RR, BGP routing on the PE routers must be configured and BGP neighbors activated. Enable global BGP routing on PE1-AS1 and PE2-AS1 routers and activate the BGP RR neighbors on the PE routers for VPNv4 route exchange only. Example 6-10 shows the configuration for defining P1-AS1-RR as the BGP neighbor on the PE router PE1-AS1. Use the same steps to configure PE2-AS1.

Example 6-10 *Configure BGP Routing on PE Routers and Activate BGP Neighbors*

```
PE1-AS1(config)#router bgp 1
PE1-AS1(config-router)#neighbor 10.10.10.100 remote-as 1
PE1-AS1(config-router)#neighbor 10.10.10.100 update-source Loopback0
PE1-AS1(config-router)#no bgp default ipv4-unicast
PE1-AS1(config-router)# address-family ipv4
PE1-AS1(config-router-af)#no neighbor 10.10.10.100 activate
PE1-AS1(config-router-af)#address-family vpnv4
PE1-AS1(config-router-af)#neighbor 10.10.10.100 activate
PE1-AS1(config-router-af)#neighbor 10.10.10.100 send-community extended
PE1-AS1(config-router-af)#exit-address-family
```

Configuration Step for P Router as RR for Only VPNv4 Prefixes

To configure the RR P1-AS1-RR, configure the P router as VPNv4 RR. Enable global BGP routing on the P router, P1-AS1-RR. Example 6-11 shows the configuration procedure to enable global BGP routing, define the BGP relationship with PE routers PE1-AS1 and PE2-AS1, activate them for VPNv4 route-exchange, and configure the PE routers as clients for the route-reflection process.

Example 6-11 *Configure Provider Router as VPNv4 RR*

```
P1-AS1-RR(config)#router bgp 1
P1-AS1-RR(config-router)#neighbor 10.10.10.101 remote-as 1
P1-AS1-RR(config-router)#neighbor 10.10.10.101 update-source Loopback0
P1-AS1-RR(config-router)#neighbor 10.10.10.102 remote-as 1
P1-AS1-RR(config-router)#neighbor 10.10.10.102 update-source Loopback0
P1-AS1-RR(config-router)#no bgp default ipv4-unicast
P1-AS1-RR(config-router)#address-family ipv4
P1-AS1-RR(config-router-af)#no neighbor 10.10.10.101 activate
P1-AS1-RR(config-router-af)#no neighbor 10.10.10.102 activate
P1-AS1-RR(config-router-af)#exit
P1-AS1-RR(config-router)#address-family vpnv4
P1-AS1-RR(config-router-af)#neighbor 10.10.10.102 route-reflector-client
P1-AS1-RR(config-router-af)#neighbor 10.10.10.102 route-reflector-client
P1-AS1-RR(config-router-af)#neighbor 10.10.10.101 activate
P1-AS1-RR(config-router-af)#neighbor 10.10.10.102 activate
```

CE Configurations

Refer to Example 6-4 for CE configurations.

P1-AS1-RR, PE1-AS1, and PE2-AS1 Final Configuration for MPLS VPN Using RRs

Example 6-12 outlines the final relevant configurations for PE1-AS1, PE2-AS1, and P1-AS1-RR implementing MPLS VPN for sites using the P router as a VPNv4 RR. Refer to Example 6-5 for the remaining configurations pertaining to each router.

Example 6-12 *Relevant Configurations*

```
hostname PE1-AS1
!
!For the remainder configuration refer to example 6-5
!
router bgp 1
 no bgp default ipv4-unicast
 bgp log-neighbor-changes
 neighbor 10.10.10.100 remote-as 1
 neighbor 10.10.10.100 update-source Loopback0
 !
 address-family vpnv4
 neighbor 10.10.10.100 activate
 neighbor 10.10.10.100 send-community extended
 exit-address-family
```

```
hostname PE2-AS1
!
!For the remainder configuration refer to example 6-5
!
router bgp 1
 no bgp default ipv4-unicast
 bgp log-neighbor-changes
 neighbor 10.10.10.100 remote-as 1
 neighbor 10.10.10.100 update-source Loopback0
 !
 address-family vpnv4
 neighbor 10.10.10.100 activate
 neighbor 10.10.10.100 send-community extended
 exit-address-family
```

```
hostname P1-AS1-RR
!
!For the remainder configuration refer to example 6-5
!
router bgp 1
 no bgp default ipv4-unicast
 bgp log-neighbor-changes
 neighbor 10.10.10.101 remote-as 1
 neighbor 10.10.10.101 update-source Loopback0
 neighbor 10.10.10.102 remote-as 1
 neighbor 10.10.10.102 update-source Loopback0
 !
 address-family vpnv4
 neighbor 10.10.10.101 activate
 neighbor 10.10.10.101 send-community extended
 neighbor 10.10.10.101 route-reflector-client
 neighbor 10.10.10.102 activate
 neighbor 10.10.10.102 send-community extended
 neighbor 10.10.10.102 route-reflector-client
 exit-address-family
```

Verifying MPLS VPNs Using RRs

The steps to verify MPLS VPNs using RRs are

Step 1   **Verify BGP neighbor relationship on PE1-AS1 and PE2-AS1—**
Verify the BGP neighbor relationship. Example 6-13 shows PE1-AS1
and PE2-AS1 have a BGP relationship with the CE routers for VRF VRF-
BGP and have received prefixes from those peers.

Example 6-13 *Verify BGP Neighbor Relationship*

```
P1-AS1-RR#show ip bgp vpnv4 all summary
<output truncated for clarity>

Neighbor        V     AS MsgRcvd MsgSent   TblVer  InQ OutQ Up/Down  State/PfxRcd
10.10.10.101    4     1      26      26        9    0    0 00:03:10           2
10.10.10.102    4     1      17      19        9    0    0 00:03:20           2
```

Step 2   **Verify BGP VPNv4 routing table on P1-AS1-RR and PE1-AS1—**
Check the BGP VPNv4 routing table to see if the routes are received as
expected. Example 6-14 shows that P1-AS1-RR and PE1-AS1 receive
the routes as expected.

Example 6-14 *Verify BGP VPNv4 Routing Table on P1-AS1-RR and PE1-AS1*

```
P1-AS1-RR#show ip bgp vpnv4 all
BGP table version is 9, local router ID is 10.10.10.100
Status codes: s suppressed, d damped, h history, * valid, > best, i - internal,
              r RIB-failure, S Stale
Origin codes: i - IGP, e - EGP, ? - incomplete

   Network          Next Hop          Metric LocPrf Weight Path
Route Distinguisher: 1:100
*>i172.16.10.0/24   10.10.10.101           0    100      0 65001 i
*>i172.16.20.0/24   10.10.10.102           0    100      0 65002 i
Route Distinguisher: 1:200
*>i192.168.10.0     10.10.10.101           0    100      0 65001 i
*>i192.168.20.0     10.10.10.102           0    100      0 65001 i
PE1-AS1#show ip bgp vpnv4 all
BGP table version is 15, local router ID is 10.10.10.101
Status codes: s suppressed, d damped, h history, * valid, > best, i - internal,
              r RIB-failure, S Stale
Origin codes: i - IGP, e - EGP, ? - incomplete

   Network          Next Hop          Metric LocPrf Weight Path
Route Distinguisher: 1:100 (default for vrf Cust_A)
*> 172.16.10.0/24   172.16.1.2             0             0 65001 i
*>i172.16.20.0/24   10.10.10.102           0    100      0 65002 i
Route Distinguisher: 1:200 (default for vrf Cust_B)
*> 192.168.10.0     192.168.1.2            0             0 65001 i
*>i192.168.20.0     10.10.10.102           0    100      0 65001 i
```

Step 3 **Verify end-to-end connectivity via ping**—Verify end-to-end connectivity between the Customer A sites as well as Customer B sites. Example 6-15 shows the result of the ping.

Example 6-15 *Verify End-to-End Connectivity via Ping*

```
CE1-A#ping 172.16.20.1 source 172.16.10.1

Type escape sequence to abort.
Sending 5, 100-byte ICMP Echos to 172.16.20.1, timeout is 2 seconds:
Packet sent with a source address of 172.16.10.1
!!!!!
Success rate is 100 percent (5/5), round-trip min/avg/max = 80/80/84 ms
```
```
CE1-B#ping 192.168.20.1 source 192.168.10.1

Type escape sequence to abort.
Sending 5, 100-byte ICMP Echos to 192.168.20.1, timeout is 2 seconds:
Packet sent with a source address of 192.168.10.1
!!!!!
Success rate is 100 percent (5/5), round-trip min/avg/max = 80/80/80 ms
```

Partitioned RRs

Existing RRs carrying VPNv4 routes will not scale to meet the demands of continually expanding MPLS VPN networks. Large MPLS VPN providers might have to resort to partitioning or segregating VPNv4 prefixes based on route targets or any other BGP attributes, for example, standard BGP communities, to accommodate a large number of VPNv4 routes.

Figure 6-13 shows a basic MPLS VPN network in which P1-RR accepts only VPN-A VPNv4 prefixes with a route-target value of 1:100, and P2-RR accepts only VPN-B VPNv4 prefixes with a route-target value of 1:200.

Figure 6-13 *Route Partitioning*

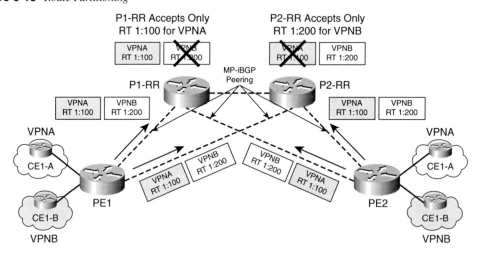

In order to receive all the routing information required for proper operation, all PE routers may need to have BGP sessions with all RRs. Further resource optimization can be achieved if the PE routers peer only with the relevant RRs. This deployment, although optimal, may lead to the providers incurring additional management and configuration complexity. Partitioning of RRs can be achieved by configuring

- **Outbound or inbound filters**—Outbound filters on the PE routers or inbound filters on RRs. In both cases, the filtering can be performed with a route-map, matching routes on any BGP attribute that is usually on route target or standard BGP community. Outbound filters (ORF) on the PE routers reduce bandwidth utilization and CPU utilization of the RRs. The disadvantage with outbound filters is that the service providers may incur additional operational burden due to constant maintenance required for these filters on all PE routers. On the other hand, inbound filters on RRs are optimal from a maintenance perspective, but may increase the CPU utilization of the RRs.

- **BGP RR groups**—Configure the inbound route-target filter on the BGP RR by using the **bgp rr-group** command. This command performs the same function as a route-map. However, it is configured under the BGP routing process and applies to all BGP neighbors. Also, another important operational detail is that the extended community access-list maintained on the RR is downloaded as an outbound filter to the PE routers through the ORF functionality. The route-map based input filter cannot be downloaded via ORF functionality.

As an alternate solution, the VPNv4 routing information can also be partitioned based on standard BGP communities. In the first design, outbound updates on the PE routers are filtered. Because the PE routers have to attach standard BGP community to the VPNv4 routes, the filtering of outbound VPNv4 routing updates based on the standard BGP community does not represent an additional maintenance burden.

The second design is to attach standard BGP communities to the VPNv4 routes on the PE routers and perform the filtering on the RRs, either in the inbound or outbound direction. This design achieves a clear separation of the marking of customer routes from the partitioning of VPNv4 routing information. Inbound filtering is preferred, because it reduces the volume of VPNv4 routing information on RRs.

RR Partitioning Using BGP Inbound Route-Target Filters

Figure 6-14 is similar to Figure 6-1 except that a second RR (P2-AS1-RR2) has been added to the topology. P1-AS1-RR1 and P2-AS1-RR2 perform both control and data plane functionality for VPNA and VPNB sites. As previously demonstrated, the configured route targets on PE1-AS1 and PE2-AS1 for VPNA and VPNB are 1:100 and 1:200, respectively. To demonstrate route partitioning, P1-AS1-RR1 will accept routes only for VPN-A (Cust_A) and P2-AS1-RR2 will accept routes only for VPN-B (Cust_B).

Figure 6-14 *MPLS Network Implementing Route Partitioning Using Inbound Route-Target Filters*

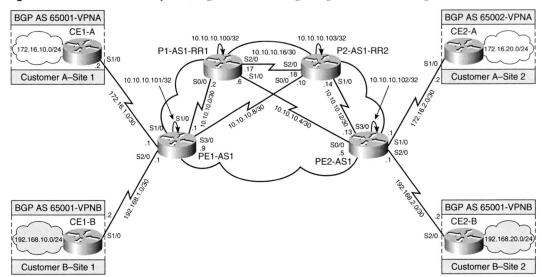

Figure 6-15 shows the flowchart to configure route partitioning using inbound route-target filters on RRs.

Figure 6-15 *Configuration Steps for Partitioning Routes Using Inbound Route-Target Filters*

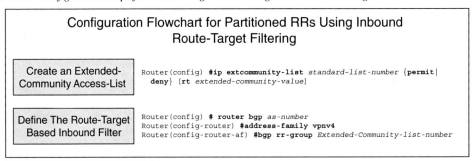

Route-Partitioning Configuration Steps on the P Routers P1-RR and P2-RR

The configurations steps for the RRs are the same as those demonstrated in the section "Configuring P Router as RR Only for VPNv4 Prefixes (Option 3)." In addition to those steps, the following steps are required to configure route partitioning on the RRs:

Step 1 **Create an extended-community access-list**—The first step is to create an extended-community access-list on the RR that permits routes with the appropriate route-target value. P1-AS1-RR1 accepts only VPNv4 routes with the route target 1:100, and P2-AS1-RR2 accepts only VPNv4 prefixes with a route-target value of 1:200. Example 6-16 illustrates the configuration steps for creating an extended-community access-list.

Example 6-16 *Create an Extended-Community Access-List*

```
P1-AS1-RR1(config)#ip extcommunity-list  standard VPNA
P1-AS1-RR1(config-extcomm-list)#permit rt 1:100
P2-AS1-RR2(config)#ip extcommunity-list  standard VPNB
P2-AS1-RR2(config-extcomm-list)#permit rt 1:200
```

Step 2   **Define the route-target based inbound filter**—In this step, you configure the **bgp rr-group** command under the BGP routing process on the RRs. The extended-community list number should match that of the access-list configured in Step 1. Example 6-17 illustrates the steps to define the route-target based inbound filter on P1-AS1-RR1 and P2-AS1-RR2.

Example 6-17 *Define the Route-Target Based Inbound Filter*

```
P1-AS1-RR1(config)#router bgp 1
P1-AS1-RR1(config-router)#address-family vpnv4
P1-AS1-RR1(config-router-af)#bgp rr-group VPNA
P2-AS1-RR2(config)#router bgp 1
P2-AS1-RR2(config-router)#address-family vpnv4
P2-AS1-RR2(config-router-af)#bgp rr-group VPNB
```

PE1-AS1, PE2-AS1, P1-AS1-RR1, and P2-AS1-RR2 Final Configuration for Partitioned RRs

Example 6-18 shows only the additional configurations on PE1-AS1, PE2-AS1, and P1-AS1-RR1. The complete configuration is shown for P2-AS1-RR2. For the remaining configurations, refer to Example 6-5.

Example 6-18 *PE1-AS1, PE2-AS1, P1-AS1-RR1, and P2-AS1-RR2 Final Configurations for Partitioned RRs*

```
hostname PE1-AS1
!
!Refer to example 6-5 for the rest of the configuration
router bgp 1
neighbor 10.10.10.103 remote-as 1
neighbor 10.10.10.103 update-source Loopback0
 !
address-family vpnv4
neighbor 10.10.10.103 activate
neighbor 10.10.10.103 send-community extended
exit-address-family
hostname PE2-AS1
!
```

continues

Example 6-18 *PE1-AS1, PE2-AS1, P1-AS1-RR1, and P2-AS1-RR2 Final Configurations for Partitioned RRs (Continued)*

```
!Refer to example 6-5 for the rest of the configuration
router bgp 1
neighbor 10.10.10.103 remote-as 1
neighbor 10.10.10.103 update-source Loopback0
 !
address-family vpnv4
neighbor 10.10.10.103 activate
neighbor 10.10.10.103 send-community extended
exit-address-family
```
```
hostname P1-AS1-RR1
 !
!Refer to example 6-5
 !
router bgp 1
 no bgp default ipv4-unicast
 neighbor 10.10.10.101 remote-as 1
 neighbor 10.10.10.101 update-source Loopback0
 neighbor 10.10.10.102 remote-as 1
 neighbor 10.10.10.102 update-source Loopback0
 neighbor 10.10.10.103 remote-as 1
 neighbor 10.10.10.103 update-source Loopback0
 !
 address-family vpnv4
 neighbor 10.10.10.101 activate
 neighbor 10.10.10.101 send-community extended
 neighbor 10.10.10.101 route-reflector-client
 neighbor 10.10.10.102 activate
 neighbor 10.10.10.102 send-community extended
 neighbor 10.10.10.102 route-reflector-client
 neighbor 10.10.10.103 activate
 neighbor 10.10.10.103 send-community extended
 neighbor 10.10.10.103 route-reflector-client
 bgp rr-group VPNA
 exit-address-family
 !
ip extcommunity-list standard VPNA permit rt 1:100
```
```
hostname P2-AS1-RR2
 !
mpls ldp router-id Loopback0
 !
interface Loopback0
 ip address 10.10.10.103 255.255.255.255
 !
interface Serial0/0
 ip address 10.10.10.10 255.255.255.252
 mpls ip
 !
interface Serial1/0
 ip address 10.10.10.14 255.255.255.252
 mpls ip
```

Example 6-18 *PE1-AS1, PE2-AS1, P1-AS1-RR1, and P2-AS1-RR2 Final Configurations for Partitioned RRs (Continued)*

```
!
interface Serial2/0
 ip address 10.10.10.18 255.255.255.252
 mpls ip
!
router ospf 1
 log-adjacency-changes
 network 10.0.0.0 0.255.255.255 area 0
!
router bgp 1
 no bgp default ipv4-unicast
 neighbor 10.10.10.101 remote-as 1
 neighbor 10.10.10.101 update-source Loopback0
 neighbor 10.10.10.102 remote-as 1
 neighbor 10.10.10.102 update-source Loopback0
 neighbor 10.10.10.100 remote-as 1
 neighbor 10.10.10.100 update-source Loopback0
 !
 address-family vpnv4
 neighbor 10.10.10.101 activate
 neighbor 10.10.10.101 send-community extended
 neighbor 10.10.10.101 route-reflector-client
 neighbor 10.10.10.102 activate
 neighbor 10.10.10.102 send-community extended
 neighbor 10.10.10.102 route-reflector-client
 neighbor 10.10.10.100 activate
 neighbor 10.10.10.100 send-community extended
 neighbor 10.10.10.100 route-reflector-client
 bgp rr-group VPNB
 exit-address-family
!
ip extcommunity-list standard VPNB permit rt 1:200
```

Verifying Partitioned RRs

The steps to verify partitioned RRs are

Step 1 **Verify BGP VPNv4 routing table on P1-AS1-RR1 and P2-AS1-RR2**—Verify the BGP VPNv4 routing table on P1-AS1-RR1 and P2-AS1-RR2. Example 6-19 shows that P1-AS1-RR1 shows VPNv4 routes for VPNA and P2-AS1-RR2 sees VPNv4 routes for VPNB.

Example 6-19 *Verify BGP VPNv4 Routing Table on P1-AS1-RR1 and P2-AS1-RR2*

```
P1-AS1-RR1# show ip bgp vpnv4 all
BGP table version is 3, local router ID is 10.10.10.100
Status codes: s suppressed, d damped, h history, * valid, > best, i - internal,
              r RIB-failure, S Stale
Origin codes: i - IGP, e - EGP, ? - incomplete
```

continues

Example 6-19 *Verify BGP VPNv4 Routing Table on P1-AS1-RR1 and P2-AS1-RR2 (Continued)*

```
   Network          Next Hop          Metric LocPrf Weight Path
Route Distinguisher: 1:100
*>i172.16.10.0/24   10.10.10.101           0    100      0 65001 i
*>i172.16.20.0/24   10.10.10.102           0    100      0 65002 i
```
```
P2-AS1-RR2#show ip bgp vpnv4 all
BGP table version is 23, local router ID is 10.10.10.103
Status codes: s suppressed, d damped, h history, * valid, > best, i - internal,
              r RIB-failure, S Stale
Origin codes: i - IGP, e - EGP, ? - incomplete

   Network          Next Hop          Metric LocPrf Weight Path
Route Distinguisher: 1:200
*>i192.168.10.0     10.10.10.101           0    100      0 65001 i
*>i192.168.20.0     10.10.10.102           0    100      0 65001 i
```

Step 2   **Verify end-to-end connectivity via ping**—Ping the edge customer
networks from CE1-A to CE2-A and CE1-B to CE2-B. Example 6-20
shows the successful ping outputs.

Example 6-20 *Verify End-to-End Connectivity via Ping*

```
CE1-A#ping 172.16.20.1 source 172.16.10.1

Type escape sequence to abort.
Sending 5, 100-byte ICMP Echos to 172.16.20.1, timeout is 2 seconds:
Packet sent with a source address of 172.16.10.1
!!!!!
Success rate is 100 percent (5/5), round-trip min/avg/max = 80/81/88 ms
```
```
CE1-B#ping 192.168.20.1 source 192.168.10.1

Type escape sequence to abort.
Sending 5, 100-byte ICMP Echos to 192.168.20.1, timeout is 2 seconds:
Packet sent with a source address of 192.168.10.1
!!!!!
Success rate is 100 percent (5/5), round-trip min/avg/max = 80/82/88 ms
```

RR Partitioning Using Standard BGP Communities

This configuration scenario demonstrates RR partitioning using standard BGP communities.
The same topology as what's shown in Figure 6-14 is used for this scenario. The objective
is to ensure that P1-AS1-RR1 will accept routes only for VPNA (Cust_A) and P2-AS1-RR2
will accept routes only for VPNB (Cust_B).

Figure 6-16 shows the steps to configure route partitioning using standard BGP
communities.

Figure 6-16 *Configuration Flowchart for Partitioning Routes Using Standard BGP Communities*

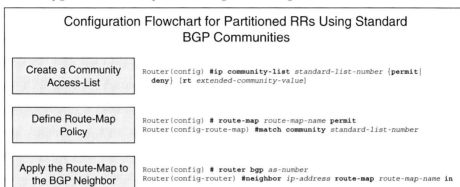

Configuration Steps on the PE Routers PE1-AS1 and PE2-AS1

On the PE routers, set the community for the CE1-A and CE1-B prefixes on PE1-AS1 and for CE2-A and CE2-B on PE2-AS1. Example 6-21 shows the additional relevant configuration on PE1-AS1. Repeat the same steps on PE2-AS1.

Example 6-21 *PE1-AS1 Configuration*

```
PE1-AS1(config)#router bgp 1
PE1-AS1(config-router)#address-family vpnv4
PE1-AS1(config-router-af)#neighbor 10.10.10.100 send-community both
PE1-AS1(config-router-af)#neighbor 10.10.10.100 route-map allow1 out
PE1-AS1(config-router-af)#neighbor 10.10.10.103 send-community both
PE1-AS1(config-router-af)#neighbor 10.10.10.103 route-map allow2 out
PE1-AS1(config-router-af)#exit-address-family
PE1-AS1(config-router)#exit
PE1-AS1(config)#ip bgp-community new-format
PE1-AS1(config)#access-list 10 permit 172.16.10.0 0.0.0.255
PE1-AS1(config)#access-list 20 permit 192.168.10.0 0.0.0.255
PE1-AS1(config)#route-map allow2 permit 10
PE1-AS1(config-route-map)# match ip address 20
PE1-AS1(config-route-map)# set community 1:200
PE1-AS1(config-route-map)#exit
PE1-AS1(config)#route-map allow1 permit 10
PE1-AS1(config-route-map)# match ip address 10
PE1-AS1(config-route-map)# set community 1:100
```

Configuration Steps on the P Routers P1-AS1-RR1 and P2-AS1-RR2

The configuration steps for the RRs are the same as demonstrated in the section "Configuration Step for PE Routers PE1-AS1 and PE2-AS1." In addition to that step, the following steps are required to configure route partitioning on the RRs using standard BGP communities:

Step 1   **Create a community access-list and route-map policy**—Create a community access-list that permits the route with the route-target value that is to be accepted by the RR. P1-RR is accepting only VPNv4 with the route target 1:100, and P2-RR is accepting only VPNv4 prefixes with the route-target value of 1:200. Prior to this, make sure that the routers are configured with **ip bgp-community new-format**. Example 6-22 shows the relevant configuration on the RRs.

Example 6-22 *Create a Community Access-List and Route-Map Policy*

```
P1-AS1-RR1(config)#ip community-list 1 permit  1:100
P1-AS1-RR1(config)#route-map allow-VPNA permit 10
P1-AS1-RR1(config-route-map)#match community 1
P2-AS1-RR2(config)#ip community-list 1 permit  1:200
P2-AS1-RR2(config)#route-map allow-VPNB permit 10
P2-AS1-RR2(config-route-map)#match community 1
```

Step 2   **Apply the route-map to the BGP PE neighbor**—In this step, apply the route-map to the relevant BGP neighbors. This is shown in Example 6-23.

Example 6-23 *Apply the Route-Map to the BGP Neighbors*

```
P1-AS1-RR1(config)#router bgp 1
P1-AS1-RR1(config-router)#address-family vpnv4
P1-AS1-RR1(config-router-af)#neighbor 10.10.10.101 route-map allow-VPNA in
P1-AS1-RR1(config-router-af)#neighbor 10.10.10.102 route-map allow-VPNA in
P1-AS1-RR1(config-router-af)#neighbor 10.10.10.103 route-map allow-VPNA in
P2-AS1-RR2(config)#router bgp 1
P2-AS1-RR2(config-router)#address-family vpnv4
P2-AS1-RR2(config-router-af)#neighbor 10.10.10.101 route-map allow-VPNB in
P2-AS1-RR2(config-router-af)#neighbor 10.10.10.102 route-map allow-VPNB in
P2-AS1-RR2(config-router-af)#neighbor 10.10.10.100 route-map allow-VPNB in
```

PE1-AS1 and PE2-AS1 Final Configuration for Partitioned RRs

Example 6-24 shows the relevant configuration on the PE1-AS1, PE2-AS1, and P routers.

Example 6-24 *Relevant Configuration on the PE1-AS1, PE2-AS1, and P Routers*

```
!PE1-AS1 Router Configuration
router bgp 1
 no bgp default ipv4-unicast
 bgp log-neighbor-changes
 neighbor 10.10.10.100 remote-as 1
 neighbor 10.10.10.100 update-source Loopback0
 neighbor 10.10.10.103 remote-as 1
 neighbor 10.10.10.103 update-source Loopback0
 !
 address-family vpnv4
 neighbor 10.10.10.100 activate
 neighbor 10.10.10.100 send-community both
```

Example 6-24 *Relevant Configuration on the PE1-AS1, PE2-AS1, and P Routers (Continued)*

```
 neighbor 10.10.10.100 route-map allow1 out
 neighbor 10.10.10.103 activate
 neighbor 10.10.10.103 send-community both
 neighbor 10.10.10.103 route-map allow2 out
 exit-address-family
!
ip bgp-community new-format
!
access-list 10 permit 172.16.10.0 0.0.0.255
access-list 20 permit 192.168.10.0 0.0.0.255
!
route-map allow1 permit 10
 match ip address 10
 set community 1:100
!
route-map allow2 permit 10
 match ip address 20
 set community 1:200
```

```
!PE2-AS1 Router Configuration
router bgp 1
 no bgp default ipv4-unicast
 bgp log-neighbor-changes
 neighbor 10.10.10.100 remote-as 1
 neighbor 10.10.10.100 update-source Loopback0
 neighbor 10.10.10.103 remote-as 1
 neighbor 10.10.10.103 update-source Loopback0
 !
 address-family vpnv4
 neighbor 10.10.10.100 activate
 neighbor 10.10.10.100 send-community both
 neighbor 10.10.10.100 route-map allow1 out
 neighbor 10.10.10.103 activate
 neighbor 10.10.10.103 send-community both
 neighbor 10.10.10.103 route-map allow2 out
 exit-address-family
!
ip bgp-community new-format
!
access-list 10 permit 172.16.20.0 0.0.0.255
access-list 20 permit 192.168.20.0 0.0.0.255
!
route-map allow1 permit 10
 match ip address 10
 set community 1:100
!
route-map allow2 permit 10
 match ip address 20
 set community 1:200
```

```
!P1-RR Router Configuration
router bgp 1
```

continues

Example 6-24 *Relevant Configuration on the PE1-AS1, PE2-AS1, and P Routers (Continued)*

```
 no bgp default ipv4-unicast
 bgp log-neighbor-changes
 neighbor 10.10.10.101 remote-as 1
 neighbor 10.10.10.101 update-source Loopback0
 neighbor 10.10.10.102 remote-as 1
 neighbor 10.10.10.102 update-source Loopback0
 neighbor 10.10.10.103 remote-as 1
 neighbor 10.10.10.103 update-source Loopback0
 !
 address-family vpnv4
 neighbor 10.10.10.101 activate
 neighbor 10.10.10.101 send-community both
 neighbor 10.10.10.101 route-reflector-client
 neighbor 10.10.10.101 route-map allow-VPNA in
 neighbor 10.10.10.102 activate
 neighbor 10.10.10.102 send-community both
 neighbor 10.10.10.102 route-reflector-client
 neighbor 10.10.10.102 route-map allow-VPNA in
 neighbor 10.10.10.103 activate
 neighbor 10.10.10.103 send-community both
 neighbor 10.10.10.103 route-map allow-VPNA in
 exit-address-family
!
ip bgp-community new-format
ip community-list 1 permit 1:100
!
route-map allow-VPNA permit 10
 match community 1

!P2-RR Router Configuration
router bgp 1
 no bgp default ipv4-unicast
 bgp log-neighbor-changes
 neighbor 10.10.10.100 remote-as 1
 neighbor 10.10.10.100 update-source Loopback0
 neighbor 10.10.10.101 remote-as 1
 neighbor 10.10.10.101 update-source Loopback0
 neighbor 10.10.10.102 remote-as 1
 neighbor 10.10.10.102 update-source Loopback0
 !
 address-family vpnv4
 neighbor 10.10.10.100 activate
 neighbor 10.10.10.100 send-community both
 neighbor 10.10.10.100 route-map allow-VPNB in
 neighbor 10.10.10.101 activate
 neighbor 10.10.10.101 send-community both
 neighbor 10.10.10.101 route-reflector-client
 neighbor 10.10.10.101 route-map allow-VPNB in
 neighbor 10.10.10.102 activate
 neighbor 10.10.10.102 send-community both
 neighbor 10.10.10.102 route-reflector-client
 neighbor 10.10.10.102 route-map allow-VPNB in
 exit-address-family
```

Example 6-24 *Relevant Configuration on the PE1-AS1, PE2-AS1, and P Routers (Continued)*

```
!
ip bgp-community new-format
ip community-list 1 permit 1:200
!
route-map allow-VPNB permit 10
 match community 1
```

Verifying Partitioned RRs Using Standard BGP Communities

The steps to verify partitioned RRs using standard BGP communities are

Step 1   **Verify BGP VPNv4 routing table on P1-RR and P2-RR**—Example 6-25 shows the VPNv4 routing table on P1-AS1-RR1 and P2-AS1-RR2.

Example 6-25 show ip bgp vpnv4 all *on P1-AS1-RR1 and P2-AS1-RR2*

```
P1-AS1-RR1# show ip bgp vpnv4 all
BGP table version is 3, local router ID is 10.10.10.100
Status codes: s suppressed, d damped, h history, * valid, > best, i - internal,
              r RIB-failure, S Stale
Origin codes: i - IGP, e - EGP, ? - incomplete

   Network          Next Hop          Metric LocPrf Weight Path
Route Distinguisher: 1:100
*>i172.16.10.0/24   10.10.10.101           0    100      0 65001 i
*>i172.16.20.0/24   10.10.10.102           0    100      0 65002 i
P2-AS1-RR2#show ip bgp vpnv4 all
BGP table version is 3, local router ID is 10.10.10.103
Status codes: s suppressed, d damped, h history, * valid, > best, i - internal,
              r RIB-failure, S Stale
Origin codes: i - IGP, e - EGP, ? - incomplete

   Network          Next Hop          Metric LocPrf Weight Path
Route Distinguisher: 1:200
*>i192.168.10.0     10.10.10.101           0    100      0 65001 i
*>i192.168.20.0     10.10.10.102           0    100      0 65001 i
```

Step 2   **Verify connectivity via ping**—Example 6-26 demonstrates this step.

Example 6-26 *Verify Connectivity via Ping*

```
CE1-A#ping 172.16.20.1 source 172.16.10.1

Type escape sequence to abort.
Sending 5, 100-byte ICMP Echos to 172.16.20.1, timeout is 2 seconds:
Packet sent with a source address of 172.16.10.1
!!!!!
Success rate is 100 percent (5/5), round-trip min/avg/max = 80/80/84 ms
CE1-B#ping 192.168.20.1 source 192.168.10.1
Type escape sequence to abort.
Sending 5, 100-byte ICMP Echos to 192.168.20.1, timeout is 2 seconds:
Packet sent with a source address of 192.168.10.1
!!!!!
Success rate is 100 percent (5/5), round-trip min/avg/max = 80/80/84 ms
```

RRs and Peer Groups

A BGP peer group is a collection of BGP neighbors that share the same outbound policies. Instead of configuring each neighbor with the same policy individually, peer groups allow the user to group the policies that can be applied to individual peers. Using BGP peer groups reduces the amount of system resources (CPU and memory) used by allowing the routing table to be checked only once and updates to be replicated to all peer group members instead of being done individually for each peer in the peer group. The reduction in system resources, however, depends on the number of peer group members, the number of prefixes in the table, and the number of prefixes that are being advertised or being imported. The other benefit of peer groups is also to help in simplifying the BGP configuration.

Figure 6-17 shows an MPLS VPN network where P1-AS1-RR and P2-AS1-RR are RRs for PE1-AS1 and PE2-AS1 PE routers. PE1-AS1 and PE2-AS1 are both members of peer group group1 and group2 on P1-AS1-RR and P2-AS1-RR, respectively.

Figure 6-17 *PE1-AS1 and PE2-AS1 Members of Peer Group group1 and group2*

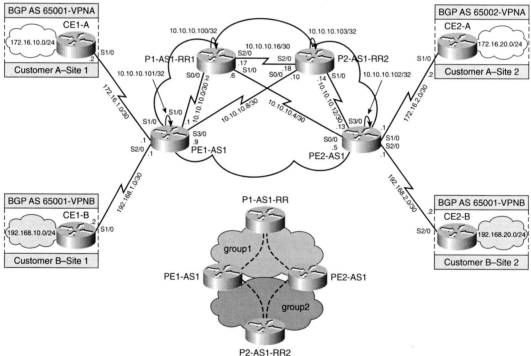

Figure 6-18 shows the steps to configure peer groups in a RR-based MPLS VPN network.

Figure 6-18 *Configuration Steps for RRs with Peer Groups*

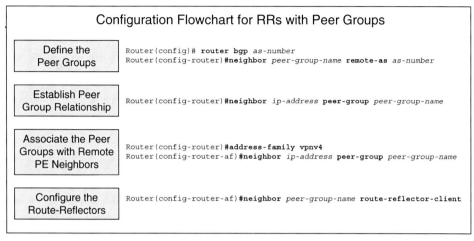

Configuration Flowchart for RRs with Peer Groups

Define the Peer Groups	`Router(config)# router bgp as-number` `Router(config-router)#neighbor peer-group-name remote-as as-number`
Establish Peer Group Relationship	`Router(config-router)#neighbor ip-address peer-group peer-group-name`
Associate the Peer Groups with Remote PE Neighbors	`Router(config-router)#address-family vpnv4` `Router(config-router-af)#neighbor ip-address peer-group peer-group-name`
Configure the Route-Reflectors	`Router(config-router-af)#neighbor peer-group-name route-reflector-client`

Configuring Peer Groups on P Routers P1-AS1-RR1 and P2-AS1-RR2

The steps to configure peer groups on P routers P1-AS1-RR1 and P2-AS1-RR2 are

Step 1 **Define the peer groups on P1-AS1-RR1 and P2-AS1-RR2**—The first step in configuring the peer groups is to define the peer group name on the P1-AS1-RR1 and P2-AS1-RR2 routers, as displayed in Example 6-27.

Example 6-27 *Define Peer Groups*

```
P1-AS1-RR1(config)#router bgp 1
P1-AS1-RR1(config-router)#neighbor group1 peer-group
P2-AS1-RR2(config)#router bgp 1
P2-AS1-RR2(config-router)#neighbor group2 peer-group
```

Step 2 **Configure the remote AS for the peer group**—In this step, the remote BGP AS is defined for the peer group. Example 6-28 shows the relevant steps.

Example 6-28 *Configure the Remote AS for the Peer Group*

```
P1-AS1-RR1(config-router)#neighbor group1 remote-as 1
P2-AS1-RR2(config-router)#neighbor group2 remote-as 1
```

Step 3 **Associate the peer group with remote BGP PE neighbors**—In this step, associate the peer group with the remote BGP PE neighbors in the VPNv4 address-family. This configuration step is shown in Example 6-29.

Example 6-29 *Associate the Peer Group with Remote BGP PE Neighbors*

```
P1-AS1-RR1(config-router)#address-family vpnv4
P1-AS1-RR1(config-router-af)#neighbor 10.10.10.101 peer-group group1
P1-AS1-RR1(config-router-af)#neighbor 10.10.10.102 peer-group group1
P2-AS1-RR2(config-router)#address-family vpnv4
P2-AS1-RR2(config-router-af)#neighbor 10.10.10.101 peer-group group2
P2-AS1-RR2(config-router-af)#neighbor 10.10.10.102 peer-group group2
```

In this case, the router is configured to serve only as a VPNv4 RR to reflect VPNv4 prefixes and, as a result, configuring the **neighbor** *peer-group* command in the VPNv4 address-family would result in the Example 6-30 configuration to be inserted in the P1-AS1-RR1 and P2-AS1-RR2 configuration.

Example 6-30 neighbor *Peer Group Command*

```
address-family ipv4
 neighbor group1 activate
 no neighbor 10.10.10.101 activate
 no neighbor 10.10.10.102 activate
```

Step 4   **Configure the routers to function as RRs**—To enable the routers for RR functionality, you need to enter the VPNv4 address-family configuration mode and use the **neighbor route-reflector-client** command. Example 6-31 demonstrates this configuration step.

Example 6-31 *Configure the Routers to Function as RRs*

```
P1-AS1-RR1(config-router)#address-family vpnv4
P1-AS1-RR1(config-router-af)# neighbor group1 route-reflector-client
P2-AS1-RR2(config-router)#address-family vpnv4
P2-AS1-RR2(config-router-af)# neighbor group2 route-reflector-client
```

Another key point to note is that the peer groups need not be activated under the VPNv4 address-family. They are automatically activated when peer-group parameters are defined. The message in Example 6-32 is shown if the peer group is activated under the VPNv4 address-family.

Example 6-32 *Message if the Peer Group Is Activated Under the VPNv4 Address-Family*

```
P1-AS1-RR12(config-router)#address-family vpnv4
P1-AS1-RR12(config-router-af)#neighbor group1 activate
% Peergroups are automatically activated when parameters are configured
```

P1-AS1-RR1 and P2-AS1-RR2 Final RR Configurations with Peer Groups

Example 6-33 shows the relevant configuration on P1-AS1-RR1 and P2-AS1-RR2.

Example 6-33 *P1-AS1-RR1 and P2-AS1-RR2 Configuration*

```
!P1-AS1-RR1 Router Configuration
router bgp 1
 no bgp default ipv4-unicast
 neighbor group1 peer-group
 neighbor group1 remote-as 1
 neighbor group1 update-source Loopback0
 neighbor 10.10.10.101 peer-group group1
 neighbor 10.10.10.102 peer-group group1
 neighbor 10.10.10.103 remote-as 1
 neighbor 10.10.10.103 update-source Loopback0
 !
 address-family vpnv4
 neighbor group1 send-community extended
 neighbor group1 route-reflector-client
 neighbor 10.10.10.101 activate
 neighbor 10.10.10.102 activate
 neighbor 10.10.10.103 activate
 neighbor 10.10.10.103 send-community extended
 exit-address-family
```
```
!P2-AS1-RR2 Router Configuration
router bgp 1
 no bgp default ipv4-unicast
 neighbor group2 peer-group
 neighbor group2 remote-as 1
 neighbor group2 update-source Loopback0
 neighbor 10.10.10.100 remote-as 1
 neighbor 10.10.10.100 update-source Loopback0
 neighbor 10.10.10.101 peer-group group2
 neighbor 10.10.10.102 peer-group group2
 !
 address-family ipv4
 no auto-summary
 no synchronization
 exit-address-family
 !
 address-family vpnv4
 neighbor group2 send-community extended
 neighbor group2 route-reflector-client
 neighbor 10.10.10.100 activate
 neighbor 10.10.10.100 send-community extended
 neighbor 10.10.10.101 activate
 neighbor 10.10.10.102 activate
 exit-address-family
```

Verifying Peer Groups and RRs

The steps to verify peer groups and RRs are

Step 1   **Verify peer group formation**—Verify if PE1-AS1 and PE2-AS1 are
part of the BGP peer groups group1 and group2. Example 6-34 shows
that PE1-AS1 and PE2-AS1 are part of peer group group1 on P1-AS1-
RR1 and part of group2 on P2-AS1-RR2.

Example 6-34 *Verify Peer Group Formation*

```
P1-AS1-RR1#show ip bgp peer-group group1
BGP peer-group is group1, remote AS 1
  BGP version 4
  Default minimum time between advertisement runs is 5 seconds

  For address family: VPNv4 Unicast
  BGP neighbor is group1, peer-group internal, members:
  10.10.10.101 10.10.10.102
  Index 0, Offset 0, Mask 0x0
  Route-Reflector Client
  Update messages formatted 0, replicated 0
  Number of NLRIs in the update sent: max 0, min 0
P2-AS1-RR2#show ip bgp peer-group group2
BGP peer-group is group2, remote AS 1
  BGP version 4
  Default minimum time between advertisement runs is 5 seconds

  For address family: VPNv4 Unicast
  BGP neighbor is group2, peer-group internal, members:
  10.10.10.101 10.10.10.102
  Index 0, Offset 0, Mask 0x0
  Route-Reflector Client
  Update messages formatted 0, replicated 0
  Number of NLRIs in the update sent: max 0, min 0
```

Step 2 **Verify BGP VPNv4 routing table on P1-AS1-RR1**—Check the BGP
VPNv4 routing table to see if routes are received as expected. Example 6-35
shows that P1-AS1-RR1 and PE1-AS1 receive the routes as expected.

Example 6-35 *Verify BGP VPNv4 Routing Table on P1-AS1-RR*

```
P1-AS1-RR1#show ip bgp vpnv4 all
BGP table version is 5, local router ID is 10.10.10.100
Status codes: s suppressed, d damped, h history, * valid, > best, i - internal,
              r RIB-failure, S Stale
Origin codes: i - IGP, e - EGP, ? - incomplete

   Network          Next Hop         Metric LocPrf Weight Path
Route Distinguisher: 1:100
 * i172.16.10.0/24  10.10.10.101          0    100      0 65001 i
 *>i                10.10.10.101          0    100      0 65001 i
 * i172.16.20.0/24  10.10.10.102          0    100      0 65002 i
 *>i                10.10.10.102          0    100      0 65002 i
Route Distinguisher: 1:200
 * i192.168.10.0    10.10.10.101          0    100      0 65001 i
 *>i                10.10.10.101          0    100      0 65001 i
 * i192.168.20.0    10.10.10.102          0    100      0 65001 i
 *>i                10.10.10.102          0    100      0 65001 i
PE1-AS1#show ip bgp vpnv4 all
BGP table version is 9, local router ID is 10.10.10.101
Status codes: s suppressed, d damped, h history, * valid, > best, i - internal,
              r RIB-failure, S Stale
```

Example 6-35 *Verify BGP VPNv4 Routing Table on P1-AS1-RR (Continued)*

```
Origin codes: i - IGP, e - EGP, ? - incomplete
   Network          Next Hop          Metric LocPrf Weight Path
Route Distinguisher: 1:100 (default for vrf Cust_A)
*> 172.16.10.0/24    172.16.1.2            0               0 65001 i
*  i172.16.20.0/24   10.10.10.102          0     100       0 65002 i
*>i                  10.10.10.102          0     100       0 65002 i
Route Distinguisher: 1:200 (default for vrf Cust_B)
*> 192.168.10.0      192.168.1.2           0               0 65001 i
*  i192.168.20.0     10.10.10.102          0     100       0 65001 i
*>i                  10.10.10.102          0     100       0 65001 i
```

Step 3   **Verify end-to-end connectivity via ping**—Verify end-to-end
connectivity between the Customer A sites as well as Customer B sites.
Example 6-36 shows the result of the ping.

Example 6-36 *Verify End-to-End Connectivity via Ping*

```
CE1-A#ping 172.16.20.1 source 172.16.10.1

Type escape sequence to abort.
Sending 5, 100-byte ICMP Echos to 172.16.20.1, timeout is 2 seconds:
Packet sent with a source address of 172.16.10.1
!!!!!
Success rate is 100 percent (5/5), round-trip min/avg/max = 80/80/84 ms
CE1-B#ping 192.168.20.1 source 192.168.10.1

Type escape sequence to abort.
Sending 5, 100-byte ICMP Echos to 192.168.20.1, timeout is 2 seconds:
Packet sent with a source address of 192.168.10.1
!!!!!
Success rate is 100 percent (5/5), round-trip min/avg/max = 80/80/80 ms
```

BGP Confederations

BGP confederation is another BGP scalability tool that can reduce the iBGP mesh inside
an AS. In BGP confederation, an AS is divided into multiple autonomous systems or sub
autonomous systems, and these are assigned to a single confederation. Each sub AS will be
fully iBGP meshed. Each sub AS will also have connections to other autonomous systems
inside the confederation. Each sub AS will be eBGP peered with other sub autonomous
systems. Although the sub autonomous systems will be eBGP peered to other autonomous
systems within the confederation, they will exchange routing as if they were using iBGP;
next hop, metric, and local preference information will be preserved. To the outside world,
the confederation (the group of autonomous systems) will look like a single AS.

Figure 6-19 shows a provider network, AS 1, which is divided into multiple sub autonomous
systems, AS 100, AS 101, and AS 102. Each sub AS is iBGP fully meshed, and there is eBGP
peering between the sub autonomous systems. To BGP CE neighbors, the confederation (the
group of autonomous systems, AS 100, 101, and 102) will look like a single BGP AS 1.

Figure 6-19 *BGP Confederation*

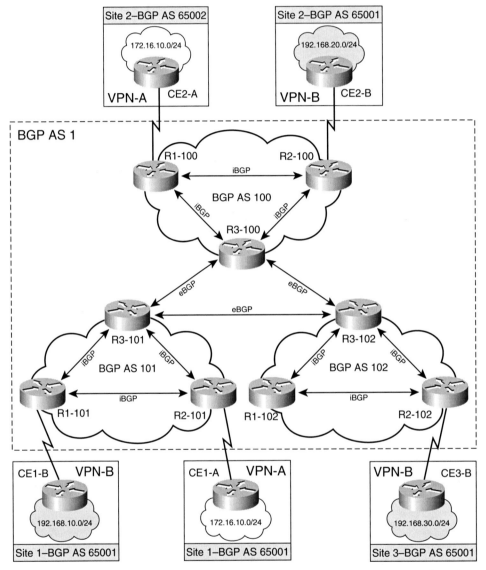

Figure 6-20 shows an MPLS VPN network in which BGP AS 1 is divided into three sub autonomous systems, AS 100, AS 101, and AS 102. P1-AS1, PE1-AS1, and PE2-AS1 are in AS 100, AS 101, and AS 102.

Configuration Flowchart to Implement BGP Confederations

Figure 6-21 shows the configuration flowchart to implement BGP confederation in the provider core.

Figure 6-20 *MPLS VPN Network Using BGP Confederations*

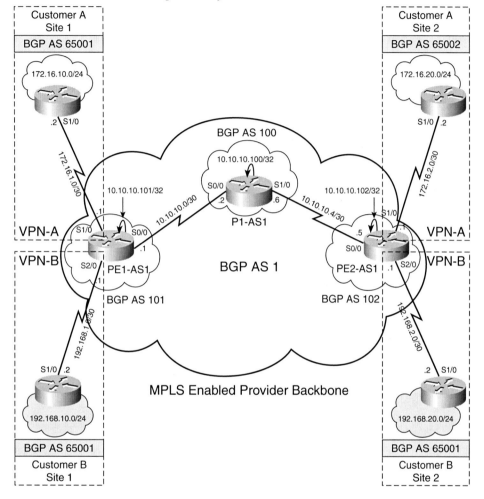

Figure 6-21 *Configuration Flowchart to Implement BGP Confederations*

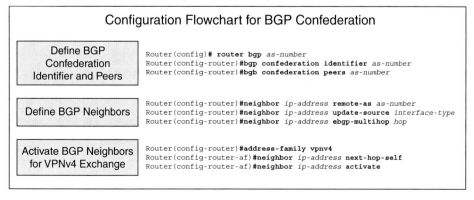

Configuring BGP Confederation for P Routers PE1-AS1, PE2-AS1, and P1-AS1

The steps to configure BGP confederation for the topology shown in Figure 6-20 are as follows. The steps are shown for PE1-AS1 and PE2-AS1. Configure P1-AS1 similarly:

Step 1 **Define BGP confederation identifier and peers**—The first step is to configure the BGP confederation identifier and peers. Example 6-37 demonstrates the step.

Example 6-37 *Define BGP Confederation Identifier and Peers*

```
PE1-AS1(config)#router bgp 101
PE1-AS1(config-router)# bgp confederation identifier 1
PE1-AS1(config-router)# bgp confederation peers 100 102
PE2-AS1(config)#router bgp 102
PE2-AS1(config-router)# bgp confederation identifier 1
PE2-AS1(config-router)#bgp confederation peers 100 101
```

Step 2 **Define BGP neighbors**—In this step, the remote BGP AS for the peer group is defined. Example 6-38 shows the relevant steps.

Example 6-38 *Define BGP Neighbors*

```
PE1-AS1(config-router)# neighbor 10.10.10.102 remote-as 102
PE1-AS1(config-router)# neighbor 10.10.10.102 ebgp-multihop 2
PE1-AS1(config-router)# neighbor 10.10.10.102 update-source Loopback0
PE1-AS1(config-router)# neighbor 10.10.10.200 remote-as 100
PE1-AS1(config-router)# neighbor 10.10.10.200 ebgp-multihop 2
PE1-AS1(config-router)# neighbor 10.10.10.200 update-source Loopback0
PE2-AS1(config-router)# neighbor 10.10.10.101 remote-as 101
PE2-AS1(config-router)# neighbor 10.10.10.101 ebgp-multihop 2
PE2-AS1(config-router)# neighbor 10.10.10.101 update-source Loopback0
PE2-AS1(config-router)# neighbor 10.10.10.200 remote-as 100
PE2-AS1(config-router)# neighbor 10.10.10.200 ebgp-multihop 2
PE2-AS1(config-router)# neighbor 10.10.10.200 update-source Loopback0
```

Step 3 **Activate the BGP neighbors for VPNv4 exchange**—In this step, activate the BGP neighbors to exchange VPNv4 prefixes. Example 6-39 demonstrates this configuration step.

Example 6-39 *Activate the BGP Neighbors for VPNv4 Exchange*

```
PE1-AS1(config-router)# address-family vpnv4
PE1-AS1(config-router-af)# neighbor 10.10.10.102 activate
PE1-AS1(config-router-af)# neighbor 10.10.10.102 next-hop-self
PE1-AS1(config-router-af)# neighbor 10.10.10.200 activate
PE1-AS1(config-router-af)# neighbor 10.10.10.200 next-hop-self
PE2-AS1(config-router)# address-family vpnv4
PE2-AS1(config-router-af)# neighbor 10.10.10.101 activate
PE2-AS1(config-router-af)# neighbor 10.10.10.101 next-hop-self
PE2-AS1(config-router-af)# neighbor 10.10.10.200 activate
PE2-AS1(config-router-af)# neighbor 10.10.10.200 next-hop-self
```

To ensure that the router sends and receives only VPNv4 prefixes, use the configuration shown in Example 6-40 in BGP router configuration mode.

Example 6-40 *Ensuring That the Router Sends and Receives Only VPNv4 Prefixes*

```
PE1-AS1(config)#router bgp 101
PE1-AS1(config-router)# no bgp default ipv4-unicast
PE1-AS1(config-router)# no address-family ipv4
```

Final BGP Confederation Configuration on PE1-AS1, P1-AS1, and PE2-AS1

Example 6-41 shows the relevant configuration on PE1-AS1, P1-AS1, and PE2-AS1.

Example 6-41 *PE1-AS1, P1-AS1, and PE2-AS1 Configuration*

```
hostname PE1-AS1
!Refer to examples on VRF, interface, and OSPF configuration
!
router bgp 101
 no bgp default ipv4-unicast
 bgp log-neighbor-changes
 bgp confederation identifier 1
 bgp confederation peers 100 102
 neighbor 10.10.10.102 remote-as 102
 neighbor 10.10.10.102 ebgp-multihop 2
 neighbor 10.10.10.102 update-source Loopback0
 neighbor 10.10.10.200 remote-as 100
 neighbor 10.10.10.200 ebgp-multihop 2
 neighbor 10.10.10.200 update-source Loopback0
 !
 address-family vpnv4
 neighbor 10.10.10.102 activate
 neighbor 10.10.10.102 send-community extended
 neighbor 10.10.10.102 next-hop-self
 neighbor 10.10.10.200 activate
 neighbor 10.10.10.200 send-community extended
 neighbor 10.10.10.200 next-hop-self
 exit-address-family
 !
 address-family ipv4 vrf Cust_B
 neighbor 192.168.1.2 remote-as 65001
 neighbor 192.168.1.2 activate
 neighbor 192.168.1.2 as-override
 no auto-summary
 no synchronization
 exit-address-family
 !
 address-family ipv4 vrf Cust_A
 neighbor 172.16.1.2 remote-as 65001
 neighbor 172.16.1.2 activate
 no auto-summary
 no synchronization
 exit-address-family

hostname P1-AS1
!Refer to examples on VRF, interface, and OSPF configuration>
```

continues

Example 6-41 *PE1-AS1, P1-AS1, and PE2-AS1 Configuration (Continued)*

```
!
router bgp 100
 no bgp default ipv4-unicast
 bgp log-neighbor-changes
 bgp confederation identifier 1
 bgp confederation peers 101 102
 neighbor 10.10.10.101 remote-as 101
 neighbor 10.10.10.101 ebgp-multihop 2
 neighbor 10.10.10.101 update-source Loopback0
 neighbor 10.10.10.102 remote-as 102
 neighbor 10.10.10.102 ebgp-multihop 2
 neighbor 10.10.10.102 update-source Loopback0
 !
 address-family vpnv4
 neighbor 10.10.10.101 activate
 neighbor 10.10.10.101 send-community extended
 neighbor 10.10.10.101 next-hop-self
 neighbor 10.10.10.102 activate
 neighbor 10.10.10.102 send-community extended
 neighbor 10.10.10.102 next-hop-self
 exit-address-family
```

```
hostname PE2-AS1
!Refer to examples on VRF, interface, and OSPF configuration>
!
router bgp 102
 no bgp default ipv4-unicast
 bgp log-neighbor-changes
 bgp confederation identifier 1
 bgp confederation peers 100 101
 neighbor 10.10.10.101 remote-as 101
 neighbor 10.10.10.101 ebgp-multihop 2
 neighbor 10.10.10.101 update-source Loopback0
 neighbor 10.10.10.200 remote-as 100
 neighbor 10.10.10.200 ebgp-multihop 2
 neighbor 10.10.10.200 update-source Loopback0
 !
 address-family vpnv4
 neighbor 10.10.10.101 activate
 neighbor 10.10.10.101 send-community extended
 neighbor 10.10.10.101 next-hop-self
 neighbor 10.10.10.200 activate
 neighbor 10.10.10.200 send-community extended
 neighbor 10.10.10.200 next-hop-self
 exit-address-family
 !
 address-family ipv4 vrf Cust_B
 neighbor 192.168.2.2 remote-as 65001
 neighbor 192.168.2.2 activate
 neighbor 192.168.2.2 as-override
 no auto-summary
 no synchronization
```

Example 6-41 *PE1-AS1, P1-AS1, and PE2-AS1 Configuration (Continued)*

```
exit-address-family
!
address-family ipv4 vrf Cust_A
neighbor 172.16.2.2 remote-as 65002
neighbor 172.16.2.2 activate
no auto-summary
no synchronization
exit-address-family
```

Verifying BGP Confederations

The steps to verify BGP confederations are

Step 1   **Verify BGP neighbors**—Example 6-42 shows that PE1-AS1 has
established a BGP neighbor relationship with PE2-AS1 in AS 102 and
P1-AS1 in AS 100.

Example 6-42 *Verify BGP Neighbor Between BGP Confederations*

```
PE1-AS1#show ip bgp vpnv4 all summary
BGP router identifier 10.10.10.101, local AS number 101
BGP table version is 21, main routing table version 21
4 network entries using 532 bytes of memory
4 path entries using 272 bytes of memory
6/4 BGP path/bestpath attribute entries using 648 bytes of memory
3 BGP AS-PATH entries using 72 bytes of memory
2 BGP extended community entries using 48 bytes of memory
0 BGP route-map cache entries using 0 bytes of memory
0 BGP filter-list cache entries using 0 bytes of memory
BGP using 1572 total bytes of memory
BGP activity 4/0 prefixes, 8/4 paths, scan interval 15 secs

Neighbor        V    AS MsgRcvd MsgSent   TblVer  InQ OutQ Up/Down   State/PfxRcd
10.10.10.102    4   102      34      34       19    0    0 00:00:25          2
10.10.10.200    4   100      27      46       19    0    0 00:00:47          0
172.16.1.2      4 65001      22      25       17    0    0 00:17:04          1
192.168.1.2     4 65001      22      25       17    0    0 00:17:03          1
```

Step 2   **Verify the BGP VPNv4 routing table on PE routers**—Check the BGP
VPNv4 routing table to see if routes are received as expected. Example 6-43
shows that PE1-AS1 and PE2-AS1 receive the routes as expected.

Example 6-43 *Verify BGP VPNv4 on PE Routers*

```
PE1-AS1#show ip bgp vpnv4 all
BGP table version is 9, local router ID is 10.10.10.101
Status codes: s suppressed, d damped, h history, * valid, > best, i - internal,
              r RIB-failure, S Stale
Origin codes: i - IGP, e - EGP, ? - incomplete
```

continues

Example 6-43 *Verify BGP VPNv4 on PE Routers (Continued)*

```
     Network          Next Hop           Metric LocPrf Weight Path
Route Distinguisher: 1:100 (default for vrf Cust_A)
*> 172.16.10.0/24    172.16.1.2                 0            0 65001 i
*> 172.16.20.0/24    10.10.10.102               0    100     0 (102) 65002 i
Route Distinguisher: 1:200 (default for vrf Cust_B)
*> 192.168.10.0      192.168.1.2                0            0 65001 i
*> 192.168.20.0      10.10.10.102               0    100     0 (102) 65001 i
```

```
PE2-AS1#show ip bgp vpnv4 all
BGP table version is 9, local router ID is 10.10.10.102
Status codes: s suppressed, d damped, h history, * valid, > best, i - internal,
              r RIB-failure, S Stale
Origin codes: i - IGP, e - EGP, ? - incomplete

     Network          Next Hop           Metric LocPrf Weight Path
Route Distinguisher: 1:100 (default for vrf Cust_A)
*> 172.16.10.0/24    10.10.10.101               0    100     0 (101) 65001 i
*> 172.16.20.0/24    172.16.2.2                 0            0 65002 i
Route Distinguisher: 1:200 (default for vrf Cust_B)
*> 192.168.10.0      10.10.10.101               0    100     0 (101) 65001 i
*> 192.168.20.0      192.168.2.2                0            0 65001 i
```

Step 3   **Verify end-to-end connectivity via ping**—Verify end-to-end connectivity between the Customer A sites and the Customer B sites. Example 6-44 shows the result of the ping.

Example 6-44 *Verify End-to-End Connectivity via Ping*

```
CE1-A#ping 172.16.20.1 source 172.16.10.1
Type escape sequence to abort.
Sending 5, 100-byte ICMP Echos to 172.16.20.1, timeout is 2 seconds:
Packet sent with a source address of 172.16.10.1
!!!!!
Success rate is 100 percent (5/5), round-trip min/avg/max = 80/80/84 ms
```

```
CE1-B#ping 192.168.20.1 source 192.168.10.1

Type escape sequence to abort.
Sending 5, 100-byte ICMP Echos to 192.168.20.1, timeout is 2 seconds:
Packet sent with a source address of 192.168.10.1
!!!!!
Success rate is 100 percent (5/5), round-trip min/avg/max = 80/80/80 ms
```

Case Study—Hub and Spoke MPLS VPN Network Using BGP PE-CE Routing for Sites Using Unique AS Numbers

Figure 6-22 shows an MPLS VPN network implementing BGP PE-CE routing in a hub and spoke environment.

Figure 6-22 *Hub and Spoke-Based MPLS VPN Network*

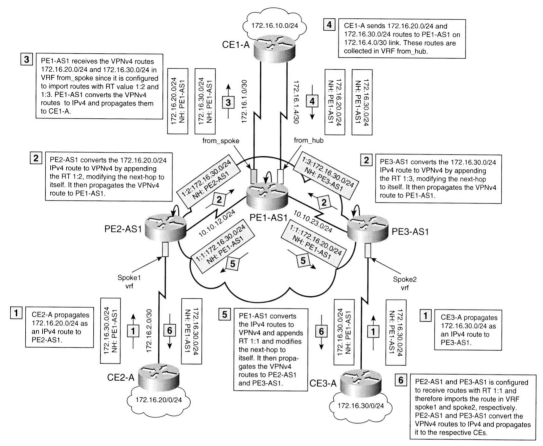

CE1-A, CE2-A, and CE3-A are CE devices. CE1-A is the hub CE for the Customer A network and is connected to PE1-AS1, which is the hub PE router for the Customer A network. CE2-A and CE3-A are spoke sites and are connected to PE2-AS1 and PE3-AS1. As shown in Figure 6-22, the PE-CE link between PE1-AS1 and CE1-A has two links. One link is configured to forward routing information for VRF from_spoke and another link for VRF from_hub. VRF from_spoke on PE1-AS1 is configured to receive routes from spoke sites CE2-A and CE3-A. VRF from_hub receives routes from CE1-A and sends that out to remote sites. The sequence of steps that takes place in the hub and spoke environment is shown in Figure 6-22.

Base MPLS VPN Configuration

Example 6-45 shows the base MPLS configuration.

Example 6-45 *Base MPLS VPN Configuration for the Provider Core*

```
hostname PE1-AS1
!
ip cef
!
mpls ldp router-id Loopback0
!
interface Loopback0
 ip address 10.10.10.101 255.255.255.255
!
interface Serial0/0
 ip address 10.10.10.1 255.255.255.252
 mpls ip
!
interface Serial1/0
 ip address 10.10.10.5 255.255.255.252
 mpls ip
!
router ospf 1
 log-adjacency-changes
 network 10.0.0.0 0.255.255.255 area 0
!
router bgp 1
 no synchronization
 bgp log-neighbor-changes
 neighbor 10.10.10.102 remote-as 1
 neighbor 10.10.10.102 update-source Loopback0
 neighbor 10.10.10.103 remote-as 1
 neighbor 10.10.10.103 update-source Loopback0
 no auto-summary
 !
 address-family vpnv4
 neighbor 10.10.10.102 activate
 neighbor 10.10.10.102 send-community extended
 neighbor 10.10.10.103 activate
 neighbor 10.10.10.103 send-community extended
 exit-address-family
```
```
hostname PE2-AS1
!
ip cef
!
mpls ldp router-id Loopback0
!
interface Loopback0
 ip address 10.10.10.102 255.255.255.255
!
interface Serial0/0
 ip address 10.10.10.2 255.255.255.252
 mpls ip
!
router ospf 1
 log-adjacency-changes
 network 10.0.0.0 0.255.255.255 area 0
```

Example 6-45 *Base MPLS VPN Configuration for the Provider Core (Continued)*

```
!
router bgp 1
 no synchronization
 bgp log-neighbor-changes
 neighbor 10.10.10.101 remote-as 1
 neighbor 10.10.10.101 update-source Loopback0
no auto-summary
!
 address-family vpnv4
 neighbor 10.10.10.101 activate
 neighbor 10.10.10.101 send-community extended
 exit-address-family
```
```
hostname PE3-AS1
!
ip cef
!
mpls ldp router-id Loopback0
!
interface Loopback0
 ip address 10.10.10.103 255.255.255.255
!
interface Serial0/0
 ip address 10.10.10.6 255.255.255.252
 mpls ip
!
router ospf 1
 log-adjacency-changes
 network 10.0.0.0 0.255.255.255 area 0
!
router bgp 1
 no synchronization
 bgp log-neighbor-changes
 neighbor 10.10.10.101 remote-as 1
 neighbor 10.10.10.101 update-source Loopback0
 no auto-summary
 !
 address-family vpnv4
 neighbor 10.10.10.101 activate
 neighbor 10.10.10.101 send-community extended
 exit-address-family
```

Hub and Spoke MPLS VPN Configuration for Sites Using Unique AS Numbers

Figure 6-23 shows the relevant configuration to implement hub and spoke MPLS VPN for sites using unique AS numbers.

Figure 6-23 *Hub and Spoke MPLS VPN Configuration for Sites Using Unique AS Numbers*

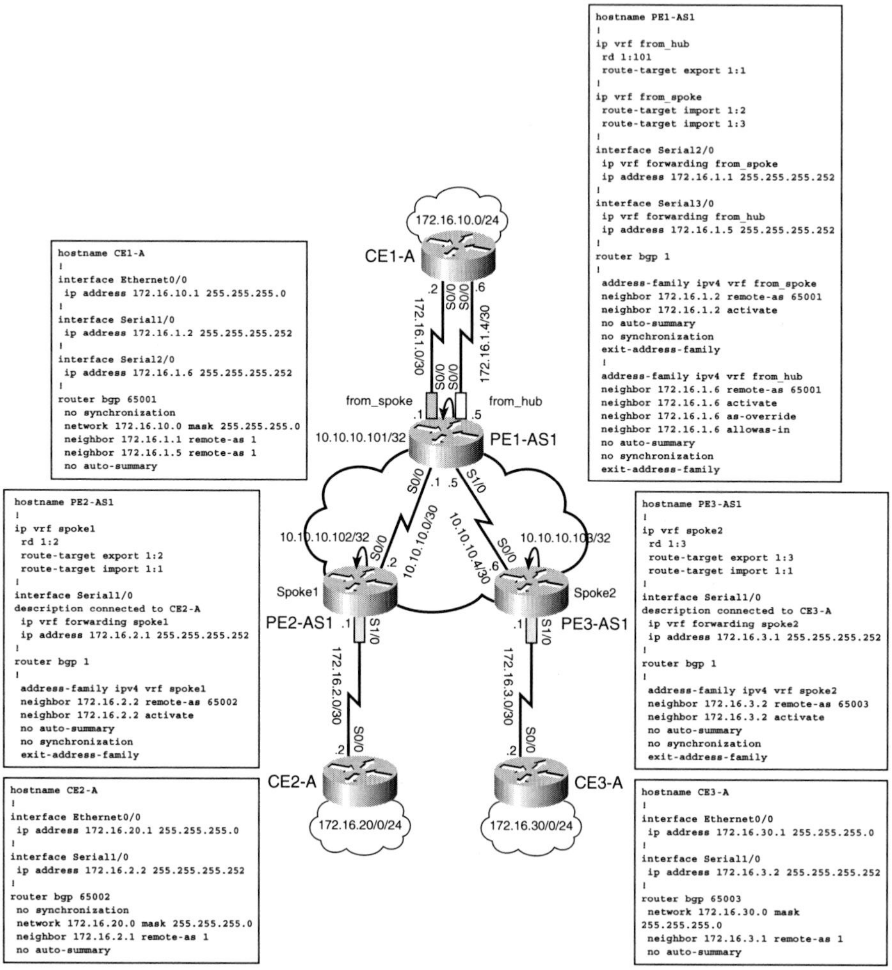
hostname PE1-AS1
!
ip vrf from_hub
 rd 1:101
 route-target export 1:1
!
ip vrf from_spoke
 route-target import 1:2
 route-target import 1:3
!
interface Serial2/0
 ip vrf forwarding from_spoke
 ip address 172.16.1.1 255.255.255.252
!
interface Serial3/0
 ip vrf forwarding from_hub
 ip address 172.16.1.5 255.255.255.252
!
router bgp 1
!
 address-family ipv4 vrf from_spoke
 neighbor 172.16.1.2 remote-as 65001
 neighbor 172.16.1.2 activate
 no auto-summary
 no synchronization
 exit-address-family
 !
 address-family ipv4 vrf from_hub
 neighbor 172.16.1.6 remote-as 65001
 neighbor 172.16.1.6 activate
 neighbor 172.16.1.6 as-override
 neighbor 172.16.1.6 allowas-in
 no auto-summary
 no synchronization
 exit-address-family
hostname CE1-A
!
interface Ethernet0/0
 ip address 172.16.10.1 255.255.255.0
!
interface Serial1/0
 ip address 172.16.1.2 255.255.255.252
!
interface Serial2/0
 ip address 172.16.1.6 255.255.255.252
!
router bgp 65001
 no synchronization
 network 172.16.10.0 mask 255.255.255.0
 neighbor 172.16.1.1 remote-as 1
 neighbor 172.16.1.5 remote-as 1
 no auto-summary
172.16.10.0/24
CE1-A
.2
.6
S0/0
S0/0
172.16.1.0/30
172.16.1.4/30
S0/0
S0/0
from_spoke
from_hub
.1
.5
10.10.10.101/32
PE1-AS1
S0/0
S1/0
.1
.5
10.10.10.102/32
10.10.10.103/32
10.10.10.0/30
10.10.10.4/30
S0/0
S0/0
.2
.6
Spoke1
Spoke2
PE2-AS1
PE3-AS1
.1
.1
S1/0
S1/0
172.16.2.0/30
172.16.3.0/30
S0/0
S0/0
.2
.2
CE2-A
CE3-A
172.16.20/0/24
172.16.30/0/24
hostname PE2-AS1
!
ip vrf spoke1
 rd 1:2
 route-target export 1:2
 route-target import 1:1
!
interface Serial1/0
description connected to CE2-A
 ip vrf forwarding spoke1
 ip address 172.16.2.1 255.255.255.252
!
router bgp 1
!
 address-family ipv4 vrf spoke1
 neighbor 172.16.2.2 remote-as 65002
 neighbor 172.16.2.2 activate
 no auto-summary
 no synchronization
 exit-address-family
hostname CE2-A
!
interface Ethernet0/0
 ip address 172.16.20.1 255.255.255.0
!
interface Serial1/0
 ip address 172.16.2.2 255.255.255.252
!
router bgp 65002
 no synchronization
 network 172.16.20.0 mask 255.255.255.0
 neighbor 172.16.2.1 remote-as 1
 no auto-summary
hostname PE3-AS1
!
ip vrf spoke2
 rd 1:3
 route-target export 1:3
 route-target import 1:1
!
interface Serial1/0
description connected to CE3-A
 ip vrf forwarding spoke2
 ip address 172.16.3.1 255.255.255.252
!
router bgp 1
!
 address-family ipv4 vrf spoke2
 neighbor 172.16.3.2 remote-as 65003
 neighbor 172.16.3.2 activate
 no auto-summary
 no synchronization
 exit-address-family
hostname CE3-A
!
interface Ethernet0/0
 ip address 172.16.30.1 255.255.255.0
!
interface Serial1/0
 ip address 172.16.3.2 255.255.255.252
!
router bgp 65003
 network 172.16.30.0 mask
255.255.255.0
 neighbor 172.16.3.1 remote-as 1
 no auto-summary

Verifying MPLS VPN Hub and Spoke Routing for Sites Using Unique AS Numbers

The steps to verify MPLS VPN hub and spoke routing are

Step 1 **Verify routing on hub PE and spoke PE**—Example 6-46 shows that VRF from_spoke on PE1-AS1 has received routes from spoke site Routers CE2-A and CE3-A via the MP-BGP session. VRF from_hub shows the routes received from CE1-A (hub CE). Similarly, PE2-AS1 and PE3-AS1 also show that routes are received by each of the VRFs configured on them.

Example 6-46 *Verify Routing on Hub PE and Spoke PE Routers*

```
PE1-AS1#show ip route vrf from_spoke
<truncated for brevity>
     172.16.0.0/16 is variably subnetted, 4 subnets, 2 masks
B       172.16.30.0/24 [200/0] via 10.10.10.103, 00:24:08
B       172.16.20.0/24 [200/0] via 10.10.10.102, 00:25:08
B       172.16.10.0/24 [20/0] via 172.16.1.2, 00:25:23
C       172.16.1.0/30 is directly connected, Serial2/0
```

```
PE1-AS1#show ip route vrf from_hub
<truncated for brevity>
     172.16.0.0/16 is variably subnetted, 4 subnets, 2 masks
B       172.16.30.0/24 [20/0] via 172.16.1.6, 00:23:58
B       172.16.20.0/24 [20/0] via 172.16.1.6, 00:24:57
B       172.16.10.0/24 [20/0] via 172.16.1.6, 00:27:13
C       172.16.1.4/30 is directly connected, Serial3/0
```

```
PE2-AS1#show ip route vrf spoke1
<truncated for brevity>
     172.16.0.0/16 is variably subnetted, 4 subnets, 2 masks
B       172.16.30.0/24 [200/0] via 10.10.10.101, 00:25:42
B       172.16.20.0/24 [20/0] via 172.16.2.2, 00:26:42
B       172.16.10.0/24 [200/0] via 10.10.10.101, 00:27:27
C       172.16.2.0/30 is directly connected, Serial1/0
```

```
PE3-AS1#show ip route vrf spoke2
<truncated for brevity>
     172.16.0.0/16 is variably subnetted, 4 subnets, 2 masks
B       172.16.30.0/24 [20/0] via 172.16.3.2, 00:34:01
B       172.16.20.0/24 [200/0] via 10.10.10.101, 00:35:02
B       172.16.10.0/24 [200/0] via 10.10.10.101, 00:34:47
C       172.16.3.0/30 is directly connected, Serial1/0
```

Step 2   **Verify routing on CE routers**—Example 6-47 shows CE routers have
received the relevant BGP routes.

Example 6-47 *Verify Routing on CE Routers*

```
CE1-A#show ip route bgp
     172.16.0.0/16 is variably subnetted, 5 subnets, 2 masks
B       172.16.30.0/24 [20/0] via 172.16.1.1, 00:29:54
B       172.16.20.0/24 [20/0] via 172.16.1.1, 00:30:56
```

```
CE1-A#show ip bgp
<truncated for brevity>
   Network          Next Hop          Metric LocPrf Weight Path
*> 172.16.10.0/24   0.0.0.0              0         32768 i
*> 172.16.20.0/24   172.16.1.1                         0 1 65002 i
*> 172.16.30.0/24   172.16.1.1                         0 1 65003 i
```

```
CE2-A#show ip route bgp
     172.16.0.0/16 is variably subnetted, 4 subnets, 2 masks
B       172.16.30.0/24 [20/0] via 172.16.2.1, 00:29:51
B       172.16.10.0/24 [20/0] via 172.16.2.1, 00:31:52
```

```
CE2-A#show ip bgp
<truncated for brevity>
   Network          Next Hop          Metric LocPrf Weight Path
*> 172.16.10.0/24   172.16.2.1                         0 1 65001 i
*> 172.16.20.0/24   0.0.0.0              0         32768 i
```

continues

Example 6-47 *Verify Routing on CE Routers (Continued)*

```
 *> 172.16.30.0/24   172.16.2.1                            0 1 65001 1 65003 i
```

```
CE3-A#show ip route bgp
     172.16.0.0/16 is variably subnetted, 4 subnets, 2 masks
B       172.16.20.0/24 [20/0] via 172.16.3.1, 00:31:17
B       172.16.10.0/24 [20/0] via 172.16.3.1, 00:30:46
```

```
CE3-A#show ip bgp
<truncated for brevity>
   Network          Next Hop          Metric LocPrf Weight Path
 *> 172.16.10.0/24   172.16.3.1                           0 1 65001 i
 *> 172.16.20.0/24   172.16.3.1                           0 1 65001 1 65002 i
 *> 172.16.30.0/24   0.0.0.0                0            32768 i
```

Step 3   **Verify connectivity between CE routers**—Example 6-48 shows CE2-A
         and CE3-A have access to each other's networks and the 172.16.10.0
         network located on CE1-A.

Example 6-48 *Verify Connectivity Between CE Routers*

```
CE2-A#ping 172.16.10.1 source 172.16.20.1
Type escape sequence to abort.
Sending 5, 100-byte ICMP Echos to 172.16.10.1, timeout is 2 seconds:
Packet sent with a source address of 172.16.20.1
!!!!!
Success rate is 100 percent (5/5), round-trip min/avg/max = 60/61/68 ms
```

```
CE2-A#ping 172.16.30.1 source 172.16.20.1
Type escape sequence to abort.
Sending 5, 100-byte ICMP Echos to 172.16.30.1, timeout is 2 seconds:
Packet sent with a source address of 172.16.20.1
!!!!!
Success rate is 100 percent (5/5), round-trip min/avg/max = 116/119/120 ms
```

```
CE3-A#ping 172.16.20.1 source 172.16.30.1
Type escape sequence to abort.
Sending 5, 100-byte ICMP Echos to 172.16.20.1, timeout is 2 seconds:
Packet sent with a source address of 172.16.30.1
!!!!!
Success rate is 100 percent (5/5), round-trip min/avg/max = 120/120/120 ms
```

```
CE3-A#ping 172.16.10.1 source 172.16.30.1
Type escape sequence to abort.
Sending 5, 100-byte ICMP Echos to 172.16.10.1, timeout is 2 seconds:
Packet sent with a source address of 172.16.30.1
!!!!!
Success rate is 100 percent (5/5), round-trip min/avg/max = 48/57/60 ms
```

Case Study—Hub and Spoke MPLS VPN Network with Sites Using Same AS Numbers

Figure 6-24 shows the relevant configuration for a similar MPLS VPN network as shown
in the previous case study except that spoke sites now use the same BGP AS as configured
on CE1-A (AS 65001). In this case study, because sites are using the same BGP AS number,
the **neighbor as-override** command is used.

Figure 6-24 *Hub and Spoke MPLS VPN Network with Sites Using Same AS Numbers*

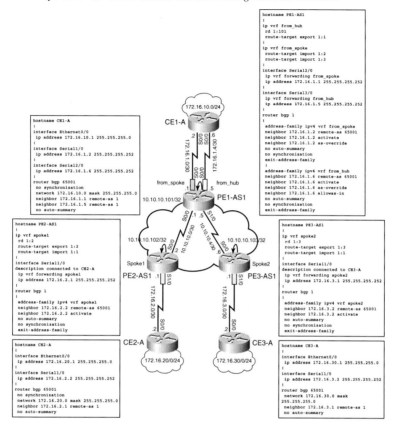

Verifying MPLS VPN Hub and Spoke Routing for Spoke Sites Using Same AS Numbers

The steps to verify MPLS VPN hub and spoke routing for spoke sites using the same AS numbers are

Step 1   **Verify routing on CE routers**—Example 6-49 shows CE routers have received the relevant BGP routes.

Example 6-49 *Verify Routing on CE Routers*

```
CE1-A#show ip route bgp
      172.16.0.0/16 is variably subnetted, 5 subnets, 2 masks
B        172.16.30.0/24 [20/0] via 172.16.1.1, 00:08:42
B        172.16.20.0/24 [20/0] via 172.16.1.1, 00:08:42
CE1-A#show ip bgp
<truncated for brevity>
   Network          Next Hop            Metric LocPrf Weight Path
*> 172.16.10.0/24   0.0.0.0                  0            32768 i
```

continues

Example 6-49 *Verify Routing on CE Routers (Continued)*

```
*> 172.16.20.0/24    172.16.1.1                              0 1 1 i
*> 172.16.30.0/24    172.16.1.1                              0 1 1 i
```
```
CE2-A#show ip route bgp
     172.16.0.0/16 is variably subnetted, 4 subnets, 2 masks
B       172.16.30.0/24 [20/0] via 172.16.2.1, 00:08:39
B       172.16.10.0/24 [20/0] via 172.16.2.1, 00:12:02
```
```
CE2-A#show ip bgp
   Network          Next Hop          Metric LocPrf Weight Path
*> 172.16.10.0/24   172.16.2.1                          0 1 1 i
*> 172.16.20.0/24   0.0.0.0                0         32768 i
*> 172.16.30.0/24   172.16.2.1                          0 1 1 1 1 i
```
```
CE3-A#sh ip route bgp
     172.16.0.0/16 is variably subnetted, 4 subnets, 2 masks
B       172.16.20.0/24 [20/0] via 172.16.3.1, 00:09:23
B       172.16.10.0/24 [20/0] via 172.16.3.1, 00:11:59
```
```
CE3-A#show ip bgp
<truncated for brevity>
   Network          Next Hop          Metric LocPrf Weight Path
*> 172.16.10.0/24   172.16.3.1                          0 1 1 i
*> 172.16.20.0/24   172.16.3.1                          0 1 1 1 1 i
*> 172.16.30.0/24   0.0.0.0                0         32768 i
```

Step 2   **Verify connectivity between CE routers**—Example 6-50 shows CE2-A
and CE3-A have access to each other's networks and the 172.16.10.0
network located on CE1-A.

Example 6-50 *Verify Connectivity Between CE Routers*

```
CE2-A#ping 172.16.30.1 source 172.16.20.1
Type escape sequence to abort.
Sending 5, 100-byte ICMP Echos to 172.16.30.1, timeout is 2 seconds:
Packet sent with a source address of 172.16.20.1
!!!!!
Success rate is 100 percent (5/5), round-trip min/avg/max = 120/120/124 ms
```
```
CE2-A#ping 172.16.10.1 source 172.16.20.1
Type escape sequence to abort.
Sending 5, 100-byte ICMP Echos to 172.16.10.1, timeout is 2 seconds:
Packet sent with a source address of 172.16.20.1
!!!!!
Success rate is 100 percent (5/5), round-trip min/avg/max = 60/61/68 ms
```
```
CE3-A#ping 172.16.20.1 source 172.16.30.1
Type escape sequence to abort.
Sending 5, 100-byte ICMP Echos to 172.16.20.1, timeout is 2 seconds:
Packet sent with a source address of 172.16.30.1
!!!!!
Success rate is 100 percent (5/5), round-trip min/avg/max = 116/119/120 ms
```
```
CE3-A#ping 172.16.10.1 source 172.16.30.1
Type escape sequence to abort.
Sending 5, 100-byte ICMP Echos to 172.16.10.1, timeout is 2 seconds:
Packet sent with a source address of 172.16.30.1
!!!!!
Success rate is 100 percent (5/5), round-trip min/avg/max = 60/62/72 ms
```

Command Reference

Command	Description
Router(config-router-af)#**neighbor** *ip-address* **as-override**	Configures a PE router to override the AS number of a site with the AS number of a provider.
Router(config-router-af)#**neighbor allowas-in** *number*	Configures a PE router to allow readvertisement of all prefixes containing duplicate AS numbers.
Router(config-router)#**neighbor** *peer-group-name* **peer-group**	Creates a BGP or multiprotocol BGP peer group.
Router(config-router)#**neighbor** {*ip-address* | *peer-group-name*} **route-map** *map-name* {**in** | **out**}	Applies a route-map to incoming or outgoing routes.
Router(config-router-af)#**neighbor** *ip-address* **route-reflector-client**	To configure the router as a BGP RR and configure the specified neighbor as its client, use the **neighbor route-reflector-client** command in address-family or router configuration mode.
Router(config-router)#**neighbor** {*ip-address* | *peer-group-name*} **send-community** [**both** | **standard** | **extended**]	Specifies that a community's attribute should be sent to a BGP neighbor.
Router(config-router)#**neighbor** {*ip-address* | *ipv6-address* | peer-group-name} **update-source** *interface-type interface-number*	Allows BGP sessions to use any operational interface for TCP connections.
Router(config-router)#**no bgp default ipv4-unicast**	Disables the IPv4 unicast address-family on all neighbors.
Router(config-router)#**bgp rr-group** {*community-list-number*}	Creates a RR group and enables automatic inbound filtering for VPNv4 updates based on the allowed route target extended communities.
Router(config)#**ip bgp-community new-format**	Displays BGP communities in the format AA:NN.
Router (config) #**ip community-list** {*standard-list-number* | *expanded-list-number* [*regular-expression*] | {**standard** | **expanded**} *community-list-name*} {**permit** | **deny**} {*community-number* | *regular-expression*}	Creates a numbered or named community list for BGP and controls access to it.
Router(config)#**ip extcommunity-list** *standard-list-number expanded-list-number* {**permit** | **deny**} [*regular-expression*] [**rt** | **soo** *extended-community-value*]	Creates an extended community access-list and controls access to it.
Router(config-map)#**set community** {*community-number* [**additive**] | **none**}	Sets the BGP communities attribute.
Router(config-map)#**set extcommunity** {**rt** *extended-community-value* [**additive**] | **soo** *extended-community-value*}	Sets BGP extended-community attributes.

CHAPTER 7

Inter-Provider VPNs

Several requirements have resulted from the sudden growth in VPN deployments. One such requirement is that VPNs need to reside on different autonomous systems in different geographic areas or extend across multiple service providers. The MPLS Inter-AS feature plays an important role in making such a requirement as seamless as possible for the end customer. The MPLS Inter-AS feature allows an MPLS VPN to span service providers and autonomous systems.

Overview of Inter-Provider VPNs

Traditional MPLS VPN networks contain customer or client VPN sites traversing a single MPLS VPN backbone. However, in a geographically dispersed network, client VPN sites might connect to different MPLS VPN backbones. Figure 7-1 shows such a network where client sites belonging to VPN-A and VPN-B are connected to different service provider networks.

Figure 7-1 *Dispersed Client Sites Belonging to Different Providers*

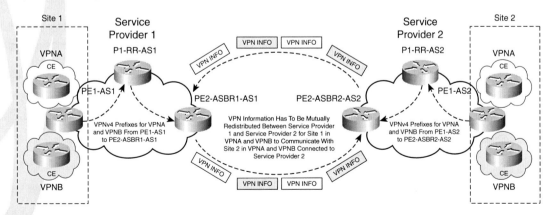

In such cases, to enable continuity of VPN services across multiple service providers, the VPN information has to be mutually redistributed. The Inter-AS or Inter-Provider VPN feature allows the VPN information to be redistributed between adjacent MPLS VPN entities so that client sites belonging to VPN-A and VPN-B that are dispersed across multiple service provider backbones can communicate with each other.

Figure 7-2 shows the MPLS VPN network in which the edge routers PE2-ASBR1-AS1 and PE2-ASBR2-AS2 serve as Autonomous System Boundary Router (ASBR) routers. The ASBR Router PE2-ASBR1-AS1 is responsible for propagating Site 1 VPN information to Site 2 and PE2-ASBR2-AS2 propagates Site 2 VPN information to Site 1.

Figure 7-2 *Inter-Provider VPN Network Using Edge Routers as ASBRs*

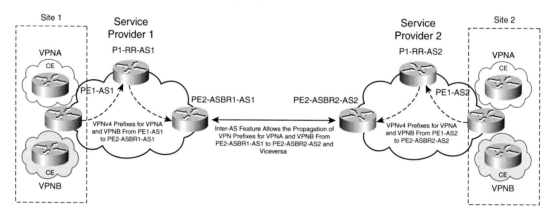

To maintain the continuity of VPN services across multiple service providers, there are four different options to distribute VPNv4 information across the ASBR routers:

- **Option 1:** Back-to-back VRF
- **Option 2:** Multiprotocol eBGP (MP-eBGP) for VPNv4
  - **Option 2a:** Using the next-hop-self method
  - **Option 2b:** Using the redistribute connected approach
  - **Option 2c:** Multi-hop MP-eBGP
- **Option 3:** Multi-hop MP-eBGP between route-reflectors (RRs)
- **Option 4:** Non-VPN transit provider

Figure 7-3 shows the various options to distribute VPNv4 information.

NOTE   Options 1, 2a, and 3 correspond to the following options mentioned in RFC 2547bis:

- VRF-to-VRF connections at the AS border routers.
- eBGP redistribution of labeled VPN-IPv4 routes from AS to neighboring AS.
- Multi-hop eBGP redistribution of labeled VPN-IPv4 routes between source and destination autonomous systems, with eBGP redistribution of labeled IPv4 routes from AS to neighboring AS.

Figure 7-3   *Inter-AS VPNv4 Distribution Options*

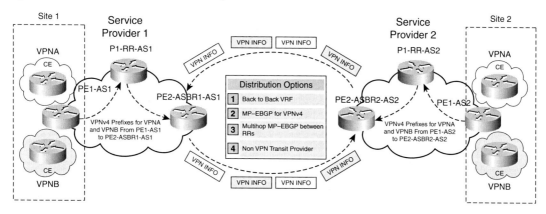

Forthcoming sections discuss each of the VPNv4 distribution options.

Option 1: Inter-Provider VPN Using Back-to-Back VRF Method

The VRF-to-VRF approach is the simplest method for allowing MPLS VPN providers to exchange VPN routing information for CE sites in different MPLS domains. In this approach, the border provider edge (PE) routers residing in different autonomous systems function as ASBRs. These ASBRs are interconnected either via a single link consisting of logical subinterfaces or via multiple physical links. VRFs are configured on the ASBRs to collect VPN client routes. Each subinterface or interface connected between the ASBRs is dedicated to a single client VRF. The single client VRF can run eBGP, RIPv2, EIGRP, OSPF, or static routing to distribute the VPN routes to its adjacent peer. The use of eBGP is, however, the most common in back-to-back VRF method because eBGP scales best to this type of application, retaining the type of the route and offering better policy, scalability, and security mechanisms. In this method, the LSP paths in adjacent MPLS VPN autonomous systems are interconnected using the IP forwarding mechanism between the AS border routers.

Figure 7-4 shows an MPLS VPN network where sites in VPN-A and VPN-B are geographically dispersed. Site 1 and Site 2 in VPN-A have CE Routers CE1-A and CE2-A, which respectively connect to PE Routers PE1-AS1 and PE1-AS2, located in Service Provider 1 and Service Provider 2. Site 1 and Site 2 in VPN-B have CE Routers CE1-B and CE2-B, which respectively connect to PE Routers PE1-AS1 and PE1-AS2 located in Service Provider 1 and Service Provider 2.

Figure 7-4 *Back-to-Back VRF Method*

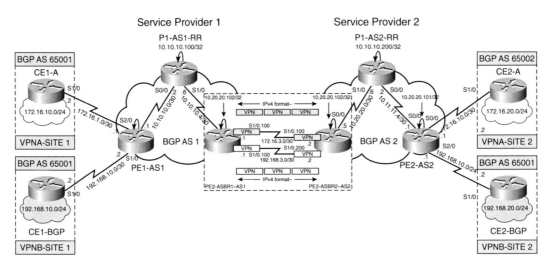

Service Provider 1 uses BGP AS 1 and Service Provider 2 uses BGP AS 2. PE1-ASBR1-AS1 and PE2-ASBR2-AS2 are ASBR routers that are connected by multiple subinterfaces. The interfaces are associated with a given VRF (Cust_A for VPN-A and Cust_B for VPN-B). Conventional routing is configured between MPLS VPN sites to distribute IPv4 routes to its peers. Therefore, the ASBR Router PE2-ASBR1-AS1 treats the other ASBR Router PE2-ASBR2-AS2 as if it was a CE router; similarly, PE2-ASBR2-AS2 also treats the PE1-ASBR1-AS1 as a CE router. This approach enhances the usability of MPLS VPN backbones; however, it also introduces greater complexity because it requires dedicated VPN links between the adjacent ASBRs. The VPN routing information that is passed between the two ASBR routers, PE2-ASBR1-AS1 and PE2-ASBR2-AS2, is in IPv4 format.

Control Plane Forwarding in Option 1

In the back-to-back VRF method, the ASBRs use the IP forwarding mechanism to interconnect the LSP path between the two different MPLS VPN entities. Figure 7-5 shows the path taken by the control packet for 172.16.10.0/24 originating from CE1-A to CE2-A.

NOTE	In this chapter, the control plane operation for VPN and LDP (IGP) label distribution is shown to occur simultaneously. This is done to provide more clarity to the entire operation and does not imply that they occur together. LDP label distribution can occur independent of the VPN label distribution.

Figure 7-5 *Control Plane Forwarding in Back-to-Back VRF Method*

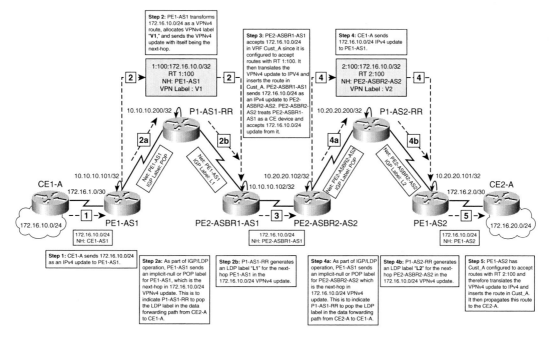

Data Forwarding in Option 1

The data forwarding path originates from the 172.16.20.0 network (assuming the source is 172.16.20.1/24) with the traffic destined to 172.16.10.0 network (assuming the destination is 172.16.10.1). The source and destination are located on two different MPLS VPN provider networks. Figure 7-6 traces the path of the data packet from the source to the destination.

Figure 7-6 *Data Forwarding in Back-to-Back VRF Method*

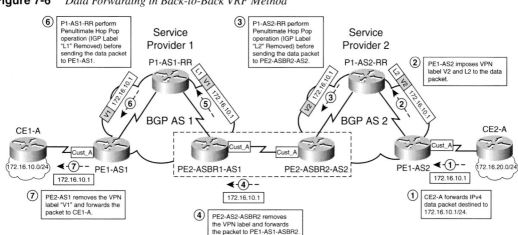

Configuring Back-to-Back VRF Method

In this chapter, the configuration steps will be shown for routers that are responsible for Inter-AS operations. The configuration for back-to-back VRF method on the ASBR routers is similar to any configuration on a PE router providing VPN services:

Step 1 **Configure VRF on the PE ASBR routers**—Configure VRF and its parameters on the PE ASBR Routers PE2-ASBR1-AS1 and PE2-ASBR2-AS2. Example 7-1 shows the configuration procedure to enable VRF Cust_A on the PE ASBR routers. Similarly, configure Cust_B VRF and associate that VRF to the second subinterface S1/0.200.

Example 7-1 *VRF Creation and Forwarding on PE ASBR Routers*

```
PE2-ASBR1-AS1(config)#ip vrf Cust_A
PE2-ASBR1-AS1(config-vrf)# rd 1:100
PE2-ASBR1-AS1(config-vrf)# route-target export 1:100
PE2-ASBR1-AS1(config-vrf)# route-target import 1:100
PE2-ASBR1-AS1(config-vrf)#interface Serial1/0.100 point-to-point
PE2-ASBR1-AS1(config-subif)# description connected to Cust_A PE2-AS
PE2-ASBR1-AS1(config-subif)# ip vrf forwarding Cust_A
PE2-ASBR1-AS1(config-subif)# ip address 172.16.3.1 255.255.255.252
PE2-ASBR1-AS1(config-subif)# frame-relay interface-dlci 100
PE2-ASBR2-AS2(config)#ip vrf Cust_A
PE2-ASBR2-AS2(config-vrf)# rd 2:100
PE2-ASBR2-AS2(config-vrf)# route-target export 2:100
PE2-ASBR2-AS2(config-vrf)# route-target import 2:100
PE2-ASBR2-AS2(config-vrf)#interface Serial1/0.100 point-to-point
PE2-ASBR2-AS2(config-subif)# description connected to Cust_A PE2-ASBR1-AS1
PE2-ASBR2-AS2(config-subif)# ip vrf forwarding Cust_A
PE2-ASBR2-AS2(config-subif)# ip address 172.16.3.2 255.255.255.252
PE2-ASBR2-AS2(config-subif)# frame-relay interface-dlci 100
```

Step 2 **Enable per VRF PE-CE routing protocol**—In this step, you enable per VRF routing protocol on ASBR routers. In this case, you will use eBGP PE-CE routing on the PE and ASBR routers, as shown in Example 7-2.

Example 7-2 *Enable per VRF PE-CE Routing Protocol*

```
PE2-ASBR1-AS1(config)#router bgp 1
PE2-ASBR1-AS1(config-router)# address-family ipv4 vrf Cust_A
PE2-ASBR1-AS1(config-router-af)# neighbor 172.16.3.2 remote-as 2
PE2-ASBR1-AS1(config-router-af)# neighbor 172.16.3.2 activate
PE2-ASBR1-AS1(config-router-af)# no auto-summary
PE2-ASBR1-AS1(config-router-af)# no synchronization
PE2-ASBR1-AS1(config-router-af)# exit-address-family
PE2-ASBR1-AS1(config-router)#address-family ipv4 vrf Cust_B
PE2-ASBR1-AS1(config-router-af)# neighbor 192.168.3.2 remote-as 2
PE2-ASBR1-AS1(config-router-af)# neighbor 192.168.3.2 activate
PE2-ASBR1-AS1(config-router-af)# no auto-summary
PE2-ASBR1-AS1(config-router-af)# no synchronization
PE2-ASBR1-AS1(config-router-af)# exit-address-family
```

Example 7-2 *Enable per VRF PE-CE Routing Protocol (Continued)*

```
PE2-ASBR2-AS2(config)# router bgp 2
PE2-ASBR2-AS2(config-router)# address-family ipv4 vrf Cust_A
PE2-ASBR2-AS2(config-router-af)# neighbor 172.16.3.1 remote-as 1
PE2-ASBR2-AS2(config-router-af)# neighbor 172.16.3.1 activate
PE2-ASBR2-AS2(config-router-af)# no auto-summary
PE2-ASBR2-AS2(config-router-af)# no synchronization
PE2-ASBR2-AS2(config-router-af)# exit-address-family
PE2-ASBR2-AS2(config-router)#address-family ipv4 vrf Cust_B
PE2-ASBR2-AS2(config-router-af)# neighbor 192.168.3.1 remote-as 1
PE2-ASBR2-AS2(config-router-af)# neighbor 192.168.3.1 activate
PE2-ASBR2-AS2(config-router-af)# no auto-summary
PE2-ASBR2-AS2(config-router-af)# no synchronization
PE2-ASBR2-AS2(config-router-af)# exit-address-family
```

CE CE1-A and CE2-A Configuration for Option 1

Example 7-3 shows the configurations on Customer A CE routers.

Example 7-3 *CE CE1-A and CE2-A Configuration*

```
hostname CE1-A
!
interface Ethernet0/0
 description Customer A Site 1 network
 ip address 172.16.10.1 255.255.255.0
 !
interface Serial1/0
 description connected to PE1-AS1
 ip address 172.16.1.2 255.255.255.252
 !
router bgp 65001
no synchronization
bgp log-neighbor-changes
network 172.16.10.0 mask 255.255.255.0
neighbor 172.16.1.1 remote-as 1
no auto-summary
```

```
hostname CE2-A
!
interface Ethernet0/0
 description Customer A Site 2 network
 ip address 172.16.20.1 255.255.255.0
 !
interface Serial1/0
 description connected to PE1-AS2
 ip address 172.16.2.2 255.255.255.252
 !
router bgp 65002
 no synchronization
 bgp log-neighbor-changes
 network 172.16.20.0 mask 255.255.255.0
 neighbor 172.16.2.1 remote-as 2
 no auto-summary
```

Example 7-4 shows the configurations on Customer B CE routers.

Example 7-4 *CE CE1-B and CE2-B Configuration*

```
hostname CE1-B
!
interface Ethernet0/0
 description Customer B Site 1 network
 ip address 192.168.10.1 255.255.255.0
 no keepalive
!
interface Serial1/0
 description connected to PE1-AS1
 ip address 192.168.1.2 255.255.255.252
!
router bgp 65001
 no synchronization
 bgp log-neighbor-changes
 network 192.168.10.0
 neighbor 192.168.1.1 remote-as 1
 no auto-summary
hostname CE2-B
!
interface Ethernet0/0
 description Customer B Site 2 network
 ip address 192.168.20.1 255.255.255.0
 no keepalive
!
interface Serial1/0
 description connected to PE1-AS2
 ip address 192.168.2.2 255.255.255.252
!
router bgp 65001
 no synchronization
 bgp log-neighbor-changes
 network 192.168.20.0
 neighbor 192.168.2.1 remote-as 2
 no auto-summary
```

Provider Router, PE, and PE ASBR Router Configurations for Option 1

Example 7-5 shows final configuration on the PE1, PE2, and P1 routers.

Example 7-5 *Provider, PE, and ASBR Router Configurations*

```
hostname PE1-AS1
!
ip cef
!
ip vrf Cust_A
 rd 1:100
 route-target export 1:100
```

Example 7-5 *Provider, PE, and ASBR Router Configurations (Continued)*

```
 route-target import 1:100
!
ip vrf Cust_B
 rd 1:101
 route-target export 1:101
 route-target import 1:101
!
mpls ldp router-id Loopback0
!
interface Loopback0
 ip address 10.10.10.101 255.255.255.255
!
interface Serial0/0
 description connected to P1-AS1
 ip address 10.10.10.1 255.255.255.252
 mpls ip
!
interface Serial1/0
 description connected to Cust_A CE1-A
 ip vrf forwarding Cust_A
 ip address 172.16.1.1 255.255.255.252
!
interface Serial2/0
 description connected to Cust_B CE1-B
 ip vrf forwarding Cust_B
 ip address 192.168.1.1 255.255.255.252
!
router ospf 1
 router-id 10.10.10.101
 network 10.0.0.0 0.255.255.255 area 0
!
router bgp 1
 no synchronization
 neighbor 10.10.10.200 remote-as 1
 neighbor 10.10.10.200 update-source Loopback0
 no auto-summary
 !
 address-family vpnv4
 neighbor 10.10.10.200 activate
 neighbor 10.10.10.200 send-community extended
 exit-address-family
 !
 address-family ipv4 vrf Cust_B
 neighbor 192.168.1.2 remote-as 65001
 neighbor 192.168.1.2 activate
 neighbor 192.168.1.2 as-override
 no auto-summary
 no synchronization
 exit-address-family
 !
 address-family ipv4 vrf Cust_A
```

continues

Example 7-5 *Provider, PE, and ASBR Router Configurations (Continued)*

```
 neighbor 172.16.1.2 remote-as 65001
 neighbor 172.16.1.2 activate
 no auto-summary
 no synchronization
 exit-address-family
hostname PE2-AS1-ASBR1
!
ip cef
!
ip vrf Cust_A
 rd 1:100
 route-target export 1:100
 route-target import 1:100
!
ip vrf Cust_B
 rd 1:101
 route-target export 1:101
 route-target import 1:101
!
mpls ldp router-id Loopback0
!
interface Loopback0
 ip address 10.10.10.102 255.255.255.255
!
interface Serial0/0
 description connected to P1-AS1
 ip address 10.10.10.5 255.255.255.252
 mpls ip
!
interface Serial1/0
 no ip address
 encapsulation frame-relay
!
interface Serial1/0.100 point-to-point
 description connected to Cust_A PE2-AS2-ASBR2
 ip vrf forwarding Cust_A
 ip address 172.16.3.1 255.255.255.252
 frame-relay interface-dlci 100
!
interface Serial1/0.200 point-to-point
 description connected to Cust_B PE2-AS2-ASBR2
 ip vrf forwarding Cust_B
 ip address 192.168.3.1 255.255.255.252
 frame-relay interface-dlci 200
!
router ospf 1
 router-id 10.10.10.102
 network 10.0.0.0 0.255.255.255 area 0
!
router bgp 1
 no synchronization
 neighbor 10.10.10.200 remote-as 1
```

Example 7-5 *Provider, PE, and ASBR Router Configurations (Continued)*

```
 neighbor 10.10.10.200 update-source Loopback0
 no auto-summary
 !
 address-family vpnv4
 neighbor 10.10.10.200 activate
 neighbor 10.10.10.200 send-community extended
 exit-address-family
 !
 address-family ipv4 vrf Cust_B
 neighbor 192.168.3.2 remote-as 2
 neighbor 192.168.3.2 activate
 no auto-summary
 no synchronization
 exit-address-family
 !
 address-family ipv4 vrf Cust_A
 neighbor 172.16.3.2 remote-as 2
 neighbor 172.16.3.2 activate
 no auto-summary
 no synchronization
 exit-address-family
hostname P1-AS1-RR
!
ip cef
!
mpls ldp router-id Loopback0
!
interface Loopback0
 ip address 10.10.10.200 255.255.255.255
!
interface Serial0/0
 description connected to PE1-AS1
 ip address 10.10.10.2 255.255.255.252
 mpls ip
!
interface Serial1/0
 description connected to PE2-AS1-ASBR1
 ip address 10.10.10.6 255.255.255.252
 mpls ip
!
router ospf 1
 router-id 10.10.10.200
 log-adjacency-changes
 network 10.0.0.0 0.255.255.255 area 0
!
router bgp 1
 no bgp default ipv4-unicast
 neighbor 10.10.10.101 remote-as 1
 neighbor 10.10.10.101 update-source Loopback0
 neighbor 10.10.10.102 remote-as 1
 neighbor 10.10.10.102 update-source Loopback0
 !
```

continues

Example 7-5 *Provider, PE, and ASBR Router Configurations (Continued)*

```
 address-family vpnv4
 neighbor 10.10.10.101 activate
 neighbor 10.10.10.101 send-community extended
 neighbor 10.10.10.101 route-reflector-client
 neighbor 10.10.10.102 activate
 neighbor 10.10.10.102 send-community extended
 neighbor 10.10.10.102 route-reflector-client
 exit-address-family
hostname P1-AS2-RR
!
ip cef
!
mpls ldp router-id Loopback0
!
interface Loopback0
 ip address 10.20.20.200 255.255.255.255
!
interface Serial0/0
 description connected to PE2-AS2-ASBR2
 ip address 10.20.20.6 255.255.255.252
 mpls ip
!
interface Serial1/0
 description connected to PE1-AS2
 ip address 10.20.20.2 255.255.255.252
 mpls ip
!
router ospf 2
 router-id 10.20.20.200
 log-adjacency-changes
 network 10.0.0.0 0.255.255.255 area 0
!
router bgp 2
 no bgp default ipv4-unicast
 neighbor 10.20.20.101 remote-as 2
 neighbor 10.20.20.101 update-source Loopback0
 neighbor 10.20.20.102 remote-as 2
 neighbor 10.20.20.102 update-source Loopback0
 !
 address-family vpnv4
 neighbor 10.20.20.101 activate
 neighbor 10.20.20.101 send-community extended
 neighbor 10.20.20.101 route-reflector-client
 neighbor 10.20.20.102 activate
 neighbor 10.20.20.102 send-community extended
 neighbor 10.20.20.102 route-reflector-client
 exit-address-family
hostname PE2-AS2-ASBR2
!
ip cef
```

Example 7-5 *Provider, PE, and ASBR Router Configurations (Continued)*

```
!
ip vrf Cust_A
 rd 2:100
 route-target export 2:100
 route-target import 2:100
!
ip vrf Cust_B
 rd 2:101
 route-target export 2:101
 route-target import 2:101
!
frame-relay switching
!
mpls ldp router-id Loopback0
!
interface Loopback0
 ip address 10.20.20.102 255.255.255.255
!
interface Serial0/0
 description connected to P1-AS2
 ip address 10.20.20.5 255.255.255.252
 mpls ip
!
interface Serial1/0
 no ip address
 encapsulation frame-relay
 frame-relay intf-type dce
!
interface Serial1/0.100 point-to-point
 description connected to Cust_A PE2-AS1-ASBR1
 ip vrf forwarding Cust_A
 ip address 172.16.3.2 255.255.255.252
 frame-relay interface-dlci 100
!
interface Serial1/0.200 point-to-point
 description connected to Cust_B PE2-AS1-ASBR1
 ip vrf forwarding Cust_B
 ip address 192.168.3.2 255.255.255.252
 frame-relay interface-dlci 200
!
router ospf 2
 router-id 10.20.20.102
 network 10.0.0.0 0.255.255.255 area 0
!
router bgp 2
 no synchronization
 neighbor 10.20.20.200 remote-as 2
 neighbor 10.20.20.200 update-source Loopback0
 no auto-summary
 !
```

continues

Example 7-5 *Provider, PE, and ASBR Router Configurations (Continued)*

```
address-family vpnv4
neighbor 10.20.20.200 activate
neighbor 10.20.20.200 send-community extended
exit-address-family
!
address-family ipv4 vrf Cust_B
neighbor 192.168.3.1 remote-as 1
neighbor 192.168.3.1 activate
no auto-summary
no synchronization
exit-address-family
!
address-family ipv4 vrf Cust_A
neighbor 172.16.3.1 remote-as 1
neighbor 172.16.3.1 activate
no auto-summary
no synchronization
exit-address-family
```

```
hostname PE1-AS2
!
ip cef
!
ip vrf Cust_A
 rd 2:100
 route-target export 2:100
 route-target import 2:100
!
ip vrf Cust_B
 rd 2:101
 route-target export 2:101
 route-target import 2:101
!
mpls ldp router-id Loopback0
!
interface Loopback0
 ip address 10.20.20.101 255.255.255.255
!
interface Serial0/0
 description connected to P1-AS2
 ip address 10.20.20.1 255.255.255.252
 mpls ip
!
interface Serial1/0
 description connected to Cust_A CE2-A
 ip vrf forwarding Cust_A
 ip address 172.16.2.1 255.255.255.252
!
interface Serial2/0
 description connected to Cust_B CE2-B
 ip vrf forwarding Cust_B
 ip address 192.168.2.1 255.255.255.252
```

Example 7-5   *Provider, PE, and ASBR Router Configurations (Continued)*

```
!
router ospf 2
 router-id 10.20.20.101
 network 10.0.0.0 0.255.255.255 area 0
!
router bgp 2
 no synchronization
 neighbor 10.20.20.200 remote-as 2
 neighbor 10.20.20.200 update-source Loopback0
 no auto-summary
 !
 address-family vpnv4
 neighbor 10.20.20.200 activate
 neighbor 10.20.20.200 send-community extended
 exit-address-family
 !
 address-family ipv4 vrf Cust_B
 neighbor 192.168.2.2 remote-as 65001
 neighbor 192.168.2.2 activate
 neighbor 192.168.2.2 as-override
 no auto-summary
 no synchronization
 exit-address-family
 !
 address-family ipv4 vrf Cust_A
 neighbor 172.16.2.2 remote-as 65002
 neighbor 172.16.2.2 activate
 no auto-summary
 no synchronization
 exit-address-family
```

Verifying Option 1

The steps to verify back-to-back VRF operation are

Step 1   **Verify control plane operation**—Figure 7-7 shows the control plane traffic traversing AS 1 and AS 2. The control plane traffic is demonstrated for the 172.16.10.0/24 update sent by CE1-A to CE2-A.

Step 2   **Verify data forwarding in back-to-back VRF method**—Figure 7-8 shows the data plane forwarding that takes place for a packet sourced from 172.16.20.1 to 172.16.10.1.

Figure 7-7 *Control Plane Forwarding in AS1 Using Back-to-Back VRF Method*

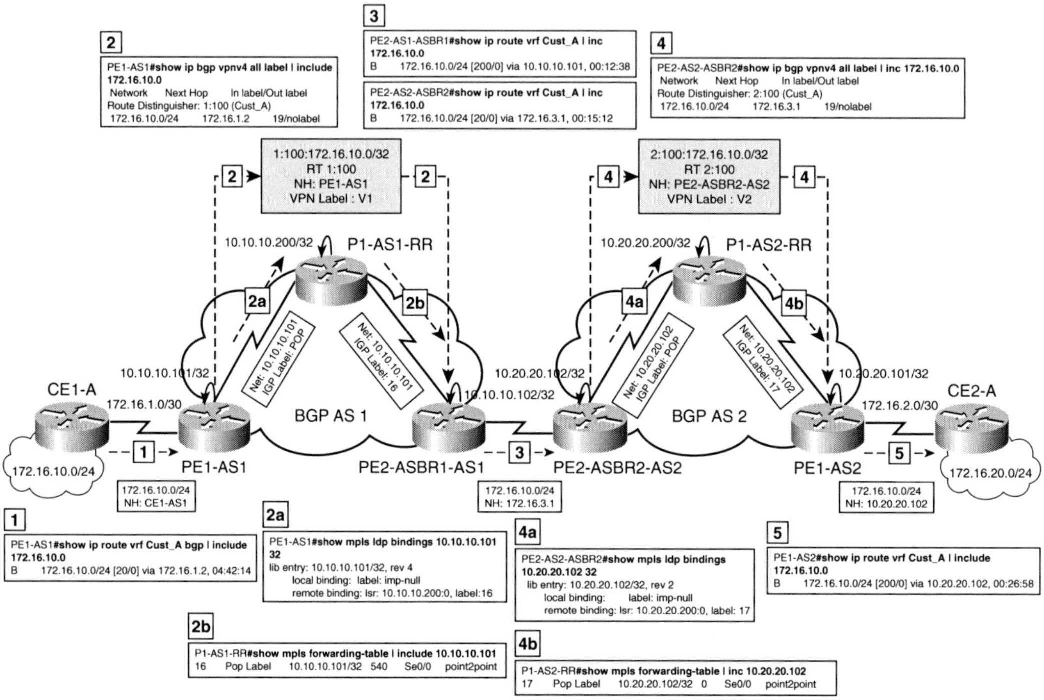

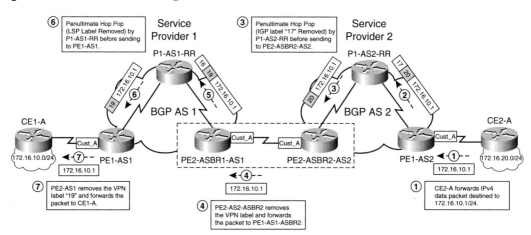

Figure 7-8 *Data Plane Forwarding in Back-to-Back VRF Method*

Step 3 **Verify end-to-end connectivity via ping**— Verify end-to-end connectivity between CE1-B and CE2-B by issuing a ping from CE1-B to network 172.16.20.1/24 on CE2-B and vice versa. Example 7-6 shows the result of the ping operation.

Example 7-6 *Verify End-to-End Connectivity*

```
CE1-A#ping 172.16.20.1 source 172.16.10.1
Type escape sequence to abort.
Sending 5, 100-byte ICMP Echos to 172.16.20.1, timeout is 2 seconds:
Packet sent with a source address of 172.16.10.1
!!!!!
Success rate is 100 percent (5/5), round-trip min/avg/max = 140/140/140 ms
CE1-B#ping 192.168.20.1 source 192.168.10.1
Type escape sequence to abort.
Sending 5, 100-byte ICMP Echos to 192.168.20.1, timeout is 2 seconds:
Packet sent with a source address of 192.168.10.1
!!!!!
Success rate is 100 percent (5/5), round-trip min/avg/max = 132/138/140 ms
```

Option 2: Inter-Provider VPNs Using ASBR-to-ASBR Approach

In the back-to-back VRF method, ASBRs use traditional IPv4 routing to integrate VPNs across two adjacent service provider networks. In the second method, the ASBRs use MP-eBGP to peer with each other to transport VPNv4 routes between autonomous systems. This is called the ASBR-to-ASBR approach, also known as MP-eBGP for VPNv4 exchange. This approach, therefore, alleviates the need to have per-VPN configuration on the ASBRs as seen in the back-to-back VRF method, and, thus, allows VPNv4 prefixes to be transported across multiple providers. However, to allow the transportation of VPNv4 prefixes, the link between the autonomous systems must support the exchange of MPLS packets because the VPNv4 updates are encapsulated in MPLS packets when they traverse an AS and so need to be encapsulated when going across (between) the autonomous systems.

To understand the concept of ASBR-to-ASBR operation, it is necessary to understand how traditional MPLS VPN forwarding takes place. In an MPLS VPN network, packet forwarding takes place only if the router specified as the BGP next hop in the incoming BGP update is the same as the router that assigned the VPN label in the MPLS VPN label stack. However, when VPNs are geographically dispersed across multiple service providers, the BGP next-hop attribute is changed when there is an eBGP session between the ASBRs. Therefore, in an ASBR-to-ASBR method, a VPN label is assigned whenever the BGP next hop is changed. The ASBR-to-ASBR approach accommodates the use of MP-eBGP between ASBRs to transport VPNv4 prefixes versus the MP-iBGP implementation in traditional VPN networks within a single AS. The only difference between MP-iBGP and MP-eBGP when transporting VPNv4 prefixes is the way the next-hop attribute is handled. Because the next hop is changed when there is an eBGP session between the ASBR, the LSP path terminates on the ASBR originating the update. As a result, the advertising ASBR has to assign a new label for the route before sending it via the MP-eBGP update to its ASBR peer.

There are some important characteristics to keep in mind when using the ASBR-to-ASBR approach:

- There is no requirement of TDP/LDP or any IGP to be enabled on the link connecting the two ASBRs. The MP-eBGP session between directly connected interfaces on the ASBRs enables the interfaces to forward labeled packets.

- **no bgp default route-target filter** needs to be configured on an ASBR that does not have any VRFs configured or is functioning as a RR. The command ensures that the ASBR accepts the BGP VPNv4 prefixes from other PE routers inside the AS. The default behavior is to deny incoming VPNv4 prefixes that are not otherwise imported into any local VRF.

Figure 7-9 shows a multiprovider MPLS VPN network. ASBR1-AS1 and ASBR2-AS2 belong to different provider networks.

Figure 7-9 *Multiprovider Network Using ASBR-ASBR Approach*

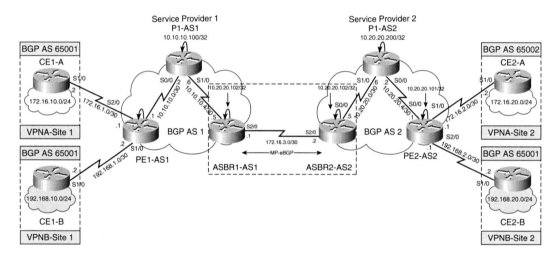

The three methods of transporting VPNv4 prefixes between the two ASBRs are as follows:

- **Option 2a**—Next-hop-self method
- **Option 2b**—Redistribute connected method
- **Option 2c**—eBGP between ASBRs and MP-eBGP between RRs

The following sections discuss each of these approaches in greater detail.

Option 2a: ASBR-ASBR Approach Using Next-Hop-Self Method

Figure 7-9 shows an Inter-AS VPN network. In this topology, when the next-hop-self approach is used, ASBR1-AS1 announces itself as the next hop to P1-AS1-RR, and, similarly, ASBR2-AS2 announces itself as the next hop to P1-AS2-RR. Because the next hop is modified, a new VPNv4 label has to be generated. The eBGP border router ASBR1-AS1 distributes the route to ASBR2-AS2 in the adjoining AS, specifying its own address as eBGP next hop, and assigns a new VPNv4 label. This label is propagated to ASBR2-AS2. ASBR2-AS2 receives the VPNv4 route on the MP-eBGP session from ASBR1-AS1. The next-hop-self is again used and, as a result, the next hop is modified from ASBR1-AS1 to ASBR2-AS2 when ASBR2-AS2 propagates these routes via the MP-iBGP session to P1-AS2-RR. Because the next hop is modified, the VPN label is modified as well and will be used by ASBR2-AS2 to map incoming traffic from PE2-AS2 into the correct LSP toward ASBR2-AS2. This is demonstrated in the following section.

Control Plane Forwarding in Option 2a

Figure 7-10 shows the control plane forwarding action that takes place for prefix 172.16.10.0/24 advertised by CE1-A to CE2-A in Customer A network.

Figure 7-10 *Control Plane Forwarding in Option 2a*

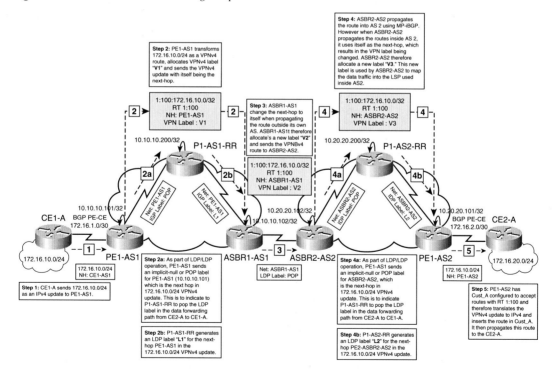

Data Forwarding in Option 2a

Figure 7-11 traces the path of the data packet from the source network, 172.16.20.0/24, to the destination network, 172.16.10.0/24.

Figure 7-11 *Data Plane Forwarding in Option 2a*

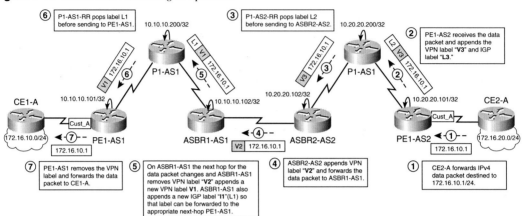

Configuration Flowchart to Implement Inter-Provider VPN Operation Using Option 2a

Figure 7-12 shows the configuration flowchart to accomplish a functional Inter-AS network using the ASBR-to-ASBR approach. As shown in the flowchart, the first step is to configure MP-eBGP between the ASBRs. The second step is to define the ASBRs as the next hop in their respective BGP autonomous systems.

Figure 7-12 *Configuration Flowchart for Option 2a*

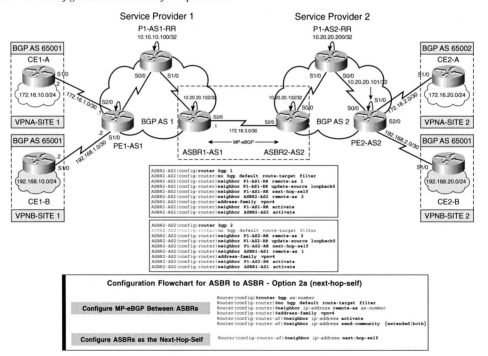

Configuration Step to Implement Inter-Provider VPN Operation Using Option 2a

To configure inter-provider VPNs using the ASBR-to-ASBR (next-hop-self) approach, configure the ASBRs for MP-eBGP exchange. Configure the ASBR Routers ASBR1 and ASBR2 for MP-eBGP exchange. Ensure **no bgp default route-target filter** is configured under the BGP routing process. Define the BGP relationship with the RR and configure the ASBR-AS1 as the next hop for all updates originating from ASBR1-AS1 to P1-AS1-RR. This is shown in Example 7-7. Repeat the same steps on ASBR2-AS2.

Example 7-7   *Configure ASBRs for MP-eBGP*

```
ASBR1-AS1(config)#router bgp 1
ASBR1-AS1(config-router)# no bgp default route-target filter
ASBR1-AS1(config-router)# neighbor 172.16.3.2 remote-as 2
ASBR1-AS1(config-router)# address-family vpnv4
ASBR1-AS1(config-router-af)# neighbor 172.16.3.2 activate
ASBR1-AS1(config-router-af)# neighbor 10.10.10.200 next-hop-self
ASBR2-AS2(config)#router bgp 2
ASBR2-AS2(config-router)# no bgp default route-target filter
ASBR2-AS2(config-router)# neighbor 172.16.3.1 remote-as 1
ASBR2-AS2(config-router)# address-family vpnv4
ASBR2-AS2(config-router-af)# neighbor 172.16.3.1 activate
ASBR2-AS2(config-router-af)# neighbor 10.20.20.200 next-hop-self
```

ASBR1-AS1 and ASBR2-AS2 Final Configurations for Option 2a

Example 7-8 shows the ASBR1-AS1 and ASBR2-AS2 configurations when using the **next-hop-self** approach. For PE1-AS1, P1-AS1-RR, P1-AS2-RR, and PE2-AS2 (PE1-AS2 in option 1) configurations, refer to configurations used in option 1—back-to-back VRF method.

Example 7-8   *ASBR1-AS1 and ASBR2-AS2 Final Configurations*

```
hostname ASBR1-AS1
!
ip cef
!
mpls ldp router-id Loopback0
!
interface Loopback0
 ip address 10.10.10.102 255.255.255.255
!
interface Serial0/0
 description connected to P1-AS1
 ip address 10.10.10.5 255.255.255.252
 mpls ip
!
interface Serial1/0
 ip address 172.16.3.1 255.255.255.252
 mpls bgp forwarding
!
router ospf 1
 router-id 10.10.10.102
```

continues

Example 7-8 *ASBR1-AS1 and ASBR2-AS2 Final Configurations (Continued)*

```
 network 10.0.0.0 0.255.255.255 area 0
!
router bgp 1
 no bgp default ipv4-unicast
 no bgp default route-target filter
 neighbor 10.10.10.200 remote-as 1
 neighbor 10.10.10.200 update-source Loopback0
 neighbor 172.16.3.2 remote-as 2
 !
 address-family ipv4
 neighbor 10.10.10.200 activate
 neighbor 172.16.3.2 activate
 no auto-summary
 no synchronization
 exit-address-family
 !
 address-family vpnv4
 neighbor 10.10.10.200 activate
 neighbor 10.10.10.200 send-community extended
 neighbor 10.10.10.200 next-hop-self
 neighbor 172.16.3.2 activate
 neighbor 172.16.3.2 send-community extended
 exit-address-family
hostname ASBR2-AS2
!
ip cef
!
mpls ldp router-id Loopback0
!
interface Loopback0
 ip address 10.20.20.102 255.255.255.255
!
interface Serial0/0
 description connected to P1-AS2
 ip address 10.20.20.5 255.255.255.252
 mpls ip
!
interface Serial1/0
 ip address 172.16.3.2 255.255.255.252
 mpls bgp forwarding
!
router ospf 2
 router-id 10.20.20.102
 network 10.0.0.0 0.255.255.255 area 0
!
router bgp 2
 no bgp default ipv4-unicast
 no bgp default route-target filter
 neighbor 10.20.20.200 remote-as 2
 neighbor 10.20.20.200 update-source Loopback0
 neighbor 172.16.3.1 remote-as 1
 !
```

Example 7-8   *ASBR1-AS1 and ASBR2-AS2 Final Configurations (Continued)*

```
address-family ipv4
neighbor 10.20.20.200 activate
neighbor 172.16.3.1 activate
no auto-summary
no synchronization
exit-address-family
!
address-family vpnv4
neighbor 10.20.20.200 activate
neighbor 10.20.20.200 send-community extended
neighbor 10.20.20.200 next-hop-self
neighbor 172.16.3.1 activate
neighbor 172.16.3.1 send-community extended
exit-address-family
```

Verifying Inter-Provider VPN Operation Using Option 2a

The steps to verify inter-provider VPN operation using next-hop-self method are

Step 1   **Verify control plane**—Figure 7-13 shows the control plane forwarding operation when the 172.16.10.0/24 prefix is propagated across the multi-provider networks AS1 and AS2 to CE2-A.

Figure 7-13   *Verify Control Plane Forwarding*

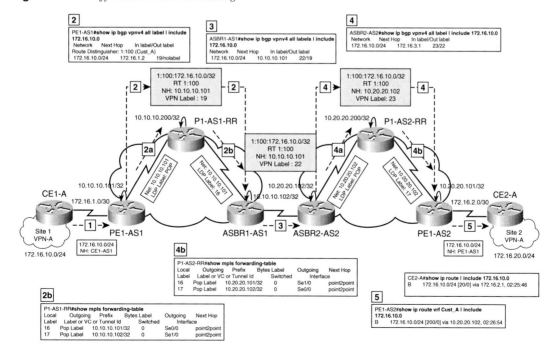

Step 2 **Verify data forwarding**—Figure 7-14 shows the data plane forwarding operation when the 172.16.10.0/24 prefix is propagated across the multi-provider networks AS1 and AS2 to CE2-A.

Figure 7-14 *Verify Data Plane Forwarding*

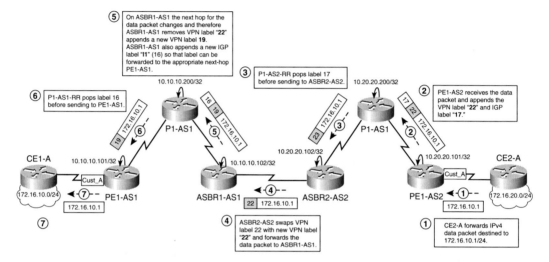

Step 3 **Verify end-to-end connectivity via ping**—Verify end-to-end connectivity between Customer A sites and Customer B sites. Example 7-9 shows the result of the ping.

Example 7-9 *Verify End-to-End Connectivity*

```
CE1-A#ping 172.16.20.1 source 172.16.10.1
Type escape sequence to abort.
Sending 5, 100-byte ICMP Echos to 172.16.20.1, timeout is 2 seconds:
Packet sent with a source address of 172.16.10.1
!!!!!
Success rate is 100 percent (5/5), round-trip min/avg/max = 140/140/140 ms
```
```
CE1-B#ping 192.168.20.1 source 192.168.10.1
Type escape sequence to abort.
Sending 5, 100-byte ICMP Echos to 192.168.20.1, timeout is 2 seconds:
Packet sent with a source address of 192.168.10.1
!!!!!
Success rate is 100 percent (5/5), round-trip min/avg/max = 132/138/140 ms
```

Option 2b: ASBR-to-ASBR Approach Using Redistribute Connected

In the redistribute connected approach, the receiving ASBR accepts the route without changing the next-hop attribute and any label information. The receiving ASBR also creates a /32 host route for its ASBR neighbor so as to access the next-hop address for the prefix. This host route must be redistributed into the IGP using the **redistribute connected** command.

Control Plane Forwarding in Option 2b

Figure 7-15 shows the control plane forwarding action that takes place for prefix 172.16.10.0/24 advertised by CE1-A to CE2-A that belongs to the same VPN CUST_A.

Figure 7-15 *Control Plane Forwarding Using Option 2b*

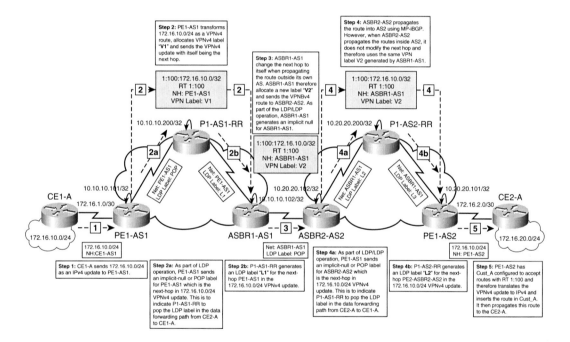

Data Forwarding in Option 2b

The source and destination networks belonging to the same VPN, VPN-A, are located on two different MPLS VPN provider networks. The data forwarding path originates from the source address of the flow, which is 172.16.20.1 destined to the 172.16.10.1. Figure 7-16 traces the path of the data packet from the source to the destination.

Figure 7-16 *Data Plane Forwarding Using Option 2b*

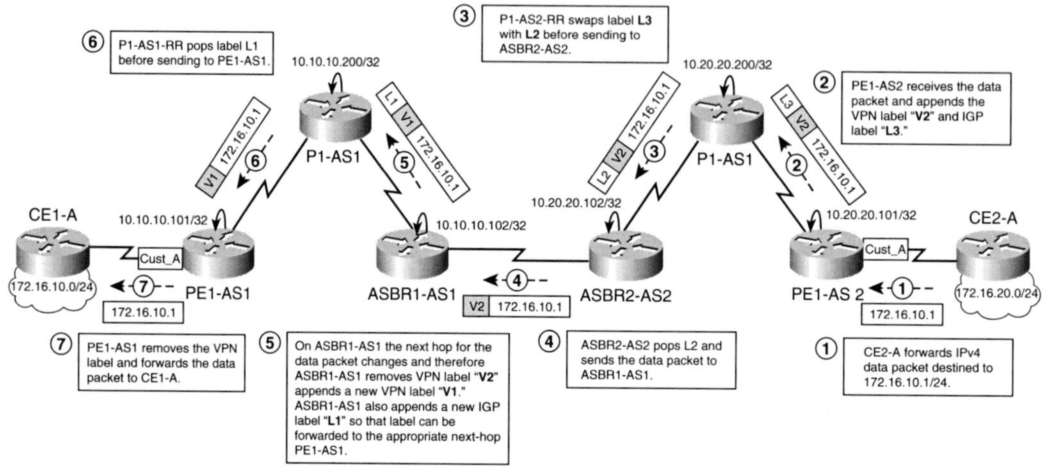

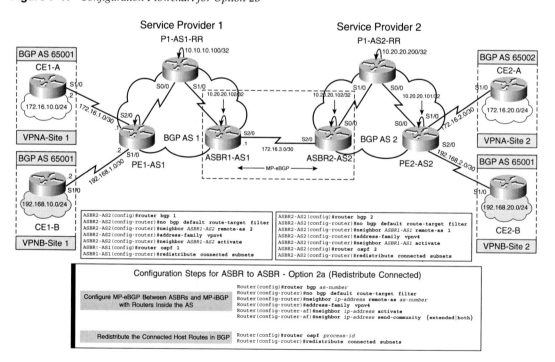

Configuration Flowchart for Implementing Option 2b

Figure 7-17 shows the configuration flowchart to configure option 2b.

Figure 7-17 *Configuration Flowchart for Option 2b*

Configuring Inter-Provider VPNs Using Option 2b

In this section, the topology shown in Figure 7-9 is used, and the configuration steps are shown only for routers that are responsible for Inter-AS operations. You can use the PE1-AS1, P1-AS1-RR, P1-AS2-RR, and PE1-AS2 configurations used in back-to-back VRF for the ASBR-to-ASBR approach. The only exceptions would be

- Hostname for PE1-AS2 changes to PE2-AS2.

- Hostname PE2-AS1-ASBR1 and PE2-AS2-ASBR2 change to ASBR1-AS1 and ASBR2-AS2, respectively, because the ASBR performs a single function of transporting VPNv4 prefixes and not the dual function of a PE router, as seen in the back-to-back VRF method.

The steps to configure inter-provider VPNs using the redistribute connected approach are

Step 1   **Configure ASBRs for MP-eBGP exchange**—Configure the ASBR Routers ASBR1 and ASBR2 for MP-eBGP exchange. Ensure **no bgp default route-target filter** is configured under the BGP routing process. This step is the same as Step 1 shown in section "Configuration Step to Implement Inter-Provider VPN Operation Using Option 2a" except the next-hop-self statement in redistribute connected approach is not used.

Step 2   **Redistribute the connected host routes in BGP**—Example 7-11 shows the step to redistribute connected routes (see Example 7-10) in OSPF. The host connected routes were created when the MP-eBGP session between the ASBRs was established.

Example 7-10 *Connected Host Routes on ASBR1-AS1 and ASBR2-AS2*

```
ASBR1-AS1#show ip route | include 172.16.3
C       172.16.3.2/32 is directly connected, Serial1/0
C       172.16.3.0/30 is directly connected, Serial1/0
ASBR2-AS2#show  ip route | include 172.16.3
C       172.16.3.1/32 is directly connected, Serial1/0
C       172.16.3.0/30 is directly connected, Serial1/0
```

Example 7-11 *Redistribute the Connected Host Routes in BGP*

```
ASBR1-AS1(config)#router ospf 1
ASBR1-AS1(config-router)#redistribute connected subnets route-map net_172.16.3.0
ASBR1-AS1(config-router)#exit
ASBR1-AS1(config)#route-map net_172.16.3.0 permit 10
ASBR1-AS1(config-route-map)# match ip address net_172.16.3.0
ASBR1-AS1(config-route-map)#exit
ASBR1-AS1(config)#ip access-list standard net_172.16.3.0
ASBR1-AS1(config-std-nacl)# permit 172.16.3.0 0.0.0.3
ASBR2-AS2(config)#router ospf 2
ASBR2-AS2(config-router)#redistribute connected subnets route-map net_172.16.3.0
ASBR2-AS2(config-router)#exit
```

continues

Example 7-11 *Redistribute the Connected Host Routes in BGP (Continued)*

```
ASBR2-AS2(config)#route-map net_172.16.3.0 permit 10
ASBR2-AS2(config-route-map)# match ip address net_172.16.3.0
ASBR2-AS2(config-route-map)#exit
ASBR2-AS2(config)#ip access-list standard net_172.16.3.0
ASBR2-AS2(config-std-nacl)# permit 172.16.3.0 0.0.0.3
```

Final Router Configurations for ASBRs in Option 2b

Example 7-12 shows ASBR1-AS1 and ASBR2-AS2 configurations when using the redistribute connected approach in ASBR-to-ASBR. They reflect only the necessary configurations required to implement this methodology. The remaining configurations are similar to ASBR1-AS1 and ASBR-AS2 configurations in option 2a, next-hop-self method, excluding the **next-hop-self** statement.

Example 7-12 *ASBR1-AS1 and ASBR2-AS2 Configurations When Using the Redistribute Connected Approach in ASBR-ASBR*

```
hostname ASBR1-AS1
!
router ospf 1
 router-id 10.10.10.102
 redistribute connected subnets route-map net_172.16.3.0
 network 10.0.0.0 0.255.255.255 area 0
!
router bgp 1
 no bgp default ipv4-unicast
 no bgp default route-target filter
 bgp log-neighbor-changes
 neighbor 10.10.10.200 remote-as 1
 neighbor 10.10.10.200 update-source Loopback0
 neighbor 172.16.3.2 remote-as 2
 !
 address-family ipv4
 neighbor 10.10.10.200 activate
 neighbor 172.16.3.2 activate
 no auto-summary
 no synchronization
 exit-address-family
 !
 address-family vpnv4
 neighbor 10.10.10.200 activate
 neighbor 10.10.10.200 send-community extended
 neighbor 172.16.3.2 activate
 neighbor 172.16.3.2 send-community extended
 exit-address-family
!
ip access-list standard net_172.16.3.0
 permit 172.16.3.0 0.0.0.3
 !
```

Example 7-12 *ASBR1-AS1 and ASBR2-AS2 Configurations When Using the Redistribute Connected Approach in ASBR-ASBR (Continued)*

```
route-map net_172.16.3.0 permit 10
 match ip address net_172.16.3.0
hostname ASBR2-AS2
!
router ospf 2
 router-id 10.20.20.102
 redistribute connected subnets route-map net_172.16.3.0
 network 10.0.0.0 0.255.255.255 area 0
!
router bgp 2
 no bgp default ipv4-unicast
 no bgp default route-target filter
 bgp log-neighbor-changes
 neighbor 10.20.20.200 remote-as 2
 neighbor 10.20.20.200 update-source Loopback0
 neighbor 172.16.3.1 remote-as 1
 !
 address-family ipv4
 neighbor 10.20.20.200 activate
 neighbor 172.16.3.1 activate
 no auto-summary
 no synchronization
 exit-address-family
 !
 address-family vpnv4
 neighbor 10.20.20.200 activate
 neighbor 10.20.20.200 send-community extended
neighbor 172.16.3.1 activate
 neighbor 172.16.3.1 send-community extended
 exit-address-family
 !
ip access-list standard net_172.16.3.0
 permit 172.16.3.0 0.0.0.3
 !
route-map net_172.16.3.0 permit 10
 match ip address net_172.16.3.0
```

Verification of Control Plane Forwarding When Using Option 2b

Figure 7-18 shows the control plane forwarding operation when the 172.16.10.0/24 prefix is propagated across the multiprovider networks AS1 and AS2 to CE2-A.

Verification of Data Forwarding in Option 2b

Figure 7-19 traces the path of the data packet from the source to the destination.

Figure 7-18 *Verification of Control Plane Forwarding When Using Option 2b*

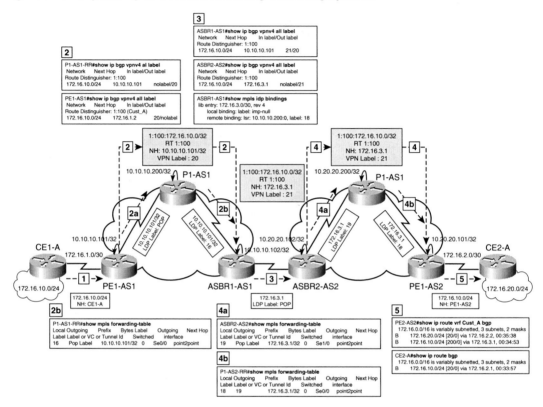

Figure 7-19 *Data Plane Forwarding Using Option 2b*

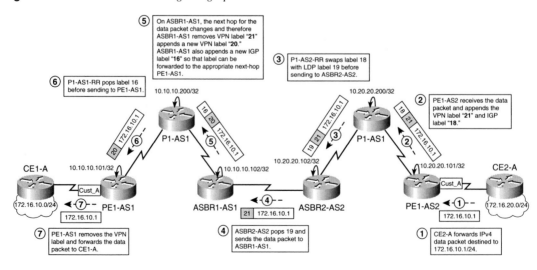

Option 2c: Multi-Hop MP-eBGP Between ASBRs

Option 2c is a variant of Option 2a and 2b where the ASBR routers provide transportation of VPNv4 prefixes from AS1 to AS2 and vice versa. Figure 7-20 shows a multiprovider VPN network that is providing VPN services to it sites belonging to Customer A. P1-AS1-RR and P1-AS2-RR are RRs that are local in each of the provider's network. An MP-eBGP session is formed between the ASBRs to transport VPNv4 information across the multiprovider network. To maintain an end-to-end LSP path, MPLS is enabled between the ASBRs.

Control Plane Forwarding in Option 2c

Figure 7-20 shows the control plane forwarding action that takes place for prefix 172.16.10.0/24 advertised by CE1-A to CE2-A that belongs to the same VPN CUST_A.

Figure 7-20 *Control Plane Forwarding in Option 2c*

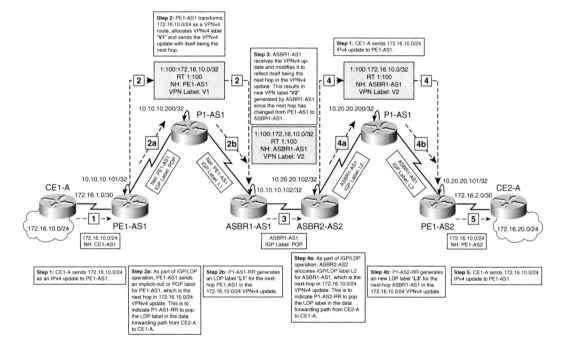

Data Plane Forwarding in Option 2c

The source and destination networks are located on two different MPLS VPN provider networks. The data forwarding path originates from the source address of the flow, which is 172.16.20.1 destined to 172.16.10.1. Figure 7-21 traces the path of the data packet from the source to the destination.

Figure 7-21 *Data Plane Forwarding in Option 2c*

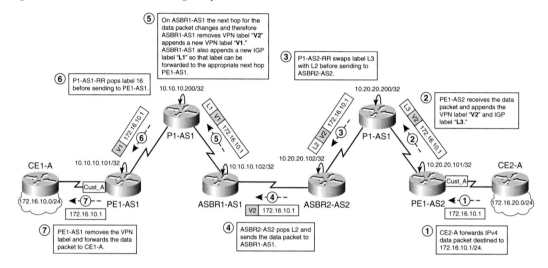

Configuring Multi-Hop MP-eBGP Between ASBRs

Figure 7-22 shows an MPLS VPN network in which sites in VPN-A are geographically dispersed. Site 1 and Site 2 in VPN-A have CE routers CE1-A and CE2-A, which connect to PE routers PE1-AS1 and PE1-AS2 located in Service Provider 1 and Service Provider 2, respectively. The network shown in Figure 7-22 has two ASBRs, ASBR1 and ASBR2, which are connected to each other via a single link.

Configuration Flowchart for Implementing Option 2c

Figure 7-22 shows the configuration steps that are involved in accomplishing a functional Inter-AS network using multi-hop MP-eBGP between ASBRs:

Step 1   Configure LDP between the ASBRs for label exchange—Enable the interface between the ASBRs for IPv4 label exchange. Example 7-13 demonstrates the step.

Example 7-13 *Configure LDP Between the ASBRs for Label Exchange*

```
ASBR1-AS1(config)#interface serial1/0
ASBR1-AS1(config-if)#mpls ip

ASBR2-AS2(config)#interface serial1/0
ASBR2-AS2(config-f)#mpls ip
```

Figure 7-22 *Configuration Steps in Option 2c*

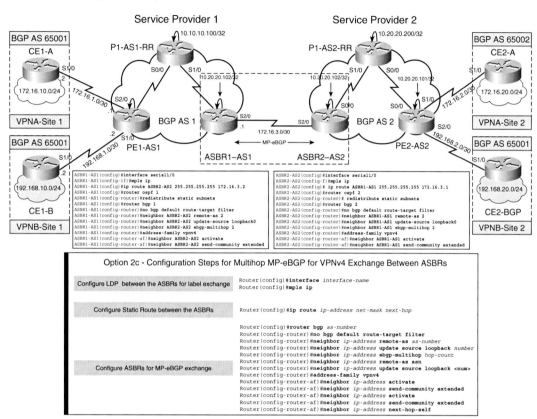

Step 2   Configure IGP for ASBR reachability—Configure static routes to the
loopback address on ASBR1-AS1 and ASBR2-AS2. Redistribute the
static routes in the OSPF. Example 7-14 shows the configuration to
ensure ASBR reachability.

Example 7-14 *Configure IGP for ASBR Reachability*

```
ASBR1-AS1(config)#interface Loopback0
ASBR1-AS1(config-if)#ip address 10.10.10.102 255.255.255.255
ASBR1-AS1(config-if)#exit
ASBR1-AS1(config)#ip route 10.20.20.102 255.255.255.255 172.16.3.2
ASBR1-AS1(config)#router ospf 1
ASBR1-AS1(config-router)#redistribute static subnets
ASBR1-AS2(config)#interface Loopback0
ASBR1-AS2(config-if)#ip address 10.20.20.102 255.255.255.255
ASBR1-AS2(config-if)#exit
ASBR2-AS2(config)# ip route 10.10.10.102 255.255.255.255 172.16.3.1
ASBR2-AS2(config)#router ospf 2
ASBR2-AS2(config-router)# redistribute static subnets
```

Step 3 **Configure multi-hop MP-eBGP between ASBRs for VPNv4 exchange**—Configure the ASBR Routers ASBR1-AS1 and ASBR2-AS2 for MP-eEBGP, as shown in Example 7-15.

Example 7-15 *Configure Multi-Hop MP-eEBGP Between ASBRs for VPNv4 Exchange*

```
ASBR1-AS1(config)#router bgp 1
ASBR1-AS1(config-router)#no bgp default route-target filter
ASBR1-AS1(config-router)#neighbor 10.20.20.102 remote-as 2
ASBR1-AS1(config-router)#neighbor 10.20.20.102 update-source loopback0
ASBR1-AS1(config-router)#neighbor 10.20.20.102 ebgp-multihop 2
ASBR1-AS1(config-router)#address-family vpnv4
ASBR1-AS1(config-router-af)#neighbor 10.20.20.102 activate
ASBR2-AS2(config)#router bgp 2
ASBR2-AS2(config-router)#no bgp default route-target filter
ASBR2-AS2(config-router)#neighbor 10.10.10.102 remote-as 2
ASBR2-AS2(config-router)#neighbor 10.10.10.102 update-source loopback0
ASBR2-AS2(config-router)#neighbor 10.10.10.102 ebgp-multihop 2
ASBR2-AS2(config-router)#address-family vpnv4
ASBR2-AS2(config-router-af)#neighbor 10.10.10.102 activate
```

ASBR1-AS1 and ASBR2-AS2 Configurations for Option 2c

Example 7-16 shows the ASBR1-AS1 and ASBR2-AS2 configurations when using multi-hop MP-eBGP between the ASBRs.

Example 7-16 *ASBR1-AS1 and ASBR2-AS2 Configurations*

```
! ASBR1-AS1
interface Serial1/0
 ip address 172.16.3.1 255.255.255.252
 mpls ip
!
router ospf 1
 router-id 10.10.10.102
 redistribute static subnets
 network 10.0.0.0 0.255.255.255 area 0
!
router bgp 1
 no bgp default ipv4-unicast
 no bgp default route-target filter
 neighbor 10.10.10.200 remote-as 1
 neighbor 10.10.10.200 update-source Loopback0
 neighbor 10.20.20.102 remote-as 2
 neighbor 10.20.20.102 ebgp-multihop 2
 neighbor 10.20.20.102 update-source Loopback0
 !
 address-family ipv4
 neighbor 10.10.10.200 activate
 no auto-summary
 no synchronization
```

Example 7-16 *ASBR1-AS1 and ASBR2-AS2 Configurations (Continued)*

```
 exit-address-family
 !
 address-family vpnv4
 neighbor 10.10.10.200 activate
 neighbor 10.10.10.200 send-community extended
 neighbor 10.20.20.102 activate
 neighbor 10.20.20.102 send-community extended
 exit-address-family
 !
ip route 10.20.20.102 255.255.255.255 172.16.3.2
! ASBR2-AS2
interface Serial1/0
 ip address 172.16.3.2 255.255.255.252
 mpls ip
 !
router ospf 2
 router-id 10.20.20.102
 redistribute connected
 redistribute static subnets
 network 10.0.0.0 0.255.255.255 area 0
 !
router bgp 2
 no bgp default ipv4-unicast
 no bgp default route-target filter
 neighbor 10.10.10.102 remote-as 1
 neighbor 10.10.10.102 ebgp-multihop 2
 neighbor 10.10.10.102 update-source Loopback0
 neighbor 10.20.20.200 remote-as 2
 neighbor 10.20.20.200 update-source Loopback0
 !
 address-family vpnv4
 neighbor 10.10.10.102 activate
 neighbor 10.10.10.102 send-community extended
 neighbor 10.20.20.200 activate
 neighbor 10.20.20.200 send-community extended
 exit-address-family
 !
ip route 10.10.10.102 255.255.255.255 172.16.3.1
```

Verifying Inter-Provider VPN Operation Option 2c

The steps to verify inter-provider VPN operation option 2c are

Step 1   Verification of control plane forwarding—Figure 7-23 shows
the control plane forwarding operation when the 172.16.10.0/24
prefix is propagated across the multiprovider networks AS1 and AS2
to CE2-A.

Figure 7-23 *Verify Control Plane Forwarding*

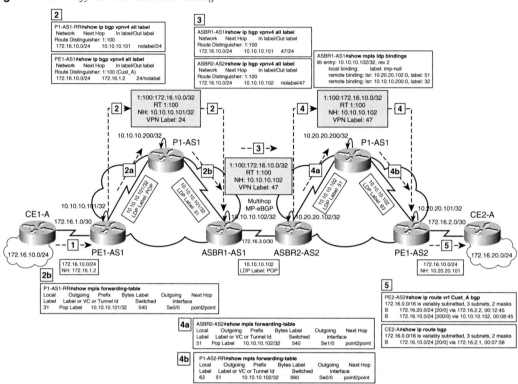

Step 2   Verification of data plane forwarding—Figure 7-24 shows the data plane forwarding operation when the 172.16.10.0/24 prefix is propagated across the multiprovider networks, AS1 and AS2, to CE2-A.

Figure 7-24 *Verify Data Plane Forwarding*

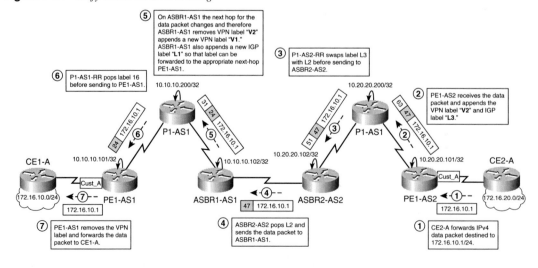

Step 3   **Verify end-to-end connectivity via ping**—Verify end-to-end connectivity between CE1-B and CE2-B by issuing a ping from CE1-B to network 172.16.20.1/24 on CE2-B and vice versa. Example 7-17 shows the result of the ping operation.

Example 7-17 *Verify End-to-End Connectivity*

```
CE1-A#ping 172.16.20.1 source 172.16.10.1
Type escape sequence to abort.
Sending 5, 100-byte ICMP Echos to 172.16.20.1, timeout is 2 seconds:
Packet sent with a source address of 172.16.10.1
!!!!!
Success rate is 100 percent (5/5), round-trip min/avg/max = 140/140/140 ms
CE1-B#ping 192.168.20.1 source 192.168.10.1
Type escape sequence to abort.
Sending 5, 100-byte ICMP Echos to 192.168.20.1, timeout is 2 seconds:
Packet sent with a source address of 192.168.10.1
!!!!!
Success rate is 100 percent (5/5), round-trip min/avg/max = 132/138/140 ms
```

Option 3: Multi-Hop MP-eBGP Between RR and eBGP Between ASBRs

This approach is considered to be more scalable than option 1 or option 2. In this option, VPNv4 information is held by the RRs. To meet this requirement, each provider needs to have local RRs for VPNv4 prefix distribution and eBGP connection to exchange prefixes with the external peer. The ASBRs in this option participate in exchange of BGP next-hop-address using IPv4 labels, and RRs form an MP-eBGP session to transport VPNv4 information. Figure 7-25 shows a multiprovider VPN network that is providing VPN services to sites belonging to Customer A.

Figure 7-25 *MPLS VPN Network Using Option 3*

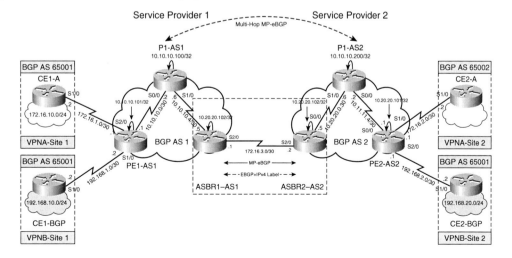

P1-AS1-RR and P1-AS2-RR are RRs that are local to each of the provider's autonomous systems. An MP-eBGP session is formed between the RRs to transport VPNv4 information across the multiprovider network. An eBGP session is formed between the ASBRs to exchange next-hop-address prefixes.

Control Plane Forwarding in Option 3

Figure 7-26 shows the control plane forwarding action that takes place for prefix 172.16.10.0/24 advertised by CE1-A to CE2-A that belongs to the same VPN, CUST_A.

Figure 7-26 *Control Plane Operation in Option 3*

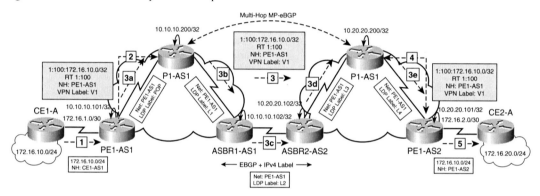

Data Forwarding in Option 3

The source and destination networks are located on two different MPLS VPN provider networks. The data forwarding path originates from the source address of the flow, which is 172.16.20.1 destined to the 172.16.10.1. Figure 7-27 traces the path of the data packet from the source to the destination.

Figure 7-27 *Data Forwarding in Option 3*

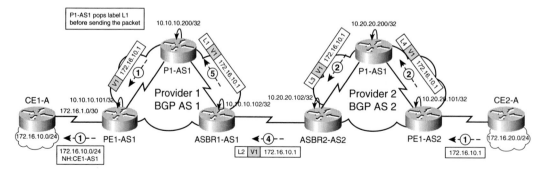

Configuration Flowchart to Implement Option 3

Figure 7-28 shows the configuration steps that are involved in accomplishing a functional Inter-AS network using option 3.

Figure 7-28 *Configuration Steps for Option 3*

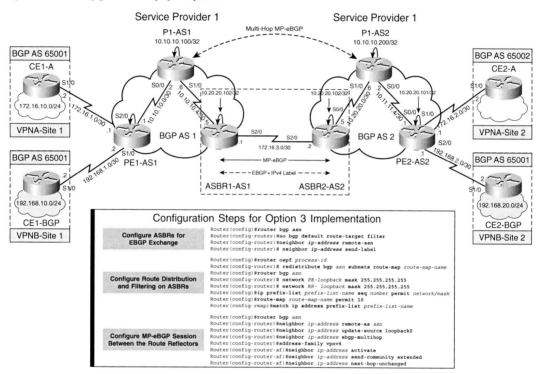

Configuration and Verification of Option 3

The steps to implement option 3 for the topology shown in Figure 7-26 are as follows:

Step 1   **Configure ASBRs for eBGP and IPv4 label exchange**—Configure the ASBR Routers ASBR1-AS1 and ASBR2-AS2 for eBGP. Use the **neighbor send-label** command to enable exchange of IPv4 label exchange between the two peers. Example 7-18 demonstrates the step.

Example 7-18 *Configure ASBRs for eBGP and IPv4 Label Exchange*

```
ASBR1-AS1(config)#router bgp 1
ASBR1-AS1(config-router)#no bgp default route-target filter
ASBR1-AS1(config-router)#neighbor 172.16.3.2 remote-as 2
ASBR1-AS1(config-router)# neighbor 172.16.3.2 send-label
ASBR2-AS2(config)#router bgp 2
```

continues

Example 7-18 *Configure ASBRs for eBGP and IPv4 Label Exchange (Continued)*

```
ASBR2-AS2(config-router)#no bgp default route-target filter
ASBR2-AS2(config-router)#neighbor 172.16.3.1 remote-as 1
ASBR2-AS2(config-router)# neighbor 172.16.3.1 send-label
```

> **Step 2** **Route redistribution and filtering on ASBR**—In this step, the
> loopbacks on PE1-AS1 (10.10.10.101) and P1-AS1 (10.10.10.200) are
> advertised in BGP so that they can be advertised to ASBR2-AS2. At
> ASBR2-AS2, PE1-AS1 and P1-AS1-RR loopbacks are redistributed in
> IGP. Example 7-19 illustrates this step.

Example 7-19 *Route Redistribution and Filtering on ASBR*

```
ASBR1-AS1(config)#router ospf 1
ASBR1-AS1(config-router)# redistribute bgp 1 subnets route-map bgp-to-ospf
ASBR1-AS1(config)#router bgp 1
ASBR1-AS1(config-router)# network 10.10.10.101 mask 255.255.255.255
ASBR1-AS1(config-router)# network 10.10.10.200 mask 255.255.255.255
ASBR1-AS1(config)#ip prefix-list pref-from-AS2 seq 1 permit 10.20.20.101/32
ASBR1-AS1(config)#ip prefix-list pref-from-AS2 seq 2 permit 10.20.20.200/32
ASBR1-AS1(config)#route-map bgp-to-ospf permit 10
ASBR1-AS1(config-rmap)#match ip address prefix-list pref-from-AS2

ASBR1-AS2(config)#router ospf 2
ASBR1-AS2(config-router)# redistribute bgp 2 subnets route-map bgp-to-ospf
ASBR2-AS2(config)#router bgp 1
ASBR2-AS2(config-router)# network 10.20.20.101 mask 255.255.255.255
ASBR2-AS2(config-router)# network 10.20.20.200 mask 255.255.255.255
ASBR2-AS2(config)#ip prefix-list pref-from-AS1 seq 1 permit 10.10.10.101/32
ASBR2-AS2(config)#ip prefix-list pref-from-AS1 seq 2 permit 10.10.10.200/32
ASBR2-AS2(config)#route-map bgp-to-ospf permit 10
ASBR2-AS2(config-rmap)#match ip address prefix-list pref-from-AS1
```

> **Step 3** **Configure MP-eBGP session between the RRs**—In this step, an MP-
> eBGP session is configured between the RR, as shown in Example 7-20.
> *Before performing this step, ensure that the loopback addresses on the
> RRs are reachable by ping.*

Example 7-20 *Configure MP-eBGP Session Between the RRs*

```
P1-AS1-RR(config)#router bgp 1
P1-AS1-RR(config-router)#neighbor 10.20.20.200 remote-as 2
P1-AS1-RR(config-router)#neighbor 10.20.20.200 update-source loopback0
P1-AS1-RR(config-router)#neighbor 10.20.20.200 ebgp-multihop
P1-AS1-RR(config-router)#address-family vpnv4
P1-AS1-RR(config-router-af)#neighbor 10.20.20.200 activate
P1-AS1-RR(config-router-af)#neighbor 10.20.20.200 send-community extended

P1-AS1-RR(config-router-af)#neighbor 10.20.20.200 next-hop-unchanged
P1-AS2-RR(config)#router bgp 1
P1-AS2-RR(config-router)#neighbor 10.10.10.200 remote-as 2
P1-AS2-RR(config-router)#neighbor 10.10.10.200 update-source loopback0
P1-AS2-RR(config-router)#neighbor 10.10.10.200 ebgp-multihop
```

Example 7-20 *Configure MP-eBGP Session Between the RRs (Continued)*

```
P1-AS2-RR(config-router)#address-family vpnv4
P1-AS2-RR(config-router-af)#neighbor 10.10.10.200 activate
P1-AS2-RR(config-router-af)#neighbor 10.10.10.200 send-community extended
P1-AS2-RR(config-router-af)#neighbor 10.10.10.200 next-hop-unchanged
```

ASBR and RR Configurations in Option 3

Example 7-21 shows the ASBR configurations for ASBR1-AS1 and ASBR2-AS2 and RR configurations for P1-AS1-RR and P1-AS2-RR.

Example 7-21 *ASBR and RR Configurations*

```
hostname P1-AS1-RR
!
ip cef
!
mpls ldp router-id Loopback0
!
interface Loopback0
 ip address 10.10.10.200 255.255.255.255
!
interface Serial0/0
 description connected to PE1-AS1
 ip address 10.10.10.2 255.255.255.252
 mpls ip
!
interface Serial1/0
 description connected to ASBR1-AS1
 ip address 10.10.10.6 255.255.255.252
 mpls ip
!
router ospf 1
 router-id 10.10.10.200
 network 10.0.0.0 0.255.255.255 area 0
!
router bgp 1
 no bgp default ipv4-unicast
 neighbor 10.10.10.101 remote-as 1
 neighbor 10.10.10.101 update-source Loopback0
 neighbor 10.20.20.200 remote-as 2
 neighbor 10.20.20.200 ebgp-multihop 255
 neighbor 10.20.20.200 update-source Loopback0
 !
 address-family vpnv4
 neighbor 10.10.10.101 activate
 neighbor 10.10.10.101 send-community extended
 neighbor 10.10.10.101 route-reflector-client
 neighbor 10.20.20.200 activate
 neighbor 10.20.20.200 send-community extended
 neighbor 10.20.20.200 next-hop-unchanged
 exit-address-family
```

continues

Example 7-21 *ASBR and RR Configurations (Continued)*

```
Hostname P1-AS2-RR
!
ip cef
!
mpls ldp router-id Loopback0
!
interface Loopback0
 ip address 10.20.20.200 255.255.255.255
!
interface Serial0/0
 description connected to PE2-AS2-ASBR2
 ip address 10.20.20.6 255.255.255.252
 mpls ip
!
interface Serial1/0
 description connected to PE1-AS2
 ip address 10.20.20.2 255.255.255.252
 mpls ip
!
router ospf 2
 router-id 10.20.20.200
 network 10.0.0.0 0.255.255.255 area 0
!
router bgp 2
 no bgp default ipv4-unicast
 neighbor 10.10.10.200 remote-as 1
 neighbor 10.10.10.200 ebgp-multihop 255
 neighbor 10.10.10.200 update-source Loopback0
 neighbor 10.20.20.101 remote-as 2
 neighbor 10.20.20.101 update-source Loopback0
 !
 address-family vpnv4
 neighbor 10.10.10.200 activate
 neighbor 10.10.10.200 send-community extended
 neighbor 10.10.10.200 next-hop-unchanged
 neighbor 10.20.20.101 activate
 neighbor 10.20.20.101 send-community extended
 neighbor 10.20.20.101 route-reflector-client
 exit-address-family
```

```
hostname ASBR1-AS1
!
ip cef
!
mpls ldp router-id Loopback0
!
interface Loopback0
 ip address 10.10.10.102 255.255.255.255
!
interface Serial0/0
 description connected to P1-AS1-RR
 ip address 10.10.10.5 255.255.255.252
 mpls ip
!
```

Example 7-21 *ASBR and RR Configurations (Continued)*

```
interface Serial1/0
 ip address 172.16.3.1 255.255.255.252
 mpls bgp forwarding
!
router ospf 1
 router-id 10.10.10.102
 redistribute bgp 1 subnets route-map bgp-to-ospf
 network 10.0.0.0 0.255.255.255 area 0
!
router bgp 1
 no synchronization
 network 10.10.10.101 mask 255.255.255.255
 network 10.10.10.200 mask 255.255.255.255
 neighbor 172.16.3.2 remote-as 2
 neighbor 172.16.3.2 send-label
 no auto-summary
!
ip prefix-list pref-from-AS2 seq 1 permit 10.20.20.101/32
ip prefix-list pref-from-AS2 seq 2 permit 10.20.20.200/32
!
route-map bgp-to-ospf permit 10
 match ip address prefix-list pref-from-AS2
hostname ASBR2-AS2
!
ip cef
!
mpls ldp router-id Loopback0
!
interface Loopback0
 ip address 10.20.20.102 255.255.255.255
!
interface Serial0/0
 description connected to P1-AS2-RR
 ip address 10.20.20.5 255.255.255.252
 mpls ip
!
interface Serial1/0
 ip address 172.16.3.2 255.255.255.252
 mpls bgp forwarding
!
router ospf 2
 router-id 10.20.20.102
 redistribute bgp 2 metric 1 subnets route-map bgp-to-ospf
 network 10.0.0.0 0.255.255.255 area 0
!
router bgp 2
 no synchronization
 network 10.20.20.101 mask 255.255.255.255
 network 10.20.20.200 mask 255.255.255.255
 neighbor 172.16.3.1 remote-as 1
 neighbor 172.16.3.1 send-label
 no auto-summary
```

continues

Example 7-21 *ASBR and RR Configurations (Continued)*

```
!
ip prefix-list pref-from-AS1 seq 1 permit 10.10.10.200/32
ip prefix-list pref-from-AS1 seq 2 permit 10.10.10.101/32
!
route-map bgp-to-ospf permit 10
 match ip address prefix-list pref-from-AS1
```

Verifying Inter-Provider VPN Operation Using Option 3

The steps to verify inter-provider VPN operation using option 3 are

Step 1 **Verify control plane forwarding**—Figure 7-29 shows the control plane forwarding operation when the 172.16.10.0/24 prefix is propagated across the multiprovider networks AS1 and AS2 to CE2-A.

Figure 7-29 *Verify Control Plane Forwarding Using Option 3*

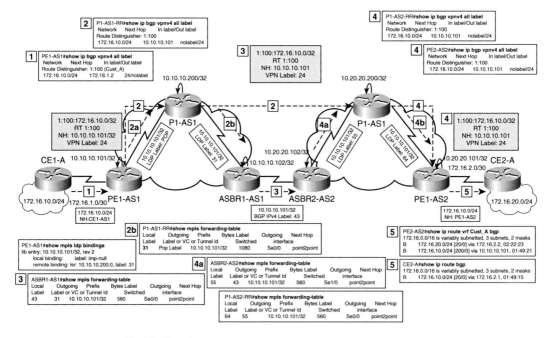

Step 2 **Verify data forwarding**—Figure 7-30 shows the data forwarding path taken by 172.16.20.1 to reach 172.16.10.1.

Figure 7-30 *Verify Data Forwarding Using Option 3*

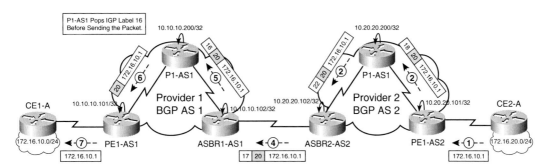

> **Step 3** **Verify end-to-end connectivity via ping**—Verify end-to-end connectivity between Customer A networks (172.16.10.0/24 and 172.16.20.0/24) and Customer B networks (192.168.10.0/24 and 192.168.20.0/24). Example 7-22 shows the result of the ping operation.

Example 7-22 *Verify End-to-End Connectivity*

```
CE1-A#ping 172.16.20.1 source 172.16.10.1
Type escape sequence to abort.
Sending 5, 100-byte ICMP Echos to 172.16.20.1, timeout is 2 seconds:
Packet sent with a source address of 172.16.10.1
!!!!!
Success rate is 100 percent (5/5), round-trip min/avg/max = 140/140/140 ms
CE1-B#ping 192.168.20.1 source 192.168.10.1
Type escape sequence to abort.
Sending 5, 100-byte ICMP Echos to 192.168.20.1, timeout is 2 seconds:
Packet sent with a source address of 192.168.10.1
!!!!!
Success rate is 100 percent (5/5), round-trip min/avg/max = 132/138/140 ms
```

Option 4: Non-VPN Transit Provider

In this approach, multiple VPN providers use another MPLS-enabled service provider as a transit backbone to exchange MPLS VPN routes. Figure 7-31 shows a multiprovider MPLS VPN network using AS100 as a transit provider to transport VPN routes.

In this option, a multi-hop MP-eBGP session is formed between the two RRs belonging to the two different providers. To implement this option, BGP next hops need to be propagated and an end-to-end LSP path needs to be maintained.

P1-AS1-RR and P1-AS2-RR are RRs that are local in each of the provider's network. An MP-eBGP session is formed between the RRs to transport VPNv4 information across the multiprovider network. An eBGP session is formed between the ASBR1-AS1 and ASBR1-AS100. Another eBGP session is formed between ASBRs in AS2 and AS100.

Figure 7-31 *Inter-AS Using a Non-VPN Transit Provider*

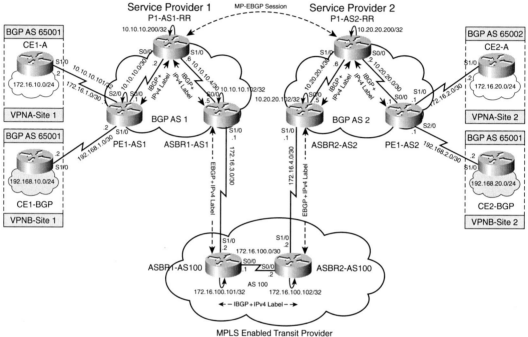

Control Plane Forwarding in Option 4

Figure 7-32 shows the control plane forwarding action that takes place for prefix 172.16.10.0/24 advertised by CE1-A to CE2-A that belongs to the same VPN, CUST_A.

Data Forwarding in Option 4

The source and destination networks are located on two different MPLS VPN provider networks. The data forwarding path originates from the source address of the flow, which is 172.16.20.1 destined to 172.16.10.1. Figure 7-33 traces the path of the data packet from the source to the destination.

Figure 7-32 *Control Plane Operation in a Non-VPN Transit Provider Network*

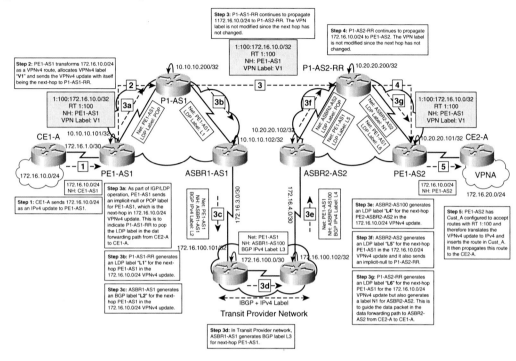

Figure 7-33 *Data Forwarding in Option 4*

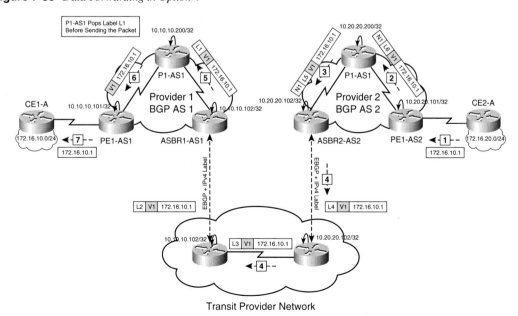

Configuration Flowchart in Option 4

Figure 7-34 shows the configuration steps that are involved in accomplishing a functional Inter-AS network using option 4.

Figure 7-34 *MPLS VPN Network Using Option 4*

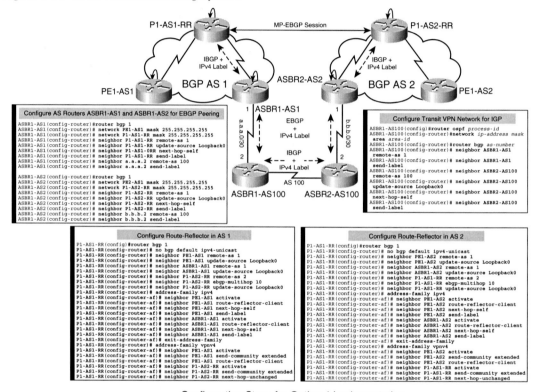

Configuration Steps for Option 4 Implementation

Configuration and Verification of Option 4

Figure 7-31 illustrated a multiprovider MPLS VPN network in which sites in VPN-A are geographically dispersed. Site 1 in VPN-A is connected to PE1-AS1 in AS1, and Site 2 in VPN-A is connected to PE1-AS2 in AS2. EBGP peering is configured between ASBRs:

- ASBR1-AS1 and ASBR1-AS100

- ASBR1-AS2 and ASBR2-AS100

The steps to configure are

Step 1 **Configure transit VPN network, AS100**—Configure the ASBR Routers ASBR1-AS100 and ASBR2-AS100 for IGP, as shown in Example 7-23. In this case, OSPF is used. Configure iBGP peering between the two ASBRs for eBGP. Use **neighbor send-label** to enable exchange of IPv4 label exchange between the two peers.

Example 7-23 *Configure Transit VPN Network, AS100*

```
ASBR1-AS100(config)#interface Loopback0
ASBR1-AS100(config-if)# ip address 172.16.100.101 255.255.255.255
ASBR1-AS100(config-if)#interface Serial0/0
ASBR1-AS100(config-if)# ip address 172.16.100.1 255.255.255.252
ASBR1-AS100(config-if)# mpls ip
ASBR1-AS100(config-if)#interface Serial1/0
ASBR1-AS100(config-if)# ip address 172.16.3.2 255.255.255.252
ASBR1-AS100(config-if)#router ospf 100
ASBR1-AS100(config-router)# network 172.16.100.0 0.0.0.255 area 0
ASBR1-AS100(config-router)#router bgp 100
ASBR1-AS100(config-router)# network 172.16.100.101 mask 255.255.255.255
ASBR1-AS100(config-router)# neighbor 172.16.3.1 remote-as 1
ASBR1-AS100(config-router)# neighbor 172.16.3.1 send-label
ASBR1-AS100(config-router)# neighbor 172.16.100.102 remote-as 100
ASBR1-AS100(config-router)# neighbor 172.16.100.102 update-source Loopback0
ASBR1-AS100(config-router)# neighbor 172.16.100.102 next-hop-self
ASBR1-AS100(config-router)# neighbor 172.16.100.102 send-label
ASBR2-AS100(config)#interface Loopback0
ASBR2-AS100(config-if)# ip address 172.16.100.102 255.255.255.255
ASBR2-AS100(config-if)#interface Serial0/0
ASBR2-AS100(config-if)# ip address 172.16.100.2 255.255.255.252
ASBR2-AS100(config-if)# mpls ip
ASBR2-AS100(config-if)#interface Serial1/0
ASBR2-AS100(config-if)# ip address 172.16.4.2 255.255.255.252
ASBR2-AS100(config-if)#router ospf 100
ASBR2-AS100(config-router)# network 172.16.100.0 0.0.0.255 area 0
ASBR2-AS100(config-router)#router bgp 100
ASBR2-AS100(config-router)# network 172.16.100.102 mask 255.255.255.255
ASBR2-AS100(config-router)# neighbor 172.16.4.1 remote-as 2
ASBR2-AS100(config-router)# neighbor 172.16.4.1 send-label
ASBR2-AS100(config-router)# neighbor 172.16.100.101 remote-as 100
ASBR2-AS100(config-router)# neighbor 172.16.100.101 update-source Loopback0
ASBR2-AS100(config-router)# neighbor 172.16.100.101 next-hop-self
ASBR2-AS100(config-router)# neighbor 172.16.100.101 send-label
```

Step 2   **Configure ASBR routers in AS1 and AS2**—In this step, the ASBR routers are configured to perform eBGP peering with transit VPN providers ASBR routers, ASBR1-AS100 and ASBR2-AS100. The loopbacks on PE and RR routers are advertised in BGP on the ASBR routers, and the BGP routes are redistributed in OSPF to ensure reachability. Example 7-24 demonstrates the step. Note that **mpls bgp forwarding** is added by default when MP-eBGP is established between ASBR1-AS1 and ASBR1-AS100. You will see this command under the serial interface in the final configurations.

Example 7-24 *Configure ASBR Routers in AS1 and AS2*

```
ASBR1-AS1(config)#interface Loopback0
ASBR1-AS1(config-if)# ip address 10.10.10.102 255.255.255.255
ASBR1-AS1(config-if)# exit
ASBR1-AS1(config)#mpls ldp router-id Loopback0
ASBR1-AS1(config)#interface Serial0/0
ASBR1-AS1(config-if)# ip address 10.10.10.5 255.255.255.252
ASBR1-AS1(config-if)# mpls ip
ASBR1-AS1(config-if)#interface Serial1/0
ASBR1-AS1(config-if)# ip address 172.16.3.1 255.255.255.252
ASBR1-AS1(config-if)# mpls bgp forwarding
ASBR1-AS1(config-if)#router ospf 1
ASBR1-AS1(config-router)# router-id 10.10.10.102
ASBR1-AS1(config-router)# network 10.0.0.0 0.255.255.255 area 0
ASBR1-AS1(config-router)#router bgp 1
ASBR1-AS1(config-router)# network 10.10.10.101 mask 255.255.255.255
ASBR1-AS1(config-router)# network 10.10.10.200 mask 255.255.255.255
ASBR1-AS1(config-router)# neighbor 10.10.10.200 remote-as 1
ASBR1-AS1(config-router)# neighbor 10.10.10.200 update-source Loopback0
ASBR1-AS1(config-router)# neighbor 10.10.10.200 next-hop-self
ASBR1-AS1(config-router)# neighbor 10.10.10.200 send-label
ASBR1-AS1(config-router)# neighbor 172.16.3.2 remote-as 100
ASBR1-AS1(config-router)# neighbor 172.16.3.2 send-label
ASBR2-AS2(config)#interface Loopback0
ASBR2-AS2(config-if)# ip address 10.20.20.102 255.255.255.255
ASBR2-AS2(config-if)#exit
ASBR2-AS2(config)#mpls ldp router-id Loopback0
ASBR2-AS2(config-if)#interface Serial0/0
ASBR2-AS2(config-if)# ip address 10.20.20.5 255.255.255.252
ASBR2-AS2(config-if)# mpls ip
ASBR2-AS2(config-if)#interface Serial1/0
ASBR2-AS2(config-if)# ip address 172.16.4.1 255.255.255.252
ASBR2-AS2(config-if)#router ospf 2
ASBR2-AS2(config-router)# router-id 10.20.20.102
ASBR2-AS2(config-router)# network 10.0.0.0 0.255.255.255 area 0
ASBR2-AS2(config-router)#router bgp 2
ASBR2-AS2(config-router)# network 10.20.20.101 mask 255.255.255.255
ASBR2-AS2(config-router)# network 10.20.20.200 mask 255.255.255.255
ASBR2-AS2(config-router)# neighbor 10.20.20.200 remote-as 2
ASBR2-AS2(config-router)# neighbor 10.20.20.200 update-source Loopback0
ASBR2-AS2(config-router)# neighbor 10.20.20.200 next-hop-self
ASBR2-AS2(config-router)# neighbor 10.20.20.200 send-label
ASBR2-AS2(config-router)# neighbor 172.16.4.2 remote-as 100
ASBR2-AS2(config-router)# neighbor 172.16.4.2 send-label
```

Step 3   **Configure MP-eBGP session between the RRs**—In this step, you
configure an MP-eBGP session between the RR as shown in
Example 7-25. Before performing this step, ensure that the loopback
addresses on the RRs are reachable. Ensure that P1-AS1-RR and
P1-AS2-RR serve both as an IPv4 and VPNv4 RR.

Example 7-25 *Configure MP-eBGP Session Between the RRs*

```
P1-AS1-RR(config)#router bgp 1
P1-AS1-RR(config-router)# no bgp default ipv4-unicast
P1-AS1-RR(config-router)# neighbor 10.10.10.101 remote-as 1
P1-AS1-RR(config-router)# neighbor 10.10.10.101 update-source Loopback0
P1-AS1-RR(config-router)# neighbor 10.10.10.102 remote-as 1
P1-AS1-RR(config-router)# neighbor 10.10.10.102 update-source Loopback0
P1-AS1-RR(config-router)# neighbor 10.20.20.200 remote-as 2
P1-AS1-RR(config-router)# neighbor 10.20.20.200 ebgp-multihop 10
P1-AS1-RR(config-router)# neighbor 10.20.20.200 update-source Loopback0
P1-AS1-RR(config-router)# address-family ipv4
P1-AS1-RR(config-router-af)# neighbor 10.10.10.101 activate
P1-AS1-RR(config-router-af)# neighbor 10.10.10.101 route-reflector-client
P1-AS1-RR(config-router-af)# neighbor 10.10.10.101 next-hop-self
P1-AS1-RR(config-router-af)# neighbor 10.10.10.101 send-label
P1-AS1-RR(config-router-af)# neighbor 10.10.10.102 activate
P1-AS1-RR(config-router-af)# neighbor 10.10.10.102 route-reflector-client
P1-AS1-RR(config-router-af)# neighbor 10.10.10.102 next-hop-self
P1-AS1-RR(config-router-af)# neighbor 10.10.10.102 send-label
P1-AS1-RR(config-router-af)# exit-address-family
P1-AS1-RR(config-router)# address-family vpnv4
P1-AS1-RR(config-router-af)# neighbor 10.10.10.101 activate
P1-AS1-RR(config-router-af)# neighbor 10.10.10.101 send-community extended
P1-AS1-RR(config-router-af)# neighbor 10.10.10.101 route-reflector-client
P1-AS1-RR(config-router-af)# neighbor 10.20.20.200 activate
P1-AS1-RR(config-router-af)# neighbor 10.20.20.200 send-community extended
P1-AS1-RR(config-router-af)# neighbor 10.20.20.200 next-hop-unchanged
P1-AS2-RR(config)#router bgp 2
P1-AS2-RR(config-router)# no bgp default ipv4-unicast
P1-AS2-RR(config-router)# neighbor 10.10.10.200 remote-as 1
P1-AS2-RR(config-router)# neighbor 10.10.10.200 ebgp-multihop 10
P1-AS2-RR(config-router)# neighbor 10.10.10.200 update-source Loopback0
P1-AS2-RR(config-router)# neighbor 10.20.20.101 remote-as 2
P1-AS2-RR(config-router)# neighbor 10.20.20.101 update-source Loopback0
P1-AS2-RR(config-router)# neighbor 10.20.20.102 remote-as 2
P1-AS2-RR(config-router)# neighbor 10.20.20.102 update-source Loopback0
P1-AS2-RR(config-router)# address-family ipv4
P1-AS2-RR(config-router-af)# neighbor 10.20.20.101 activate
P1-AS2-RR(config-router-af)# neighbor 10.20.20.101 route-reflector-client
P1-AS2-RR(config-router-af)# neighbor 10.20.20.101 next-hop-self
P1-AS2-RR(config-router-af)# neighbor 10.20.20.101 send-label
P1-AS2-RR(config-router-af)# neighbor 10.20.20.102 activate
P1-AS2-RR(config-router-af)# neighbor 10.20.20.102 route-reflector-client
P1-AS2-RR(config-router-af)# neighbor 10.20.20.102 next-hop-self
P1-AS2-RR(config-router-af)# neighbor 10.20.20.102 send-label
P1-AS2-RR(config-router-af)# exit-address-family
P1-AS2-RR(config-router)# address-family vpnv4
P1-AS2-RR(config-router-af)# neighbor 10.10.10.200 activate
P1-AS2-RR(config-router-af)# neighbor 10.10.10.200 send-community extended
P1-AS2-RR(config-router-af)# neighbor 10.10.10.200 next-hop-unchanged
P1-AS2-RR(config-router-af)# neighbor 10.20.20.101 activate
P1-AS2-RR(config-router-af)# neighbor 10.20.20.101 send-community extended
P1-AS2-RR(config-router-af)# neighbor 10.20.20.101 route-reflector-client
```

ASBR and RR Configurations in Option 4

Example 7-26 shows the ASBR1, ASBR2, and RR configurations when using option 4.

Example 7-26 *ASBR and RR Configurations*

```
hostname ASBR1-AS1
!
ip cef
!
mpls ldp router-id Loopback0
!
interface Loopback0
 ip address 10.10.10.102 255.255.255.255
!
interface Serial0/0
 ip address 10.10.10.5 255.255.255.252
 mpls ip
!
interface Serial1/0
 ip address 172.16.3.1 255.255.255.252
 mpls bgp forwarding
!
router ospf 1
 router-id 10.10.10.102
 redistribute bgp 1 metric 1 subnets route-map from_AS100
 network 10.0.0.0 0.255.255.255 area 0
!
router bgp 1
 no synchronization
 network 10.10.10.101 mask 255.255.255.255
 network 10.10.10.102 mask 255.255.255.255
 network 10.10.10.200 mask 255.255.255.255
 network 100.100.100.100 mask 255.255.255.255
 neighbor 172.16.3.2 remote-as 100
 neighbor 172.16.3.2 send-label
 no auto-summary
!
ip access-list standard from_AS100
 permit 10.20.20.102
 permit 10.20.20.101
 permit 172.16.100.101
 permit 172.16.100.102
 permit 10.20.20.200
!
route-map from_AS100 permit 10
 match ip address from_AS100
hostname ASBR2-AS2
!
ip cef
!
mpls ldp router-id Loopback0
!
 interface Loopback0
```

Example 7-26 *ASBR and RR Configurations (Continued)*

```
 ip address 10.20.20.102 255.255.255.255
 !
interface Serial0/0
 ip address 10.20.20.5 255.255.255.252
 mpls ip
 !
interface Serial1/0
 ip address 172.16.4.1 255.255.255.252
 mpls bgp forwarding
 !
router ospf 2
 router-id 10.20.20.102
 redistribute bgp 2 metric 1 subnets route-map from_AS100
 network 10.0.0.0 0.255.255.255 area 0
 !
router bgp 2
 no synchronization
 network 10.20.20.101 mask 255.255.255.255
 network 10.20.20.102 mask 255.255.255.255
 network 10.20.20.200 mask 255.255.255.255
 network 100.100.100.101 mask 255.255.255.255
 neighbor 172.16.4.2 remote-as 100
 neighbor 172.16.4.2 send-label
 no auto-summary
 !
ip access-list standard from_AS100
 permit 10.10.10.102
 permit 10.10.10.101
 permit 172.16.100.101
 permit 172.16.100.102
 permit 10.10.10.200
 !
route-map from_AS100 permit 10
 match ip address from_AS100
hostname ASBR1-AS100
 !
ip cef
 !
interface Loopback0
 ip address 172.16.100.101 255.255.255.255
 !
interface Serial0/0
 ip address 172.16.100.1 255.255.255.252
 mpls ip
 !
interface Serial1/0
 ip address 172.16.3.2 255.255.255.252
 mpls bgp forwarding
 !
router ospf 100
  network 172.16.100.0 0.0.0.255 area 0
```

continues

Example 7-26 *ASBR and RR Configurations (Continued)*

```
!
router bgp 100
 no synchronization
 network 172.16.100.101 mask 255.255.255.255
 neighbor 172.16.3.1 remote-as 1
 neighbor 172.16.3.1 send-label
 neighbor 172.16.100.102 remote-as 100
neighbor 172.16.100.102 next-hop-self
 neighbor 172.16.100.102 update-source Loopback0
 neighbor 172.16.100.102 send-label
 no auto-summary
hostname ASBR2-AS100
!
ip cef
!
interface Loopback0
 ip address 172.16.100.102 255.255.255.255
!
interface Serial0/0
 ip address 172.16.100.2 255.255.255.252
  mpls ip
!
interface Serial1/0
 ip address 172.16.4.2 255.255.255.252
 mpls bgp forwarding
!
router ospf 100
network 172.16.100.0 0.0.0.255 area 0
!
router bgp 100
 no synchronization
 network 172.16.100.102 mask 255.255.255.255
 neighbor 172.16.4.1 remote-as 2
 neighbor 172.16.4.1 send-label
 neighbor 172.16.100.101 remote-as 100
 neighbor 172.16.100.101 update-source Loopback0
neighbor 172.16.100.101 next-hop-self
 neighbor 172.16.100.101 send-label
 no auto-summary
hostname P1-AS1-RR
!
ip cef
!
mpls ldp router-id Loopback0
!
interface Loopback0
 ip address 10.10.10.200 255.255.255.255
!
interface Serial0/0
 ip address 10.10.10.2 255.255.255.252
 mpls ip
!
```

Example 7-26 *ASBR and RR Configurations (Continued)*

```
interface Serial1/0
 ip address 10.10.10.6 255.255.255.252
 mpls ip
!
router ospf 1
 router-id 10.10.10.200
 network 10.0.0.0 0.255.255.255 area 0
!
router bgp 1
 no bgp default ipv4-unicast
 neighbor 10.10.10.101 remote-as 1
 neighbor 10.10.10.101 update-source Loopback0
 neighbor 10.20.20.200 remote-as 2
 neighbor 10.20.20.200 ebgp-multihop 255
 neighbor 10.20.20.200 update-source Loopback0
 !
 address-family vpnv4
 neighbor 10.10.10.101 activate
 neighbor 10.10.10.101 route-reflector-client
 neighbor 10.10.10.101 send-community extended
 neighbor 10.20.20.200 activate
 neighbor 10.20.20.200 next-hop-unchanged
 neighbor 10.20.20.200 send-community extended
 exit-address-family
hostname P1-AS2-RR
!
ip cef
!
mpls ldp router-id Loopback0
!
interface Loopback0
 ip address 10.20.20.200 255.255.255.255
!
interface Serial0/0
 ip address 10.20.20.6 255.255.255.252
  mpls ip
!
interface Serial1/0
 ip address 10.20.20.2 255.255.255.252
  mpls ip
!
router ospf 2
 router-id 10.20.20.200
 network 10.0.0.0 0.255.255.255 area 0
!
router bgp 2
 no bgp default ipv4-unicast
 neighbor 10.10.10.200 remote-as 1
 neighbor 10.10.10.200 ebgp-multihop 255
 neighbor 10.10.10.200 update-source Loopback0
 neighbor 10.20.20.101 remote-as 2
```

continues

Example 7-26 *ASBR and RR Configurations (Continued)*

```
neighbor 10.20.20.101 update-source Loopback0
!
address-family vpnv4
neighbor 10.10.10.200 activate
neighbor 10.10.10.200 next-hop-unchanged
neighbor 10.10.10.200 send-community extended
neighbor 10.20.20.101 activate
neighbor 10.20.20.101 route-reflector-client
neighbor 10.20.20.101 send-community extended
exit-address-family
```

Verifying Inter-Provider VPN Operation Using Option 4

The steps to verify inter-provider VPN operation using option 4 are

Step 1 **Verify control plane forwarding with option 4**—Figure 7-35 shows the control plane forwarding operation when the 172.16.10.0/24 prefix is propagated across the multiprovider networks AS1 and AS2 to CE2-A.

Figure 7-35 *Control Plane Forwarding in Option 4*

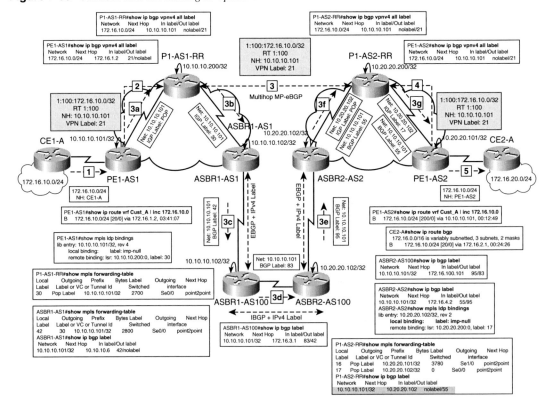

Step 2   **Verify data forwarding in option 4**—Figure 7-36 shows the data plane forwarding operation when a packet is sent from 172.16.20.1 to 172.16.10.1.

Figure 7-36   *Data Forwarding in Option 4*

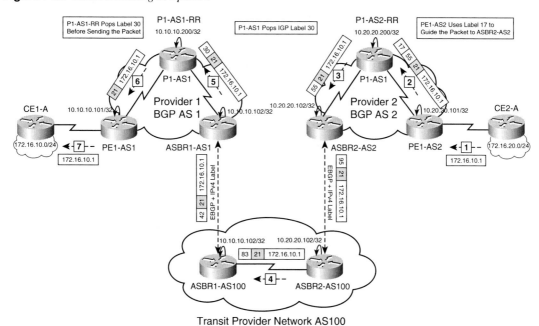

Step 3   **Verify end-to-end connectivity via ping**—Verify end-to-end connectivity between Customer A networks (172.16.10.0/24 and 172.16.20.0/24) and Customer B networks (192.168.10.0/24 and 192.168.20.0/24). Example 7-27 shows the result of the ping operation.

Example 7-27 *Verify End-to-End Connectivity*

```
CE1-A#ping 172.16.20.1 source 172.16.10.1
Type escape sequence to abort.
Sending 5, 100-byte ICMP Echos to 172.16.20.1, timeout is 2 seconds:
Packet sent with a source address of 172.16.10.1
!!!!!
Success rate is 100 percent (5/5), round-trip min/avg/max = 140/140/140 ms
CE1-B#ping 192.168.20.1 source 192.168.10.1
Type escape sequence to abort.
Sending 5, 100-byte ICMP Echos to 192.168.20.1, timeout is 2 seconds:
Packet sent with a source address of 192.168.10.1
!!!!!
Success rate is 100 percent (5/5), round-trip min/avg/max = 132/138/140 ms
```

Case Study—Inter-AS Implementing Route-Reflector and BGP Confederation in Provider Networks

Figure 7-37 shows an Inter-AS network topology in which SP1 and SP2 are providing MPLS VPN services to geographically dispersed Customer A and Customer B sites.

Figure 7-37 *Inter-AS Providers Implementing RR and BGP Confederation*

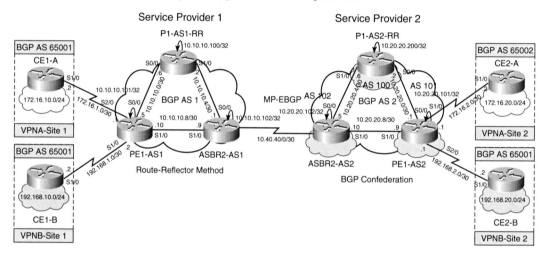

Provider 1 uses the RR method to reduce iBGP mesh while Provider 2 uses BGP confederation to minimize the number of BGP sessions. ASBR2-AS1 in the provider network uses the Inter-AS redistribute connected option to distribute the next-hop to devices in Provider Network 1, while ASBR2-AS2 uses the Inter-AS next-hop-self method to distribute next-hop information to devices in Provider Network 2. Example 7-28 shows the ASBR, PE router, and RR configurations. Refer to Example 7-3 and Example 7-4 for CE configurations.

Example 7-28 *ASBR and RR Configurations*

```
hostname ASBR2-AS1
!
ip cef
!
mpls ldp router-id Loopback0
!
interface Loopback0
 ip address 10.10.10.102 255.255.255.255
!
interface Ethernet0/0
 ip address 10.10.10.5 255.255.255.252
 mpls ip
!
interface Ethernet1/0
 ip address 10.10.10.10 255.255.255.252
```

Example 7-28 *ASBR and RR Configurations (Continued)*

```
 mpls ip
!
interface Serial2/0
 ip address 10.40.40.1 255.255.255.252
 mpls bgp forwarding
!
router ospf 1
 redistribute connected subnets route-map adv-conn
 network 10.10.10.0 0.0.0.255 area 0
!
router bgp 1
 no bgp default ipv4-unicast
 no bgp default route-target filter
 neighbor 10.10.10.100 remote-as 1
 neighbor 10.10.10.100 update-source Loopback0
 neighbor 10.40.40.2 remote-as 2
 !
 address-family vpnv4
 neighbor 10.10.10.100 activate
 neighbor 10.10.10.100 send-community extended
 neighbor 10.40.40.2 activate
 neighbor 10.40.40.2 send-community extended
 exit-address-family
!
access-list 10 permit 10.40.40.2
!
route-map adv-conn permit 10
 match ip address 10
```

```
hostname ASBR2-AS2
!
ip cef
!
mpls ldp router-id Loopback0
!
interface Loopback0
 ip address 10.20.20.102 255.255.255.255
!
interface Ethernet0/0
 ip address 10.20.20.5 255.255.255.252
 mpls ip
!
interface Ethernet1/0
 ip address 10.20.20.10 255.255.255.252
 mpls ip
!
interface Serial2/0
 ip address 10.40.40.2 255.255.255.252
 mpls bgp forwarding
!
router ospf 2
 network 10.20.20.0 0.0.0.255 area 0
```

continues

Example 7-28 *ASBR and RR Configurations (Continued)*

```
!
router bgp 102
 no bgp default ipv4-unicast
 no bgp default route-target filter
 bgp confederation identifier 2
 bgp confederation peers 100 101
 neighbor 10.20.20.100 remote-as 100
 neighbor 10.20.20.100 ebgp-multihop 2
 neighbor 10.20.20.100 update-source Loopback0
 neighbor 10.20.20.101 remote-as 101
 neighbor 10.20.20.101 ebgp-multihop 2
 neighbor 10.20.20.101 update-source Loopback0
 neighbor 10.40.40.1 remote-as 1
 !
 address-family vpnv4
 neighbor 10.20.20.100 activate
 neighbor 10.20.20.100 send-community extended
 neighbor 10.20.20.100 next-hop-self
 neighbor 10.20.20.101 activate
 neighbor 10.20.20.101 send-community extended
 neighbor 10.20.20.101 next-hop-self
 neighbor 10.40.40.1 activate
 neighbor 10.40.40.1 send-community extended
 exit-address-family
hostname PE1-AS1
!
ip cef
!
ip vrf Cust_A
 rd 1:100
 route-target export 1:100
  route-target import 2:100
!
ip vrf Cust_B
 rd 1:101
 route-target export 1:101
route-target import 2:101
!
mpls ldp router-id Loopback0
!
interface Loopback0
 ip address 10.10.10.101 255.255.255.255
!
interface Ethernet0/0
 ip address 10.10.10.1 255.255.255.252
 mpls ip
!
interface Ethernet1/0
 ip address 10.10.10.9 255.255.255.252
 mpls ip
!
interface Serial2/0
```

Example 7-28 *ASBR and RR Configurations (Continued)*

```
  description connected to Cust_A CE1-A
  ip vrf forwarding Cust_A
  ip address 172.16.1.1 255.255.255.252
 !
 interface Serial3/0
  description connected to Cust_B CE1-B
  ip vrf forwarding Cust_B
  ip address 192.168.1.1 255.255.255.252
 !
 router ospf 1
  network 10.10.10.0 0.0.0.255 area 0
 !
 router bgp 1
  no bgp default ipv4-unicast
  neighbor 10.10.10.100 remote-as 1
  neighbor 10.10.10.100 update-source Loopback0
  !
  address-family vpnv4
  neighbor 10.10.10.100 activate
  neighbor 10.10.10.100 send-community extended
  exit-address-family
  !
  address-family ipv4 vrf Cust_B
  neighbor 192.168.1.2 remote-as 65001
  neighbor 192.168.1.2 activate
  neighbor 192.168.1.2 as-override
  no auto-summary
  no synchronization
  exit-address-family
  !
  address-family ipv4 vrf Cust_A
  neighbor 172.16.1.2 remote-as 65001
  neighbor 172.16.1.2 activate
  no auto-summary
  no synchronization
  exit-address-family
hostname PE1-AS2
!
ip cef
!
ip vrf Cust_A
 rd 2:100
 route-target export 2:100
 route-target import 1:100
!
ip vrf Cust_B
 rd 2:101
 route-target export 2:101
 route-target import 1:101
!
mpls ldp router-id Loopback0
```

continues

Example 7-28 *ASBR and RR Configurations (Continued)*

```
!
interface Loopback0
 ip address 10.20.20.101 255.255.255.255
!
interface Ethernet0/0
 ip address 10.20.20.1 255.255.255.252
 mpls ip
!
interface Ethernet1/0
 ip address 10.20.20.9 255.255.255.252
 mpls ip
!
interface Serial2/0
 description connected to Cust_A CE2-A
 ip vrf forwarding Cust_A
 ip address 172.16.2.1 255.255.255.252
!
interface Serial3/0
 description connected to Cust_B CE2-B
 ip vrf forwarding Cust_B
 ip address 192.168.2.1 255.255.255.252
!
router ospf 2
 network 10.20.20.0 0.0.0.255 area 0
!
router bgp 101
 no bgp default ipv4-unicast
 bgp confederation identifier 2
 bgp confederation peers 100 102
 neighbor 10.20.20.100 remote-as 100
 neighbor 10.20.20.100 ebgp-multihop 2
 neighbor 10.20.20.100 update-source Loopback0
 neighbor 10.20.20.102 remote-as 102
 neighbor 10.20.20.102 ebgp-multihop 2
 neighbor 10.20.20.102 update-source Loopback0
 !
 address-family vpnv4
 neighbor 10.20.20.100 activate
 neighbor 10.20.20.100 send-community extended
 neighbor 10.20.20.100 next-hop-self
 neighbor 10.20.20.102 activate
 neighbor 10.20.20.102 send-community extended
 neighbor 10.20.20.102 next-hop-self
 exit-address-family
 !
 address-family ipv4 vrf Cust_B
 neighbor 192.168.2.2 remote-as 65001
 neighbor 192.168.2.2 activate
 neighbor 192.168.2.2 as-override
 no auto-summary
 no synchronization
 exit-address-family
```

Example 7-28 *ASBR and RR Configurations (Continued)*

```
 !
 address-family ipv4 vrf Cust_A
 neighbor 172.16.2.2 remote-as 65002
 neighbor 172.16.2.2 activate
 no auto-summary
 no synchronization
 exit-address-family
hostname P1-AS1-RR
 !
 ip cef
 !
 mpls ldp router-id Loopback0
 !
 interface Loopback0
  ip address 10.10.10.100 255.255.255.255
 !
 interface Ethernet0/0
  ip address 10.10.10.2 255.255.255.252
  mpls ip
 !
 interface Ethernet1/0
  ip address 10.10.10.6 255.255.255.252
  mpls ip
 !
 router ospf 1
  network 10.10.10.0 0.0.0.255 area 0
 !
 router bgp 1
  no bgp default ipv4-unicast
  neighbor 10.10.10.101 remote-as 1
  neighbor 10.10.10.101 update-source Loopback0
  neighbor 10.10.10.102 remote-as 1
  !
  address-family vpnv4
  neighbor 10.10.10.101 activate
  neighbor 10.10.10.101 send-community extended
  neighbor 10.10.10.101 route-reflector-client
  neighbor 10.10.10.101 next-hop-self
  neighbor 10.10.10.102 activate
  neighbor 10.10.10.102 send-community extended
  neighbor 10.10.10.102 route-reflector-client
  neighbor 10.10.10.102 next-hop-self
  exit-address-family
hostname P1-AS2
 !
 ip cef
 !
 mpls ldp router-id Loopback0
 !
 interface Loopback0
  ip address 10.20.20.100 255.255.255.255
```

continues

Example 7-28 *ASBR and RR Configurations (Continued)*

```
!
interface Ethernet0/0
 ip address 10.20.20.2 255.255.255.252
 mpls ip
!
interface Ethernet1/0
 ip address 10.20.20.6 255.255.255.252
 mpls ip
!
router ospf 2
 network 10.20.20.0 0.0.0.255 area 0
!
router bgp 100
 no bgp default ipv4-unicast
 bgp confederation identifier 2
 bgp confederation peers 101 102
 neighbor 10.20.20.101 remote-as 101
 neighbor 10.20.20.101 ebgp-multihop 2
 neighbor 10.20.20.101 update-source Loopback0
 neighbor 10.20.20.102 remote-as 102
 neighbor 10.20.20.102 ebgp-multihop 2
 neighbor 10.20.20.102 update-source Loopback0
 !
 address-family vpnv4
 neighbor 10.20.20.101 activate
 neighbor 10.20.20.101 send-community extended
 neighbor 10.20.20.101 next-hop-self
 neighbor 10.20.20.102 activate
 neighbor 10.20.20.102 send-community extended
 neighbor 10.20.20.102 next-hop-self
 exit-address-family
```

Example 7-29 shows that CE1-A and CE1-B see local and remote routes for VPN-A and VPN-B networks.

Example 7-29 *Verifying End-to-End Connectivity*

```
CE1-A#show ip bgp
<truncated>
   Network          Next Hop          Metric LocPrf Weight Path
*> 172.16.10.0/24   0.0.0.0                0          32768 i
*> 172.16.20.0/24   172.16.1.1                            0 1 2 65002 i
CE1-B#show ip bgp
<truncated>
   Network          Next Hop          Metric LocPrf Weight Path
*> 192.168.10.0     0.0.0.0                0          32768 i
*> 192.168.20.0     192.168.1.1                          0 1 2 1 i
```

Example 7-30 shows the result of the ping operation.

Example 7-30 *Verify End-to-End Connectivity*

```
CE1-A#ping 172.16.20.1 source 172.16.10.1
Type escape sequence to abort.
Sending 5, 100-byte ICMP Echos to 172.16.20.1, timeout is 2 seconds:
Packet sent with a source address of 172.16.10.1
!!!!!
Success rate is 100 percent (5/5), round-trip min/avg/max = 60/61/68 ms
CE1-B#ping 192.168.20.1 source 192.168.10.1
Type escape sequence to abort.
Sending 5, 100-byte ICMP Echos to 192.168.20.1, timeout is 2 seconds:
Packet sent with a source address of 192.168.10.1
!!!!!
Success rate is 100 percent (5/5), round-trip min/avg/max = 60/60/64 ms
```

Case Study—Multi-Homed Inter-AS Provider Network

Figure 7-38 shows an Inter-AS network topology in which Service Provider 1 and Service Provider 2 are providing MPLS VPN services to geographically dispersed Customer A and B sites.

Figure 7-38 *Multi-Homed Inter-AS Provider Network*

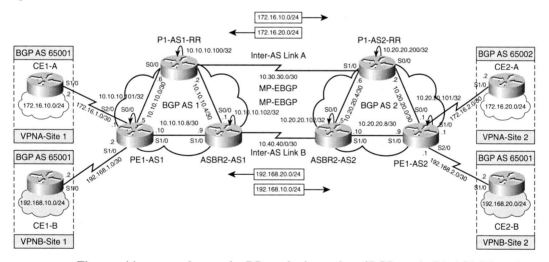

The provider network uses the RR method to reduce iBGP mesh. P1-AS1-RR and P1-AS2-RR serve as both an ASBR and a RR in the provider network. In this case study, ASBR1-AS1 and ASBR2-AS2 in the provider network use the Inter-AS redistribute connected option to distribute the next hop to devices in Provider Network 1, while P1-AS1-RR and P1-AS2-RR use the Inter-AS next-hop-self method to distribute next-hop information to devices in Provider Network 2. Provider 2, in this case study, also wants to ensure that Customer A traffic uses the Inter-AS Link A and Customer B traffic uses the Inter-AS Link B, and, in case any link goes down, both customers' traffic should be routed across the other operational link. Example 7-31 shows the ASBR and PE router configuration. Refer to Example 7-3 and Example 7-4 for CE configurations.

Example 7-31 *Multi-Homed Inter-AS Provider Network Router Configurations*

```
hostname ASBR2-AS1
!
ip cef
!
mpls ldp router-id Loopback0
!
interface Loopback0
 ip address 10.10.10.102 255.255.255.255
!
interface Ethernet0/0
 ip address 10.10.10.5 255.255.255.252
 mpls ip
!
interface Ethernet1/0
 ip address 10.10.10.10 255.255.255.252
 mpls ip
!
interface Serial2/0
 ip address 10.40.40.1 255.255.255.252
 mpls bgp forwarding
!
router ospf 1
 redistribute connected subnets route-map adv-conn
 network 10.10.10.0 0.0.0.255 area 0
!
router bgp 1
 no bgp default ipv4-unicast
 no bgp default route-target filter
 neighbor 10.10.10.100 remote-as 1
 neighbor 10.10.10.100 update-source Loopback0
 neighbor 10.40.40.2 remote-as 2
 !
 address-family vpnv4
 neighbor 10.10.10.100 activate
 neighbor 10.10.10.100 send-community extended
 neighbor 10.40.40.2 activate
 neighbor 10.40.40.2 send-community extended
 exit-address-family
!
access-list 1 permit 172.16.10.0
access-list 2 permit 192.168.10.0
access-list 10 permit 10.40.40.2
!
route-map adv-conn permit 10
 match ip address 10
hostname ASBR2-AS2
!
ip cef
!
```

Example 7-31 *Multi-Homed Inter-AS Provider Network Router Configurations (Continued)*

```
mpls ldp router-id Loopback0
!
interface Loopback0
 ip address 10.20.20.102 255.255.255.255
!
interface Ethernet0/0
 ip address 10.20.20.5 255.255.255.252
 mpls ip
!
interface Ethernet1/0
 ip address 10.20.20.10 255.255.255.252
 mpls ip
!
interface Serial2/0
 ip address 10.40.40.2 255.255.255.252
mpls bgp forwarding
!
router ospf 2
 network 10.20.20.0 0.0.0.255 area 0
!
router bgp 2
 no synchronization
 no bgp default route-target filter
 neighbor 10.20.20.100 remote-as 2
 neighbor 10.20.20.100 update-source Loopback0
 neighbor 10.40.40.1 remote-as 1
 no auto-summary
 !
 address-family vpnv4
 neighbor 10.20.20.100 activate
 neighbor 10.20.20.100 send-community extended
 neighbor 10.20.20.100 next-hop-self
 neighbor 10.40.40.1 activate
 neighbor 10.40.40.1 send-community extended
 neighbor 10.40.40.1 route-map pref_192 in
 neighbor 10.40.40.1 route-map pref_192_local out
 exit-address-family
!
access-list 1 permit 192.168.10.0
access-list 2 permit 172.16.10.0
access-list 3 permit 192.168.20.0
access-list 4 permit 172.16.20.0
!
route-map pref_192_local permit 10
 match ip address 3
!
route-map pref_192_local permit 20
 match ip address 4
 set as-path prepend 65501 65501 65501
!
```

continues

Example 7-31 *Multi-Homed Inter-AS Provider Network Router Configurations (Continued)*

```
route-map pref_192 permit 10
 match ip address 1
 set metric 50
!
route-map pref_192 permit 20
 match ip address 2
 set metric 100
hostname PE1-AS1
!
ip cef
!
ip vrf Cust_A
 rd 1:100
 route-target export 1:100
 route-target import 2:100
!
ip vrf Cust_B
 rd 1:101
 route-target export 1:101
route-target import 2:101
!
mpls ldp router-id Loopback0
!
interface Loopback0
 ip address 10.10.10.101 255.255.255.255
!
interface Ethernet0/0
 ip address 10.10.10.1 255.255.255.252
 mpls ip
!
interface Ethernet1/0
 ip address 10.10.10.9 255.255.255.252
 mpls ip
!
interface Serial2/0
 description connected to Cust_A CE1-A
 ip vrf forwarding Cust_A
 ip address 172.16.1.1 255.255.255.252
!
interface Serial3/0
 description connected to Cust_B CE1-B
 ip vrf forwarding Cust_B
 ip address 192.168.1.1 255.255.255.252
!
router ospf 1
 network 10.10.10.0 0.0.0.255 area 0
!
router bgp 1
 no bgp default ipv4-unicast
 neighbor 10.10.10.100 remote-as 1
 neighbor 10.10.10.100 update-source Loopback0
 !
```

Example 7-31 *Multi-Homed Inter-AS Provider Network Router Configurations (Continued)*

```
 address-family vpnv4
 neighbor 10.10.10.100 activate
 neighbor 10.10.10.100 send-community extended
 exit-address-family
 !
 address-family ipv4 vrf Cust_B
 neighbor 192.168.1.2 remote-as 65001
 neighbor 192.168.1.2 activate
 neighbor 192.168.1.2 as-override
 no auto-summary
 no synchronization
 exit-address-family
 !
 address-family ipv4 vrf Cust_A
 neighbor 172.16.1.2 remote-as 65001
 neighbor 172.16.1.2 activate
  no auto-summary
 no synchronization
 exit-address-family
hostname PE1-AS2
!
ip cef
!
ip vrf Cust_A
 rd 2:100
 route-target export 2:100
 route-target import 1:100
!
ip vrf Cust_B
 rd 2:101
 route-target export 2:101
 route-target import 1:101
!
mpls ldp router-id Loopback0
!
interface Loopback0
 ip address 10.20.20.101 255.255.255.255
!
interface Ethernet0/0
 ip address 10.20.20.1 255.255.255.252
 mpls ip
!
interface Ethernet1/0
 ip address 10.20.20.9 255.255.255.252
 mpls ip
!
interface Serial2/0
 description coonected to Cust_A CE2-A
 ip vrf forwarding Cust_A
 ip address 172.16.2.1 255.255.255.252
```

continues

Example 7-31 *Multi-Homed Inter-AS Provider Network Router Configurations (Continued)*

```
!
interface Serial3/0
 description coonected to Cust_B CE2-B
 ip vrf forwarding Cust_B
 ip address 192.168.2.1 255.255.255.252
!
router ospf 2
 network 10.20.20.0 0.0.0.255 area 0
!
router bgp 2
 no bgp default ipv4-unicast
 neighbor 10.20.20.100 remote-as 2
 neighbor 10.20.20.100 update-source Loopback0
 !
 address-family vpnv4
 neighbor 10.20.20.100 activate
 neighbor 10.20.20.100 send-community extended
 exit-address-family
 !
 address-family ipv4 vrf Cust_B
 neighbor 192.168.2.2 remote-as 65001
 neighbor 192.168.2.2 activate
 neighbor 192.168.2.2 as-override
 no auto-summary
 no synchronization
 exit-address-family
 !
 address-family ipv4 vrf Cust_A
 neighbor 172.16.2.2 remote-as 65002
 neighbor 172.16.2.2 activate
 no auto-summary
 no synchronization
 exit-address-family
```
```
hostname ASBR1-AS1-RR
!
ip cef
!
mpls ldp router-id Loopback0
!
interface Loopback0
 ip address 10.10.10.100 255.255.255.255
!
interface Ethernet0/0
 ip address 10.10.10.2 255.255.255.252
 mpls ip
!
interface Ethernet1/0
 ip address 10.10.10.6 255.255.255.252
 mpls ip
!
interface Serial2/0
 ip address 10.30.30.1 255.255.255.252
```

Example 7-31 *Multi-Homed Inter-AS Provider Network Router Configurations (Continued)*

```
 mpls bgp forwarding
 !
router ospf 1
 redistribute connected subnets route-map adv-conn
 network 10.10.10.0 0.0.0.255 area 0
 !
router bgp 1
 no bgp default ipv4-unicast
 no bgp default route-target filter
 neighbor 10.10.10.101 remote-as 1
 neighbor 10.10.10.101 update-source Loopback0
 neighbor 10.10.10.102 remote-as 1
 neighbor 10.30.30.2 remote-as 2
 !
 address-family vpnv4
 neighbor 10.10.10.101 activate
 neighbor 10.10.10.101 send-community extended
 neighbor 10.10.10.101 route-reflector-client
 neighbor 10.10.10.102 activate
 neighbor 10.10.10.102 send-community extended
 neighbor 10.10.10.102 route-reflector-client
 neighbor 10.30.30.2 activate
 neighbor 10.30.30.2 send-community extended
 exit-address-family
 !
access-list 10 permit 10.30.30.2
 !
route-map adv-conn permit 10
 match ip address 10
```
```
hostname ASBR1-AS2-RR
 !
ip cef
 !
mpls ldp router-id Loopback0
 !
interface Loopback0
 ip address 10.20.20.100 255.255.255.255
 !
interface Ethernet0/0
 ip address 10.20.20.2 255.255.255.252
 mpls ip
 !
interface Ethernet1/0
 ip address 10.20.20.6 255.255.255.252
 mpls ip
 !
interface Serial2/0
 ip address 10.30.30.2 255.255.255.252
 mpls bgp forwarding
 !
```

continues

Example 7-31 *Multi-Homed Inter-AS Provider Network Router Configurations (Continued)*

```
router ospf 2
 network 10.20.20.0 0.0.0.255 area 0
!
router bgp 2
 no synchronization
 no bgp default route-target filter
 neighbor 10.20.20.101 remote-as 2
 neighbor 10.20.20.101 update-source Loopback0
 neighbor 10.20.20.102 remote-as 2
 neighbor 10.20.20.102 update-source Loopback0
 neighbor 10.30.30.1 remote-as 1
 no auto-summary
 !
 address-family vpnv4
 neighbor 10.20.20.101 activate
 neighbor 10.20.20.101 send-community extended
 neighbor 10.20.20.101 route-reflector-client
 neighbor 10.20.20.101 next-hop-self
 neighbor 10.20.20.102 activate
 neighbor 10.20.20.102 send-community extended
 neighbor 10.20.20.102 route-reflector-client
 neighbor 10.20.20.102 next-hop-self
 neighbor 10.30.30.1 activate
 neighbor 10.30.30.1 send-community extended
 neighbor 10.30.30.1 route-map pref_172 in
 neighbor 10.30.30.1 route-map pref_172_local out
 exit-address-family
!
access-list 1 permit 172.16.10.0
access-list 2 permit 192.168.10.0
access-list 3 permit 172.16.20.0
access-list 4 permit 192.168.20.0
!
route-map pref_172_local permit 10
 match ip address 3
!
route-map pref_172_local permit 20
 match ip address 4
 set as-path prepend 65501 65501 65501
!
route-map pref_172 permit 10
 match ip address 1
 set metric 50
!
route-map pref_172 permit 20
 match ip address 2
 set metric 100
```

Example 7-32 shows that, on PE1-AS1, 172.16.20.0/24 is reachable via Inter-AS Link A, and 192.168.20.0/24 is reachable via Inter-AS Link B. Based on the output shown in

Example 7-32, traffic between Customer A sites take Inter-AS Link A and traffic between Customer B sites take Inter-AS Link B.

Example 7-32 *Verifying End-to-End Connectivity*

```
PE1-AS1#show ip bgp vpnv4 all
<truncated>
*>i172.16.20.0/24    10.30.30.2              0      100      0 2 65002 i
*>i192.168.20.0      10.40.40.2              0      100      0 2 65001 i
```
```
PE1-AS2#show ip bgp vpnv4 all
<truncated>
*>i172.16.10.0/24    10.20.20.100           50      100      0 1 65001 i
*>i192.168.10.0      10.20.20.102           50      100      0 1 65001 i
```

Example 7-33 shows the result of the ping operation.

Example 7-33 *Verify End-to-End Connectivity*

```
CE1-A#ping 172.16.20.1 source 172.16.10.1

Type escape sequence to abort.
Sending 5, 100-byte ICMP Echos to 172.16.20.1, timeout is 2 seconds:
Packet sent with a source address of 172.16.10.1
!!!!!
Success rate is 100 percent (5/5), round-trip min/avg/max = 60/60/60 ms
```
```
CE1-B#ping 192.168.20.1 source 192.168.10.1

Type escape sequence to abort.
Sending 5, 100-byte ICMP Echos to 192.168.20.1, timeout is 2 seconds:
Packet sent with a source address of 192.168.10.1
!!!!!
Success rate is 100 percent (5/5), round-trip min/avg/max = 60/60/60 ms
```

Command Reference

Command	Description
Router(config-router)#**no bgp default route-target filter**	Using the **no** form of this command causes all received VPN-IPv4 routes to be accepted by the router. In an Inter-AS environment, accepting VPN-IPv4 routes is the desired behavior for a router configured as an autonomous system border edge router.
Router(config-router)#**neighbor** *ip-address* **send-label**	Enables a router to use BGP to distribute MPLS labels along with the IPv4 routes to a peer router. This command has to be enabled on both the BGP routers peering to each other.

CHAPTER 8

Carrier Supporting Carriers

In Chapter 7, "Inter-Provider VPNs," you saw that two MPLS VPN provider networks belonging to different BGP autonomous systems use MP-eBGP to transport routing information for VPN clients connected to them. In this chapter, the concept of MPLS VPN provider networks providing transport of routing information to their VPN customers, who are carriers themselves, is introduced. This chapter covers the following subjects:

- Carrier supporting carriers overview
- Deployment scenarios with CSC architecture
- CSC architecture benefits

Carrier Supporting Carriers Overview

Carrier supporting carriers (CSC) is implemented in circumstances in which one service provider needs to use the transport services provided by another service provider. The service provider providing the transport is called the *backbone carrier* and the service provider using the services provided by the backbone carrier is called a *customer carrier*. The customer carrier can either be an ISP provider or an MPLS VPN service provider.

Figure 8-1 shows a network topology in which ISPX is the customer carrier and has two POP sites, ISPX-POP1 and ISPX-POP2.

The customer carrier ISPX is using MPLS VPN services provided by the backbone carrier to route traffic between user sites. In the CSC model, the links between the backbone and customer carrier are MPLS enabled to provide an end-to-end LSP path between the two POP sites located in the customer carrier network. In the CSC model, the backbone carrier providing MPLS VPN services to the customer carrier has knowledge of only the customer carrier's internal routes. These routes are relevant for building the LSP path between the two POP sites and for forming the iBGP or MP-iBGP session between the POP sites. User networks will then be transported across this iBGP or MP-iBGP session.

Figure 8-1   *CSC Architecture*

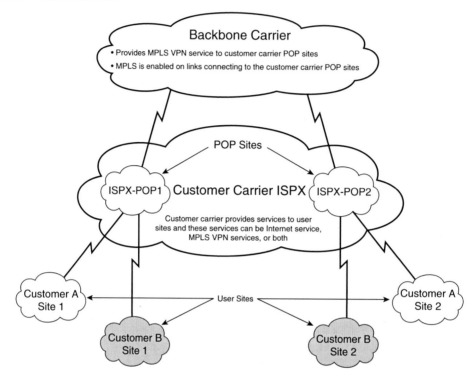

Label Exchange Methods in CSC Architecture

There are two ways of exchanging IGP labels in an MPLS VPN network:

- Using IGP for label exchange
- Using BGP for label exchange

Using IGP for Label Exchange

This method employs the traditional approach of using an IGP to exchange routes between PE-CE routers. Label exchange is performed using TDP/LDP protocols. Figure 8-2 shows the configuration steps for enabling MPLS on PE-CE routers.

Control Plane Forwarding Operation—Customer Carrier Not Running MPLS

Figure 8-5 shows the control plane forwarding operation that takes place in the customer carrier not running the MPLS deployment model. Path a-b-c-d-e shows the control plane propagation for network 172.16.10.0/24, and path 1-2-2a-2b-3 shows the control plane propagation for 10.20.20.102/32, which is the next hop in the 172.16.10.0/24 update.

Figure 8-5 *Control Plane Forwarding Operation—Customer Carrier ISPX POP Sites Not Running MPLS*

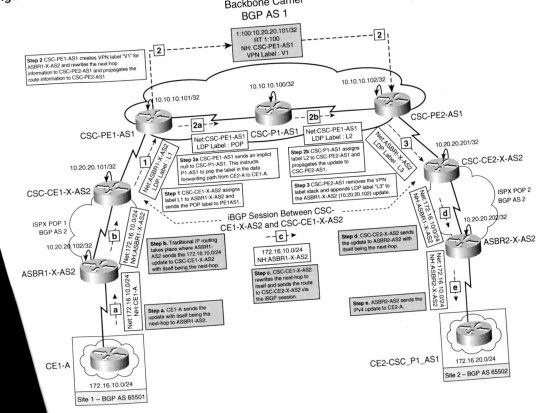

Forwarding Operation—Customer Carrier Not Running MPLS

Figure 8-6 shows the data plane forwarding operation that takes place in the customer carrier not running the MPLS deployment model for a packet destined for network 172.16.10.0/24 originated by CE2-A.

Figure 8-2 *Label Exchange by Enabling MPLS on the Interface*

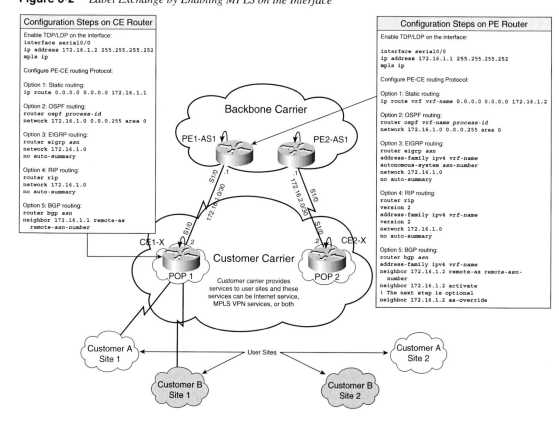

Using BGP for Label Exchange

In this method, BGP is used for routing and for label exchange. When using EBGP for label exchange, **mpls bgp forwarding** is automatically configured under the interface. Prior to that, ensure that TDP/LDP Protocol (mpls ip) is not enabled on the interface.

Figure 8-3 shows the steps to configure BGP for IPv4 label distribution.

NOTE   Check Cisco.com for IOS versions supporting this method.

Figure 8-3   *Using BGP for IPv4 Label Distribution*

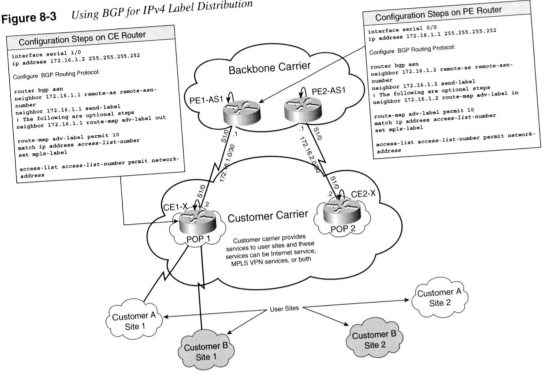

Deployment Scenarios with CSC Architecture

Three deployment scenarios are possible with CSC architecture:

- Customer carrier is not running MPLS inside its POP sites.
- Customer carrier is running MPLS inside its POP sites.
- Customer carrier is providing MPLS VPN services to user sites.

The following sections delve into each of the deployment scenarios in greater detail.

CSC Network—Customer Carrier Not Running MPLS

In this deployment model, devices in the customer carrier ISPX do not use MPLS and no IGP/LDP label exchange takes place inside the customer carrier network. MPLS is enabled only on the CE router (CSC-CE1-X-AS2 and CSC-CE2-X-AS2) interface peering with the PE router located in the backbone carrier network. The backbone carrier only has knowledge of the customer carrier's internal networks. To allow exchange of external networks belonging to the user sites (customer carrier clients like Customer A), an internal BGP (iBGP) session needs to be enabled on the customer edge (CE) routers located in the customer carrier network.

Figure 8-4 shows an example case study of this deployment model in which CSC-CE1-X-AS2 and CSC-CE2-X-AS2 are CE routers belonging to different ISPX POP sites, ISPX-POP1 and ISPX-POP2, in the customer carrier network.

Figure 8-4   *Customer Carrier ISPX POP Sites Not Running MPLS*

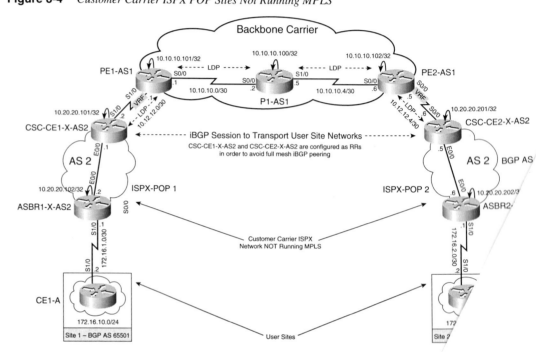

PE1-AS1 and PE2-AS1 are provider edge (PE) routers in the back
OSPF PE-CE routing is used between PE routers, PE1-AS1 and PF
carrier and CE routers, CSC-CE1-X-AS2 and CSC-CE2-X-AS
network. The ASBR routers, ASBR1-X-AS2 and ASBR2-X-/
user sites or Customer A sites, Site 1 and Site 2. MPLS is enab
to facilitate label exchange so that an end-to-end label swi'
between the CE routers, CSC-CE1-X-AS2 and CSC-CE2
on interfaces connecting the CE and ASBR devices in t'
iBGP session is established between the CE routers, C'
AS2, to allow Customer A Sites 1 and 2 to exchang
deployment model, because the ISPX-POP1 and IS
and need to have iBGP peering between, it is alwa
configured to avoid iBGP peering mesh. In this '
X-AS2 act as RRs.

Figure 8-6 *Data Forwarding Operation—Customer Carrier ISPX POP Sites Not Running MPLS*

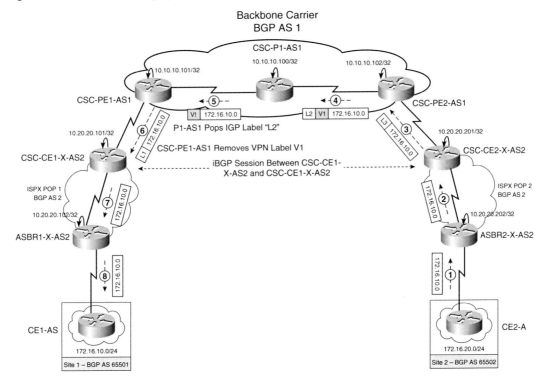

Configuring the CSC Model—Customer Carrier Not Running MPLS

The steps to configure the CSC model in which the customer carrier is not running MPLS are as follows. Refer to the topology shown in Figure 8-4:

Step 1 Provision the MPLS VPN backbone carrier network—In this step, you configure the backbone carrier's PE and provider core routers, CSC-PE1-AS1, CSC-PE2-AS1, and CSC-P1-AS1, to provide MPLS VPN services to the carrier network. IS-IS is used as an IGP protocol in the backbone carrier's core. The PE-CE routing protocol is OSPF. Example 8-1 shows the configuration for CSC-PE1-AS1, CSC-PE2-AS1, and CSC-P1-AS1. Ensure that MPLS is enabled on the VRF enabled interfaces.

Example 8-1 *CSC-PE1-AS1, CSC-PE2-AS1, and CSC-P1-AS1 Configurations*

```
hostname CSC-PE1-AS1

!
ip cef
```

continues

Example 8-1 *CSC-PE1-AS1, CSC-PE2-AS1, and CSC-P1-AS1 Configurations (Continued)*

```
!
ip vrf VRFX
 route-target export 1:100
 route-target import 1:100
!
mpls ldp router-id Serial1/0
!
interface Loopback0
 ip address 10.10.10.101 255.255.255.255
!
interface Serial0/0
 ip address 10.10.10.1 255.255.255.252
  ip router isis
 mpls ip
!
interface Serial1/0
 ip vrf forwarding VRFX
 ip address 10.12.12.1 255.255.255.252
  mpls ip
!
router ospf 2 vrf VRFX
 redistribute bgp 1 subnets
 network 10.12.12.0 0.0.0.255 area 0
!
router isis
 net 49.0001.0000.0000.0001.00
 passive-interface Loopback0
!
router bgp 1
 no synchronization
 neighbor 10.10.10.102 remote-as 1
 neighbor 10.10.10.102 update-source Loopback0
 no auto-summary
 !
 address-family vpnv4
 neighbor 10.10.10.102 activate
 neighbor 10.10.10.102 send-community extended
 exit-address-family
 !
 address-family ipv4 vrf VRFX
 redistribute ospf 2 vrf VRFX match internal external 1 external 2
 no auto-summary
 no synchronization
 exit-address-family
hostname CSC-PE2-AS1
!
ip cef
!
ip vrf VRFX
 route-target export 1:100
 route-target import 1:100
!
mpls ldp router-id Serial1/0
```

Figure 8-2   *Label Exchange by Enabling MPLS on the Interface*

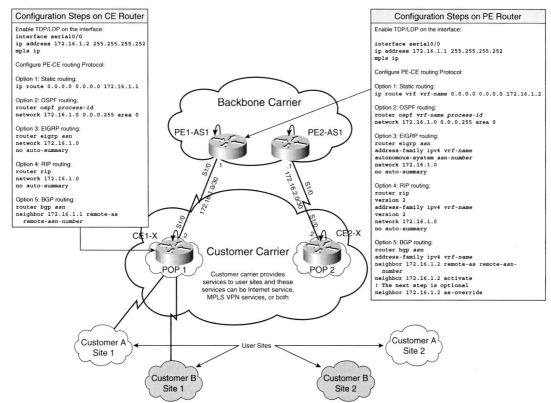

Using BGP for Label Exchange

In this method, BGP is used for routing and for label exchange. When using EBGP for label exchange, **mpls bgp forwarding** is automatically configured under the interface. Prior to that, ensure that TDP/LDP Protocol (mpls ip) is not enabled on the interface.

Figure 8-3 shows the steps to configure BGP for IPv4 label distribution.

NOTE	Check Cisco.com for IOS versions supporting this method.

Figure 8-3 *Using BGP for IPv4 Label Distribution*

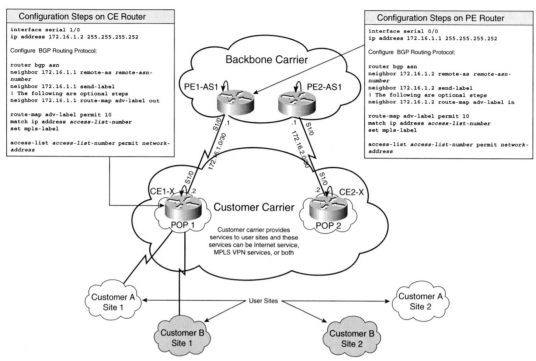

Deployment Scenarios with CSC Architecture

Three deployment scenarios are possible with CSC architecture:

- Customer carrier is not running MPLS inside its POP sites.
- Customer carrier is running MPLS inside its POP sites.
- Customer carrier is providing MPLS VPN services to user sites.

The following sections delve into each of the deployment scenarios in greater detail.

CSC Network—Customer Carrier Not Running MPLS

In this deployment model, devices in the customer carrier ISPX do not use MPLS and no IGP/LDP label exchange takes place inside the customer carrier network. MPLS is enabled only on the CE router (CSC-CE1-X-AS2 and CSC-CE2-X-AS2) interface peering with the PE router located in the backbone carrier network. The backbone carrier only has knowledge of the customer carrier's internal networks. To allow exchange of external networks belonging to the user sites (customer carrier clients like Customer A), an internal BGP (iBGP) session needs to be enabled on the customer edge (CE) routers located in the customer carrier network.

Figure 8-4 shows an example case study of this deployment model in which CSC-CE1-X-AS2 and CSC-CE2-X-AS2 are CE routers belonging to different ISPX POP sites, ISPX-POP1 and ISPX-POP2, in the customer carrier network.

Figure 8-4 *Customer Carrier ISPX POP Sites Not Running MPLS*

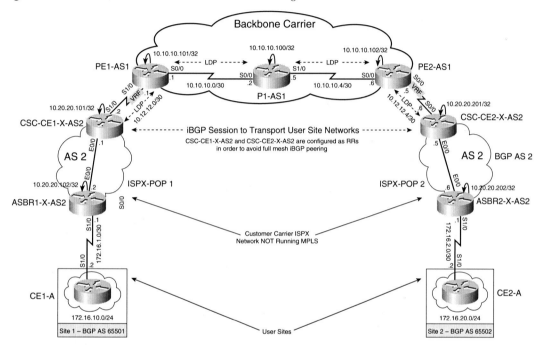

PE1-AS1 and PE2-AS1 are provider edge (PE) routers in the backbone carrier network. OSPF PE-CE routing is used between PE routers, PE1-AS1 and PE2-AS1, in the backbone carrier and CE routers, CSC-CE1-X-AS2 and CSC-CE2-X-AS2, in the customer carrier network. The ASBR routers, ASBR1-X-AS2 and ASBR2-X-AS2, provide services to user sites or Customer A sites, Site 1 and Site 2. MPLS is enabled on the PE-CE interfaces to facilitate label exchange so that an end-to-end label switched path (LSP) is formed between the CE routers, CSC-CE1-X-AS2 and CSC-CE2-X-AS2. MPLS is not enabled on interfaces connecting the CE and ASBR devices in the customer carrier network. An iBGP session is established between the CE routers, CSC-CE1-X-AS2 and CSC-CE2-X-AS2, to allow Customer A Sites 1 and 2 to exchange routing information. In this deployment model, because the ISPX-POP1 and ISPX-POP2 sites run BGP internally and need to have iBGP peering between, it is always practical to have route-reflector (RR) configured to avoid iBGP peering mesh. In this case, CSC-CE1-X-AS2 and CSC-CE2-X-AS2 act as RRs.

Control Plane Forwarding Operation—Customer Carrier Not Running MPLS

Figure 8-5 shows the control plane forwarding operation that takes place in the customer carrier not running the MPLS deployment model. Path a-b-c-d-e shows the control plane propagation for network 172.16.10.0/24, and path 1-2-2a-2b-3 shows the control plane propagation for 10.20.20.102/32, which is the next hop in the 172.16.10.0/24 update.

Figure 8-5 *Control Plane Forwarding Operation—Customer Carrier ISPX POP Sites Not Running MPLS*

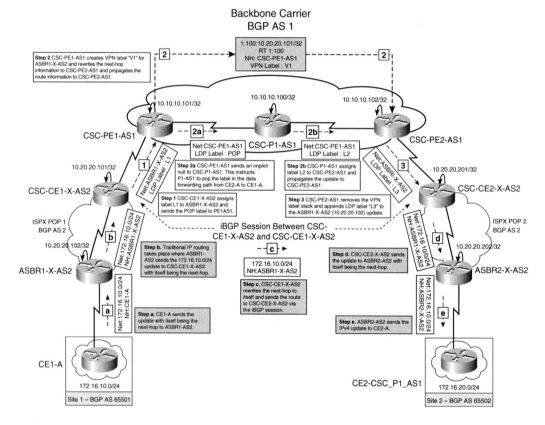

Data Forwarding Operation—Customer Carrier Not Running MPLS

Figure 8-6 shows the data plane forwarding operation that takes place in the customer carrier not running the MPLS deployment model for a packet destined for network 172.16.10.0/24 originated by CE2-A.

Figure 8-6 *Data Forwarding Operation—Customer Carrier ISPX POP Sites Not Running MPLS*

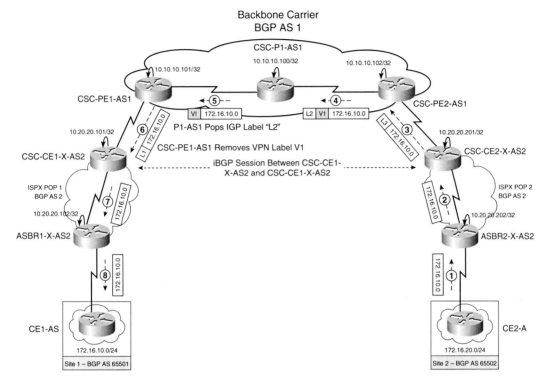

Configuring the CSC Model—Customer Carrier Not Running MPLS

The steps to configure the CSC model in which the customer carrier is not running MPLS
are as follows. Refer to the topology shown in Figure 8-4:

Step 1 Provision the MPLS VPN backbone carrier network—In this step, you
configure the backbone carrier's PE and provider core routers,
CSC-PE1-AS1, CSC-PE2-AS1, and CSC-P1-AS1, to provide MPLS
VPN services to the carrier network. IS-IS is used as an IGP protocol in
the backbone carrier's core. The PE-CE routing protocol is OSPF.
Example 8-1 shows the configuration for CSC-PE1-AS1, CSC-PE2-
AS1, and CSC-P1-AS1. Ensure that MPLS is enabled on the VRF
enabled interfaces.

Example 8-1 *CSC-PE1-AS1, CSC-PE2-AS1, and CSC-P1-AS1 Configurations*

```
hostname CSC-PE1-AS1
!
ip cef
```

continues

Example 8-1 *CSC-PE1-AS1, CSC-PE2-AS1, and CSC-P1-AS1 Configurations (Continued)*

```
!
ip vrf VRFX
 route-target export 1:100
 route-target import 1:100
!
mpls ldp router-id Serial1/0
!
interface Loopback0
 ip address 10.10.10.101 255.255.255.255
!
interface Serial0/0
 ip address 10.10.10.1 255.255.255.252
  ip router isis
 mpls ip
!
interface Serial1/0
 ip vrf forwarding VRFX
 ip address 10.12.12.1 255.255.255.252
  mpls ip
!
router ospf 2 vrf VRFX
 redistribute bgp 1 subnets
 network 10.12.12.0 0.0.0.255 area 0
!
router isis
 net 49.0001.0000.0000.0001.00
 passive-interface Loopback0
!
router bgp 1
 no synchronization
 neighbor 10.10.10.102 remote-as 1
 neighbor 10.10.10.102 update-source Loopback0
 no auto-summary
 !
 address-family vpnv4
 neighbor 10.10.10.102 activate
 neighbor 10.10.10.102 send-community extended
 exit-address-family
 !
 address-family ipv4 vrf VRFX
 redistribute ospf 2 vrf VRFX match internal external 1 external 2
 no auto-summary
 no synchronization
 exit-address-family
hostname CSC-PE2-AS1
!
ip cef
!
ip vrf VRFX
 route-target export 1:100
 route-target import 1:100
!
mpls ldp router-id Serial1/0
```

Example 8-1 *CSC-PE1-AS1, CSC-PE2-AS1, and CSC-P1-AS1 Configurations (Continued)*

```
!
interface Loopback0
 ip address 10.10.10.102 255.255.255.255
!
interface Serial0/0
 ip address 10.10.10.5 255.255.255.252
  ip router isis
 mpls ip
!
interface Serial1/0
 ip vrf forwarding VRFX
 ip address 10.12.12.5 255.255.255.252
  mpls ip
!
router ospf 2 vrf VRFX
 redistribute bgp 1 subnets
 network 10.12.12.0 0.0.0.255 area 0
!
router isis
 net 49.0001.0000.0000.0003.00
 passive-interface Loopback0
!
router bgp 1
 no synchronization
 neighbor 10.10.10.101 remote-as 1
 neighbor 10.10.10.101 update-source Loopback0
 no auto-summary
 !
 address-family vpnv4
 neighbor 10.10.10.101 activate
 neighbor 10.10.10.101 send-community extended
 exit-address-family
 !
 address-family ipv4 vrf VRFX
 redistribute ospf 2 vrf VRFX match internal external 1 external 2
 no auto-summary
 no synchronization
 exit-address-family
```

```
hostname CSC-P1-AS1
!
ip cef
mpls ldp router-id Loopback0
!
interface Loopback0
 ip address 10.10.10.100 255.255.255.255
!
interface Serial0/0
 ip address 10.10.10.2 255.255.255.252
 ip router isis
 mpls ip
!
```

continues

Example 8-1 *CSC-PE1-AS1, CSC-PE2-AS1, and CSC-P1-AS1 Configurations (Continued)*

```
interface Serial1/0
 ip address 10.10.10.6 255.255.255.252
 ip router isis
 mpls ip
!
router isis
 net 49.0001.0000.0000.0002.00
 passive-interface Loopback0
```

Step 2 **Configure the customer carrier network**—In this step, CSC-CE1-X-AS2 and ASBR1-X-AS2 belonging to ISPX-POP1 and CSC-CE2-X-AS2 and ASBR2-X-AS2 belonging to ISPX-POP2 in the ISPX network are configured. In each POP site, OSPF is used as an IGP routing protocol. Example 8-2 shows the configuration for ISPX-POP1 and ISPX-POP2 devices.

Example 8-2 *ISPX-POP1 and ISPX-POP2 Device Configurations*

```
hostname CSC-CE1-X-AS2
!
ip cef
!
interface Loopback0
 ip address 10.20.20.101 255.255.255.255
!
interface Ethernet0/0
 ip address 10.20.20.1 255.255.255.252
!
interface Serial1/0
 ip address 10.12.12.2 255.255.255.252
  mpls ip
!
router ospf 2
 network 10.12.12.0 0.0.0.255 area 0
 network 10.20.20.0 0.0.0.255 area 0
!
router bgp 2
 no synchronization
 bgp cluster-id 1
 neighbor 10.20.20.102 remote-as 2
 neighbor 10.20.20.102 update-source Loopback0
 neighbor 10.20.20.102 route-reflector-client
 neighbor 10.20.20.102 next-hop-self
 neighbor 10.20.20.201 remote-as 2
 neighbor 10.20.20.201 update-source Loopback0
 neighbor 10.20.20.201 next-hop-self
 no auto-summary
hostname CSC-CE2-X-AS2
!
ip cef
!
interface Loopback0
```

Example 8-2 *ISPX-POP1 and ISPX-POP2 Device Configurations (Continued)*

```
 ip address 10.20.20.201 255.255.255.255
 !
interface Ethernet0/0
 ip address 10.20.20.5 255.255.255.252
 !
interface Serial1/0
 ip address 10.12.12.6 255.255.255.252
 mpls ip
 !
router ospf 2
 network 10.12.12.0 0.0.0.255 area 0
 network 10.20.20.0 0.0.0.255 area 0
 !
router bgp 2
 no synchronization
 bgp cluster-id 2
 neighbor 10.20.20.101 remote-as 2
 neighbor 10.20.20.101 update-source Loopback0
 neighbor 10.20.20.101 next-hop-self
  neighbor 10.20.20.202 remote-as 2
 neighbor 10.20.20.202 update-source Loopback0
 neighbor 10.20.20.202 route-reflector-client
 neighbor 10.20.20.202 next-hop-self
 no auto-summary
```

```
hostname ASBR1-X-AS2
 !
interface Loopback0
 ip address 10.20.20.102 255.255.255.255
 !
interface Ethernet0/0
 ip address 10.20.20.2 255.255.255.252
 !
interface Serial1/0
 ip address 172.16.1.1 255.255.255.252
 !
router ospf 2
network 10.20.20.0 0.0.0.255 area 0
 !
router bgp 2
 no synchronization
 neighbor 10.20.20.101 remote-as 2
 neighbor 10.20.20.101 update-source Loopback0
 neighbor 10.20.20.101 next-hop-self
 neighbor 10.20.20.201 remote-as 2
 neighbor 10.20.20.201 update-source Loopback0
 neighbor 10.20.20.201 next-hop-self
 neighbor 172.16.1.2 remote-as 65001
 no auto-summary
```

```
hostname ASBR2-X-AS2
 !
interface Loopback0
 ip address 10.20.20.202 255.255.255.255
```

continues

Example 8-2 *ISPX-POP1 and ISPX-POP2 Device Configurations (Continued)*

```
!
interface Ethernet0/0
 ip address 10.20.20.6 255.255.255.252
!
interface Serial1/0
 ip address 172.16.2.1 255.255.255.252
!
router ospf 2
 network 10.20.20.0 0.0.0.255 area 0
!
router bgp 2
 no synchronization
 neighbor 10.20.20.101 remote-as 2
 neighbor 10.20.20.101 update-source Loopback0
 neighbor 10.20.20.101 next-hop-self
 neighbor 10.20.20.201 remote-as 2
 neighbor 10.20.20.201 update-source Loopback0
 neighbor 10.20.20.201 next-hop-self
 neighbor 172.16.2.2 remote-as 65002
 no auto-summary
```

Step 3 **Provision customer carrier's user sites**—In this step, Customer A sites that are customer carrier ISPX user sites are configured. The customer carrier network runs eBGP with Customer A sites belonging to BGP AS 65001 and 65002, respectively. Example 8-3 shows the configuration for user devices CE1-A and CE2-A, respectively.

Example 8-3 *Customer A CE1-A and CE2-A Configurations*

```
hostname CE1-A
!
interface Ethernet0/0
description Customer A Site 1
 ip address 172.16.10.1 255.255.255.0
!
interface Serial1/0
 ip address 172.16.1.2 255.255.255.252
 !
router bgp 65001
 no synchronization
 network 172.16.10.0 mask 255.255.255.0
 neighbor 172.16.1.1 remote-as 2
 no auto-summary
hostname CE2-A
!
interface Ethernet0/0
description Customer A Site 2
 ip address 172.16.20.1 255.255.255.0
!
interface Serial1/0
 ip address 172.16.2.2 255.255.255.252
 !
router bgp 65002
```

Example 8-3   *Customer A CE1-A and CE2-A Configurations (Continued)*

```
no synchronization
network 172.16.20.0 mask 255.255.255.0
neighbor 172.16.2.1 remote-as 2
no auto-summary
```

Verify CSC Model—Customer Carrier Not Running MPLS

In this section, you verify

- Control plane operation
- Data forwarding operation
- Connectivity between the sites

The steps are as follows:

Step 1   Verify control plane operation—Figure 8-7 shows the control plane
operation. Path a-b-c-d-e shows the control plane propagation for network
172.16.10.0/24, and path 1-2-2a-2b-3 shows the control plane propagation
for 10.20.20.102/32, which is the next hop in the 172.16.10.0/24 update.

Figure 8-7   *Control Plane Forwarding*

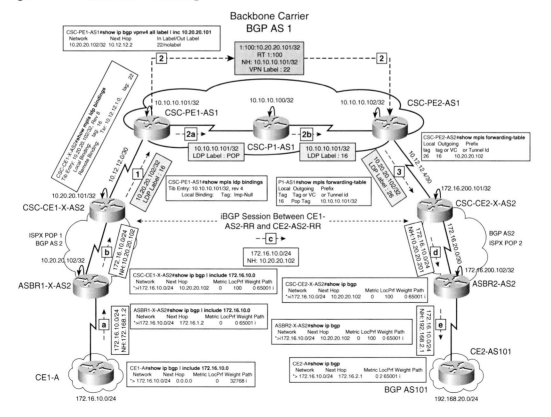

Step 2   **Verify data forwarding**—Figure 8-8 shows the data forwarding
operation that takes place for a packet sourced from 172.16.20.1 to
172.16.10.1.

Figure 8-8   *Data Forwarding*

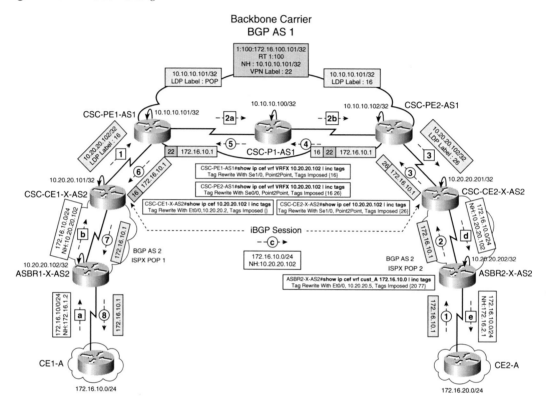

Step 3   **Verify end-to-end connectivity via ping**—Verify end-to-end
connectivity between CE1-A and CE2-A by issuing a ping from CE1-A
to network 172.16.20.1/24 on CE2-A and vice versa. Example 8-4 shows
the result of the ping operation.

Example 8-4   *Verify End-to-End Connectivity*

```
CE1-A#ping 172.16.10.1 source 172.16.20.1
Type escape sequence to abort.
Sending 5, 100-byte ICMP Echos to 172.16.10.1, timeout is 2 seconds:
Packet sent with a source address of 172.16.20.1
!!!!!
Success rate is 100 percent (5/5), round-trip min/avg/max = 140/140/140 ms
```

CSC Network—Customer Carrier Running MPLS

The only difference between this CSC model and the one shown in the previous section is that in this deployment scenario, the customer carrier is running MPLS in its POP sites. Therefore, internal routes in the customer carrier's network will be assigned labels and label switched paths (LSPs) will be built inside each POP site.

Figure 8-9 shows the components in the CSC network in which the customer carrier is running MPLS. This figure is similar to the one shown in Figure 8-4 except that the iBGP session is now formed between ASBR1-X-AS2 and ASBR2-X-AS2. LDP is enabled on the ISPX-POP1 and ISPX-POP2 devices.

Figure 8-9   *CSC Model with Customer Carrier Running MPLS*

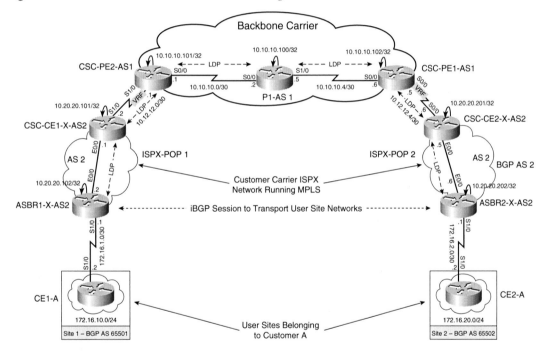

Control Plane Forwarding Operation—Customer Carrier Running MPLS

Figure 8-10 shows the control plane forwarding operation that takes place in the customer carrier running MPLS deployment model. Path a-b-c shows the control plane propagation for network 172.16.10.0/24, and path 1-2-3-3a-3b-4-5 shows the control plane propagation for 10.20.20.102/32, which is the next hop in the 172.16.10.0/24 update.

Figure 8-10 *Control Plane Forwarding Operation—Customer Carrier ISPX POP Sites Running MPLS*

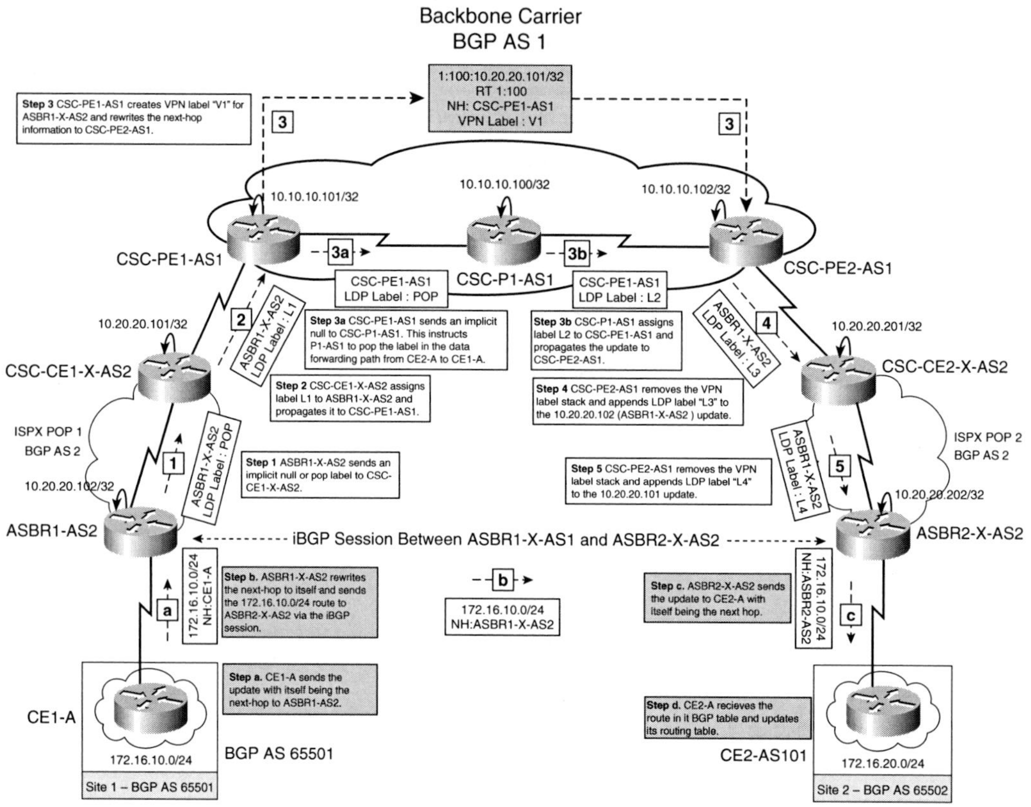

Data Forwarding Operation—Customer Carrier Running MPLS

Figure 8-11 shows the data plane forwarding operation that takes place in the customer carrier running MPLS deployment model.

Configuring the CSC Model—Customer Carrier Running MPLS

The steps to configure the CSC model in which the customer carrier is running MPLS are as follows:

Step 1   Provision the MPLS VPN backbone carrier network—This step is similar to the one shown in the section "Configuring the CSC Model—Customer Carrier Not Running MPLS."

Figure 8-11 *Data Forwarding Operation—Customer Carrier ISPX POP Sites Running MPLS*

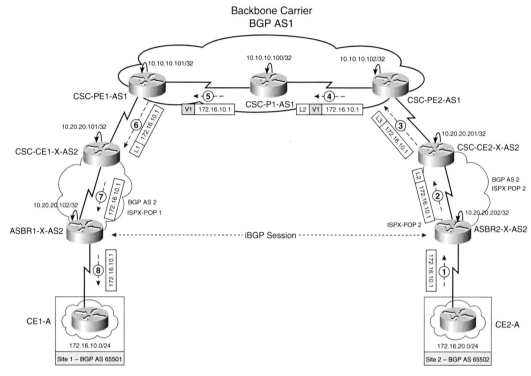

Step 2 **Configure the customer carrier network**—In this step, configure
CSC-CE1-X-AS2 and ASBR1-X-AS2 belonging to the ISPX-POP1 site,
and CSC-CE2-X-AS2 and ASBR2-X-AS2 belonging to the ISPX-POP2
site in the ISPX network. Each of the POP sites is running OSPF as an
IGP protocol. Example 8-5 shows the configuration for the POP1 and
POP2 site devices.

Example 8-5 *ISPX-POP1 and ISPX-POP2 Device Configurations*

```
hostname CSC-CE1-X-AS2
!
ip cef
!
interface Loopback0
 ip address 10.20.20.101 255.255.255.255
!
interface Ethernet0/0
 ip address 10.20.20.1 255.255.255.252
 mpls ip
!
interface Serial1/0
 ip address 10.12.12.2 255.255.255.252
```

continues

Example 8-5 *ISPX-POP1 and ISPX-POP2 Device Configurations (Continued)*

```
 mpls ip
 !
 router ospf 2
  network 10.12.12.0 0.0.0.255 area 0
  network 10.20.20.0 0.0.0.255 area 0
 !
 router bgp 2
  no synchronization
  bgp cluster-id 1
  bgp log-neighbor-changes
  neighbor 10.20.20.201 remote-as 2
  neighbor 10.20.20.201 update-source Loopback0
  neighbor 10.20.20.201 next-hop-self
```
```
hostname CSC-CE2-X-AS2
 !
 ip cef
 !
 interface Loopback0
  ip address 10.20.20.201 255.255.255.255
 !
 interface Ethernet0/0
  ip address 10.20.20.5 255.255.255.252
  mpls ip
 !
 interface Serial1/0
  ip address 10.12.12.6 255.255.255.252
 mpls ip
 !
 router ospf 2
 network 10.12.12.0 0.0.0.255 area 0
  network 10.20.20.0 0.0.0.255 area 0
 !
 router bgp 2
  no synchronization
  bgp cluster-id 2
  bgp log-neighbor-changes
  neighbor 10.20.20.101 remote-as 2
  neighbor 10.20.20.101 update-source Loopback0
  neighbor 10.20.20.101 next-hop-self
  no auto-summary
```
```
hostname ASBR1-X-AS2
 !
 ip cef
 !
 interface Loopback0
  ip address 10.20.20.102 255.255.255.255
 !
 interface Ethernet0/0
  ip address 10.20.20.2 255.255.255.252
  mpls ip
```

Example 8-5 *ISPX-POP1 and ISPX-POP2 Device Configurations (Continued)*

```
!
interface Serial1/0
 ip address 172.16.1.1 255.255.255.252
!
router ospf 2
 network 10.20.20.0 0.0.0.255 area 0
!
router bgp 2
 no synchronization
 neighbor 10.20.20.202 remote-as 2
 neighbor 10.20.20.202 update-source Loopback0
 neighbor 10.20.20.202 next-hop-self
 neighbor 172.16.1.2 remote-as 65001
 no auto-summary
```

```
hostname ASBR2-X-AS2
!
ip cef
!
interface Loopback0
 ip address 10.20.20.202 255.255.255.255
!
interface Ethernet0/0
 ip address 10.20.20.6 255.255.255.252
   mpls ip
!
interface Serial1/0
 ip address 172.16.2.1 255.255.255.252
!
router ospf 2
 network 10.20.20.0 0.0.0.255 area 0
!
router bgp 2
 no synchronization
 neighbor 10.20.20.102 remote-as 2
 neighbor 10.20.20.102 update-source Loopback0
 neighbor 10.20.20.102 next-hop-self
 neighbor 172.16.2.2 remote-as 65002
 no auto-summary
```

Step 3 **Provision customer carrier's user sites**—This step is similar to Step 3 shown in the section "Configuring the CSC Model—Customer Carrier Not Running MPLS." Refer to Example 8-3 for configurations.

Verify CSC Model—Customer Carrier Running MPLS

In this section, you verify

- Control plane operation
- Data forwarding operation
- Connectivity between the sites

The steps are as follows:

Step 1 **Verify control plane operation**—Figure 8-12 shows the control plane traffic for the CSC model with customer carrier running MPLS. Path a-b-c shows the control plane propagation for network 172.16.10.0/24, and path 1-2-2a-2b-3-4-5 shows the control plane propagation for 10.20.20.102/32, which is the next hop in the 172.16.10.0/24 update.

Figure 8-12 *Control Plane Forwarding*

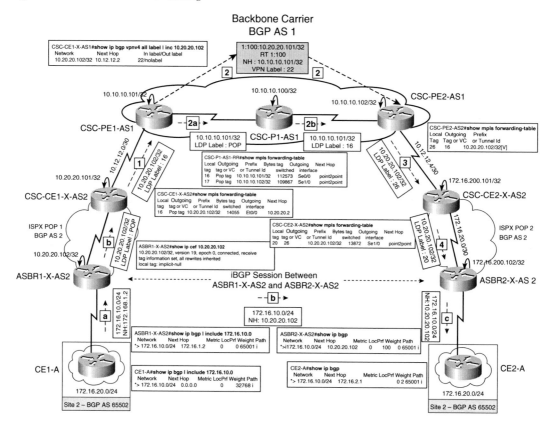

Step 2 **Verify data forwarding operation**—Figure 8-13 shows the data forwarding that takes place for a packet sourced from 172.16.20.1 to 172.16.10.1.

Step 3 **Verify end-to-end connectivity via ping**—Verify end-to-end connectivity between CE1-A and CE2-A by issuing a ping from CE2-A to network 172.16.10.1/24 on CE1-A. Example 8-6 shows the result of the ping operation.

Figure 8-13 *Data Plane Forwarding*

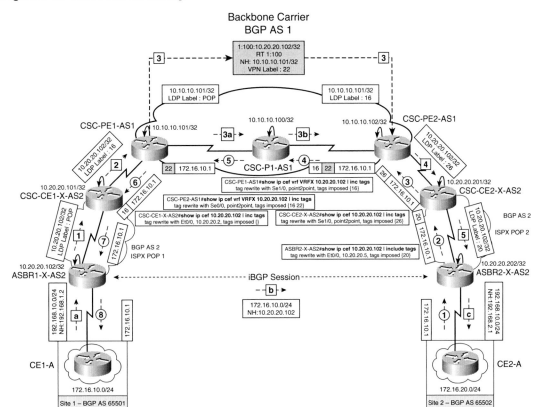

Example 8-6 *Verify End-to-End Connectivity*

```
CE2-A#ping 172.16.10.1 source 172.16.20.1
Type escape sequence to abort.
Sending 5, 100-byte ICMP Echos to 172.16.10.1, timeout is 2 seconds:
Packet sent with a source address of 172.16.20.1
!!!!!
Success rate is 100 percent (5/5), round-trip min/avg/max = 140/140/140 ms
```

CSC Network—Customer Carrier Providing MPLS VPN Service

In this deployment scenario, the customer carrier provides MPLS VPN services to its clients. In order to provide MPLS VPN services, an MP-iBGP session is required between the customer carrier routers located at different POP sites to transport VPNv4 information. The VPNv4 label exchange is transparent to the backbone carrier. The backbone carrier holds only the internal routes of the customer carrier and not that of the customer carrier's clients. Figure 8-14 shows a CSC network in which the customer carrier ISPX provides MPLS VPN services to Customer A sites, Site 1 and Site 2, belonging to BGP AS 65501 and 65502, respectively. The sites belong to the same VPN.

Figure 8-14 *Customer Carrier Providing MPLS VPN Services*

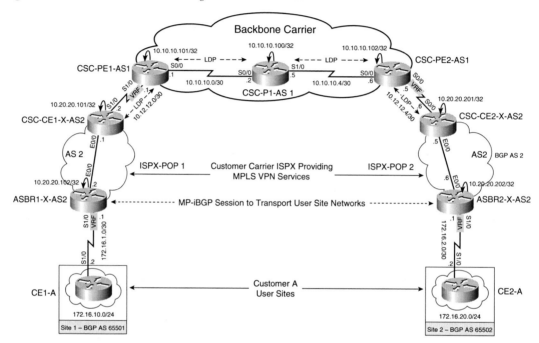

The customer carrier's ASBRs, ASBR1-X-AS2 and ASBR2-X-AS2, hold the VRF routing information for its clients and use MP-iBGP sessions between the ASBRs to transport VPNv4 information between the two sites. Because the backbone carrier is providing MPLS VPN service to the customer carrier, which in turn is also providing MPLS VPN service to Customer A sites, this type of deployment scenario is also known as *hierarchical VPN*.

Control Plane Forwarding Operation—Customer Carrier Providing MPLS VPN Service

Figure 8-15 shows the control plane forwarding operation that takes place in the customer carrier providing MPLS VPN services model. Path a-b-c shows the control plane propagation for network 172.16.10.0/24, and path 1-2-3-3a-3b-4-5 shows the control plane propagation for 10.20.20.102/32, which is the next hop in the 172.16.10.0/24 update.

Figure 8-15 *Control Plane Forwarding Operation—Customer Carrier ISPX POP Sites Providing MPLS VPN Services*

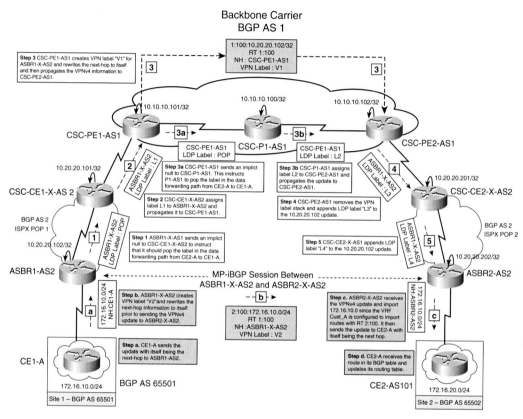

Data Forwarding Operation—Customer Carrier Providing MPLS VPN Service

Figure 8-16 shows the data forwarding operation that takes place in the customer carrier providing MPLS VPN services model.

Configuring the CSC Model—Customer Carrier Providing MPLS VPN Service

The steps to configure the CSC model in which the customer carrier is providing MPLS VPN services are as follows. Refer to the topology shown in Figure 8-14:

Step 1 **Provision the MPLS VPN backbone carrier network**—This step is similar to the one shown in the section "Configuring the CSC Model— Customer Carrier Not Running MPLS."

Figure 8-16 *Data Forwarding Operation—Customer Carrier ISPX POP Sites Providing MPLS VPN Services*

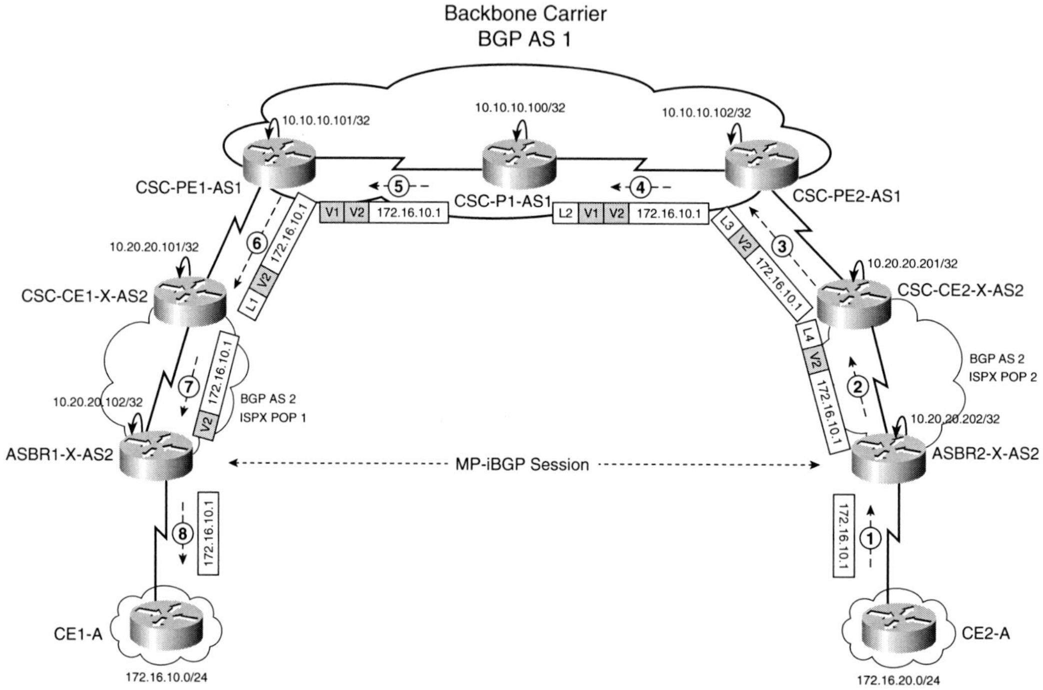

Step 2 **Configure the customer carrier network**—In this step, you configure the MP-iBGP session between ASBR1-X-AS2 and ASBR2-X-AS2 to transport VPNv4 belonging to the ISPX-POP2 site in the ISPX network. Each of the POP sites is running OSPF as the IGP routing protocol. Example 8-7 shows the configuration for POP1 and POP2 site devices. Refer to Example 8-5 for configurations related to CSC-CE1-X-AS2 and CSC-CE2-X-AS2.

Example 8-7 *ASBR Configurations*

```
hostname ASBR1-X-AS2
!
ip cef
!
ip vrf Cust_A
 rd 2:100
 route-target export 2:100
 route-target import 2:100
!
interface Loopback0
 ip address 10.20.20.102 255.255.255.255
!
```

Example 8-7 *ASBR Configurations (Continued)*

```
interface Ethernet0/0
 ip address 10.20.20.2 255.255.255.252
  mpls ip
!
interface Serial1/0
 ip vrf forwarding Cust_A
 ip address 172.16.1.1 255.255.255.252
 !
router ospf 2
 network 10.20.20.0 0.0.0.255 area 0
!
router bgp 2
 no synchronization
 neighbor 10.20.20.202 remote-as 2
 neighbor 10.20.20.202 update-source Loopback0
 neighbor 10.20.20.202 next-hop-self
 no auto-summary
 !
 address-family vpnv4
 neighbor 10.20.20.202 activate
 neighbor 10.20.20.202 send-community extended
 exit-address-family
 !
 address-family ipv4 vrf Cust_A
 neighbor 172.16.1.2 remote-as 65001
 neighbor 172.16.1.2 activate
 no auto-summary
 no synchronization
 exit-address-family
```

```
hostname ASBR2-X-AS2
!
ip cef
!
ip vrf Cust_A
 rd 2:100
 route-target export 2:100
 route-target import 2:100
 !
interface Loopback0
 ip address 10.20.20.202 255.255.255.255
 !
interface Ethernet0/0
 ip address 10.20.20.6 255.255.255.252
  mpls ip
 !
interface Serial1/0
 ip vrf forwarding Cust_A
 ip address 172.16.2.1 255.255.255.252
```

continues

Example 8-7 *ASBR Configurations (Continued)*

```
!
router ospf 2
network 10.20.20.0 0.0.0.255 area 0
!
router bgp 2
 no synchronization
  neighbor 10.20.20.102 remote-as 2
 neighbor 10.20.20.102 update-source Loopback0
 neighbor 10.20.20.102 next-hop-self
 no auto-summary
 !
 address-family vpnv4
 neighbor 10.20.20.102 activate
 neighbor 10.20.20.102 send-community extended
 exit-address-family
 !
 address-family ipv4 vrf Cust_A
 neighbor 172.16.2.2 remote-as 65002
 neighbor 172.16.2.2 activate
 no auto-summary
 no synchronization
 exit-address-family
```

Step 3 **Provision customer carrier's user sites**—This step is similar to Step 3 in the section "Configuring the CSC Model—Customer Carrier Not Running MPLS." Refer to Example 8-3 for configurations related to CE1-A and CE2-A.

Verify CSC Model—Customer Carrier Providing MPLS VPN Service

In this section, you verify

- Control plane operation
- Data forwarding operation
- Connectivity between the sites

The steps are as follows:

Step 1 **Verify control plane operation**—Figure 8-17 shows the control plane traffic for the CSC model with the customer carrier providing MPLS VPN services. Path a-b-c shows the control plane propagation for network 172.16.10.0/24, and path 1-2-2a-2b-3-4-5 shows the control plane propagation for 10.20.20.102/32, which is the next hop in the 172.16.10.0/24 update.

Figure 8-17 *Control Plane Forwarding*

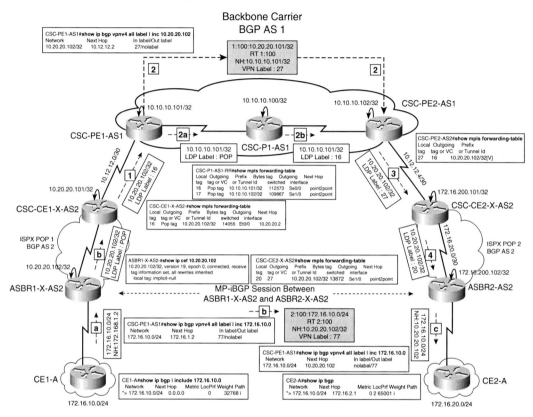

Step 2   Verify data forwarding—Figure 8-18 shows the data forwarding that takes place for a packet sourced from 172.16.20.1 to 172.16.10.1.

Step 3   Verify end-to-end connectivity via ping—Verify end-to-end connectivity between CE1-A and CE2-A by issuing a ping from CE1-A to 172.16.20.1 belonging to network 172.16.20.0/24 on CE2-A and vice versa. Example 8-8 shows the result of the ping operation.

Example 8-8 *Verify End-to-End Connectivity*

```
CE2-A#ping 172.16.10.1 source 172.16.20.1
Type escape sequence to abort.
Sending 5, 100-byte ICMP Echos to 172.16.10.1, timeout is 2 seconds:
Packet sent with a source address of 172.16.20.1
!!!!!
Success rate is 100 percent (5/5), round-trip min/avg/max = 140/140/140 ms
```

Figure 8-18 *Data Forwarding*

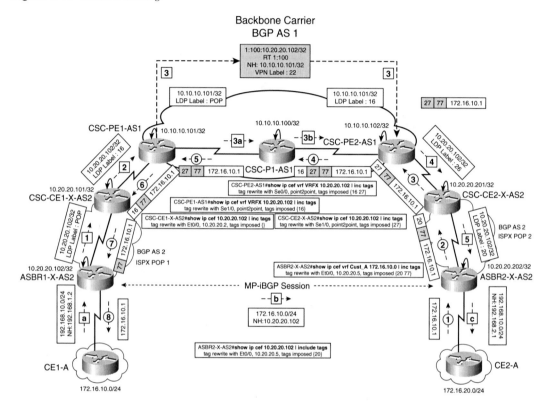

CSC Architecture Benefits

The CSC architecture can provide several benefits:

- The CSC backbone carrier can be used by the customer carrier to connect multiple point-to-point POP sites.

- MPLS VPN can be used to separate traffic from different carriers' POP sites.

- A single CSC backbone can provide multiple services, such as MPLS VPN or Internet service, to the customer carrier.

- The MPLS VPN backbone CSC feature removes from the customer carrier the burden of configuring, operating, and maintaining its own backbone.

- The customer carrier can use any addressing scheme because MPLS VPN is used to separate customer carriers.

Command Reference

Command	Description
Router(config-router)# **neighbor** *ip-address* **send-label**	Enables a BGP router to send MPLS labels with BGP routes to a neighboring BGP router. This command is configured in router configuration mode.
Router(config-route-map)# **set mpls-label**	Can be used only with the **neighbor route-map out** command to manage outbound route maps for a BGP session. Use the **route-map** global configuration command with **match** and **set route-map** configuration commands to define the conditions for redistributing routes from one routing protocol into another.
Router(config-route-map)# **match mpls-label**	Use this command in a route-map to select those routes that carry match labels.

CHAPTER 9

MPLS Traffic Engineering

MPLS Traffic Engineering (MPLS TE) is a growing implementation in today's service provider networks. MPLS adoption in service provider networks has increased manifold due to its inherent TE capabilities. MPLS TE allows the MPLS-enabled network to replicate and expand upon the TE capabilities of Layer 2 ATM and Frame Relay networks. MPLS uses the reachability information provided by Layer 3 routing protocols and operates like a Layer 2 ATM network. With MPLS, TE capabilities are integrated into Layer 3, which can be implemented for efficient bandwidth utilization between routers in the SP network.

This chapter provides you with information on the operation and configuration of MPLS TE on Cisco routers.

TE Basics

TE is the process of steering traffic across to the backbone to facilitate efficient use of available bandwidth between a pair of routers. Prior to MPLS TE, traffic engineering was performed either by IP or by ATM, depending on the protocol in use between two edge routers in a network. Though the term "traffic engineering" has attained popularity and is used more in the context of MPLS TE today, traditional TE in IP networks was performed either by IP or by ATM.

TE with IP was mostly implemented by manipulation of interface cost when multiple paths existed between two endpoints in the network. In addition, static routes enabled traffic steering along a specific path to a destination. Figure 9-1 outlines a basic IP network with two customers, A and B, connected to the same service provider.

As illustrated in Figure 9-1, two paths exist between customer routers CE1-A and CE2-A via the provider network. If all links between the routers in Figure 9-1 were of equal cost, the preferred path between customer routers CE1-A and CE2-A would be the one with the minimum cost (via routers PE1-AS1, P3-AS1, and PE2-AS1) or *PATH1*. The same would apply for the customer routers CE1-B and CE2-B belonging to Customer B. If all the links were T3 links, for example, in the event of CE1-A sending 45 Mbps of traffic and CE1-B simultaneously sending 10 Mbps of traffic, some packets will be dropped at PE1-AS1 because the preferred path for both customers is using *PATH1*. The path *PATH2* will not be utilized for traffic forwarding; therefore, TE can utilize this available bandwidth. To implement TE using IP whereby the paths *PATH1* and *PATH2* are either load balanced or used equally, we will need to implement IGP features such as maximum paths with variance or change the cost associated with the suboptimal path, *PATH2*, to make it equal to the current optimal path, *PATH1*. In an SP environment, this is often cumbersome to implement as the number of routers is much larger.

Figure 9-1   *Traditional IP Networks*

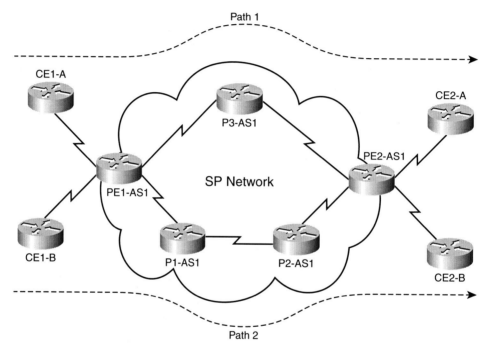

With ATM networks, the solution is a lot more feasible; PVCs can be configured between routers PE1-AS1 and PE2-AS1 with the same cost, but this would create a full mesh of PVCs between a group of routers. Implementing ATM for TE, however, has an inherent problem when a link or a node goes down. During link or node failure used in conjunction with ATM for TE, messages are flooded on the network. The Layer 3 topology must be predominantly fully meshed to take advantage of the Layer 2 TE implementation. Often, this might prove to be a scalability constraint for the IGP in use, due to issues with reconvergence at Layer 3.

The main advantage of implementing MPLS TE is that it provides a combination of ATM's TE capabilities along with the class of service (CoS) differentiation of IP. In MPLS TE, the headend router in the network controls the path taken by traffic to any particular destination in the network. The requirement to implement a full mesh of VCs, as in ATM, does not exist when implementing MPLS TE. Therefore, when MPLS TE is implemented, the IP network depicted in Figure 9-1 transforms into the label switched domain, as shown in Figure 9-2, in which the TE label switched paths or TE tunnels (Tunnel1 and Tunnel2) define paths that can be used by traffic between PE1-AS1 and PE2-AS1.

Figure 9-2   *MPLS TE*

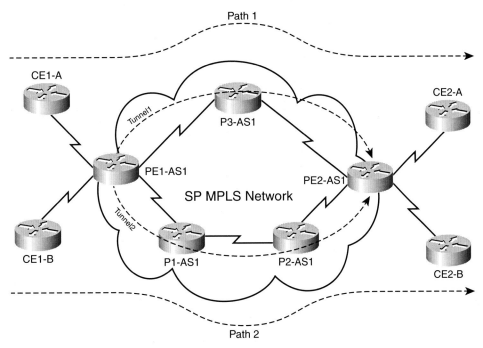

MPLS TE Theory

This section introduces you to the theoretical nuances in the implementation of MPLS TE. The primary topics covered will be the components of MPLS TE as well as RSVP and its function in the implementation of MPLS TE.

MPLS TE Overview

In a traditional IP forwarding paradigm, packets are forwarded on a per-hop basis where a route lookup is performed on each router from source to destination. As cited earlier, the destination-based forwarding paradigm leads to suboptimal use of available bandwidth between a pair of routers in the service provider network. Predominantly, the suboptimal paths are under-utilized in IP networks. To avoid packet drops due to inefficient use of available bandwidth and to provide better performance, TE is employed to steer some of the traffic destined to follow the optimal path to a suboptimal path to enable better bandwidth management and utilization between a pair of routers. TE, hence, relieves temporary congestion in the core of the network on the primary or optimal cost links. TE maps flows between two routers appropriately to enable efficient use of already available bandwidth in the core of the network. The key to implementing a scalable and efficient TE methodology in the core of the network is to gather information on the traffic patterns as they traverse the core of the network so that bandwidth guarantees can be established. As illustrated in Figure 9-2, TE tunnels, *Tunnel1 and Tunnel2,* can be configured on PE1-AS1 that can map to separate paths *(PATH1, PATH2),* enabling efficient bandwidth utilization.

TE tunnels configured on routers are unidirectional. Therefore, to implement bidirectional TE deployment between routers PE1-AS1 and PE2-AS1 in Figure 9-2, a pair of tunnels must also be configured on PE2-AS1 in addition to *Tunnel1 and Tunnel2* configured on PE1-AS1. In an MPLS network, all pertinent tunnel configurations are always performed or provider edge (PE) routers. The TE tunnels or LSPs will be used to link the edge routers across the core of the service provider network.

MPLS TE can also map to certain classes of traffic versus destinations. If Customer A CE routers are connected into the SP network using OC3 links versus Customer B connecting into the SP network using a 64 K dialup link, preferential treatment can be configured on TE tunnels so that TE *Tunnel1* can carry Customer A traffic and Tunnel2 can carry Customer B traffic. This is shown in Figure 9-3. Also note that Figure 9-3 illustrates tunnels configured on both PE1-AS1 and PE2-AS1.

Figure 9-3　*TE Tunnels Based on Customer CoS*

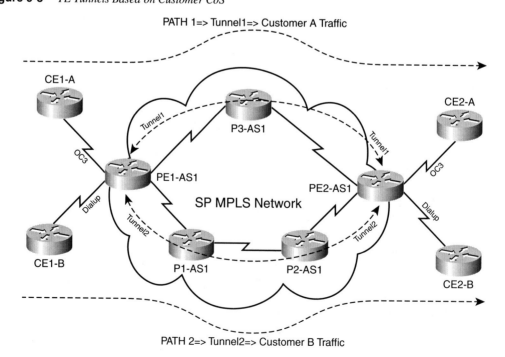

TE tunnels are, thus, data flows between a specific source and destination that might have properties or attributes associated with them. The attributes associated with a tunnel, in addition to the ingress (headend) and egress (tailend) points of the network, can include the bandwidth requirements and the CoS for data that will be forwarded utilizing this tunnel. Traffic is forwarded along the path defined as the TE tunnel by using MPLS label switching. Hence, TE tunnels are assigned specific label switched paths (LSPs) in the network from source to destination, which are usually PE routers. MPLS LSPs have a one-to-one mapping with TE tunnels, and TE tunnels are not bound to a specific path through the SP network to a destination PE router. Unless configured explicitly, TE tunnels can reroute packets via any path through the network associated with an MPLS LSP. This path might be defined by the IGP used in the core, which are discussed in the section on MPLS TE extensions.

The primary reason for the implementation of MPLS TE is to control paths along which traffic flows through a network. MPLS TE also lends itself to a resilient design in which a secondary path can be used when the primary path fails between two routers in a network. Data plane information is forwarded using label switching; a packet arriving on a PE from the CE router is applied labels and forwarded to the egress PE router. The labels are removed at the egress router and forwarded out to the appropriate destination as an IP packet.

OSPF or IS-IS with extensions for TE is used to carry information pertaining to the tunnel configured on a router. The extensions carry information on available resources for building a tunnel, like bandwidth on a link. As a result, a link that does not have the requested resources (like bandwidth) is not chosen to be a part of the LSP tunnel or TE tunnel. Signaling in an MPLS TE environment uses resource reservation protocol (RSVP) with extensions to support TE tunnel features.

The data plane ingress (headend) router in the MPLS domain requires information pertaining to the resource availability on all links capable of being a part of the MPLS TE tunnel. This information is provided by IGPs like OSPF and IS-IS due to the inherent operation of flooding information about links to all routers in the IGP domain. In IS-IS, a new TLV (type 22) has been developed to transmit information pertaining to resource availability and link status in the LS-PDUs. In OSPF, the type 10 LSA provides resource and links status information. When this information is flooded in IGP updates, the ingress (headend) router gathers information on all the available resources in the network along with the topology, which defines tunnels through the network between a set of MPLS-enabled routers.

The inspiration behind MPLS TE is *Constraint Based Routing (CBR)*, which takes into account the possibility of multiple paths between a specific source/destination pair in a network. With CBR, the operation of an IP network is enhanced so the least cost routing can be implemented as well as variables to find paths from a source to destination. CBR requires an IGP, like OSPF or IS-IS, for its operation. CBR is the backbone of the TE tunnel definition and is defined on the ingress routers to the MPLS domain when implementing MPLS TE. Resource availability and link status information are calculated using a *constrained SPF* calculation in which factors such as the bandwidth, policies, and topology are taken into consideration to define probable paths from a source to destination.

CSPF calculation results with an ordered set of IP addresses that map to next-hop IP addresses of routers forming an LSP, in turn mapping to the TE tunnel. This ordered set is defined by the headend router that is propagated to other routers in the LSP. The intermediate routers, thus, do not perform the function of path selection. RSVP with TE extensions is used to reserve resources in the LSP path as well as label association to the TE tunnel. The operation of RSVP for MPLS TE is introduced in the next section.

RSVP with TE Extensions: Signaling

RSVP reserves bandwidth along a path from a specific source to destination. RSVP messages are sent by the headend router in a network to identify resource availability along the path from a specific source to destination. The headend router is always the source of the MPLS TE tunnel, and the tailend router is the router that functions as the endpoint for the TE tunnel. After the RSVP messages are sent, the status of routers in the path (resource availability) information is stored in the path message as it traverses the network. RSVP, therefore, communicates the requirements of a specific traffic flow to the network and gathers information about whether the requirements can be fulfilled by the network.

The four main messages used in implementation of RSVP for TE are the *RSVP PATH message,* the *RSVP RESERVATION message, RSVP error messages,* and *RSVP tear messages.* In MPLS TE, RSVP is used to ensure and verify resource availability, as well as apply the MPLS labels to form the MPLS TE LSP through the routers in the network:

- **RSVP PATH message**—Generated by the headend router and is forwarded through the network along the path of a future TE LSP. At each hop, the PATH message checks the availability of requested resources and stores this information. In our network, shown in Figure 9-4, the PATH message is generated by Router PE1-AS1, the headend router, and is forwarded downstream where it checks resource availability at each hop (P1-AS1 and PE2-AS1). The RSVP PATH message functions as a label request in MPLS TE domain. Because all TE domains function with downstream-on-demand label allocation mode, the request to assign a label is generated at the headend router and propagated downstream.

Figure 9-4   *RSVP PATH and RESERVATION Messages*

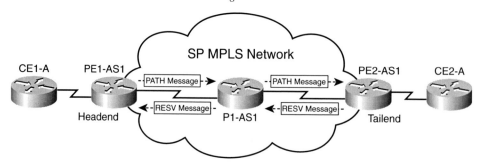

- **RSVP RESERVATION message**—Created by the tailend router in the MPLS TE domain and used to confirm the reservation request that was sent earlier with the PATH messages. In the network depicted in Figure 9-4, PE2-AS1 will generate the RSVP RESERVATION message in response to the PATH message. Therefore, PATH messages function as reservation requests and RESERVATION messages function as reservation confirmations for the availability of requested resources. The RSVP RESERVATION message performs the function of label assignment for a particular LSP mapping to the TE tunnel. As the MPLS domain label allocation and distribution is performed downstream-on-demand, the label mapping to a TE LSP is first generated by the tailend router or egress Edge LSR and then propagated upstream. This process is repeated at each hop upstream where local labels mapping to a TE tunnel are assigned and propagated upstream until the headend router is reached.

- **RSVP error messages**—In the event of unavailability of the requested resources, the router generates RSVP error messages and sends them to the router from which the request or reply was received. If Router P1-AS1 is unable to accommodate requested resources as defined in the PATH message generated by PE1-AS1 (headend router), the router generates a PATH ERROR (PATHERR) message and sends it to its upstream LSR PE1-AS1, as depicted in Figure 9-5.

Figure 9-5 *RSVP PATH Error and RESERVATION Error Messages*

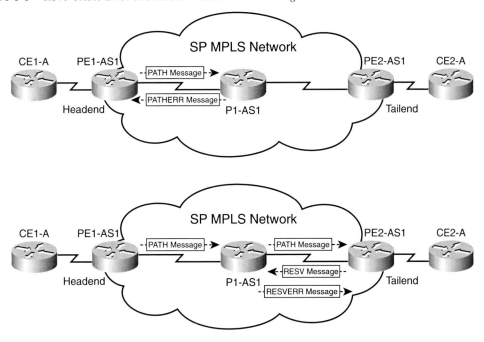

If the RSVP PATH message successfully reaches the tailend router, the tailend Router PE2-AS1 generates a RESERVATION message. If in the time lapsed between P1-AS1 receiving the PATH message from PE1-AS1 to receiving the RESERVATION message from PE2-AS1, P1-AS1 identifies a lack of resources to confirm the request, P1-AS1 will send a RESERVATION ERROR (RESVERR) message to its downstream LSR PE2-AS1 denying the reservation, as depicted in Figure 9-5.

- **RSVP tear messages**—RSVP creates two types of tear messages, namely, the PATH tear message and the RESERVATION tear message. These tear messages clear the PATH or RESERVATION states on the router instantaneously. The process of clearing a PATH or RESERVATION state on a router using tear messages enables the reuse of resources on the router for other requests. The PATH tear messages are usually generated in inter-area LSP creation where the inter-area LSP is not configured to be fast reroutable, and if a link failure occurs within an area, the LSR to which the failed link is directly attached will generate an RSVP PATH error and an RESV tear message to the headend. The headend will then generate an RSVP PATH tear message. The corresponding path option will be marked as invalid for a certain amount of time and the next path option will be immediately evaluated if it exists.

RSVP Operation in MPLS TE

As mentioned earlier, the result of a CSPF or CBR calculation on the headend router is an ordered list of IP addresses that identifies the next hops along the path of the TE tunnel or LSP. This list of routers is computed and is known only to the headend router that is the source of the TE tunnel. Other routers in the domain do not perform a CBR calculation. The headend router provides information to the routers in the TE tunnel path via RSVP signaling to request and confirm resource availability for the tunnel. RSVP with extensions for TE reserves appropriate resources on each LSR in the path defined by the headend router and assigns labels mapping to the TE tunnel LSP.

The RSVP extensions to enable RSVP use for signaling in an MPLS environment to implement TE are defined in Table 9-1. The functions of each of these extensions/objects in the messages are also outlined.

Table 9-1 *RSVP Objects*

Object	Message	Function
LABEL_REQUEST	PATH	Used to request a label mapping to the TE tunnel or LSP; generated by the headend router in the PATH message.
LABEL	RESERVATION	Used to allocate labels mapping to the TE tunnel or LSP; generated by the tailend router in the RESERVATION message and propagated upstream.

Table 9-1   *RSVP Objects (Continued)*

Object	Message	Function
EXPLICIT_ROUTE	PATH	Carried in PATH messages and is used to either request or confirm a specific path/route for the tunnel.
RECORD_ROUTE	PATH, RESERVATION	Similar to a record option with ICMP ping. It is added to the PATH or RESERVATION messages to notify the originating node about the actual route/path that the LSP TE tunnel traverses.
SESSION_ATTRIBUTE	PATH	Used to define specific session parameters local to the TE LSP tunnel.

During the path setup process for LSP TE tunnels, RSVP messages containing one or more of these extensions are used to identify the significance of each message type and its contents.

The path message contains the information outlined in Table 9-2.

Table 9-2   *RSVP Objects in Path Message*

Object	Message
SESSION	Defines the source and the destination of the LSP tunnel. Usually identified by IP addresses of corresponding loopback interfaces on headend and tailend routers.
SESSION_ATTRIBUTE	Defines the characteristics of the specific LSP tunnel, such as the bandwidth requirements and resources that would need to be allocated to the tunnel.
EXPLICIT_ROUTE	Populated by the list of next hops that are either manually specified or calculated using constraint-based SPF. The previous hop (PHOP) is set to the router's outgoing interface address. The Record_Route (RRO) is populated with the same address as well.
RECORD_ROUTE	Populated with the local router's outgoing interface address in the path of the LSP tunnel.
SENDER_TEMPLATE	In addition to the previously mentioned attributes, the sender template object in the path message depicts the interface address that will be used as the LSP-ID for the tunnel. This value is defined by the headend router.

The steps in the PATH and RESV message propagation in Figure 9-6 are depicted here:

Step 1   The appropriate values for the fields mentioned in Table 9-1 applied by the headend Router PE1-AS1 and the PATH message is sent to the next-hop router in the LSP tunnel path.

Step 2 When P1-AS1 receives this PATH message, the router checks the EXPLICIT_ROUTE object to see if the next hop is a directly connected network. This is checked in the *L-bit* of the RSVP path message. If the L-bit is set, the local router is not directly connected to the next hop in the LSP tunnel path. Therefore, the router would perform a constrained-SPF calculation to identify the next hop in the tunnel path.

If the L-bit is unset, the Router P1-AS1 knows that it is directly connected to the next hop in the LSP tunnel path. It then removes all entries in the EXPLICIT_ROUTE mapping to the local router (P1-AS1) and forwards the PATH message to the next hop as defined in the EXPLICIT_ROUTE object. In addition, P2-AS1 updates and appends the RECORD_ROUTE object to depict the local outgoing interface in the path of the LSP tunnel. Figure 9-6 depicts the PATH message values as the PATH message is forwarded from P1-AS1 to P2-AS1 after the appropriate values are updated. As previously mentioned, P1-AS1 removes references to its local interface in the EXPLICIT_ROUTE object and adds the outgoing interface in the RECORD_ROUTE object.

Figure 9-6 *RSVP PATH/RESERVATION Messages and Object Values*

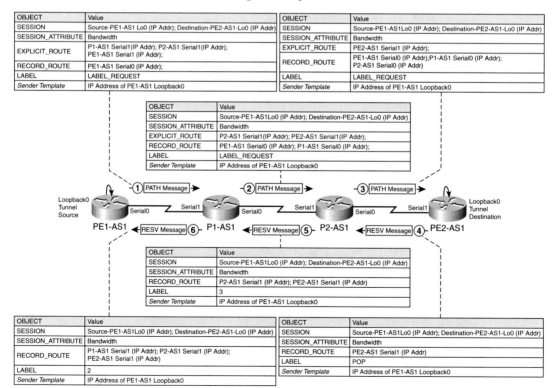

Step 3   The process is repeated at P2-AS1 in which references to its local interface in the EXPLICIT_ROUTE object are removed and appends the outgoing interface in the RECORD_ROUTE object.

Step 4   After the RSVP PATH message is received by the tailend Router PE2-AS1, it triggers the creation of a RESERVATION message. The key concept to note is that the *label allocation* process begins at the tailend router upon generation of the RESERVATION message upstream. Therefore, when PE2-AS1 generates a RESERVATION message, the router assigns a POP label to the LSP tunnel (penultimate hop popping). The RESERVATION message now has the RECORD_ROUTE object pointing to the outgoing interface on the tailend router toward the headend router. Therefore, the RECORD_ROUTE object is reinitiated in the RESERVATION message. The values are depicted in Figure 9-6.

Step 5   When this reservation message reaches P2-AS1, the RECORD_ROUTE is *prepended* with the outgoing interface and the local label mapping to the LSP is also generated and mapped in the LABEL object. An arbitrary value of 3 has been depicted for this LABEL value in Figure 9-6.

Step 6   This process is again repeated on P1-AS1 and the RESERVATION message is then received by PE1-AS1.

Step 7   When PE1-AS1 receives the RESERVATION message, the RECORD_ROUTE identifies the traffic engineered LSP associated to a specific bandwidth or resource requirement as defined in the SESSION object. The labels mapped to the LSP are thus used as in regular MPLS in which a local label is mapped to a next-hop label at each router that now maps to an RSVP-learned TE LSP versus a normal LSP.

In the implementation of RSVP for MPLS TE, RSVP with extensions for TE requests as well as confirms the LSP, reserves resources as requested on all LSP path routers, and applies MPLS labels to form the MPLS LSP through the network. Note that the routers store a copy of the PATH request as the request is forwarded to the next-hop LSR. This information identifies the interface as reservation messages are received on the same LSR to an egress interface to the headend router. In the next section, you will be introduced to the constraint-based SPF calculation process and the need for a link-state protocol to enable MPLS TE dynamically in a service provider core.

Constraint-Based Routing and Operation in MPLS TE

The most important requirement of TE is that the characteristics, as well as resource availability, on links on the network (in addition to bandwidth that would be used for cost computations) be propagated across the network to allow efficient choice of possible TE LSP paths. In link-state routing protocols, the preferred path still predominantly takes into consideration the bandwidth on the link between any two routers to compute the cost or metric associated with that path, prior to preferred path allocation. Enabling the use of link-state routing protocols to efficiently propagate information pertaining to resource availability in their routing updates is performed by additional extensions to the actual operation of the link-state routing protocol. The mechanics of operation of a link-state routing protocol involves the flooding of updates in the network upon link-state or metric change or, in better terms, bandwidth availability from a TE perspective. The resource attributes are flooded by the routers in the network to make them available by the headend router in the TE tunnel during LSP path computation (dynamic tunnels). Link-state announcements carry information that lists that router's neighbors, attached networks, network resource information, and other relevant information pertaining to the actual resource availability that might be later required to perform a constraint-based SPF calculation. OSPF and IS-IS have been provided with extensions to enable their use in an MPLS TE environment to propagate information pertaining to resource availability and in dynamic LSP path selection.

Maximum Versus Available Bandwidth

Available bandwidth (AB) is a key value taken into consideration during the LSP path computation process to identify the preferred path for the TE tunnel. The available bandwidths on interfaces are configured on a priority basis. The number of priorities that can be configured in conjunction with the available bandwidth is 8: 0–7, where 0 represents the *highest* priority. *When the available bandwidth for a certain priority level on an interface is configured, it is subtracted from the available bandwidth on all priority levels below the one it is configured on.*

If Router PE1-AS1 has a serial interface (T1-1.544 Mbps), 1 Ethernet interface (10 Mbps) and one Fast Ethernet interface (100 Mbps), the actual bandwidths on the interfaces map to the *maximum bandwidth* (MB) values on the respective links. The *available bandwidth is usually the bandwidth of the required reservation subtracted from the maximum bandwidth.* However, this does not hold true if the available bandwidth value on the link is configured to be higher than the maximum bandwidth value on the link. Though the available bandwidth on the link can be configured to be higher than the max-bandwidth value, reservations exceeding the maximum bandwidth value are rejected.

When Router PE1-AS1 initially propagates information on the maximum bandwidth and the available bandwidth on all its links, the values for the available bandwidth at each priority level (P) for each link would be equal to their maximum bandwidth values (1.544 Mbps for serial, 10 Mbps for Ethernet, and 100 Mbps for Fast Ethernet).

When a tunnel request is accepted and the bandwidth deducted from the available bandwidth at a certain priority, it is also deducted from all the priorities lower than the priority at which the resource request was performed. If an LSP tunnel creation on PE1-AS1 consumes 40 Mbps of bandwidth on the Fast Ethernet interface at a priority level of 5, the available bandwidth values at the appropriate priorities on the Fast Ethernet interface would change for priorities 5 and above (100 – 40 = 60 Mbps).

Let us now consider the following sequence of requests:

1 Request for 10 Mbps of bandwidth on Ethernet interface at priority 1

2 Request for 20 Mbps of bandwidth on Fast Ethernet interface at priority 0

3 Request for 1 Mbps of bandwidth on serial interface at priority 0

4 Request for 2 Mbps of bandwidth on Ethernet interface at priority 3

This sequence will reduce the AB values, as depicted in Table 9-3.

Table 9-3   *PE1-AS1: Maximum Bandwidth and Available Bandwidth—All Interfaces*

Interface	AB P = 0 (Mbps)	AB P = 1 (Mbps)	AB P = 2 (Mbps)	AB P = 3 (Mbps)	AB P = 4 (Mbps)	AB P = 5 (Mbps)	AB P = 6 (Mbps)	AB P = 7 (Mbps)
Serial	1.544 − 1 = .544	1.544 − 1 = .544	1.544 − 1 = .544	1.544 − 1 = .544	1.544 − 1 = .544	1.544 − 1 = .544	1.544 − 1 = .544	1.544 − 1 = .544
Ethernet	10	10 − 10 = 0	10 − 10 = 0	10 − 10 = 0	10 − 10 = 0	10 − 10 = 0	10 − 10 = 0	10 − 10 = 0
Fast Ethernet	100 − 20 = 80	100 − 20 = 80	100 − 20 = 80	100 − 20 = 80	100 − 20 = 80	60 − 20 = 40	60 − 20 = 40	60 − 20 = 40

The outputs of Table 9-3 do not reflect the request for 2 Mbps of bandwidth on the Ethernet interface at priority 3. This request is rejected due to unavailable bandwidth at this priority level on the interface when the request is received. Link-state updates pertaining to resource availability are flooded when the status of the link changes, during manual reconfiguration of parameters mapping to the resource availability on the link, periodic updates on links and their status, and when the LSP path setup fails due to unavailability of requested resources for the LSP TE tunnel.

If the resources pertaining to the link change constantly, it will trigger update generation, which clearly must be avoided. During the instant when the resources pertaining to the links change constantly, the headend router might view the link as a probable link in the LSP path. Therefore, this probable nonupdated link might be used in path computation even though the link might not have the resources required for LSP path setup. However, after LSP path computation when the LSP path establishment is attempted, the router containing the link with the unavailable resources generates an update with information affirming a lack of resources.

Thresholds can be set up on a per interface or link basis on a router whereby updates are generated within a configured range of resource availabilities. Therefore, the upper limit, as well as the lower limit, when an update will be generated on the router containing the link, can be configured. For example, if the lower limit was configured to be 50% of link bandwidth with steps at 60, 70, 80, and 90 with the upper limit configured at 100%, updates with regards to link resource availability are generated and flooded in the network when 50%, 60%, 70%, 80%, 90%, and 100% of bandwidth are achieved.

Constraint-Based SPF

In the normal SPF calculation process, a router places itself at the head of the tree with shortest paths calculated to each of the destinations, only taking into account the least metric or cost route to the destination.

During regular SPF operation in the network, illustrated in Figure 9-7, only the cost is taken into consideration, and the least cost path from a loopback on PE1-AS1 to a loopback on PE2-AS1 is PE1-AS1->P1-AS1->PE2-AS1. In this calculation, a key concept to note is no consideration to the bandwidth of the links on the other paths from PE1-AS1 to PE2-AS1, namely via routers P3-AS1->P4-AS1 and P2-AS1. The bandwidth of the links is shown as an ordered pair in Figure 9-7 with the first value showing the cost of the link and the second showing the bandwidth across the link.

Figure 9-7 *SPF*

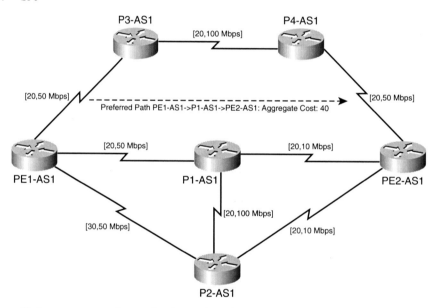

If the parameters chosen for the preferred path are not the least cost alone but also a requirement to support a bandwidth of 50 Mbps in Figure 9-7, we can eliminate the links that do not allow for the mentioned requirement. The network capable of supporting the requirement would look like what's shown in Figure 9-8.

With the just mentioned constraints, the only path capable of being used as an LSP for TE is the path from PE1-AS1 to PE2-AS1 via P3-AS1 and P4-AS1. If any of the links between P1-AS1, P2-AS1, and PE2-AS1 were to support a bandwidth more than the requirement, they would become a part of the CSPF tree structure with Router PE1-AS1 or the headend router as the root of the tree.

Figure 9-8   *CSPF*

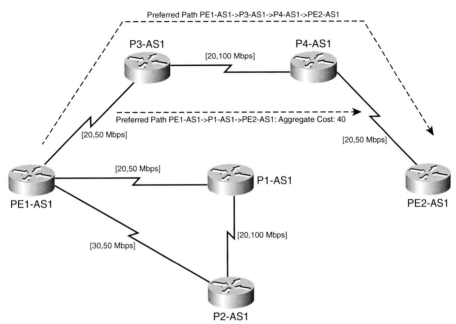

With CSPF, we use more than the link cost to identify the probable paths that can be used for TE LSP paths. The decision as to which path is chosen to set up a TE LSP path is performed at the headend router after ruling out all links that do not meet a certain criteria, such as bandwidth requirements in addition to the cost of the link. The result of the CSPF calculation at the headend router is an ordered set of IP addresses that maps to the next-hop addresses of routers that form the TE LSP. Therefore, multiple TE LSPs could be used by the use of CSPF to identify probable links in the network that meet the criteria. In addition, the user can configure a static TE tunnel or LSP on the headend router that outlines the next hops in the TE LSP path and, therefore, can use the statically defined LSP as the backup LSP path in the event of the primary TE LSP failing.

The result of the CSPF calculation is then passed over to the RSVP process to begin the RSVP request and reservation process, as mentioned in the earlier section. RSVP thus is used along with the result computed by CSPF or list of next hops configured by the user for LSP signaling and final establishment of the TE LSP. Note the TE LSP formed as a result of this process is unidirectional in nature.

Constraint-based SPF can use either administrative weights or IGP metric (also called TE metric) during the constraint-based computation. In the event of a tie, the path with the highest minimum bandwidth takes precedence, followed by the least number of hops along the path. If all else is equal, CSPF picks a path at random and chooses the same to be the TE LSP path of preference.

Therefore, the sequence of steps in the creation of an MPLS TE tunnel LSP in the network is as follows:

Step 1 CSPF calculation is performed from the headend router based on the constraints defined in the tunnel definition and requirements. This calculation is performed by the IGP in use, either OSPF or IS-IS.

Step 2 After the LSP path is calculated using the CSPF process, the output of the CSPF process, which is an ordered set of IP addresses mapping to next-hop addresses in the TE LSP, is passed to RSVP.

Step 3 RSVP now performs the resource reservation request and confirmation on the LSP, as defined by the CSPF process, to determine if the LSP meets the requirements of the specific resources requested by the tunnel definition.

Step 4 After the RSVP process receives a reservation message, it signals that the LSP is now established.

Step 5 At this juncture, the TE tunnel is available for the IGP to use. By default, the tunnel information is not added into the routing table; however, the router can be configured so that the tunnel interface is added to the routing table. You will be introduced to the configurations involved for TE on Cisco routers in the next section.

Link admission control performs a check at each hop in the desired LSP path to see if the resources requested are available prior to TE tunnel creation. The link admission control function is performed on a per hop basis with each router in the LSP path checking resource availability. If the requested resources are available, bandwidth is reserved and the router waits for the RESERVATION message to confirm this resource allocation. If, however, the resources requested are unavailable, the IGP in use sends messages stating resource unavailability. Link admission control then informs RSVP about lack of resources, and RSVP sends PATHERR messages to the headend requesting the resources and notifying a lack of resources.

When setting up TE LSP paths in link admission control, it is important that the priorities assigned to the available bandwidths are checked. Therefore, if the requested bandwidth is in use by a lower priority session (priorities 0–7, with 0 having highest priority), the lower priority session can be *preempted*. If preemption is supported, each preempted reservation leads to creation of PATHERR and RESVERR messages because the preempted session no longer fits the profile of the resource allocation.

OSPF Extension for MPLS TE

OSPF can be used as the link-state protocol of choice in MPLS TE for resource allocation information flooding through the network by implementing OSPF extensions or *Opaque LSAs*. The type of Opaque LSA in use is defined by the flooding scope of the LSA. OSPF also now possesses TLV and sub-TLV attributes that can be configured to propagate resource availability information in link-state routing updates.

Opaque LSAs are of Type 9, 10, and 11 and differ in the flooding scope. Type 9 LSAs are not flooded beyond the local subnet and are of link-local scope. Type 10 LSAs are not flooded beyond the ABR and have an area-local scope. Type 11 LSAs are flooded throughout the autonomous system (AS). Cisco currently supports only Type 10 LSAs that have area-local scopes and are flooded within the area.

The Type 10 LSA, which is used in MPLS TE, has a number of TLV and sub-TLV values that map to specific resources in a TE domain. Figure 9-9 depicts the TLV and sub-TLV values and the appropriate values that they map to enable OSPF use for MPLS TE.

Figure 9-9   *OSPF TLV/Sub-TLV TE Extensions*

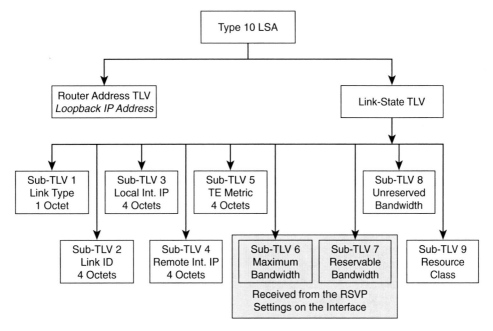

The most important sub-TLV values pertaining to TE are 6, 7, and 8. Values for sub-TLVs 6 and 7 are received from the RSVP configuration on the specific interface. Sub-TLV 8 defines the bandwidth available for reservation on each of the eight priorities. The value for sub-TLV 8 is received from the reservations active on the specific interface.

IS-IS Extensions for MPLS TE

Similar to OSPF, IS-IS can also be used as the link-state protocol of choice in the TE domain. IS-IS with extensions and newly defined TLVs can be used to propagate information pertaining to resource allocation in an MPLS TE domain. The following TLVs have been defined for the use of IS-IS as the link-state IGP in a MPLS TE domain:

- **TLV22: Extended IS reachability**—This TLV propagates information about the state of links in the network and allows the use of "wide" metrics. In addition, this TLV provides information on resource availability, like link bandwidths.

- **TLV134: Router ID**—This TLV is used to identify the router with a distinct IP address, usually a loopback address. The source and destination IP addresses used to identify and define the tunnel endpoints must match the router ID.

- **TLV135: Extended IP reachability**—This TLV uses "wide" metrics and determines if a prefix is a level-1 or level-2 prefix. It also allows the flagging of routes when a prefix is leaked from level 2 into level 1.

In addition to the just mentioned TLVs, sub-TLVs have been defined that affix information pertaining to TE resource allocations to updates. Each sub-TLV consists of three octets except those explicitly mentioned in Figure 9-10. Most of the sub-TLVs are defined in draft-ietf-isis-traffic-xx.txt. Figure 9-10 depicts the TLVs and sub-TLVs in use by IS-IS to support MPLS TE functionality.

Figure 9-10 *IS-IS TLV/Sub-TLVs for MPLS TE*

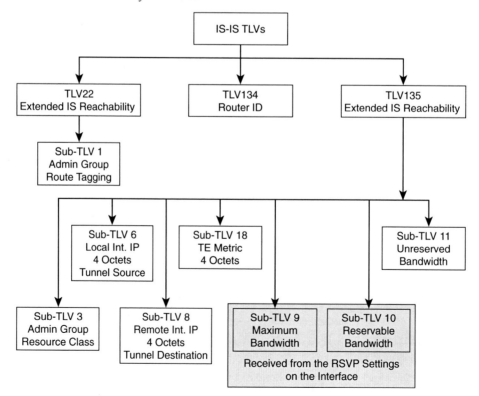

The key TLVs to note are Sub-TLV 6 and 8, which map to the tunnel endpoints or source and destination IP addresses that are usually loopback addresses; Sub-TLV 9 and 10, which map to the RSVP settings on a specific interface; and Sub-TLV 11, which maps to the unreserved bandwidth per priority on an interface after current resource allocations for active sessions have been established.

Configuring MPLS TE

This section introduces you to the steps involved in the configuration of Cisco routers to implement MPLS TE. The first subsection identifies the stepwise procedure involved in the configuration of Cisco routers for TE. It is then followed by a subsection depicting the actual configuration process on a topology consisting of six routers in which multiple paths can be used for TE purposes from a headend to tailend router.

MPLS TE Configuration Flowchart

The configuration of Cisco routers for MPLS TE support can be described in a systematic flowchart as depicted in the top row of Figure 9-11. It is assumed that the network is already configured with an IGP for NLRI exchange as well as MPLS forwarding on the appropriate interfaces prior to performing the following steps:

Step 1   Configure a loopback interface for tunnel association to the TE tunnel, as depicted in Figure 9-11.

Figure 9-11   *MPLS TE Configuration: Step 1*

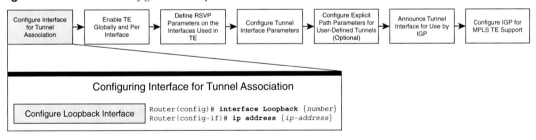

Step 2   The next step is the first configuration performed in relevance to enabling TE on the Cisco router. Figure 9-12 outlines the configurations performed on the Cisco router to enable TE functions globally on the router as well as interfaces that are possible candidates to be chosen for TE LSP paths.

Figure 9-12 *MPLS TE Configuration: Step 2*

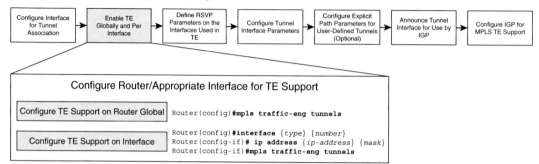

Step 3 Configure RSVP bandwidth parameters that will be used on the interface for signaling purposes and resource allocation for traffic engineered sessions. Figure 9-13 outlines the configurations that need to be performed on the interface.

Figure 9-13 *MPLS TE Configuration: Step 3*

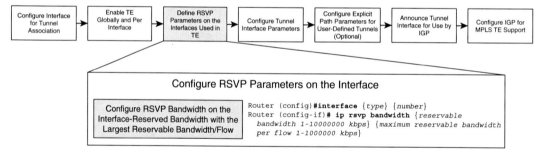

Step 4 After the interfaces that can be chosen to be a part of the LSP have been enabled for TE as well as RSVP parameters configured, the next step is to configure the tunnel interface. The main configurations of the tunnel interface would be association of the tunnel interface IP address to the loopback address configured earlier, the mode of the tunnel operation, and the destination address of the tunnel endpoint, which would map to the IP address of a loopback on the tailend router as well as the process by which the tunnel LSP path is chosen. In this step, if the path chosen for the LSP is done using the IGP and CSPF, the path option is chosen to be dynamic. Figure 9-14 depicts the configuration involved in setting up the tunnel interface.

Step 5 In addition to using the IGP for LSP path setup, the user can also define an **explicit-path** that will be used for the TE LSP. This optional step can be performed on the headend router so that the dynamic tunnel can be chosen to be the tunnel of choice for traffic forwarding and the explicit-path tunnel or user-defined static tunnel can be the backup path. In some cases, load balancing can also be achieved between the two types. Figure 9-15 depicts the configurations to set up an explicit-path LSP.

Figure 9-14 *MPLS TE Configuration: Step 4*

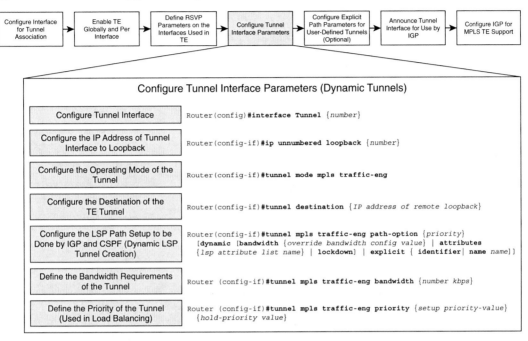

Figure 9-15 *MPLS TE Configuration: Step 5*

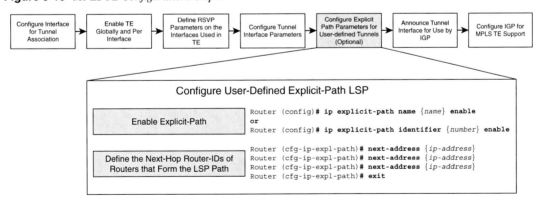

Step 6 By default, the tunnel interface is not announced into the IGP for use in the routing table. This will have to be configured explicitly for the tunnel interface to be used as the next hop in the routing table by the IGP. Figure 9-16 outlines the configurations that will have to be performed on the headend router to enable tunnel interface use as the next-hop address in the routing table for TE.

Figure 9-16 *MPLS TE Configuration: Step 6*

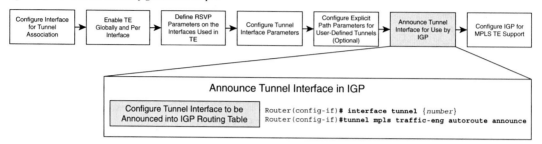

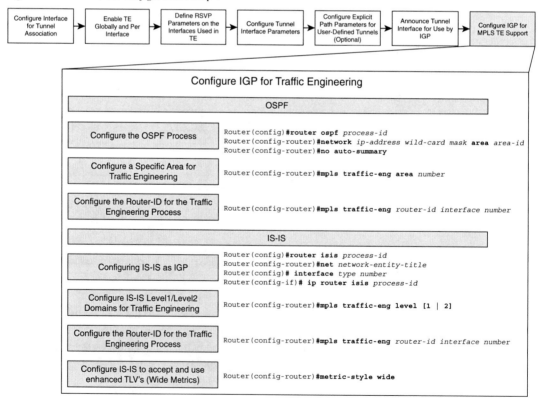

Step 7   The final step in the configuration of MPLS TE is the configuration of the
IGP for TE support. The IGP in use can be either OSPF or IS-IS. The IGP
process used for TE is the same as what's defined for NLRI reachability.
The configurations involved for enabling TE extensions for both these
protocols are outlined in Figure 9-17.

Figure 9-17 *MPLS TE Configuration: Step 7*

Configuring Dynamic Paths and Explicit Paths with MPLS TE

Figure 9-18 outlines the layout of the devices in the network that will be used to configure MPLS TE using dynamic and explicit paths. Prior to the following configurations, the devices shown in Figure 9-18 are configured with appropriate IP addresses on the interfaces as well as OSPF as the IGP. In addition, MPLS forwarding has been enabled on all interfaces in the network, as shown in Figure 9-18.

Figure 9-18 *MPLS TE Configuration Topology*

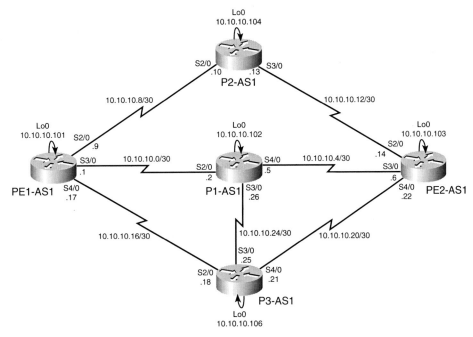

The following steps show how to configure dynamic paths and explicit paths with MPLS TE:

Step 1   Configure a loopback interface for tunnel association. This IP address can be used as the router ID in the various processes on the router (see Example 9-1).

Example 9-1 *Configure Loopback Interface for Tunnel Association*

```
PE1-AS1(config)#interface loopback 0
PE1-AS1(config-if)# ip address 10.10.10.101 255.255.255.255
```

Step 2   Enable TE globally on the router and per interface. Because we want the headend router to take all links in the network as possible links for LSP path setup, this interface-specific configuration is performed on all links in the network topology shown in Figure 9-18. Only the configuration pertaining to PE1-AS1 is shown in Example 9-2.

Example 9-2 *Enable TE on the Router and per Interface*

```
PE1-AS1(config)#mpls traffic-eng tunnels
PE1-AS1(config)#interface serial 2/0
PE1-AS1(config-if)#mpls traffic-eng tunnels
PE1-AS1(config-if)#interface serial 3/0
PE1-AS1(config-if)#mpls traffic-eng tunnels
PE1-AS1(config-if)#interface serial 4/0
PE1-AS1(config-if)#mpls traffic-eng tunnels
```

Step 3 **Configuring RSVP bandwidth parameters**—Because we have chosen to include all interfaces in the network topology to be considered for LSP path setup, this configuration is performed on all interfaces. The chosen RSVP bandwidth configured on all interfaces is 256 K with the maximum that can be allotted to a single flow also 256 K. The configuration of headend Router PE1-AS1 is shown in Example 9-3.

Example 9-3 *Configure RSVP Parameters per Interface*

```
PE1-AS1(config)#interface serial 2/0
PE1-AS1(config-if)#ip rsvp bandwidth 256 256
PE1-AS1(config-if)#interface serial 3/0
PE1-AS1(config-if)#ip rsvp bandwidth 256 256
PE1-AS1(config-if)#interface serial 4/0
PE1-AS1(config-if)#ip rsvp bandwidth 256 256
```

Step 4 **Configuring tunnel interface parameters on the headend router**—On headend Router PE1-AS1, the tunnel destination is the loopback on Router PE2-AS1 (10.10.10.103). First, dynamic tunnels are configured in which the IGP performs a CSPF calculation and identifies the appropriate LSP path. Therefore, the path-option for this tunnel creation would be **dynamic**. The tunnel is defined with a priority of *1* and a bandwidth requirement of *100 K*. In addition, the tunnel is also provided a setup and hold priority of *1* to define that this is the most preferred tunnel LSP in the domain. See Example 9-4.

Example 9-4 *Configure Tunnel Interface Parameters on PE1-AS1*

```
PE1-AS1(config)#interface Tunnel0
PE1-AS1(config-if)# ip unnumbered Loopback0
PE1-AS1(config-if)# tunnel destination 10.10.10.103
PE1-AS1(config-if)# tunnel mode mpls traffic-eng
PE1-AS1(config-if)# tunnel mpls traffic-eng priority 1 1
PE1-AS1(config-if)# tunnel mpls traffic-eng bandwidth  100
PE1-AS1(config-if)# tunnel mpls traffic-eng path-option 1 dynamic
```

Step 5 **Configuring dynamic tunnel announcement into IGP**—In this step, the tunnel interface is configured to be added into the IGP routing table to enable traffic forwarding along the tunnel. See Example 9-5.

Example 9-5 *Announce Tunnel Interface into IGP*

```
PE1-AS1(config)#interface Tunnel0
PE1-AS1(config-if)#tunnel mpls traffic-eng autoroute announce
```

Step 6   **Configure explicit-path tunnel**—In this step, an explicit-path tunnel named *LSP1* is configured via P2-AS1 between PE1-AS1 and PE2-AS1. Configure the tunnel interface with appropriate parameters. The tunnel is configured with association to the same loopback address as used earlier with the same destination address on PE2-AS1. The resource requirements of the tunnel are also maintained. However, the tunnel priorities are configured to be 2 versus 1 in the prior dynamic tunnel configuration so that the dynamic tunnel is not chosen over the explicit tunnel for establishing primary LSP. Also, the path-option maps to the name of an explicit-path are configured on the headend router that maps to next-hop addresses in the LSP path. See Example 9-6.

Example 9-6 *Configure Tunnel Interface on PE1-AS1*

```
PE1-AS1(config)#interface Tunnel1
PE1-AS1(config-if)# ip unnumbered Loopback0
PE1-AS1(config-if)# tunnel destination 10.10.10.103
PE1-AS1(config-if)# tunnel mode mpls traffic-eng
PE1-AS1(config-if)# tunnel mpls traffic-eng priority 2 2
PE1-AS1(config-if)# tunnel mpls traffic-eng bandwidth  100
PE1-AS1(config-if)# tunnel mpls traffic-eng path-option 1 explicit name LSP1
```

Step 7   Configure the explicit-path with next-hop IP addresses of routers in the LSP path, as depicted in Example 9-7.

Example 9-7 *Configuration of Explicit LSP Path*

```
PE1-AS1(config)#ip explicit-path name LSP1
PE1-AS1(cfg-ip-expl-path)#next-address 10.10.10.10
Explicit Path name LSP1:
    1: next-address 10.10.10.10
PE1-AS1(cfg-ip-expl-path)#next-address 10.10.10.14
Explicit Path name LSP1:
    1: next-address 10.10.10.10
    2: next-address 10.10.10.14
PE1-AS1(cfg-ip-expl-path)#next-address 10.10.10.103
Explicit Path name LSP1:
    1: next-address 10.10.10.10
    2: next-address 10.10.10.14
    3: next-address 10.10.10.103
```

Step 8   Configure the tunnel interface to be announced into IGP to be the preferred path for traffic engineered traffic in the domain. See Example 9-8.

Example 9-8   *Announce Tunnel Interface into IGP*

```
PE1-AS1(config)#interface Tunnel1
PE1-AS1(config-if)# tunnel mpls traffic-eng autoroute announce
```

Step 9   **Enable IGP for MPLS TE**—The configurations on Router PE1-AS1 to enable OSPF for MPLS TE are shown in Example 9-9. The router ID configured under the MPLS TE module in OSPF and IS-IS is the loopback interface on the local router. This configuration needs to be performed on all routers in the TE domain.

Example 9-9   *Configure IGP for MPLS TE*

```
PE1-AS1(config)#router ospf 100
PE1-AS1(config-router)#mpls traffic-eng area 0
PE1-AS1(config-router)#mpls traffic-eng router-id loopback 0
```

Verification of MPLS TE Tunnel Creation

The following steps outline the various commands that can be entered on PE1-AS1 (after the just mentioned configuration) to determine if the TE tunnel has been created successfully on the router (headend):

Step 1   Perform a **show mpls traffic-eng tunnels brief** on the headend Routers PE1-AS1 and P1-AS1 in the LSP path, as well as the tailend Router PE2-AS1 to verify the tunnel state is up/up. The output of the command also gives us information on the LSP path in the tunnel setup. **UP IF** defines the upstream interface for the tunnel, and **DOWN IF** defines the downstream interface for the tunnel. See Example 9-10.

Example 9-10 show mpls traffic-eng tunnels brief *on Tunnel LSP Path Routers*

```
PE1-AS1#show mpls traffic-eng tunnels brief
Signalling Summary:
    LSP Tunnels Process:          running
    RSVP Process:                 running
    Forwarding:                   enabled
    Periodic reoptimization:      every 3600 seconds, next in 3206 seconds
    Periodic FRR Promotion:       Not Running
    Periodic auto-bw collection:  every 300 seconds, next in 206 seconds
TUNNEL NAME                       DESTINATION       UP IF    DOWN IF    STATE/PROT
PE1-AS1_t0                        10.10.10.103      -        Se3/0      up/up
PE1-AS1_t1                        10.10.10.103      -        Se2/0      up/up
Displayed 2 (of 2) heads, 0 (of 0) midpoints, 0 (of 0) tails
PE1-AS1#show mpls traffic-eng tunnels brief
Signalling Summary:
    LSP Tunnels Process:          running
    RSVP Process:                 running
    Forwarding:                   enabled
    Periodic reoptimization:      every 3600 seconds, next in 2951 seconds
    Periodic FRR Promotion:       Not Running
    Periodic auto-bw collection:  every 300 seconds, next in 251 seconds
```

Example 9-10 **show mpls traffic-eng tunnels brief** *on Tunnel LSP Path Routers (Continued)*

```
TUNNEL NAME                          DESTINATION      UP IF    DOWN IF   STATE/PROT
PE1-AS1_t0                           10.10.10.103     Se2/0    Se4/0     up/up
Displayed 1 (of 1) heads, 1 (of 1) midpoints, 0 (of 0) tails
PE2-AS1#show mpls traffic-eng tunnels brief
Signalling Summary:
    LSP Tunnels Process:             running
    RSVP Process:                    running
    Forwarding:                      enabled
    Periodic reoptimization:         every 3600 seconds, next in 2857 seconds
    Periodic FRR Promotion:          Not Running
    Periodic auto-bw collection:     every 300 seconds, next in 157 seconds
TUNNEL NAME                          DESTINATION      UP IF    DOWN IF   STATE/PROT
PE1-AS1_t0                           10.10.10.103     Se3/0    -         up/up
PE1-AS1_t1                           10.10.10.103     Se2/0    -         up/up
```

Step 2   A view of the actual parameters of the tunnel can be retrieved by performing a **show mpls traffic-eng tunnels destination** *ip-address* (only Tunnel 0 depicted in Example 9-8) or a **show mpls traffic-eng tunnels tunnel** *interface-number*. As illustrated in Example 9-11, the output shows the status of the tunnel and the information about the parameters associated with the tunnel. In addition, it shows the preferred path chosen by the CSPF process under the explicit-path field in the output of the command, as shaded in Example 9-11.

Example 9-11 *MPLS TE Verification: Tunnel Parameters*

```
PE1-AS1#show mpls traffic-eng tunnels destination 10.10.10.103

Name: PE1-AS1_t0                                    (Tunnel0) Destination: 10.10.10.103
  Status:
    Admin: up         Oper: up      Path: valid       Signalling: connected

    path option 1, type dynamic (Basis for Setup, path weight 20)

  Config Parameters:
    Bandwidth: 100        kbps (Global) Priority: 1  1   Affinity: 0x0/0xFFFF
    Metric Type: TE (default)
    AutoRoute: enabled   LockDown: disabled Loadshare: 100       bw-based
    auto-bw: disabled
  Active Path Option Parameters:
    State: dynamic path option 1 is active
    BandwidthOverride: disabled  LockDown: disabled  Verbatim: disabled

  InLabel  :  -
  OutLabel : Serial3/0, 26
  RSVP Signalling Info:
       Src 10.10.10.101, Dst 10.10.10.103, Tun_Id 0, Tun_Instance 71
    RSVP Path Info:
      My Address: 10.10.10.101
      Explicit Route: 10.10.10.2 10.10.10.6 10.10.10.103
```

continues

Example 9-11 *MPLS TE Verification: Tunnel Parameters (Continued)*

```
       Record   Route:   NONE
       Tspec: ave rate=100 kbits, burst=1000 bytes, peak rate=100 kbits
     RSVP Resv Info:
       Record   Route:   NONE
       Fspec: ave rate=100 kbits, burst=1000 bytes, peak rate=100 kbits
   History:
     Tunnel:
       Time since created: 3 hours, 42 minutes
       Time since path change: 33 minutes, 26 seconds
     Current LSP:
       Uptime: 33 minutes, 26 seconds
PE1-AS1#show mpls traffic-eng tunnels tunnel 0

Name: PE1-AS1_t0                              (Tunnel0) Destination: 10.10.10.103
  Status:
    Admin: up          Oper: up      Path: valid      Signalling: connected

    path option 1, type dynamic (Basis for Setup, path weight 20)

  Config Parameters:
    Bandwidth: 100       kbps (Global)  Priority: 1  1   Affinity: 0x0/0xFFFF
    Metric Type: TE (default)
    AutoRoute:  enabled   LockDown: disabled  Loadshare: 100      bw-based
    auto-bw: disabled
  Active Path Option Parameters:
    State: dynamic path option 1 is active
    BandwidthOverride: disabled  LockDown: disabled  Verbatim: disabled

  InLabel  :  -
  OutLabel : Serial3/0, 26
  RSVP Signalling Info:
       Src 10.10.10.101, Dst 10.10.10.103, Tun_Id 0, Tun_Instance 71
    RSVP Path Info:
      My Address: 10.10.10.101
      Explicit Route: 10.10.10.2 10.10.10.6 10.10.10.103
      Record   Route:   NONE
      Tspec: ave rate=100 kbits, burst=1000 bytes, peak rate=100 kbits
    RSVP Resv Info:
      Record   Route:   NONE
      Fspec: ave rate=100 kbits, burst=1000 bytes, peak rate=100 kbits
  Shortest Unconstrained Path Info:
    Path Weight: 20 (TE)
    Explicit Route: 10.10.10.2 10.10.10.6 10.10.10.103
  History:
    Tunnel:
      Time since created: 3 hours, 42 minutes
      Time since path change: 33 minutes, 47 seconds
    Current LSP:
      Uptime: 33 minutes, 47 seconds
```

Step 3   Verify that the next hop to the destination IP address points to the tunnel interfaces in the IGP routing table. Only routes to network 10.l0.10.103 (destination) pointing to the tunnel interface as the next hop are shown for brevity. See Example 9-12. Because we have two tunnels configured on Router PE1-AS1 (dynamic and explicit) with the same parameters, the traffic to destination 10.10.10.103 is *load balanced equally* among the two paths, as shown in Example 9-12, because the bandwidths configured on the TE tunnels are the same. Traffic from PE1-AS1 to PE2-AS1 is *equally* load balanced across the two tunnels.

Example 9-12 *Verify Next-Hop Mapping to Tunnel Interface (Truncated)*

```
PE1-AS1#show ip route 10.10.10.103
Routing entry for 10.10.10.103/32
  Known via "ospf 100", distance 110, metric 97, type intra area
  Routing Descriptor Blocks:
  * directly connected, via Tunnel0
     Route metric is 97, traffic share count is 1
    directly connected, via Tunnel1
     Route metric is 97, traffic share count is 1
```

Step 4   By performing an extended ping to the destination loopback address on PE2-AS1, we see that the packets are load balanced across the two tunnel paths. See Example 9-13.

Example 9-13 *Extended Ping Verification for MPLS TE Tunnel Path*

```
PE2-AS1#ping
Protocol [ip]:
Target IP address: 10.10.10.103
Repeat count [5]: 2
Datagram size [100]:
Timeout in seconds [2]:
Extended commands [n]: y
Source address or interface: 10.10.10.101
Type of service [0]:
Set DF bit in IP header? [no]:
Validate reply data? [no]:
Data pattern [0xABCD]:
Loose, Strict, Record, Timestamp, Verbose[none]: r
Number of hops [ 9 ]: 4
Loose, Strict, Record, Timestamp, Verbose[RV]:
Sweep range of sizes [n]:
Type escape sequence to abort.
Sending 2, 100-byte ICMP Echos to 10.10.10.103, timeout is 2 seconds:
Reply to request 0 (28 ms).  Received packet has options
 Total option bytes= 40, padded length=40
 Record route:
   (10.10.10.103)
   (10.10.10.6)
```

continues

Example 9-13 *Extended Ping Verification for MPLS TE Tunnel Path (Continued)*

```
     (10.10.10.2)
     (10.10.10.101) <*>
 End of list

 Reply to request 1 (28 ms).  Received packet has options
  Total option bytes= 40, padded length=40
  Record route:
    (10.10.10.103)
    (10.10.10.14)
    (10.10.10.10)
    (10.10.10.101) <*>
 End of list
```

Final Configurations for Dynamic and Explicit Tunnels with MPLS TE

Example 9-14 and Example 9-15 outline the final configurations for all devices in Figure 9-18 for implementation of dynamic and explicit tunnels from PE1-AS1 to PE2-AS1.

Example 9-14 *Final Configurations for PE1-AS1 and PE2-AS1 to Implement Dynamic and Explicit Tunnels*

```
hostname PE1-AS1
!
ip cef
!
mpls traffic-eng tunnels
!
interface Loopback0
 ip address 10.10.10.101 255.255.255.255
!
interface Tunnel0
 ip unnumbered Loopback0
 tunnel destination 10.10.10.103
 tunnel mode mpls traffic-eng
 tunnel mpls traffic-eng autoroute announce
 tunnel mpls traffic-eng priority 1 1
 tunnel mpls traffic-eng path-option 1 dynamic
 tunnel MPLS traffic-eng bandwidth 100
!
interface Tunnel1
 ip unnumbered Loopback0
 tunnel destination 10.10.10.103
 tunnel mode mpls traffic-eng
 tunnel mpls traffic-eng autoroute announce
 tunnel mpls traffic-eng priority 2 2
 tunnel mpls traffic-eng path-option 1 explicit name LSP1
 tunnel MPLS traffic-end bandwidth 100
!
interface Serial2/0
 ip address 10.10.10.9 255.255.255.252
 mpls traffic-eng tunnels
```

Example 9-14 *Final Configurations for PE1-AS1 and PE2-AS1 to Implement Dynamic and Explicit Tunnels (Continued)*

```
 tag-switching ip
 fair-queue 64 256 48
 ip rsvp bandwidth 1000
!
interface Serial3/0
 ip address 10.10.10.1 255.255.255.252
mpls traffic-eng tunnels
mpls ip
ip rsvp bandwidth 1000
!
interface Serial4/0
 ip address 10.10.10.17 255.255.255.252
 mpls traffic-eng tunnels
 MPLS ip
 ip rsvp bandwidth 1000
!
router ospf 100
 mpls traffic-eng router-id Loopback0
 mpls traffic-eng area 0
 network 10.0.0.0 0.255.255.255 area 0
!
ip explicit-path name LSP1 enable
 next-address 10.10.10.10
 next-address 10.10.10.14
 next-address 10.10.10.103
!
end
```

```
hostname PE2-AS1
!
ip cef
!
mpls traffic-eng tunnels
!
interface Loopback0
 ip address 10.10.10.103 255.255.255.255
!
interface Serial2/0
 ip address 10.10.10.14 255.255.255.252
mpls traffic-eng tunnels
mpls ip
ip rsvp bandwidth 1000
!
interface Serial3/0
 ip address 10.10.10.6 255.255.255.252
 mpls traffic-eng tunnels
 mpls ip
 ip rsvp bandwidth 1000
!
interface Serial4/0
 ip address 10.10.10.22 255.255.255.252
```

continues

Example 9-14 *Final Configurations for PE1-AS1 and PE2-AS1 to Implement Dynamic and Explicit Tunnels (Continued)*

```
 mpls traffic-eng tunnels
 mpls ip
ip rsvp bandwidth 1000
!
router ospf 100
mpls traffic-eng router-id Loopback0
 mpls traffic-eng area 0
 network 10.0.0.0 0.255.255.255 area 0
 !
end
```

Example 9-15 *Final Configurations for P1-AS1, P2-AS1, and P3-AS1 to Implement Dynamic and Explicit Tunnels*

```
hostname P1-AS1
!
ip cef
!
mpls traffic-eng tunnels
!
interface Loopback0
 ip address 10.10.10.102 255.255.255.255
 !
interface Serial2/0
 ip address 10.10.10.2 255.255.255.252
mpls traffic-eng tunnels
 mpls ip
 ip rsvp bandwidth 1000
 !
interface Serial3/0
 ip address 10.10.10.26 255.255.255.252
 mpls traffic-eng tunnels
 mpls ip
ip rsvp bandwidth 1000
 !
interface Serial4/0
 ip address 10.10.10.5 255.255.255.252
 mpls traffic-eng tunnels
 mpls ip
ip rsvp bandwidth 1000
 !
router ospf 100
 mpls traffic-eng router-id Loopback0
 mpls traffic-eng area 0
 network 10.0.0.0 0.255.255.255 area 0
 !
end
hostname P2-AS1
!
ip cef
```

Example 9-15 *Final Configurations for P1-AS1, P2-AS1, and P3-AS1 to Implement Dynamic and Explicit Tunnels (Continued)*

```
!
mpls traffic-eng tunnels
!
interface Loopback0
 ip address 10.10.10.104 255.255.255.255
!
interface Serial2/0
 ip address 10.10.10.10 255.255.255.252
 mpls traffic-eng tunnels
 MPLS ip
 ip rsvp bandwidth 1000
!
interface Serial3/0
 ip address 10.10.10.13 255.255.255.252
 mpls traffic-eng tunnels
 mpls ip
 ip rsvp bandwidth 1000
!
router ospf 100
 mpls traffic-eng router-id Loopback0
 mpls traffic-eng area 0
 network 10.0.0.0 0.255.255.255 area 0
!
end
```

```
hostname P3-AS1
!
ip cef
!
mpls traffic-eng tunnels
!
interface Loopback0
 ip address 10.10.10.105 255.255.255.255
!
interface Serial2/0
 ip address 10.10.10.18 255.255.255.252
 mpls traffic-eng tunnels
 mpls ip
 ip rsvp bandwidth 1000
!
interface Serial3/0
 ip address 10.10.10.25 255.255.255.252
 no ip directed-broadcast
 mpls traffic-eng tunnels
 mpls ip
ip rsvp bandwidth 1000
!
interface Serial4/0
 ip address 10.10.10.21 255.255.255.252
```

continues

Example 9-15 *Final Configurations for P1-AS1, P2-AS1, and P3-AS1 to Implement Dynamic and Explicit Tunnels (Continued)*

```
 mpls traffic-eng tunnels
 mpls ip
 ip rsvp bandwidth 1000
!
router ospf 100
 mpls traffic-eng router-id Loopback0
 mpls traffic-eng area 0
 network 10.0.0.0 0.255.255.255 area 0
!
end
```

Unequal Cost Load Balancing Across Multiple TE Tunnels

In this section, we will configure another tunnel via the path PE1-AS1, P3-AS1, and PE2-AS1 with bandwidth requirements of 50 kbps versus 100 kbps. In every five packets, load balancing is performed so that two packets are sent on Tunnel 0, two on Tunnel 1, and one packet on Tunnel 2. In this case, if the source and destination of the tunnel interfaces are the same, the traffic between the sites performs unequal cost load balancing among the various tunnels between Routers PE1-AS1 and PE2-AS1. The configuration on PE1-AS1 (headend router) for another explicit LSP path setup via the path PE1-AS1, P3-AS1, and PE2-AS1 is shown in Example 9-16.

Example 9-16 *Unequal Cost Load Balancing Configuration on PE1-AS1*

```
PE1-AS1(config)#interface Tunnel2
PE1-AS1(config-if)# ip unnumbered Loopback0
PE1-AS1(config-if)# tunnel destination 10.10.10.103
PE1-AS1(config-if)# tunnel mode mpls traffic-eng
PE1-AS1(config-if)# tunnel mpls traffic-eng autoroute announce
PE1-AS1(config-if)# tunnel mpls traffic-eng priority 3 3
PE1-AS1(config-if)# tunnel mpls traffic-eng bandwidth  50
PE1-AS1(config-if)# tunnel mpls traffic-eng path-option 1 explicit name LSP2

PE1-AS1(config)#ip explicit-path name LSP2 enable
PE1-AS1(cfg-ip-expl-path)# next-address 10.10.10.18
Explicit Path name LSP2:
    1: next-address 10.10.10.18
PE1-AS1(cfg-ip-expl-path)# next-address 10.10.10.22
Explicit Path name LSP2:
    1: next-address 10.10.10.18
    2: next-address 10.10.10.22
PE1-AS1(cfg-ip-expl-path)# next-address 10.10.10.103
Explicit Path name LSP2:
    1: next-address 10.10.10.18
    2: next-address 10.10.10.22
    3: next-address 10.10.10.103
PE1-AS1(cfg-ip-expl-path)#end
```

After the configuration is performed, the output of the routing table entry for 10.10.10.103/32 shows the unequal cost load balancing in effect (see Example 9-17).

Example 9-17 *Verification of Unequal Cost Load Balancing*

```
PE1-AS1#show ip route 10.10.10.103
Routing entry for 10.10.10.103/32
  Known via "ospf 100", distance 110, metric 97, type intra area
  Routing Descriptor Blocks:
  * directly connected, via Tunnel0
      Route metric is 97, traffic share count is 2
    directly connected, via Tunnel1
      Route metric is 97, traffic share count is 2
    directly connected, via Tunnel2
      Route metric is 97, traffic share count is 1
```

Therefore, the final configuration for PE1-AS1 includes, in addition to Example 9-14, the configuration shown in Example 9-18.

Example 9-18 *Additional Configuration on PE1-AS1 for Unequal Cost Load Balancing*

```
interface Tunnel2
 ip unnumbered Loopback0
 no ip directed-broadcast
 tunnel destination 10.10.10.103
 tunnel mode mpls traffic-eng
 tunnel mpls traffic-eng autoroute announce
 tunnel mpls traffic-eng priority 3 3
 tunnel mpls traffic-eng bandwidth  50
 tunnel mpls traffic-eng path-option 1 explicit name LSP2
```

MPLS TE Fast ReRoute Link Protection

Fast ReRoute (FRR) is a procedure used in conjunction with MPLS TE to reroute around a link in the case of link failure. Protection in networks can be provided by SONET, optical protection, or, more recently, MPLS FRR. With MPLS FRR, we can implement both link and node protection. In addition, different protection policies can be applied to different classes of traffic traversing the MPLS backbone. In FRR operation, a *backup tunnel* is configured to be used if the primary tunnel LSP fails. The backup tunnel must be configured so that the LSP can get to the next-hop LSR downstream without attempting to use the failed link.

The configuration for implementing FRR for link protection is simple to implement. If you use a subset of the network shown in Figure 9-18 to implement link protection, as illustrated in Figure 9-19, you can configure a backup tunnel on the LSR P1-AS1. If the primary tunnel from PE1-AS1 via P1-AS1 to PE2-AS1 fails due to link failure between P1-AS1 and PE2-AS1, the backup tunnel is used to forward traffic.

Figure 9-19 *MPLS FRR Network Topology, Configuration, and Verification*

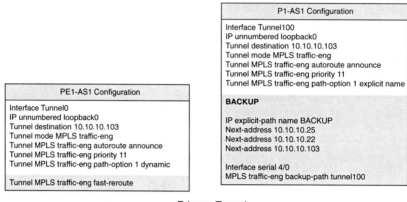

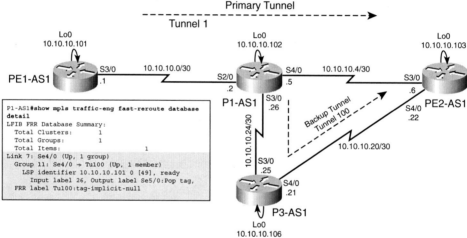

Configuration of the tunnel (Tunnel0 on PE1-AS1) to be protected from a link failure includes the **tunnel mpls traffic-eng fast-reroute** command under the tunnel interface configuration on the headend router (PE1-AS1) to enable FRR protection on the tunnel. In addition, a backup tunnel, Tunnel100, is configured on the downstream LSR (in our case, P1-AS1) to reroute traffic if the link between P1-AS1 and PE2-AS1 fails. Configuration is performed following the procedure shown in the earlier sections with an explicit path from P1-AS1 to PE2-AS1 via P3-AS1. Finally, this tunnel (Tunnel100) on P1-AS1 is associated to the link to be protected by using the command **mpls traffic-eng backup-path tunnel tunnel100** under the interface to be protected (Serial 4/0 on P1-AS1).

Verification of FRR capabilities can be performed by issuing the **show mpls traffic-eng fast-reroute database detail** command on the downstream LSR configured with a backup tunnel, as shown in Figure 9-19.

Implementing MPLS VPNs over MPLS TE

MPLS was initially adopted due to its inherent properties to deliver VPNs. However, in recent years, MPLS TE has gained popularity due to the robust TE capabilities it provides. In this section, we will discuss the configurations involved in the implementation of MPLS VPN over TE tunnels. TE tunnels can be configured between PE to PE routers as well as from PE to provider core or P routers. The configurations involved in both of these implementations of MPLS TE in the provider core are introduced. The network used to implement MPLS VPN over TE tunnels is shown in Figure 9-20.

Figure 9-20 *MPLS VPN Over TE Network Topology/Configuration*

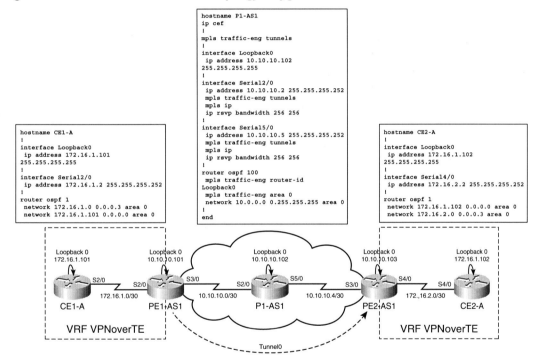

For simplicity, the OSPF PE-CE connectivity implementation is used on both PE Routers PE1-AS1 and PE2-AS1 in Figure 9-20. For this section, the IGP used in the core is OSPF with process-id 100. The process-id for the PE to CE connections is configured under OSPF 1. All networks are in area 0.

The configurations on Routers P1-AS1, CE1-A, and CE2-A are illustrated in Figure 9-20. Configurations for PE1-AS1 and PE2-AS1 are illustrated in Example 9-19. A tunnel is already configured with a dynamic path-option between PE1-AS1 and PE2-AS1.

Example 9-19 *PE1-AS1 and PE2-AS1 Configuration: MPLS VPN Over TE with PE to PE Tunnels*

```
hostname PE1-AS1
!
ip cef
!
ip vrf VPNoverTE
 rd 1:100
 route-target export 1:100
 route-target import 1:100
!
mpls traffic-eng tunnels
!
interface Loopback0
 ip address 10.10.10.101 255.255.255.255
!
interface Tunnel0
 ip unnumbered Loopback0
 tunnel destination 10.10.10.103
 tunnel mode mpls traffic-eng
 tunnel mpls traffic-eng autoroute announce
 tunnel mpls traffic-eng priority 1 1
 tunnel mpls traffic-eng bandwidth  100
 tunnel mpls traffic-eng path-option 1 dynamic
!
interface Serial2/0
 ip vrf forwarding VPNoverTE
 ip address 172.16.1.1 255.255.255.252
!
interface Serial3/0
 ip address 10.10.10.1 255.255.255.252
 mpls traffic-eng tunnels
 mpls ip
 ip rsvp bandwidth 256 256
!
router ospf 1 vrf VPNoverTE
 redistribute bgp 100 metric 10 subnets
 network 172.16.1.0 0.0.0.3 area 0
!
router ospf 100
 mpls traffic-eng router-id Loopback0
 mpls traffic-eng area 0
 network 10.10.10.0 0.0.0.3 area 0
 network 10.10.10.101 0.0.0.0 area 0
!
router bgp 100
 bgp router-id 10.10.10.101
 neighbor 10.10.10.103 remote-as 100
 neighbor 10.10.10.103 update-source Loopback0
 no auto-summary
 !
 address-family vpnv4
 neighbor 10.10.10.103 activate
 neighbor 10.10.10.103 send-community extended
 exit-address-family
 !
```

Example 9-19 *PE1-AS1 and PE2-AS1 Configuration: MPLS VPN Over TE with PE to PE Tunnels (Continued)*

```
 address-family ipv4 vrf VPNoverTE
 redistribute ospf 1 vrf VPNoverTE metric 2
exit-address-family
!
end
hostname PE2-AS1
!
ip cef
!
ip vrf VPNoverTE
 rd 1:100
 route-target export 1:100
 route-target import 1:100
!
mpls traffic-eng tunnels
!
interface Loopback0
 ip address 10.10.10.103 255.255.255.255
!
interface Serial3/0
 ip address 10.10.10.6 255.255.255.252
 mpls traffic-eng tunnels
 mpls ip
 ip rsvp bandwidth 256 256
!
interface Serial4/0
 ip vrf forwarding VPNoverTE
 ip address 172.16.2.1 255.255.255.252
!
router ospf 1 vrf VPNoverTE
 redistribute bgp 100 metric 2 subnets
 network 172.16.2.0 0.0.0.3 area 0
!
router ospf 100
 mpls traffic-eng router-id Loopback0
 mpls traffic-eng area 0
 network 10.10.10.4 0.0.0.3 area 0
 network 10.10.10.103 0.0.0.0 area 0
!
router bgp 100
 bgp router-id 10.10.10.103
 neighbor 10.10.10.101 remote-as 100
 neighbor 10.10.10.101 update-source Loopback0
 !
 address-family vpnv4
 neighbor 10.10.10.101 activate
 neighbor 10.10.10.101 send-community extended
 exit-address-family
 !
 address-family ipv4 vrf VPNoverTE
 redistribute ospf 1 vrf VPNoverTE metric 2
 exit-address-family
 !
 end
```

Verification of MPLS VPN over TE with PE to PE Tunnels

Figure 9-21 outlines the various verification steps for identifying the operation of MPLS VPNs over TE with PE to PE tunnels.

Figure 9-21   *MPLS VPN over TE Verification—PE to PE Tunnels*

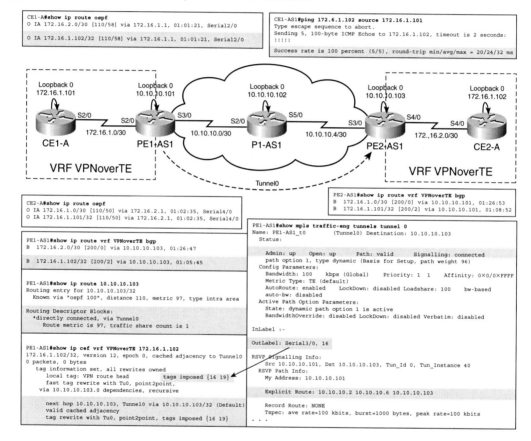

Figure 9-21 illustrates the routing tables on CE routers in which the CE routers learn the routes from the remote CEs via the MPLS backbone and place them in their local routing tables as OSPF IA routes, though all CE routes are in area 0 because sham-links are not configured.

Figure 9-21 also shows the routing table on the respective PE routers for the VRF VPNoverTE to check for route propagation in the MPLS VPN domain. As can be derived from the output, the appropriate VPN routes obtained from the remote CEs are learned from the next hop that maps to the remote PE loopback.

A closer look at the prefix 172.16.1.102 (loopback0 on CE2-A), learned across the MPLS domain one PE1-AS1, indicates a next-hop address of the remote PE loopback 10.10.10.103 (lo0 on PE2-AS1). In the global routing table, if this VPN forwards traffic over the MPLS TE tunnel configured on PE1-AS1, the next-hop address of 10.10.10.103 must point to the tunnel interface (Tunnel0) as shown in Figure 9-21 by the output of **show ip route 10.10.10.103** on PE1-AS1. In addition, note that in the label-stack imposed on the packets in the MPLS domain when implementing MPLS VPN over TE (one label for MPLS VPN and the top label for TE), the top label maps to the label assigned by RSVP for the traffic engineered LSP path. Therefore, the out-label value in the output of **show MPLS traffic-eng tunnels tunnel0** (16) maps to the top label in the label stack, as highlighted in the output of **show ip cef vrf VPNoverTE 172.16.1.102** in Figure 9-21.

For final verification of connectivity, an extended ping is performed between loopback interfaces on CE routers, as shown in Figure 9-21.

Configuration of MPLS VPN over TE with PE to P Tunnels

In the preceding section, MPLS VPN was configured over TE tunnels in which the TE tunnel was configured between the two PE routers in the MPLS domain. Another possibility that might arise while deploying MPLS VPN over a TE enabled domain is a tunnel existing between a PE router and a provider core router. In our existing setup, the tunnel interface, Tunnel 0, configured on the PE Router PE1, is changed so that the destination of the tunnel is the loopback address on P1 or 10.10.10.102/32 (see Example 9-20). This configuration might be used in conjunction with FRR to enable link protection in the SP backbone for MPLS forwarded traffic belonging to a customer.

Example 9-20 *Configuration on PE1-AS1: Tunnel Destination Changed to 10.10.10.102/32*

```
PE1-AS1(config)#interface tunnel 0
PE1-AS1(config-if)# tunnel destination 10.10.10.102
```

If no other changes in configuration are made on any router, the CE routers no longer have connectivity to one another because the LSP is broken, as shown in Example 9-21.

Example 9-21 *CE1-AS1 Cannot Reach CE2 Because LSP Is Broken*

```
CE1-AS1#ping 172.16.1.102 source 172.16.1.101
Type escape sequence to abort.
Sending 5, 100-byte ICMP Echos to 172.16.1.102, timeout is 2 seconds:
.....
Success rate is 0 percent (0/5)
```

To enable a complete LSP, MPLS is enabled on the tunnel interface on PE1-AS1. Also, P1-AS1 is configured to accept directed hellos, as shown in Example 9-22.

Example 9-22 *Enabling MPLS on the Tunnel Interface and Configuring Directed-Hello Accept on P1-AS1*

```
PE1-AS1(config)#interface tunnel 0
PE1-AS1(config-if)#mpls ip
P1-AS1(config)#mpls ldp discovery targeted-hello accept
```

Because the P1-AS1 router can accept directed hellos from neighbors who are not directly connected, the LSP is now established using the tunnel. This is shown in Figure 9-22 where the next hop for the remote CE loopback interfaces point to the interface tunnel 0 on PE1-AS1.

Figure 9-22 *MPLS VPN Over TE Verification—PE to P Tunnels*

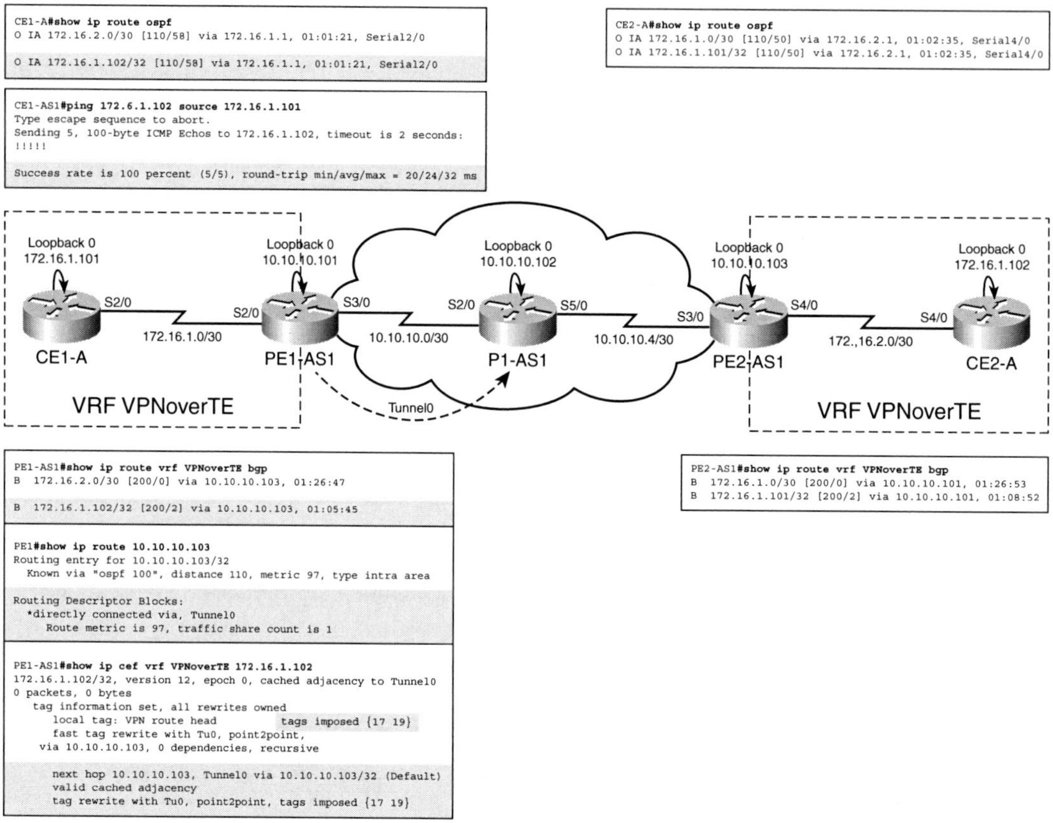
CE1-A#show ip route ospf
O IA 172.16.2.0/30 [110/58] via 172.16.1.1, 01:01:21, Serial2/0
O IA 172.16.1.102/32 [110/58] via 172.16.1.1, 01:01:21, Serial2/0
CE2-A#show ip route ospf
O IA 172.16.1.0/30 [110/50] via 172.16.2.1, 01:02:35, Serial4/0
O IA 172.16.1.101/32 [110/50] via 172.16.2.1, 01:02:35, Serial4/0
CE1-AS1#ping 172.6.1.102 source 172.16.1.101
Type escape sequence to abort.
Sending 5, 100-byte ICMP Echos to 172.16.1.102, timeout is 2 seconds:
!!!!!
Success rate is 100 percent (5/5), round-trip min/avg/max = 20/24/32 ms
Loopback 0
172.16.1.101
S2/0
172.16.1.0/30
CE1-A
VRF VPNoverTE
Loopback 0
10.10.10.101
S2/0
S3/0
PE1-AS1
10.10.10.0/30
Tunnel0
Loopback 0
10.10.10.102
S2/0
S5/0
P1-AS1
10.10.10.4/30
Loopback 0
10.10.10.103
S3/0
S4/0
PE2-AS1
172.,16.2.0/30
Loopback 0
172.16.1.102
S4/0
CE2-A
VRF VPNoverTE
PE1-AS1#show ip route vrf VPNoverTE bgp
B 172.16.2.0/30 [200/0] via 10.10.10.103, 01:26:47
B 172.16.1.102/32 [200/2] via 10.10.10.103, 01:05:45
PE2-AS1#show ip route vrf VPNoverTE bgp
B 172.16.1.0/30 [200/0] via 10.10.10.101, 01:26:53
B 172.16.1.101/32 [200/2] via 10.10.10.101, 01:08:52
PE1#show ip route 10.10.10.103
Routing entry for 10.10.10.103/32
Known via "ospf 100", distance 110, metric 97, type intra area
Routing Descriptor Blocks:
*directly connected via, Tunnel0
Route metric is 97, traffic share count is 1
PE1-AS1#show ip cef vrf VPNoverTE 172.16.1.102
172.16.1.102/32, version 12, epoch 0, cached adjacency to Tunnel0
0 packets, 0 bytes
tag information set, all rewrites owned
local tag: VPN route head
tags imposed {17 19}
fast tag rewrite with Tu0, point2point,
via 10.10.10.103, 0 dependencies, recursive
next hop 10.10.10.103, Tunnel0 via 10.10.10.103/32 (Default)
valid cached adjacency
tag rewrite with Tu0, point2point, tags imposed {17 19}

Connectivity between CE routers is verified using extended pings between loopback interfaces on CE routers, as shown in Figure 9-22.

Command Reference

Command	Description
Router(config)#**mpls traffic-eng tunnels**	Configures TE support on router in the global configuration mode.
Router(config-if)#**mpls traffic-eng tunnels**	Configures MPLS TE support per interface.
Router(config-if)# **ip rsvp bandwidth** {*reservable bandwidth 1-10000000 kbps*} {*maximum reservable bandwidth per flow 1-1000000 kbps*}	Configures RSVP bandwidth on the interface-reserved bandwidth with the largest reservable bandwidth/flow.
Router(config)#**interface tunnel** {*number*}	Configures tunnel interface.

(Continued)

Command	Description
Router(config-if)#**ip unnumbered loopback** {*number*}	Configures the loopback interface IP address to be associated with the tunnel interface under tunnel interface configuration.
Router(config-if)#**tunnel mode mpls traffic-eng**	Configures the tunnel mode to be an MPLS traffic-engineered tunnel.
Router(config-if)#**tunnel destination** {*IP address of remote loopback*}	Configures the MPLS traffic-engineered tunnel's destination or end-point.
Router(config-if)#**tunnel mpls traffic-eng path-option** {*priority*} **dynamic [bandwidth** {*override bandwidth config value*} | **attributes** {*lsp attribute list name*} | **lockdown]**	Configures the LSP path setup to be done by IGP and CSPF (dynamic LSP tunnel creation). The tunnels can be configured with the associated priority and attributes.
Router(config)# **ip explicit-path name** {*name*} **enable** or Router(config)# **ip explicit-path identifier** {*number*} **enable**	Configures an explicit path to be associated with a TE tunnel.
Router(cfg-ip-expl-path)#**next-address** {*ip-address*} Router(cfg-ip-expl-path)#**exit**	Configures the IP next-hop addresses for the explicit MPLS traffic engineered tunnel.
Router(config-if)#**tunnel mpls traffic-eng priority** {*setup priority-value*} {*hold-priority value*}	Defines the priority of the tunnel (used in load balancing).
Router(config-if)#**tunnel mpls traffic-eng autoroute announce**	Configures tunnel interface to be announced into IGP routing table (configured under tunnel interface configuration).
Router(config-router)#**mpls traffic-eng area** *number*	Enables OSPF for TE (under router OSPF configuration).
Router(config-router)#**mpls traffic-eng** *router-id interface number*	Configures the router ID for the TE process under OSPF or IS-IS.
Router(config-router)#**mpls traffic-eng level [1 | 2]**	Configures IS-IS Level1/Level2 domains for TE.
Router(config-router)#**metric-style wide**	Configures IS-IS to accept and use enhanced TLVs (wide metrics).
Router(config-if)# **tunnel mpls traffic-eng fast-reroute**	Enables the MPLS tunnel for FRR protection.
Router(config-if)# **mpls traffic-eng backup-path tunnel** {*interface-number*}	Configures the backup tunnel to be used during interface failure.

CHAPTER 10

Implementing VPNs with Layer 2 Tunneling Protocol Version 3

In prior chapters, the implementation of Layer 3 VPN technologies and deployment scenarios was discussed. VPNs can also be deployed at Layer 2 using various technologies. Tunneling is a technology that allows a network transport protocol to carry information for other protocols within its own packets. For example, IPX data packets can be encapsulated in IP packets for transport across the Internet, and these packets are delivered unmodified to a remote device. The packets can be secured using data encryption, authentication, or integrity functions. In this chapter, the operation and configuration of Layer 2 tunneling protocol version 3 (L2TPv3) will be discussed.

L2TPv3 Overview

L2TPv3 is the successor to the Cisco proprietary implementation of universal tunnel interface (UTI) for Layer 2 tunneling and implementation of Layer 2 VPNs. L2TPv3 accounts for signaling capabilities that were not implemented in the initial UTI implementations. In addition, L2TPv3 is a standardized implementation, depicted in the L2TPv3 draft *draft-ietf-l2tpext-l2tp-base-xx*, that defines the control protocol as well as the encapsulation procedures for tunneling multiple Layer 2 connections between two IP connected nodes. This extension to L2TP provides the capabilities to tunnel Layer 2 payloads over L2TP. L2TPv3 provides a scalable solution to deploy multiple Layer 2 VPNs over existing IP infrastructure and is emerging as the core tunneling technology for next generation IP core networks. With inherent ease of migration from existing UTI tunnels to L2TPv3, service providers implementing Layer 2 VPN services with UTI have migrated to L2TPv3 as the protocol of choice for implementing transparent Layer 2 services.

Operation of L2TPv3

If two routers, PE1-AS1 and PE2-AS1, are already connected through an IP network as illustrated in Figure 10-1, L2TPv3 can be used to provide Layer 2 VPN services between interfaces connecting to routers PE1-AS1 and PE2-AS1 that belong to Customer A. Therefore, the CE Routers CE1-A and CE2-A can be connected via the SP network where

L2TPv3 can be used to provide a transparent tunnel or Layer 2 VPN between these two customer routers.

Figure 10-1 *Implementing L2TPv3 Layer 2 Transparent Services*

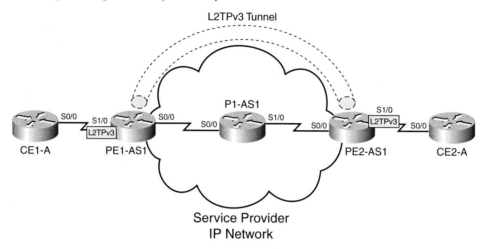

Figure 10-1 also highlights the interfaces that are part of the tunnel. On PE1-AS1, the interface connecting to CE1-A is configured as part of the L2TPv3 tunnel, and, on PE2-AS1, the interface connecting to CE2-A is configured as part of the L2TPv3 tunnel. Traffic from CE1-A to CE2-A entering Serial1/0 on PE1-AS1 is encapsulated in an L2TPv3 tunnel and forwarded to PE2-AS1. PE2-AS1, upon packet reception, decapsulates the packet and transmits the same on Serial1/0, which is configured as an endpoint of the tunnel. The routers in the core of the IP network forward this information as they would a regular IP packet, and the payload containing the information being transmitted across the tunnel is processed only on egress from the IP network.

When L2TPv3 is implemented, the physical interfaces that are connected to the customer's networks are used as the tunnel ingress and egress interfaces. L2TPv3 can also provide transparent LAN services between customer LAN segments connecting to different service provider routers. L2TPv3 can thus be used to tunnel traffic between the two separated LANs across the SP network.

L2TPv3 can also be used on serial and POS interfaces and on VLAN-based subinterfaces on certain platforms supporting L2TPv3. Frame Relay encapsulation on serial interfaces is supported for L2TPv3 tunneling based Layer 2 connectivity. For more information on supported interfaces for implementation of L2TPv3 tunnels and line card support, refer to Cisco documentation at Cisco.com.

NOTE   L2TPv3 is supported as a tunneling protocol on the following Cisco routers:

- Cisco 12000 gigabit switch routers

- Cisco 7500 series routers

- Cisco 7200 series routers

- Cisco 10700 Internet routers

For more information on platform and software support, refer to Cisco.com for the latest information and updates.

L2TPv3 Modes of Operation

The following modes of operation are supported when implementing L2TPv3 as the tunneling mechanism to deploy Layer 2 transparent services:

- **Raw mode**—In raw mode, information received on a physical interface is tunneled without regard to the type of information. Therefore, in raw mode, a *physical interface* is associated with the endpoints of the tunnel. The key to this implementation is that the physical interfaces associated with the tunnel as the endpoints must be of the same type. The interfaces supported in raw mode are serial, Packet over SONET, and Ethernet interfaces.

- **Ethernet**—Ethernet interfaces or virtual LAN segments can be extended from one site to another by using L2TPv3 tunneling technology. Therefore, either the physical interface (raw mode) or the VLAN subinterfaces can be mapped to L2TPv3 tunnels, and, thus, connectivity at Layer 2 is established across the SP infrastructure. *Support for VLAN subinterfaces at this juncture is only provided on Cisco 10720 Internet routers. All other chassis support only raw mode where the physical interface is mapped to an L2TPv3 tunnel.*

- **Frame relay**—If a Frame Relay subinterface is associated with an L2TPv3 tunnel, the tunnel parameters must be unique in relation to the subinterface; that is, a one-to-one mapping *must* exist between the Frame Relay subinterface to the tunnel. In addition, the DLCI used at the ingress and egress routers for interfaces mapped to the same L2TPv3 tunnel must be the same. The support for Frame Relay encapsulation on the physical interface is similar to the raw mode operation, wherein a packet arriving on an ingress router's physical interface is encapsulated and sent to the egress router's physical interface mapped to the tunnel without regard to the actual contents of the payload.

- **ATM modes**—*ATM AAL5 OAM Emulation over L2TPv3* binds the PVC to an *xconnect* attachment circuit to forward ATM AAL5 frames over an established L2TPv3 pseudowire. *ATM port mode cell relay over L2TPv3* enables ATM cells coming into an ingress ATM interface to be packed into the L2TP packets and transported to the egress

ATM interface (tunnel endpoint). *ATM Cell Packing over L2TPv3* enhances throughput and uses bandwidth more efficiently than the ATM cell relay function. Instead of packing a single ATM cell into each L2TPv3 data packet, multiple ATM cells can be packed into a single L2TPv3 data packet. ATM cell packing is supported for port mode, VP mode, and VC mode. Cell packing must be configured on the PE devices, and no additional configuration is required on the CE routers connecting into the SP infrastructure. *ATM Single Cell Relay VC Mode over L2TPv3* enables mapping of a single VC to an L2TPv3 session. All ATM cells arriving on the ATM interface with the specified VPI and VCI are encapsulated into a single L2TP packet. ATM single cell relay VC mode can carry any type of AAL traffic over the Layer 2 VPN tunnel.

L2TPv3 Prerequisites

To implement L2TPv3 on Cisco routers, the following general prerequisites apply:

- CEF must be enabled on the interfaces that function as L2TPv3 endpoints.
- A loopback interface must be configured as the source and destination interface associated with the L2TPv3 tunnel.
- The number of tunnels that can be configured on a router that map to a PPP, HDLC, Ethernet, or dot1q VLAN is limited by the number of interface descriptor blocks that the router can support as each tunnel consumes an IDB.
- A tunnel server card is a requirement on a Cisco 12000 series router for implementing L2TPv3 tunnels. Cisco recommends the use of the OC48 POS Line Card for use as the tunnel server card for implementing L2TPv3 tunnels.

In addition to these general prerequisites, restrictions exist for the implementation of L2TPv3 on Cisco high-end platforms, depending on the platform in use (Cisco 12000, 7200, 7500, or 10720 Internet routers). Refer to the online documentation at Cisco.com for more information on platform and interface encapsulation specific restrictions.

Tunnel Server Card Operation on GSR 12000 Series Routers When Implementing L2TPv3

The tunnel server card performs the action of packet encapsulation and decapsulation when L2TPv3 is implemented on a Cisco 12000 series router. The data plane operations of the tunnel server card on a Cisco 12000 series router, both ingress into the tunnel (encapsulation) as well as egress out of the tunnel (decapsulation), are described in Figure 10-2.

Figure 10-2 outlines the stages and the operation of a tunnel server card in a GSR 12000 series router on the ingress PE router PE1-AS1. The stages are

1 An IP packet enters the interface that is part of the L2TPv3 tunnel (interface connected to customer router CE1-A).

2 The IP packet is forwarded to the tunnel server card for encapsulation.

3 The tunnel server card receives the IP packet and applies an L2TPv3 header on the IP packet on ingress into the tunnel server card. The contents of the L2TPv3 header and the format of the same will be discussed in the next section. The encapsulated packet is forwarded to the egress line card.

4 The egress line card receives the encapsulated packet and forwards the encapsulated packet to the tunnel destination.

Figure 10-2 *Tunnel Server Card Operation—Ingress and Egress*

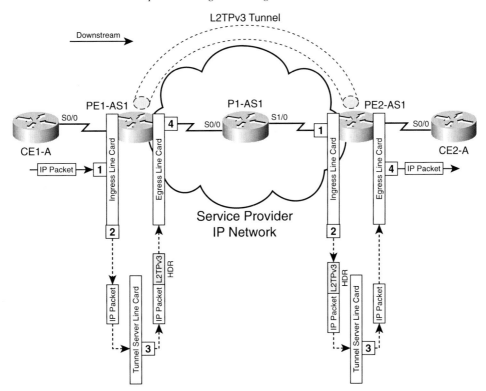

The stages in the operation of a tunnel server card on the egress router PE2-AS1 (L2TPv3 destination) are as follows:

1 When the packet arrives at the ingress line card, a regular IP lookup is performed on the packet. If the lookup points to the loopback address that is used for the IP address of the tunneled interface, then the packet is forwarded to the tunnel server card.

2 The L2TPv3 encapsulated packet is forwarded to the tunnel server card after IP lookup.

3 The tunnel server card receives the encapsulated packet, and the packet is checked for a valid session ID and matching L2TPv3 key (part of the L2TPv3 header that will be covered in the next section). If the parameters match, the tunnel server card

removes the IP and L2TPv3 headers and forwards the decapsulated packet to the egress line card.

4 The packet is forwarded out the interface that is a part of the customer network (interface connected to customer Router CE2-A).

L2TPv3 Header Format

Figure 10-3 shows the L2TPv3 header used to encapsulate packets when using L2TPv3 tunnels.

Figure 10-3 *L2TPv3 Header Format*

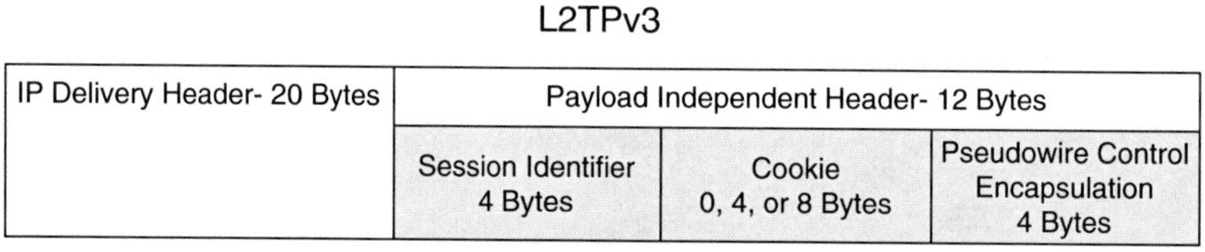

L2TPv3

IP Delivery Header- 20 Bytes	Payload Independent Header- 12 Bytes		
	Session Identifier 4 Bytes	Cookie 0, 4, or 8 Bytes	Pseudowire Control Encapsulation 4 Bytes

In the L2TPv3 header, the *session identifier* identifies the tunnel context at the decapsulating router. The session ID of 0 is reserved for use by the protocol. Static L2TPv3 sessions need manual configuration of session ID on the PE routers. However, for dynamic L2TPv3 tunnel setup, the session IDs can be chosen depending on the number of tunnels that are supported by the router in question. Therefore, a smaller number of bits might be used by the router to depict a session ID to support a larger number of unique sessions.

The *cookie* contains the key for the L2TPv3 session. The cookie length can be configured on a router, but the default value for the cookie length is 4 bytes. When the originating and terminating routers are different platforms, the cookie length needs to be configured manually to be 4 bytes.

Pseudowire control encapsulation consists of 4 bytes and implements sequencing with the L2TPv3 tunnel. It uses only the first bit and bits 8 through 31. The value of the first bit defines if bits 8 through 31 contain a sequence number and if it needs to be updated.

Configuring L2TPv3 Tunnels for Layer 2 VPN

The configuration steps involved in the implementation of L2TPv3 on Cisco routers is outlined in Figure 10-4. All steps in the configurations outlined here are performed on the routers in the provider network that connect to the customer network using either Ethernet, serial, ATM, or POS interfaces. To implement L2TPv3, there is no configuration requirement on either the CE routers or the provider core routers. All configurations are performed only on the PE routers, that is, the routers containing the tunnel endpoints for the L2TPv3 tunnel.

Figure 10-4 *L2TPv3 Configuration Flowchart*

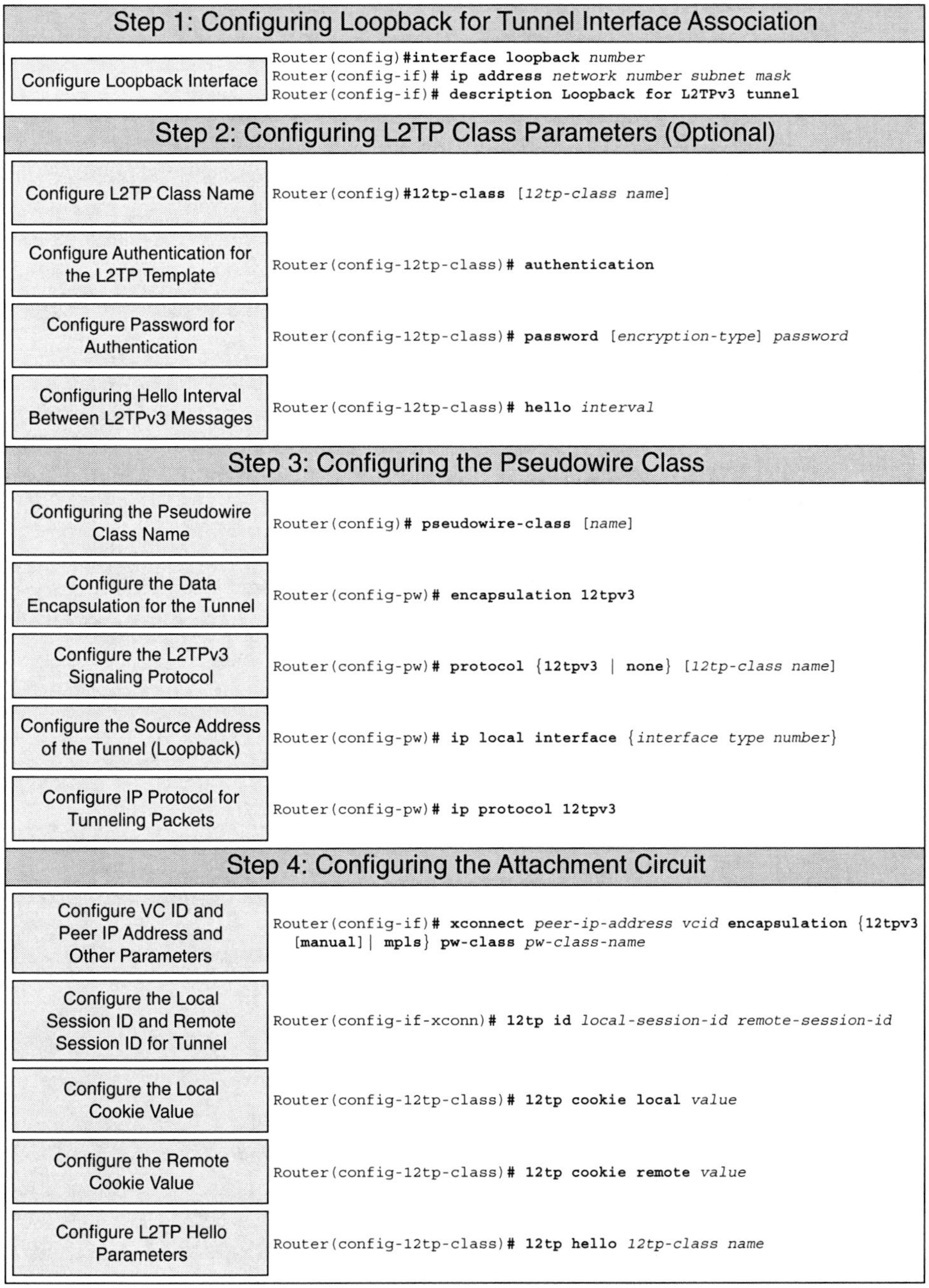

Step 1: Configuring Loopback for Tunnel Interface Association	

Configure Loopback Interface	`Router(config)#interface loopback number`
	`Router(config-if)# ip address network number subnet mask`
	`Router(config-if)# description Loopback for L2TPv3 tunnel`

Step 2: Configuring L2TP Class Parameters (Optional)	
Configure L2TP Class Name	`Router(config)#l2tp-class [l2tp-class name]`
Configure Authentication for the L2TP Template	`Router(config-l2tp-class)# authentication`
Configure Password for Authentication	`Router(config-l2tp-class)# password [encryption-type] password`
Configuring Hello Interval Between L2TPv3 Messages	`Router(config-l2tp-class)# hello interval`
Step 3: Configuring the Pseudowire Class	
Configuring the Pseudowire Class Name	`Router(config)# pseudowire-class [name]`
Configure the Data Encapsulation for the Tunnel	`Router(config-pw)# encapsulation l2tpv3`
Configure the L2TPv3 Signaling Protocol	`Router(config-pw)# protocol {l2tpv3	none} [l2tp-class name]`
Configure the Source Address of the Tunnel (Loopback)	`Router(config-pw)# ip local interface {interface type number}`
Configure IP Protocol for Tunneling Packets	`Router(config-pw)# ip protocol l2tpv3`
Step 4: Configuring the Attachment Circuit	
Configure VC ID and Peer IP Address and Other Parameters	`Router(config-if)# xconnect peer-ip-address vcid encapsulation {l2tpv3` `[manual]| mpls} pw-class pw-class-name`
Configure the Local Session ID and Remote Session ID for Tunnel	`Router(config-if-xconn)# l2tp id local-session-id remote-session-id`
Configure the Local Cookie Value	`Router(config-l2tp-class)# l2tp cookie local value`
Configure the Remote Cookie Value	`Router(config-l2tp-class)# l2tp cookie remote value`
Configure L2TP Hello Parameters	`Router(config-l2tp-class)# l2tp hello l2tp-class name`

The optional *L2TP Class* configuration creates a template of L2TP control channel parameters that can be used by different pseudowire classes. If configured, the *same* L2TP class must be invoked by the pseudowire classes used on the endpoints of the tunnel.

The *pseudowire class* configuration creates a configuration template for the pseudowire. The pseudowire class configuration is used as a template for session level information for L2TPv3 sessions. This information is used to transport Layer 2 circuit traffic over the pseudowire. The pseudowire configuration specifies the characteristics of the L2TPv3 signaling mechanism, including the data encapsulation type, the control protocol, sequencing, fragmentation, payload-specific options, and IP information. The configuration of manual sessions versus dynamic sessions is also performed in the pseudowire class configuration. The source IP address of the Layer 2 tunnel is also specified in this configuration and is usually a loopback interface.

Binding the interface that is part of the L2TPv3 tunnel to the pseudowire template and the L2TP class is the final step in the L2TPv3 tunnel configuration. The virtual circuit identifier that you configure creates the binding between a pseudowire configured on a PE router and an attachment circuit, and the virtual circuit identifier configured on the PE router at one end of the L2TPv3 control channel must also be configured on the peer PE router at the other end.

In addition to the just mentioned steps, if the PE routers are GSR 12000 series routers, a line card will need to be configured as a tunnel server card. The configuration of a line card on the GSR series as a tunnel server card is outlined in Figure 10-5.

Figure 10-5 *L2TPv3—Configuring Line Card as Tunnel Server*

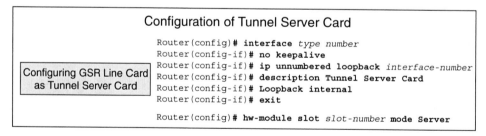

Configuring L2TPv3 Static Tunnels

In this section, you will be provided with the configuration procedure for manual or static L2TPv3 tunnels in the network topology shown in Figure 10-6. Figure 10-6 shows an SP network with two PE routers, PE1-AS1 and PE2-AS1, connected to Customer A Routers CE1-A and CE2-A, respectively. The devices used in the test setup are GSR 12000 series routers for the provider cloud devices (PE1-AS1, PE2-AS1, and P1-AS1) and 7200 series routers for the CE devices. The GSRs were chosen for the provider cloud devices to depict tunnel server card configuration that does not apply to other platforms that support L2TPv3 functionality (7200s, 7500s, and 10700 routers).

Figure 10-6 *L2TPv3—Static Tunnels Topology and Base Configuration*

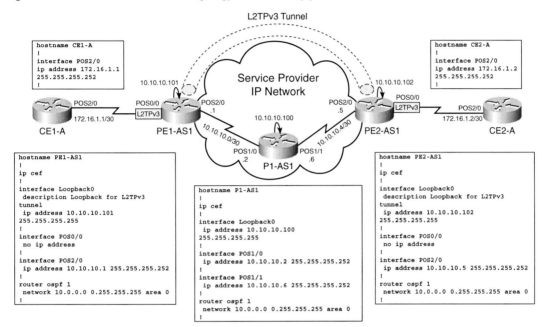

For the GSR 12000 series routers functioning as PE1-AS1 and PE2-AS1 in the network topology, Slot 3 contains an OC48 POS line card that functions as the tunnel server card for the L2TPv3 tunnel. Therefore, all configurations pertaining to implementing a line card on a Cisco 12000 series router as the tunnel server card will be performed with perspective to Slot 3 on Routers PE1-AS1 and PE2-AS1. The following steps outline the configuration process to implement the L2TPv3 tunnel. The basic configuration for all devices in the setup prior to L2TPv3 tunnel configuration is also shown in Figure 10-6. The L2TPv3 specific configuration is illustrated in the following steps:

Step 1   Configure the L2TP class on each PE router. The L2TP class implements a template for control channel parameters that can be applied to different pseudowire classes on the router. For simplicity, the L2TP class is configured with a name "manual" and cookie size of 4 bytes, as shown in Example 10-1.

Example 10-1 *Configuration of L2TP Class Parameters*

```
PE1-AS1(config)#l2tp-class manual
PE1-AS1(config-l2tp-class)# cookie size 4
PE2-AS1(config)#l2tp-class manual
PE2-AS1(config-l2tp-class)#cookie size 4
```

Step 2 Configure the pseudowire class to define the session level parameters of the L2TPv3 sessions. For simplicity, the only configurations performed under the pseudowire class are the configurations of the encapsulation protocol (**l2tpv3**) and the local interface that will be used as the source of the tunnel. In addition, because static endpoints will be configured with the L2TPv3 tunnel, disable the use of any IP protocol for signaling (the default being the use of L2TPv3 for dynamic session establishment), as shown in Example 10-2.

Example 10-2 *Pseudowire Class Configuration*

```
PE1-AS1(config)#pseudowire-class manual
PE1-AS1(config-pw-class)# encapsulation l2tpv3
PE1-AS1 (config-pw-class)# protocol none
PE1-AS1 (config-pw-class)# ip local interface Loopback0
PE2-AS1(config)#pseudowire-class manual
PE2-AS1(config-pw-class)# encapsulation l2tpv3
PE2-AS1 (config-pw-class)# protocol none
PE2-AS1 (config-pw-class)# ip local interface Loopback0
```

Step 3 The next step is to associate the interface that will be a part of the tunnel with the parameters of the pseudowire. In addition, configurations need to be performed for the local and remote session IDs and the cookie values. In the configurations, a VC ID of 1 with a local session, remote session value of 1, and the cookie values of 1 are used. The configuration is shown in Example 10-3.

Example 10-3 *Attachment Circuit Configuration*

```
PE1-AS1(config)#interface pos 0/0
PE1-AS1(config-if)#xconnect 10.10.10.102 1 encapsulation l2tpv3 manual pw-class
  manual
PE1-AS1(config-if-xconn)# l2tp id 1 1
PE1-AS1(config-if-xconn)# l2tp cookie local 4 1
PE1-AS1(config-if-xconn)# l2tp cookie remote 4 1
PE2-AS1(config)#interface pos 0/0
PE2-AS1(config-if)#xconnect 10.10.10.101 1 encapsulation l2tpv3 manual pw-class
  manual
PE2-AS1(config-if-xconn)#l2tp id 1 1
PE2-AS1(config-if-xconn)#l2tp cookie local 4 1
PE2-AS1(config-if-xconn)# l2tp cookie remote 4 1
```

Step 4 This step applies only to Cisco GSR 12000 series routers. Configure the appropriate line card and slot on the GSR 12000 series router as the tunnel server card for processing L2TPv3 tunneled packets on the chassis. In our network, the configuration is performed on Routers PE1-AS1 and PE2-AS1 where the L2TPv3 tunnels are originated and terminated. This is shown in Example 10-4.

Example 10-4 *Tunnel Server Card Configuration*

```
PE1-AS1(config)#interface POS3/0
PE1-AS1(config-if)# ip unnumbered Loopback0
PE1-AS1(config-if)# loopback internal

PE1-AS1(config)#hw-module slot 3 mode server
PE2-AS1(config)#interface POS3/0
PE2-AS1(config-if)# ip unnumbered Loopback0
PE2-AS1(config-if)# loopback internal

PE2-AS1(config)#hw-module slot 3 mode server
```

Verification of Static L2TPv3 Tunnel Operation

The following verification steps are performed on the PE routers to validate L2TPv3 tunnel and Layer 2 VPN operation:

Step 1   Verify if the state of the tunnel is established, as shown in Example 10-5 in the output of the **show l2tun tunnel all** and **show l2tun session all** commands.

Example 10-5 *L2TPv3 Tunnel State Verification*

```
PE1-AS1#show l2tun tunnel all
 Tunnel Information Total tunnels 1 sessions 1

Tunnel id 31529 is up, remote id is 56005, 0 active sessions
  Tunnel state is established, time since change 00:30:56
  Tunnel transport is IP (115)
  Remote tunnel name is PE2
    Internet Address 10.10.10.102, port 0
  Local tunnel name is PE1
    Internet Address 10.10.10.101, port 0
  Tunnel domain is
  VPDN group for tunnel is -
  L2TP class for tunnel is manual
  0 packets sent, 0 received
  0 bytes sent, 0 received
  Control Ns 31, Nr 31
  Local RWS 8192 (default), Remote RWS 8192 (max)
  Tunnel PMTU checking disabled
  Retransmission time 1, max 1 seconds
  Unsent queuesize 0, max 0
  Resend queuesize 0, max 1
  Total resends 0, ZLB ACKs sent 30
  Current nosession queue check 0 of 5
  Retransmit time distribution: 0 0 0 0 0 0 0 0 0
  Sessions disconnected due to lack of resources 0
```

continues

Example 10-5 *L2TPv3 Tunnel State Verification (Continued)*

```
PE1-AS1#show l2tun session all
  Session Information Total tunnels 1 sessions 1

 Session id 1 is up, tunnel id 31529
 Call serial number is 0
 Remote tunnel name is PE2-AS1
   Internet address is 10.10.10.102
   Session is manually signalled
   Session state is established, time since change 00:24:21
     197 Packets sent, 173 received
     18252 Bytes sent, 11252 received
     Receive packets dropped:
       out-of-order:          0
       total:                 0
     Send packets dropped:
       exceeded session MTU:  0
       total:                 0
   Session vcid is 1
   Session Layer 2 circuit, type is HDLC, name is POS0/0
   Circuit state is UP
     Remote session id is 1, remote tunnel id 56005
   DF bit off, ToS reflect disabled, ToS value 0, TTL value 255
   Session cookie information:
     local cookie, size 4 bytes, value 00 00 00 01
     remote cookie, size 4 bytes, value 00 00 00 01
   SSS switching enabled
   Sequencing is off
```

Step 2 Perform a ping from one CE router interface to the other CE router
interface across the L2VPN tunnel. If all configurations have been
performed correctly, connectivity is established between the CE routers
and the customer sites, as shown in Example 10-6.

Example 10-6 *Verify IP Connectivity Between CE Routers*

```
CE1-A#ping 172.16.1.2
Type escape sequence to abort.
Sending 5, 100-byte ICMP Echos to 172.16.1.2, timeout is 2 seconds:
!!!!!
Success rate is 100 percent (5/5), round-trip min/avg/max = 1/1/4 ms
```

Final Device Configuration for L2TPv3 Static Tunnels

Figure 10-7 depicts the final configuration for devices to implement L2TPv3 static
tunnels.

Figure 10-7 *L2TPv3 Static Tunnels—Final Configuration*

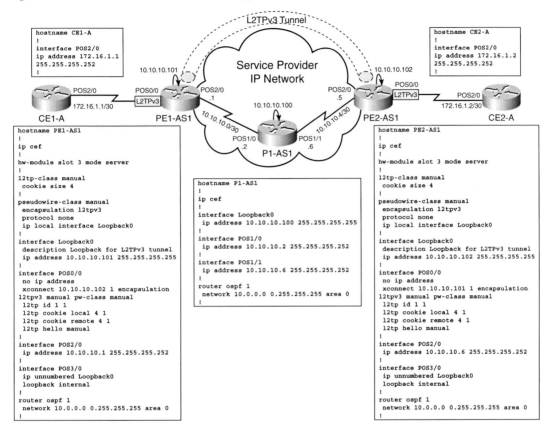

Configuring L2TPv3 Dynamic Tunnels

In this section, you will be provided with the configuration process to configure dynamic L2TPv3 tunnels in the network topology shown earlier in Figure 10-6. The same endpoints are used for implementing the dynamic L2TPv3 tunnels. The only differences are in the configuration of the pseudowire class or template as well as the attachment circuit configuration. The following steps outline the configuration process to implement the dynamic L2TPv3 tunnel. The initial interface configurations and the configuration of the L2TP class/template are not repeated for conciseness:

Step 1   Configure the pseudowire class/template with the protocol to be used for control channel information exchange to be L2TPv3. The only configuration change in comparison to implementation of static/manual L2TPv3 tunnel configuration is the configuration of a protocol for signaling the control channel parameters as shown in Example 10-7.

Example 10-7 *Configuring Pseudowire Class for Dynamic L2TPv3 Tunnels*

```
PE1-AS1(config)#pseudowire-class dynamic
PE1-AS1(config-pw-class)# encapsulation l2tpv3
PE1-AS1(config-pw-class)# ip local interface Loopback0
PE2-AS1(config)#pseudowire-class dynamic
PE2-AS1(config-pw-class)# encapsulation l2tpv3
PE2-AS1(config-pw-class)# ip local interface Loopback0
```

> **Step 2** The next step is the association of an attachment circuit by the use of **xconnect** commands under the interface configuration to associate the pseudowire class with the physical or logical interface that is part of the tunnel. To differentiate between the manual VC and the new dynamic configuration VC, configure the **xconnect** commands with a VC ID of 2 and a mapping to the pseudowire template configured in Step 1, as shown in Example 10-8.

Example 10-8 *Configuration of Attachment Circuit*

```
PE1-AS1(config)#int pos 0/0
PE1-AS1(config-if)# xconnect 10.10.10.102 2 pw-class dynamic
PE2-AS1(config)#int pos 0/0
PE2-AS1(config-if)# xconnect 10.10.10.101 2 pw-class dynamic
```

> **Step 3** In addition to the previous steps, you need to configure a tunnel server card on the PE routers that are GSR series chassis, as depicted in Example 10-9.

Example 10-9 *Configuring the Tunnel Server Card for the PE Routers (GSR)*

```
PE1-AS1(config)#interface POS3/0
PE1-AS1(config-if)# ip unnumbered Loopback0
PE1-AS1(config-if)# loopback internal

PE1-AS1(config)#hw-module slot 3 mode server
PE2-AS1(config)#interface POS3/0
PE2-AS1(config-if)# ip unnumbered Loopback0
PE2-AS1(config-if)# loopback internal

PE2-AS1(config)#hw-module slot 3 mode server
```

Verification of Dynamic L2TPv3 Tunnel Operation

The following verification steps are performed on the PE routers to validate L2TPv3 tunnel and Layer 2 VPN operation:

> **Step 1** Verify if the state of the tunnel is established, as shown in Example 10-10 in the output of the **show l2tun tunnel all** and **show l2tun session all** commands.

Example 10-10 *Verification of L2TPv3 Dynamic Tunnel Status*

```
PE1-AS1#show l2tun tunnel all
 Tunnel Information Total tunnels 1 sessions 1

Tunnel id 50899 is up, remote id is 54048, 1 active sessions
   Tunnel state is established, time since change 5d21h
   Tunnel transport is IP (115)
   Remote tunnel name is PE2-AS1
     Internet Address 10.10.10.102, port 0
   Local tunnel name is PE1-AS1
     Internet Address 10.10.10.101, port 0
   Tunnel domain is
   VPDN group for tunnel is -
   L2TP class for tunnel is l2tp_default_class
   0 packets sent, 0 received
   0 bytes sent, 0 received
   Control Ns 8483, Nr 8486
   Local RWS 8192 (default), Remote RWS 8192 (max)
   Tunnel PMTU checking disabled
   Retransmission time 1, max 1 seconds
   Unsent queuesize 0, max 0
   Resend queuesize 0, max 1
   Total resends 0, ZLB ACKs sent 8484
   Current nosession queue check 0 of 5
   Retransmit time distribution: 0 0 0 0 0 0 0 0
Sessions disconnected due to lack of resources 0
PE1-AS1#show l2tun session all
 Session Information Total tunnels 1 sessions 1

Session id 3544 is up, tunnel id 50899
Call serial number is 2130200000
Remote tunnel name is PE2
   Internet address is 10.10.10.102
   Session is L2TP signalled
   Session state is established, time since change 5d21h
      67894 Packets sent, 59399 received
      6263779 Bytes sent, 3565000 received
      Receive packets dropped:
        out-of-order:           0
        total:                  0
      Send packets dropped:
        exceeded session MTU:   0
        total:                  0
   Session vcid is 2
   Session Layer 2 circuit, type is HDLC, name is POS0/0
   Circuit state is UP
      Remote session id is 10589, remote tunnel id 54048
   DF bit off, ToS reflect disabled, ToS value 0, TTL value 255
   No session cookie information available
   SSS switching enabled
   Sequencing is off
PE2-AS1#show l2tun tunnel all
 Tunnel Information Total tunnels 1 sessions 1
```

continues

Example 10-10 *Verification of L2TPv3 Dynamic Tunnel Status (Continued)*

```
Tunnel id 54048 is up, remote id is 50899, 1 active sessions
  Tunnel state is established, time since change 5d21h
  Tunnel transport is IP (115)
  Remote tunnel name is PE1
    Internet Address 10.10.10.101, port 0
  Local tunnel name is PE2
    Internet Address 10.10.10.102, port 0
  Tunnel domain is
  VPDN group for tunnel is -
  L2TP class for tunnel is
  0 packets sent, 0 received
  0 bytes sent, 0 received
  Control Ns 8487, Nr 8484
  Local RWS 8192 (default), Remote RWS 8192 (max)
  Tunnel PMTU checking disabled
  Retransmission time 1, max 1 seconds
  Unsent queuesize 0, max 0
  Resend queuesize 0, max 2
  Total resends 0, ZLB ACKs sent 8482
  Current nosession queue check 0 of 5
  Retransmit time distribution: 0 0 0 0 0 0 0 0
  Sessions disconnected due to lack of resources 0
PE2-AS1#show l2tun session all
  Session Information Total tunnels 1 sessions 1

Session id 10589 is up, tunnel id 54048
Call serial number is 2130200000
Remote tunnel name is PE1-AS1
  Internet address is 10.10.10.101
  Session is L2TP signalled
  Session state is established, time since change 5d21h
    59409 Packets sent, 67908 received
    4278376 Bytes sent, 5450303 received
    Receive packets dropped:
      out-of-order:          0
      total:                 0
    Send packets dropped:
      exceeded session MTU:  0
      total:                 0
  Session vcid is 2
  Session Layer 2 circuit, type is HDLC, name is POS0/0
  Circuit state is UP
    Remote session id is 3544, remote tunnel id 50899
  DF bit off, ToS reflect disabled, ToS value 0, TTL value 255
  No session cookie information available
  SSS switching enabled
  Sequencing is off
```

Step 2 Perform a ping from one CE router interface to the other CE router interface across the L2VPN tunnel. If all configurations have been performed correctly, connectivity is established between the CE routers and the customer sites. (See Example 10-11.)

Example 10-11 *Verify IP Connectivity Between CE Routers*

```
CE1-A#ping 172.16.1.2
Type escape sequence to abort.
Sending 5, 100-byte ICMP Echos to 172.16.1.2, timeout is 2 seconds:
!!!!!
Success rate is 100 percent (5/5), round-trip min/avg/max = 1/1/4 ms
```

Final Device Configurations for L2TPv3 Dynamic Tunnels

Figure 10-8 depicts the final configuration for the PE Routers PE1-AS1 and PE2-AS1 to implement dynamic L2TPv3 tunnel configuration.

Figure 10-8 *Final Device Configuration for Implementation of L2TPv3 Dynamic Tunnels*

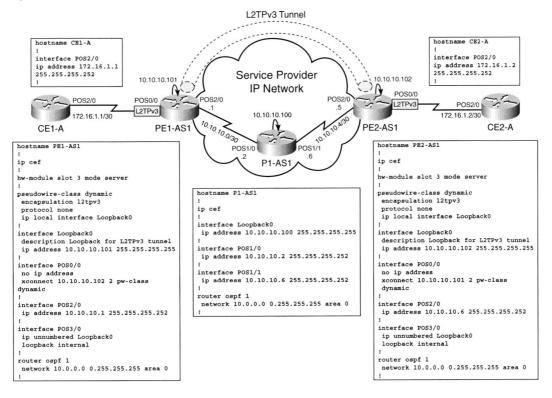

Implementing Layer 3 VPNs over L2TPv3 Tunnels

Layer 3 VPNs can be implemented in conjunction with L2TPv3 tunnels. The solution lends itself to implementation where the SP does not implement MPLS transport mechanism in the core to forward packets. Implementation of L2TPv3 tunnels creates a tunnel network as an overlay to the IP backbone, which interconnects the PE routers to transport VPN traffic. The multipoint tunnel uses BGP to distribute VPNv4 information between PE routers. The advertised next hop in BGP VPNv4 triggers tunnel endpoint discovery. Dynamic L3 VPN implementation over multipoint L2TPv3 tunnels provides the ability for multiple service providers to cooperate and offer a joint VPN service with traffic tunneled directly from the ingress PE router at one service provider directly to the egress PE router at a different service provider site.

When implementing dynamic L3VPNs over L2TPv3 tunnels, the addition of new remote VPN peers is simplified because only the new router needs to be configured. The new address is learned dynamically and propagated to the other nodes in the network.

In Figure 10-9, Customer A routers CE1-A, CE2-A, and CE3-A are to be connected using dynamic Layer 3 VPN over L2TPv3 tunnels by the service provider routers PE1-AS1, PE2-AS1, and PE3-AS1. Static PE to CE is configured for the Customer A CE routers. In addition, no MPLS is configured in the core transport network, and all traffic between Customer A sites is propagated using L2TPv3 tunnels between the PE routers in the SP network.

Figure 10-9 *Topology for L3VPN Over L2TPv3 Tunnels*

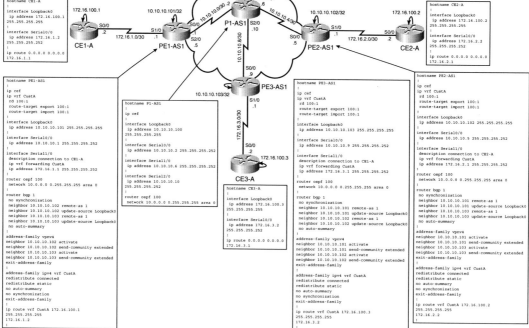

Figure 10-9 shows the base configuration of devices prior to the implementation of L3VPN over L2TPv3 tunnels. All configurations on the PE routers are the same as in the case of regular static PE to CE configurations. The only difference is that no MPLS is enabled on the core interfaces, and L2TPv3 tunnels are configured to enable route propagation between PE routers that belong to Customer A.

Configuring L3VPN over L2TPv3 Tunnels

Figure 10-10 shows the configuration flowchart for the PE routers in addition to the configuration shown in Figure 10-9. The steps shown in the flowchart are explained here:

Step 1   Configure an additional VRF that will be used to transport mGRE.

Step 2   Configure a tunnel interface and assign the tunnel interface as part of the mGRE associated VRF. Configure an IP address and a tunnel mode to be **l3vpn l2tpv3 multipoint**.

Step 3   Configure a default route for the mGRE VRF pointing to the tunnel interface.

Step 4   Configure route-map to set the next-hop resolution to the L2TPv3 VRF.

Step 5   Associate the route-map inbound for VPNv4 routes learned from MP-BGP neighbors.

Step 6   Configure the IPV4 tunnel SAFI for the MP-BGP peers. Configuration of this SAFI allows BGP to advertise the tunnel endpoints and SAFI-specific attributes (which contain the tunnel type and the tunnel capabilities) between the PE routers.

Figure 10-11 shows the L3VPN over L2TPv3 tunnels configuration for PE1-AS1, PE2-AS1, and PE3-AS1 routers. The highlighted portion depicts the important configuration steps with relation to implementation of L3VPN over L2TPv3 tunnels.

Figure 10-10 *L3VPN Over L2TPv3 Configuration Flowchart*

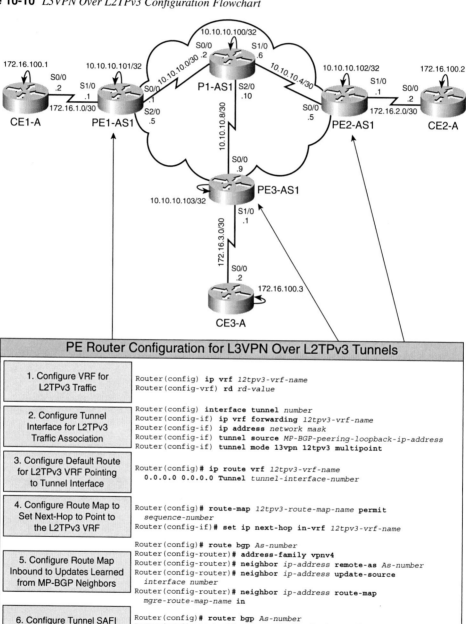

PE Router Configuration for L3VPN Over L2TPv3 Tunnels	
1. Configure VRF for L2TPv3 Traffic	`Router(config) ip vrf l2tpv3-vrf-name` `Router(config-vrf) rd rd-value`

2. Configure Tunnel Interface for L2TPv3 Traffic Association	`Router(config) interface tunnel number`
	`Router(config-if) ip vrf forwarding l2tpv3-vrf-name`
	`Router(config-if) ip address network mask`
	`Router(config-if) tunnel source MP-BGP-peering-loopback-ip-address`
	`Router(config-if) tunnel mode l3vpn l2tpv3 multipoint`

3. Configure Default Route for L2TPv3 VRF Pointing to Tunnel Interface	`Router(config)# ip route vrf l2tpv3-vrf-name` `  0.0.0.0 0.0.0.0 Tunnel tunnel-interface-number`

4. Configure Route Map to Set Next-Hop to Point to the L2TPv3 VRF	`Router(config)# route-map l2tpv3-route-map-name permit`
	`  sequence-number`
	`Router(config-if)# set ip next-hop in-vrf l2tpv3-vrf-name`

5. Configure Route Map Inbound to Updates Learned from MP-BGP Neighbors	`Router(config)# route bgp As-number`
	`Router(config-router)# address-family vpnv4`
	`Router(config-router)# neighbor ip-address remote-as As-number`
	`Router(config-router)# neighbor ip-address update-source`
	`  interface number`
	`Router(config-router)# neighbor ip-address route-map`
	`  mgre-route-map-name in`

6. Configure Tunnel SAFI for MP-BGP Peers	`Router(config)# router bgp As-number`
	`Router(config-router)# address-family ipv4 tunnel`
	`Router(config-router)# neighbor ip-address activate`

Figure 10-11 *Layer 3 VPN Over L2TPv3 Configuration*

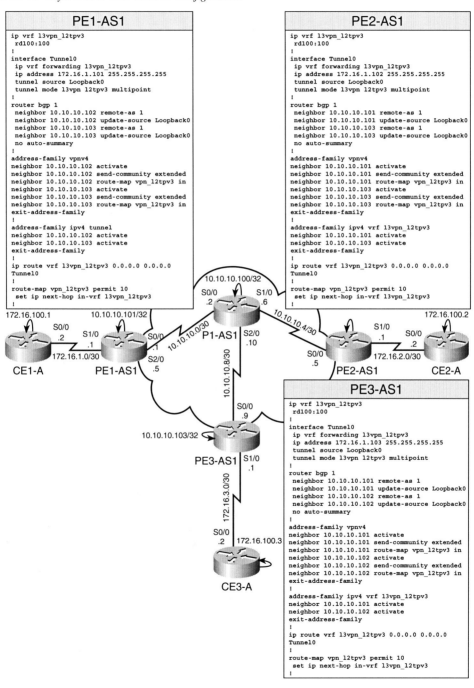

Verification for L3VPN over L2TPv3 Tunnels

The following steps outline the verification steps for implementation of L3VPN over L2TPv3 tunnels:

Step 1 Verify the tunnel's operational state using the **show tunnel endpoints** command on the PE routers, as shown in Example 10-12.

Example 10-12 *Verify Tunnel Endpoints of L2TPv3 Tunnel*

```
PE1-AS1#show tunnel endpoints
 Tunnel0 running in Multi-L2TPv3 (L3VPN) mode
  RFC2547/L3VPN Tunnel endpoint discovery is active on Tu0
  Transporting l3vpn traffic to all routes recursing through "l3vpn_l2tpv3"

 Endpoint 10.10.10.102 via destination 10.10.10.102
  Session 1025, High Cookie 0x4C9DDF2F Low Cookie 0xA82C4E76
 Endpoint 10.10.10.103 via destination 10.10.10.103
  Session 1025, High Cookie 0xC2689B74 Low Cookie 0x1A58AE6C

 Tunnel Endpoint Process Active
 MGRE L3VPN Summary
   Active Tunnel: None
 L2tpv3 L3VPN Summary
   Active Tunnel Tunnel0: Current receive session 1025
   L2TPv3 cookie mismatch counters: 0
PE2-AS1#show tunnel endpoints
 Tunnel0 running in Multi-L2TPv3 (L3VPN) mode
  RFC2547/L3VPN Tunnel endpoint discovery is active on Tu0
  Transporting l3vpn traffic to all routes recursing through "l3vpn_l2tpv3"

 Endpoint 10.10.10.101 via destination 10.10.10.101
  Session 1025, High Cookie 0x0DB50E05 Low Cookie 0x44281295
 Endpoint 10.10.10.103 via destination 10.10.10.103
  Session 1025, High Cookie 0xC2689B74 Low Cookie 0x1A58AE6C

 Tunnel Endpoint Process Active
 MGRE L3VPN Summary
   Active Tunnel: None
 L2tpv3 L3VPN Summary
   Active Tunnel Tunnel0: Current receive session 1025
   L2TPv3 cookie mismatch counters: 0
PE3-AS1#show tunnel endpoints
 Tunnel0 running in Multi-L2TPv3 (L3VPN) mode
  RFC2547/L3VPN Tunnel endpoint discovery is active on Tu0
  Transporting l3vpn traffic to all routes recursing through "l3vpn_l2tpv3"

 Endpoint 10.10.10.101 via destination 10.10.10.101
  Session 1025, High Cookie 0x0DB50E05 Low Cookie 0x44281295
 Endpoint 10.10.10.102 via destination 10.10.10.102
  Session 1025, High Cookie 0x4C9DDF2F Low Cookie 0xA82C4E76
```

Example 10-12 *Verify Tunnel Endpoints of L2TPv3 Tunnel (Continued)*

```
Tunnel Endpoint Process Active
MGRE L3VPN Summary
  Active Tunnel: None
L2tpv3 L3VPN Summary
  Active Tunnel Tunnel0: Current receive session 1025
  L2TPv3 cookie mismatch counters: 0
```

Step 2   Verify that routes are received on the Customer A VRF using the L2TPv3
L3VPN VRF, as shown in Example 10-13.

Example 10-13 *Verify Routes in Customer A VRF*

```
PE1-AS1#show ip route vrf CustA bgp
     172.16.0.0/16 is variably subnetted, 6 subnets, 2 masks
B       172.16.2.0/30 [200/0] via 10.10.10.102 (l3vpn_l2tpv3), 00:29:24
B       172.16.3.0/30 [200/0] via 10.10.10.103 (l3vpn_l2tpv3), 00:24:20
B       172.16.100.2/32 [200/0] via 10.10.10.102 (l3vpn_l2tpv3), 00:20:53
B       172.16.100.3/32 [200/0] via 10.10.10.103 (l3vpn_l2tpv3), 00:20:23
PE2-AS1#show ip route vrf CustA bgp
     172.16.0.0/16 is variably subnetted, 6 subnets, 2 masks
B       172.16.1.0/30 [200/0] via 10.10.10.101 (l3vpn_l2tpv3), 00:23:00
B       172.16.3.0/30 [200/0] via 10.10.10.103 (l3vpn_l2tpv3), 00:23:00
B       172.16.100.1/32 [200/0] via 10.10.10.101 (l3vpn_l2tpv3), 00:23:00
B       172.16.100.3/32 [200/0] via 10.10.10.103 (l3vpn_l2tpv3), 00:21:00
PE3-AS1#show ip route vrf CustA bgp
     172.16.0.0/16 is variably subnetted, 6 subnets, 2 masks
B       172.16.1.0/30 [200/0] via 10.10.10.101 (l3vpn_l2tpv3), 00:00:21
B       172.16.2.0/30 [200/0] via 10.10.10.102 (l3vpn_l2tpv3), 00:28:40
B       172.16.100.1/32 [200/0] via 10.10.10.101 (l3vpn_l2tpv3), 00:00:21
B       172.16.100.2/32 [200/0] via 10.10.10.102 (l3vpn_l2tpv3), 00:27:24
```

Step 3   Verify reachability between the CE routers using pings, as illustrated in
Example 10-14.

Example 10-14 *Verify Reachability Using Pings*

```
CE1-A#ping 172.16.100.2
Type escape sequence to abort.
Sending 5, 100-byte ICMP Echos to 172.16.100.2, timeout is 2 seconds:
!!!!!
Success rate is 100 percent (5/5), round-trip min/avg/max = 20/20/20 ms
CE1-A#ping 172.16.100.3
Type escape sequence to abort.
Sending 5, 100-byte ICMP Echos to 172.16.100.3, timeout is 2 seconds:
!!!!!
Success rate is 100 percent (5/5), round-trip min/avg/max = 20/24/36 ms
```

Final Configurations for L3VPN over L2TPv3 Tunnels for PE Routers

Example 10-15 shows the final configuration of the PE routers for the implementation of L3VPN over L2TPv3 tunnels. For configurations of the CE routers and the P1-AS1 router, refer to Figure 10-9.

Example 10-15 *Configurations for PE Routers*

```
hostname PE1-AS1
!
ip cef
ip vrf CustA
 rd 100:1
 route-target export 100:1
 route-target import 100:1
!
ip vrf l3vpn_l2tpv3
 rd 100:100
!
interface Loopback0
 ip address 10.10.10.101 255.255.255.255
!
interface Tunnel0
 ip vrf forwarding l3vpn_l2tpv3
 ip address 172.16.1.101 255.255.255.255
 tunnel source Loopback0
 tunnel mode l3vpn l2tpv3 multipoint
!
interface Serial0/0
 ip address 10.10.10.1 255.255.255.252
!
interface Serial1/0
 description connection to CE1-A
 ip vrf forwarding CustA
 ip address 172.16.1.1 255.255.255.252
!
router ospf 100
 network 10.0.0.0 0.255.255.255 area 0
!
router bgp 1
 no synchronization
 neighbor 10.10.10.102 remote-as 1
 neighbor 10.10.10.102 update-source Loopback0
 neighbor 10.10.10.103 remote-as 1
 neighbor 10.10.10.103 update-source Loopback0
 no auto-summary
 !
 address-family ipv4 tunnel
 neighbor 10.10.10.102 activate
 neighbor 10.10.10.103 activate
 exit-address-family
```

Example 10-15 *Configurations for PE Routers (Continued)*

```
!
address-family vpnv4
neighbor 10.10.10.102 activate
neighbor 10.10.10.102 send-community extended
neighbor 10.10.10.102 route-map vpn_l2tpv3 in
neighbor 10.10.10.103 activate
neighbor 10.10.10.103 send-community extended
neighbor 10.10.10.103 route-map vpn_l2tpv3 in
exit-address-family
!
address-family ipv4 vrf CustA
redistribute connected
redistribute static
no auto-summary
no synchronization
exit-address-family
!
ip route vrf CustA 172.16.100.1 255.255.255.255 172.16.1.2
ip route vrf l3vpn_l2tpv3 0.0.0.0 0.0.0.0 Tunnel0
!
route-map vpn_l2tpv3 permit 10
 set ip next-hop in-vrf l3vpn_l2tpv3
hostname PE2-AS1
!
ip cef
ip vrf CustA
 rd 100:1
 route-target export 100:1
 route-target import 100:1
!
ip vrf l3vpn_l2tpv3
 rd 100:100
!
interface Loopback0
 ip address 10.10.10.102 255.255.255.255
!
interface Tunnel0
 ip vrf forwarding l3vpn_l2tpv3
 ip address 172.16.1.102 255.255.255.255
 tunnel source Loopback0
 tunnel mode l3vpn l2tpv3 multipoint
!
interface Serial0/0
 ip address 10.10.10.5 255.255.255.252
!
interface Serial1/0
 description connection to CE2-A
 ip vrf forwarding CustA
 ip address 172.16.2.1 255.255.255.252
```

continues

Example 10-15 *Configurations for PE Routers (Continued)*

```
!
router ospf 100
 network 10.0.0.0 0.255.255.255 area 0
!
router bgp 1
 no synchronization
 neighbor 10.10.10.101 remote-as 1
 neighbor 10.10.10.101 update-source Loopback0
 neighbor 10.10.10.103 remote-as 1
 neighbor 10.10.10.103 update-source Loopback0
 no auto-summary
 !
 address-family ipv4 tunnel
 neighbor 10.10.10.101 activate
 neighbor 10.10.10.103 activate
 exit-address-family
 !
 address-family vpnv4
 neighbor 10.10.10.101 activate
 neighbor 10.10.10.101 send-community extended
 neighbor 10.10.10.101 route-map vpn_l2tpv3 in
 neighbor 10.10.10.103 activate
 neighbor 10.10.10.103 send-community extended
 neighbor 10.10.10.103 route-map vpn_l2tpv3 in
 exit-address-family
 !
 address-family ipv4 vrf CustA
 redistribute connected
 redistribute static
 no auto-summary
 no synchronization
 exit-address-family
!
ip route vrf CustA 172.16.100.2 255.255.255.255 172.16.2.2
ip route vrf l3vpn_l2tpv3 0.0.0.0 0.0.0.0 Tunnel0
!
route-map vpn_l2tpv3 permit 10
 set ip next-hop in-vrf l3vpn_l2tpv3
hostname PE3-AS1
!
ip cef
ip vrf CustA
 rd 100:1
 route-target export 100:1
 route-target import 100:1
!
ip vrf l3vpn_l2tpv3
 rd 100:100
```

Example 10-15 *Configurations for PE Routers (Continued)*

```
!
interface Loopback0
 ip address 10.10.10.103 255.255.255.255
!
interface Tunnel0
 ip vrf forwarding l3vpn_l2tpv3
 ip address 172.16.1.103 255.255.255.255
 tunnel source Loopback0
 tunnel mode l3vpn l2tpv3 multipoint
!
interface Serial0/0
 ip address 10.10.10.9 255.255.255.252
!
interface Serial1/0
 description connection to CE1-A
 ip vrf forwarding CustA
 ip address 172.16.3.1 255.255.255.252
!
router ospf 100
 network 10.0.0.0 0.255.255.255 area 0
!
router bgp 1
 no synchronization
 neighbor 10.10.10.101 remote-as 1
 neighbor 10.10.10.101 update-source Loopback0
 neighbor 10.10.10.102 remote-as 1
 neighbor 10.10.10.102 update-source Loopback0
 no auto-summary
 !
 address-family ipv4 tunnel
 neighbor 10.10.10.101 activate
 neighbor 10.10.10.102 activate
 exit-address-family
 !
 address-family vpnv4
 neighbor 10.10.10.101 activate
 neighbor 10.10.10.101 send-community extended
 neighbor 10.10.10.101 route-map vpn_l2tpv3 in
 neighbor 10.10.10.102 activate
 neighbor 10.10.10.102 send-community extended
 neighbor 10.10.10.102 route-map vpn_l2tpv3 in
 exit-address-family
 !
 address-family ipv4 vrf CustA
 redistribute connected
 redistribute static
 no auto-summary
 no synchronization
 exit-address-family
```

continues

Example 10-15 *Configurations for PE Routers (Continued)*

```
!
ip route vrf CustA 172.16.100.3 255.255.255.255 172.16.3.2
ip route vrf l3vpn_l2tpv3 0.0.0.0 0.0.0.0 Tunnel0
!
route-map vpn_l2tpv3 permit 10
 set ip next-hop in-vrf l3vpn_l2tpv3
```

Command Reference

Command	Description
Router(config)#**l2tp-class** [*l2tp-class name*]	Configures an L2TP class to define the L2TP template
Router(config-l2tp-class)# **authentication**	Configures authentication for the L2TP template
Router(config-l2tp-class)# **password** [*encryption-type*] *password*	Configures a password for L2TP template authentication
Router(config-l2tp-class)# **hello** *interval*	Configures the interval between L2TPv3 hello packets
Router(config)# **pseudowire-class** [*name*]	Defines/configures the pseudowire class
Router(config-pw)# **encapsulation l2tpv3**	Configures the encapsulation type of the pseudowire to be L2TPv3
Router(config-pw)# **protocol** {**l2tpv3** | **none**} [*l2tp-class name*]	Configures the protocol for L2TPv3 signaling
Router(config-pw)# **ip local interface** *interface type number*	Defines the source interface for the tunnel
Router(config-pw)# **ip protocol l2tpv3**	Defines the IP protocol for tunneling packets
Router(config-if)# **xconnect** *peer-ip-address* **vcid encapsulation** {**l2tpv3** [**manual**] | **mpls**} **pw-class** *pw-class-name*	Configures the attachment circuit parameters
Router(config-if-xconn)# **l2tp id** *local-session-id remote-session-id*	Configures the local and remote session IDs for the tunnel
Router(config-l2tp-class)# **l2tp cookie local** *value*	Configures the local L2TP cookie values
Router(config-l2tp-class)# **l2tp cookie remote** *value*	Configures the remote L2TP cookie value

(Continued)

Command	Description
Router(config-l2tp-class)# **l2tp hello** *l2tp-class name*	Configures the L2TP hello parameters
Router(config)# **hw-module slot** *slot-number* **mode server**	Configures a specific card on a GSR 12000 series router as a tunnel server card
Router(config-if)# **tunnel mode l3vpn l2tpv3 multipoint**	Configures the tunnel mode to dynamic multipoint L2TPv3

CHAPTER 11

Any Transport over MPLS (AToM)

In Chapter 10, "Implementing VPNs with Layer 2 Tunneling Protocol Version 3," you were introduced to the configuration and benefits of implementing L2TPv3 in IP-enabled networks to deliver Layer 2 VPNs. In this chapter, you will be introduced to the configuration of Layer 2 VPN implementations in an MPLS-enabled network and how it has played an important role in service provider environments. This chapter covers the following topics:

- Introduction to Layer 2 VPNs
- Implementing AToM for like to like circuits
- Implementing AToM for any to any circuits
- Local switching

Introduction to Layer 2 VPNs

Layer 2 VPNs were originally implemented using Layer 2 technologies like Frame Relay and ATM. However, there has been a considerable shift in technology; service provider (SP) networks are transitioning from circuit-switched networks to packet-switched networks. This shift is primarily due to increased revenue generation opportunities and improved management of current network resources. Overall, Layer 2 VPNs help reduce the cost for the provider because the cost of managing separate networks (TDM, FR, ATM, IP) is much higher from both a CAPEX and OPEX perspective than managing one larger aggregate network.

SPs can support both Layer 2 VPNs and Layer 3 MPLS VPNs over a single infrastructure because MPLS-enabled networks allow seamless integration of Layer 2 and Layer 3 services. Layer 2 VPNS provide several benefits, such as

- Consolidation of multiple Layer 2 networks within enterprise or SP environments into one core network with Layer 2 services running over a common IP/MPLS core. This enables the SP to deliver transparent services to end customers.
- The ability to seamlessly extend LANs as private virtual LANs across a SP's network and to deliver multipoint Ethernet services.

A Layer 2 VPN is defined as a VPN comprising switched connections between subscriber endpoints over a shared network. Figure 11-1 shows an MPLS-based provider that offers Layer 2 VPN services.

Figure 11-1   *Layer 2 VPNs*

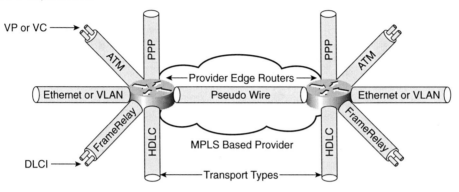

VPWS and VPLS

Virtual Private LAN Service (VPLS) and Virtual Private Wire Service (VPWS) are packet-switched VPN solutions that unify Layer 2 and Layer 3 services.

VPLS is designed for applications that require multipoint or broadcast access. It uses Layer 2 architecture to offer multipoint Ethernet VPNs that connect several sites over a metropolitan-area network (MAN) or wide-area network (WAN).

In VPWS, the two pseudo-wire technologies that enable point-to-point Layer 2 services are as follows:

- **AToM**—A pseudo-wire technology that uses MPLS-enabled networks to provide Layer 2 services.
- **L2TPv3**—A pseudo-wire technology for non-MPLS enabled networks or purely native IP-based networks. This has been covered extensively in Chapter 10.

Both AToM and L2TPv3 support the transport of Frame Relay, ATM, High-Level Data Link Control (HDLC), PPP, and Ethernet traffic over an MPLS or IP core.

Figure 11-2 (page 451) shows the various pseudo-wire technologies used in Layer 2 VPN networks.

Pseudo Wire Reference Model

AToM uses the Pseudo Wire Reference Model, shown in Figure 11-3, to transport Layer 2 traffic across an MPLS backbone. The Pseduo Wire Reference Model is based on the workings of the IETF PWE3 (Pseudo-Wire Emulation Edge to Edge) group that provides the framework for edge to edge wire emulation over a packet-based provider network.

Figure 11-2 *Layer 2 VPN Model*

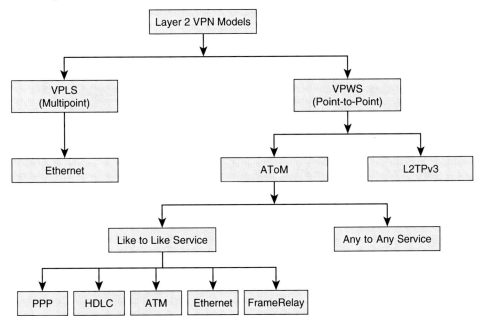

Figure 11-3 *Pseudo Wire Reference Model*

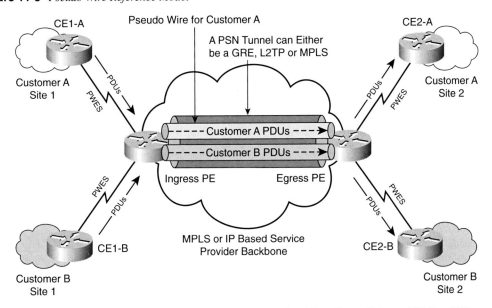

A PWES Is Either an Ethernet Link or VLAN Link or ATM VC or VP or Frame Relay or HDLC or PPP

A **pseudo wire** is a logical connection between two provider edge (PE) devices that connects two pseudo-wire end-services (PWES) of the same type. **PWES** can be either one of the following used between the PE and CE device:

- Ethernet, VLAN, or 802.1Q tunneling (QinQ)
- ATM VC or VP
- Frame Relay VC
- HDLC
- PPP

The PE routers are configured as the endpoints of a pseudo-wire connection. After the formation of the pseudo wire, Layer 1 or Layer 2 PDUs are encapsulated at the ingress PW (pseudo wire) device. The encapsulated PDU is then sent over the PW to the egress PW device where the L2 or L3 headers are reconstructed and the frames are sent in its original format to the other CE device.

AToM Terminology

The following terminology is often used in AToM-based VPN networks:

- Attachment circuit (AC)
- Packet switched network (PSN)
- Emulated VC

Figure 11-4 shows the AToM terminology used.

Figure 11-4 *Pseudo Wire Reference Model*

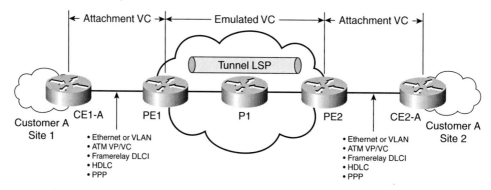

An *attachment circuit (AC)* is a physical or virtual circuit (VC) that attaches a CE to a PE. An AC can be, among other things, a VC (for example, Frame Relay or ATM), an Ethernet port, a VLAN, an HDLC link, or a PPP connection.

A *packet switched network (PSN)* uses IP or MPLS as the mechanism for packet forwarding. The endpoints of a pseudo wire are two PE routers connected to ACs of the same type. PWE3 is a mechanism that emulates the essential attributes of a service (such as Frame Relay or ATM PVC) over a PSN.

An *emulated VC* is used to provide a Layer 2 connection between the two CE devices. The emulated circuits use three layers of encapsulation:

- **Tunnel header**—This is implemented as an MPLS label or LSP label, which is learned via LDP inside the provider backbone. It is the first or outer label in the MPLS label stack. The label is implemented so that the PDU can be transported from the ingress PE to the egress PE device.

- **Demultiplexer field**—The function of this label is to identify individual circuits in the tunnel. This is implemented as a VC label, is the second or inner label in the stack, and is learned via the directed LDP session between the PE routers.

- **Emulated VC encapsulation**—This is implemented as a 32-bit control word and identifies information inside the enclosed Layer 2 PDU.

Protocol data units (PDUs) received from customer sites are encapsulated at the ingress PE router. In AToM architecture, encapsulation implies attaching a certain label stack and special control word. The encapsulated customer PDU is then label switched across the service provider backbone toward the remote PE. The pseudo-wire PDU contains all data and control information stored, if needed, in the control word that is necessary to provide Layer 2 service. Some information might be stored as a state at the pseudo-wire setup—for example, the mapping between label and outgoing interface.

How AToM Works

In an MPLS-based network providing AToM services, Layer 2 frames are received on the ingress interface of the ingress PE router. This Layer 2 frame is encapsulated into an MPLS packet using a label stack by the ingress PE router. The ingress PE encapsulates the frame into the MPLS label stack and tunnels it across the backbone to the egress PE. Figure 11-5 shows the operation of AToM in SP networks.

The egress PE decapsulates the packet and reproduces the Layer 2 frame on the appropriate egress interface. As mentioned earlier, the AToM frames are carried across the MPLS backbone using a label stack of two labels. In the AToM framework, the outer label is called the *tunnel label*. This outer label propagates the packet from the ingress PE to the correct egress PE router. This outer tunnel label is used for the PE-to-PE LSP.

The second label (inner label), known as the *VC label*, is used by the egress PE router to forward the packet out on the appropriate egress interface. This procedure is somewhat similar to MPLS VPN, where the egress PE router uses a VPN label. An IGP protocol similar to MPLS VPN implementation is required in the provider backbone between the PE routers so that they can exchange the VC labels. However, in L2 VPN, unlike MPLS VPN, extended communities in BGP are not used to carry VC labels.

Figure 11-5 *Tunnel LSP and Directed LDP*

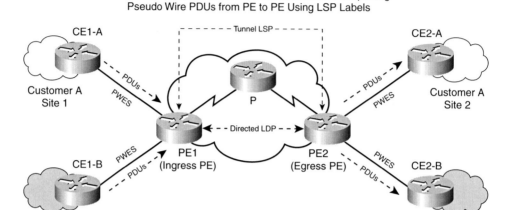

In case of AToM, VC label exchange is achieved by establishing a directed multihop LDP session between the PE routers. The egress PE router sends an LDP Label Mapping Message that indicates the label value to use for a VC Forwarding Equivalence Class (VC-FEC). *VC FEC* is a new LDP element type defined for this purpose. The VC information exchange uses downstream unsolicited label distribution procedures. This label value is then used by the ingress PE router as the second label in the label stack imposed to the frames of the indicated VC-FEC.

LDP Label Mapping Procedure

An emulated VC is an LSP tunnel between the ingress and egress PE. The emulated VC consists of two unidirectional LSPs used to transport Layer 2 PDUs in each direction. A two-level label stack consisting of the tunnel label (top label) and the bottom label (VC label) is used to switch packets back and forth between the ingress and egress PE. The VC label is provided to the ingress PE by the egress PE of a particular LSP to direct traffic to a particular egress interface on the egress PE. A VC label is assigned by the egress PE during the VC setup and represents the binding between the egress interface and a given VC ID. A VC is identified by a unique and configurable VC ID that is recognized by both the ingress and egress PE. During a VC setup, the ingress and egress PE exchange VC label bindings for the specified VC ID. Figure 11-6 shows the LDP label mapping procedure that takes place in an MPLS-based AToM network.

Figure 11-6 *LDP Label Mapping Procedure*

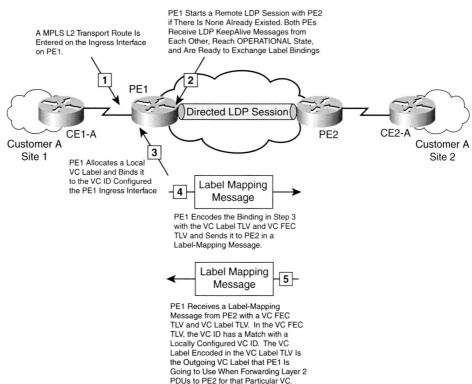

The following procedure of setting the VC between the PE routers is independent of the transport:

Step 1 An MPLS L2 transport route is entered on the ingress interface on PE1 (**xconnect** *remote-PE-ip-address VCID* **encapsulation mpls**).

Step 2 PE1 starts a remote LDP session with PE2 if it does not already exist.

Step 3 The physical layer of the ingress interface on PE1 comes up. PE1 recognizes a VC configured for the ingress interface over which Layer 2 PDUs received from CE1 are forwarded, and, hence, allocates a local VC label and binds it to the VC ID configured under the ingress interface.

Step 4 PE1 encodes this binding with the VC-label TLV and VC FEC TLV and sends it to PE2 in a label-mapping message.

Step 5 PE1 receives a label-mapping message from PE2 with a VC FEC TLV and VC-label TLV. In the VC FEC TLV, the VC ID has a match with a locally configured VC ID. The VC label encoded in the VC-label TLV is the outgoing VC label that PE1 is going to use when forwarding Layer 2 PDUs to PE2 for that particular VC.

Step 6 PE1 might receive a label-request message from some other PE with a specific VC FEC TLV at any time during the OPERATIONAL state. PE1 examines the VC ID encoded in the FEC element and responds to the peer with a label mapping with the local VC label corresponding to the VC ID.

Step 7 After Steps 1 through 6, the LSP between PE1 to PE2 is up and unidirectional. PE2 now performs Steps 1 through 6 as it did with PE1. After both exchange the VC labels for a particular VC ID, the VC ID is considered established.

Step 8 When the VC is taken down for some reason, for example, the CE-PE link goes down or the VC configuration is removed from one PE router, the PE router must send a label-withdraw message to its remote LDP peer to withdraw the VC label it previously advertised.

PSN Tunnel and VC Label Distribution

This section covers the control and data plane forwarding operation that takes place in a provider network delivering AToM services.

Control Plane Operation

Figure 11-7 shows an MPLS backbone network that provides AToM services to the Customer A sites, CE1-A and CE2-A.

Figure 11-7 *Control Plane—PSN Tunnel and VC Label Distribution*

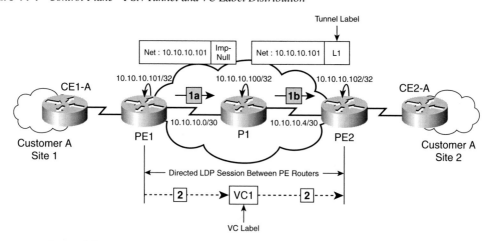

To establish the LSP between the PE routers, PE1 and PE2, for control plane traffic from PE1 to PE2, the IGP or LDP label propagation process begins when PE1 advertises the pop label (implicit-null) for its own loopback address (10.10.10.101). The backbone router P1-AS1 advertises a label value of L1 to the PE2 router. This is shown in Steps 1a and 1b in Figure 11-7. An LSP from PE1 to PE2 is now established.

A directed LDP session will also be created between the PE1 and PE2 routers to exchange the VC label. To provide AToM services, any PE pair requires a similar directed LDP session. The PE1 router allocates a local label of VC1 to be the VC label for the specific circuit. The VC label, VC1, is advertised to the PE2 router using the directed LDP session between PE1 and PE2. The PE2 router now forms a label stack. The top-most label, the tunnel label, has the value L1 and forwards the packets to the PE1.

Data Plane Operation

Figure 11-8 shows the data plane forwarding operation for traffic originating from CE2-A to CE1-A.

Figure 11-8 *Data Plane Operation*

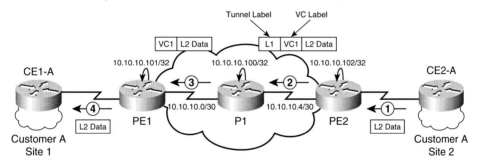

Layer 2 data from CE2-A is received by PE2. PE2 does label imposition on the data packet with tunnel label L1 and VC label VC1. PE2 uses the outer or tunnel label L1 to forward the data packets to PE1. At P1, the tunnel label L1 is popped, and the resulting packet is forwarded to PE1. PE1 uses the inner label, or VC label, VC1 to forward the packets on the correct outgoing interface on PE1.

VC Label Withdrawal Procedure

If a PE router detects a condition that affects normal service, it must withdraw the corresponding VC label using the LDP protocol. Figure 11-9 (page 458) shows an MPLS-based AToM network in which a link failure between PE2 and CE2-A results in the VC label withdrawal message being sent by PE2 to PE1.

Control Word

The ingress PE router will use a label stack to encapsulate the Layer 2 frames into MPLS by removing any preamble, frame checksums, and also some header information. Essential header information is carried across the MPLS backbone in a control word, or shim-header. The control word is also used for sequence numbering to guarantee sequenced delivery, if required.

Figure 11-9 *VC Label Withdrawal Procedure*

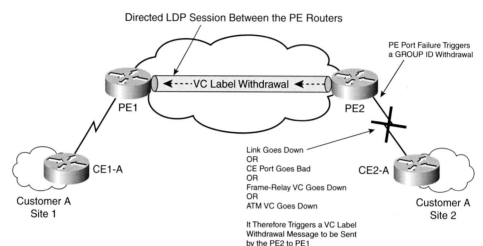

Sequence number zero indicates that no sequencing is done. Small packets may need to be padded if the minimum maximum transmission unit (MTU) of the medium is larger than actual packet size. Control bits carried in the header of the Layer 2 frame may need to be transported in flag fields.

The control word is optional. Some Layer 2 protocols make use of it, while others do not. Both endpoints (ingress PE and egress PE) must, of course, agree to use or not to use the control word. When the control word is used, it is transmitted after the label stack but before the Layer 2 PDU.

The control word is 32 bits. It is divided into 4 fields. The first field is 4 reserved bits that must always be set to 0. The next field is a 4-bit flag field. The flags have different uses depending on the Layer 2 protocol being forwarded. The next 2 bits are always set to 0 when transmitting. The third field is a 6-bit field that is only used if the Layer 2 PDU is shorter than the minimum MPLS packet and padding is required. If no padding is required, the length field is not used. The fourth field is a 16-bit sequence number. Sequence numbering is only used on Layer 2 protocols, which guarantees ordered delivery. The special value 0 in the sequence field indicates that there is no guaranteed sequenced delivery.

When AToM is used for Frame Relay over MPLS, the Frame Relay header is removed and the FECN, BECN, DE, and C/R (CRC) bits are carried in the control word flag field. When AToM is used for ATM over MPLS, the first flag in the control word flag field indicates whether AAL5 frames or raw ATM cells are being transported by AToM. The other three flags are used for Explicit Forward Congestion Indicator (EFCI), Cell Loss Priority (CLP), and C/R.

If one of these flags is set in any of the ATM cells being transported in the MPLS packet, then the corresponding flag is set in the control word.

Implementing AToM for Like to Like Circuits

AToM supports the following Layer 2 technologies over MPLS:

- Ethernet
- 802.1Q VLAN
- ATM AAL5 frames
- ATM cells
- Frame Relay
- PPP
- HDLC

In this section, you will configure AToM for the following like to like circuits:

- ATM over MPLS
  - AAL5 over MPLS
  - ATM Cell Relay over MPLS
- Ethernet over MPLS
  - Router-based port mode
  - Router-based VLAN mode
  - Switch-based port mode
  - Switch-based VLAN mode
  - Switch-based Dot1q tunnel mode
- PPP over MPLS
- HDLC over MPLS
- Frame Relay over MPLS

ATM over MPLS

In ATM over MPLS, two modes of encapsulation are supported to transport ATM cells over MPLS:

- AAL5 over MPLS
- ATM Cell Relay over MPLS

AAL5 over MPLS

In AAL5 over MPLS operation, the entire AAL5 frame is encapsulated and label switched across the MPLS backbone. The ingress PE router is required to reassemble all AAL5 CPCS-SDUs from the incoming VC and transport each CPCS-SDU as a single packet. The AAL5 trailer is not encapsulated and, therefore, not transported across the MPLS backbone. The use of the control word is required although its use is optional. The PE router can choose whether to use the control word. If the router chooses not to use it, it must set the flags in the control word to 0. The egress PE router must also follow similar procedure and must set the ATM control bits to 0 if it chooses to ignore the control word. The EFCI and CLP bits are carried across the network in the control word. The PE routers can change the EFCI and CLP bits from 0 to 1, during encapsulation and decapsulation. The AAL5 CPCS SDU is prepended with the header shown in Figure 11-10.

Figure 11-10 *Control Word*

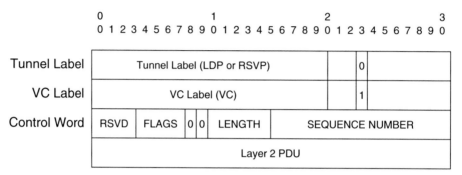

Figure 11-11 shows a provider network providing AAL5 service to CE1-A and CE2-A. These customer devices exchange ATM cells on a permanent virtual circuit (PVC) with the PE Router PE1 and PE2.

Figure 11-11 *AAL5 over MPLS*

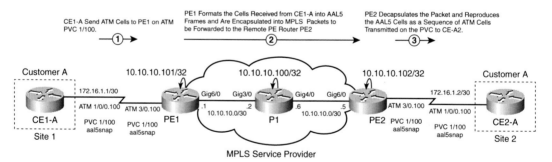

When the ATM cells on the PVC from CE1-A arrive on PE1's interface, PE1 reassembles the cells into AAL5 CPCS-SDU. These AAL5 CPCS-SDUs are encapsulated and forwarded across the MPLS backbone to the PE2 router. The encapsulation may contain a control word incorporating the EFCI and CLP bits and VPI/VCI information. PE2 decapsulates the packet and reproduces the AAL5 CPCS-DSU as a sequence of ATM cells to be transmitted on the PVC to CE-A2. Similar functions take place in the other direction from PE2 to PE1.

PE and Provider Router Configuration

The first step prior to provisioning Layer 2 VPN services is to ensure that the provider network is enabled for MPLS. Figure 11-12 shows the configuration for the PE Routers PE1 and PE2, and provider core Router P1 for MPLS forwarding. These basic configurations apply to all configuration scenarios in this chapter.

Figure 11-12 *PE and Provider Router Configuration*

```
hostname P1
!
ip cef
!
mpls ldp router-id Loopback0
!
interface Loopback0
 ip address 10.10.10.100 255.255.255.255
!
interface GigabitEthernet3/0
 ip address 10.10.10.2 255.255.255.252
mpls ip
!
interface GigabitEthernet4/0
 ip address 10.10.10.6 255.255.255.252
 mpls ip
!
router ospf 1
network 10.0.0.0 0.255.255.255 area 0
```

```
hostname PE1
!
ip cef
!
mpls ldp router-id Loopback0
!
interface Loopback0
 ip address 10.10.10.101 255.255.255.255
!
interface GigabitEthernet6/0
 ip address 10.10.10.1 255.255.255.252
 mpls ip
!
router ospf 1
 network 10.0.0.0 0.255.255.255 area 0
```

```
hostname PE2
!
ip cef
!
mpls ldp router-id Loopback0
!
interface Loopback0
 ip address 10.10.10.102 255.255.255.255
!
interface GigabitEthernet6/0
 ip address 10.10.10.5 255.255.255.252
mpls ip
!
router ospf 1
network 10.0.0.0 0.255.255.255 area 0
```

Configuration Flowchart for AAL5 over MPLS

Figure 11-13 shows the flowchart to configure AAL5 over MPLS.

Figure 11-13 *Configuration Flowchart for AAL5 over MPLS*

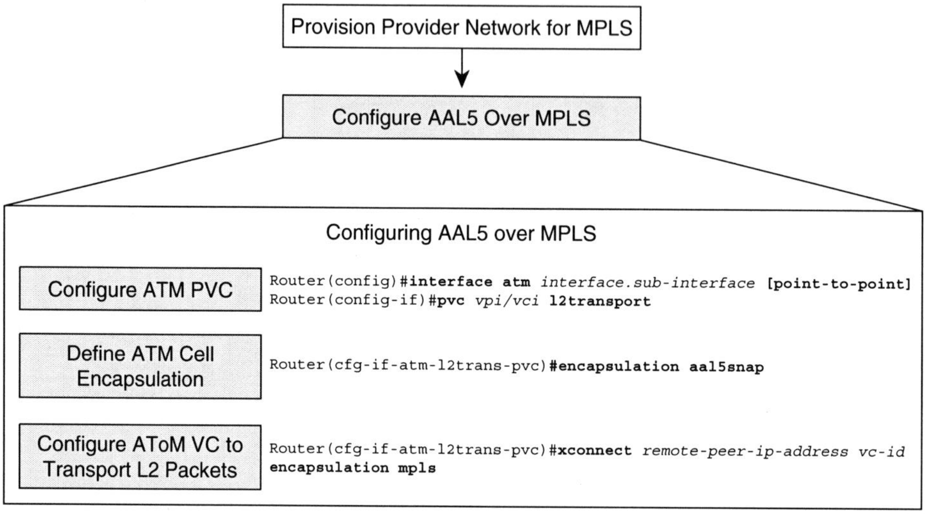

Configuring AAL5 over MPLS

The steps to configure AAL5 over MPLS for the network topology shown in Figure 11-11 are

Step 1   **Configure ATM PVCs**—In this step, you configure the ATM PVC on
the ATM interface by defining the VPI and VCI value and defining the
ATM encapsulation type. The command **pvc** {*vpi/vci*} **l2transport**
assigns a VPI and VCI and enters the PVC configuration mode. The
l2transport keyword indicates that the PVC is a switched PVC instead
of a terminated PVC. AAL5 can be configured on only PVCs and cannot
be configured on main interfaces. When defining the encapsulation type,
ensure that the encapsulation type is the same on the PE and the CE
routers connected to each other. See Example 11-1.

Example 11-1 *Enable Transport of AAL5 Cells over MPLS on PE Routers*

```
PE1(config)#interface ATM3/0.100 point-to-point
PE1(config-subif)# pvc 1/100 l2transport
PE1(cfg-if-atm-l2trans-pvc)#  encapsulation aal5snap

PE2(config)#interface ATM3/0.100 point-to-point
PE2(config-subif)# pvc 1/100 l2transport
PE2(cfg-if-atm-l2trans-pvc)#  encapsulation aal5snap
```

Step 2   **Configure AToM VC to transport L2 packets**—Example 11-2 shows
the creation of an AToM VC to enable transportation of the AAL5 cells
over MPLS. As illustrated in Example 11-2, VC ID 100 is used. The

xconnect command is used under the PVC configuration for the ATM interface.

Example 11-2 *Configure AToM VC to Transport Layer 2 Packet*

```
PE1(cfg-if-atm-l2trans-pvc)#xconnect 10.10.10.102 100 encapsulation mpls
PE2(cfg-if-atm-l2trans-pvc)#xconnect 10.10.10.101 100 encapsulation mpls
```

AAL5 over MPLS Configuration

Figure 11-14 shows the final relevant configuration for AAL5 over MPLS. Refer to Figure 11-12 for provider network configuration.

Figure 11-14 *AAL5 over MPLS Configuration*

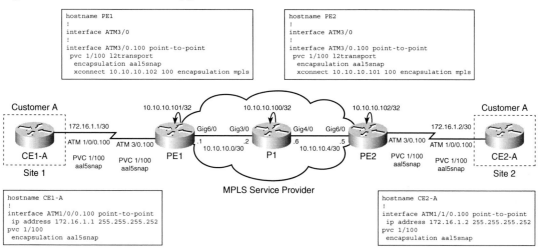

Verification of AAL5 over MPLS

Step 1   **Verify AToM VC is operational**—Example 11-3 depicts the output of **show mpls l2transport vc** on PE1. The output indicates that the AToM VC is functional to transport L2 packets across the MPLS backbone.

Example 11-3 *Verify if AToM VC Is Up*

```
PE1#show mpls l2transport vc
Local intf     Local circuit      Dest address     VC ID      Status
-------------  -----------------  ---------------  ---------  ----------
AT3/0.100      ATM AAL5 1/100     10.10.10.102     100        UP
```

Step 2   **Verify control plane and data forwarding operation**—Figure 11-15 shows the control and data plane operation in AAL5 over MPLS.

Figure 11-15 *Control and Data Plane Operation for AAL5 over MPLS Service*

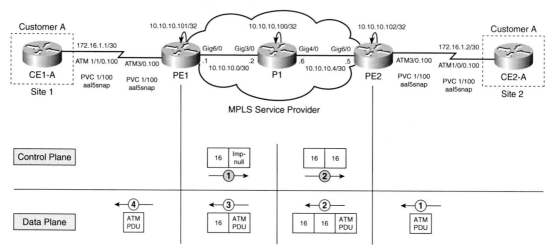

The steps to verify control plane operations are

Step 1 PE1 assigns VC label **16** to the attachment circuit connected to CE1-A, as shown in Example 11-4. PE1 propagates VC label **16** to PE2. To ensure that PE2 has reachability to PE1, PE1, as part of its IGP label operation, sends an implicit-null to P1 to instruct P1 to pop the IGP label in the data forwarding path from CE2-A to CE1-A.

Example 11-4 *LFIB on PE1*

```
PE1#show mpls forwarding-table
Local   Outgoing      Prefix          Bytes Label    Outgoing    Next Hop
Label   Label or VC   or Tunnel Id    Switched       interface
16      No Label      l2ckt(100)      540            none        point2point
17      Pop Label     10.10.10.4/30   0              Gi6/0       10.10.10.2
18      Pop Label     10.10.10.100/32 0              Gi6/0       10.10.10.2
19      17            10.10.10.102/32 0              Gi6/0       10.10.10.2
```

Step 2 P1 assigns a local IGP or tunnel label of 16 to PE1 (10.10.10.101/32) and propagates the same to PE2. See Example 11-5.

Example 11-5 *LFIB on P1*

```
P1#show mpls forwarding-table
Local   Outgoing      Prefix          Bytes Label    Outgoing    Next Hop
Label   Label or VC   or Tunnel Id    Switched       interface
16      Pop Label     10.10.10.101/32 92682          Gi3/0       10.10.10.1
17      Pop Label     10.10.10.102/32 92772          Gi4/0       10.10.10.5
```

In the data forwarding path from CE2-A to CE1-A,

Step 1   CE2-A sends data in the form of ATM cells to PE2.

Step 2   PE2 receives the ATM cells and reassembles the cells to form an AAL5
SDU in a single packet over the MPLS network. As shown in Example 11-6,
it appends the VC label 16 and the tunnel (IGP) label 16 to the packet and
sends it to P1.

Step 3   P1 receives the AAl5 SDU and pops the tunnel label as part of
penultimate hop popping function and sends the data packet to PE1.

Example 11-6 *Verify MPLS and VC Label*

```
PE2#show mpls l2transport vc 100 detail
Local interface: AT3/0.100 up, line protocol up, ATM AAL5 1/100 up
  Destination address: 10.10.10.101, VC ID: 100, VC status: up
    Output interface: Gi6/0, imposed label stack {16 16}
    Preferred path: not configured
    Default path: active
    Tunnel label: 16, next hop 10.10.10.6
  Create time: 00:26:08, last status change time: 00:26:04
  Signaling protocol: LDP, peer 10.10.10.101:0 up
    MPLS VC labels: local 16, remote 16
    Group ID: local 0, remote 0
    MTU: local 4470, remote 4470
    Remote interface description:
  Sequencing: receive disabled, send disabled
  VC statistics:
    packet totals: receive 5, send 5
    byte totals:   receive 540, send 670
    packet drops:  receive 0, send 0
```

Step 4   PE1 receives the packet from P1 and finds the VC label 16 associated
with the AC connected to CE1-A. PE1 removes the VC-label 16 and
forwards the data packet to CE1-A.

ATM Cell Relay over MPLS

In ATM Cell Relay over MPLS, there is no concept of ATM adaptation layers, and, therefore,
the raw ATM cells are transported individually without invoking the Segmentation and
Reassembly (SAR) process. As a result, raw ATM cells are received on the PE interface
and are not reassembled into AAL frames at the PE device. The raw ATM cells may be
encapsulated with a control word. The usage of the control word is optional. The control
word includes the EFCI and CLP bits, and these are copied at the PE router from the ATM
header into the control word. Figure 11-16 shows an MPLS provider providing Cell Relay
over MPLS services to CE1-A and CE2-A.

Figure 11-16 *ATM Cell Relay over MPLS Service*

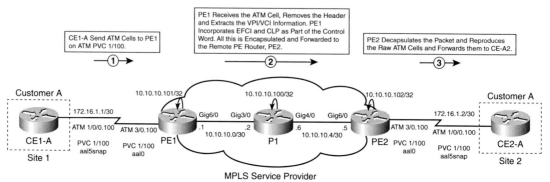

CE1-A and CE2-A exchange raw ATM cells over the MPLS backbone. PE1 receives the ATM cells from CE1-A and encapsulates the cell into an MPLS packet to be transported to PE2. Assuming the use of CONTROL WORD, the MPLS packet at the PE Router PE1 copies the EFCI and CLP information and appends the tunnel LSP label and VC label that was received from the remote PE Router PE2, indicating the outgoing interface on the remote PE Router PE2. At PE2, the raw cells are derived and forwarded to CE2-A.

Configuration Flowchart for ATM Cell over MPLS

Figure 11-17 shows the flowchart for configuring ATM Cell Relay over MPLS.

Figure 11-17 *ATM Cell Relay over MPLS service*

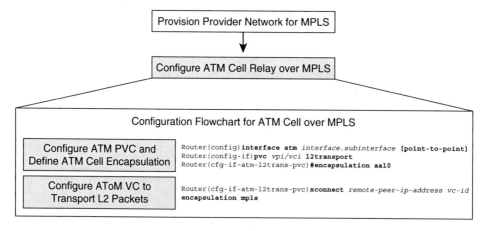

Configuring ATM Cell over MPLS

The steps to configure ATM cell relay services over MPLS are

Step 1   **Configure ATM PVCs**—This step is similar to that shown in the section on AAL5 over MPLS. In this case, the encapsulation type is aal0. In Cell Relay over MPLS, the PE-CE encapsulation can differ; however, the

ATM encapsulation on the CE routers on both ends should be the same. See Example 11-7.

Example 11-7 *Enable Transport of AAL5 Cells over MPLS on PE Routers*

```
PE1(config)#interface ATM3/0.100 point-to-point
PE1(config-subif)# pvc 1/100 l2transport
PE1(cfg-if-atm-l2trans-pvc)#  encapsulation aal0
PE2(config)#interface ATM3/0.100 point-to-point
PE2(config-subif)# pvc 1/100 l2transport
PE2(cfg-if-atm-l2trans-pvc)#  encapsulation aal0
```

Step 2 **Configure AToM VC to transport L2 packets**—In this step, you configure the AToM VC to enable transportation of the ATM cells over MPLS. This step is the same as shown in Example 11-2.

ATM Cell Relay over MPLS Configuration

Figure 11-18 shows the final relevant configuration for ATM Cell Relay over MPLS.

Figure 11-18 *ATM Cell Relay over MPLS Configuration*

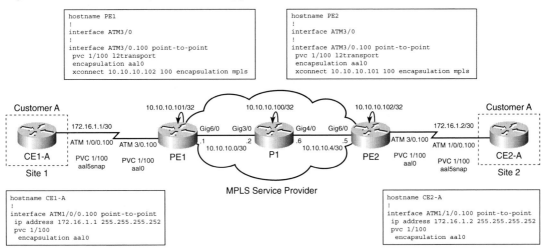

Verification of ATM Cell Relay over MPLS

Step 1 **Ensure that AToM VC is functional**—Example 11-8 shows the output of **show mpls l2transport vc**. The output indicates that the AToM VC is functional to transport L2 packets across the MPLS backbone.

Example 11-8 *Verify if AToM VC Is Functional*

```
PE1#show mpls l2transport vc

Local intf     Local circuit        Dest address      VC ID      Status
-----------    ----------------     ---------------    ---------  ---------
AT3/0.100      ATM VCC CELL 1/100   10.10.10.102       100        UP
```

Step 2 **Verify MPLS transport bindings**—Example 11-9 shows the maximum
number of concatenated cells, which means the maximum total number
of packed cells that the egress PE router can process in a single AToM
packet. In other words, it involves concatenating multiple cells into a
single AToM packet. The value of the maximum number of concatenated
cells value defaults to 1, which means that by default only one ATM cell
is packed in an AToM packet. Another detail to note from the output is
that the AToM pseudo wire is functional irrespective of the MTU used. In
other words, MTU value is not applied when ATM cells are transported
over MPLS.

Example 11-9 *Verify MPLS Transport Bindings*

```
PE1#show mpls l2transport binding
  Destination Address: 10.10.10.102,  VC ID: 100
    Local Label:  20
        Cbit: 1,     VC Type: ATM VCC CELL,     GroupID: 7
        MTU: n/a,    Interface Desc: n/a
        Max Concatenated ATM Cells: 1
        VCCV Capabilities: None
    Remote Label: 20
        Cbit: 1,     VC Type: ATM VCC CELL,     GroupID: 7
        MTU: n/a,    Interface Desc: n/a
        Max Concatenated ATM Cells: 1
        VCCV Capabilities: None
```

OAM in ATM AAL5 and ATM Cell Relay over MPLS

Operations, Administration, and Maintenance (OAM) provides VC/VP integrity, fault, and
performance management. The system supports F4 and F5 ATM OAM fault management,
loopback, and continuity check (CC) cells. These cells perform fault detection and
notification, loopback testing, and link integrity. ATM uses F4 and F5 cell flows as follows:

- F4 is used in VPs and inside each virtual path; the F4 OAM flow carries operation and
  maintenance information related to the virtual path. Cells belonging to this OAM flow
  have a VPI value of the VP and a Virtual Circuit Identifier (VCI) value of 3 (segment
  OAM) or 4 (multisegment OAM) respectively.

- F5 is used in VCs and is responsible for OAM information on the virtual circuit level.
  Cells belonging to this OAM flow are marked with the VPI/VCI value of the VC they
  are responsible for as well as the Payload Type (PT) value of either 100 (segment
  OAM) or 101 (end-to-end OAM). When encapsulating ATM over MPLS (either
  AAL5 over MPLS or Cell Relay over MPLS), these OAM flows need to be transported
  across an MPLS backbone for proper operation.

OAM support is implemented in AAL5 over MPLS and Cell Relay over MPLS. The OAM
cells are always encapsulated in a single label-switched packet during transport across an
MPLS backbone.

In Cell Relay over MPLS, the F5 OAM flow is passed through transparently. The cells belonging to this OAM flow are distinguished by a specific VCI value, so no additional action is needed. Cells belonging to the F5 OAM flow carry the same VPI/VCI value as other user cells, but are distinguished by a specific PT value. During label imposition, the PT value is copied into the control word, maintaining end-to-end OAM flow. The copying of PT values in the control word is automatic and needs no specific configuration.

In AAL5 over MPLS operation, the entire AAL5 frame is label-encapsulated and switched across the MPLS backbone. It is not possible to forward the OAM cells across the MPLS backbone because forwarding individual cells (OAM cells in this case) is not supported when AAL5 frames (SDUs) are reassembled and forwarded in a single MPLS packet. However, it is possible to generate the OAM cells between local loopbacks.

To enable OAM cell emulation on AAL5 over MPLS, use the **oam-ac emulation-enable** command in the ATM VC configuration mode on both PE routers. To disable OAM cell emulation, use the **no** form of this command on both routers.

In case the AToM device does not support NNI signaling, the segment F4-OAM flow needs to be disabled to ensure proper operation. This inhibits the creation of F4 OAM VPs with the **no-f4-oam** keyword.

Ethernet over MPLS

In Ethernet over MPLS environment, Ethernet frames are exchanged between customer sites using the SP backbone as the medium of transport. Ethernet over MPLS is implemented in two different modes:

- Port mode
- VLAN mode

Forthcoming subsections will show you configuration and verification of EoMPLS on routers and switches.

Router-Based Ethernet over MPLS—Port Mode

In port mode, the entire Ethernet frame without the preamble or FCS is transported as a single AToM packet. The use of the control word is optional. If the control word is not used, the flag bits are set to zero when the packet is MPLS encapsulated and ignored when it is decapsulated on the receiving side. Ethernet frames with hardware level CRC errors, framing errors, and runt packets that arrive at the PE router are discarded. In port mode, the interface uses VC type 5 or 0x0005. Figure 11-19 shows an MPLS provider network that provides a Layer 2 Ethernet port-to-port connection for Customer A sites CE1-A and CE2-A.

Figure 11-19 *Ethernet over MPLS—Port Mode*

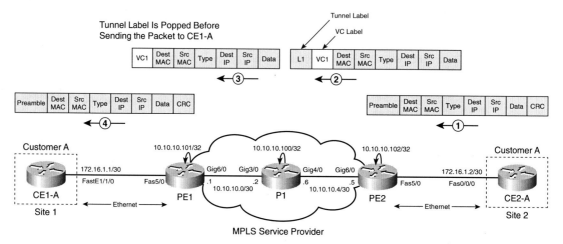

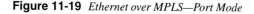

As shown in Figure 11-19, CE1-A and CE2-A exchange Ethernet frames over the provider backbone. PE2 receives the Ethernet frame from CE2-A and encapsulates that frame into an MPLS packet. This frame is then forwarded across the provider backbone to PE1. PE1 removes the MPLS headers and reproduces the Ethernet frame and forwards it to the CE1-A.

Configuration Flowchart for Router-Based Ethernet over MPLS—Port Mode

The configuration flowchart for Ethernet over MPLS in port mode is shown in Figure 11-20.

Figure 11-20 *Configuration Flowchart for Ethernet over MPLS—Port Mode*

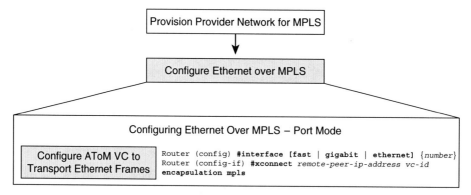

Configuring Router-Based Ethernet over MPLS—Port Mode

The step to configure port mode Ethernet over MPLS is illustrated in Example 11-10 in which the **xconnect** statement is defined under the Ethernet interface to enable transportation of Ethernet frames from end CE devices over the MPLS network.

Example 11-10 *Enable Transport of Ethernet over MPLS on PE Router*

```
PE1(config)#interface FastEthernet5/0
PE1(config-if)#xconnect 10.10.10.102 100 encapsulation mpls
PE2(config)#interface FastEthernet5/0
PE2(config-if)#xconnect 10.10.10.101 100 encapsulation mpls
```

Device Configuration for Router-Based Ethernet over MPLS—Port Mode

The final relevant configuration for Ethernet over MPLS in port mode is shown in Figure 11-21.

Figure 11-21 *Configuration for Ethernet over MPLS—Port Mode*

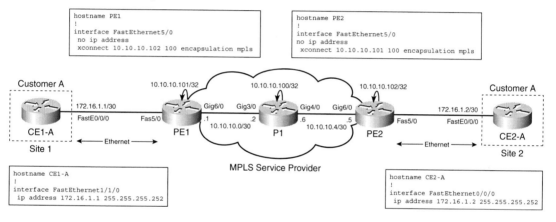

Verification of Ethernet over MPLS—Port Mode

Verify if AToM VC is functional. Example 11-11 shows the output of **show mpls l2transport vc** where the VC between the PE routers is up and running.

Example 11-11 *Enable Transport of Ethernet over MPLS on PE Router*

```
PE1#show mpls l2transport vc
Local intf     Local circuit          Dest address      VC ID    Status
-------------  -------------------    ---------------   -------- ----------
Fa5/0          Ethernet               10.10.10.102      100      UP
```

Control Plane and Data Plane—Ethernet over MPLS (Port Mode)

Figure 11-22 shows the control and data plane operation for Ethernet over MPLS in port mode configuration.

As shown in Figure 11-22, during the control plane operation, PE1 allocates VC label 16 for the AC connected to CE1-A. This VC label is propagated via the MPLS network to PE2, which uses this VC label 16 in the data forwarding for the packet originating from

CE2-A destined to CE1-A. The tunnel label or IGP label 16, which is assigned by P1 for PE1 loopback 10.10.10.101, guides the packet from PE2 to PE1 for a data packet originating from CE2-A to CE1-A.

Figure 11-22 *Control and Data Plane EoMPLS—Port Mode*

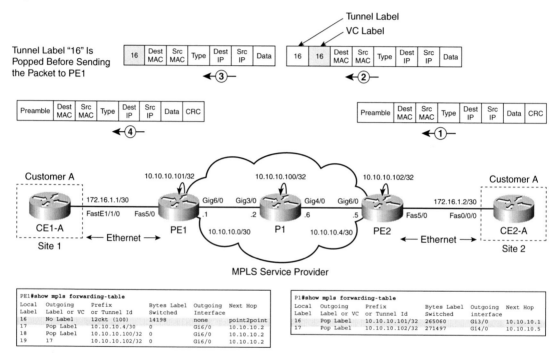

Router-Based Ethernet over MPLS—VLAN Mode

In the VLAN mode, PE devices do not filter any frames based on the MAC addresses. In other words, there is no support for MAC layer address learning and filtering. In EoMPLS, the Spanning-Tree Protocol is not used, and BPDUs are propagated transparently but not processed.

Figure 11-23 shows an MPLS provider network where PE devices PE1 and PE2 are connected to CE devices CE1-A and CE2-A. The interface encapsulation between the CE and the PE routers supports VLANs. Different subinterfaces in the PE routers connect different VLANs. The PE1 interface connected to CE1-A is configured as a VLAN subinterface. This VLAN subinterface is used for AToM forwarding.

Figure 11-23 *Ethernet over MPLS—VLAN Mode*

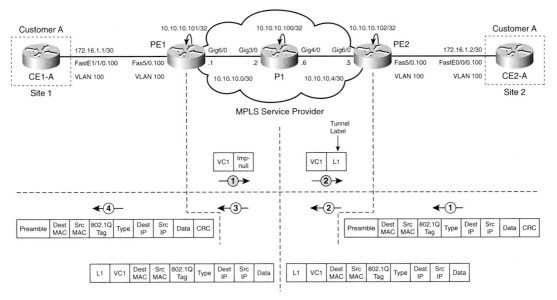

In Figure 11-23, PE1 and PE2 are configured for EoMPLS to propagate VLAN 100 across the backbone. PE1 and PE2 have loopback interfaces with IP address 10.10.10.101 and 10.10.10.102, respectively. These two addresses are used as LDP peer IDs. The subinterface fas5/0.100 is configured for VLAN 100 on both PE1 and PE2. This subinterface is configured for EoMPLS. The Ethernet frames are MPLS-encapsulated and forwarded to the PE router with IP address 10.10.10.101, which is PE1. The VC identifier, value 100, associates the connection with the other end. It is required that both endpoints use the same VC identifier value. There is no requirement that the VLAN identifier should be the same at both the ends. The most important detail is the VC identifier. The value 100 is used on both PE1 and PE2. From the end-user perspective, the EoMPLS service appears as an extension of their Ethernet segment (or in this case, a VLAN). There is no awareness of the MPLS backbone to the end-user routers. The backbone devices in the provider network are also oblivious to end-user activities. As shown in the example network in Figure 11-23, the Ethernet frame arrives on the PE2's VLAN subinterface; it is encapsulated into MPLS and forwarded across the backbone to PE1. PE1 decapsulates the packet and reproduces the Ethernet frame on the outgoing VLAN subinterface.

Configuration Flowchart for Router-Based Ethernet over MPLS—VLAN Mode

Figure 11-24 shows the configuration flowchart relevant to configuring Ethernet over MPLS in VLAN mode.

Figure 11-24 *Configuration Flowchart for Ethernet over MPLS—VLAN Mode*

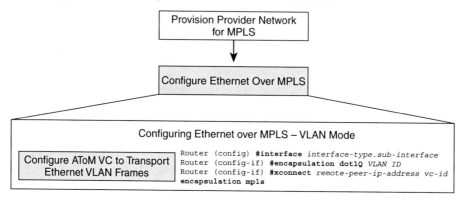

Configuring Ethernet over MPLS—VLAN Mode

Example 11-12 depicts the configuration of Ethernet over MPLS in VLAN mode in which interface fas5/0.100 is configured for VLAN 100. The **xconnect** statement is defined under the Ethernet subinterface to enable transportation of Ethernet frames from end CE devices over MPLS network.

Example 11-12 *Enable Transport of Ethernet over MPLS on PE Router*

```
PE1(config)#interface FastEthernet5/0.100
PE1(config-subif)# encapsulation dot1Q 100
PE1(config-subif)# no cdp enable
PE1(config-subif)# xconnect 10.10.10.102 100 encapsulation mpls
PE2(config)#interface FastEthernet5/0.100
PE2(config-subif)# encapsulation dot1Q 100
PE2(config-subif)# no cdp enable
PE2(config-subif)# xconnect 10.10.10.101 100 encapsulation mpls
```

Device Configuration for Router-Based Ethernet over MPLS—VLAN Mode

Figure 11-25 shows the relevant configuration for Ethernet over MPLS in VLAN mode.

Verification of Ethernet over MPLS—VLAN Mode

Step 1   **Verify if AToM VC is operational**—Example 11-13 shows the output of **show mpls l2transport vc**. The output indicates that the AToM VC is functional to transport L2 packets across the MPLS backbone.

Example 11-13 *Transport of Ethernet over MPLS on PE Router*

```
PE1#show mpls l2transport vc

Local intf     Local circuit        Dest address      VC ID      Status
------------   ------------------   ---------------   ---------   ----------
Fa5/0.100      Eth VLAN 100         10.10.10.102      100         UP
```

Figure 11-25 *Configuration for Ethernet over MPLS—VLAN Mode*

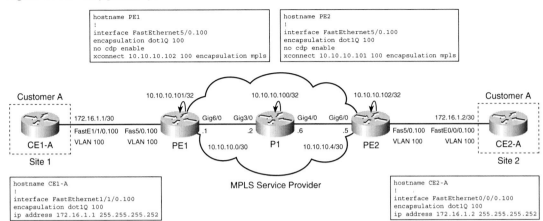

> Step 2   **Verify MPLS and VC label**—Example 11-14 shows the directed LDP
> peer is 10.10.10.101 for PE2. The example also shows the output of **show
> mpls l2transport** *vc-id* **detail**. The output indicates that the AToM VC is
> functional to transport L2 packets across the MPLS backbone. The VC
> ID is **100** and tunnel label is **16**. This tunnel label is derived from LDP.
> The VC label on PE1 for outgoing interface on PE2 connected to CE2-A
> is **16**, and PE1 allocates VC label **20** for the interface connected to CE1-A.

Example 11-14 *Verify VC Label and Tunnel Label*

```
PE2#show mpls l2transport vc 100 detail
Local interface: Fa5/0.100 up, line protocol up, Eth VLAN 100 up
  Destination address: 10.10.10.101, VC ID: 100, VC status: up
    Output interface: Gi6/0, imposed label stack {16 16}
    Preferred path: not configured
    Default path: active
    Tunnel label: 16, next hop 10.10.10.6
  Create time: 00:13:42, last status change time: 00:10:32
  Signaling protocol: LDP, peer 10.10.10.101:0 up
    MPLS VC labels: local 20, remote 16
    Group ID: local 0, remote 0
    MTU: local 1500, remote 1500
    Remote interface description:
  Sequencing: receive disabled, send disabled
  VC statistics:
    packet totals: receive 20, send 10
    byte totals:   receive 4802, send 1382
    packet drops:  receive 0, send 0
```

Figure 11-26 shows the data plane forwarding operation for an MPLS-enabled provider
network providing Ethernet over MPLS using the VLAN mode.

Figure 11-26 *Data Plane Operation—Ethernet over MPLS: VLAN Mode*

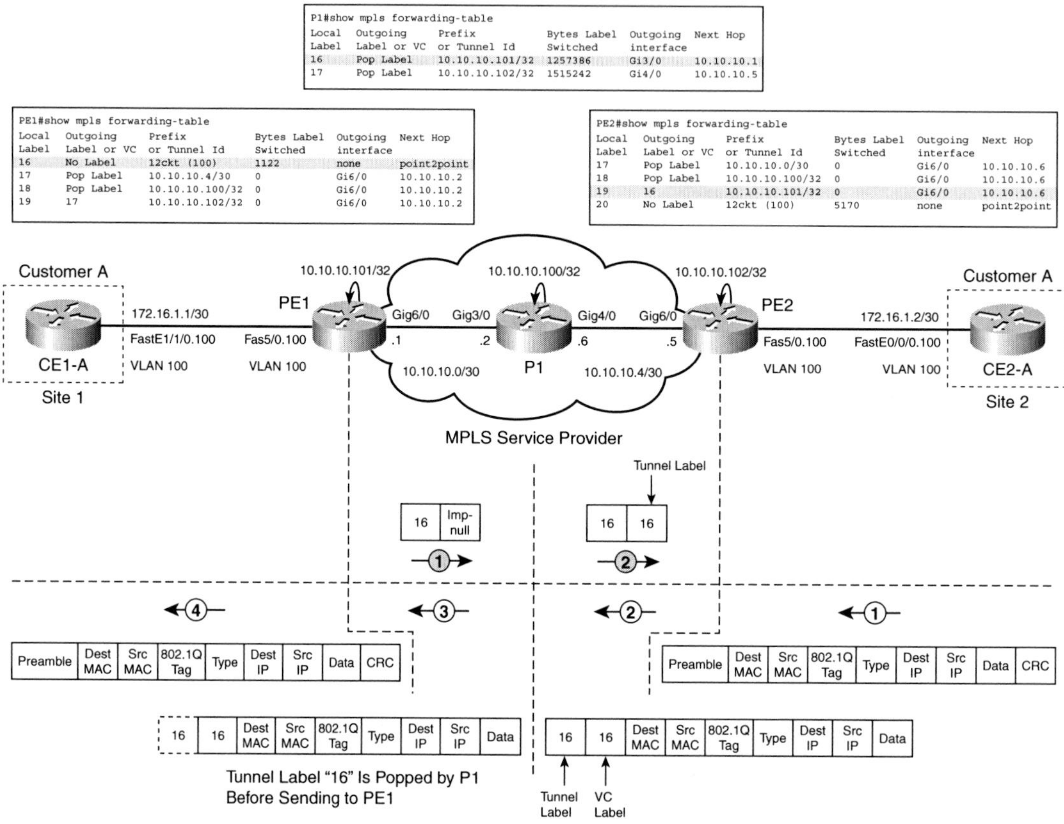

Router-Based EoMPLS—VLAN Rewrite

Figure 11-27 depicts the configurations for the individual devices if the VLANs connected at each of the customer sites are not equal. Therefore, in this scenario, CE1-A is connected to PE1 using VLAN 100, and CE2-A is connected to PE2 using VLAN 200. As mentioned earlier, the VLAN mapping does not have to be consistent across sites to implement router-based Ethernet over MPLS VLAN mode.

Switch-Based Ethernet over MPLS—Port Mode

Figure 11-28 shows an MPLS-enabled, switch-based provider network providing Ethernet port mode services to CE1-A and CE2-A. PE1 and PE2 are Supervisor 2 (Catalyst 6500 series) based switches running Cisco IOS (native).

Figure 11-27 *Ethernet over MPLS—VLAN Mode: VLAN Rewrite*

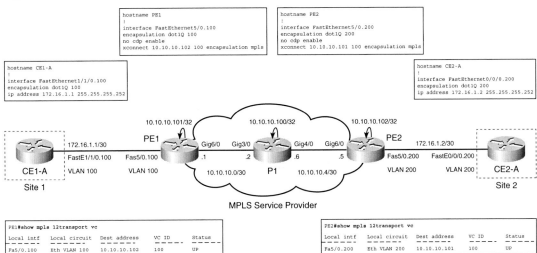

```
hostname PE1
!
interface FastEthernet5/0.100
encapsulation dot1Q 100
no cdp enable
xconnect 10.10.10.102 100 encapsulation mpls
```

```
hostname PE2
!
interface FastEthernet5/0.200
encapsulation dot1Q 200
no cdp enable
xconnect 10.10.10.101 100 encapsulation mpls
```

```
hostname CE1-A
!
interface FastEthernet1/1/0.100
encapsulation dot1Q 100
ip address 172.16.1.1 255.255.255.252
```

```
hostname CE2-A
!
interface FastEthernet0/0/0.200
encapsulation dot1Q 200
ip address 172.16.1.2 255.255.255.252
```

```
PE1#show mpls l2transport vc

Local intf    Local circuit    Dest address    VC ID    Status
----------    -------------    ------------    -----    ------
Fas5/0.100    Eth VLAN 100     10.10.10.102    100      UP
```

```
PE2#show mpls l2transport vc

Local intf    Local circuit    Dest address    VC ID    Status
----------    -------------    ------------    -----    ------
Fas5/0.200    Eth VLAN 200     10.10.10.101    100      UP
```

Figure 11-28 *Switch-Based Ethernet over MPLS—Port Mode*

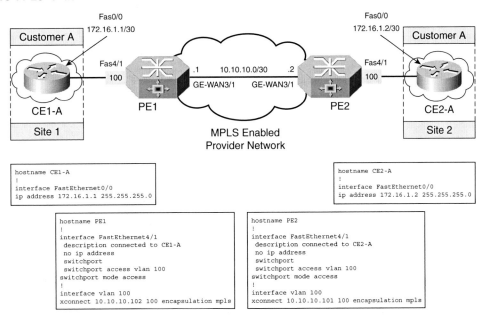

```
hostname CE1-A
!
interface FastEthernet0/0
ip address 172.16.1.1 255.255.255.0
```

```
hostname CE2-A
!
interface FastEthernet0/0
ip address 172.16.1.2 255.255.255.0
```

```
hostname PE1
!
interface FastEthernet4/1
 description connected to CE1-A
 no ip address
 switchport
 switchport access vlan 100
switchport mode access
!
interface vlan 100
xconnect 10.10.10.102 100 encapsulation mpls
```

```
hostname PE2
!
interface FastEthernet4/1
 description connected to CE2-A
 no ip address
 switchport
 switchport access vlan 100
switchport mode access
!
interface vlan 100
xconnect 10.10.10.101 100 encapsulation mpls
```

Configuration Flowchart for Ethernet over MPLS—Port, Dot1Q, and Tunnel Mode

Figure 11-29 shows the configuration flowchart relevant to configuring Ethernet over MPLS in Port mode.

Figure 11-29 *Configuration Flowchart for Ethernet over MPLS—VLAN Mode*

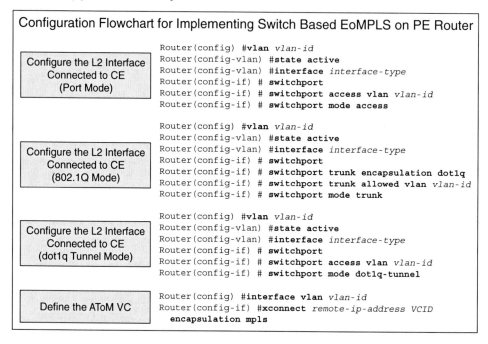

Backbone Configuration for PE1 and PE2

Example 11-15 outlines the basic configuration on the PE Routers PE1 and PE2 used for the switch-based AToM implementations.

Example 11-15 *Backbone Configuration for PE1 and PE2*

```
hostname PE1
!
mpls label protocol ldp
mpls ldp discovery targeted-hello accept
mpls ldp router-id Loopback0 force
!
interface Loopback0
 ip address 10.10.10.101 255.255.255.255
!
interface GE-WAN3/1
description connected to PE2
 ip address 10.10.10.1 255.255.255.252
 negotiation auto
 mpls ip
 mls qos trust dscp
!
router ospf 1
 network 10.0.0.0 0.255.255.255 area 0
hostname PE2
```

Example 11-15 *Backbone Configuration for PE1 and PE2 (Continued)*

```
!
mpls label protocol ldp
mpls ldp discovery targeted-hello accept
mpls ldp router-id Loopback0 force
!
interface Loopback0
 ip address 10.10.10.102 255.255.255.255
!
interface GE-WAN3/1
description connected to PE1
 ip address 10.10.10.2 255.255.255.252
 negotiation auto
 mpls ip
 mls qos trust dscp
!
router ospf 1
 network 10.0.0.0 0.255.255.255 area 0
```

Configuring Ethernet over MPLS—Port Mode

Example 11-16 depicts the configuration of switch-based Ethernet over MPLS in port mode where interface fas4/1 on PE1 is configured as an access port connected to CE1-A. The **xconnect** statement is defined under the VLAN interface to enable transportation of Ethernet frames from end CE devices over MPLS network.

Example 11-16 *Enable Transport of Ethernet over MPLS on PE Router*

```
PE1(config)#vlan 100
PE1(config-vlan)#state active
PE1(config-vlan)#exit
PE1(config)#interface fastEthernet 4/1
PE1(config-if)#switchport
PE1(config-if)#switchport access vlan 100
PE1(config-if)#switchport mode access
PE1(config-if)#exit
PE1(config)#interface vlan 100
PE1(config-if)#xconnect 10.10.10.102 100 encapsulation mpls
PE2(config)#vlan 100
PE2(config-vlan)#state active
PE2(config-vlan)#exit
PE2(config)#interface fastEthernet 4/1
PE2(config-if)#switchport
PE2(config-if)#switchport access vlan 100
PE2(config-if)#switchport mode access
PE2(config-if)#exit
PE2(config)#interface vlan 100
PE2(config-if)#xconnect 10.10.10.101 100 encapsulation mpls
```

Switch-Based Ethernet over MPLS—Port Mode Configuration

Figure 11-30 shows the relevant configuration for Ethernet over MPLS in VLAN mode.

Figure 11-30 *Configuration for Ethernet over MPLS—Port Mode*

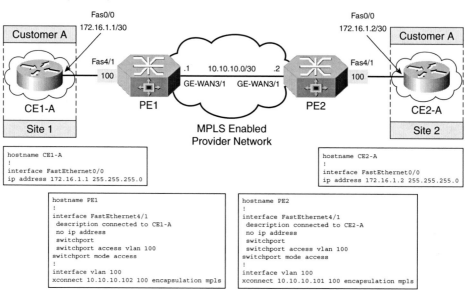

```
hostname CE1-A
!
interface FastEthernet0/0
ip address 172.16.1.1 255.255.255.0
```

```
hostname CE2-A
!
interface FastEthernet0/0
ip address 172.16.1.2 255.255.255.0
```

```
hostname PE1
!
interface FastEthernet4/1
 description connected to CE1-A
 no ip address
 switchport
 switchport access vlan 100
switchport mode access
!
interface vlan 100
xconnect 10.10.10.102 100 encapsulation mpls
```

```
hostname PE2
!
interface FastEthernet4/1
 description connected to CE2-A
 no ip address
 switchport
 switchport access vlan 100
switchport mode access
!
interface vlan 100
xconnect 10.10.10.101 100 encapsulation mpls
```

Verification of Ethernet over MPLS—Port Mode

Step 1 **Verify that AToM VC is up**—Example 11-17 illustrates the output of
show mpls l2transport vc. The output indicates that the AToM VC is
functional to transport L2 packets across the MPLS backbone.

Example 11-17 *Transport of Ethernet over MPLS on PE Router*

```
PE1#show mpls l2transport vc

Local intf     Local circuit      Dest address     VC ID     Status
-------------  ----------------   --------------   ---------  ----------
Vl100          Eth VLAN 100       10.10.10.102     100       UP
PE2#show mpls l2transport vc

Local intf     Local circuit      Dest address     VC ID     Status
-------------  ----------------   --------------   ---------  ----------
Vl100          Eth VLAN 100       10.10.10.101     100       UP
```

Step 2 **Verify connectivity**—Example 11-18 shows the verification of
connectivity between the CE routers.

Example 11-18 *Verify Connectivity*

```
CE1-A#ping 172.16.1.2 source 172.16.1.1

Type escape sequence to abort.
Sending 5, 100-byte ICMP Echos to 172.16.1.2, timeout is 2 seconds:
Packet sent with a source address of 172.16.1.1
!!!!!
Success rate is 100 percent (5/5), round-trip min/avg/max = 1/2/4 ms
```

Switch-Based Ethernet over MPLS—VLAN Mode

Figure 11-31 shows an MPLS-enabled, switch-based provider network providing Ethernet port mode services to CE1-A and CE2-A. PE1 and PE2 are Supervisor 2-based switches running Cisco IOS.

Figure 11-31 *Switch-Based Ethernet over MPLS—VLAN Mode*

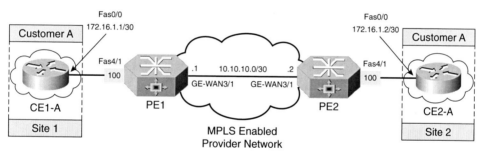

Configuration Flowchart for Ethernet over MPLS—VLAN Mode

Figure 11-32 shows the configuration flowchart relevant to configuring Ethernet over MPLS in VLAN mode.

Configuring Ethernet over MPLS—VLAN Mode

Example 11-19 shows the steps to configure Ethernet over MPLS in VLAN mode. The **xconnect** statement is defined under the VLAN interface to enable transportation of Ethernet VLAN frames from end CE devices over the MPLS network.

Figure 11-32 *Configuration Flowchart for Ethernet over MPLS—VLAN Mode*

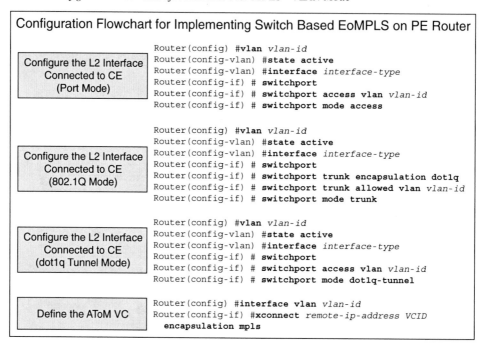

Example 11-19 *Enable Transport of Ethernet over MPLS on PE Router*

```
PE1(config)#vlan 100
PE1(config-vlan)#state active
PE1(config-vlan)#exit
PE1(config)#interface fastEthernet 4/1
PE1(config-if)#switchport
PE1(config-if)# switchport trunk encapsulation dot1q
PE1(config-if)# switchport trunk allowed vlan 100
PE1(config-if)# switchport mode trunk
PE1(config-if)#exit
PE1(config)#interface vlan 100
PE1(config-if)#xconnect 10.10.10.102 100 encapsulation mpls
PE2(config)#vlan 100
PE2(config-vlan)#state active
PE2(config-vlan)#exit
PE1(config)#interface fastEthernet 4/1
PE1(config-if)#switchport
PE1(config-if)# switchport trunk encapsulation dot1q
PE1(config-if)# switchport trunk allowed vlan 100
PE1(config-if)# switchport mode trunk
PE2(config-if)#exit
PE2(config)#interface vlan 100
PE2(config-if)#xconnect 10.10.10.101 100 encapsulation mpls
```

Final Configurations for Switch-Based Ethernet over MPLS—VLAN Mode

Figure 11-33 shows the relevant configuration for Ethernet over MPLS in VLAN mode.

Figure 11-33 *Configuration for Ethernet over MPLS—VLAN Mode*

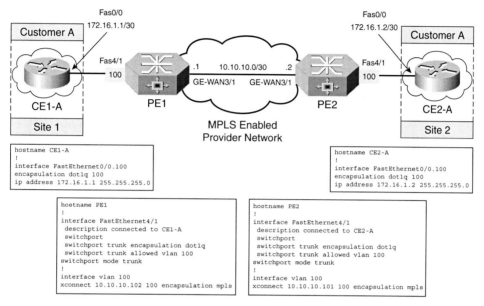

```
hostname CE1-A
!
interface FastEthernet0/0.100
 encapsulation dot1q 100
 ip address 172.16.1.1 255.255.255.0
```

```
hostname CE2-A
!
 interface FastEthernet0/0.100
 encapsulation dot1q 100
 ip address 172.16.1.2 255.255.255.0
```

```
hostname PE1
!
interface FastEthernet4/1
 description connected to CE1-A
 switchport
 switchport trunk encapsulation dot1q
 switchport trunk allowed vlan 100
switchport mode trunk
!
interface vlan 100
xconnect 10.10.10.102 100 encapsulation mpls
```

```
hostname PE2
!
interface FastEthernet4/1
 description connected to CE2-A
 switchport
 switchport trunk encapsulation dot1q
 switchport trunk allowed vlan 100
switchport mode trunk
!
interface vlan 100
xconnect 10.10.10.101 100 encapsulation mpls
```

Verification of Ethernet over MPLS—VLAN Mode

Step 1   **Verify that AToM VC is up**—Example 11-20 shows the output of **show mpls l2transport vc**. The output indicates that the AToM VC is functional to transport L2 packets across the MPLS backbone.

Example 11-20 *Transport of Ethernet over MPLS on PE Router*

```
PE1#show mpls l2transport vc

Local intf     Local circuit        Dest address      VC ID       Status
------------   -------------------  ---------------   ---------   ----------
Vl100          Eth VLAN 100         10.10.10.102      100         UP
PE2#show mpls l2transport vc

Local intf     Local circuit        Dest address      VC ID       Status
------------   -------------------  ---------------   ---------   ----------
Vl100          Eth VLAN 100         10.10.10.101      100         UP
```

Step 2   **Verify connectivity**—Example 11-21 illustrates the verification for connectivity between the CE routers.

Example 11-21 *Verify Connectivity*

```
CE1-A#ping 172.16.1.2 source 172.16.1.1

Type escape sequence to abort.
Sending 5, 100-byte ICMP Echos to 172.16.1.2, timeout is 2 seconds:
Packet sent with a source address of 172.16.1.1
!!!!!
Success rate is 100 percent (5/5), round-trip min/avg/max = 1/2/4 ms
```

Switch-Based Ethernet over MPLS—dot1q Tunnel Mode

Figure 11-34 shows an MPLS-enabled, switch-based provider network providing Ethernet port mode services to CE1-A and CE2-A. PE1 and PE2 are Supervisor 2 based switches running Cisco IOS.

Figure 11-34 *Switch-Based Ethernet over MPLS—Port Mode*

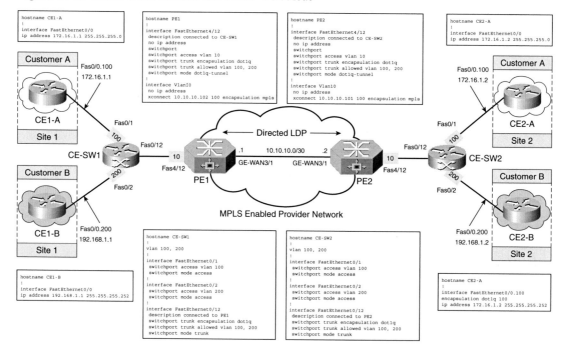

Configuration Flowchart for Ethernet over MPLS—dot1Q Mode

Figure 11-35 shows the configuration flowchart relevant to configuring Ethernet over MPLS in VLAN mode.

Figure 11-35 *Configuration Flowchart for Ethernet over MPLS—VLAN Mode*

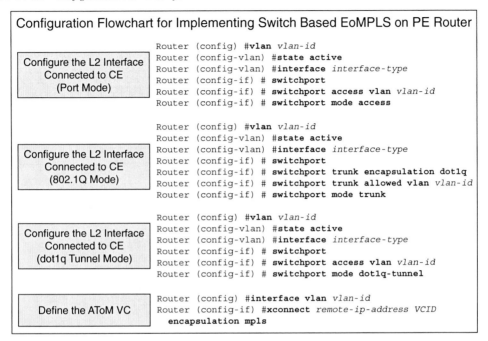

Configuring Ethernet over MPLS—dot1q Mode

Example 11-22 shows the steps to configure Ethernet over MPLS in dot1q mode. Example 11-23 shows the configuration steps on CE switch CE-Sw1 and CE-Sw2.

Example 11-22 *Enable Transport of Ethernet over MPLS on PE Router*

```
PE1(config)#vlan 10
PE1(config-vlan)#state active
PE1(config-vlan)#exit
PE1(config)#interface FastEthernet4/12
PE1(config-if)#switchport
PE1(config-if)# switchport access vlan 10
PE1(config-if)# switchport trunk encapsulation dot1q
PE1(config-if)# switchport trunk allowed vlan 100,200
PE1(config-if)# switchport mode dot1q-tunnel
PE1(config-if)#exit
PE1(config)#interface vlan 10
PE1(config-if)#xconnect 10.10.10.102 100 encapsulation mpls
PE2(config)#vlan 10
PE2(config-vlan)#state active
PE2(config-vlan)#exit
PE2(config)#int fastEthernet 4/12
PE2(config-if)#switchport
```

continues

Example 11-22 *Enable Transport of Ethernet over MPLS on PE Router (Continued)*

```
PE2(config-if)# switchport trunk encapsulation dot1q
PE2(config-if)# switchport trunk allowed vlan 100,200
PE2(config-if)# switchport mode dot1q-tunnel
PE2(config-if)#exit
PE2(config)#interface vlan 10
PE2(config-if)#xconnect 10.10.10.101 100 encapsulation mpls
```

Example 11-23 *Configuration Steps on CE Switch CE-Sw1 and CE-Sw2*

```
CE-SW1(config)#vlan 100
CE-SW1(config-vlan)#state active
CE-SW1(config)#vlan 200
CE-SW1(config-vlan)#state active
CE-SW1(config-vlan)#exit
CE-SW1(config-if)#interface FastEthernet0/1
CE-SW1(config-if)# switchport access vlan 100
CE-SW1(config-if)# switchport mode access
CE-SW1(config-if)#interface FastEthernet0/2
CE-SW1(config-if)# switchport access vlan 200
CE-SW1(config-if)# switchport mode access
CE-SW1(config-if)#interface FastEthernet0/12
CE-SW1(config-if)# switchport trunk encapsulation dot1q
CE-SW1(config-if)# switchport trunk allowed vlan 100,200
CE-SW1(config-if)# switchport mode trunk
CE-SW2(config)#vlan 100
CE-SW2(config-vlan)#state active
CE-SW2(config)#vlan 200
CE-SW2(config-vlan)#state active
CE-SW2(config-vlan)#exit
CE-SW2(config-if)#interface FastEthernet0/1
CE-SW2(config-if)# switchport access vlan 100
CE-SW2(config-if)# switchport mode access
CE-SW2(config-if)#interface FastEthernet0/2
CE-SW2(config-if)# switchport access vlan 200
CE-SW2(config-if)# switchport mode access
CE-SW2(config-if)#interface FastEthernet0/12
CE-SW2(config-if)# switchport trunk encapsulation dot1q
CE-SW2(config-if)# switchport trunk allowed vlan 100,200
CE-SW2(config-if)# switchport mode trunk
```

Switch-Based Ethernet over MPLS—Dot1q Tunnel Mode

Figure 11-36 shows the relevant configuration for switch based Ethernet over MPLS in Dot1q Tunnel mode.

Figure 11-36 *Configuration for Ethernet over MPLS—VLAN Mode*

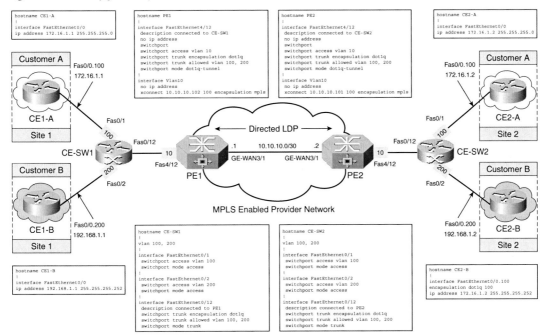

Verification of Ethernet over MPLS—VLAN Mode

Step 1   **Verify that AToM VC is up**—Example 11-24 shows the output of **show mpls l2transport vc**. The output indicates that the AToM VC is functional to transport L2 packets across the MPLS backbone.

Example 11-24 *Transport of Ethernet over MPLS on PE Router*

```
PE1#show mpls l2transport vc

Local intf     Local circuit          Dest address      VC ID      Status
-------------  ---------------------  ----------------  ---------  ----------
Vl10           Eth VLAN 10            10.10.10.102       100        UP
PE2#show mpls l2transport vc

Local intf     Local circuit          Dest address      VC ID      Status
-------------  ---------------------  ----------------  ---------  ----------
Vl10           Eth VLAN 10            10.10.10.101       100        UP
```

Step 2   **Verify connectivity**—Example 11-25 shows the steps to verify connectivity between the CE routers.

Example 11-25 *Verify VC Label and Tunnel Label*

```
CE1-A#ping 172.16.1.2 source 172.16.1.1

Type escape sequence to abort.
Sending 5, 100-byte ICMP Echos to 172.16.1.2, timeout is 2 seconds:
Packet sent with a source address of 172.16.1.1
!!!!!
Success rate is 100 percent (5/5), round-trip min/avg/max = 1/2/4 ms
CE1-B#ping 192.168.1.2 source 192.168.1.1

Type escape sequence to abort.
Sending 5, 100-byte ICMP Echos to 192.168.1.2, timeout is 2 seconds:
Packet sent with a source address of 192.168.1.1
!!!!!
Success rate is 100 percent (5/5), round-trip min/avg/max = 1/2/4 ms
```

PPP over MPLS

PPP mode provides point-to-point transport of PPP-encapsulated traffic. The PPP PDU is transported in its entirety, including the protocol field, but excluding any media-specific framing information, such as HDLC address and control fields or FCS. The sequencing control word is optional, and its usage is signaled during the VC label binding distribution.

The protocol field is transmitted intact, regardless of the two PPP peers negotiated Protocol Field Compression (PFC).

The HDLC address and control fields, if present in the PPP header, are always removed from the PPP PDU received from ingress interface by the ingress PE router. Even if the two peering CE routers might have negotiated Address and Control Field Compression (ACFC), the egress PE router has no way of identifying this unless it sniffs the PPP LCP negotiation, which is not part of the end-to-end PPP peering model. Therefore, the egress PE router always adds HDLC address and control fields back to the PPP PDU before sending it out to the egress interface, if the CE-PE link uses HDLC-like framing. This is perfectly legitimate because a PPP implementation must prepare to receive PPP PDU with uncompressed address and control field at all times regardless of ACFC. For CE-PE links that do not use HDLC-like framing, such as PPPoE, PPPoATM, and PPPoFR, there is no need to add the address and control fields at the egress PE.

Figure 11-37 shows a detail level of MPLS labels being used in PPP over MPLS.

The following steps outline the data plane operation of PPP over MPLS:

Step 1 When the device driver of the ingress interface on ingress PE (PE1) receives PPP packets at the interrupt level, it classifies the packets based on the protocol field in the PPP header and interface configuration.

Step 2   At the ingress PE (PE1), a two-level label stack is precalculated for each VC where the top label is the tunnel label and the bottom label is the VC label. The address and control fields in the PPP header are removed if present, and the protocol field is uncompressed if compressed. To switch received PPP packets into the VC, the label stack and the MAC string of the outgoing MPLS interface are prepended to the packets.

Step 3   While labeled PPP packets traverse the MPLS backbone via standard label switching, the tunnel label may be swapped or popped. If the penultimate LSR on the LSP from the ingress (PE1) to egress PE (PE2) supports label popping, the egress PE binds an implicit-null label to its host route FEC and advertises this label binding to the penultimate LSR. This causes the penultimate LSR to pop the tunnel label when switching the packets to the egress PE (PE2). With penultimate hop popping, the packet arrives at the egress PE with only the VC label. PE2 pops the VC label and determines the egress interface based on the VC label.

Step 4   The egress PE router, PE2, adds the address and control fields back to the PPP PDU before it is switched to the egress interface to the CE device CE2-A.

Figure 11-37 *Data Plane Operation in PPP over MPLS*

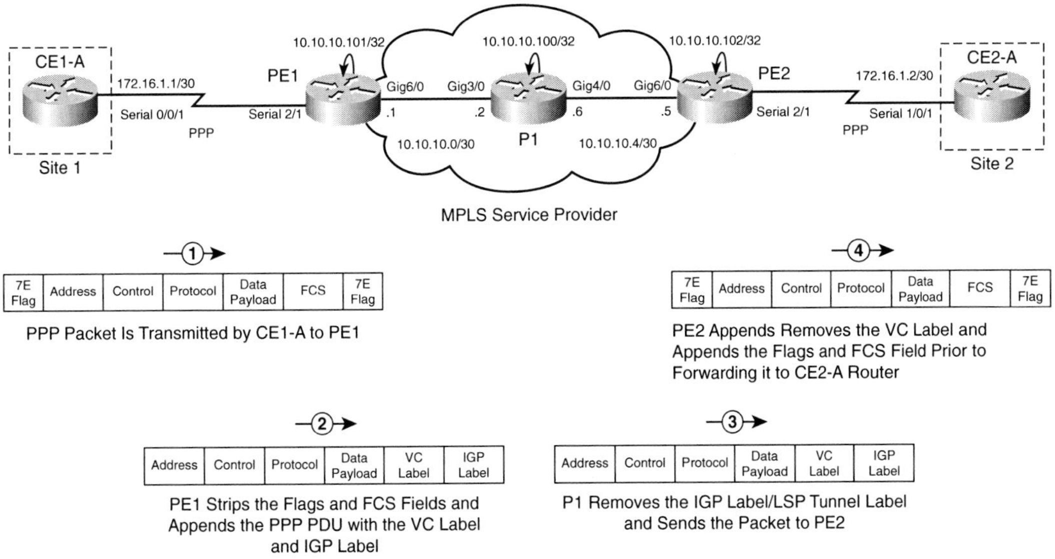

Configuration Flowchart for PPP over MPLS

Figure 11-38 shows the configuration steps relevant to configuring PPP over MPLS.

Figure 11-38 *Configuration Flowchart for PPP over MPLS*

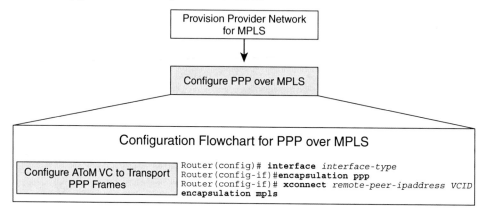

Configuring PPP over MPLS

The step to configure PPP over MPLS for the topology shown in Figure 11-37 is to first define PPP encapsulation and configure the VCID on each of the PE routers' interface connected to the CE routers, so that the directed LDP session can be formed to enable transportation of PPP packets from end CE devices over MPLS. See Example 11-26.

Example 11-26 *Enable PPP over MPLS on PE Routers*

```
PE1(config)# interface Serial2/1
PE1(config-if)#encapsulation ppp
PE1(config-if)# xconnect 10.10.10.102 100 encapsulation mpls
PE2(config)# interface Serial2/1
PE2(config-if)#encapsulation ppp
PE2(config-if)# xconnect 10.10.10.102 100 encapsulation mpls
```

Device Configuration for PPP over MPLS

Figure 11-39 shows the relevant device configuration for PPP over MPLS. PE1 and PE2 are PE routers in the MPLS provider network.

Verification of PPP over MPLS

Step 1   **Verify directed LDP session**—This step verifies that the AToM VC is functional to transport PPP over MPLS. See Example 11-27.

Example 11-27 *Verify AToM VC Is Operational*

```
PE1#show mpls l2transport vc
Local intf      Local circuit        Dest address      VC ID      Status
------------    -------------------  ---------------   ---------  ----------
Se2/1           PPP                  10.10.10.102      100        UP
```

Figure 11-39 *MPLS-Enabled Network Providing PPP over MPLS*

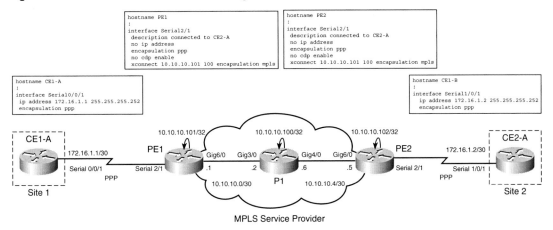

Step 2 **Verify Layer 2 transport label bindings**—In this step, you verify the local and remote label bindings. As shown in Example 11-28, the VC type is PPP, the control word is set and local, and remote MTU is 1500.

Example 11-28 *Verify Label Bindings*

```
PE2#show mpls l2transport binding
  Destination Address: 10.10.10.101,  VC ID: 100
    Local Label:  20
        Cbit: 1,    VC Type: PPP,    GroupID: 0
        MTU: 1500,   Interface Desc: connected to CE2-A
        VCCV Capabilities: None
    Remote Label: 16
        Cbit: 1,    VC Type: PPP,    GroupID: 0
        MTU: 1500,   Interface Desc: connected to CE1-A
        VCCV Capabilities: None
```

MTUs need to match; otherwise, the circuit will not come up, as shown in Example 11-29.

Example 11-29 *L2 Transport Down in Case of MTU Mismatch*

```
PE2#show mpls l2transport binding
  Destination Address: 10.10.10.101,  VC ID: 100
    Local Label:  16
        Cbit: 1,    VC Type: PPP,    GroupID: 0
        MTU: 512,   Interface Desc: connected to CE2-A
        VCCV Capabilities: None
    Remote Label: 16
        Cbit: 1,    VC Type: PPP,    GroupID: 0
        MTU: 1500,   Interface Desc: connected to CE1-A
        VCCV Capabilities: None
```

continues

Example 11-29 *L2 Transport Down in Case of MTU Mismatch (Continued)*

```
PE2#show mpls l2transport vc
Local intf     Local circuit          Dest address    VC ID      Status
------------   --------------------   --------------  ---------  ----------
Se2/1          PPP                    10.10.10.101    100        DOWN
```

Data Plane Forwarding for PPP over MPLS

Figure 11-40 shows the data forwarding operation that takes place for traffic originating from CE2-A to CE1-A.

Figure 11-40 *Data Forwarding for PPP over MPLS*

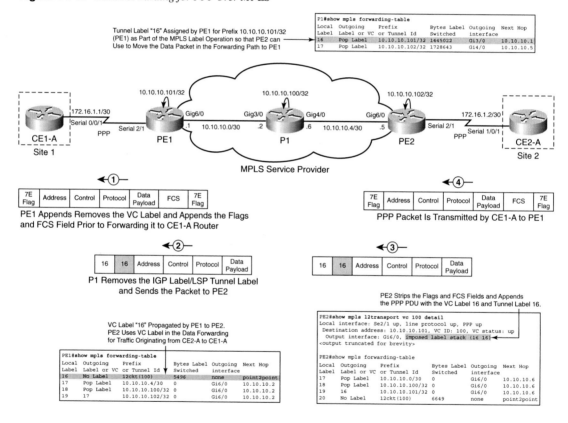

HDLC over MPLS

HDLC mode provides port-to-port transport of HDLC-encapsulated traffic. The HDLC PDU is transported in its entirety, including the HDLC address, control, and protocol fields, but excluding HDLC flags and the FCS. Bit/byte stuffing is undone. The control word is optional and when the control word is used, then the flag bits in the control word are set to 0 when transmitted and ignored on receipt. In Cisco implementation of HDLC over MPLS, the C bit is set by default. Figure 11-41 shows the control word when HDLC is used for transporting over MPLS.

Figure 11-41 *Control Word—HDLC over MPLS*

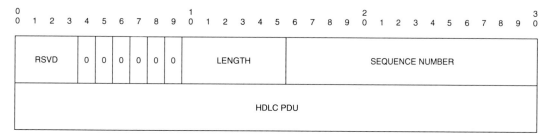

The process of encapsulating the HDLC PDU is shown in Figure 11-42.

Figure 11-42 *Data Plane—HDLC over MPLS*

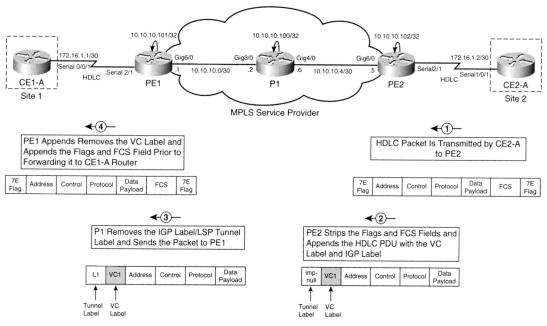

The data plane operation process when CE2-A sends an HDLC packet to CE1-A is explained in the following steps:

Step 1   CE2-A sends an HDLC packet to PE2.

Step 2   PE2 receives the HDLC packet and removes the flag and FCS fields from the packet. The remnants of the HDLC packet are used as L2 PDU, and the VC label and IGP label are appended to the packet. The modified packet is then sent to P1-AS1.

Step 3 P1 performs PHP function on the packet and removes the IGP label or LSP tunnel label and forwards the packet to PE1.

Step 4 PE1 does a lookup on the VC label and appends the HDLC PDU with HDLC flags and FCS fields prior to forwarding it to CE1-A.

Configuration Flowchart for HDLC over MPLS

Figure 11-43 shows the configuration flowchart relevant to configuring HDLC over MPLS.

Figure 11-43 *Configuration Steps for HDLC over MPLS*

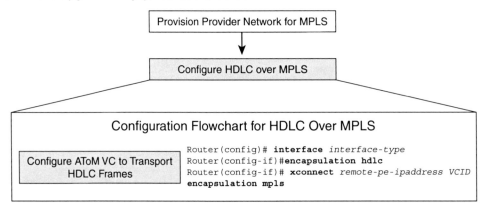

Configuring HDLC over MPLS

The objective for the L2 transport provider is to provide transparent L2 services to customer sites. Figure 11-44 shows an MPLS-enabled service provider network providing L2 transport service to Customer A sites, CE1-A and CE2-A.

Figure 11-44 *Network Providing HDLC over MPLS Service*

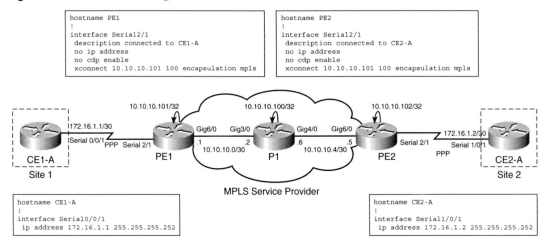

To configure HDLC over MPLS, enable transport of HDLC over MPLS. In this step, the HDLC encapsulation is defined and the VCID configured on each of the PE routers' interface connected to the CE routers, so that the directed LDP session can be formed to enable transportation of PPP packets from end CE devices over MPLS. See Example 11-30.

Example 11-30 *Enable HDLC over MPLS on PE Routers*

```
PE1(config)# interface Serial2/1
PE1(config-if)#encapsulation hdlc
PE1(config-if)# xconnect 10.10.10.102 100 encapsulation mpls

PE2(config)# interface Serial2/1
PE2(config-if)#encapsulation hdlc
PE2(config-if)# xconnect 10.10.10.101 100 encapsulation mpls
```

Verify HDLC over MPLS

To verify HDLC over MPLS, follow these steps:

Step 1   Verify directed LDP session—In this step, you verify if the AToM VC is functional to transport PPP over MPLS. See Example 11-31.

Example 11-31 *Verification of ATOM VC*

```
PE1#show mpls l2transport vc

Local intf     Local circuit          Dest address     VC ID     Status
-------------  ---------------------  ---------------  --------- ----------
Se2/1          HDLC                   10.10.10.102     100       UP
```

Step 2   Verify Layer 2 transport label bindings—In this step, the local and remote label bindings are verified. As shown in Example 11-32, the VC type is PPP, the control word is set and local, and remote MTU is 1500.

Example 11-32 *Verification of Layer 2 Transport Label Bindings*

```
PE1#show mpls l2transport binding
  Destination Address: 10.10.10.102,  VC ID: 100
    Local Label:  16
        Cbit: 1,    VC Type: HDLC,    GroupID: 0
        MTU: 1500,   Interface Desc: connected to CE1-A
        VCCV Capabilities: None
    Remote Label: 20
        Cbit: 1,    VC Type: HDLC,    GroupID: 0
        MTU: 1500,   Interface Desc: connected to CE2-A
        VCCV Capabilities: None
```

Final Configuration for HDLC over MPLS

Figure 11-44 shows the relevant device configuration for HDLC over MPLS. PE1 and PE2 are PE routers in the MPLS provider network.

Frame Relay over MPLS

Frame Relay over MPLS can work in either data-link connection identifier (DLCI)-to-DLCI mode or port-to-port mode. Frame Relay frames are received by the PE1 router from CE1-A, encapsulated into an MPLS, and forwarded across the backbone to PE2, where they are decapsulated and reproduced on the interface to CE2-A.

The main difference between DLCI-to-DLCI mode and port-to-port mode is the devices on which the Local Management Interface (LMI) procedures run. In port-to-port mode, the CE routers run the LMI between themselves, and the PE routers do not participate in the LMI. In port-to-port mode, the PE routers use the HDLC as a transport mode on the interface facing the CE router. In DLCI-to-DLCI mode, the PE routers actively participate in the LMI procedures, so the LMI runs between the PE and CE routers. Figure 11-45 shows the network used to depict implementation of Frame Relay over MPLS.

Figure 11-45 *Network Providing Frame Relay over MPLS Service*

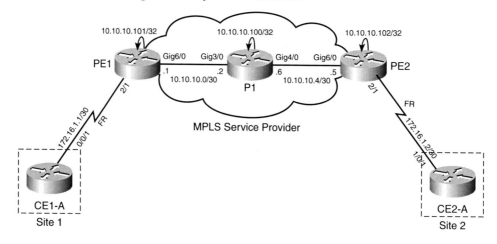

Configuration Steps for Frame Relay over MPLS—DLCI Mode

Figure 11-46 shows the steps to configure Frame Relay over MPLS in DLCI mode.

Configuring Frame Relay over MPLS—DLCI Mode

In this step, you configure the VCID on each of the PE routers' interface connected to the CE routers, so that the directed LDP session can be formed to enable transportation of Frame Relay frames from end CE devices over MPLS network. See Example 11-33.

Figure 11-46 *Network Providing Frame Relay over MPLS Service*

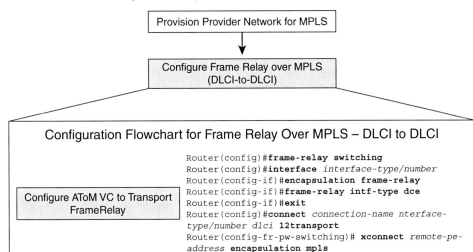

Example 11-33 *Enable Transport of Ethernet over MPLS on PE Routers*

```
PE1(config)#frame-relay switching
PE1(config)#interface Serial2/1
PE1(config-if)# encapsulation frame-relay
PE1(config-if)# frame-relay intf-type dce
PE1(config-if)#exit
PE1(config)#connect FR Serial2/1 100 l2transport
PE1(config-fr-pw-switching)# xconnect 10.10.10.102 100 encapsulation mpls
PE2(config)#frame-relay switching
PE2(config)#interface Serial2/1
PE2(config-if)# encapsulation frame-relay
PE2(config-if)# frame-relay intf-type dce
PE2(config-if)#exit
PE2(config)#connect FR Serial2/1 100 l2transport
PE2(config-fr-pw-switching)# xconnect 10.10.10.101 100 encapsulation mpls
```

Verification of Frame Relay over MPLS—DLCI Mode

To verify Frame Relay over MPLS in DLCI mode, follow these steps:

Step 1   **Ensure that AToM VC is up**—Example 11-34 shows the output of **show MPLS l2transport vc**. The output indicates that the AToM VC is functional to transport L2 packets across the MPLS backbone.

Example 11-34 show mpls l2transport vc *on PE1*

```
PE1#show mpls l2transport vc
Local intf      Local circuit        Dest address     VC ID      Status
------------    ------------------   --------------   --------   --------
Se2/1           FR DLCI 100          10.10.10.102     100        UP
```

Step 2 **Verify pseudo wire status**—Example 11-35 shows the output of the **show connection all** command where the Frame Relay switched connection has two segments:

— **Segment 1**—The local attachment circuit out of Serial 2/1 DLCI 100.

— **Segment 2**—The remote endpoint of the pseudo wire is PE2 (10.10.10.102).

Example 11-35 *Verification of Pseudo Wire Status—DLCI Mode*

```
PE1#show connection all

ID    Name              Segment 1            Segment 2              State
===============================================================================
1     FR              Se2/1 100            10.10.10.102 100       UP
PE1#show connection id 1

FR/Pseudo-Wire Connection: 1 - FR
  Status   - UP
  Segment 1 - Serial2/1 DLCI 100
    Segment status: UP
    Line status: UP
    PVC status: ACTIVE
    NNI PVC status: ACTIVE
  Segment 2 - 10.10.10.102 100
    Segment status: UP
    Requested AC state: UP
    PVC status: ACTIVE
    NNI PVC status: ACTIVE
```

Step 3 **Verify MPLS and VC label**—Example 11-36 shows the output of show **MPLS l2transport binding**. The output indicates that the VC type is Frame Relay DLCI mode as well as the local and remote-label bindings.

Example 11-36 *Verification of MPLS and VC Label Bindings*

```
PE1#show mpls l2transport binding
  Destination Address: 10.10.10.102,  VC ID: 100
    Local Label:  16
        Cbit: 1,    VC Type: FR DLCI,    GroupID: 0
        MTU: 1500,   Interface Desc: connected to CE1-A
        VCCV Capabilities: None
    Remote Label: 20
        Cbit: 1,    VC Type: FR DLCI,    GroupID: 0
        MTU: 1500,   Interface Desc: connected to CE2-A
        VCCV Capabilities: None
```

Final Configuration for Frame Relay over MPLS (DLCI Mode)

Figure 11-47 shows the final configurations for the devices to implement Frame Relay over MPLS (DLCI mode).

Figure 11-47 *Configurations for Frame Relay over MPLS (DLCI Mode)*

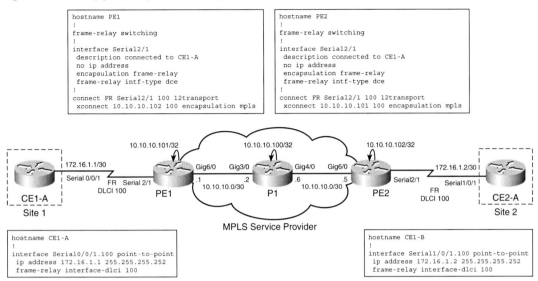

L2 VPN—Any to Any Interworking

You have seen that Layer 2 VPN is possible with like-to-like ACs such as HDLC-to-HDLC. In the forthcoming subsections, you will be introduced to L2 VPN implementation between different types of attachment circuits like Ethernet-to-PPP and so on. This function of translating different Layer 2 encapsulations is also called L2 VPN Interworking. L2 VPN Interworking, therefore, provides service providers with the ability to interconnect sites using different transport mediums on a common infrastructure. The common infrastructure is the MPLS backbone, which facilitates the interworking functionality of translating between various Layer 2 technologies. The L2 VPN Interworking feature supports Ethernet, 802.1Q (VLAN), Frame Relay, ATM AAL5, and PPP attachment circuits over MPLS.

The L2 VPN Interworking function is implemented in two modes.

Bridged Interworking Mode

In bridged interworking mode, Ethernet frames are extracted from the AC and sent over the pseudo wire. AC frames that are not Ethernet are dropped. In the case of a VLAN, the VLAN tag is removed, leaving an untagged Ethernet frame. This interworking functionality is implemented by configuring the **interworking ethernet** command under the pseudo-wire class configuration mode.

Figure 11-48 shows a Layer 2 VPN network using bridged interworking mode between Ethernet and 802.1Q VLAN.

Figure 11-48 *Bridged Interworking Mode*

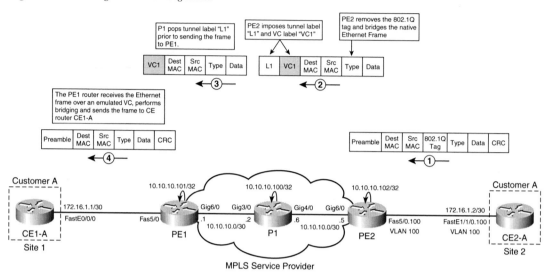

The steps are outlined as follows:

Step 1   The CE2-A generates an 802.1Q encapsulated frame. This 802.1Q frame is forwarded to PE2.

Step 2   PE2 removes the VLAN tag and performs bridging of the native Ethernet frames into the emulated VC (pseudo wire) established between PE routers. The Ethernet frame is encapsulated using a standard AToM encapsulation, which means the label header of two labels is attached.

The outer label, or tunnel label (L1), is the label that switches the frame across the MPLS backbone toward the PE1 router, and this label is to be assigned either by standard LDP or RSVP-TE in case an MPLS TE tunnel has been established between the PE routers. The inner label, or the VC label (VC1), is the label that distinguishes between multiple emulated VCs (pseudo wires) between the PE routers.

Step 3   The P1 router, upon receiving this frame, removes the top label (tunnel label) and forwards the packet to PE1.

Step 4   The PE1 router, after receiving the Ethernet frame over an emulated VC, performs bridging and sends the frame to CE router CE1-A.

Routed Interworking Mode

In routed interworking, IP packets are extracted from the AC and sent over the pseudo wire. AC frames are dropped if they do not contain the IPv4 packets. This interworking functionality is implemented by configuring the **interworking ip** command under the pseudo-wire class configuration mode.

Figure 11-49 shows an L2 VPN network implementing routed interworking where the CE2-A router generates an IP packet, which is encapsulated using 802.1Q encapsulation.

Figure 11-49 *Routed Interworking Mode*

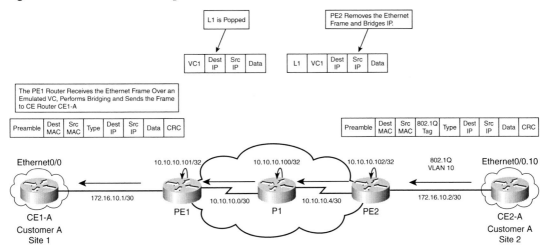

The steps are outlined as follows:

Step 1   CE2-A router generates an IP packet, which is encapsulated using 802.1Q encapsulation.

Step 2   PE2 receives the frame for further processing. In routed interworking, PE2 strips out the Layer 2 frame and bridges IP packets instead of bridging frames. Next, an AToM header (L1 and VC1) is attached to the decapsulated IP packet. Control Word 2 (CW2), an additional control word, is attached to carry information about the L2 protocol type. This control word is needed to resolve ARP requests, because the L2 circuit is terminated at the PE router.

Step 3   P1 pops the top label and forwards the resulting packet to PE1.

Step 4   The PE1 router, after receiving the Ethernet frame over an emulated VC, routes the IP packet to CE router CE1-A.

L2 VPN Interworking Limitations

L2 VPN Interworking has limitations to be considered when implementing interworking functionality between different Layer 2 technologies. The following are some of the limitations pertaining to the relevant Layer 2 technology.

L2 VPN Interworking Limitations for Ethernet/VLAN

Multipoint configurations are not supported. Care should be taken when configuring routing protocols for Ethernet to Frame Relay interworking. For example, in case of OSPF, one site operating in broadcast and the other site on nonbroadcast or point-to-point would result in OSPF adjacency not forming across the pseudo wire. It is, therefore, necessary to ensure that OSPF operates in a single mode on both ends. The PE router acts as a proxy ARP server and responds with its own MAC address to CE router's ARP requests. When you change the interworking configuration on the Ethernet PE router, ensure that the ARP entry on the adjacent CE router is cleared, so that it can learn the new MAC address. Otherwise, you might encounter traffic drops.

L2 VPN Interworking Limitations for Frame Relay

Inverse ARP is not supported with IP interworking. CE routers must use the point-to-point subinterfaces or static maps. The AC maximum transmission unit (MTU) sizes must match when you connect them over an MPLS. To avoid reduction of the interface MTUs to the lowest common denominator (1500 bytes in this case), you can specify the MTU for individual DLCIs using the **mtu** command. The PE router automatically supports the translation of both Cisco and IETF encapsulations coming from the CE, but translates only to IETF when sending to the CE router. This is not a problem for the Cisco CE router because it can handle the IETF encapsulation on receipt, even if it is configured to send Cisco encapsulation.

L2 VPN Interworking Limitations for AAL5

Only ATM AAL5 VC mode is supported. ATM VP and port mode are not supported. SVCs are not supported. Inverse ARP is not supported with IP interworking. CE routers must use point-to-point subinterfaces or static maps. Both AAL5MUX and AAL5SNAP encapsulations are supported.

Configuring Layer 2 VPN Interworking

Figure 11-50 shows the configuration flowchart to configure Layer 2 VPN Interworking for various Layer 2 access technologies.

Ethernet to VLAN Interworking

Figure 11-51 shows an MPLS provider network providing L2 VPN Interworking for Customer A site devices CE1-A and CE2-A. PE1 and PE2 are the PE routers in the MPLS provider network. CE1-A is connected via Ethernet to PE1, and CE2-A is connected via 802.1Q VLAN to PE2.

Figure 11-50 *Configuring L2 VPN Interworking*

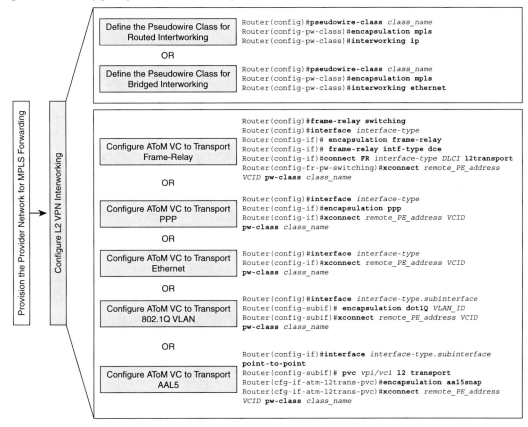

Figure 11-51 *Configuring L2 VPN Interworking—Ethernet to VLAN*

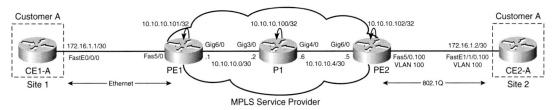

Configuration Steps—Ethernet to VLAN Interworking

The steps to configure Ethernet to VLAN Interworking between CE1-A and CE2-A are as follows:

Step 1 **Define pseudo-wire class on PE routers**—In this step, a pseudo-wire class called **Eth-VLAN** is defined on PE1 and **VLAN-Eth** on PE2. The configuration is shown in Example 11-37. This class configures the pseudo wire between the PE Routers PE1 and PE2. Ensure that the parameters of the pseudo-wire class are the same on both PEs to enable pseudo-wire establishment. Example 11-37 shows that AToM encapsulation (**encapsulation mpls**) and bridged interworking mode (**interworking ethernet**) will be used by the pseudo-wire class on the PE Routers PE1 and PE2.

Example 11-37 *Define Pseudo-Wire Class on PE Routers*

```
PE1(config)#pseudowire-class Eth-VLAN
PE1(config-pw-class)# encapsulation mpls
PE1(config-pw-class)# interworking ethernet

PE2(config)#pseudowire-class VLAN-Eth
PE2(config-pw-class)# encapsulation mpls
PE2(config-pw-class)# interworking ethernet
```

Step 2   **Define AToM VC to transport Layer 2 frames**—In this step, use the **xconnect** statement to define the AToM VC to carry the Layer 2 frames from CE1-A to CE2-A, and vice versa. Associate the pseudo-wire class defined in Step 1 with the AToM VC. See Example 11-38.

Example 11-38 *Define AToM VC to Transport Layer 2 Frames*

```
PE1(config)#interface Ethernet0/0
PE1(config-if)#xconnect 10.10.10.102 100  pw-class Eth-VLAN

PE2(config)#interface Ethernet0/0.10
PE2(config-subif)# encapsulation dot1Q 10
PE2(config-subif)# xconnect 10.10.10.101 100 pw-class VLAN-Eth
```

Final Configuration for Ethernet to VLAN Interworking

Figure 11-52 shows the final relevant configuration for customer and PE routers.

Figure 11-52 *Final Configuration—Ethernet to VLAN*

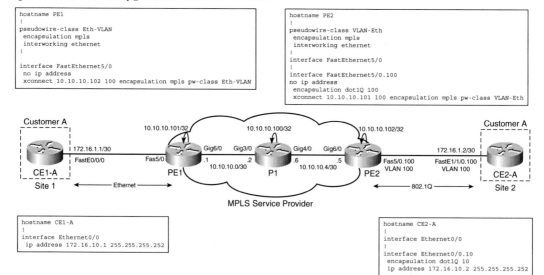

Verification of Ethernet to VLAN Interworking over MPLS

Verify AToM VC is up. Example 11-39 shows the output of **show mpls l2transport vc** in which the L2 transport VC is operational. The local circuit on PE1 is shown to be Ethernet on PE1 and Ethernet VLAN on PE2.

Example 11-39 *Verify AToM VC Is Up*

```
PE1#show mpls l2transport vc

Local intf     Local circuit         Dest address      VC ID      Status
-------------  --------------------  ---------------   ---------  ----------
Et0/0          Ethernet              10.10.10.102      100        UP
PE2#show mpls l2transport vc

Local intf     Local circuit         Dest address      VC ID      Status
-------------  --------------------  ---------------   ---------  ----------
Et0/0.10       Eth VLAN 10           10.10.10.101      100        UP
```

Control Plane and Data Forwarding Operation

Figure 11-53 shows the control and data forwarding operation for Ethernet to VLAN inter-working. From a control plane perspective, PE1 allocates VC label 18 for the Ethernet circuit connected to CE1-A. PE1 propagates this VC label 18 to PE2. As part of the IGP label operation, P1 assigns an LDP label 16 for PE1 (10.10.10.101) and propagates this to PE2. PE2 uses IGP label 16 to guide the data packet originating from CE2-A to CE1-A across the MPLS backbone.

Figure 11-53 *Control and Data Plane Forwarding: Ethernet to VLAN*

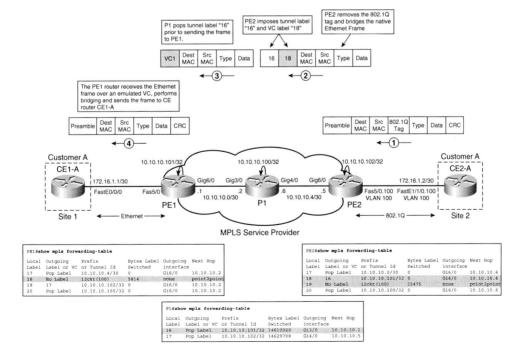

Frame Relay to AAL5 Interworking

Figure 11-54 shows an MPLS provider network providing L2 VPN Interworking for Customer A site devices CE1-A and CE2-A. PE1 and PE2 are the PE routers in the MPLS provider network. CE1-A is connected via ATM to PE1, and CE2-A is connected via Frame Relay to PE2.

Figure 11-54 *L2 VPN Network—Frame Relay to AAL5*

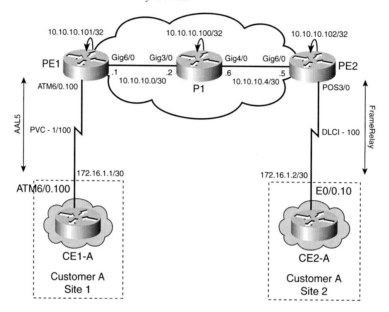

Configuration Steps—Frame Relay to AAL5 Interworking

The steps to configure Frame Relay to AAL5 Interworking between CE1-A and CE2-A are as follows:

Step 1   **Define pseudo-wire class on PE routers**—In this step, a pseudo-wire class called AAL5-FR is defined on PE1 and Fr-AAL5 on PE2. Example 11-40 shows that the AToM encapsulation (**encapsulation mpls**) and routed interworking model (**interworking ip**) is used by the pseudo-wire class on the PE routers PE1 and PE2.

Example 11-40 *Define Pseudo-Wire Class on PE Routers*

```
PE1(config)#pseudowire-class AAL5-FR
PE1(config-pw-class)# encapsulation mpls
PE1(config-pw-class)# interworking ip
PE2(config)#pseudowire-class FR-AAL5
PE2(config-pw-class)# encapsulation mpls
PE2(config-pw-class)# interworking ip
```

Step 2   **Define AToM VC to transport Layer 2 frames**—In Example 11-41, use
the **xconnect** statement to define the AToM VC to carry the Layer 2
frames from CE1-A to CE2-A and vice versa. Associate the pseudo-wire
class defined in Step 1 with the AToM VC.

Example 11-41 *Define AToM VC to Transport Layer 2 Frames*

```
PE1(config-subif)#interface ATM6/0.100 point-to-point
PE1(config-subif)# pvc 1/100 l2transport
PE1(cfg-if-atm-l2trans-pvc)#encapsulation aal5snap
PE1(cfg-if-atm-l2trans-pvc)#xconnect 10.10.10.102 100 pw-class AAL5-FR
PE2(config)#frame-relay switching
PE2(config)#interface POS3/0
PE2(config-if)# no ip address
PE2(config-if)# encapsulation frame-relay
PE2(config-if)# clock source internal
PE2(config-if)# frame-relay intf-type dce
PE2(config-if)#connect FR POS3/0 100 l2transport
PE2(config-fr-pw-switching)#xconnect 10.10.10.101 100 pw-class FR-AAL5
```

Verification of Frame Relay to AAL5 Interworking over MPLS

To verify Frame Relay to AAL5 interworking over MPLS, follow these steps:

Step 1   **Verify if AToM VC is up**—Example 11-42 shows the output of **show
mpls l2transport vc.** The output indicates that the AToM VC is
functional to transport L2 packets across the MPLS backbone.

Example 11-42 *Verification of ATOM VC Status*

```
PE1#show mpls l2transport vc

Local intf     Local circuit           Dest address      VC ID      Status
------------   ----------------------  ---------------   ---------  ----------
AT6/0.100      ATM AAL5 1/100          10.10.10.102      100        UP
PE1#show mpls l2transport vc

Local intf     Local circuit           Dest address      VC ID      Status
------------   ----------------------  ---------------   ---------  ----------
PO3/0          FR DLCI 100             10.10.10.101      100        UP
```

Step 2   **Verify tunnel and VC label**—Example 11-43 shows the output of **show
mpls l2transport vc detail**. The output indicates the directed LDP peer
is 10.10.10.102 and that the AToM VC is functional to transport L2
packets across the MPLS backbone. The VC ID is 100 and tunnel label
is 17. This tunnel label is derived from LDP. The VC label on PE1 for
outgoing interface on PE2 connected to CE2-A is 17, and it allocates VC
label 23 for the interface connected to CE1-A.

Example 11-43 *Verification of Tunnel and VC Labels*

```
PE1#show mpls l2transport vc detail
Local interface: AT6/0.100 up, line protocol up, ATM AAL5 1/100 up
  MPLS VC type is IP, interworking type is IP
  Destination address: 10.10.10.102, VC ID: 100, VC status: up
    Preferred path: not configured
    Default path: active
    Next hop: 10.10.10.2
    Output interface: Gi0/1, imposed label stack {17 17}
  Create time: 00:27:12, last status change time: 00:18:58
  Signaling protocol: LDP, peer 10.10.10.102:0 up
    MPLS VC labels: local 23, remote 17
    Group ID: local 6, remote 0
    MTU: local 4470, remote 4470
    Remote interface description:
  Sequencing: receive disabled, send disabled
  Sequence number: receive 0, send 0
  VC statistics:
    packet totals: receive 15, send 15
    byte totals:   receive 1620, send 1620
    packet drops:  receive 0, seq error 0, send 0
PE2#show mpls l2transport vc detail
Local interface: PO3/0 up, line protocol up, FR DLCI 100 up
  MPLS VC type is IP, interworking type is IP
  Destination address: 10.10.10.101, VC ID: 100, VC status: up
    Preferred path: not configured
    Default path: active
    Next hop: 10.10.10.6
    Output interface: Gi0/1, imposed label stack {16 23}
  Create time: 00:18:39, last status change time: 00:18:35
  Signaling protocol: LDP, peer 10.10.10.101:0 up
    MPLS VC labels: local 17, remote 23
    Group ID: local 0, remote 6
    MTU: local 4470, remote 4470
    Remote interface description:
  Sequencing: receive disabled, send disabled
  Sequence number: receive 0, send 0
  VC statistics:
    packet totals: receive 15, send 15
    byte totals:   receive 1620, send 1620
    packet drops:  receive 0, seq error 0, send 0
```

Step 3 **Verify MPLS forwarding table on the PE and P routers**—Example 11-44
shows the LFIB on the PE routers in which PE1 allocates VC label 23 and
PE2 allocates VC label 17.

Example 11-44 *Data Plane Forwarding Verification*

```
PE1#show mpls forwarding-table
Local  Outgoing    Prefix        Bytes tag  Outgoing   Next Hop
tag    tag or VC   or Tunnel Id  switched   interface
16     Pop tag     10.10.10.4/30     0      Gi0/1      10.10.10.2
17     17          10.10.10.102/32   0      Gi0/1      10.10.10.2
21     Pop tag     10.10.10.100/32   0      Gi0/1      10.10.10.2
23     Untagged    l2ckt(100)     1620      none       point2point
P1#show mpls forwarding-table
Local  Outgoing    Prefix          Bytes Label  Outgoing   Next Hop
Label  Label or VC or Tunnel Id    Switched     interface
16     Pop Label   10.10.10.101/32  29489374    Gi0/1      10.10.10.1
17     Pop Label   10.10.10.102/32   5134192    Gi0/2      10.10.10.5
PE2#show mpls forwarding-table
Local  Outgoing    Prefix        Bytes tag  Outgoing   Next Hop
tag    tag or VC   or Tunnel Id  switched   interface
17     Untagged    l2ckt(100)     1620      none       point2point
18     Pop tag     10.10.10.0/30     0      Gi0/1      10.10.10.6
19     Pop tag     10.10.10.100/32   0      Gi0/1      10.10.10.6
20     16          10.10.10.101/32   0      Gi0/1      10.10.10.6
```

Frame Relay to PPP Interworking

Figure 11-55 shows an MPLS provider network using L2 VPN Interworking for Customer A sites with devices CE1-A and CE2-A. PE1 and PE2 are the PE routers in the MPLS provider network. CE1-A is connected using PPP encapsulation to PE1 and CE2-A is connected via Frame Relay to PE2.

Figure 11-55 *Configuring L2 VPN Interworking—PPP to Frame Relay*

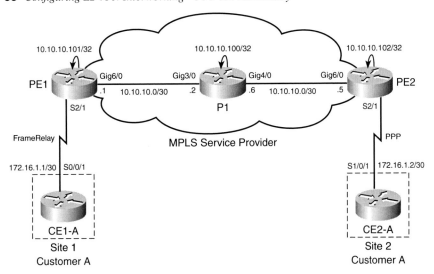

Configuration Steps—Ethernet to VLAN Interworking

The steps to configure Ethernet to VLAN Interworking between CE1-A and CE2-A are as follows:

Step 1   **Define pseudo-wire class on PE routers**—In this step, pseudo-wire classes called **PPP-FR** and **FR-PPP** are defined on PE1 and PE2, respectively. The configuration is shown in Example 11-45. Ensure that the parameters of the pseudo-wire class are the same on both PEs; otherwise, the pseudo wire will not be established.

Example 11-45 *Define Pseudo-Wire Class on PE Routers*

```
PE1(config)#pseudowire-class FR-PPP
PE1(config-pw-class)# encapsulation mpls
PE1(config-pw-class)# interworking ip

PE2(config)#pseudowire-class PPP-FR
PE2(config-pw-class)# encapsulation mpls
PE2(config-pw-class)# interworking ip
```

Step 2   **Define AToM VC to transport Layer 2 frames**—Use the **xconnect** statement to define the AToM VC to carry the Layer 2 frames from CE1-A to CE2-A and vice versa. Associate the pseudo-wire class defined in Step 1 with the AToM VC. See Example 11-46.

Example 11-46 *Define ATOM VC to Transport Layer 2 Frames*

```
PE1(config-if)#interface Serial1/0
PE1(config-if)#no ip address
PE1(config-if)#encapsulation frame-relay
PE1(config-if)#frame-relay intf-type dce
PE1(config-if)#exit
PE1(config)#connect FR Serial1/0 100 l2transport
PE1(config-fr-pw-switching)#xconnect 10.10.10.101 100 pw-class FR-PPP

PE2(config-if)#interface Serial1/0
PE2(config-subif)#encapsulation ppp
PE2(config-subif)#xconnect 10.10.10.102 100 pw-class PPP-FR
```

Verification of Frame Relay to PPP Interworking

To verify Frame Relay to PPP interworking, follow these steps:

Step 1   **Ensure that AToM VC is up**—Example 11-47 shows the output of **show mpls l2transport vc**. The output indicates that the AToM VC is functional to transport L2 packets across the MPLS backbone.

Example 11-47 *Verification of Atom VC Status*

```
PE1#show mpls l2transport vc

Local intf     Local circuit       Dest address     VC ID    Status
-----------    ---------------     --------------   -----    ---------
Se2/1          FR DLCI 100         10.10.10.102     100      UP
```

Example 11-47 *Verification of Atom VC Status (Continued)*

```
PE2#show mpls l2transport vc

Local intf     Local circuit        Dest address     VC ID      Status
-------------  -------------------- ---------------  ---------- ----------
Se2/1          PPP                  10.10.10.101     100        UP
```

Step 2   **Verify tunnel and VC label**—Example 11-48 shows the output of **show MPLS l2transport binding**. The output indicates the directed LDP peer is 10.10.10.102 and that the AToM VC is functional to transport L2 packets across the MPLS backbone.

Example 11-48 *Verification of Label Mappings*

```
PE1#show mpls l2transport binding
  Destination Address: 10.10.10.102,  VC ID: 100
    Local Label:  21
        Cbit: 1,    VC Type: IP,    GroupID: 0
        MTU: 1500,    Interface Desc: connected to CE1-A
        VCCV Capabilities: None
    Remote Label: 16
        Cbit: 1,    VC Type: IP,    GroupID: 0
        MTU: 1500,    Interface Desc: connected to CE2-A
        VCCV Capabilities: None
```

Step 3   Example 11-49 shows the output of the **show connection all** command in which the Frame Relay switched connection is shown with Layer 2 VPN Interworking configured as well as the status of the segments.

Example 11-49 **show connection all** *Output on PE Router*

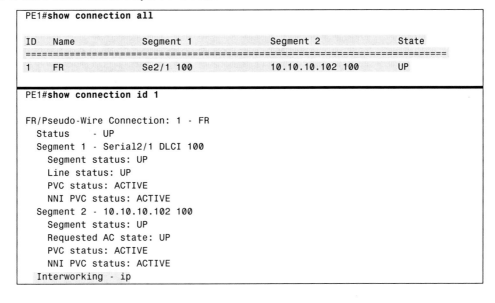

```
PE1#show connection all

ID   Name         Segment 1             Segment 2              State
================================================================================
1    FR           Se2/1 100             10.10.10.102 100       UP

PE1#show connection id 1

FR/Pseudo-Wire Connection: 1 - FR
  Status    - UP
  Segment 1 - Serial2/1 DLCI 100
    Segment status: UP
    Line status: UP
    PVC status: ACTIVE
    NNI PVC status: ACTIVE
  Segment 2 - 10.10.10.102 100
    Segment status: UP
    Requested AC state: UP
    PVC status: ACTIVE
    NNI PVC status: ACTIVE
  Interworking - ip
```

Final Configurations for Devices to Implement Frame Relay to PPP Interworking

Figure 11-56 outlines the final configurations for the devices to implement L2 VPN Interworking between Frame Relay and PPP.

Figure 11-56 *Final Device Configurations for L2 VPN Interworking: PPP to Frame Relay*

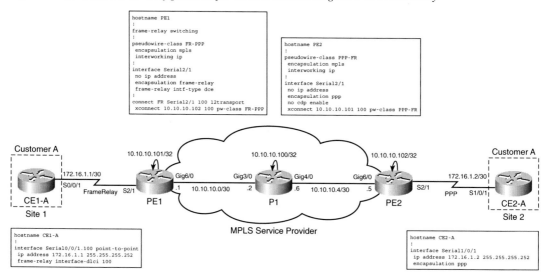

Frame Relay to VLAN Interworking

Figure 11-57 shows an MPLS provider network using L2 VPN Interworking for Customer A sites with devices CE1-A and CE2-A as CE routers. PE1 and PE2 are the PE routers in the MPLS provider network. CE1-A is connected via 802.1Q VLAN to PE1, and CE2-A is connected via Frame Relay to PE2.

Figure 11-57 *Frame Relay to VLAN Interworking Topology*

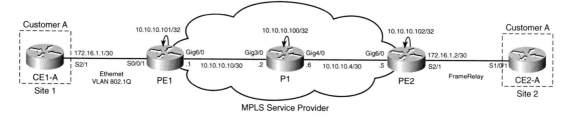

Configuration Steps for Frame Relay to VLAN Interworking

The steps to configure Ethernet to VLAN interworking between CE1-A and CE2-A are as follows:

Step 1 **Define pseudo-wire class on PE routers**—In this step, a pseudo-wire class called VLAN-FR is defined on PE1 and Fr-VLAN on PE2. The configuration is shown in Example 11-50.

Example 11-50 *Step 1: Define Pseudo-Wire Class on PE Routers*

```
PE1(config)#pseudowire-class FR-VLAN
PE1(config-pw-class)# encapsulation mpls
PE1(config-pw-class)# interworking ip

PE2(config)#pseudowire-class VLAN-FR
PE2(config-pw-class)# encapsulation mpls
PE2(config-pw-class)# interworking ip
```

Step 2 **Define AToM VC to transport Layer 2 frames**—In this example, you use the **xconnect** statement to define the AToM VC to carry the Layer 2 frames from CE1-A to CE2-A and vice versa. Associate the pseudo-wire class defined in Step 1 with the AToM VC. See Example 11-51.

Example 11-51 *Step 2: Create AToM VC on PE Routers*

```
PE1(config-pw-class)#interface Serial2/1
PE1(config-if)# no ip address
PE1(config-if)# encapsulation frame-relay
PE1(config-if)# frame-relay intf-type dce
PE1(config-if)#connect FR Serial2/1 100 l2transport
PE1(config-fr-pw-switching)#xconnect 10.10.10.101 100 pw-class FR-VLAN

PE2(config-pw-class)#interface Ethernet0/0.10
PE2(config-subif)# encapsulation dot1Q 10
PE2(config-subif)#xconnect 10.10.10.102 100 pw-class VLAN-FR
```

Verification of Frame Relay to VLAN Interworking over MPLS

To verify Frame Relay to VLAN Interworking over MPLS, follow these steps:

Step 1 **Ensure that AToM VC is up**—Example 11-52 shows the output of **show MPLS l2transport vc**. The output indicates that the AToM VC is functional to transport L2 packets across the MPLS backbone.

Example 11-52 *Verification of AToM VC Status*

```
PE1#show mpls l2transport vc

Local intf     Local circuit          Dest address      VC ID      Status
------------   --------------------   ---------------   ----------  ----------
Se2/1          FR DLCI 100            10.10.10.102      100         UP

PE2#show mpls l2transport vc

Local intf     Local circuit          Dest address      VC ID      Status
------------   --------------------   ---------------   ----------  ----------
Fa5/0.100      Eth VLAN 100           10.10.10.101      100         UP
```

Step 2 **Verify tunnel and VC label**—Example 11-53 shows the output of **show mpls l2transport binding**. The output indicates the directed LDP peer is 10.10.10.102 and that the AToM VC is functional to transport L2 packets across the MPLS backbone.

Example 11-53 *Verify AToM Label Bindings*

```
PE1#show mpls l2transport binding
  Destination Address: 10.10.10.102,  VC ID: 100
    Local Label:  21
        Cbit: 1,    VC Type: IP,     GroupID: 0
        MTU: 1500,   Interface Desc: connected to CE1-A
        VCCV Capabilities: None
    Remote Label: 20
        Cbit: 1,    VC Type: IP,     GroupID: 0
        MTU: 1500,   Interface Desc: connected to CE2-A
        VCCV Capabilities: None
```

Step 3 Example 11-54 shows the output of the **show connection all** command where the Frame Relay switched connection is depicted with Layer 2 VPN Interworking configured as well as the status of the segments.

Example 11-54 *Verification of L2 VPN Interworking Connections on PE Router*

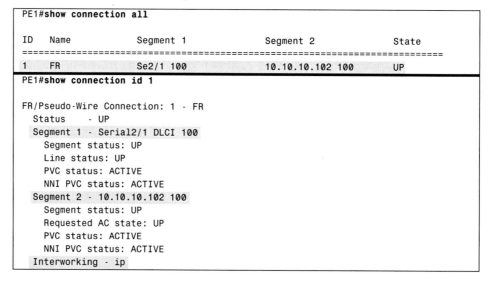

```
PE1#show connection all

ID   Name            Segment 1            Segment 2              State
===============================================================================
1    FR              Se2/1 100            10.10.10.102 100       UP
PE1#show connection id 1

FR/Pseudo-Wire Connection: 1 - FR
  Status    - UP
  Segment 1 - Serial2/1 DLCI 100
    Segment status: UP
    Line status: UP
    PVC status: ACTIVE
    NNI PVC status: ACTIVE
  Segment 2 - 10.10.10.102 100
    Segment status: UP
    Requested AC state: UP
    PVC status: ACTIVE
    NNI PVC status: ACTIVE
  Interworking - ip
```

Final Configuration for Frame Relay to VLAN Interworking

Figure 11-58 shows the final configurations for implementing Frame Relay to VLAN interworking.

Figure 11-58 *Final Configurations for Frame Relay to VLAN Interworking*

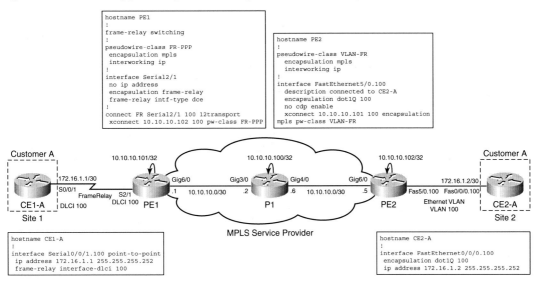

AAL5 to VLAN Interworking

Figure 11-59 shows an MPLS provider network that provides L2 VPN Interworking for Customer A sites with CE1-A and CE2-A as the CE devices. PE1 and PE2 are the PE routers in the MPLS provider network. CE1-A is connected via ATM to PE1, and CE2-A is connected via 802.1Q VLAN to PE2.

Figure 11-59 *L2 VPN Interworking—ATM to VLAN Topology*

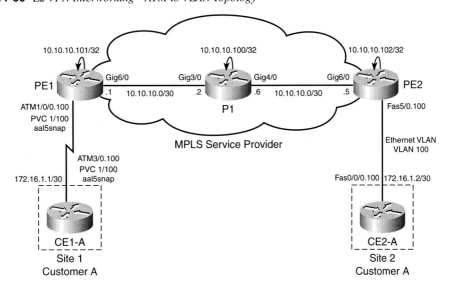

Configuration Steps—VLAN to AAL5 Interworking

The steps to configure VLAN to AAL5 interworking between CE1-A and CE2-A are as follows:

Step 1 **Define pseudo-wire class on PE routers**—In this step, a pseudo-wire class, called **Eth-VLAN**, is defined on PE1 and **VLAN-Eth** on PE2. The configuration is shown in Example 11-55.

Example 11-55 *Step 1: Define Pseudo-Wire Class on PE Routers*

```
PE1(config)#pseudowire-class AAL5-VLAN
PE1(config-pw-class)# encapsulation mpls
PE1(config-pw-class)# interworking ip

PE2(config)#pseudowire-class VLAN-AAL5
PE2(config-pw-class)# encapsulation mpls
PE2(config-pw-class)# interworking ip
```

Step 2 **Define AToM VC to transport Layer 2 frames**—Use the **xconnect** statement to define the AToM VC to carry the Layer 2 frames from CE1-A to CE2-A and vice versa. Associate the pseudo-wire class defined in Step 1 with the AToM VC. See Example 11-56.

Example 11-56 *Step 2: Create AToM VC on PE Routers*

```
PE1(config)#interface ATM3/0.100 point-to-point
PE1(config)#mtu 1500
PE1(config-subif)# pvc 1/100 l2transport
PE1(cfg-if-atm-l2trans-pvc)# encapsulation aal5snap
PE1(cfg-if-atm-l2trans-pvc)#xconnect 10.10.10.102 100 pw-class AAL5-VLAN

PE2(config)#interface FastEthernet5/0.100
PE2(config-subif)# encapsulation dot1Q 100
PE2(config-subif)# xconnect 10.10.10.102 100 pw-class VLAN-AAL5
```

Verification of AAL5 to VLAN Interworking over MPLS

To verify AAL5 to VLAN Interworking over MPLS, follow these steps:

Step 1 **Ensure that AToM VC is up**—Example 11-57 shows the output of **show mpls l2transport vc**. The output indicates that the AToM VC is functional to transport L2 packets across the MPLS backbone.

Example 11-57 *Verification of AToM VC Status*

```
PE1#show mpls l2transport vc

Local intf     Local circuit       Dest address     VC ID      Status
------------   -----------------   --------------   ---------- ----------
AT3/0.100      ATM AAL5 1/100      10.10.10.102     100        UP

PE2#show mpls l2transport vc

Local intf     Local circuit       Dest address     VC ID      Status
------------   -----------------   --------------   ---------- ----------
Fa5/0.100      Eth VLAN 100        10.10.10.101     100        UP
```

Step 2 **Verify tunnel and VC label**—Example 11-58 shows the output of **show mpls l2transport binding**. The output indicates the directed LDP peer is 10.10.10.102 and that the AToM VC is functional to transport L2 packets across the MPLS backbone.

Example 11-58 *Verify Label Assignment*

```
PE1#show mpls l2transport binding
  Destination Address: 10.10.10.102,  VC ID: 100
    Local Label:  16
        Cbit: 1,    VC Type: IP,    GroupID: 0
        MTU: 1500,   Interface Desc: connected to CE1-A
        VCCV Capabilities: None
    Remote Label: 20
        Cbit: 1,    VC Type: IP,    GroupID: 0
        MTU: 1500,   Interface Desc: connected to CE2-A
        VCCV Capabilities: None
```

Final Device Configurations to Implement ATM to Ethernet VLAN Interworking

Figure 11-60 depicts the final configurations on the devices to implement ATM to Ethernet VLAN interworking.

Figure 11-60 *Final Device Configurations for L2 VPN Interworking—ATM to VLAN*

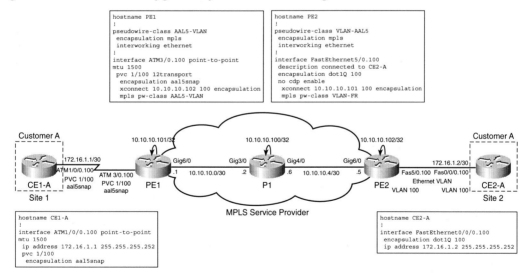

Local Switching

Layer 2 switching permits you to switch Layer 2 frames between two ACs located on the same PE. These ACs can be of the same encapsulation type or different. In this section, you will configure and verify Layer 2 local switching for

- Ethernet to Ethernet
- ATM to ATM

- Frame Relay to Frame Relay
- Ethernet to Frame Relay

Configuration Flowchart for Local Switching Among Like Circuits

Figure 11-61 shows the configuration flowchart for local switching among like circuits.

Figure 11-61 *Configuration Flowchart for Local Switching*

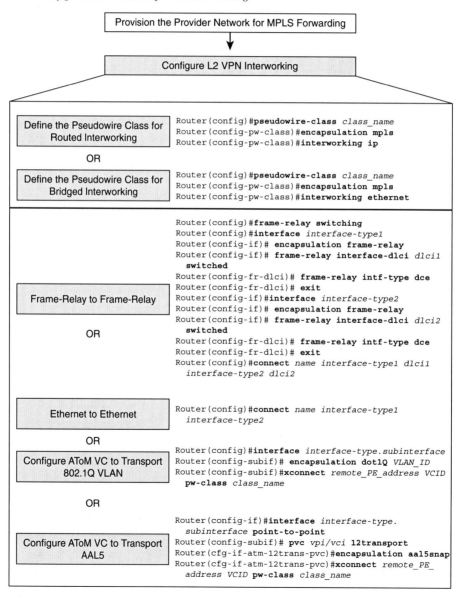

Local Switching—Frame Relay to Frame Relay

Figure 11-62 shows the network topology where PE1 is connected to CE1-A and CE2-A via Frame Relay circuits. To allow CE1-A to communicate with CE2-A, PE1 needs to be configured for local switching.

Figure 11-62 *Frame Relay to Frame Relay Local Switching Topology*

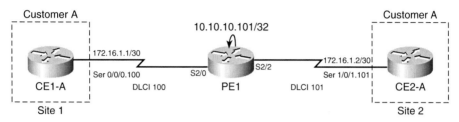

Configuring Frame Relay to Frame Relay Local Switching

To configure the topology shown in Figure 11-62, configure local switching on PE. Configure the PE router for Frame Relay switching. Configure the interfaces to CE routers for Frame Relay encapsulation and DLCI value. Note that configuring the switched DLCI using **frame-relay interface-dlci** *dlci* **switched** is optional. Use the connect IOS command to configure local switching between two Frame Relay circuits. Example 11-59 shows the steps to configure local switching on PE1.

Example 11-59 *Configuring Frame Relay to Frame Relay Local Switching*

```
PE1(config)#frame-relay switching
PE1(config)#interface Serial2/0
PE1(config-if)# no ip address
PE1(config-if)# encapsulation frame-relay
PE1(config-if)# frame-relay interface-dlci 100 switched
PE1(config-fr-dlci)# frame-relay intf-type dce
PE1(config-fr-dlci)# exit
PE1(config-if)#interface Serial2/2
PE1(config-if)# no ip addressPE1(config-if)# encapsulation frame-relay
PE1(config-if)# frame-relay interface-dlci 101 switched
PE1(config-fr-dlci)# frame-relay intf-type dce
PE1(config-fr-dlci)# exit
PE1(config)#connect FR Serial2/0 100 Serial2/2 101
```

Frame Relay to Frame Relay Local Switching Configuration

The final relevant configuration for local switching between Frame Relay circuits is shown in Figure 11-63.

Figure 11-63 *Frame Relay to Frame Relay Local Switching Configurations*

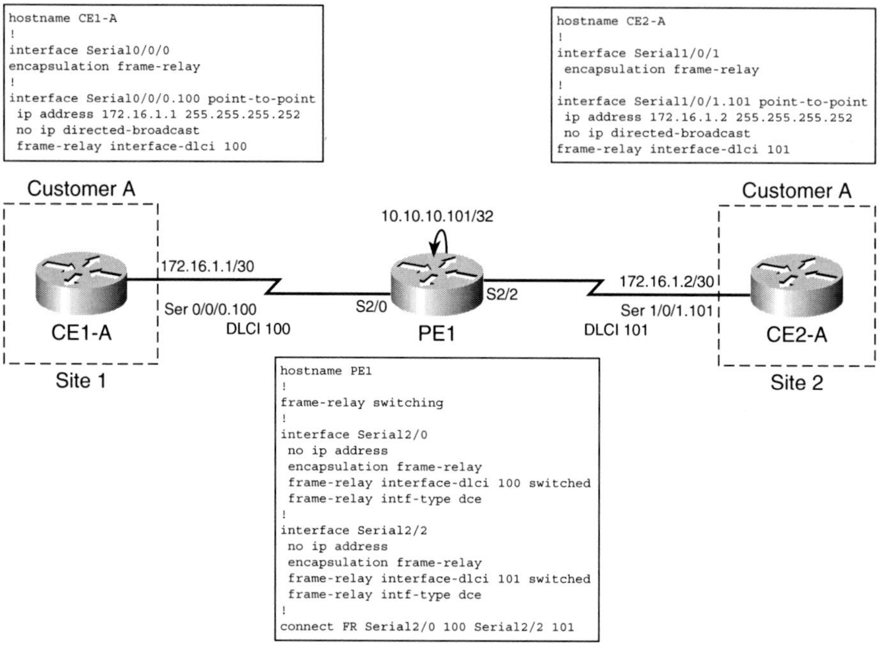

Verify Frame Relay to Frame Relay Local Switching

To verify Frame Relay to Frame Relay local switching, follow these steps:

Step 1 **Verify Frame Relay connection**—Example 11-60 shows the output of **show connection all**, which shows that local switching is up and operational.

Example 11-60 *Configuring Frame Relay to Frame Relay Local Switching*

```
PE1#show connection all

ID   Name          Segment 1           Segment 2           State
=================================================================================
2    FR            Se2/0 100           Se2/2 101             UP
```

Step 2 **Verify connectivity using ping**—Example 11-61 shows that CE1-A has connectivity to CE2-A.

Example 11-61 *Verifying Local Switching Connectivity*

```
CE1-A#ping 172.16.1.2

Type escape sequence to abort.
Sending 5, 100-byte ICMP Echos to 172.16.1.2, timeout is 2 seconds:
!!!!!
Success rate is 100 percent (5/5), round-trip min/avg/max = 4/4/4 ms
```

Local Switching—Ethernet to Ethernet

Figure 11-64 shows the network topology where PE1 is connected to CE1-A and CE2-A via Ethernet. To allow CE1-A to communicate with CE2-A, PE1 needs to be configured for local switching.

Figure 11-64 *Configuration for Local Switching*

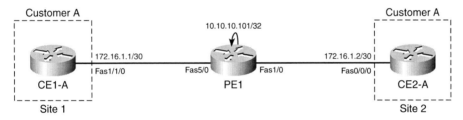

Configuring Ethernet to Ethernet Local Switching

To configure the topology shown in Figure 11-64, configure local switching on PE. Use the **connect** IOS command to configure local switching between two Ethernet interfaces. Example 11-62 shows the step to configure local switching for Ethernet on PE1.

Example 11-62 *Configuring Local Switching for Ethernet on PE1*

```
PE1(config)# connect Ethernet fastEthernet 5/0 fastEthernet 1/0
```

Ethernet to Ethernet Switching Configuration

The final relevant configuration for local switching between Frame Relay circuits is shown in Figure 11-65.

Figure 11-65 *Final Configuration for Ethernet to Ethernet Local Switching*

```
hostname CE1-A
!
interface FastEthernet1/1/0
 ip address 172.16.1.1 255.255.255.252
```

```
hostname CE2-A
!
interface FastEthernet0/0/0
 ip address 172.16.1.2 255.255.255.252
```

Customer A

Customer A

10.10.10.101/32

172.16.1.1/30

172.16.1.2/30

Fas1/1/0

Fas5/0

Fas1/0

Fas0/0/0

CE1-A

PE1

CE2-A

Site 1

Site 2

```
hostname PE1
!
connect Ethernet fastEthernet 5/0
fastEthernet 1/0
```

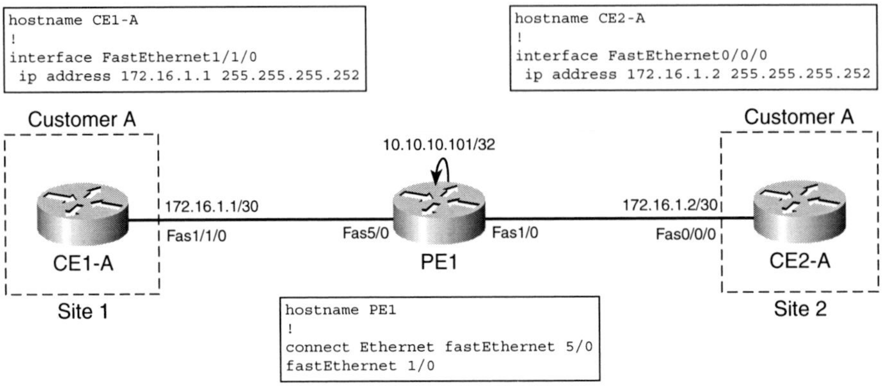

Verification of Ethernet to Ethernet Local Switching

To verify Ethernet to Ethernet local switching, follow these steps:

Step 1   **Verify Ethernet connection**—Example 11-63 shows the output of **show connection all**, which shows that local switching is up and operational.

Example 11-63 *Verify Ethernet Connectivity*

```
PE1#show connection all

ID   Name          Segment 1          Segment 2          State
===============================================================================
3    Ethernet      Fa5/0              Fa1/0              UP
```

Step 2   **Verify connectivity using ping**—Example 11-64 shows that CE1-A has connectivity to CE2-A.

Example 11-64 *Verify Connectivity Using Ping*

```
CE1-A#ping 172.16.1.2

Type escape sequence to abort.
Sending 5, 100-byte ICMP Echos to 172.16.1.2, timeout is 2 seconds:
!!!!!
Success rate is 100 percent (5/5), round-trip min/avg/max = 4/4/4 ms
```

Local Switching—ATM to ATM

Figure 11-66 shows the network topology in which PE1 is connected to CE1-A and CE2-A via ATM AAL5 circuits. In order to allow CE1-A to communicate with CE2-A, PE1 needs to be configured for local switching.

Figure 11-66 *ATM to ATM Local Switching Topology*

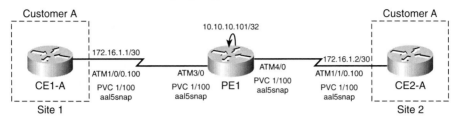

Configuring ATM to ATM Local Switching

To configure the topology shown in Figure 11-66, configure local switching on PE.
Example 11-65 shows the steps to configure local switching on PE1.

Example 11-65 *Configuring ATM to ATM Local Switching*

```
PE1(config)#interface atm3/0
PE1(config-if)#pvc 1/100 l2transport
PE1(config-if)#exit
PE1(config)#interface atm 4/0
PE1(config-if)# pvc 1/100 l2transport
PE1(config-if)#exit
PE1(config)#connect ATM atm 3/0 1/100 atm 4/0 1/100
```

Final Configurations for ATM to ATM Local Switching

The final relevant configuration for local switching between Frame Relay circuits is shown
in Figure 11-67.

Figure 11-67 *ATM to ATM Local Switching Final Configurations*

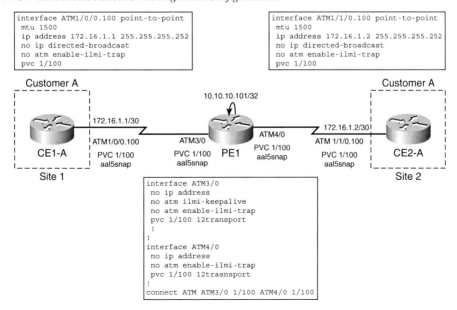

Verify ATM to ATM Local Switching

To verify ATM to ATM local switching, follow these steps:

Step 1 **Verify ATM connection**—Example 11-66 shows the output of **show connection all**, which shows that local switching is up and operational.

Example 11-66 *Verifying ATM to ATM Local Switching*

```
PE1#show connection all

ID   Name        Segment 1            Segment 2            State
=================================================================
4    ATM         AT3/0 AAL5 1/100     AT4/0 AAL5 1/100     UP
```

Step 2 **Verify connectivity using ping**—Example 11-67 shows that CE1-A has connectivity to CE2-A.

Example 11-67 *Verification of ATM to ATM Local Switching*

```
CE1-A#ping 172.16.1.2

Type escape sequence to abort.
Sending 5, 100-byte ICMP Echos to 172.16.1.2, timeout is 2 seconds:
!!!!!
Success rate is 100 percent (5/5), round-trip min/avg/max = 4/4/4 ms
```

Local Switching—Ethernet to Frame Relay

Figure 11-68 shows the network topology where PE1 is connected to CE1-A and CE2-A via Ethernet and Frame Relay circuits, respectively. To allow CE1-A to communicate with CE2-A, PE1 needs to be configured for local switching.

Figure 11-68 *Ethernet to Frame Relay Local Switching Topology*

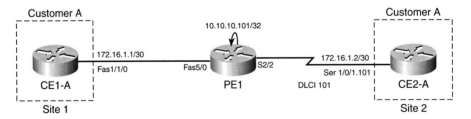

Configuring Ethernet to Frame Relay Local Switching

To configure the topology shown in Figure 11-68, configure local switching on PE. Example 11-68 shows the steps to configure local switching on PE1.

Example 11-68 *Configuring Frame Relay to Ethernet Local Switching*

```
PE1(config)#frame-relay switching
PE1(config-if)#interface Serial2/2
PE1(config-if)# no ip address
PE1(config-if)# encapsulation frame-relay
PE1(config-fr-dlci)# frame-relay intf-type dce
PE1(config-fr-dlci)# exit
PE1(config)# connect ETH-FR fastEthernet 5/0 s2/2 100 interworking ip
```

Final Configurations for Implementation of Ethernet to Frame Relay Local Switching

The final relevant configuration for local switching between Ethernet and Frame Relay circuits is illustrated in Figure 11-69.

Figure 11-69 *Configuration for Local Switching Between Ethernet and Frame Relay Circuits*

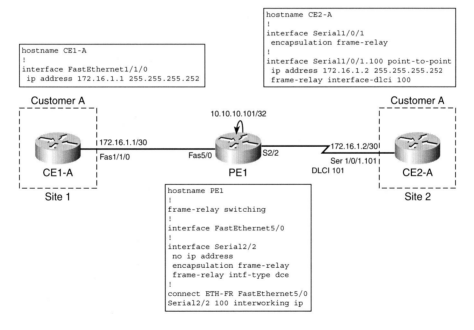

Verify Ethernet to Frame Relay Local Switching

To verify Ethernet to Frame Relay local switching, follow these steps:

Step 1 **Verify Frame Relay connection**—Example 11-69 shows the output of **show connection all**, which shows that local switching is up and operational.

Example 11-69 *Verify Frame Relay to Ethernet Local Switching*

```
PE1#show connection all

ID   Name            Segment 1             Segment 2             State
==========================================================================
11   ETH-FR          Fa5/0                 Se2/2 100             UP
```

Step 2   **Verify connectivity using ping**—Example 11-70 shows that CE1-A has
connectivity to CE2-A.

Example 11-70 *Verify Connectivity in Frame Relay to Ethernet Local Switching*

```
CE1-A#ping 172.16.1.2

Type escape sequence to abort.
Sending 5, 100-byte ICMP Echos to 172.16.1.2, timeout is 2 seconds:
!!!!!
Success rate is 100 percent (5/5), round-trip min/avg/max = 4/4/4 ms
```

Command Reference

Command	Description
Router(config-if)# **pvc** *vpi/vci* **l2transport**	Creates an ATM PVC to specify the encapsulation type on an ATM PVC. **l2transport** is used to specify that the PVC is switched and not terminated.
Router(config-if)#**xconnect** *destination vc-id* **encapsulation mpls**	Enables routing of AToM packets over a specified VC.
Router(config)#**connect** *connection-name interface dlci* {*interface dlci* | **l2transport**}	Defines connections between Frame Relay PVCs in global configuration mode.
Router(config)#**pseudowire-class** *class-name*	Creates a pseudo-wire class.
Router(config-pw-class)# **interworking** {**ethernet** | **ip**}	Enables L2 VPN Interworking. Use the **interworking** command in pseudo-wire class configuration mode.

(Continued)

Command	Description
Router(config)#**connect** *connection-name interface [dlci	pvc	pvp] interface [dlci	pvc	pvp]* [**interworking** *interworking-type*]	Creates Layer 2 data connections between two ports on the same router in global configuration mode.
Router#**show mpls l2transport vc** [**vcid** *vc-id*]	[*vc-id-min vc-id-max*] [**interface** *name* [*local-circuit-id*]] [**destination** *ip-address	name*] [**detail**]	Displays information about AToM VCs that have been enabled to route Layer 2 packets on a router.

CHAPTER 12

Virtual Private LAN Service (VPLS)

In Chapter 11, "Any Transport over MPLS (AToM)," you were introduced to the implementation of Layer 2 VPN using like to like or any to any, point-to-point Layer 2 circuits using AToM. This chapter introduces you to the implementation of multipoint Ethernet Layer 2 VPNs using virtual private LAN services (VPLS). This chapter focuses on

- VPLS overview, components, and operation
- VPLS topology—Single PE or direct attachment
- Hierarchical VPLS—Distributed PE architecture
- VPLS configuration and verification

VPLS Overview

VPLS allows multiple Ethernet LANs from different customer sites to be connected together across the service provider (SP) network, thereby emulating a single Ethernet LAN segment for that customer. Figure 12-1 shows an SP network providing VPLS services in which multiple customer sites (belonging to Customer A) can communicate as if they are connected as a private Ethernet LAN segment. VPLS uses Multiprotocol Label Switching (MPLS) to offer multipoint Ethernet connectivity over a mesh of logical circuits or tunnels, with the added benefits of Traffic Engineering (TE), resilience, and failover. VPLS enables carriers and SPs to offer managed Ethernet VPN services easily and cost effectively.

VPLS Components

The six components that are part of VPLS are as follows:

- **Attachment circuit**—A point-to-point, Layer 2 circuit between a CE router at the customer site to the connected provider edge (PE) router in the provider network. In VPLS, the currently supported attachment circuits are Ethernet in

  - **Port mode**—In port mode, the interface only sends and accepts untagged Ethernet packets.
  - **802.1Q VLAN or trunk mode**—In this mode, the interface is configured as 802.1Q trunk, and it sends and receives only tagged Ethernet VLAN and native VLAN packets.

— **Dot1q tunnel mode**—In this mode, an 802.1Q tunnel is configured and an access VLAN tag is added to the packet at the ingress tunnel interface and removed at the egress tunnel interface. Packets irrespective of being tagged or untagged are forwarded through the 802.1Q tunnel.

Figure 12-1   *VPLS—Emulated LAN Service*

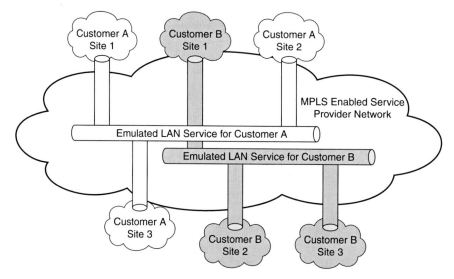

Figure 12-2 depicts attachment circuits for Customer A and Customer B VPLS networks that function in Ethernet port mode (Customer A) and 802.1Q mode (Customer B).

- **Packet Switched Network (PSN) tunnels**—PSN tunnels are built between two PE devices in a PSN to provide transport services for one or more pseudo wires (emulated VCs). In VPLS architecture, the transport is provided over MPLS label switch path (LSP).

- **Pseudo wires**—A pseudo wire is an emulated virtual circuit that connects two attachment circuits (AC) on two different PE routers across an MPLS-enabled provider network. Figure 12-2 shows the pseudo wire between the PE routers, PE1, PE2, and PE3 for Customer A CE sites.

- **Auto-discovery**—Auto-discovery is a mechanism that enables multiple PE routers participating in a VPLS domain to find each other. Auto-discovery, as a result, automates the creation of the LSP mesh. In the absence of auto-discovery, the SP must explicitly identify PEs that are part of a VPLS instance. Therefore, for every VPLS instance on a PE, the SP would have to configure the PE with addresses of all other PEs in that VPLS instance.

- **Auto configuration**—Auto configuration is a mechanism that automatically establishes pseudo wires (emulated VCs) for newly discovered CEs.

- **Virtual Switching Instance (VSI) or Virtual Forwarding Instance (VFI)**—The VSI or VFI is a virtual Layer 2 forwarding entity that defines the VPLS domain membership and resembles virtual switches on PE routers. A VPLS domain consists of Ethernet interfaces or VLANs that belong to the same (virtual) LAN but are connected to multiple PE devices. For example, Customer A's VPLS domain consists of Ethernet interfaces connected to Customer A's CE routers at different sites. The VSI learns remote MAC addresses and is responsible for proper forwarding of the customer traffic to the appropriate end nodes. It is also responsible for guaranteeing that each VPLS domain is loop free. The VSI is responsible for several functions, namely MAC address management, dynamic learning of MAC addresses on physical ports and VCs, aging of MAC addresses, MAC address withdrawal, flooding, and data forwarding.

Figure 12-2 *VPLS Components*

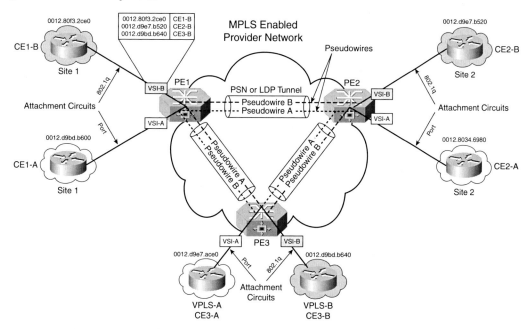

VPLS Operation

VPLS provides an Ethernet multipoint service and typically would involve the following:

- MAC address learning
- MAC address withdrawal

MAC Address Learning

Using a directed LDP session, each PE advertises a VC label mapping that is used as part of the label stack imposed on the Ethernet frames by the ingress PE during packet forwarding. Cisco VPLS learns MAC addresses by using the standard 802.1d (spanning tree) mechanism to learn, age, and filter MAC addresses. Figure 12-3 shows an MPLS-enabled provider network delivering VPLS service to Customer A sites.

Figure 12-3 *MAC Address Learning*

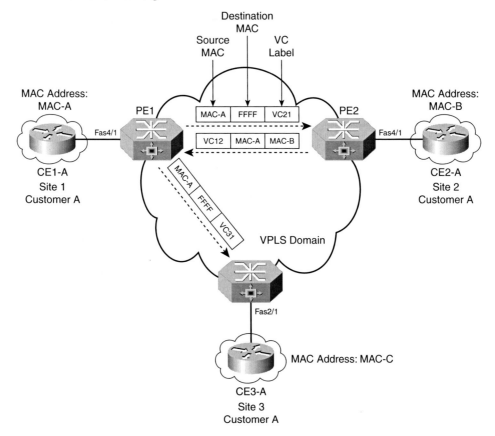

The VPLS network for Customer A is a full mesh of Ethernet pseudo wires. The VPLS instance per customer is assigned a unique Virtual Circuit Identifier (VCI). The emulated VC formed between the PE routers consists of bidirectional LSPs. MAC addresses are learned via the directed LDP label mappings between the PE routers:

1 PE1 and PE2 have IGP reachability and can communicate via the LSP tunnel. As shown in Figure 12-3, PE1 allocates a local Label VC12 for its attached circuit, and this label is propagated to PE2. PE2 allocates Label VC21 and sends this VC label to PE1.

2 A packet from CE1-A destined for CE2-A requires knowledge of the CE2-A MAC address, MAC-B. PE1 and PE2 do not have the information on the location of MAC-B (CE2-A) and MAC-A (CE1-A). Therefore, when the packet leaves CE1-A, the source MAC address is MAC-A, and, because CE1-A does not have knowledge of CE2-A (MAC-B), a broadcast is sent and relayed by PE1 to PE2 and PE3. As shown in

Figure 12-4, PE1 sends a broadcast packet with the source MAC address of CE1-A (MAC-A) to other peers PE2 and PE3 in the VPLS domain. This broadcast packet is sent with the VC Label VC21 to PE2, which was learned from PE2 during the formation of the directed LDP session between PE1 and PE2. Similarly, this broadcast packet is also sent with VC Label VC31 to PE3.

3 PE2 receives the packet from PE1 and associates the source MAC address MAC-A with the inner label (VC label) VC21 and, therefore, concludes that the source MAC address MAC-A is behind PE1 network. Because VC21 was initially assigned and propagated by PE2 to PE1 during the directed LDP session establishment, PE2 can now associate MAC-A with VC21.

As described previously, MAC address learning is done based on the traffic monitoring of customer Ethernet frames. The Forwarding Information Base (FIB) keeps track of the mapping of customer MAC addresses and their associated pseudo wires (VC labels). There are two modes of the MAC address learning process: unqualified and qualified.

In *unqualified learning*, all customer VLANs are handled by a single VSI, essentially sharing a single broadcast domain and MAC address space. This implies that MAC addresses need to be unique and nonoverlapping among customer VLANs; otherwise, they cannot be differentiated within the VSI, which can result in loss of customer frames. An application of unqualified learning is port-based VPLS service for a given customer (for example, where the all traffic received over the CE-PE interface is mapped to a single VSI).

In *qualified learning*, each customer VLAN is assigned its own VSI, which means each customer VLAN has its own broadcast domain and MAC address space. Therefore, in qualified learning, MAC addresses among customer VLANs may overlap with each other, but will be handled correctly because each customer VLAN has its own FIB (i.e., each customer VLAN has its own MAC address space). Because VSI broadcasts multicast frames, qualified learning offers the advantage of limiting the broadcast scope to a given customer VLAN.

MAC Address Withdrawal

MAC address withdrawal occurs during failure of the PE to CE link or when the CE is dual-homed to two different PE routers and the primary link fails. Figure 12-4 shows an example in which the CE is multihomed to a SP and connected via a primary and backup link to different PE routers.

In the absence of the MAC address withdrawal process, the following sequence of events takes place:

1 CE2-A sends traffic to CE1-A.

2 During this process, the primary link fails, and the traffic flow to CE1-A is still being forwarded to PE1 until the entry in the FIB ages out.

3 The primary PE router PE1 would, however, drop the traffic because the link between PE1 and CE1-A is not operational.

Figure 12-4 *VPLS Network Without MAC Address Withdrawal Process*

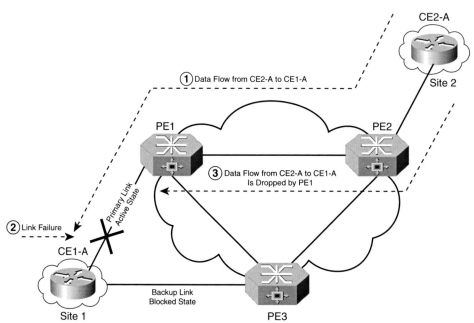

To avoid this situation, an optional MAC Type-Length-Value (TLV) is used to specify a list of MAC addresses that can be removed or relearned, and it is included in the LDP Address Withdraw message. The MAC TLV is an optional TLV and expedites removal of MAC addresses as the result of a topology change when there is a link failure between CE1-A and PE1.

Figure 12-5 shows that PE1 removes any locally learned MAC addresses on failure of the primary link and sends an LDP Withdraw message to remote PEs in the VPLS.

If a notification message with a list of MAC entries to be relearned is sent on the backup (blocked) link, which has transitioned into an active state (e.g., similar to the Topology Change Notification message of 802.1w Rapid STP), the PE will update the MAC entries in its FIB for that VSI and send the LDP Address Withdraw message to other PEs over the corresponding directed LDP sessions.

If the message contains an empty list, the receiving PE removes all the MAC addresses learned for the specified VSI except those learned from the sending PE (MAC address removal is required for all VSI instances that are affected). This mechanism guarantees consistency in MAC address withdrawal under all circumstances.

Figure 12-5 *With MAC Address Withdrawal Process*

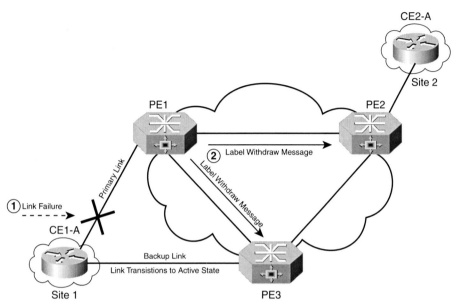

VPLS Topology—Single PE or Direct Attachment

The single PE or direct attachment architecture uses a flat architecture and supports Ethernet port, 802.1Q VLAN, and dot1q tunnel modes. The CEs are directly connected to the PE routers, and this architecture involves the creation of a separate VSI for each customer. Customer traffic originating from the CE in native Ethernet or VLAN tagged frames are MPLS encapsulated with an AToM stack. Direct attachment VPLS also uses a full mesh of directed LDP and tunnel LSPs between all the PE routers. Although this creates signaling overhead, the real detriment to large-scale deployment is the packet replication requirements for each provisioned VC on a PE router. Due to scalability constraints, this solution is suitable only for simple implementations. Figure 12-6 shows a direct attachment VPLS architecture providing VPLS services to Customers A and B.

Customer A's network has CE routers CE1-A, CE2-A, and CE3-A connected to PEs PE1, PE2, and PE3, respectively. Links to CE1-A, CE2-A, and CE3-A are configured as switch access ports on PE1, PE2, and PE3. Customer B's CE devices, CE1-B, CE2-B, and CE3-B, are configured as 802.1Q trunk ports to PE1, PE2, and PE3, respectively. Figure 12-7 shows the data forwarding that takes place in a direct attachment VPLS architecture using port and 802.1Q modes.

Figure 12-6 *Direct Attachment VPLS Network*

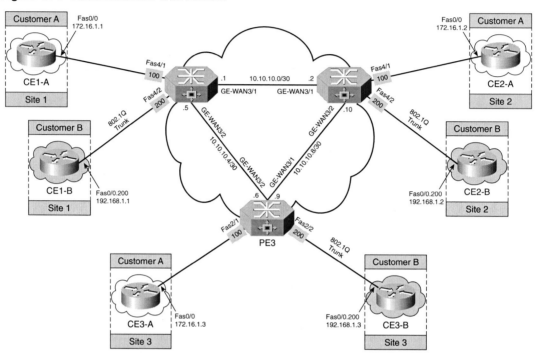

Figure 12-7 *VPLS Data Forwarding in Port and 802.1Q Mode*

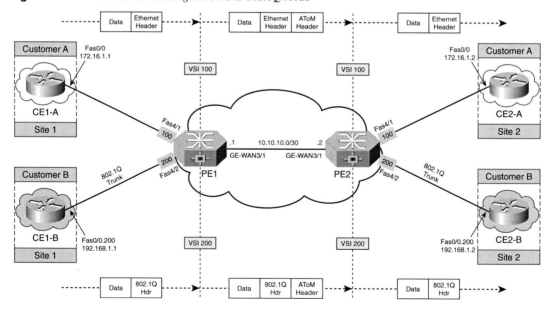

Configuration Flowchart for Direct Attachment VPLS

To achieve a functional VPLS network, there are two important steps. The first step is to ensure that the SP's network comprising PE1, PE2, and PE3 is enabled for MPLS forwarding. Example 12-1 shows the provider network configurations for PE1, PE2, and PE3. Throughout this chapter, you will use these as provider network configurations.

Example 12-1 *Provider Network Configuration for MPLS Forwarding*

```
!PE1
hostname PE1
!
mpls label protocol ldp
mpls ldp discovery targeted-hello accept
mpls ldp router-id Loopback0 force
!
interface Loopback0
 ip address 10.10.10.101 255.255.255.255
!
interface GE-WAN3/1
description connected to PE2
 ip address 10.10.10.1 255.255.255.252
 negotiation auto
 mpls ip
 mls qos trust dscp
!
interface GE-WAN3/2
description connected to PE3
 ip address 10.10.10.5 255.255.255.252
 negotiation auto
 mpls ip
 mls qos trust dscp
!
router ospf 1
 network 10.0.0.0 0.255.255.255 area 0
!PE2
hostname PE2
!
mpls label protocol ldp
mpls ldp discovery targeted-hello accept
mpls ldp router-id Loopback0 force
!
interface Loopback0
 ip address 10.10.10.102 255.255.255.255
!
interface GE-WAN3/1
description connected to PE1
 ip address 10.10.10.2 255.255.255.252
 negotiation auto
 mpls ip
 mls qos trust dscp
```

continues

Example 12-1 *Provider Network Configuration for MPLS Forwarding (Continued)*

```
!
interface GE-WAN3/2
description connected to PE3
 ip address 10.10.10.9 255.255.255.252
 negotiation auto
 mpls ip
 mls qos trust dscp
!
router ospf 1
 network 10.0.0.0 0.255.255.255 area 0
!PE3
hostname PE3
!
mpls label protocol ldp
mpls ldp router-id Loopback0
!
interface Loopback0
 ip address 10.10.10.103 255.255.255.255
!
interface GE-WAN3/1
description connected to PE2
 ip address 10.10.10.10 255.255.255.252
 negotiation auto
 mpls ip
 mls qos trust dscp
!
interface GE-WAN3/2
description connected to PE1
 ip address 10.10.10.6 255.255.255.252
 negotiation auto
 mpls ip
 mls qos trust dscp
!
router ospf 1
 network 10.0.0.0 0.255.255.255 area 0
```

The second step is to configure the VPLS service, and Figure 12-8 illustrates the configuration flowchart on the PE router to provision Ethernet port mode, Ethernet 802.1Q VLAN, and Ethernet dot1Q tunnel mode.

Direct Attachment VPLS Configuration
Scenario 1—Using Port and 802.1Q VLAN Modes

The objective of this configuration scenario is to demonstrate VPLS network using port and 802.1Q VLAN mode. As shown in Figure 12-7, Customer A VPLS network uses port mode and Customer B VPLS network uses 802.1Q VLAN mode.

Figure 12-8 *VPLS Service Configuration Flowchart on PE Router*

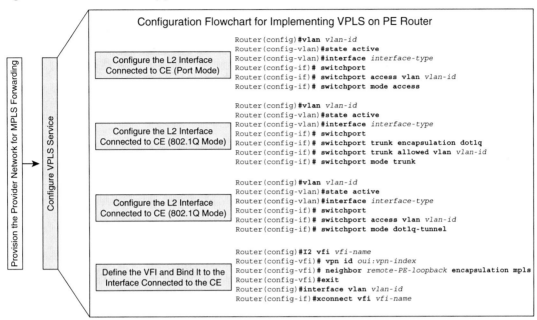

Table 12-1 shows the MAC address associated with CE routers.

Table 12-1 *MAC Address for CE Routers*

Router	MAC Address
Customer A	
CE1-A	0012.d9bd.b600
CE2-A	0012.8034.6980
CE3-A	0012.d9e7.ace0
Customer B	
CE1-B	0012.80f3.2ce0
CE2-B	0012.d9e7.b520
CE3-B	0012.d9bd.b640

The steps to configure the topology shown in Figure 12-6 are as follows:

Step 1   **Configure the interface connected to CE device**—In this step, you
configure the interfaces on the PE router connected to the CE routers for
Customer A as an access port (untagged)and Customer B as an 802.1Q
trunk port (tagged). See Example 12-2.

Example 12-2 *Configure the Two Interfaces Connected to CE Device*

```
PE1(config)#vlan 100
PE1(config-vlan)#state active
PE1(config-vlan)#vlan 200
PE1(config-vlan)#state active
PE1(config)#interface fastEthernet 4/1
PE1(config-if)#description VPLS Customer A (CE1-A)
PE1(config-if)#switchport
PE1(config-if)#switchport access vlan 100
PE1(config-if)#switchport mode access
PE1(config-if)#interface FastEthernet4/2
PE1(config-if)#description VPLS Customer B (CE1-B)
PE1(config-if)#switchport
PE1(config-if)#switchport trunk encapsulation dot1q
PE1(config-if)#switchport trunk allowed vlan 200
PE1(config-if)#switchport mode trunk
```

Step 2   **Define the VFI and bind it to the interface connected to the CE**—In this step, the VFI is configured. After defining the VFI, it is associated to one or more attachment circuits (interfaces, subinterfaces, or virtual circuits). The VFI specifies the VPN ID of a VPLS domain, the addresses of other PE routers in this domain, and the type of tunnel signaling and encapsulation (currently only MPLS is supported) mechanism for each peer.

An MPLS VPN ID is used to identify VPNs by a VPN identification number, as described in RFC 2685. This MPLS VPN ID is implemented to identify a VPN. The MPLS VPN ID feature does not control the distribution of routing information or associate IP addresses with MPLS VPN ID numbers in routing updates. Multiple VPNs can be configured in a router. You can use a VPN name (a unique ASCII string) to reference a specific VPN configured in the router. Alternately, you can use a VPN ID to identify a particular VPN in the router. The VPN ID follows a standard specification (RFC 2685). To ensure that the VPN has a consistent VPN ID, assign the same VPN ID to all the routers in the SP network that services that VPN. Each VPN ID defined by RFC 2685 consists of the following two elements:

- **Organizational unique identifier (OUI)**—A three-octet hex number that is assigned by the IEEE Registration Authority to any company that manufactures components under the ISO/IEC 8802 standard. The OUI generates universal LAN MAC addresses and protocol identifiers for use in LAN and MAN applications. For example, an OUI for Cisco Systems is 00-03-6B (hex).

- **VPN index**—A four-octet hexadecimal number, which identifies the VPN within the company. Use the **vpn id** command and specify the VPN ID in the following format:

  vpn id *oui:vpn-index*

  A colon separates the OUI from the VPN index.

Example 12-3 shows the steps to configure VFI and associate it to the attachment circuit.

Example 12-3 *Step 3: Define the VFI and Associate It to the Attachment Circuit*

```
PE1(config)#l2 vfi Cust_A manual
PE1(config-vfi)# vpn id 100
PE1(config-vfi)# neighbor 10.10.10.102 encapsulation mpls
PE1(config-vfi)# neighbor 10.10.10.103 encapsulation mpls
PE1(config-vfi)#l2 vfi Cust_B manual
PE1(config-vfi)#vpn id 200
PE1(config-vfi)#neighbor 10.10.10.102 encapsulation mpls
PE1(config-vfi)#neighbor 10.10.10.103 encapsulation mpls
PE1(config)#interface vlan 100
PE1(config-if)#xconnect vfi Cust_A
PE1(config-if)#interface vlan 200
PE1(config-if)#xconnect vfi Cust_B
```

Verification of VPLS Connectivity

To verify VPLS connectivity, follow these steps:

Step 1 **Ensure that directed LDP session is operational**—Example 12-4 shows the output of the **show mpls l2transport vc** command. The output indicates the pseudo wire is functional for transporting Layer 2 packets across the MPLS backbone.

Example 12-4 *Output of* **show mpls l2transport vc** *on PE1*

```
PE1#show mpls l2transport vc
Local intf      Local circuit      Dest address      VC ID      Status
-----------     ----------------   ---------------   --------   ----------
VFI Cust_A      VFI                10.10.10.102      100        UP
VFI Cust_B      VFI                10.10.10.102      200        UP
VFI Cust_A      VFI                10.10.10.103      100        UP
VFI Cust_B      VFI                10.10.10.103      200        UP
```

Step 2 **Verify MPLS and VC label**—Example 12-5 shows the output of **show mpls l2transport vc** *vc-number* **detail** where the VC ID is 100, and the directed LDP peer is 10.10.10.102 and 10.10.10.103. The VC label on PE1 for the outgoing interface on PE2 connected to CE2-A is 21, and it allocates VC Label 21 for the interface connected to CE1-A. With the directed LDP peer 10.10.10.103, the VC label on PE1 for the outgoing interface on PE2 connected to CE3-A is 17, and it allocates VC Label 22 for the interface connected to CE1-A.

Example 12-5 **show mpls l2transport vc** *on PE1*

```
PE1#show mpls l2transport vc 100 detail
Local interface: VFI Cust_A up
  Destination address: 10.10.10.102, VC ID: 100, VC status: up
    Tunnel label: imp-null, next hop 10.10.10.2
      Output interface: GE3/1, imposed label stack {21}
```

continues

Example 12-5 **show mpls l2transport vc** *on PE1 (Continued)*

```
        Create time: 10:13:08, last status change time: 10:06:25
        Signaling protocol: LDP, peer 10.10.10.102:0 up
          MPLS VC labels: local 21, remote 21
          Group ID: local 0, remote 0
          MTU: local 1500, remote 1500
          Remote interface description:
        Sequencing: receive disabled, send disabled
        VC statistics:
          packet totals: receive 973, send 971
          byte totals:   receive 77383, send 77244
          packet drops:  receive 0, send 0

  Local interface: VFI Cust_A up
    Destination address: 10.10.10.103, VC ID: 100, VC status: up
        Tunnel label: imp-null, next hop 10.10.10.6
        Output interface: GE3/2, imposed label stack {17}
        Create time: 10:13:09, last status change time: 10:06:45
        Signaling protocol: LDP, peer 10.10.10.103:0 up
          MPLS VC labels: local 22, remote 17
          Group ID: local 0, remote 0
          MTU: local 1500, remote 1500
          Remote interface description:
        Sequencing: receive disabled, send disabled
        VC statistics:
          packet totals: receive 90, send 977
          byte totals:   receive 8560, send 77712
          packet drops:  receive 0, send 0
```

In Example 12-6, **show mpls l2transport summary** shows the total number of the VCs that are active.

Example 12-6 *Output of* **show mpls l2 summary** *on PE3*

```
PE1#show mpls l2transport summary
Destination address: 10.10.10.102, total number of vc: 2
  0 unknown, 2 up, 0 down, 0 admin down
  2 active vc on MPLS interface GE3/1
Destination address: 10.10.10.103, total number of vc: 2
  0 unknown, 2 up, 0 down, 0 admin down
  2 active vc on MPLS interface GE3/2
```

In Example 12-7, **show vfi** shows the remote PE neighbors to which the pseudo wires are configured. The command will show the neighbors even if the pseudo wire is down.

Example 12-7 *Output of* **show vfi** *on PE1*

```
PE1#show vfi Cust_A
VFI name: Cust_A, state: up
  Local attachment circuits:
    Vlan100
  Neighbors connected via pseudowires: 10.10.10.102  10.10.10.103
```

Example 12-8 shows the MAC addresses learned by PE Router PE1.

Example 12-8 *Output of* **show mac-address-table vlan** *on PE1*

```
PE1#show mac-address-table vlan 100
Legend: * - primary entry

  vlan   mac address     type     learn          ports
------+---------------+--------+-----+------------------------
*  100   0012.d9e7.ace0  dynamic  Yes
*  100   0012.8034.6980  dynamic  Yes
*  100   0012.d9bd.b600  dynamic  Yes    Fa4/1

PE1#show mac-address-table vlan 200
Legend: * - primary entry

  vlan   mac address     type     learn          ports
------+---------------+--------+-----+------------------------
*  200   0012.d9e7.b520  dynamic  Yes
*  200   0012.80f3.2ce0  dynamic  Yes    Fa4/2
*  200   0012.d9bd.b640  dynamic  Yes
```

VPLS Configurations on PE Router

Example 12-9 shows the relevant VPLS configurations on PE Routers PE1, PE2, and PE3.

Example 12-9 *VPLS Configurations on PE1, PE2, and PE3*

```
!PE1
hostname PE1
!
l2 vfi Cust_A manual
 vpn id 100
 neighbor 10.10.10.102 encapsulation mpls
 neighbor 10.10.10.103 encapsulation mpls
!
l2 vfi Cust_B manual
 vpn id 200
 neighbor 10.10.10.102 encapsulation mpls
 neighbor 10.10.10.103 encapsulation mpls
!
interface FastEthernet4/1
 description VPLS Customer A - CE1-A
 no ip address
 switchport
 switchport access vlan 100
 switchport mode access
!
interface FastEthernet4/2
 description VPLS Customer B
 no ip address
 switchport
 switchport trunk encapsulation dot1q
```

continues

Example 12-9 *VPLS Configurations on PE1, PE2, and PE3 (Continued)*

```
 switchport trunk allowed vlan 200
 switchport mode trunk
!
interface Vlan100
 no ip address
 xconnect vfi Cust_A
!
interface Vlan200
 no ip address
 xconnect vfi Cust_B
!PE2
hostname PE2
!
l2 vfi Cust_A manual
 vpn id 100
 neighbor 10.10.10.101 encapsulation mpls
 neighbor 10.10.10.103 encapsulation mpls
!
l2 vfi Cust_B manual
 vpn id 200
 neighbor 10.10.10.101 encapsulation mpls
 neighbor 10.10.10.103 encapsulation mpls
!
interface FastEthernet4/1
 description VPLS Customer A
 no ip address
 switchport
 switchport access vlan 100
 switchport mode access
!
interface FastEthernet4/2
 description VPLS Customer B
 no ip address
 switchport
 switchport trunk encapsulation dot1q
 switchport trunk allowed vlan 200
 switchport mode trunk
!
interface Vlan100
 no ip address
 xconnect vfi Cust_A
!
interface Vlan200
 no ip address
xconnect vfi Cust_B
!PE3
hostname PE3
!
l2 vfi Cust_A manual
 vpn id 100
 neighbor 10.10.10.101 encapsulation mpls
 neighbor 10.10.10.102 encapsulation mpls
```

Example 12-9   *VPLS Configurations on PE1, PE2, and PE3 (Continued)*

```
!
l2 vfi Cust_B manual
 vpn id 200
 neighbor 10.10.10.101 encapsulation mpls
 neighbor 10.10.10.102 encapsulation mpls
!
interface FastEthernet2/1
 description VPLS Customer A
 no ip address
 switchport
 switchport access vlan 100
 switchport mode access
!
interface FastEthernet2/2
 description VPLS Customer B
 no ip address
 switchport
 switchport trunk encapsulation dot1q
 switchport trunk allowed vlan 200
 switchport mode trunk
!
interface Vlan100
 no ip address
 xconnect vfi Cust_A
!
interface Vlan200
 no ip address
 xconnect vfi Cust_B
```

CE Router Configurations for Customer A and Customer B

Example 12-10 shows the configurations for Customer A's and Customer B's CE devices.

Example 12-10   *CE Router Configurations*

```
!CE1-A
hostname CE1-A
!
interface FastEthernet0/0
ip address 172.16.1.1 255.255.255.0
```

```
!CE1-B
hostname CE1-B
!
interface FastEthernet0/0.200
 encapsulation dot1Q 200
 ip address 192.168.1.1 255.255.255.0
```

```
!CE2-A
hostname CE2-A
!
interface FastEthernet0/0
ip address 172.16.1.2 255.255.255.0
```

continues

Example 12-10 *CE Router Configurations (Continued)*

```
!CE2-B
hostname CE2-B
!
interface FastEthernet0/0.200
 encapsulation dot1Q 200
 ip address 192.168.1.2 255.255.255.0
!CE3-A
hostname CE3-A
!
interface FastEthernet0/0
 ip address 172.16.1.3 255.255.255.0
!CE3-B
hostname CE3-B
!
interface FastEthernet0/0.200
 encapsulation dot1Q 200
 ip address 192.168.1.3 255.255.255.0
```

Direct Attachment VPLS Configuration Scenario 2—Using Dot1q Tunnel Mode and Layer 2 Protocol Tunneling

Figure 12-9 shows a direct attachment VPLS network that is providing VPLS service to Customer A and B networks. The objective of this configuration scenario is to demonstrate dot1q tunnel mode configuration and the usage of Layer 2 tunnel protocol for CDP in Customer A's VPLS network. Customer B's VPLS network has Site 2 dual-homed to the SP network via user PE (u-PE23). Customer B network is used primarily to demonstrate how STP is tunneled and to prevent Layer 2 loops when a site has redundant links to the provider network. Figure 12-9 shows the VPLS topology used to demonstrate

- Layer 2 tunnel protocol for CDP and STP
- VPLS redundancy

Prior to configuring this scenario, you will be introduced to the following basic concepts:

- **Cisco 802.1Q tunneling** (also called Cisco 802.1Q-in-Q)—802.1Q tunneling enables SPs to use a single VLAN to securely transport most or all of a customer's VLANs across the MAN or WAN backbone. In 802.1Q tunneling, IOS adds an additional 802.1Q tag to customer traffic in the switch at the edge of the SP's network to keep each customer's VLAN traffic segregated and private. The tag, therefore, allows customer VLANs to be backhauled across a single SP VLAN through the use of a tunnel port that is assigned to each customer site. All of a single customer's VLANs that are configured in the tunnel port on the SP's WAN edge switch are aggregated and backhauled over a single VLAN.

Figure 12-9 *Direct Attachment VPLS Using Dot1q Tunnel Mode and Layer 2 Protocol Tunneling*

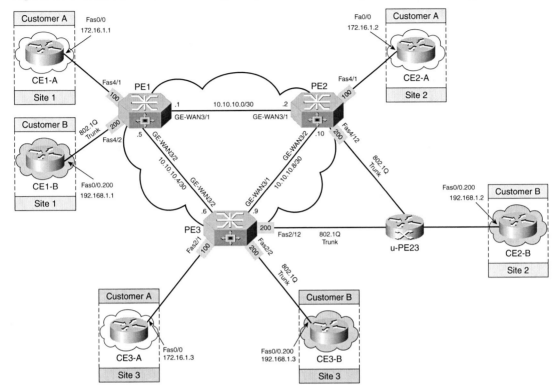

Service providers, therefore, do not have to assign a unique VLAN ID number to each individual customer VLAN, which quickly consumes the 4094 VLAN space supported by Ethernet's 802.1Q technology. In this way, encapsulating multiple customer 802.1Q VLANs into a single SP 802.1Q VLAN affords SPs a scalable approach to offering Ethernet services.

- **Dot1q tunnel mode**—In the VPLS network when using the dot1q tunnel mode, the 802.1Q tag is not used because the provider's MPLS network is used as a transit network in which the tunnel label is used to transport data packets from ingress PE to egress PE. Therefore, the tunnel label replaces the 802.1Q tag when the Layer 2 switch interface is configured to use the dot1q tunnel mode. Example 12-11 shows the configuration to enable dot1q tunnel mode on a switch port interface.

Example 12-11 *Dot1q Tunnel Mode Configuration*

```
Router(config-if)#switchport mode dot1q-tunnel
```

- **Layer 2 protocol tunneling**—In VPLS networks, Layer 2 switch ports by default drop STP and VTP packets. To avoid this, Layer 2 protocol tunneling allows Layer 2 protocol data units (PDUs), like CDP, STP, and VTP, to be tunneled through a network. As shown in Figure 12-9, if Layer 2 protocol tunneling is not enabled, CE1-A will not see CE2-A and CE3-A as CDP neighbors. Example 12-12 shows the configuration to enable Layer 2 protocol tunneling for CDP on switch port interfaces.

Example 12-12 *Configuring Layer 2 Protocol Tunneling*

```
Router(config-if)#l2protocol-tunnel cdp
```

The steps to configure the topology shown in Figure 12-9 are as follows:

Step 1 **Configure the switch port interface connected to CE device**—In this step, you configure the interfaces on the PE router connected to the CE routers for Customer A in dotq tunnel mode (untagged). Also, enable the interface for Layer 2 protocol tunneling. Example 12-13 shows the configuration on PE1 for interface 4/1 connected to CE1-A. Similarly, enable dot1q tunnel mode and Layer 2 protocol tunneling for CDP on 4/1 and 2/1 on PE2 and PE3, respectively.

Example 12-13 *Configure the Layer 2 Interface Connected to CE Device*

```
PE1(config)#interface fastEthernet 4/1
PE1(config-if)#description VPLS Customer A (CE1-A)
PE1(config-if)#switchport
PE1(config-if)# switchport access vlan 100
PE1(config-if)#switchport mode dot1q-tunnel
PE1(config-if)#l2protocol-tunnel cdp
PE2(config)#vlan 20
PE2(config-vlan)#state active
PE2(config-vlan)#no spanning-tree vlan 20,200
PE2(config)#interface FastEthernet4/12
PE2(config-if)# switchport
PE2(config-if)# switchport trunk encapsulation dot1q
PE2(config-if)# switchport trunk native vlan 20
PE2(config-if)# switchport trunk allowed vlan 20,200
PE3(config)#vlan 20
PE3(config-vlan)#state active
PE3(config-vlan)#no spanning-tree vlan 20,200
PE3(config)#interface FastEthernet2/12
PE3(config-if)# switchport
PE3(config-if)# switchport trunk encapsulation dot1q
PE3(config-if)# switchport trunk native vlan 20
PE3(config-if)# switchport trunk allowed vlan 20,200
```

For Customer B, the configurations for switch interface 4/2 on PE1 and PE2 are the same as shown in the earlier section. However, CE2B is connected to u-PE23, and u-PE23 is dual-homed to the provider network at PE2 (4/12) and PE3 (2/12). The configuration on u-PE23 is shown in Example 12-14.

Example 12-14 *Configuration of u-PE23*

```
u-PE23(config)#spanning-tree mode mst
u-PE23(config)#spanning-tree mst configuration
u-PE23(config-mst)# name instance1
u-PE23(config-mst)# revision 1
u-PE23(config-mst)# instance 1 vlan 200
u-PE23(config)#interface FastEthernet0/11
u-PE23(config-if)# description connected to n-PE3
u-PE23(config-if)# switchport trunk encapsulation dot1q
u-PE23(config-if)# switchport trunk native vlan 20
u-PE23(config-if)# switchport trunk allowed vlan 20,200
u-PE23(config-if)# switchport mode trunk
u-PE23(config-if)#interface FastEthernet0/12
u-PE23(config-if)# description connected to n-PE2
u-PE23(config-if)# switchport trunk encapsulation dot1q
u-PE23(config-if)# switchport trunk native vlan 20
u-PE23(config-if)# switchport trunk allowed vlan 20,200
u-PE23(config-if)# switchport mode trunk
u-PE23(config-if)#interface FastEthernet0/2
u-PE23(config-if)# description connected to CE2-B
u-PE23(config-if)# switchport trunk encapsulation dot1q
u-PE23(config-if)# switchport trunk allowed vlan 200
u-PE23(config-if)# switchport mode trunk
```

Step 2   **Define the VFI and bind it to the interface connected to the CE**—For
Customer A and Customer B, the VFI configuration step is similar to
section "Direct Attachment VPLS Configuration Scenario 1—Using Port
and 802.1Q VLAN Modes." Because the u-PE23 router multihomes with
PE2 and PE3, spanning tree needs to be configured on the u-PE23 for
pseudo wires that exist between the u-PE23 and PE2 and u-PE23 and
PE3 routers, respectively. It is optional to configure spanning tree
on PE Routers PE2 and PE3. In this case, PE2 and PE3 routers do not
process BPDUs and only forward or relay them. Assuming spanning
tree is configured on PE2 and PE3, they exchange and process BPDUs
with each other and with u-PE23. To make PE2 and PE3 relay BPDUs
an additional VFI, STP is configured to relay the BPDUs for MST
instance configured on u-PE23. Example 12-15 shows the steps to
configure VFI and associate it to the attachment circuit (in this case,
native VLAN 20).

Example 12-15 *Define the VFI and Associate It to the Attachment Circuit*

```
PE2(config)#l2 vfi STP manual
PE2(config-vfi)# vpn id 20
PE2(config-vfi)# neighbor 10.10.10.103 encapsulation mpls
PE2(config)#interface vlan 20
PE2(config-if)#xconnect vfi STP
```
```
PE3(config)#l2 vfi STP manual
PE3(config-vfi)#vpn id 20
```

continues

Example 12-15 *Define the VFI and Associate It to the Attachment Circuit (Continued)*

```
PE3(config-vfi)#neighbor 10.10.10.102 encapsulation mpls
PE3(config)#interface vlan 20
PE3(config-if)#xconnect vfi STP
```

Verify Layer 2 Protocol Tunneling for CDP and MSTP

To verify Layer 2 protocol tunneling for CDP and MSTP, follow these steps:

Step 1   Verify Layer 2 protocol tunneling—Example 12-16 provides the status of Layer 2 protocol tunneling on PE Routers PE2 and PE3. It also shows that Layer 2 protocols, CDP and STP, are being tunneled.

Example 12-16 *Verify Layer 2 Protocol Tunneling*

```
PE2#show l2protocol-tunnel summary
COS for Encapsulated Packets: 5
Drop Threshold for Encapsulated Packets: 0

Port     Protocol    Shutdown            Drop                Status
                     Threshold           Threshold
                     (cdp/stp/vtp)       (cdp/stp/vtp)
-------  ----------  ----------------    ----------------    ----------
Fa4/1    cdp --- ---  ----/----/----      ----/----/----     up
Fa4/12   --- stp ---  ----/----/----      ----/----/----     up
PE3#show l2protocol-tunnel summary
COS for Encapsulated Packets: 5
Drop Threshold for Encapsulated Packets: 0

Port     Protocol    Shutdown            Drop                Status
                     Threshold           Threshold
                     (cdp/stp/vtp)       (cdp/stp/vtp)
-------  ----------  ----------------    ----------------    ----------
Fa2/1    cdp --- ---  ----/----/----      ----/----/----     up
Fa2/12   --- stp ---  ----/----/----      ----/----/----     up
```

Step 2   Layer 2 protocol tunneling (CDP)—Example 12-17 shows the output of the **show cdp neighbors** command in which CE1-A sees CE2-A and CE3-A as CDP neighbors, and CE2-A sees CE1-A and CE3-A as CDP neighbors.

Example 12-17 **show cdp neighbor** *on CE1-A and CE2-A*

```
CE1-A#show cdp neighbors
Capability Codes: R - Router, T - Trans Bridge, B - Source Route Bridge
                 S - Switch, H - Host, I - IGMP, r - Repeater
Device ID       Local Intrfce     Holdtme    Capability  Platform  Port ID
CE2-A           Fas 0/0           132          R S       2611XM    Fas 0/0
CE3-A           Fas 0/0           170          R S       2621XM    Fas 0/0
```

Example 12-17 show cdp neighbor *on CE1-A and CE2-A (Continued)*

```
CE2-A#show cdp neighbors
Capability Codes: R - Router, T - Trans Bridge, B - Source Route Bridge
                  S - Switch, H - Host, I - IGMP, r - Repeater
Device ID        Local Intrfce     Holdtme    Capability  Platform  Port ID
CE3-A            Fas 0/0           130            R S      2621XM    Fas 0/0
CE1-A            Fas 0/0           158            R S      2621XM    Fas 0/0
```

Step 3   **Verify spanning tree**—Example 12-18 shows that fas0/11 on u-PE23 is in forwarding state, and fas0/12 is in blocking state. This shows that STP is being tunneled through and that the forwarding loop no longer exists.

Example 12-18 show spanning-tree mst *on u-PE23*

```
u-PE23#show spanning-tree mst 1
###### MST01         vlans mapped:    200
Bridge       address 000b.fd2a.6b00  priority  32769 (32768 sysid 1)
Root         this switch for MST01


Interface        Role Sts Cost      Prio.Nbr Type
---------------- ---- --- --------- -------- --------------------------------
Fa0/2            Desg FWD 200000    128.2    P2p
Fa0/11           Desg FWD 200000    128.11   P2p
Fa0/12           Back BLK 200000    128.12   P2p
```

PE Configurations

Example 12-19 shows the configurations on the PE router.

Example 12-19 *Configurations on PE Routers, PE1, PE2, PE3, and u-PE23*

```
!PE1
hostname PE1
!
l2 vfi Cust_A manual
 vpn id 100
 neighbor 10.10.10.102 encapsulation mpls
 neighbor 10.10.10.103 encapsulation mpls
!
l2 vfi Cust_B manual
 vpn id 200
 neighbor 10.10.10.102 encapsulation mpls
 neighbor 10.10.10.103 encapsulation mpls
!
vlan internal allocation policy ascending
vlan dot1q tag native
!
!
interface Loopback0
 ip address 10.10.10.101 255.255.255.255
!
interface FastEthernet4/1
 description VPLS Customer A (CE1-A)
```

continues

Example 12-19 *Configurations on PE Routers, PE1, PE2, PE3, and u-PE23 (Continued)*

```
 no ip address
 switchport
 switchport access vlan 100
 switchport mode dot1q-tunnel
 l2protocol-tunnel cdp
 no cdp enable
 spanning-tree bpdufilter enable
!
interface FastEthernet4/2
 description VPLS Customer B (CE1-B)
 no ip address
 switchport
 switchport trunk encapsulation dot1q
 switchport trunk allowed vlan 200
 switchport mode trunk
!
interface Vlan20
 no ip address
xconnect vfi STP

interface Vlan100
 no ip address
xconnect vfi Cust_A
!
interface Vlan200
 no ip address
 no ip igmp snooping
 xconnect vfi Cust_B
```

```
!PE2
hostname PE2
!
l2 vfi Cust_A manual
 vpn id 100
 neighbor 10.10.10.101 encapsulation mpls
 neighbor 10.10.10.103 encapsulation mpls
!
l2 vfi Cust_B manual
 vpn id 200
 neighbor 10.10.10.101 encapsulation mpls
 neighbor 10.10.10.103 encapsulation mpls
!
l2 vfi STP manual
 vpn id 20
 neighbor 10.10.10.103 encapsulation mpls
!
interface FastEthernet4/1
 description VPLS Customer A
 no ip address
 switchport
 switchport access vlan 100
 switchport mode dot1q-tunnel
 l2protocol-tunnel cdp
```

Example 12-19 *Configurations on PE Routers, PE1, PE2, PE3, and u-PE23 (Continued)*

```
 no cdp enable
 spanning-tree bpdufilter enable
!
interface FastEthernet4/12
 no ip address
 switchport
 switchport trunk encapsulation dot1q
 switchport trunk native vlan 20
 switchport trunk allowed vlan 20,200
 l2protocol-tunnel stp
 spanning-tree bpdufilter enable
!
interface Vlan20
 no ip address
xconnect vfi STP
!
interface Vlan100
 no ip address
xconnect vfi Cust_A
!
interface Vlan200
 no ip address
 no ip igmp snooping
 xconnect vfi Cust_B
```

```
!PE3
hostname PE3
!
l2 vfi Cust_A manual
 vpn id 100
 neighbor 10.10.10.101 encapsulation mpls
 neighbor 10.10.10.102 encapsulation mpls
!
l2 vfi Cust_B manual
 vpn id 200
 neighbor 10.10.10.101 encapsulation mpls
 neighbor 10.10.10.102 encapsulation mpls
!
l2 vfi STP manual
 vpn id 20
 neighbor 10.10.10.102 encapsulation mpls
!
interface FastEthernet2/1
 description VPLS Customer A
 no ip address
 switchport
 switchport access vlan 100
 switchport mode dot1q-tunnel
 l2protocol-tunnel cdp
 no cdp enable
 spanning-tree bpdufilter enable
```

continues

Example 12-19 *Configurations on PE Routers, PE1, PE2, PE3, and u-PE23 (Continued)*

```
!
interface FastEthernet2/2
 description VPLS Customer B
 no ip address
 switchport
 switchport trunk encapsulation dot1q
 switchport trunk allowed vlan 200
 switchport mode trunk
!
interface FastEthernet2/12
 no ip address
 switchport
 switchport trunk encapsulation dot1q
 switchport trunk native vlan 20
 switchport trunk allowed vlan 20,200
 l2protocol-tunnel stp
 spanning-tree bpdufilter enable
!
interface Vlan20
 no ip address
 no ip igmp snooping
 xconnect vfi STP
!
interface Vlan100
 no ip address
 xconnect vfi Cust_A
!
interface Vlan200
 no ip address
 xconnect vfi Cust_B
!u-PE2
hostname u-PE2
!
ip subnet-zero
!
vtp domain Cust_B
vtp mode transparent
!
spanning-tree mode mst
spanning-tree extend system-id
!
spanning-tree mst configuration
 name instance1
 revision 1
 instance 1 vlan 200
!
interface FastEthernet0/2
 description connected to CE2-B
 switchport trunk encapsulation dot1q
 switchport trunk allowed vlan 200
 switchport mode trunk
 spanning-tree bpdufilter enable
```

Example 12-19 *Configurations on PE Routers, PE1, PE2, PE3, and u-PE23 (Continued)*

```
!
interface FastEthernet0/11
 description connected to n-PE3
 switchport trunk encapsulation dot1q
 switchport trunk native vlan 20
 switchport trunk allowed vlan 20,200
 switchport mode trunk
!
interface FastEthernet0/12
 description connected to n-PE2
 switchport trunk encapsulation dot1q
 switchport trunk native vlan 20
 switchport trunk allowed vlan 20,200
 switchport mode trunk
```

CE Configurations for Customers A and B

Refer to Example 12-10 for configurations of Customer A's and B's CE devices.

Hierarchical VPLS—Distributed PE Architecture

A hierarchical VPLS (H-VPLS) model allows SPs to interconnect geographically dispersed Ethernet LAN networks. A hierarchical VPLS service is implemented by splitting the physical PE device into many separate physical devices (distributed PE). Therefore, in this architecture, there are two types of PE devices:

- **User facing PE (u-PE)**—CE devices connect to u-PEs directly. A u-PE typically has a single connection to the network PE (n-PE) device placed in the MPLS backbone. The u-PE aggregates the VPLS traffic received from CEs prior to forwarding the same to the n-PE where VPLS forwarding takes place based on the VSI (MAC address learning and switching).

- **Network PE (n-PE)**—u-PEs in an H-VPLS network connect to n-PEs where VPLS information is forwarded based on the VSI. The most common form of implementation uses IEEE 802.1Q encapsulation and tunneling. A double 802.1Q encapsulation, also called Q-in-Q encapsulation, can be implemented to aggregate traffic between u-PE and n-PE. The Q-in-Q trunk, therefore, becomes an access port to a VPLS instance on an n-PE. The network PE devices are connected in a basic VPLS full mesh. For each VPLS service, a single-spoke pseudo wire is set up between the u-PE and n-PE. These pseudo wires get terminated on a virtual bridge instance on the u-PE and the network PE devices. Spoke pseudo wires can be implemented using any L2 tunneling mechanism, such as MPLS (AToM) or Q-in-Q (double tagging with 802.1Q VLAN tags). The network PE devices can function as a hub, with the user PE forming the spokes. The architecture, therefore, evolves itself to form a two-tier H-VPLS

network because the VPLS core pseudo wire, formed between the network PE
devices, is augmented with access pseudo wires formed between the network PE and
u-PE devices.

Figure 12-10 shows a H-VPLS network with Q-in-Q tunnels between n-PE and u-PE
devices. In this architecture, a full mesh of directed LDP sessions is maintained between
n-PE routers. The u-PEs, u-PE1, u-PE2, and u-PE3, connect to the CE devices as well as
to the n-PEs.

Figure 12-10 *H-VPLS Using Q-in-Q Tunnels*

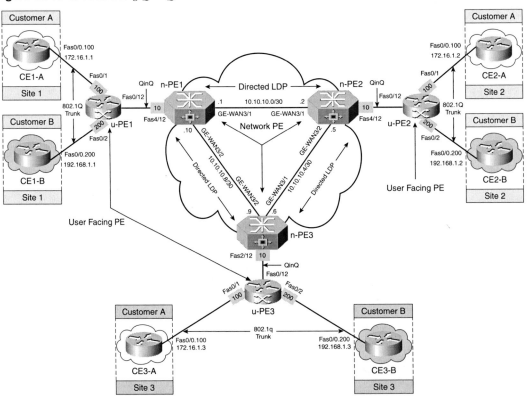

The spoke pseudo wires are Q-in-Q encapsulated (an 802.1Q VLAN frame encapsulated in
another 802.1Q VLAN frame), which allows for customer separation while maintaining
customer-specific VLAN information intact. The customer VLAN-tagged traffic is
encapsulated in the MPLS backbone with AToM stack and tunneled as Q-in-Q tunnels
between u-PE and n-PE.

Figure 12-10 illustrates two customers, Customer A and Customer B, having CE devices
located at different sites that are connected to the VPLS provider using Q-in-Q access
tunnels. Each customer has its own internal VLANs for workgroup separation. Customer A

belongs to VLAN 100 and Customer B to VLAN 200. The objective is to ensure VLAN-to-VLAN connectivity between the different sites belonging to Customer A and Customer B. In the data forwarding and encapsulation process, customers locally generate traffic on each of their workgroup VLANs. The traffic is tagged by customer LAN switches, with appropriate VLAN tags for workgroup isolation, and is sent toward the SP (VLAN tag 100 for Customer A and VLAN tag 200 for Customer B). The u-PE places an additional VLAN tag (VLAN Tag 10) for the traffic originating from the CE device. This traffic is then sent by the u-PE to the network PE, where it is processed according to the VSI for that customer. Outer VLAN tags 100 and 200 are replaced by AToM label stack (LSP label, VC label) and sent across the MPLS backbone.

H-VPLS deployment, therefore, eliminates the need for a full mesh of tunnels as well as a full mesh of pseudo wires per service between all devices participating in the VPLS implementation. It minimizes packet replication and signaling overhead because fewer pseudo wires are required for the VPLS service.

Figure 12-11 shows the data plane forwarding for VPLS architecture using Q-in-Q mode.

Figure 12-11 *Data Plane Forwarding for Network Using Q-in-Q Mode*

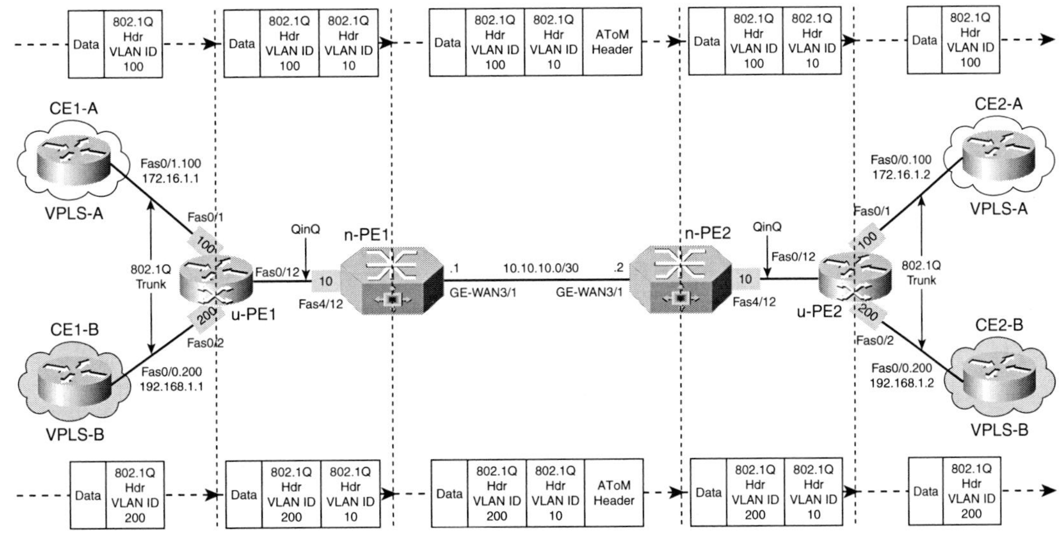

Configuration Flowchart for H-VPLS Using Q-in-Q Mode

Refer to Example 12-1 for configuration related to the provider network.

Figure 12-12 shows the steps to configure H-VPLS using Q-in-Q mode.

Figure 12-12 *Configuration Flowchart: H-VPLS Q-in-Q Mode*

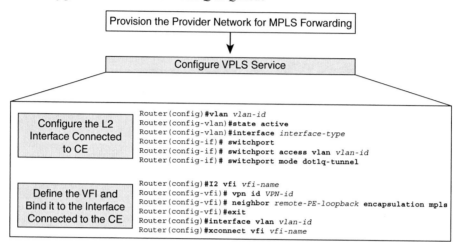

H-VPLS Configuration Scenario 1—802.1Q Tunneling (Q-in-Q)

The steps to configure the network topology shown in Figure 12-10 are

Step 1 **Configure the Layer 2 interface connected to u-PE device for 802.1Q**—In this step, the interface on the n-PE routers connected to the u-PE device for 802.1Q tunneling is configured. This is illustrated in Example 12-20.

Example 12-20 *Configuring the Layer 2 Interface Connected to u-PE Device*

```
PE1(config)#vlan 10
PE1(config-vlan)#state active
PE1(config-vlan)#interface FastEthernet4/12
PE1(config-if)# description link to u-PE1
PE1(config-if)# switchport
PE1(config-if)# switchport access vlan 10
PE1(config-if)# switchport mode dot1q-tunnel
PE2(config)#vlan 10
PE2(config-vlan)#state active
PE2(config-if)#interface FastEthernet4/12
PE2(config-if)# description link to u-PE2
PE2(config-if)# switchport
PE2(config-if)# switchport access vlan 10
PE2(config-if)# switchport mode dot1q-tunnel
PE3(config)#vlan 100
PE3(config-vlan)#state active
PE3(config-if)#interface FastEthernet4/12
```

Example 12-20 *Configuring the Layer 2 Interface Connected to u-PE Device (Continued)*

```
PE3(config-if)# description link to u-PE3
PE3(config-if)# switchport
PE3(config-if)# switchport access vlan 10
PE3(config-if)# switchport mode dot1q-tunnel
```

Step 2   **Define the VFI and bind it to the interface connected to the CE**—In
this step, the VFI is configured. After defining the VFI, you must bind it
to one or more attachment circuits (interfaces, subinterfaces, or virtual
circuits). The VFI on the n-PE specifies the VPN ID of a VPLS domain,
the addresses of other PE routers in this domain, and the type of tunnel
signaling and encapsulation (currently, only MPLS encapsulation is
supported) mechanism for each peer (shown in Example 12-21).

Example 12-21 *Define the VFI and Associate It to the Attachment Circuit*

```
n-PE1(config-vfi)#l2 vfi QinQ manual
n-PE1(config-vfi)# vpn id 10
n-PE1(config-vfi)# neighbor 10.10.10.101 encapsulation mpls
n-PE1(config-vfi)# neighbor 10.10.10.103 encapsulation mpls
n-PE1(config-vlan)#interface vlan 10
n-PE1(config-if)#xconnect vfi QinQ
n-PE2(config-vfi)#l2 vfi QinQ manual
n-PE2(config-vfi)# vpn id 10
n-PE2(config-vfi)# neighbor 10.10.10.101 encapsulation mpls
n-PE2(config-vfi)# neighbor 10.10.10.103 encapsulation mpls
n-PE2(config-vlan)#interface vlan 10
n-PE2(config-if)#xconnect vfi QinQ
n-PE3(config)#l2 vfi QinQ manual
n-PE3(config-vfi)# vpn id 10
n-PE3(config-vfi)# neighbor 10.10.10.101 encapsulation mpls
n-PE3(config-vfi)# neighbor 10.10.10.102 encapsulation mpls
n-PE3(config-vlan)#interface vlan 10
n-PE3(config-if)#xconnect vfi QinQ
```

Verification of VPLS Service

The steps to verify VPLS for the topology shown in Figure 12-10 are as
follows:

Step 1   **Ensure that the directed LDP session is operational**—Example 12-22
shows the output of **show mpls l2transport vc**. The output indicates that
the AToM VC is functional to transport L2 packets across the MPLS
backbone. Example 12-22 shows the output of **show mpls l2transport
vc** on the n-PEs.

Example 12-22 show mpls l2transport vc *Output on n-PE1, n-PE2, and n-PE3*

```
n-PE1#show mpls l2transport vc
Local intf     Local circuit          Dest address      VC ID      Status
-------------  --------------------   ---------------   ----------  ----------
VFI QinQ       VFI                    10.10.10.102       10         UP
VFI QinQ       VFI                    10.10.10.103       10         UP
n-PE2#show mpls l2transport vc
Local intf     Local circuit          Dest address      VC ID      Status
-------------  --------------------   ---------------   ----------  ----------
VFI QinQ       VFI                    10.10.10.101       10         UP
VFI QinQ       VFI                    10.10.10.103       10         UP
n-PE3#show mpls l2transport vc
Local intf     Local circuit          Dest address      VC ID      Status
-------------  --------------------   ---------------   ----------  ----------
VFI QinQ       VFI                    10.10.10.101       10         UP
VFI QinQ       VFI                    10.10.10.102       10         UP
```

Step 2 **Verify data plane forwarding information**—Issue the **show mpls forwarding-table** command on the n-PEs, as shown in Example 12-23.

Example 12-23 show mpls forwarding-table *Output on n-PE1, n-PE2, and n-PE3*

```
n-PE1#show mpls forwarding-table
Local  Outgoing    Prefix           Bytes tag  Outgoing   Next Hop
tag    tag or VC   or Tunnel Id     switched   interface
16     Untagged    l2ckt(10)        44744      Et2        point2point
17     Untagged    l2ckt(10)        10612      Et2        point2point
18     Pop tag     10.10.10.8/30    0          GE3/2      10.10.10.6
       Pop tag     10.10.10.8/30    0          GE3/1      10.10.10.2
19     Pop tag     10.10.10.103/32  0          GE3/2      10.10.10.6
20     Pop tag     10.10.10.102/32  0          GE3/1      10.10.10.2
n-PE2#show mpls forwarding-table
Local  Outgoing    Prefix           Bytes tag  Outgoing   Next Hop
tag    tag or VC   or Tunnel Id     switched   interface
16     Pop tag     10.10.10.101/32  0          GE3/1      10.10.10.1
17     Untagged    l2ckt(10)        44404      Et2        point2point
18     Pop tag     10.10.10.4/30    0          GE3/2      10.10.10.10
       Pop tag     10.10.10.4/30    0          GE3/1      10.10.10.1
19     Untagged    l2ckt(10)        5734       Et2        point2point
20     Pop tag     10.10.10.103/32  0          GE3/2      10.10.10.10
n-PE3#show mpls forwarding-table
Local  Outgoing    Prefix           Bytes tag  Outgoing   Next Hop
tag    tag or VC   or Tunnel Id     switched   interface
16     Untagged    l2ckt(10)        45373      Et3        point2point
17     Untagged    l2ckt(10)        39407      Et3        point2point
19     Pop tag     10.10.10.101/32  0          GE3/2      10.10.10.5
20     Pop tag     10.10.10.102/32  0          GE3/1      10.10.10.9
```

Step 3 **Verify MPLS bindings, VC type, and pseudo-wire neighbors**—
Example 12-24 shows the output of **show mpls l2transport binding** on
n-PE1 where the VC type is Ethernet, which is default unless the remote
PE supports only VC type 4 (Ethernet VLAN).

Example 12-24 show mpls l2transport binding *on n-PE1*

```
n-PE1#show mpls l2transport binding
  Destination Address: 10.10.10.102,  VC ID: 10
    Local Label:  16
        Cbit: 0,     VC Type: Ethernet,      GroupID: 0
        MTU: 1500,     Interface Desc: n/a
    Remote Label: 16
        Cbit: 0,     VC Type: Ethernet,      GroupID: 0
        MTU: 1500,     Interface Desc: n/a
  Destination Address: 10.10.10.103,  VC ID: 10
    Local Label:  17
        Cbit: 0,     VC Type: Ethernet,      GroupID: 0
        MTU: 1500,     Interface Desc: n/a
    Remote Label: 17
        Cbit: 0,     VC Type: Ethernet,      GroupID: 0
        MTU: 1500,     Interface Desc: n/a
```

Example 12-25 shows the output of **show mpls l2transport summary** outlining the total number of active VCs. Comparing this output with Example 12-6, it shows that a single VC is required to establish Layer 2 connectivity as compared to two VCs, shown in Example 12-6. In H-VPLS, a single pseudo wire is required irrespective of the number of customers.

Example 12-25 *Output of* **show mpls l2transport summary** *on n-PE1*

```
n-PE1#show mpls l2transport summary
Destination address: 10.10.10.102, total number of vc: 1
  0 unknown, 1 up, 0 down, 0 admin down
  1 active vc on MPLS interface GE3/1
Destination address: 10.10.10.103, total number of vc: 1
  0 unknown, 1 up, 0 down, 0 admin down
  1 active vc on MPLS interface GE3/2
```

PE Configurations

The configurations for n-PE devices, n-PE1, n-PE2, and n-PE3, are shown in Example 12-26.

Example 12-26 *n-PE Configurations*

```
!n-PE1
hostname n-PE1
!
mpls label protocol ldp
mpls ldp discovery targeted-hello accept
mpls ldp router-id Loopback0
!
l2 vfi QinQ
 vpn id 10
 neighbor 10.10.10.102 encapsulation mpls
```

continues

Example 12-26 *n-PE Configurations (Continued)*

```
 neighbor 10.10.10.103 encapsulation mpls
 !
vlan internal allocation policy ascending
vlan dot1q tag native
 !
interface Loopback0
 ip address 10.10.10.101 255.255.255.255
 !
interface FastEthernet4/12
 no ip address
 switchport
 switchport access vlan 10
 switchport mode dot1q-tunnel
 !
interface Vlan10
 no ip address
 xconnect vfi QinQ
!n-PE2
hostname n-PE2
 !
mpls label protocol ldp
mpls ldp discovery targeted-hello accept
mpls ldp router-id Loopback0
 !
l2 vfi QinQ
 vpn id 10
 neighbor 10.10.10.101 encapsulation mpls
 neighbor 10.10.10.103 encapsulation mpls
 !
vlan internal allocation policy ascending
vlan dot1q tag native
 !
interface Loopback0
 ip address 10.10.10.102 255.255.255.255
 !
interface FastEthernet4/12
 no ip address
 switchport
 switchport access vlan 10
 switchport mode dot1q-tunnel
 !
interface Vlan10
 no ip address
 xconnect vfi QinQ
!n-PE3
hostname n-PE3
 !
mpls label protocol ldp
mpls ldp discovery targeted-hello accept
mpls ldp router-id Loopback0
 !
l2 vfi QinQ
```

Example 12-26 *n-PE Configurations (Continued)*

```
vpn id 10
 neighbor 10.10.10.101 encapsulation mpls
 neighbor 10.10.10.102 encapsulation mpls
!
vlan internal allocation policy ascending
vlan dot1q tag native
!
interface Loopback0
 ip address 10.10.10.103 255.255.255.255
!
interface FastEthernet2/12
 no ip address
 switchport
 switchport access vlan 10
 switchport mode dot1q-tunnel
!
interface Vlan10
 no ip address
 xconnect vfi QinQ
```

u-PE Configurations

Example 12-27 shows configurations on the u-PE devices, u-PE1, u-PE2, and u-PE3.

Example 12-27 *u-PE Configurations*

```
!u-PE1
hostname u-PE1
!
vlan 100,200
!
interface FastEthernet0/1
description connected to CE1-A
 switchport access vlan 100
 switchport trunk encapsulation dot1q
 switchport mode dot1q-tunnel
 no cdp enable
 spanning-tree bpdufilter enable
!
interface FastEthernet0/2
description connected to CE1-B
 switchport access vlan 200
 No switchport trunk encapsulation dot1q
 switchport mode dot1q-tunnel
 no cdp enable
 spanning-tree bpdufilter enable
!
interface FastEthernet0/12
description connected to n-PE1
 no switchport trunk encapsulation dot1q
```

continues

Example 12-27 *u-PE Configurations (Continued)*

```
 switchport trunk allowed vlan 100,200
 switchport mode trunk
!u-PE2
hostname u-PE2
!
vlan 100,200
!
interface FastEthernet0/1
description connected to CE2-A
 switchport access vlan 100
 No switchport trunk encapsulation dot1q
 switchport mode dot1q-tunnel
 no cdp enable
 spanning-tree bpdufilter enable
!
interface FastEthernet0/2
description connected to CE2-B
 switchport access vlan 200
 No switchport trunk encapsulation dot1q
 switchport mode dot1q-tunnel
 no cdp enable
 spanning-tree bpdufilter enable
!
interface FastEthernet0/12
description connected to n-PE2
 switchport trunk encapsulation dot1q
 switchport trunk allowed vlan 100,200
 switchport mode trunk
!u-PE3
hostname u-PE3
!
vlan 100,200
!
interface FastEthernet0/1
description connected to CE3-A
 switchport access vlan 100
 No switchport trunk encapsulation dot1q
 switchport mode dot1q-tunnel
 no cdp enable
 spanning-tree bpdufilter enable
!
interface FastEthernet0/2
description connected to CE3-B
 switchport access vlan 200
 No switchport trunk encapsulation dot1q
 switchport mode dot1q-tunnel
 no cdp enable
 spanning-tree bpdufilter enable
!
interface FastEthernet0/12
description connected to n-PE3
```

Example 12-27 *u-PE Configurations (Continued)*

```
switchport trunk encapsulation dot1q
switchport trunk allowed vlan 100,200
switchport mode trunk
```

CE Configurations for Customer A and Customer B

The configurations for Customer A and Customer B CE devices are shown in
Example 12-28.

Example 12-28 *CE Configurations for Customer A and B*

```
!CE1-A
hostname CE1-A
!
interface FastEthernet0/0.100
 encapsulation dot1Q 100
 ip address 172.16.1.1 255.255.255.0
!CE1-B
hostname CE1-B
!
interface FastEthernet0/0.200
 encapsulation dot1Q 200
 ip address 192.168.1.1 255.255.255.0
!CE2-A
hostname CE2-A
!
interface FastEthernet0/0.100
 encapsulation dot1Q 100
 ip address 172.16.1.1 255.255.255.0
!CE2-B
hostname CE2-B
!
interface FastEthernet0/0.200
 encapsulation dot1Q 200
 ip address 192.168.1.2 255.255.255.0
!CE3-A
hostname CE3-A
!
interface FastEthernet0/0.100
encapsulation dot1Q 100
ip address 172.16.1.1 255.255.255.0
!CE3-B
hostname CE3-B
!
interface FastEthernet0/0.200
 encapsulation dot1Q 200
 ip address 192.168.1.3 255.255.255.0
```

Command Reference

Command	Description
Router(config)#**l2 vfi** *vfi-name* **manual**	Enables the L2 VFI manual configuration mode.
Router(config-vfi)#**vpn id** *oui:vpn-index*	Configures a VPN ID for a VPLS domain. The emulated VCs bound to this L2 VRF use this VPN ID for signaling.
Router(config-vfi)#**neighbor** *remote-router-id* **encapsulation mpls**	Specifies the remote peering router ID and the tunnel encapsulation type or the pseudo-wire property to be used to set up the emulated VC.
Router(config-vfi)#**xconnect vfi** *vfi name*	Specifies the L2 VFI that you are binding.
Router(config-vfi)#**shutdown**	Disconnects all emulated VCs previously established under the L2VFI and prevents the establishment of new attachment circuits.
Router(config)#**mpls label protocol** **{ldp	tdp}**	Specifies the default label distribution protocol for a platform.
Router(config)#**mpls ldp logging** **neighbor-changes** (optional)	Determines logging neighbor changes.
Router(config)#**mpls ldp discovery {hello	targeted-hello}** *{holdtime	interval}* **seconds**	Configures the interval between transmission of LDP (TDP) discovery hello messages or the hold time for a LDP transport connection.
Router(config)#**mpls ldp router-id** **loopback0 force**	Assigns the loopback as the source of TDP/LDP messages.
Router(config)#**mpls ip**	Enables label switching of IPv4 packets on an interface.
Router(config-if)#**mls qos trust** **[cos	dscp	ip-precedence]**	Sets the trusted state of an interface to specify that the ToS bits in the incoming packets contain a DSCP value.
Router(config-if)#**switchport**	Modifies the switching characteristics of the Layer 2-switched interface.
Router(config-if)#**switchport trunk** **encapsulation dot1q**	Sets the switch port encapsulation format to 802.1Q. Modifies the switching characteristics of the Layer 2-switched interface.
Router(config-if)#**switchport mode trunk** **switchport trunk allowed** *vlan*	Sets the interface to a trunking VLAN Layer 2 interface. Sets the list of allowed VLANs.

(Continued)

Command	Description
Router(config-if)#**switchport access vlan** *vlan-id*	Sets the VLAN when the interface is in access mode.
Router(config-if)#**switchport mode** [**access**l **trunk**l **dot1q-tunnel**]	Sets the interface as an 802.1Q tunnel port.
Router(config-if)#**l2protocol-tunnel** [**cdp** l **stp** l **vtp**]	Enables protocol tunneling on an interface.

CHAPTER 13

Implementing Quality of Service in MPLS Networks

Quality of service (QoS) is an integral part of large networks to enable service differentiation as well as to determine the priorities assigned to a variety of traffic classes. With an increase in the adoption of technologies such as Voice over IP (VoIP) by large enterprises around the world, the need for service differentiation by the service provider offering Internet or intranet services has achieved greater significance. This chapter deals with QoS theory and configuration applicable to MPLS networks using the Differentiated Services (Diff-Serv) model.

Introduction to QoS—Classification and Marking

In its simplistic form, *QoS is the ability to differentiate diverse classes of traffic based on predefined or user-defined criteria and assign priorities based on traffic variables that affect the treatment of traffic on each router in the network.* QoS, when implemented, becomes a requirement for end-to-end service delivery. In some cases, QoS might not be chosen for implementation in networks with excess bandwidth on links. However, it is recommended practice to implement QoS where different classes of traffic are to be transported across the SP network.

The first and foremost step in the deployment of QoS is to identify the various traffic classes that need to be supported by the network. Traffic can be classified based on type of traffic (voice, applications, data, etc.) and on properties of the traffic pattern. After traffic has been classified into different classes, the next step is to identify what QoS operations will be performed on each of these classes on the local router. *Note that although QoS is an end-to-end implementation, it is traditionally configured on all routers in the path from one end to the other.* However, various portions of the network can be configured with different QoS schemes to handle different types of traffic. The process of defining the QoS operations for a certain traffic class is also called Service Policy definition. Finally, after the policies are defined, they are *applied* on the device interface. Implementation of QoS, therefore, involves the following steps:

Step 1   Classification of traffic based on predefined or user-defined criteria

Step 2   Configuration of device for QoS policies for each of the predefined or identified classes

Step 3   Association of QoS policy/policies to an interface

In the Diff-Serv model, the routers or L3 switches in the network are configured for QoS policies that can be applied to a traffic class traversing the router. Simplistically, traffic classes can be defined by the type of traffic, such as voice, video, and data. Data traffic can also be segregated into different traffic classes based on the type of data (application versus best effort) using QoS. This mechanism where the router classifies and then applies a QoS policy based on the classification is often called the *Per-Hop-Behavior* (PHB) of the router.

Classification and Marking

Classification is the first step in the implementation of QoS. The criteria used to classify data can be based on the IP header values such as the IP address ranges, IP Precedence, DSCP, CoS, or, more recently, MPLS EXP bits. In the classification stage, the router identifies traffic that will map to each of the classes to be configured.

Following classification, the router can also perform *marking* of packets that map to a certain class. In the marking action, the router associates the packet with a unique parameter after identification of traffic pertaining to a class. This unique parameter will be used in subsequent routers to identify or, in QoS terms, classify the traffic. The common marking options available on Cisco routers and switches are IP Precedence, DSCP, CoS, ToS bits, QoS group, and MPLS EXP values.

IP Precedence, DSCP, and ToS Relationships

Figure 13-1 shows the IPv4 packet header with an 8-bit *type of service* (ToS) field. The ToS field was conventionally used to provide QoS in IP networks. However, since the advent of the Diff-Serv model, it has been replaced by the implementation of IP Precedence or DSCP values.

The higher order 3 bits in the TOS field, shown in Figure 13-1, map to the IP Precedence value assigned to the IP packet. The predefined values used to identify the IP Precedence are shown in Table 13-1.

The most important values for IP Precedence in the implementation of QoS are the *Critical, Flash Overrides, and Flash* priorities. It is common practice to implement an IP Precedence of Critical (5) for VoIP traffic or time-sensitive/real-time traffic, Flash override (4) for video traffic, and Flash (3) for higher class data traffic. All other traffic is usually mapped into best-effort or routine (0) traffic.

DSCP, as shown in Figure 13-1, is an extension of IP Precedence and can be still coded in context to the ToS value in an IP header. The DSCP value is the IP Precedence implemented along with a *Delay, Throughput, and Reliability* variable. DSCP is 6 bits in length and functions as the higher order 6 bits of the ToS byte. Therefore, the higher order 3 bits of the ToS byte as well as DSCP map to IP Precedence. In the implementation of DSCP, the delay and throughput variables collectively are called the *drop probability*. The reliability bit is not used in DSCP implementations today and is usually set to a value of 0. The most common values of DSCP that you will implement are the expedited forwarding (EF) as well as the assured forwarding (AF) classes.

Figure 13-1 *IP Packet Header*

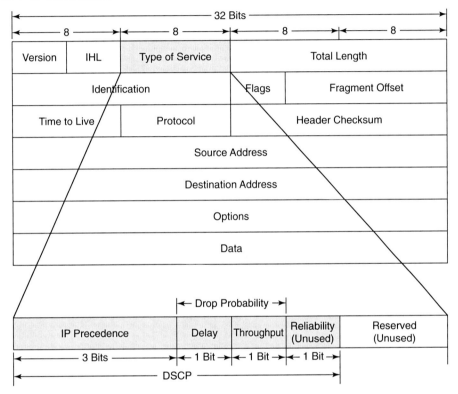

Table 13-1   *IP Precedence Values*

IP Precedence Value	Binary Value	Priority
0	000	Routine
1	001	Priority
2	010	Immediate
3	011	Flash
4	100	Flash Override
5	101	Critical
6	110	Internetwork Control
7	111	Network Control

The drop probability bits can be set to three values, as shown in Table 13-2: low drop (01), medium drop (10), or high drop (11).

Table 13-2 *Drop Probability Values in DSCP*

Drop Probability	Value
Low drop	01
Medium drop	10
High drop	11

DSCP accommodates additional granularity by implementation of 6 bits versus 3 in IP Precedence and ToS. As shown in Figure 13-2, the EF class directly maps to the IP Precedence value of 5, which is used for real-time traffic patterns. Figure 13-2 also shows the AF class where the IP Precedence value of 4 is used as the top-most 3 bits of the AF class. Further granularity is provided by classification of the traffic as either low drop (AF41), medium drop (AF42), or high drop (AF43) within the AF class.

Figure 13-2 *DSCP Classes*

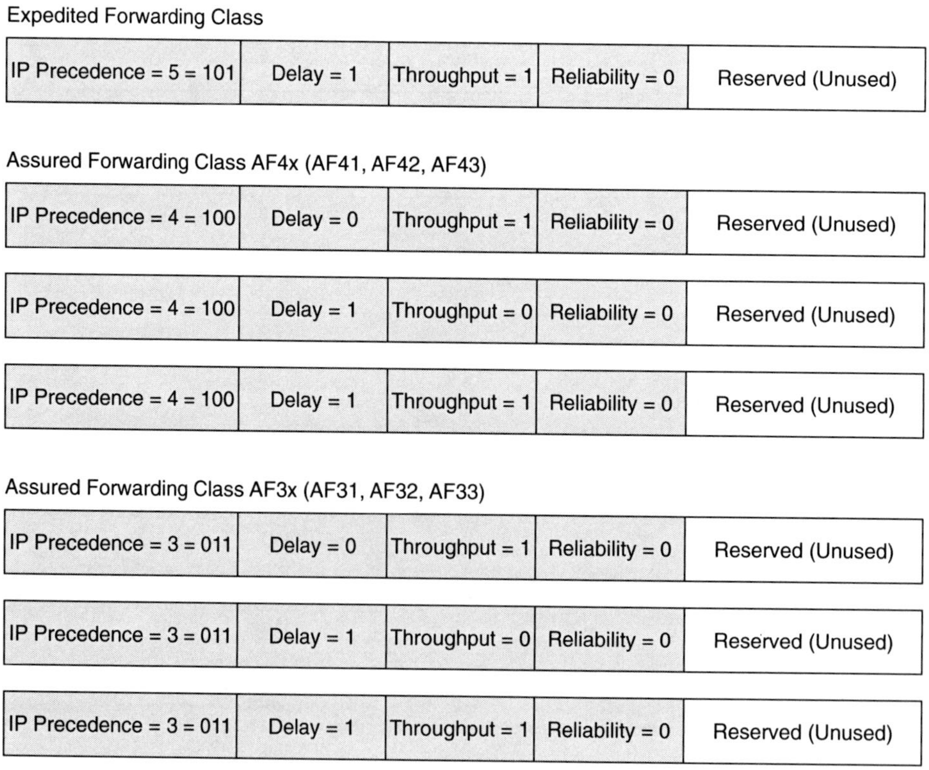

Expedited Forwarding Class

IP Precedence = 5 = 101	Delay = 1	Throughput = 1	Reliability = 0	Reserved (Unused)

Assured Forwarding Class AF4x (AF41, AF42, AF43)

IP Precedence = 4 = 100	Delay = 0	Throughput = 1	Reliability = 0	Reserved (Unused)

IP Precedence = 4 = 100	Delay = 1	Throughput = 0	Reliability = 0	Reserved (Unused)

IP Precedence = 4 = 100	Delay = 1	Throughput = 1	Reliability = 0	Reserved (Unused)

Assured Forwarding Class AF3x (AF31, AF32, AF33)

IP Precedence = 3 = 011	Delay = 0	Throughput = 1	Reliability = 0	Reserved (Unused)

IP Precedence = 3 = 011	Delay = 1	Throughput = 0	Reliability = 0	Reserved (Unused)

IP Precedence = 3 = 011	Delay = 1	Throughput = 1	Reliability = 0	Reserved (Unused)

The AF classes for IP Precedence 2 and 1 can be derived by replacing the IP Precedence bits with 010 or 001, respectively. (For brevity, Figure 13-2 does not depict this).

MPLS EXP Bit Marking

When traversing from an IP domain to an MPLS domain, IP QoS can be mapped to MPLS QoS using the MPLS EXP bits in the MPLS labels. As mentioned in Chapter 1, "MPLS Overview," the 3 bits map one-to-one with IP Precedence values. Therefore, when transitioning an IP domain containing DSCP markings versus IP Precedence markings, if more than one DSCP value is used per AF class, care must be taken to preserve granularity of the IP QoS as it traverses the MPLS domain because more than one AF subclass (for example, AF41, AF42) might map to the same MPLS EXP bit marking. The format of the MPLS label has been depicted in Figure 13-3.

Figure 13-3 *MPLS Label Format*

It is important to note that in the implementation of label stacks, matching of data pertaining to a premarked MPLS EXP value can be done only on the top label in the label stack. You will be provided with more information in the following sections on how label stacks and QoS implementations work in tandem.

Congestion Management, Congestion Avoidance, Traffic Shaping, and Policing

When implementing QoS, a common term used is *queuing*. Cisco offers a variety of queuing strategies that manage resources where congestion might occur. In traditional networks, the transition from a LAN (10/100/1000 Mbps) to a WAN (T1/T3/OC-x) makes the gateway in between a congestion point. In such cases, queuing might be configured on the gateway at the network edge where the enterprise network connects to the SP network for intersite or Internet connectivity.

Congestion management is the process of selectively queuing packets on routers so that the higher priority packets associated to a class are transmitted first during congestion. It is assumed that the reader understands various queuing strategies such as priority queuing (PQ), custom queuing (CQ), weighted fair queuing (WFQ), class-based weighted fair queuing (CBWFQ), low latency queuing (LLQ), and modified and weighted deficit round robin (only on Cisco 12000 series). Coverage of the nuances of these queuing strategies is beyond the scope of this book. For more information on these queuing strategies, visit the Cisco Systems website at Cisco.com.

Congestion avoidance is the process of selectively dropping packets prior to the queues reaching 100% of their maximum queue depth, at which time all subsequent packets are dropped. This process of dropping all packets when the queue is full is called *tail-drop*. Within each queue, depending on the queuing strategy, a minimum and maximum threshold can be configured so that, between these thresholds, the packets are dropped at increasing probability. The mechanism used for congestion avoidance is called *Weighted Random Early Detection* (WRED), which to a large extent overcomes tail-drop issues per queue on a router. When queuing is performed on a router interface, tail-drop occurs per queue in the absence of random early detection. With random early detection, the queue never reaches 100 percent of its depth and, therefore, no tail-dropping of packets occurs. Different WRED probabilities can also be associated to various queues on a per interface basis that enables differential dropping of packets per class associated with a certain queue.

The process of enforcing a policy by discarding packets in accordance to a traffic profile associated with a class is done using policing and/or shaping. In its most generic form, policing and shaping are alike except that policing drops *all* packets that do not conform to a policy whereas shaping *buffers* packets that do not conform to a QoS policy. Therefore, policing is an aggressive procedure where all packets that exceed a certain bandwidth limitation are dropped.

The following congestion management and avoidance schemes can be used in conjunction with MPLS:

- FIFO—Congestion management
- Modified deficit round robin on GSR 12000 series—Congestion management
- CBWFQ with LLQ—Congestion management
- WRED—Congestion avoidance
- Traffic shaping and policing

In summary, the QoS mechanisms that are performed on a packet, also called the PHB or per-hop behavior, can consist of the following functions:

- Classification
- Marking
- Congestion management—Queuing
- Congestion avoidance—Selective dropping
- Traffic policing and shaping

Figure 13-4 outlines these QoS functions and how they can be implemented on a router.

As shown in Figure 13-4, classification and marking are traditionally performed on ingress. In some cases, classification can also be done on egress. Congestion management, avoidance, and traffic shaping and policing are usually performed on egress. Note that policing can also be performed on ingress, but shaping cannot be implemented on ingress.

Figure 13-4 *QoS Mechanisms*

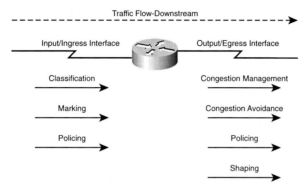

MPLS QoS Implementation

When implementing QoS over MPLS infrastructure, the Edge LSR between the IP and MPLS domains performs translation from the IP QoS domain to the MPLS QoS domain or vice versa. Specifically, an IP packet can enter a MPLS domain (for example, CE-PE); this is called the IP2MPLS condition. In some cases, the packet can be applied a label stack, and one of the labels in the label stack might have the EXP bit manipulated; this is called a MPLS2MPLS condition. Finally, a labeled packet might be converted to an appropriate IP packet (as in the case of an egress LSR in PE-CE conditions), and this is referred to as the MPLS2IP condition.

In the IP2MPLS condition, the IP packet is given a MPLS label. During this procedure, if the incoming IP packet has an associated IP Precedence, this value is copied to the MPLS EXP field, as shown in Figure 13-5. Cisco routers copy IP Precedence bits from the L3 header into MPLS EXP bits on label imposition when functioning as an ingress PE router.

In the MPLS2MPLS condition, the incoming packet is a labeled packet. Therefore, in the MPLS2MPLS condition, three actions, namely Push, Pop, or Swap, can be performed. As illustrated in Figure 13-5, in the MPLS2MPLS Push condition, an incoming labeled packet is given another label. In the MPLS2MPLS Pop operation, the incoming labeled packet is stripped off the top-most label in the label stack, resulting in a labeled packet. In the swap condition, an incoming labeled packet's top-most label is swapped with a new label. Cisco routers by default copy the top label's EXP value onto the underlying label in a label stack during label disposition in an MPLS2MPLS condition.

Figure 13-5 *MPLS QoS Implementation and Functions*

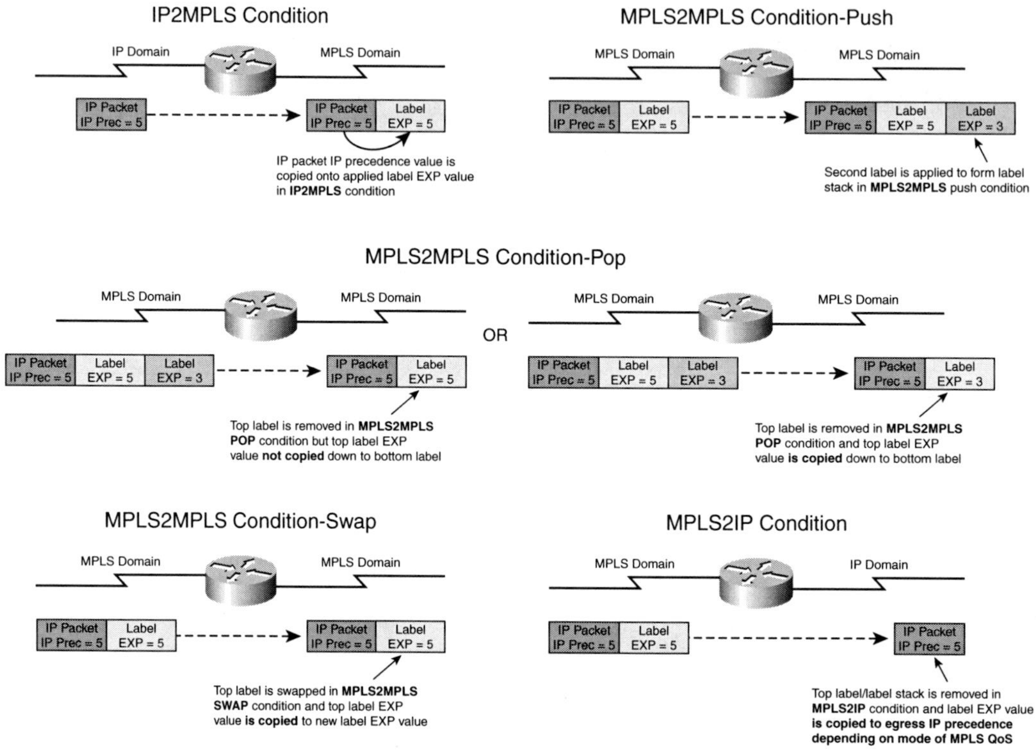

In the MPLS2IP condition, the incoming packet is a labeled packet and the outgoing packet is a pure IP packet. In the MPLS2IP condition, the EXP value is copied back onto the underlying IP Precedence value of the IP packet depending on the tunnel mode implementation in use. The different tunnel mode implementations are explained in the next section. All three conditions discussed have been illustrated in Figure 13-5.

MPLS QoS Operating Modes

Multiple modes of operation can exist when implementing QoS using MPLS. These are called the *MPLS QoS tunnel modes* of operation. The main tunneling modes in the MPLS QoS implementation are

- Uniform mode
- Pipe mode
- Short Pipe mode
- Long Pipe mode

Uniform Mode

In Uniform mode, all changes made to the class of a packet, IP Precedence, DSCP, MPLS EXP values, as the packet traverses the SP infrastructure is maintained as the packet is propagated downstream. The IP packet's IP Precedence value is copied onto the imposed label EXP value when the packet undergoes an IP2MPLS condition. When the packet undergoes a MPLS2IP condition, the top-most label EXP value (because there is a possibility of a labeled packet having more than one label, essentially a label stack) is copied onto the IP Precedence value of the IP packet.

The most important operation of Uniform mode implementation is in the MPLS2MPLS condition when a label is applied to an already labeled packet. In the MPLS2MPLS condition, when a label is swapped, the new label is given the same EXP value as the top-most received label. In the case of an MPLS2MPLS POP, the MPLS EXP value is copied downward in the label stack (top label to bottom label). The operation of Uniform mode is shown in Figure 13-6.

Figure 13-6 *Uniform Tunnel Mode Implementation*

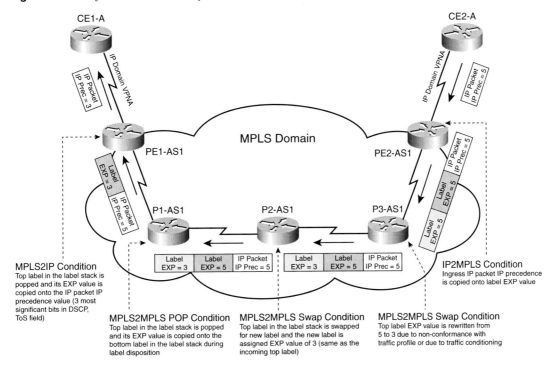

Figure 13-6 depicts a simple MPLS VPN network with two PE routers, PE1-AS1 and PE2-AS1, connected to CE routers, CE1-A and CE2-A, providing MPLS VPN services. Uniform mode is used in a managed CE scenario where the SP controls QoS from CE to CE via the MPLS domain. When implementing Uniform mode, an IP packet destined for CE1-A from CE2-A is given a label stack (MPLS VPN label stack), the labels are marked with an EXP value of 5 mapping to the ingress IP packet's IP Precedence on PE2-AS1. In some situations, as in the case of traffic engineering or non-conformance to traffic profile, the EXP value might be rewritten in the LSP path. P3-AS1 performs such a function by reassigning the top label's EXP value from 5 to 3 during the label swapping process. P2-AS1 performs a simple MPLS2MPLS swap function and forwards the labeled packet to P1-AS1 while preserving the EXP value at 3. P1-AS1 removes the top label in the label stack (penultimate hop popping). During this process, the top label's EXP value is copied onto the bottom label (MPLS2MPLS POP condition in Uniform mode). PE1-AS1 receives the labeled packet and rewrites the outgoing IP packets IP precedence to 3 to map to the ingress labeled packet's EXP value. In the Uniform mode of operation, the PEs and CEs function as a single differential services domain as the QoS associated with a packet is carried across the MPLS domain as well as the remote CE's IP domain. Therefore, as mentioned earlier, this procedure is mainly implemented in a managed CE scenario.

Pipe Mode

The working of Pipe mode is similar to the working of Uniform mode except that in the MPLS2IP condition, the EXP value of the top-most label is *not* copied as the IP Precedence value of the IP packet. This mode is used if the QoS implemented by the SP is required to be independent of the customer's QoS policy. In Pipe mode, the IP Precedence of the underlying IP packet is unchanged. The IP packet IP Precedence is not copied onto the MPLS EXP value in the IP2MPLS condition. The IP packet PHB or QoS implementation on the router as the packet undergoes an MPLS2IP condition is based on the EXP value of the label on the egress LSR. During label disposition, the egress LSR maintains a copy of the EXP value in memory as the *qos-group* value of the packet. This QoS group value is then used to define the PHB on the egress LSR. Figure 13-7 illustrates the operation of Pipe mode.

In comparison to Uniform mode, when implementing Pipe mode, as shown in Figure 13-7, PE1-AS1 does not copy the ingress label EXP value onto the egress IP packet's IP Precedence value. However, the queuing characteristics of the labeled packet on PE1-AS1 still depend on the ingress label EXP value that is copied onto the *qos-group* value. This implementation is used when the SP would like to implement the PHB based on the QoS policy implementation in the SP core versus the customer's QoS policy when forwarding data to the attached CE routers. Hence, the QoS PHB of the same packet in the IP and the MPLS domain are independent of one another.

Figure 13-7 *Pipe Mode Implementation*

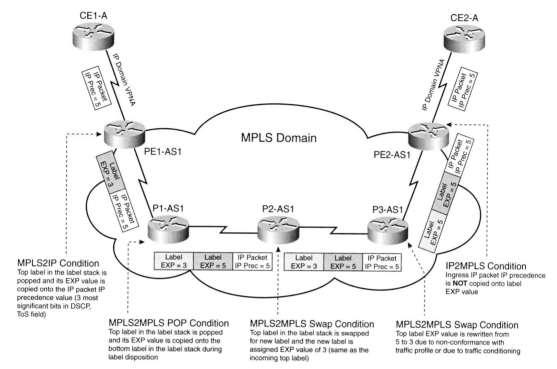

Short Pipe Mode

In Short Pipe mode, the difference occurs on egress from the MPLS to the IP domain (MPLS2IP condition). In Short Pipe mode, the packet's PHB is not associated to the ingress labeled packet's EXP value but only on the underlying IP packet's IP Precedence/DSCP value. The egress LSR does not maintain a copy of the ingress labeled packet's EXP value in the *qos-group* variable, which can be used to identify the egress PHB of the IP packet. This procedure is implemented when the QoS associated with the packet needs to conform to the customer's QoS policy.

Long Pipe Mode

Long Pipe tunnel mode is a variation of the Pipe tunnel mode; the difference being that, on the PE-CE links, the packets are forwarded using label (or label stack) marking and those links are also part of MPLS QoS domain. The CE router receiving traffic from the MPLS backbone can apply its outbound policy toward the VPN site based on MPLS experimental bits or original DSCP bits. The CE router might also copy EXP values to

IP Precedence if required. This model is mainly applicable to the carrier supporting carrier (CSC) architecture, as shown in Figure 13-8.

Figure 13-8 *Long Pipe Tunnel Implementation*

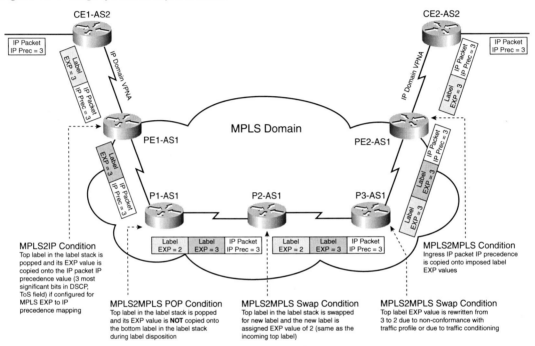

In Figure 13-8, when a labeled packet is received by CE2-AS2 destined for CE1-AS2, the label is associated with the destination, and the label EXP value is copied as the ingress IP packet's IP Precedence value. When PE2-AS1 receives the ingress labeled packet, the label stack is applied with EXP value equal to the ingress label's EXP value. Note that although P3-AS1 rewrites the top label's EXP value to 2 (from 3) upon label disposition at P1-AS1, this value is not copied back down the label stack. PE1-AS1 performs the MPLS2MPLS label swapping function with direct mapping of EXP bits. On receiving the labeled packet on CE1-AS2, the router can perform PHB based on the ingress labeled packets EXP value or underlying IP packet's IP Precedence value.

Summary of MPLS QoS Modes

Figure 13-9 shows the final summary diagram that illustrates all these MPLS QoS modes.

Figure 13-9 *Summary Diagram for Different MPLS QoS Modes*

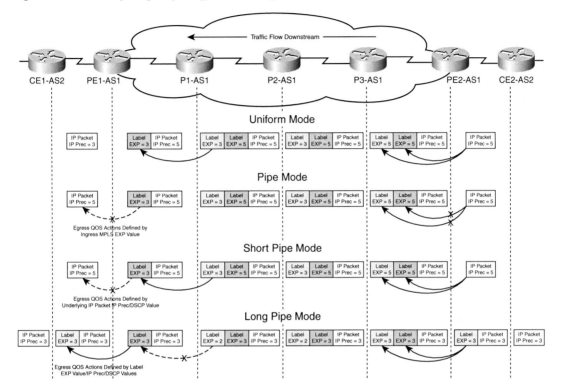

Modular QoS CLI: Configuration of QoS on Cisco Routers

Modular QoS CLI (MQC) is the Cisco implementation for configuration of QoS on its routers. Prior to the implementation of MQC on Cisco routers, all configurations were performed at the interface level for QoS policies. In the event that the router had a large number of networking interfaces, this configuration was often cumbersome and time-consuming. With MQC, the actual QoS policy has been decoupled from the interface on which it is applied. Therefore, multiple policies can be configured and do not take effect until they are applied to an interface. The modular QoS CLI implements a simple architecture to configure QoS by the definition of the following:

Step 1 **Identify the interesting traffic (classification) that will map to a traffic class using the configuration of class maps**—Interesting traffic definition can be defined to match based on many properties of an IP or an MPLS packet. However, refer to the documentation for the particular product as well as the IOS version prior to implementation and configuration of QoS policy using MQC.

In the class map, the interesting traffic is defined using **match** commands under the class-map configuration. Figure 13-10 outlines the basic options available as well as the configuration procedure on a GSR chassis with 12.0 version of code. Note that the options available on the router might vary depending on the type of chassis and the revision of IOS that you are running on router.

Figure 13-10 *Identify Interesting Traffic*

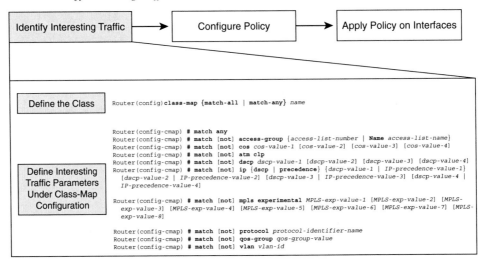

Note that a large number of options are available under the **match** keyword for the class-map configuration. The most commonly used ones have been shown in Figure 13-9. Refer to the documentation pertaining to your particular chassis as well as the IOS version for more information on options available at Cisco.com. Note that the **not** keyword can be used in conjunction with most options available under the interesting traffic definition.

Step 2 **Define the QoS policy to be applied per class using policy maps**— The QoS policy applied per class is defined as the PHB for that specific class. This usually includes the functions of congestion management, congestion avoidance, and traffic shaping and policing on a per class basis. It will also define if the specified class requires preferential treatment as in the case of LLQ. Therefore, this is often where you will find the **police**, **shape**, **priority**, **bandwidth**, and **random-detect** commands per class.

Figure 13-11 illustrates the configuration pertaining to the implementation of a QoS policy using policy maps and outlines the configuration options available for each class under the policy-map configuration.

Figure 13-11 *Configure Policy*

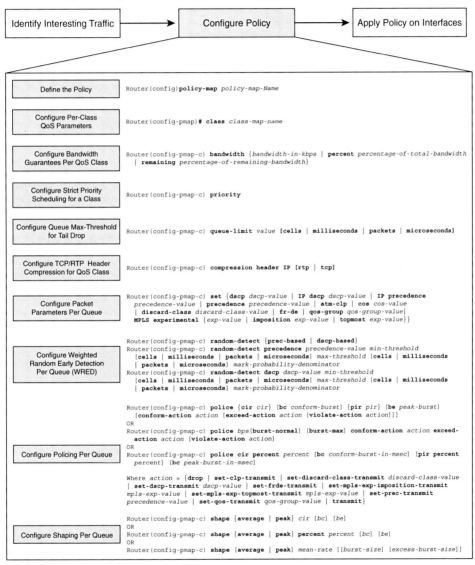

With random-detection, the queue can be configured to selectively drop packets to avoid the queue from filling up leading to tail-drop scenarios. Therefore, the minimum threshold at which the selective drop begins and the maximum threshold before the tail drop are to be configured along with the drop probability denominator, which defines the ratio of packets to be dropped at the maximum threshold. Note that the smaller the drop probability denominator, the more aggressive the congestion avoidance scheme. The most common variables are that the **bandwidth** command needs to be configured prior to random-detect configuration, as well as random-detect cannot be performed on an LLQ as defined by the **priority** command mentioned earlier. Hence, random-detection can be done based on Precedence values or DSCP values, and drops can be done selectively or more aggressively based on the Precedence or DSCP values.

Policing is the process of identifying if traffic conforms to a certain profile. Traffic not conforming to the profile can be either reconfigured (lowered in priority and class) and transmitted or simply dropped. The important difference between traffic shaping and policing is that packets are not dropped that do not match a traffic profile. In shaping, out-of-profile packets are queued and perhaps re-marked and sent at a later time interval. The shaping can be performed using peak or average rates and usually forms a single token bucket model, but, in some higher end routers manufactured by Cisco, the dual token bucket model is used in which a separate bucket is maintained for tokens matching the committed burst rate and the excess burst rates. The key item to note is that shaping is always performed on egress and not on ingress whereas policing can be performed on ingress as well.

Step 3 **Apply PHB QoS policy per interface using service-policy commands**—This final step in the MQC structure involves the application of a QoS policy on an interface (policy map) using the **service-policy** command. The PHB can be defined either on input or output and can map to different PHBs in either operation. The configuration step is identified in Figure 13-12.

Figure 13-12 *Applying Policy to an Interface*

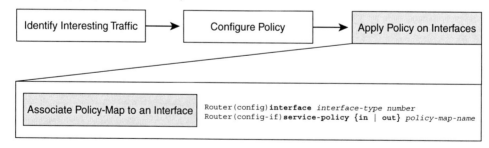

In this section, you were provided an overview of the configurations possible with the Cisco MQC architecture. For more information on configuration of classification, marking, congestion management, congestion avoidance, traffic shaping, and policing, visit the

Cisco online documentation at http://www.cisco.com/univercd/cc/td/doc/product/software/
ios120/12cgcr/qos_c/index.htm.

Configuration and Implementation of MPLS QoS in Uniform Mode and Short Pipe Mode Operation

The topology that depicts the configuration and implementation of Uniform and Short
Pipe modes is shown in Figure 13-13. The network consists of two CE routers, CE1-A and
CE2-A, belonging to Customer A's VPN (VPNA). The SP network consists of two PE
routers, PE1-AS1 and PE2-AS1, connected to CE1-A and CE2-A, respectively. OSPF PE
to CE has been implemented on these routers, and it is assumed that the VPN has been
configured prior to implementing the QoS parameters. Only the configurations pertaining
to QoS have been depicted for brevity.

Figure 13-13 *MPLS QoS Configuration Topology*

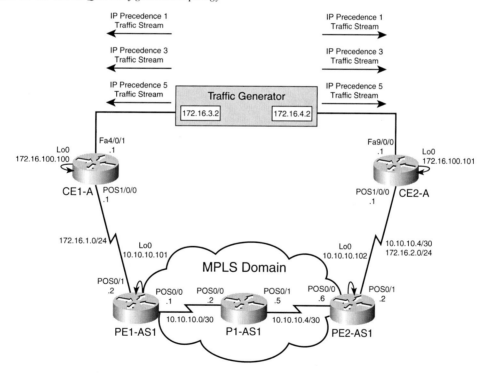

The traffic profile from the traffic generator consists of three simultaneous streams, each
with different IP Precedence values, as shown in Figure 13-13. Each traffic generator port
sends packets at an aggregate rate of 1 Mbps and each stream consists of 100,000 packets

for an aggregate of 300,000 packets generated per port on the traffic generator. The CE routers, upon receiving this traffic, either police or perform CBWFQ-LLQ and forward the packets to their attached PE routers. The PE routers classify ingress packets from the CE routers based on their associated IP Precedence values. Upon classification, the PE router then marks each IP packet with a corresponding MPLS EXP value on egress to map QoS in the IP domain to MPLS QoS. All changes (re-marking) in the core from a MPLS EXP perspective are propagated in the label stack and into the IP packet in *Uniform mode operation*. In *Pipe Mode operation*, all packets are handled on ingress similar to Uniform mode, but changes in QoS are implemented in the core and not propagated into the IP packet on the egress from PE to CE. Therefore, in Short Pipe mode operation, the MPLS domain QoS changes are not propagated upward to the IP QoS domain.

The traffic generator generates five streams between the same set of IP addresses from 172.16.3.2 to 172.16.4.2, each stream with different IP Precedence values attached to the IP packet.

Implementing Uniform Mode

The following steps outline the configurations on the appropriate routers to implement Uniform mode QoS implementation with MPLS:

Step 1   **CE router configuration**—CE routers, CE1-A and CE2-A, accept traffic from the traffic generator ports directly connected to them and implement QoS functionality based on the class of traffic for each of the five streams. CBWFQ with LLQ is implemented on the CE routers egress to the PE routers. The CE router, therefore, requires the configuration of a class map for each class to identify the characteristics of the class. In addition, each CE router also requires the definition of a QoS policy to be associated with these classes by configuration of a policy map. Finally, the configured policy map is applied to the interface connecting the CE to the PE routers using the **service-policy** command. Configuration of the CE Router CE1-A is shown in Example 13-1. In LLQ, the Precedence 5 (EF) traffic is given strict priority by the implementation of the **priority** command for the class *precedence5*. Note that in the configuration shown in Example 13-1, bandwidth not associated to any of the classes will be applied to best-effort traffic or non-marked (IP Precedence) traffic.

Example 13-1 *CE1-A Configuration*

```
CE1-A(config)#class-map precedence5
CE1-A(config-cmap)#match ip precedence 5
CE1-A(config)#class-map precedence3
CE1-A(config-cmap)#match ip precedence 3
CE1-A(config)#class-map precedence1
CE1-A(config-cmap)#match ip precedence 1
```

Example 13-1 *CE1-A Configuration (Continued)*

```
CE1-A(config)#policy-map CEQoS
CE1-A(config-pmap)#class precedence5
CE1-A(config-pmap-c)#priority
CE1-A(config-pmap-c)#class precedence3
CE1-A(config-pmap-c)#bandwidth percent 30
CE1-A(config-pmap-c)#random-detect
CE1-A(config-pmap-c)#class precedence1
CE1-A(config-pmap-c)#bandwidth percent 20
CE1-A(config)#interface pos 1/1/0
CE1-A(config-if)#service-policy output CEQoS
```

Step 2   PE routers—IP to MPLS domain configuration—On the PE routers, packets are received with different IP Precedence values from the attached CE routers. Therefore, the PE routers can map or assign class based on ingress packet IP Precedence. A class map is configured on the PE routers to match packets based on IP Precedence of 5, 3, and 1, and a policy map is configured for a QoS *action* of setting the MPLS EXP bits mapping to ingress IP Precedence. Depending on the version of IOS and platform in use, the *action* can be either **set mpls experimental topmost** or the **set mpls experimental imposition**. However, note that to use the **set mpls experimental imposition** command, the service policy should be applied on input and, therefore, must be associated to the PE-CE interface on PE routers. While using the **set mpls experimental topmost** command, the policy can be applied on the ingress interface into the MPLS domain (PE to P router interface). Example 13-2 outlines the configuration of PE Router PE1-AS1. The configuration is broken down into ingress (from CE) actions and egress (to P) actions as well as classification, marking, and QoS operations.

Example 13-2 *PE1-AS1 IP2MPLS Condition Configuration*

```
! PE1-AS1 ingress configuration:
PE1-AS1(config)#class-map match-all precedence1
PE1-AS1(config-cmap)#  match ip precedence 1
PE1-AS1(config-cmap)#class-map match-all precedence3
PE1-AS1(config-cmap)#  match ip precedence 3
PE1-AS1(config-cmap)#class-map match-all precedence5
PE1-AS1(config-cmap)#  match ip precedence 5

PE1-AS1(config)#Policy-map ip2mplsin
PE1-AS1(config-pmap)#description Marking ingress traffic into QoS-group
PE1-AS1(config-pmap)#class precedence5
PE1-AS1(config-pmap-c)#set qos-group 5
PE1-AS1(config-pmap-c)#class precedence3
PE1-AS1(config-pmap-c)#set qos-group 3
PE1-AS1(config-pmap-c)#class precedence1
PE1-AS1(config-pmap-c)#set qos-group 1
```

continues

Example 13-2 *PE1-AS1 IP2MPLS Condition Configuration (Continued)*

```
PE1-AS1(config)#interface pos 0/1
PE1-AS1(config-if)#service-policy in ip2mplsin
! PE1-AS1 Egress configuration:
PE1-AS1(config)#class-map qosgroup5
PE1-AS1(config-cmap)#match qos-group 5
PE1-AS1(config-cmap)#class-map qosgroup3
PE1-AS1(config-cmap)#match qos-group 3
PE1-AS1(config-cmap)#class-map qosgroup1
PE1-AS1(config-cmap)#match qos-group 1

PE1-AS1(config)#Policy-map ip2mplsout
PE1-AS1(config-pmap)#class qosgroup5
PE1-AS1(config-pmap-c)#set mpls experimental topmost 5
PE1-AS1(config-pmap-c)#priority
PE1-AS1(config-pmap-c)#Police 10000000 1000000
PE1-AS1(config-pmap-c)#class qosgroup3
PE1-AS1(config-pmap-c)#set mpls experimental topmost 3
PE1-AS1(config-pmap-c)#bandwidth 10000
PE1-AS1(config-pmap-c)#random-detect
PE1-AS1(config-pmap-c)#class qosgroup1
PE1-AS1(config-pmap-c)#set mpls experimental topmost 1
PE1-AS1(config-pmap-c)#bandwidth 10000
PE1-AS1(config-pmap-c)#random-detect
PE1-AS1(config-if)#interface pos 0/0
PE1-AS1(config-if)#service-policy out ip2mplsout
```

Step 3 **P router—MPLS EXP rewrite**—To demonstrate Uniform mode
operation, the P1-AS1 router is configured to rewrite the MPLS EXP bit
to 1 for all traffic coming in with EXP value of 3. This is done using a
class map matching all packets with MPLS EXP bit value of 3 (as marked
by the PE routers) and rewriting the same with the use of a policy map.
Because QoS from CE1 to CE2 is being demonstrated with these
examples, the service policy is implemented on the ingress interface from
PE1-AS1 to P1-AS1 where the MPLS EXP bits match and QoS group
setting is performed. On egress to PE2, the QoS group is matched and is
mapped to the topmost label EXP value on the egress labeled packets.
Example 13-3 outlines the configuration of P1-AS1 router.

Example 13-3 *P1-AS1 MPLS2MPLS Condition Configuration*

```
! P1-AS1 ingress configuration:
P1-AS1(config)#class-map mplsexp3
P1-AS1(config-cmap)#match mpls experimental 3

P1-AS1(config-cmap)#policy-map mpls2mplsin
P1-AS1(config-pmap)#class mplsexp3
P1-AS1(config-pmap-c)#set qos-group 3

P1-AS1(config-pmap-c)#interface pos 0/0
P1-AS1(config-if)#service-policy input mpls2mplsin
```

Example 13-3 *P1-AS1 MPLS2MPLS Condition Configuration (Continued)*

```
! P1-AS1 Egress configuration:
P1-AS1(config)#class-map qosgroup3
P1-AS1(config-cmap)#match qos-group 3

P1-AS1(config-cmap)#policy-map mpls2mplsout
P1-AS1(config-pmap)#class qosgroup3
P1-AS1(config-pmap-c)#set mpls experimental topmost 1

P1-AS1(config)#interface pos 0/1
P1-AS1(config-if)#service-policy output mpls2mplsout
```

Step 4   **PE router configuration—MPLS to IP domain**—In Uniform mode operation, when the packet transits the MPLS domain into the IP domain, the EXP value of the top-most label is propagated into the IP domain from the MPLS domain and is written as the IP Precedence value of the IP packet. A class map is configured matching all packets with MPLS EXP of 5 and 1. A corresponding policy map is configured to configure qos-group value of the packet to the corresponding IP Precedence value. This is applied on the ingress from P1-AS1 to PE2-AS1. A class map matching the QoS group is then configured, and a policy map is configured to mark the IP Precedence value to the QoS group value. This policy map is then applied on egress from PE2-AS1 to CE2-A. Example 13-4 outlines the MPLS to IP domain configuration on the PE Router PE2-AS1.

Example 13-4 *PE2-AS1 MPLS2IP Condition Configuration*

```
! PE2-AS1 ingress configuration

PE2-AS1(config)#class-map match-all mplsexp5
PE2-AS1(config-cmap)#match mpls experimental 5
PE2-AS1(config-cmap)#class-map mplsexp1
PE2-AS1(config-cmap)#match mpls experimental 1

PE2-AS1(config-cmap)#policy-map mpls2ipin
PE2-AS1(config-pmap)#class mplsexp5
PE2-AS1(config-pmap-c)#set qos-group 5
PE2-AS1(config-pmap-c)#class mplsexp1
PE2-AS1(config-pmap-c)#set qos-group 1

PE2-AS1(config-pmap-c)#interface pos 0/0
PE2-AS1(config-if)#service-policy input mpls2ipin
! PE2-AS1 Egress configuration:

PE2-AS1(config)#class-map qosgroup5
PE2-AS1(config-cmap)#match qos-group 5
PE2-AS1(config-cmap)#class-map qosgroup1
PE2-AS1(config-cmap)#match qos-group 1
```

continues

Example 13-4 *PE2-AS1 MPLS2IP Condition Configuration (Continued)*

```
PE2-AS1(config-cmap)#policy-map mpls2ipout
PE2-AS1(config-pmap)#class qosgroup5
PE2-AS1(config-pmap-c)#set ip precedence 5
PE2-AS1(config-pmap-c)#class qosgroup1
PE2-AS1(config-pmap-c)#set ip precedence 1
PE2-AS1(config)#interface pos 0/1
PE2-AS1(config-if)#service-policy output mpls2ipout
```

> **Step 5** **Verification of Uniform Mode Operation**—Example 13-5 outlines the
> **show** commands as performed on the different routers in the path from
> CE1-A to CE2-A via the MPLS domain. A total number of 100,000
> packets per class (individual IP Precedence values) are transmitted via the
> network prior to performing the verification. A truncated output has been
> performed for all routers in the path for brevity. However, the actual
> classes that are mapped on each router are shown in Example 13-5.

Example 13-5 *Verification of Uniform Mode*

```
CE1-A#show policy-map interface pos 1/1/0 out | include packets
      queue limit 11632 (packets)
      100000 packets, 5000000 bytes-------------class precedence5
      100000 packets, 5000000 bytes-------------class precedence3
      queue limit 2326 (packets)
        Mean queue depth: 0 packets
      100000 packets, 5000000 bytes-------------class precedence1
      queue limit 697 (packets)
      28 packets, 2352 bytes------------------class class-default
        28 packets, 2352 bytes
      queue limit 2791 (packets)
PE1-AS1#show policy-map interface pos 0/1 in | include packets
      100000 packets, 4600000 bytes-------------class precedence5
      100000 packets, 4600000 bytes-------------class precedence3
      100000 packets, 4600000 bytes-------------class precedence1
PE1-AS1#show policy-map interface pos 0/0 out | include packets
      100000 packets, 5400000 bytes-------------class qosgroup5
      Queue-limit: 8192 packets (default)
      Current queue-depth: 0 packets, Maximum queue-depth: 0 packets
        conformed 100000 packets, 5400000 bytes; actions:
        exceeded 0 packets, 0 bytes; actions:
      100000 packets, 5400000 bytes-------------class qosgroup3
      Queue-limit: 1024 packets (default)
      Current queue-depth: 0 packets, Maximum queue-depth: 0 packets
      100000 packets, 5400000 bytes-------------class qosgroup1
      Queue-limit: 1024 packets (default)
      Current queue-depth: 0 packets, Maximum queue-depth: 0 packets
      0 packets, 0 bytes
      Queue-limit: 16384 packets (default)
      Current queue-depth: 0 packets, Maximum queue-depth: 0 packets
P1-AS1#show policy-map interface pos 0/0 in | include packets
      100000 packets, 5000000 bytes-------------class mplsexp3
      16 packets, 780 bytes
```

Example 13-5 *Verification of Uniform Mode (Continued)*

```
P1-AS1#show policy-map interface pos 0/1 out | include packets
        100000 packets, 5000000 bytes-------------class qosgroup1
        8 packets, 396 bytes
        Queue-limit: 16384 packets (default)
        Current queue-depth: 0 packets, Maximum queue-depth: 0 packets
PE2-AS1#show policy-map interface pos 0/0 in | include packets
        100000 packets, 4600000 bytes-------------class mplsexp5
        200000 packets, 9200000 bytes-------------class mplsexp1
        12 packets, 585 bytes
PE2-AS1#show policy-map interface pos 0/1 out | include packets
        100000 packets, 4600000 bytes-------------class qosgroup5
        200000 packets, 9200000 bytes-------------class qosgroup1
        0 packets, 0 bytes
        Queue-limit: 16384 packets (default)
        Current queue-depth: 0 packets, Maximum queue-depth: 0 packets
```

Note that on PE2-AS1 ingress and egress interfaces, the number of packets matching the MPLS EXP value of 1 is twice the number of packets matching the MPLS EXP value of 5 due to the rewrite of EXP value performed at P1-AS1. This verifies that in the implementation of Uniform mode, the MPLS EXP values are copied back onto the IP packet IP Precedence values as they traverse the MPLS domain back into the IP domain of the customer. To further verify Uniform mode implementation, a generic service policy is configured on the CE2 ingress interface, and, upon verification, it is evident that the IP Precedence value has been rewritten based on the MPLS EXP bit rewrite in the MPLS domain. The configuration of CE2 is shown in Example 13-6.

Example 13-6 *CE2-A Configuration and Verification*

```
class-map match-all precedence1
  match ip precedence 1
class-map match-all precedence5
  match ip precedence 5
!
policy-map verify
  class precedence5
    police 10000000 1000000 1000000 conform-action transmit exceed-action drop
  class precedence1
    police 10000000 1000000 1000000 conform-action transmit exceed-action drop
interface POS1/0/0
 ip address 172.16.2.1 255.255.255.0
 service-policy input verify
CE2-A#show policy-map interface pos1/0/0 in | include packets
        100000 packets, 5000000 bytes-------------class precedence5
          conformed 100000 packets, 5000000 bytes; action: transmit
          exceeded 0 packets, 0 bytes; action: drop
        200000 packets, 10000000 bytes-------------class precedence1
          conformed 100000 packets, 5000000 bytes; action: transmit
          exceeded 0 packets, 0 bytes; action: drop
        0 packets, 0 bytes
          0 packets, 0 bytes
```

Note that all the previous configurations depicted unidirectional QoS with the implementation of QoS and Uniform mode downstream toward 172.16.4.2 from 172.16.3.2. In real-world networks, QoS is bidirectional between a set of devices, networks, or customer sites. The configurations to implement the QoS for traffic flowing downstream to 172.16.3.2 can be easily derived by mirroring the configurations illustrated earlier in Example 13-1 through Example 13-5. Example 13-7 through Example 13-10 illustrate the complete configurations for all devices for bidirectional QoS.

Example 13-7 *CE1-A Final Configuration for Uniform Mode Implementation*

```
class-map match-all precedence5
  match ip precedence 5
class-map match-all  precedence3
  match ip precedence 3
class-map  match-all precedence1
  match ip precedence 1
!
policy-map CEQoS
  class precedence5
    priority
  class precedence3
    bandwidth percent 30
    random-detect
  class precedence1
    bandwidth percent 20
!
class-map match-all precedence1
  match ip precedence 1
class-map match-all precedence5
  match ip precedence 5
!
policy-map verify
  class precedence5
    police 10000000 1000000 1000000 conform-action transmit exceed-action drop
  class precedence1
    police 10000000 1000000 1000000 conform-action transmit exceed-action drop
!
interface pos 1/1/0
service-policy output CEQoS
service-policy input verify
```

Example 13-8 *PE1-AS1 and PE2-AS1 Final Configurations for Uniform Mode Implementation*

```
! PE1-AS1 configuration
class-map match-all qosgroup50
  match qos-group 50
class-map match-all qosgroup10
  match qos-group 10
!
class-map match-all qosgroup3
  match qos-group 3
class-map match-all qosgroup1
  match qos-group 1
```

Example 13-8 *PE1-AS1 and PE2-AS1 Final Configurations for Uniform Mode Implementation (Continued)*

```
class-map match-all qosgroup5
  match qos-group 5
!
class-map match-all precedence1
  match ip precedence 1
class-map match-all precedence3
  match ip precedence 3
class-map match-all precedence5
  match ip precedence 5
!
class-map match-all mplsexp5
  match mpls experimental  5
class-map match-all mplsexp1
  match mpls experimental  1
!
policy-map ip2mplsin
  class precedence5
   set qos-group 5
  class precedence3
   set qos-group 3
  class precedence1
   set qos-group 1
!
policy-map mpls2ipin
  class mplsexp5
   set qos-group 50
  class mplsexp1
   set qos-group 10
!
policy-map mpls2ipout
  class qosgroup50
   set precedence 5
  class qosgroup10
   set precedence 1
!
policy-map ip2mplsout
  class qosgroup5
   set mpls experimental topmost 5
   priority
  class qosgroup3
   set mpls experimental topmost 3
   bandwidth 10000
   random-detect
  class qosgroup1
   set mpls experimental topmost 1
   bandwidth 10000
   random-detect
!
interface POS0/0
 description connection to P1
 service-policy input mpls2ipin
 service-policy output ip2mplsout
```

continues

Example 13-8 *PE1-AS1 and PE2-AS1 Final Configurations for Uniform Mode Implementation (Continued)*

```
!
interface POS0/1
 ip vrf forwarding VPNA
 service-policy input ip2mplsin
 service-policy output mpls2ipout
 !
! PE2-AS1 configuration
class-map match-all qosgroup30
  match qos-group 30
class-map match-all qosgroup10
  match qos-group 10
class-map match-all qosgroup50
  match qos-group 50
 !
class-map match-all qosgroup1
  match qos-group 1
class-map match-all qosgroup5
  match qos-group 5
 !
class-map match-all precedence1
  match ip precedence 1
class-map match-all precedence3
  match ip precedence 3
class-map match-all precedence5
  match ip precedence 5
 !
class-map match-all mplsexp5
  match mpls experimental  5
class-map match-all mplsexp1
  match mpls experimental  1
 !
policy-map ip2mplsin
  class precedence5
   set qos-group 50
  class precedence3
   set qos-group 30
  class precedence1
   set qos-group 10

policy-map mpls2ipin
  class mplsexp5
   set qos-group 5
  class mplsexp1
   set qos-group 1

policy-map mpls2ipout
  class qosgroup5
   set precedence 5
  class qosgroup1
   set precedence 1

policy-map ip2mplsout
  class qosgroup50
```

Example 13-8 *PE1-AS1 and PE2-AS1 Final Configurations for Uniform Mode Implementation (Continued)*

```
       set mpls experimental topmost 5
        priority
     class qosgroup30
       set mpls experimental topmost 3
         bandwidth 10000
         random-detect
     class qosgroup10
       set mpls experimental topmost 1
         bandwidth 10000
         random-detect
   !
   interface POS0/0
    description connection to P1
    service-policy input mpls2ipin
    service-policy output ip2mplsout
   !
   interface POS0/1
    ip vrf forwarding VPNA
    service-policy input ip2mplsin
    service-policy output mpls2ipout
```

Example 13-9 *P1-AS1 Final Configuration for Uniform Mode Implementation*

```
class-map match-all qosgroup2
match qos-group 2
class-map match-all qosgroup3
match qos-group 3
class-map match-all qosgroup1
match qos-group 1
!
class-map match-any mplsexp3
match mpls experimental  3
!
policy-map mpls2mplsin
class mplsexp3
set qos-group 3
!
policy-map mpls2mplsout
class qosgroup3
set mpls experimental topmost 1
!
interface POS0/0
description connection to PE1-AS1
ip address 10.10.10.2 255.255.255.252
service-policy input mpls2mplsin
service-policy output mpls2mplsout
!
interface POS0/1
description connection to PE2-AS1
service-policy input mpls2mplsin
service-policy output mpls2mplsout
```

Example 13-10 *CE2-A Final Configuration for Uniform Mode Implementation*

```
class-map match-all precedence5
  match ip precedence 5
class-map match-all  precedence3
  match ip precedence 3
class-map  match-all precedence1
  match ip precedence 1

policy-map CEQoS
  class precedence5
    priority
  class precedence3
    bandwidth percent 30
    random-detect
  class precedence1
    bandwidth percent 20

class-map match-all precedence1
  match ip precedence 1
class-map match-all precedence5
  match ip precedence 5
!
policy-map verify
  class precedence5
    police 10000000 1000000 1000000 conform-action transmit exceed-action drop
  class precedence1
    police 10000000 1000000 1000000 conform-action transmit exceed-action drop
!
interface pos 1/1/0
service-policy output CEQoS
service-policy input verify
```

Implementing Short Pipe Mode

Short Pipe mode is implemented the same as Uniform mode except on the egress MPLS2IP condition. In Short Pipe mode, the label EXP value is not copied back onto the IP packet Precedence or DSCP values in the egress MPLS2IP condition. Therefore, in comparison to the Uniform mode configurations shown in the prior section, the only changes in configuration will have to be on Routers PE1-AS1 and PE2-AS1 where the MPLS EXP bit rewrite in the core is not propagated back into the IP packet IP Precedence values. Consequently, in Short Pipe mode, the configuration of the PE1-AS1 and PE2-AS1 routers will *not* involve any IP Precedence rewrite based on ingress MPLS EXP bit values from the MPLS to the IP domain. Example 13-11 outlines the configurations of Routers PE1-AS1 and PE2-AS1 for the implementation of Short Pipe mode. Note the absence of the *mpls2ipin* and *mpls2ipout* policies mapping the ingress MPLS EXP values to egress IP Precedence values in comparison to Example 13-8 for PE1-AS1 and PE2-AS1. Only QoS-related configurations have been shown for brevity.

Example 13-11 *PE1-AS1 and PE2-AS1 Configurations for Short Pipe Mode*

```
! PE1-AS1 configuration
class-map match-all qosgroup3
  match qos-group 3
class-map match-all qosgroup1
  match qos-group 1
class-map match-all qosgroup5
  match qos-group 5
!
class-map match-all precedence1
  match ip precedence 1
class-map match-all precedence3
  match ip precedence 3
class-map match-all precedence5
  match ip precedence 5
!
policy-map ip2mplsin
  class precedence5
   set qos-group 5
  class precedence3
   set qos-group 3
  class precedence1
   set qos-group 1
!
policy-map ip2mplsout
  class qosgroup5
   set mpls experimental topmost 5
   priority
  class qosgroup3
   set mpls experimental topmost 3
    bandwidth 10000
    random-detect
  class qosgroup1
   set mpls experimental topmost 1
    bandwidth 10000
    random-detect
!
interface POS0/0
 description connection to P1
 service-policy output ip2mplsout
!
interface POS0/1
 ip vrf forwarding VPNA
 service-policy input ip2mplsin
! PE2-AS1 configuration
class-map match-all qosgroup30
  match qos-group 30
class-map match-all qosgroup10
  match qos-group 10
class-map match-all qosgroup50
  match qos-group 50
!
```

continues

Example 13-11 *PE1-AS1 and PE2-AS1 Configurations for Short Pipe Mode (Continued)*

```
class-map match-all precedence1
  match ip precedence 1
class-map match-all precedence3
  match ip precedence 3
class-map match-all precedence5
  match ip precedence 5
!
policy-map ip2mplsin
  class precedence5
   set qos-group 50
  class precedence3
   set qos-group 30
  class precedence1
   set qos-group 10


 policy-map ip2mplsout
  class qosgroup50
   set mpls experimental topmost 5
    priority
  class qosgroup30
   set mpls experimental topmost 3
    bandwidth 10000
    random-detect
  class qosgroup10
   set mpls experimental topmost 1
    bandwidth 10000
    random-detect
 !
interface POS0/0
 description connection to P1
 service-policy output ip2mplsout
 !
interface POS0/1
 ip vrf forwarding VPNA
 service-policy input ip2mplsin
```

As seen in the configurations for the PE routers, the only difference in the implementation of Short Pipe mode and Uniform mode is that on egress from the PE to CE routers, any changes in the MPLS EXP bits as the packets traverse the core are not propagated back into the IP header precedence bits. This mode is implemented if the QoS implemented by the SP is required to be independent of the customer's QoS policy. The IP packet PHB or QoS implementation on the router as the packet undergoes an MPLS2IP condition is based on the resulting IP packet's DSCP/IP Precedence value. Short Pipe and Pipe modes are different only on the basis of what criteria are used to implement the egress QoS PHB from the PE to the CE.

Implementing MPLS QoS for Layer 2 VPN Implementations

As mentioned in earlier chapters, SPs are beginning to use the same IP backbone to provide both Layer 3 as well as Layer 2 VPN services, meaning the usage of AToM, VPWS, VPLS, or L2TPv3 to implement Layer 2 VPN architectures. The procedure to incorporate QoS into each of these Layer 2 VPN implementations is briefly discussed here.

Implementing QoS with AToM

In the implementation of AToM, the emulated circuits use three layers of encapsulation:

- **Tunnel header**—Cisco implements this as the MPLS label or LSP label, which is learned via LDP inside the provider backbone. This is the first label in the MPLS label stack. The label is implemented so that the PDU can be transported from the ingress PE to the egress PE device.

- **Demultiplexer field**—The function of this label is to identify individual circuits within the tunnel. This is implemented as a VC label and is the second label in the stack; this is learned via the directed LDP session between the PE routers.

- **Emulated VC encapsulation**—This is implemented as a 32 bit control word and identifies information inside the enclosed Layer 2 PDU.

As illustrated in Chapter 11, "Any Transport Over MPLS (AToM)," and Chapter 12, "Virtual Private LAN Service (VPLS)," Layer 2 VPNs can be implemented over an MPLS backbone using the same principles as Layer 3 VPNs: by the implementation of label stacks. In Layer 3 VPNs, the label stack contains an LDP/IGP label as well as a VPN label as the packet traverses the MPLS backbone. The LDP/IGP label is used to transport the packet to the next hop in the LSP. This transport label, which is the top label in the label stack, is then popped at the penultimate hop. The VPN label is then read at the egress PE router to identify the interface on which the packet will be transmitted out of the PE router.

Layer 2 VPNs are implemented using the label stack implementation in which a label stack identifies the tunnel label, the VC ID, and the control word. By encapsulation in Layer 2 VPNs, the application of a label stack to a received packet (either labeled or IP packets) is implied. The tunnel label performs the same functions as the IGP/LDP label, and the VC label performs the same functions as the VPN label to identify the egress interface on the egress PE router. Finally, a control word carries essential header information across the MPLS backbone in a shim-header. The ingress PE router will use a label stack to encapsulate the Layer 2 frames into MPLS by removing any preamble, frame checksums, and also some header information. Figure 13-14 shows the label stack implementation in AToM.

Figure 13-14 *AToM Label Stack*

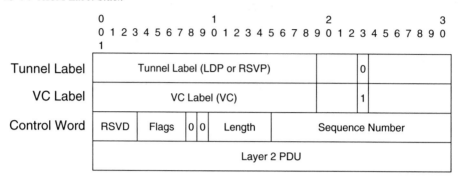

Because the same label formats for the tunnel and VC labels are used, the EXP bits on these labels can be manipulated to implement QoS for Layer 2 VPNs similar to that shown in the earlier sections of this chapter. For the various options available to configure QoS with AToM, refer to the latest Cisco documentation located at Cisco.com.

The different implementations of Layer 2 VPN using AToM and their corresponding configurations to implement QoS are shown in Figure 13-15. Configurations for a single PE router have been depicted and can be extrapolated to appropriate device interfaces on actual deployment. The CE routers and provider core routers will contain only generic interface configurations with no special configurations for implementation of AToM and AToM QoS. Examples 13-12 through Example 13-18 show the configurations for implementation of ingress AToM QoS for the different AToM implementations. Figure 13-15 depicts the setup that is used for the configuration of AToM QoS.

Figure 13-15 *AToM QoS Configuration Topology*

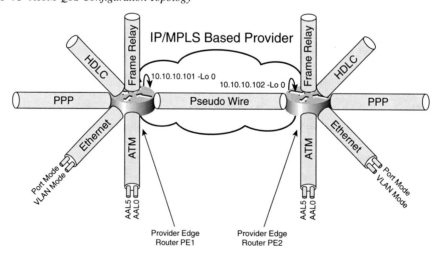

Example 13-12 *Configuration of L2VPN QoS: AAL5 over MPLS*

```
PE1(config)#class-map AToMQoS
PE1(config-cmap)#match any
PE1(config)#policy-map AToMQoS
PE1(config-pmap)#class AToMQoS
PE1(config-pmap-c)#set mpls experimental 5
PE1(config)# interface ATM6/0.100 point-to-point
PE1(config-subif)# pvc  1/100 l2transport
PE1(cfg-if-atm-l2trans-pvc)#encapsulation aal5snap
PE1(cfg-if-atm-l2trans-pvc)#xconnect 10.10.10.102 100 encapsulation mpls
PE1(cfg-if-atm-l2trans-pvc)#service-policy input AToMQoS
```

Example 13-13 *Configuration of L2VPN QoS: ATM Cell Relay over MPLS*

```
PE1(config)#class-map AToMQoS
PE1(config-cmap)#match any
PE1(config)#policy-map AToMQoS
PE1(config-pmap)#class AToMQoS
PE1(config-pmap-c)#set mpls experimental 5
PE1(config)# interface ATM6/0.100 point-to-point
PE1(config-subif)# pvc 1/100 l2transport
PE1(cfg-if-atm-l2trans-pvc)#encapsulation aal0
PE1(cfg-if-atm-l2trans-pvc)#xconnect 10.10.10.102 100 encapsulation mpls
PE1(cfg-if-atm-l2trans-pvc)#service-policy input AtoMQoS
```

Example 13-14 *Configuration of L2VPN QoS: Ethernet over MPLS Port Mode*

```
PE1(config)#class-map AToMQoS
PE1(config-cmap)#match any
PE1(config)#policy-map AToMQoS
PE1(config-pmap)#class AToMQoS
PE1(config-pmap-c)#set mpls experimental 5
PE1(config)# interface Ethernet0/0
PE1(config-if)# xconnect 10.10.10.102 100 encapsulation mpls
PE1(config-if)# service-policy input AToMQoS
```

Example 13-15 *Configuration of L2VPN QoS: Ethernet over MPLS VLAN Mode*

```
PE1(config)#class-map AToMQoS
PE1(config-cmap)#match any
PE1(config)#policy-map AToMQoS
PE1(config-pmap)#class AToMQoS
PE1(config-pmap-c)#set mpls experimental 5
PE1(config)# interface FastEthernet0/0.100
PE1(config-if)#encapsulation dot1q 100
PE1(config-if)# xconnect 10.10.10.102 100 encapsulation mpls
PE1(config-if)# service-policy input AToMQoS
```

Example 13-16 *Configuration of L2VPN QoS: PPP over MPLS*

```
PE1(config)#class-map AToMQoS
PE1(config-cmap)#match any
```

continues

Example 13-16 *Configuration of L2VPN QoS: PPP over MPLS (Continued)*

```
PE1(config)#policy-map AToMQoS
PE1(config-pmap)#class AToMQoS
PE1(config-pmap-c)#set mpls experimental 5
PE1(config)# interface Serial1/0
PE1(config-if)#encapsulation ppp
PE1(config-if)# xconnect 10.10.10.102 100 encapsulation mpls
PE1(config-if)#service-policy input AToMQoS
```

Example 13-17 *Configuration of L2VPN QoS: HDLC over MPLS*

```
PE1(config)#class-map AToMQoS
PE1(config-cmap)#match any
PE1(config)#policy-map AToMQoS
PE1(config-pmap)#class AToMQoS
PE1(config-pmap-c)#set mpls experimental 5
PE1(config)# interface Serial1/0
PE1(config-if)#encapsulation hdlc
PE1(config-if)# xconnect 10.10.10.102 100 encapsulation mpls
PE1(config-if)#service-policy input AToMQoS
```

Example 13-18 *Configuration of L2VPN QoS: Frame Relay over MPLS*

```
PE1(config)#frame-relay switching
PE1(config)#connect FR Serial1/0 100 l2transport
PE1(config-fr-pw-switching)# xconnect 10.10.10.102 100 encapsulation mpls

PE1(config)#class-map FRoverMPLS
PE1(config-cmap)#match any
PE1(config)#policy-map FRoverMPLS
PE1(config-pmap)#class FRoverMPLS
PE1(config-pmap-c)#set mpls experimental 5

PE1(config)#interface Serial1/0
PE1(config-if)# encapsulation frame-relay
PE1(config-if)# frame-relay intf-type dce
PE1(config-if)# frame-relay interface-dlci 100
PE1(config-fr-dlci)#class FRoverMPLS
```

Implementing QoS with VPLS

VPLS simplified is multipoint Ethernet over MPLS. Therefore, the configuration of QoS for VPLS is similar to that, as mentioned earlier, where the QoS configurations are performed and are applied to the appropriate interfaces. Example 13-19 shows the configuration of a PE router implementing VPLS with three other neighbors as depicted in the L2 VFI configuration of the router. The PE router implementing VPLS can perform most QoS actions and map them appropriately to the customer's VFI and, thus, implement Layer 2 Ethernet QoS and map them to the appropriate MPLS EXP bits in the MPLS domain.

Example 13-19 *Configuration of QoS for VPLS*

```
PE1(config)#l2 vfi VPLS manual
PE1(config-vfi)# vpn id 100
PE1(config-vfi)# neighbor 10.10.10.102 encapsulation mpls
PE1(config-vfi)# neighbor 10.10.10.103 encapsulation mpls

PE1(config)#interface gigabitethernet 1/1
PE1(config-if)#mls qos trust cos
PE1(config-if)#switchport
PE1(config-if)#switchport access vlan 100
PE1(config-if)#switchport mode access

PE1(config)#class-map VPLScos5
PE1(config-cmap)#match cos 5
PE1(config)#policy-map VPLS
PE1(config-pmap)#class VPLScos5
PE1(config-pmap-c)#set mpls experimental 5

PE1(config)#interface vlan 100
PE1(config-if)#xconnect vfi 100
PE1(config-if)#service-policy input VPLS
```

Figure 13-16 shows the VPLS setup for implementation of QoS with VPLS. For brevity, only the PE1 router's configuration has been depicted in Example 13-19, and it can be applied to other PE routers appropriately.

Figure 13-16 *VPLS QoS Configuration Topology*

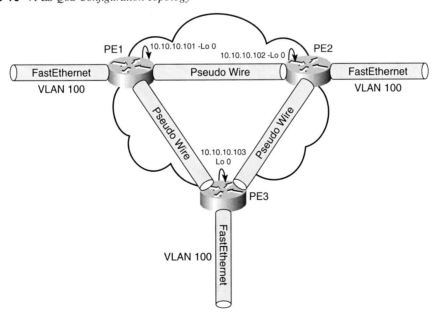

Implementing QoS with L2TPv3

Tunnel marking for L2TPv3 tunnels can be configured to associate QoS for incoming customer traffic on the PE router in a SP network. Tunnel marking enables marking of incoming customer traffic mapping to L2TPv3 tunnels with IP Precedence or DSCP values in an L2TPv3 tunnel. The marking of an IP Precedence or DSCP value for a tunnel is performed under the **policy-map** configuration with a **set ip precedence tunnel** *value* or **set ip dscp tunnel** *value* commands.

Note that the tunnel marking for L2TPv3 tunnels can only be performed on packets marked on ingress using an ingress policy map. Example 13-20 shows the configuration of an L2TPv3 marking for traffic generated with either IP Precedence of 5 or DSCP of EF on the ingress PE interface mapping to an L2TPv3 tunnel.

Example 13-20 *Implementing Tunnel Marking with L2TPv3 on PE Router*

```
PE1(config)#class-map match-any L2TPv3-marking
PE1(config-cmap)#match ip precedence 5
PE1(config-cmap)#match ip dscp ef
PE1(config)#policy-map L2TPv3-marking
PE1(config-pmap)#class L2TPv3-marking
PE1(config-pmap-c)#set ip precedence tunnel 5

PE1(config)# l2tp-class manual
PE1(config-l2tp-class)# cookie size 4

PE1(config)# pseudowire-class manual
PE1(config-pw-class)# encapsulation l2tpv3
PE1(config-pw-class)# protocol none
PE1(config-pw-class)# ip local interface Loopback0

PE1(config)# interface Loopback0
PE1(config-if)# description Loopback for L2TPv3 tunnel
PE1(config-if)# ip address 10.10.10.101 255.255.255.255

PE1(config)# interface POS0/0
PE1(config-if)# service-policy input L2Tpv3-marking
PE1(config-if)# xconnect 10.10.10.102 1 encapsulation l2tpv3 manual pw-class manual
PE1(config-if)# l2tp id 1 1
PE1(config-if)#  l2tp cookie local 4 1
PE1(config-if)#  l2tp cookie remote 4 1
PE1(config-if)#  l2tp hello manual
```

Command Reference

Command	Description
Router(config)# **class-map {match-all |** **match-any}** *name*	Configures a class map to associate class of traffic
Router(config-cmap)# **match any**	Associates any packet into this class
Router(config-cmap)# **match [not]** **access-group** {*Access-list-number* | **Name** *Access-list-name*}	Associates packets defined by predefined access list into traffic class
Router(config-cmap)# **match [not]** **cos** *cos-value-1* [*cos-value-2*] [*cos-value-3*] [*cos-value-4*]	Associates packets with certain CoS value into traffic class
Router(config-cmap)# **match [not]** **atm clp**	Associates packets by ATM CLP
Router(config-cmap)# **match [not]** **dscp** *dscp-value-1* [*dscp-value-2*] [*dscp-value-3*] [*dscp-value-4*]	Associates packets with certain DSCP value(s) to traffic class
Router(config-cmap)# **match [not] ip** {**dscp**	**precedence**} {*dscp-value-1* | *IP-precedence-value-1*} [*dscp-value-2* | *IP-precedence-value-2*] [*dscp-value-3* | *IP-precedence-value-3*] [*dscp-value-4* | *IP-precedence-value-4*]	Associates packets with certain IP Precedence or DSCP value to traffic class
Router(config-cmap)# **match [not]** **mpls experimental** *MPLS-exp-value-1* [*MPLS-exp-value-2*] [*MPLS-exp-value-3*] [*MPLS-exp-value-4*] [*MPLS-exp-value-5*] [*MPLS-exp-value-6*] [*MPLS-exp-value-7*] [*MPLS-exp-value-8*]	Matches packets with specific MPLS EXP value to traffic class
Router(config-cmap)# **match [not]** **protocol** *protocol-identifier-name*	Matches packets based on protocol ID
Router(config-cmap)# **match** **[not] qos-group** *qos-group-value*	Matches packets based on locally defined QoS group values
Router(config-cmap)# **match [not]** **vlan** *vlan-id*	Matches packets based on VLAN ID values in L2 header
Router(config)**policy-map** *policy-map-name*	Configures QOS policy
Router(config-pmap)# **class** *class-map-name*	Configures per-class PHB under policy map

continues

(Continued)

Command	Description
Router(config-pmap-c)# **bandwidth** {*bandwidth-in-kbps* I **percent** *percentage-of-total-bandwidth* I **remaining** *percentage-of-remaining-bandwidth*}	Configures the bandwidth allocation per class
Router(config-pmap-c)# **priority**	Identifies the class to be treated with LLQ
Router(config-pmap-c)# **set** {**dscp** *dscp-value* I **IP dscp** *dscp-value* I **IP precedence** *precedence-value* I **precedence** *precedence-value* I **atm-clp** I **cos** *cos-value* I **discard-class** *discard-class-value* I **fr-de** I **qos-group** *qos-group-value* I **MPLS experimental** {*exp-value* I **imposition** *exp-value* I **topmost** *exp-value*}}	Configures the PHB marking parameters for DSCP and IP Precedence per class under policy-map configuration
Router(config-pmap-c)# **random-detect** {**prec-based** I **dscp-based**} Router(config-pmap-c)# **random-detect precedence** *precedence-value min-threshold* [**cells** I **milliseconds** I **packets** I **microseconds**] *max-threshold* [**cells** I **milliseconds** I **packets** I **microseconds**] *mark-probability-denominator* Router(config-pmap-c)# **random-detect dscp** *dscp-value min-threshold* [**cells** I **milliseconds** I **packets** I **microseconds**] *max-threshold* [**cells** I **milliseconds** I **packets** I **microseconds**] *mark-probability-denominator*	Configures WRED under each class (either Precedence based or DSCP based) for congestion avoidance
Router(config-pmap-c)# **police** {**cir** *cir*} [**bc** *conform-burst*] {**pir** *pir*} [**be** *peak-burst*] [**conform-action** *action* [**exceed-action** *action* [**violate-action** *action*]]] OR Router(config-pmap-c)# **police** *bps* [**burst-normal**] [**burst-max**] **conform-action** *action* **exceed-action** *action* [**violate-action** *action*] OR Router(config-pmap-c)# **police cir percent** *percent* [**bc** *conform-burst-in-msec*] [**pir percent** *percent*] [**be** *peak-burst-in-msec*]	Configures policing per class under policy-map configuration Where *action* = {**drop** I **set-clp-transmit** I **set-discard-class-transmit** *discard-class-value* I **set-dscp-transmit** *dscp-value* I **set-frde-transmit** I **set-mpls-exp-imposition-transmit** *mpls-exp-value* I **set-mpls-exp-topmost-transmit** *mpls-exp-value* I **set-prec-transmit** *precedence-value* I **set-qos-transmit** *qos-group-value* I **transmit**}

(Continued)

Command	Description
Router(config-pmap-c)# **shape** {**average** I **peak**} *cir* [*bc*] [*be*] OR Router(config-pmap-c)# **shape** {**average** I **peak**} **percent** *percent* [*bc*] [*be*] OR Router(config-pmap-c)# **shape** [**average** I **peak**] *mean-rate* [[*burst-size*] [*excess-burst-size*]]	Configures shaping per class under policy-map configuration
Router(config)# **interface** *interface-type number* Router(config-if)# **service-policy** {**in** I **out** } *policy-map-name*	Associates the policy map with an interface, either ingress or egress

CHAPTER 14

MPLS Features and Case Studies

This chapter concentrates on the implementation of various features in correlation with MPLS deployments. Layer 3 VPNs, Layer 2 VPNs (AToM), and VPLS are the predominant implementations of MPLS in networks today. However, a large number of features have been introduced in conjunction with MPLS that enable a crisper service delivery to end customers as well as more services that can be revenue generators for service providers (SPs). The following features will be covered by means of case studies in this chapter:

- Multicast VPN support for MPLS VPN
- Multi-VRF CE (with multicast support)
- VRF selection based on source IP address
- VRF selection using policy-based routing
- NAT and HSRP support in MPLS VPN
- Layer 2 VPN pseudo-wire switching
- Providing L3 VPN over L2 VPN circuits with L2 VPN pseudo-wire redundancy
- Implementing dynamic L3 VPN over mGRE tunnels
- Class-based tunnel selection with MPLS TE
- Implementing L3 VPN hub and spoke with OSPF and EIGRP
- VPLS support on the GSR 12000 series routers
- BGP Site-Of-Origin (SOO)

Case Study 1: Implementing Multicast Support for MPLS VPNs

Multicast VPN or an MPLS VPN capable of supporting multicast packet forwarding does not use MPLS forwarding or a control mechanism but uses MPLS VPN architecture and its associated Multicast Border Gateway Protocol (MBGP) route distribution process. This architecture requires that multicast routing be enabled in the SP core network. The multicast VPN solution provides a reduction in the amount of state information while retaining optimal routing. It maps all the particular VPN multicast groups to a single unique group called the *Default Multicast Distribution Tree (Default MDT)* in the provider network.

Control and low bandwidth data traffic flows through the default MDT. The solution allows the creation of additional distribution groups called *Data Multicast Distribution Trees (Data MDTs)* in the SP network to transport high bandwidth sources to points in the network that are signaled to receive traffic. This solution includes the support of multicast routing and forwarding in the context of VPN Routing and Forwarding (VRF) and the use of multicast tunnels over the provider network for control and data connectivity.

Routers in the customer sites that will be a part of the multicast tree will have to be enabled for multicast forwarding on the appropriate interfaces. The provider edge (PE) routers maintain PIM adjacency with the CE routers. The customer can run any multicast routing protocol (SSM or PIM) independent of the multicast protocol running in the provider network. PE routers build a *per-VRF default MDT* that will be used to distribute data packets and control messages for low bandwidth traffic.

Operation of Multicast MPLS VPN

The operation of a multicast MPLS VPN is as follows:

1. Default MDT is enabled per customer VRF on every PE router that will forward multicast packets between customer sites. The VRF on the PE routers thus enabled for multicast forwarding is also called the *multicast VRF* (mVRF).

2. *Default MDT* enables multicast forwarding for all PEs where the VRF resides.

3. Control and data packets are transported per VRF over default MDT. Therefore, all low bandwidth data that is transported over the default MDT will be delivered to PEs where the VRFs reside. Hence, the default MDT is always present.

4. A *Data MDT* for higher bandwidth sources can be created on the PE routers per VRF, and only routers that are part of the multicast tree for the high bandwidth source receive the multicast packets generated by the high bandwidth source. The data MDT is created on demand for mVPN (S, G) higher bandwidth traffic.

MDT group addresses are defined by the provider and are unrelated to the groups used by the customer. Access to the MDT is via a *multicast tunnel interface* on PE routers where the PE router always functions as the root of the MDT if it is connected to the CE router containing the multicast source.

Figure 14-1 shows an SP network with the default MDT and data MDT concepts highlighted.

Figure 14-1   *Multicast MPLS VPN Support Concepts and Operation*

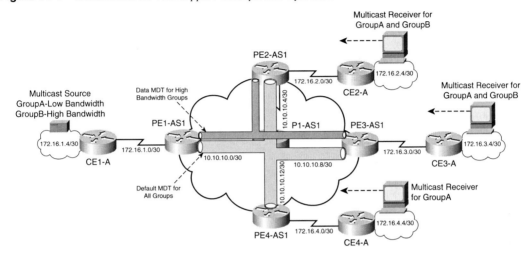

As shown in Figure 14-1, Site 1 sources multicast packets for GroupA and GroupB where GroupA is a low bandwidth source and GroupB is a high bandwidth source. Sites 2 and 3 belonging to Customer A, as well as PE Routers PE2-AS1 and PE3-AS1, receive traffic destined for both groups. As shown in Figure 14-1, the default MDT is formed between all PE routers, and the data MDT is formed only with PE routers connected to sources/receivers of high bandwidth traffic.

Configuration of Multicast Support for MPLS VPN

Configuration to enable multicast support for MPLS VPN is shown in Figure 14-2. The configurations involve enabling multicast as well as a multicast protocol on the interfaces in the customer domain, as well as the provider domain, to forward multicast packets. In addition, the VRF mapping to the customer is enabled for multicast routing using the **ip multicast-routing vrf** command, and the default and data MDTs are configured under the VRF definition.

Figure 14-2 *Multicast MPLS VPN Configuration Flowchart*

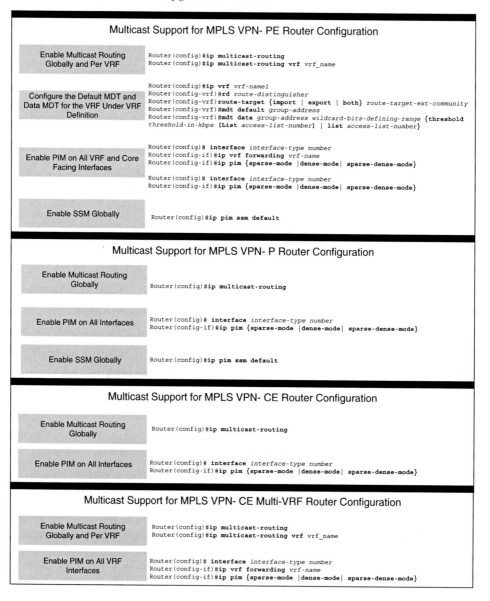

Implementing Multicast Support for MPLS VPNs

Figure 14-3 shows a SP network providing MPLS VPN services to Customer A sites. Customer A, after prior deployment of intersite connectivity using MPLS VPN, would like to also have support for multicast traffic propagation to other sites with receivers that are members of a multicast group.

Figure 14-3   *Case Study 1: Multicast MPLS VPN Topology*

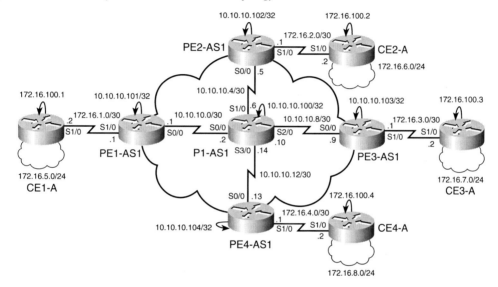

The additional complete configurations on the devices to enable multicast support for MPLS VPN are shown in Figure 14-4. Configurations for PE3-AS1 and PE4-AS1 have not been depicted for brevity and can be derived using the same process as the depicted PE router configurations. As illustrated, the default MDT is configured with a group address of 232.10.0.1, and the data MDT is configured with a group address range of 232.0.0.1 to 232.0.0.255.

Figure 14-4 *Case Study 1: Multicast MPLS VPN Configuration*

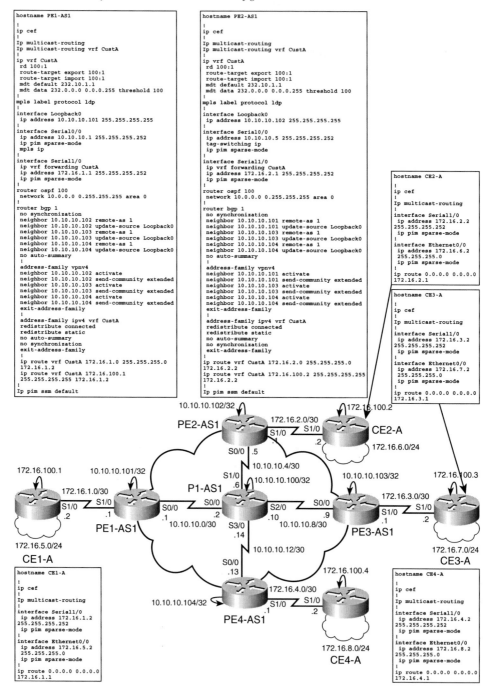

Verifications for Case Study 1

Figure 14-5 shows the verification for the implementation of multicast support for MPLS VPN by performing a **show ip mroute** on the appropriate devices. As shown in Figure 14-5, the multicast states are propagated via the MP-BGP backbone to CE2-A for the group 232.10.1.1 due to a receiver being connected in Customer A Site 2 for the group.

Figure 14-5   *Case Study 1: Multicast MPLS VPN Verification*

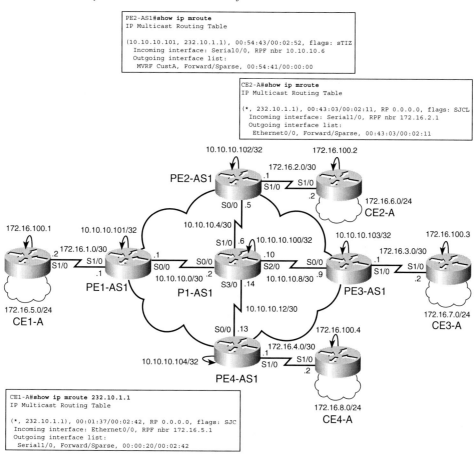

Case Study 2: Implementing Multi-VRF CE, VRF Selection Using Source IP Address, VRF Selection Using Policy-Based Routing, NAT and HSRP Support in MPLS VPN, and Multicast VPN Support over Multi-VRF CE

Service provider SP provides VPN connectivity between multiple sites belonging to Customers A and B, as depicted by CustA and CustB VRFs on the appropriate PE routers illustrated in Figure 14-6.

Figure 14-6 *Case Study 2 Topology*

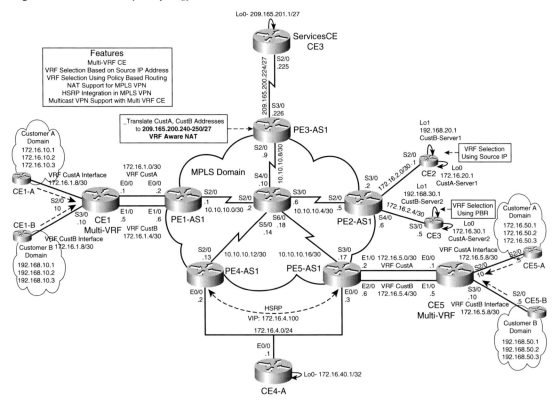

Some sites belonging to Customer A and Customer B are connected into a managed CE offering provided by the service provider *SP*. The service provider implements *multi-VRF CE* to enable the same managed CE router to be used for connecting domains belonging to both Customer A and Customer B. CE1 and CE5 routers are managed CEs that run the multi-VRF CE feature and, thus, enable connectivity of both Customer A and Customer B sites into the MPLS domain using a single SP managed-CE router.

In addition, CE Routers CE2 and CE3, connecting to PE Router PE2-AS1, provide connectivity to servers that are to be selectively reachable by Customer A and Customer B domains. Figure 14-6 depicts loopback interfaces on CE2 and CE3 that are used to emulate servers attached to these CE routers. As illustrated in Figure 14-6, one server on each of these CE routers is to be made reachable to Customer A and Customer B, respectively.

The SP implements these requirement using *VRF selection using source IP address* in relationship to servers connected to CE2 and *VRF selection using policy-based routing* to enable connectivity to servers connected to CE3 for the Customer A and Customer B domains.

SP is looking for improved methods to offer shared services to customers being offered MPLS VPN services. To enable Internet access for multiple customer VPNs, the IP addressing space pertaining to Internet access needs to be unique, though possibilities of overlapping customer addresses exist between multiple VPN domains. Therefore, *SP* implements NAT to enable such shared services to multiple customers. The *NAT Integration with MPLS VPNs* feature enables the implementation of NAT on a PE router in a MPLS cloud.

In Figure 14-6, PE3-AS1 has Router ServicesCE (CE3) connected that provides shared services to both VPNs CustA and CustB, which is part of VRF *Services*. NAT is implemented on the Router PE3-AS1 such that CustA and CustB networks (IP addresses in the ranges 172.16.x.x and 192.168.x.x for customers A and B, respectively) can access the shared services CE after undergoing an NAT translation from the private address space to the real IP address space range of 209.165.200.240-250/27.

In redundant CE to PE connections in which the same CE is connected to multiple PE routers, like in the case of CE4-A being connected to PE4-AS1 as well as PE5-AS1 using HSRP, CE4-A has a default route pointing to the virtual IP address of the HSRP group. In addition, there are also possibilities that hosts in the customer domain might have a default gateway configured to the HSRP virtual IP address. With *HSRP support for MPLS VPN*, the PE routers enable the addition of ARP entries for the virtual IP address to the VRF routing table associated with the interfaces connected to the CE routers. CE4-A belonging to CustA VRF has a default route pointing to the HSRP virtual IP address 172.16.4.100/24 to reach other hosts belonging to the CustA and other domain networks.

Finally, Customer A has posed an additional requirement for the SP to support transport of multicast to enable intersite multicast traffic to enable different sites to view web training using VOD or IP/TV. Therefore, the SP supports this requirement by enabling the VRF CustA for *multicast MPLS VPN support*. Multicast MPLS VPN support is implemented for Customer A multi-VRF CE connected routers, namely CE1-A and CE2-A, connecting to CE1 and CE5, respectively.

Configuration of Core Devices in Case Study 2

Figure 14-7 outlines the basic configurations for the devices in the SP domain, namely PE1-AS1, PE2-AS1, PE3-AS1, PE4-AS1, and PE5-AS1. It is assumed that MPLS forwarding has been enabled on the appropriate interfaces and IP addressing performed as shown earlier in Figure 14-6. Only VRF-related definitions and configurations of IGP and MP-BGP on the PE routers are shown in Figure 14-7. Configuration of P1-AS1 involving OSPF as the IGP, as well as all interfaces enabled for MPLS forwarding, are not depicted in Figure 14-7 for brevity.

Figure 14-7 *Case Study 2 Topology: SP Routers Base Configurations*

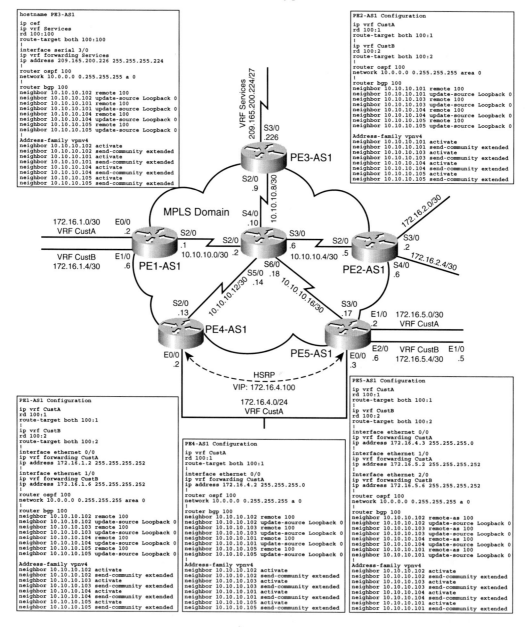

Theory and Configuration of Features in Case Study 2

This section outlines the theory and configurations behind the operation of the just mentioned features.

Multi-VRF CE

Multi-VRF CE enables the same CE router to connect to multiple customer domains and still provide transparency of customer traffic across the MPLS backbone. The caveat with multi-VRF CE is that a dedicated interface (either physical or logical) is required per customer between the PE and CE router for the CE router to implement multi-VRF CE. With multi-VRF CE, the CE router can implement separated routing tables for different services that need to be configured on the customer. However, no label exchange occurs between the PE and the connected CE, though the CE router has VRFs configured on it. Depending on the protocol in use between PE and CE routers, the configuration of the PE and CE routers vary. The protocols currently supporting multi-VRF CE are RIPv2, OSPFv2, and BGP.

Figure 14-8 outlines the steps in the configuration of multi-VRF CE on the managed CE router connecting multiple customer domains and the attached PE router.

Figure 14-8   *Multi-VRF CE Configuration Flowchart*

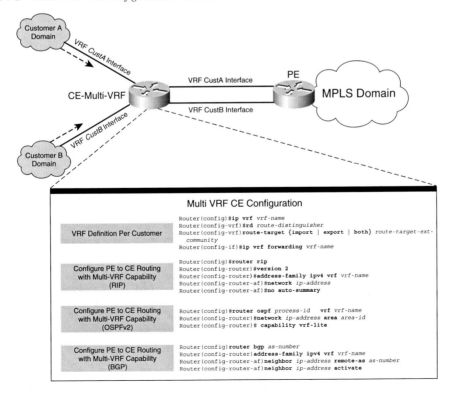

A similar configuration is to be performed on the SP-managed CE Routers CE1 and CE5 connected to PE1-AS1 and PE2-AS1, respectively. The multi-VRF related configurations for the devices are shown in Figure 14-9. The configurations illustrate the CE1-A, CE1-B, CE2-A, and CE2-B customer routers connected to the multi-vrf CE Routers CE1 and CE5. Note that multi-VRF CE with OSPF PE-CE has been implemented in this case study and can be implemented using other protocols following the configuration flowchart shown in Figure 14-8.

Figure 14-9 *Multi-VRF CE Configurations for Case Study 2*

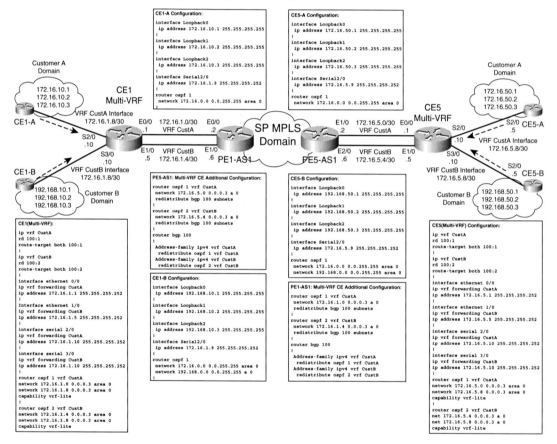

VRF Selection Based on Source IP Address and Policy-Based Routing

VRF selection based on source IP address is a method to decouple the actual interface connecting the PE and CE routers from the VPN. Therefore, a subset of IP addresses belonging to the customer domain can be associated with one VPN versus another. In traditional VPN operation and configuration, each logical or physical interface connected to a CE router is assigned as part of a VRF. With VRF selection on source IP address, this is no longer a requirement. There can be a range of IP addresses assigned to different VRFs. However, care must be taken to perform accurate IP addressing. This solution makes it lucrative to offer Internet access to a subset of users from the same customer CE attached domain. Figure 14-10 depicts the configurations to be performed on the associated CE and PE routers to enable VRF selection based on source IP address. In the case study, access to servers (simulated by loopbacks on CE router CE2) will be provided for Customer A (172.16.20.1) using the VRF selection on source IP address.

Figure 14-10 *VRF Selection Based on Source IP Configuration Flowchart*

VRF Selection Based on Source IP Address- PE Configuration	
Configure the IP Addresses to be Associated with a Specific VRF Table on the PE Router	`Router(config)# vrf selection source source-IP-address source-IP-mask` `  vrf vrf_name`
Enable VRF Selection Based on Source IP Address on the Interface Connected to CE Router	`Router(config)#interface interface-type-connected-to-ce number` `Router(config-if)#ip vrf select source`
Add All the IP Addresses that Are Associated with an Interface into a VRF Table	`Router(config-if)#ip vrf receive vrf-name`

Add Static VRF Routes to the Networks Associated with VRF Tables Mapped Using VRF Selection on Source IP Address	`Router(config)# ip route vrf vrf_name prefix mask [ce-next-hop-address]`
	`  [interface-connected-to-ce {interface-number}] [global] [distance] [permanent]`
	`  [tag tag]`

Redistribute VRF Specific Static Routes Into Appropriate IPv4 Address-Families Under MP-BGP Configuration	`Router(config)router bgp as-number`
	`Router(config-router)address-family ipv4 vrf vrf-name`
	`Router(config-router-af)redistribute static`

VRF Selection Based on Source IP Address- CE Configuration	
Add Static/Default Route to the PE Router for Reachability to Remote Networks	`Router(config)# ip route prefix mask [pe-next-hop-address] [interface-` `  connected-to-pe {interface-number}] [global] [distance] [permanent] [tag tag]`

The key configurations involve identification of IP address ranges that apply to a certain VPN on the PE as well as configuration of static routes pointing to those prefixes from the PE to the CE routers. In addition, the interface that will be used for VRF selection based on source IP address needs to be enabled for the feature; the VPNs that will be used on that interface also need to be defined.

VRF selection based on policy-based routing (PBR) is similar in operation and configuration to VRF selection based on source IP address. Note, however, that *an interface configured for VRF selection based on source IP cannot be also configured for VRF selection based on PBR.* In VRF selection based on PBR, policy routing of VPN traffic is based on match criteria. Match criteria is defined in a prefix list, in an IP access list, or based on packet length. Policy routing is defined in the route-map. The route-map is applied to the incoming interface with the **ip policy route-map** interface configuration command.

The flowchart for the implementation of VRF selection using PBR is shown in Figure 14-11.

Figure 14-11 *VRF Selection Using PBR Configuration Flowchart*

VRF Selection Based on PBR- PE Configuration	
Configure Traffic to Map to VRF's Using Access-Lists	`Router(config)#ip access-list {standard|extended} [access-list-name|access-list-number]` `Router(config-[std/ext]-nacl)#[sequence-number]permit	deny protocol source source-wildcard destination destination-wildcard [option option-value] [precedence precedence] [tos tos] [log] [time-range time-range-name] [fragments]`
Configure Traffic to Map to VRF's Using Prefix-Lists	`Router(config)#ip prefix-list prefix-list-name [seq seq-value] {deny network/length	permit network/length} [ge ge-value] [le le-value]`
Add all the IP Addresses that Are Associated with an Interface into a VRF Table	`Router(config)#interface interface-type-connected-to-ce number` `Router(config-if)#ip vrf receive vrf-name`
Add Static VRF Routes to the Networks Associated with VRF Tables Mapped Using VRF Selection on Source IP Address	`Router(config)# ip route vrf vrf_name prefix mask [ce-next-hop-address] [interface-connected-to-ce {interface-number}] [global] [distance] [permanent] [tag tag]`

Redistribute VRF Specific Static Routes into Appropriate IPv4 Address-Families Under MP-BGP Configuration	`Router(config)router bgp as-number`
	`Router(config-router)address-family ipv4 vrf vrf-name`
	`Router(config-router-af)redistribute static`

VRF Selection Based on PBR- CE Configuration	
Add Static/Default Route to the PE Router for Reachability to Remote Networks	`Router(config)# ip route prefix mask [ce-next-hop-address] [interface-connected-to-ce {interface-number}] [global] [distance] [permanent] [tag tag]`

By following the steps shown in Figure 14-10 and Figure 14-11, the devices PE2-AS1, CE2, and CE3 are configured to implement VRF selection. The configurations of only PE2-AS1 shows VRF selection using source IP address in relationship to CE2 and VRF selection using PBR in relationship to CE3. Configurations of PE2-AS1 for implementing these two features on the interfaces connecting to CE2 and CE3 are illustrated separately in Figure 14-12 for clarity. Configurations do not show the IGP, MP-BGP, and VRF definitions as they are already shown in Figure 14-7.

Figure 14-12 *VRF Selection Using PBR and Source IP: Configurations for Case Study 2*

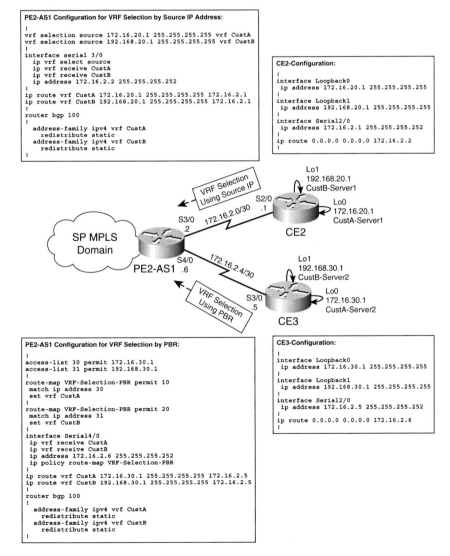

HSRP Integration with MPLS VPN

With HSRP support for MPLS VPN, the CE4-A router can be connected to PE Routers PE4-AS1 and PE5-AS1 and, thus, enables the addition of ARP entries for the virtual IP address to the VRF routing table associated with the interfaces connected to the CE router.

The configuration flowchart for the implementation of HSRP integration to MPLS VPN is shown in Figure 14-13.

Figure 14-13 *HSRP Integration to MPLS VPN: Configuration Flowchart*

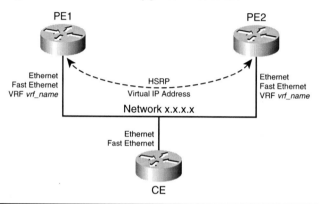

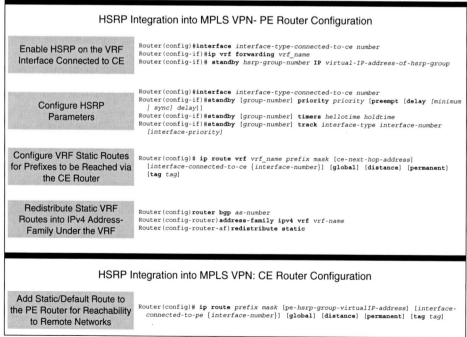

HSRP integration is configured on PE4-AS1 and PE5-AS1 with a virtual IP address of 172.16.4.100. CE Router CE4-A has a static default route pointing to this VIP address. PE4-AS1 and PE5-AS1 are also configured with static VRF routes pointing to CE4-A networks. The configurations for HSRP integration are shown in Figure 14-14.

Figure 14-14 *HSRP Integration to MPLS VPN: Configurations for Case Study 2*

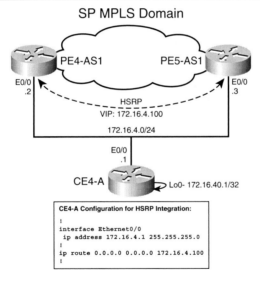

PE4-AS1 Configuration for HSRP Integration:
```
!
interface Ethernet0/0
 ip vrf forwarding CustA
 ip address 172.16.4.2 255.255.255.0
 standby ip 172.16.4.100
 standby 1 preempt delay minimum 10
 standby 1 track Serial2/0
!
ip route vrf CustA 172.16.40.1 255.255.255.255 172.16.4.1
!
router bgp 100
!
   address-family ipv4 vrf CustA
     redistribute static
!
```

PE5-AS1 Configuration for HSRP Integration:
```
!
interface Ethernet0/0
 ip vrf forwarding CustA
 ip address 172.16.4.3 255.255.255.0
 standby ip 172.16.4.100
 standby 1 preempt delay minimum 10
 standby 1 track Serial3/0
!
ip route vrf CustA 172.16.40.1 255.255.255.255 172.16.4.1
!
router bgp 100
!
   address-family ipv4 vrf CustA
     redistribute static
!
```

CE4-A Configuration for HSRP Integration:
```
!
interface Ethernet0/0
 ip address 172.16.4.1 255.255.255.0
!
ip route 0.0.0.0 0.0.0.0 172.16.4.100
!
```

NAT Integration to MPLS VPN

NAT can be implemented to enable shared services to multiple customers. The NAT Integration with MPLS VPNs feature enables the implementation of NAT on a PE router in an MPLS cloud. Configurations for the implementation of NAT integration to MPLS VPN are only required on the PE router performing NAT integration. In the case study, this function is provided by PE Router PE3-AS1, which connects the VRFs, CustA and CustB, to the services VRF configured on PE3-AS1 after undergoing an NAT translation. The configuration flowchart for the implementation of NAT integration to MPLS VPN is shown in Figure 14-15.

Figure 14-15 *NAT Integration to MPLS VPN Configuration Flowchart*

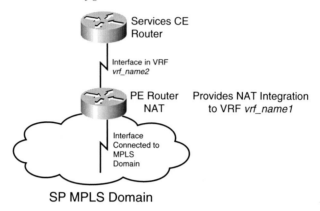

NAT Integration into MPLS VPN- PE NAT Router Configuration	

Configure VRF's for NAT Integration	`Router(config)#`**`ip vrf`** `vrf-name1`
	`Router(config-vrf)#`**`rd`** `route-distinguisher`
	`Router(config-vrf)`**`route-target {import
		export	both}`** `route-target-ext-community`

Configure Common Services VRF to be Enabled for NAT and Associate Interfaces	`Router(config)#`**`ip vrf`** `vrf-name2` `Router(config-vrf)#`**`rd`** `route-distinguisher` `Router(config-vrf)`**`route-target {import	export	both}`** `route-target-ext-community` `Router(config)#` **`interface`** `interface-type number` `Router(config-if)#`**`ip vrf forwarding`** `vrf-name`

Configure NAT Inside and Outside Interfaces	`Router(config)#` **`interface`** `interface-connected-to-services-ce-type number`
	`Router(config)#` **`ip nat outside`**
	
	`Router(config)#` **`interface`** `interface-connected-to-MPLS-domain-type number`
	`Router(config-if)#` **`ip nat inside`**

Configure Static Routes for VRF vrf-name1 Pointing to Networks that can be Reached by the Services CE	`Router(config)#` **`ip route vrf`** `vrf_name1 prefix mask` `[services-ce-next-hop-address]` `[interface-connected-to-services-ce {interface-number}]` **`[global]`** **`[distance]`** **`[permanent]`** **`[tag`** `tag`**`]`**
Configure NAT Pool for Interfaces Undergoing NAT Translation	`Router(config)#` **`ip nat pool`** `nat-pool-name start-range-of-IP-addresses end-range-` `of-IP-addresses` **`netmask`** `netmask`
Configure Access-lists to define Routes that Are To Be NAT Translated	`Router(config)#`**`ip access-list {standard|extended}`** `[access-list-name|access-list-` `number]` `Router(config-[std/ext]-nacl)#`*`[sequence-number]`***`permit	deny`** `protocol source` `source-wildcard destination destination-wildcard` **`[option`** `option-value`**`]`** **`[precedence`** `precedence]` **`[tos`** `tos`**`]`** **`[log]`** **`[time-range`** `time-range-name`**`]`** **`[fragments]`**
Associate NAT Pool with Customer VPN VRF's	`Router(config)#`**`ip nat inside source-list`** `[access-list-name|access-list-number]` **`pool`** `nat-pool-name` **`vrf`** `vrf_name2`

Redistribute Static VRF Routes Into IPv4 Address-Family Under the VRF	`Router(config)`**`router bgp`** `as-number`
	`Router(config-router)`**`address-family ipv4 vrf`** `vrf-name2`
	`Router(config-router-af)`**`redistribute static`**

The configurations for PE Router PE3-AS1 performing NAT translation for networks 172.16.x.x from CustA and 192.168.x.x from CustB are shown in Figure 14-16.

Figure 14-16 *NAT Integration to MPLS VPN Configuration for Case Study 2*

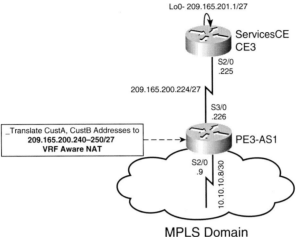

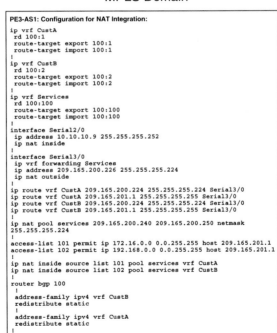

```
PE3-AS1: Configuration for NAT Integration:

ip vrf CustA
 rd 100:1
 route-target export 100:1
 route-target import 100:1
!
ip vrf CustB
 rd 100:2
 route-target export 100:2
 route-target import 100:2
!
ip vrf Services
 rd 100:100
 route-target export 100:100
 route-target import 100:100
!
interface Serial2/0
 ip address 10.10.10.9 255.255.255.252
 ip nat inside
!
interface Serial3/0
 ip vrf forwarding Services
 ip address 209.165.200.226 255.255.255.224
 ip nat outside
!
ip route vrf CustA 209.165.200.224 255.255.255.224 Serial3/0
ip route vrf CustA 209.165.201.1 255.255.255.255 Serial3/0
ip route vrf CustB 209.165.200.224 255.255.255.224 Serial3/0
ip route vrf CustB 209.165.201.1 255.255.255.255 Serial3/0
!
ip nat pool services 209.165.200.240 209.165.200.250 netmask
255.255.255.224
!
access-list 101 permit ip 172.16.0.0 0.0.255.255 host 209.165.201.1
access-list 102 permit ip 192.168.0.0 0.0.255.255 host 209.165.201.1
!
ip nat inside source list 101 pool services vrf CustA
ip nat inside source list 102 pool services vrf CustB
!
router bgp 100
 !
 address-family ipv4 vrf CustB
 redistribute static
 !
 address-family ipv4 vrf CustA
 redistribute static
 !
```

Multicast VPN Support over Multi-VRF CE

Multicast VPN support enables the SP to provide for Customer A's requirement of transport of multicast traffic between its sites. Multicast VPN support is configured by enabling the core VRFs needed to support multicast traffic transport with a default multicast distribution tree that transports all customer multicast frames between sites. In addition, source specific multicast (SSM) is enabled on all routers in the SP domain to enable transport of multicast information between SP domain routers.

In the case study, a source connected to CE1-A router sends multicast frames to group 232.1.1.1. PIM (protocol-independent-multicast) sparse-dense mode is configured on all interfaces in the customer and provider domains to enable transport of customer multicast traffic. A default MDT of 239.1.1.1 is configured for VRF CustA on all PE routers to enable tunneling of multicast frames between PE routers. Finally, a receiver is connected to CE5-A that joins the 232.1.1.1 group and, thus, has to receive traffic destined for the group.

The configuration flowchart for SP domain routers and CE routers has already been shown as part of Case Study 1 in Figure 14-2. In this setup, the implementation involves multicast VPN over multi-VRF CE where the multi-VRF CE has VRF definitions. However, no MDT configuration is required on the multi-VRF CE under the VRF definition to enable transport of multicast frames.

Configurations for the devices in Case Study 2 to support multicast traffic forwarding between CE1-A and CE2-A Customer A routers are illustrated in Figure 14-17.

Figure 14-17 *Multicast VPN Support: Configurations for Devices in Case Study 2*

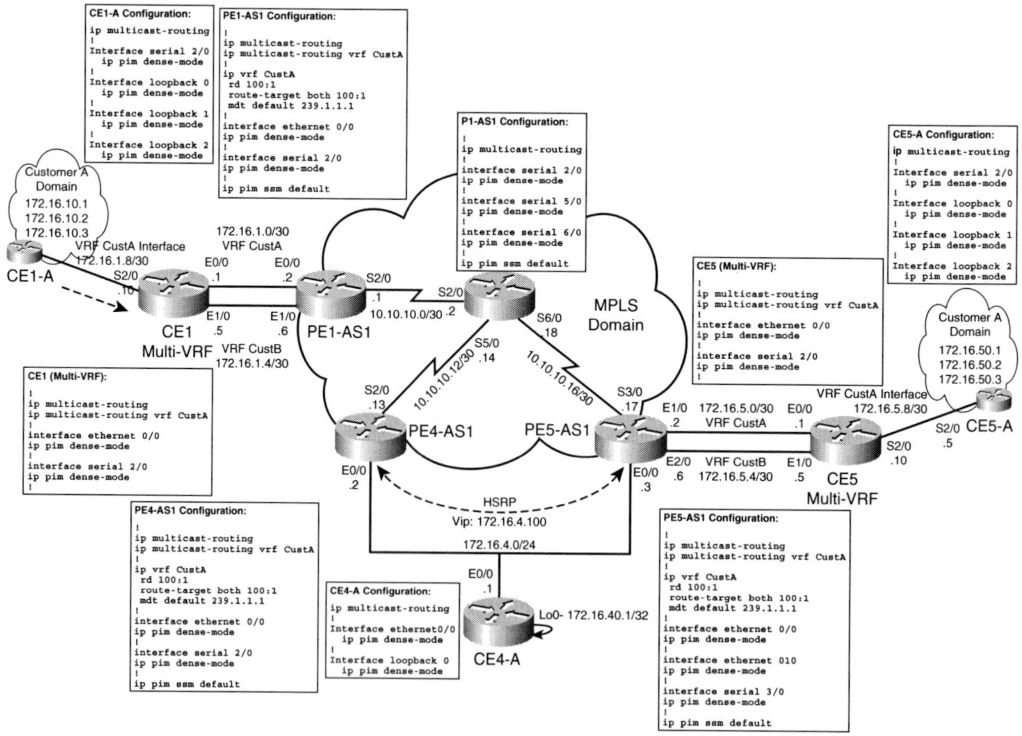

Verifications for Case Study 2

Figure 14-18 shows the verifications associated with the implementation of Case Study 2. Only verifications for VRF CustA have been shown for brevity.

Figure 14-18 *Verifications for Case Study 2*

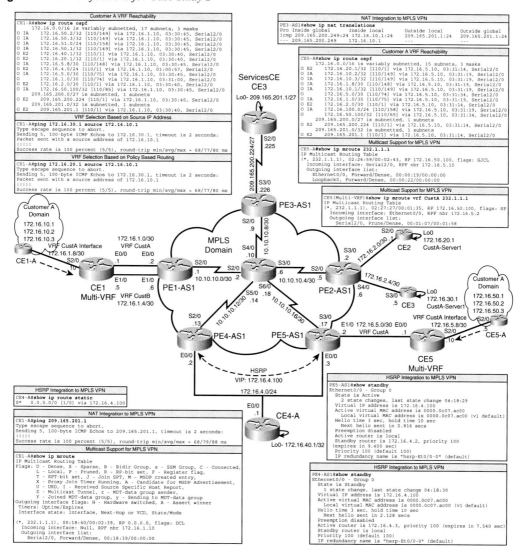

Final Configurations for Case Study 2

Figure 14-19, Figure 14-20, and Figure 14-21 show the final configurations for the CE and PE devices in Case Study 2.

Figure 14-19 *Final Configurations for CE Routers in Case Study 2*

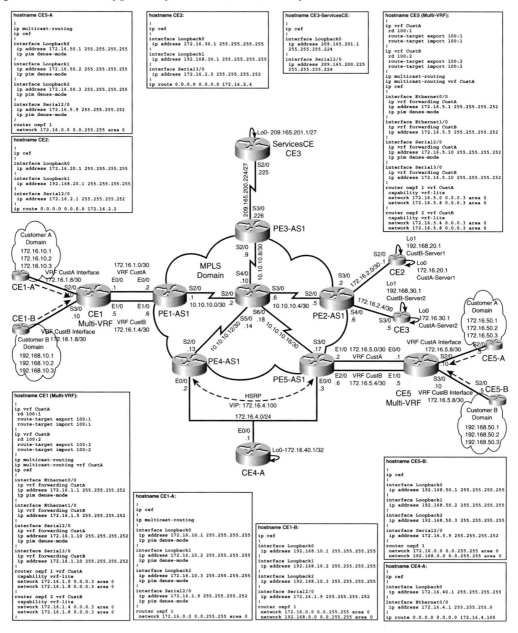

Figure 14-20 *Final Configurations for PE1-AS1, PE2-AS1, and P1-AS1 in Case Study 2*

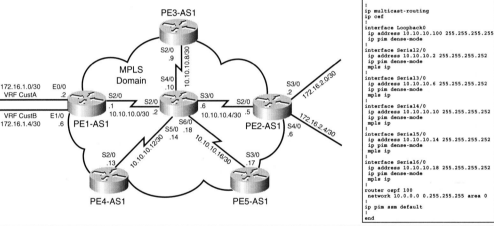

```
hostname PE1-AS1                        ip address 172.16.1.6 255.255.255.252          neighbor 10.10.10.105 remote-as 100
!                                       !                                              neighbor 10.10.10.105 update-source Loopback0
ip vrf CustA                            interface Serial2/0                            no auto-summary
 rd 100:1                                ip address 10.10.10.1 255.255.255.252         !
 route-target export 100:1               ip pim dense-mode                            address-family vpnv4
 route-target import 100:1               mpls ip                                       neighbor 10.10.10.102 activate
 mdt default 239.1.1.1                   no fair-queue                                 neighbor 10.10.10.102 send-community extended
!                                       !                                              neighbor 10.10.10.103 activate
ip vrf CustB                            router ospf 1 vrf CustA                        neighbor 10.10.10.103 send-community extended
 rd 100:2                                log-adjacency-changes                         neighbor 10.10.10.104 activate
 route-target export 100:2               redistribute bgp 100 subnets                  neighbor 10.10.10.104 send-community extended
 route-target import 100:2               network 172.16.1.0 0.0.0.3 area 0             neighbor 10.10.10.105 activate
!                                       !                                              neighbor 10.10.10.105 send-community extended
ip multicast-routing                    router ospf 2 vrf CustB                        exit-address-family
ip multicast-routing vrf CustA           log-adjacency-changes                         !
ip cef                                   redistribute bgp 100 subnets                  address-family ipv4 vrf CustB
!                                        network 172.16.1.4 0.0.0.3 area 0              redistribute ospf 2 vrf CustB
interface Loopback0                     !                                              no auto-summary
 ip address 10.10.10.101 255.255.255.255 router ospf 100                               no synchronization
 ip pim dense-mode                       log-adjacency-changes                         exit-address-family
!                                        network 10.0.0.0 0.255.255.255 area 0         !
interface Ethernet0/0                   !                                             address-family ipv4 vrf CustA
 ip vrf forwarding CustA                router bgp 100                                 redistribute ospf 1 vrf CustA
 ip address 172.16.1.2 255.255.255.252   no synchronization                           no auto-summary
 ip pim dense-mode                       bgp log-neighbor-changes                      no synchronization
!                                        neighbor 10.10.10.102 remote-as 100           exit-address-family
interface Ethernet1/0                    neighbor 10.10.10.102 update-source Loopback0 !
 ip vrf forwarding CustB                 neighbor 10.10.10.103 remote-as 100          ip pim ssm default
                                         neighbor 10.10.10.103 update-source Loopback0 !
                                         neighbor 10.10.10.104 remote-as 100          end
                                         neighbor 10.10.10.104 update-source Loopback0
```

```
hostname P1-AS1
!
ip multicast-routing
ip cef
!
interface Loopback0
 ip address 10.10.10.100 255.255.255.255
 ip pim dense-mode
!
interface Serial2/0
 ip address 10.10.10.2 255.255.255.252
 ip pim dense-mode
 mpls ip
!
interface Serial3/0
 ip address 10.10.10.6 255.255.255.252
 ip pim dense-mode
 mpls ip
!
interface Serial4/0
 ip address 10.10.10.10 255.255.255.252
 ip pim dense-mode
 mpls ip
!
interface Serial5/0
 ip address 10.10.10.14 255.255.255.252
 ip pim dense-mode
 mpls ip
!
interface Serial6/0
 ip address 10.10.10.18 255.255.255.252
 ip pim dense-mode
 mpls ip
!
router ospf 100
 network 10.0.0.0 0.255.255.255 area 0
!
ip pim ssm default
end
```

Diagram labels:

PE3-AS1

MPLS Domain

S2/0 .9   10.10.10.8/30

S4/0 .10

172.16.1.0/30 VRF CustA E0/0 .2

VRF CustB E1/0 172.16.1.4/30 .6   PE1-AS1

S2/0 .1   S2/0 10.10.10.0/30 .2   S3/0 .6

S6/0 .18   S5/0 .18 .14   10.10.10.12/30

10.10.10.16/30

S2/0 .13   PE4-AS1

S2/0 .5   S3/0 .2   172.16.2.0/30

10.10.10.4/30   PE2-AS1   S4/0 .6   172.16.2.4/30

S3/0 .17   PE5-AS1

```
hostname PE2-AS1                        interface Serial4/0                            address-family ipv4 vrf CustB
!                                        ip address 172.16.2.6 255.255.255.252          redistribute static
ip vrf CustA                             ip pim sparse-mode                             no auto-summary
 rd 100:1                                ip policy route-map VRF-Selection-PBR          no synchronization
 route-target export 100:1               ip vrf receive CustA                           exit-address-family
 route-target import 100:1               ip vrf receive CustB                           !
 mdt default 239.1.1.1                  !                                              address-family ipv4 vrf CustA
!                                       router ospf 100                                 redistribute static
ip vrf CustB                             log-adjacency-changes                          no auto-summary
 rd 100:2                                network 10.0.0.0 0.255.255.255 area 0          no synchronization
 route-target export 100:2              !                                               exit-address-family
 route-target import 100:2              router bgp 100                                 !
!                                        no synchronization                           ip route vrf CustA 172.16.20.1 255.255.255.255 172.16.2.1
ip multicast-routing                     bgp log-neighbor-changes                      ip route vrf CustA 172.16.30.1 255.255.255.255 172.16.2.5
ip multicast-routing vrf CustA           neighbor 10.10.10.101 remote-as 100           ip route vrf CustB 192.168.20.1 255.255.255.255 172.16.2.1
ip cef                                   neighbor 10.10.10.101 update-source Loopback0 ip route vrf CustB 192.168.30.1 255.255.255.255 172.16.2.5
!                                        neighbor 10.10.10.103 remote-as 100           !
interface Loopback0                      neighbor 10.10.10.103 update-source Loopback0 ip pim ssm default
 ip address 10.10.10.102 255.255.255.255 neighbor 10.10.10.104 remote-as 100           !
 ip pim sparse-mode                      neighbor 10.10.10.104 update-source Loopback0 vrf selection source 172.16.20.1 255.255.255.255 vrf CustA
!                                        neighbor 10.10.10.105 remote-as 100           vrf selection source 192.168.20.1 255.255.255.255 vrf CustB
interface Serial2/0                      neighbor 10.10.10.105 update-source Loopback0 !
 ip address 10.10.10.5 255.255.255.252   no auto-summary                              access-list 30 permit 172.16.30.1
 ip pim sparse-mode                     !                                             access-list 31 permit 192.168.30.1
 mpls ip                                address-family vpnv4                           !
!                                        neighbor 10.10.10.101 activate                route-map VRF-Selection-PBR permit 10
interface Serial3/0                      neighbor 10.10.10.101 send-community extended  match ip address 30
 ip vrf select source                    neighbor 10.10.10.103 activate                set vrf CustA
 ip vrf receive CustA                    neighbor 10.10.10.103 send-community extended !
 ip vrf receive CustB                    neighbor 10.10.10.104 activate                route-map VRF-Selection-PBR permit 20
 ip address 172.16.2.2 255.255.255.252   neighbor 10.10.10.104 send-community extended  match ip address 31
 ip pim sparse-mode                      neighbor 10.10.10.105 activate                 set vrf CustB
!                                        neighbor 10.10.10.105 send-community extended !
                                         exit-address-family                          end
                                         !
```

Figure 14-21 *Final Configurations for PE3-AS1, PE4-AS1, and PE5-AS1 in Case Study 2*

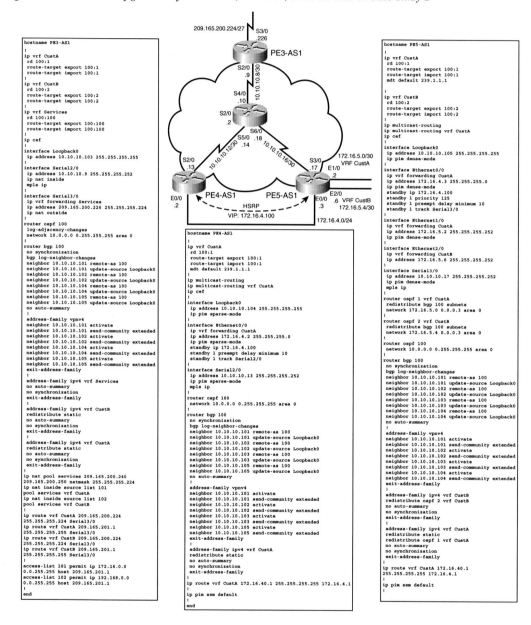

Case Study 3: Implementing Layer 2 VPNs over Inter-AS Topologies Using Layer 2 VPN Pseudo-Wire Switching

Service providers SP1 and SP2 are required by Customer A to provide Layer 2 VPN connectivity between multiple sites belonging to Customer A, as illustrated in Figure 14-22.

Figure 14-22 *Case Study 3 Topology and Base Configurations*

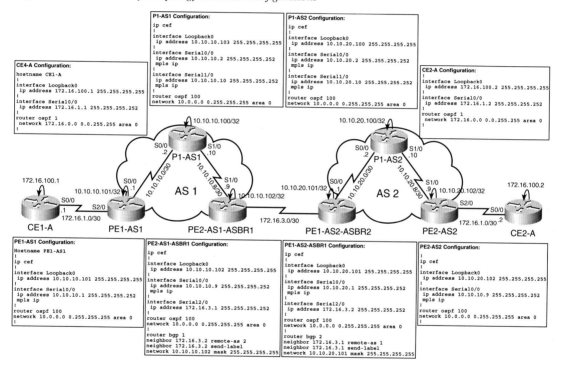

To enable the implementation of Layer 2 VPN (AToM) over an Inter-AS topology, as shown in Figure 14-22, the ASBR Routers PE2-AS1-ASBR1 and PE1-AS2-ASBR1 are configured for *layer2vpn pseudo-wire switching*.

Figure 14-22 also outlines the basic configurations for the devices in the SP domain, namely, PE1-AS1, PE2-AS1-ASBR1, P1-AS1, PE2-AS2, PE1-AS2-ASBR1, P1-AS2, and CE routers CE1-A and CE2-A. It is assumed that MPLS forwarding has been enabled on the appropriate interfaces, and IP addressing performed as illustrated in Figure 14-22. The PE routers are configured for OSPF as the IGP. The ASBR routers are configured for Inter-AS implementation between one another. CE routers CE1-A and CE2-A are configured with OSPF process of 10 with all networks in area 0. Only the configurations on the routers to implement Inter-AS have been depicted. Note that the Inter-AS implementation uses IPv4 BGP for label distribution between AS boundaries. Configurations pertaining to the implementation of Layer 2 VPN pseudo-wire switching are shown later in this section.

Layer 2 VPN Pseudo-Wire Switching Theory and Configuration

Layer 2 VPN pseudo-wire switching enables extension of Layer 2 VPN pseudo-wires across an Inter-AS boundary or across two separate MPLS networks. Layer 2 VPN pseudo-wire switching connects two or more contiguous pseudo-wire segments to form an end-to-end multi-hop pseudo-wire. This end-to-end pseudo-wire functions as a single point-to-point pseudo-wire. Layer 2 VPN pseudo-wire switching enables the SP to keep the IP addresses of the edge PE routers private across Inter-AS boundaries, using the IP addresses of the ASBRs, the ASBRs join the pseudo wires of the two domains.

AToM packets forwarded between two pseudo wires are treated the same as any other MPLS packet excluding the following exceptions:

- The outgoing virtual circuit (VC) label replaces the incoming VC label in the packet. New Internal Gateway Protocol (IGP) labels and Layer 2 encapsulation are added.

- The incoming VC label Time To Live (TTL) field is decremented by one and copied to the outgoing VC label TTL field.

- The incoming VC label EXP value is copied to the outgoing VC label EXP field.

- The outgoing VC label "Bottom of Stack" S bit in the outgoing VC label is set to 1.

- AToM control word processing is not performed at the Layer 2 VPN pseudo-wire switching aggregation point or ASBR. Sequence numbers are not validated.

The configurations required on the PE routers in either domain, as well as the ASBRs implementing Inter-AS, are shown in the configuration flowchart in Figure 14-23.

Following the configuration flowchart shown in Figure 14-23, the additional configurations for the PE and PE-ASBR devices in Figure 14-22 are as illustrated in Figure 14-24.

Verifications for Case Study 3

Figure 14-25 outlines the verification involved in the implementation of L2 VPN pseudo-wire switching on the PE, PE-ASBR, and CE routers in Case Study 3.

Figure 14-23 *Configuration Flowchart for PE and ASBR Routers to Implement Layer 2 VPN Pseudo-Wire Switching*

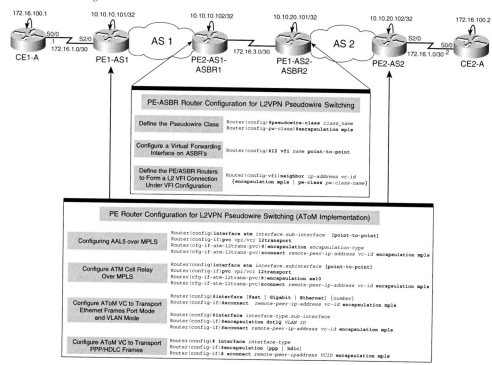

Figure 14-24 *Configuration in Case Study 3 for PE and ASBR Routers to Implement Layer 2 VPN Pseudo-Wire Switching*

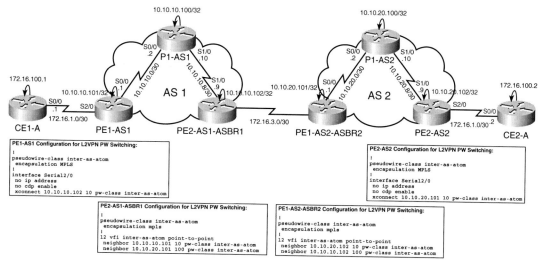

Figure 14-25 *Case Study 3: Layer 2 VPN Pseudo-Wire Switching Verification*

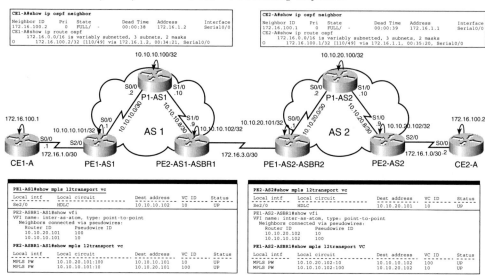

Final Configurations for Case Study 3

The final configurations for the devices in Case Study 3 are shown in Figure 14-26.

Figure 14-26 *Case Study 3: Final Configurations*

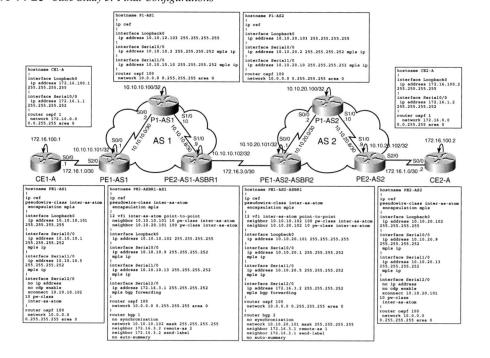

Case Study 4: Implementing Layer 3 VPNs over Layer 2 VPN Topologies and Providing L2 VPN Redundancy

Figure 14-27 illustrates the topology used for this case study. The requirements posed by Customer A to the SP are as follows:

- Customer A requires Layer 2 VPN connectivity between Routers PE1-A and PE2-A via the SP backbone.

- Customer A requires the ability to provide other Layer 3 services using the connectivity provided by the SP. This includes the ability to provide Layer 3 VPN connectivity between two sites belonging to Customer B by implementing MPLS VPN over the Layer 2 VPN service provided by the SP.

- Customer A requires redundancy between Routers PE1-A and PE2-A connected via the SP infrastructure at Layer 2, enabling fast recovery during primary path failure between PE1-A and PE2-A using L2 VPN redundancy.

Figure 14-27 *Case Study 4 Topology*

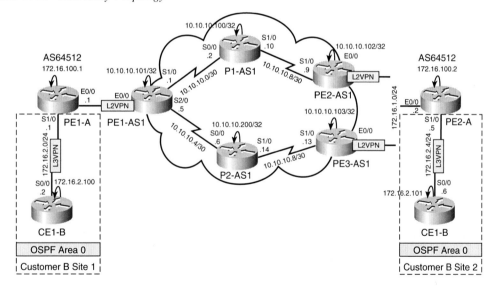

Layer 3 VPN over L2 VPN Configuration

Figure 14-28 outlines the basic configurations for devices to implement Layer 3 VPNs for Customer B traffic (by Customer A), as well as implementation of Layer 2 AToM tunnels between PE1-A and PE2-A over the SP infrastructure.

Figure 14-28 *Case Study 4: Layer 3 VPN for Customer B over Customer A Layer 2 VPN Configuration*

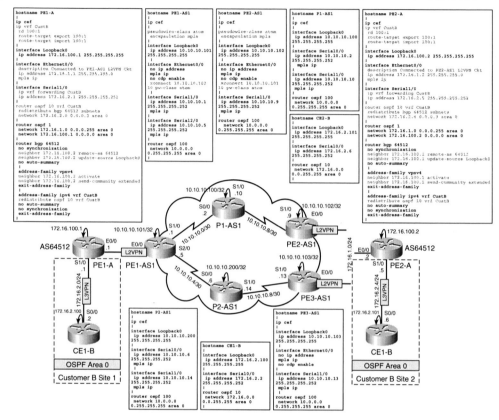

The highlighted portions in Figure 14-28 outline the pertinent configurations for the implementation of the following:

- L2 VPN Ethernet AToM configuration on PE1-AS1 and PE2-AS1 for L2 VPN connectivity between PE1-A and PE2-A

- Configurations on the Customer A PE Routers PE1-A and PE2-A to implement Layer 3 VPN using OSPF PE to CE for Customer B Sites 1 and 2 between Routers CE1-B and CE2-B

Implementing L2 VPN Redundancy

Customer A's final requirement is the ability to provide Layer 2 VPN redundancy between Sites PE1-A and PE2-A. To enable Layer 2 VPN redundancy, a third PE Router PE3-AS1 is connected to the same segment as between PE2-AS1 and PE2-A to provide Layer 2 VPN redundancy in the event of the primary VC failure between PE1-AS1 and PE2-AS1.

In the event of failure, all traffic from Customer A Site PE1-A must failover to the redundant path via PE3-AS1 to reach PE2-A. This is accomplished by configuration of a backup tunnel VC between PE1-AS1 and PE3-AS1 to the primary pseudo wire between PE1-AS1 and PE2-AS1.

Therefore, Layer 2 VPN redundancy when configured provides protection for the following failures:

- Failure of PE2-AS1 router
- Failure of link between P1-AS1 and PE2-AS1 routers
- Failure of link between PE2-AS1 and PE2-A

Layer 2 VPN Pseudo-Wire Redundancy enables you to configure a backup pseudo wire in case the primary pseudo wire fails. When the primary pseudo wire fails, the PE router can switch to the backup pseudo wire. Traffic can be switched back to the primary pseudo wire after the path is operational again.

Configuration of Layer 2 VPN pseudo-wire redundancy and verification of its operation are performed using the procedure illustrated in Figure 14-29.

Figure 14-29 *Layer 2 VPN Pseudo-Wire Redundancy Configuration Flowchart*

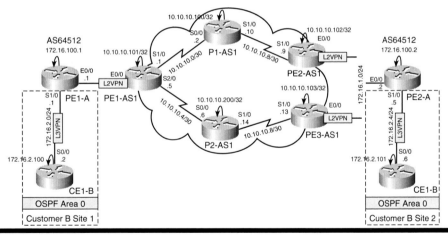

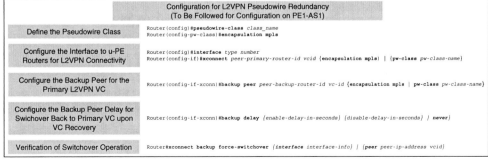

Layer 2 VPN Pseudo-Wire Redundancy Configuration for Customer A Traffic from PE1-A to PE2-A

Layer 2 VPN pseudo-wire redundancy for Customer A traffic originating from PE1-A to PE2-A is configured by the association of a backup VC between PE1-AS1 and PE3-AS1 for the primary tunnel between PE1-AS1 and PE2-AS1. The configuration of the PE routers to implement L2 VPN pseudo-wire redundancy is shown in Figure 14-30. In addition, for quicker IGP convergence OSPF, fast hellos are configured on the SP router interfaces for immediate failover to redundant paths. Configurations of all other devices remain the same as shown earlier.

Figure 14-30 *Case Study 4: L2 VPN Pseudo-Wire Redundancy Configuration*

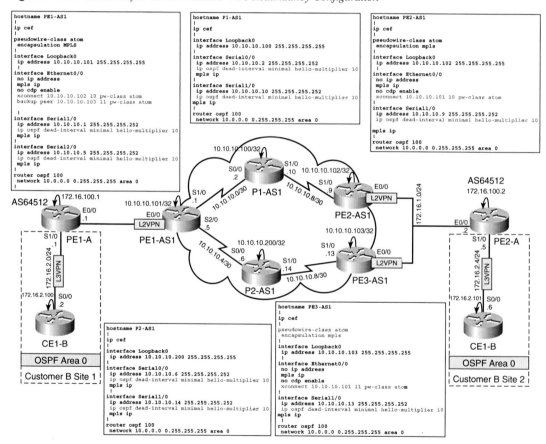

Verifications for Case Study 4

Figure 14-31 outlines the verifications performed on the various devices for Case Study 4. Verification operation of Layer 2 VPN circuits on PE1-AS1 and PE2-AS1 are done by performing **show mpls l2transport vc** on the routers, as shown in the figure. The output of PE1-AS1 must depict the primary Layer 2 VPN circuit as UP and the backup circuit as DOWN.

In addition, verification of Layer 3 VPN over Layer 2 VPN is performed as shown in Figure 14-31 by issuing **show ip bgp vpnv4 all** on the u-PE Routers PE1-A and PE2-A.

Finally, verify operation of the Layer 2 VPN pseudo-wire redundancy by performing an extended ping between the CE1-B and CE2-B loopback address and simultaneously performing **xconnect backup force-switchover peer 10.10.10.103 11** on the PE1-AS1 router to force traffic between PE1-A and PE2-A to switch over to the backup pseudo wire, as illustrated in Figure 14-31. The outputs depict the loss of a single ping packet when pinging between CE2-B and CE1-B when the switchover is performed. The output also depicts the active pseudo wire after switchover.

Figure 14-31 *Case Study 4: Verifications*

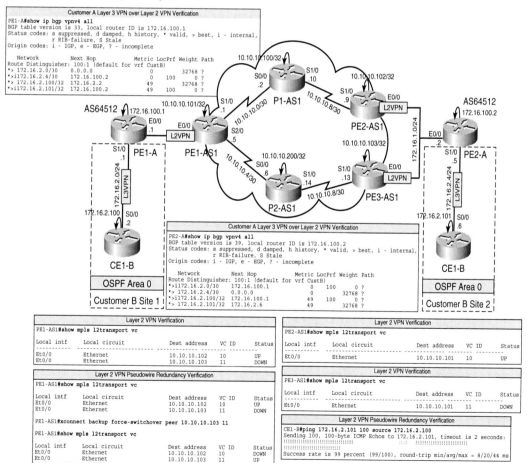

Final Configurations for Case Study 4

Final configurations for devices in Case Study 4 are shown in Figure 14-32.

Figure 14-32 *Case Study 4: Final Configurations*

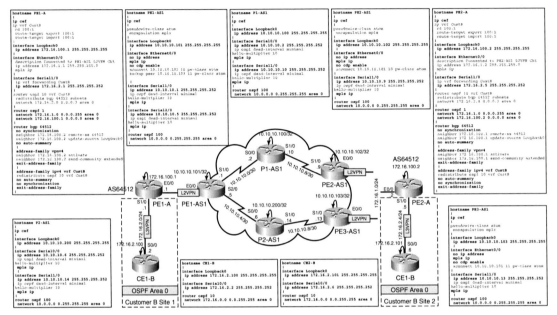

Case Study 5: Implementing Dynamic Layer 3 VPNs Using mGRE Tunnels

This case study delves into the implementation of dynamic Layer 3 VPNs using mGRE tunnels. Implementation of mGRE tunnels creates a multipoint tunnel network as an overlay to the IP backbone that interconnects the PE routers to transport VPN traffic. The multipoint tunnel uses BGP to distribute VPNv4 information between PE routers. The advertised next hop in BGP VPNv4 triggers tunnel endpoint discovery. Dynamic L3 VPN implementation over mGRE tunnels provides the ability for multiple SPs to cooperate and offer a joint VPN service with traffic tunneled directly from the ingress PE router at one service provider directly to the egress PE router at a different SP site.

When implementing dynamic Layer 3 VPNs over mGRE tunnels, the addition of new remote VPN peers is simplified because only the new router needs to be configured. The new address is learned dynamically and propagated to the other nodes in the network.

In Figure 14-33, Customer A Routers CE1-A, CE2-A, and CE3-A are to be connected using dynamic Layer 3 VPNs over mGRE tunnels, by the SP routers PE1-AS1, PE1-AS2, and PE1-AS3. Static PE to CE is configured for the Customer A CE routers. In addition, no MPLS is configured in the core transport network and all traffic between Customer A sites is propagated using mGRE tunnels between the PE routers in the SP network.

Figure 14-33 *Case Study 5: Topology and basic configuration for Layer 3 VPN over mGRE*

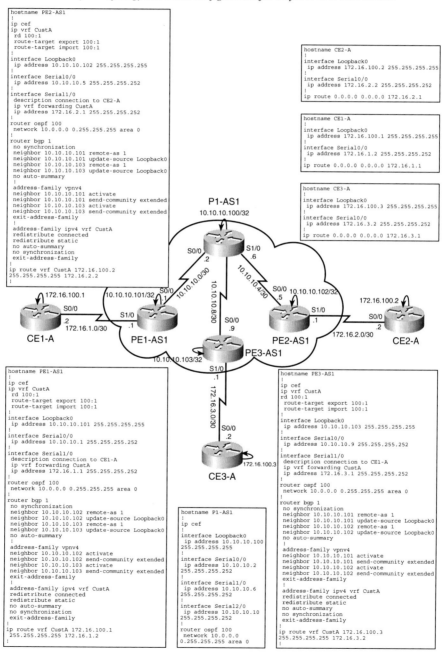

Figure 14-33 shows the base configuration of devices prior to the implementation of Layer 3 VPN over mGRE tunnels. All configurations on the PE routers are similar to regular static PE to CE configurations except no MPLS is enabled on the core interfaces; mGRE tunnels are configured next to enable route propagation between PE routers that belong to Customer A.

Configuring Layer 3 VPN over mGRE Tunnels

Figure 14-34 shows the flowchart for configuration of the PE routers in addition to the configuration shown in Figure 14-33. The steps in the flowchart are outlined here:

Step 1   Configure an additional VRF to transport mGRE.

Step 2   Configure a tunnel interface and assign it as part of the mGRE-associated VRF. Configure an IP address and a tunnel mode to be **gre multipoint l3vpn**. Also, configure the tunnel key.

Step 3   Configure a default route for the mGRE VRF pointing to the tunnel interface.

Step 4   Configure route-map to set the next-hop resolution to the mGRE VRF.

Step 5   Associate the route-map inbound for VPNv4 routes learned from MP-BGP neighbors.

Figure 14-34 *Case Study 5: Layer 3 VPN over mGRE Configuration Flowchart*

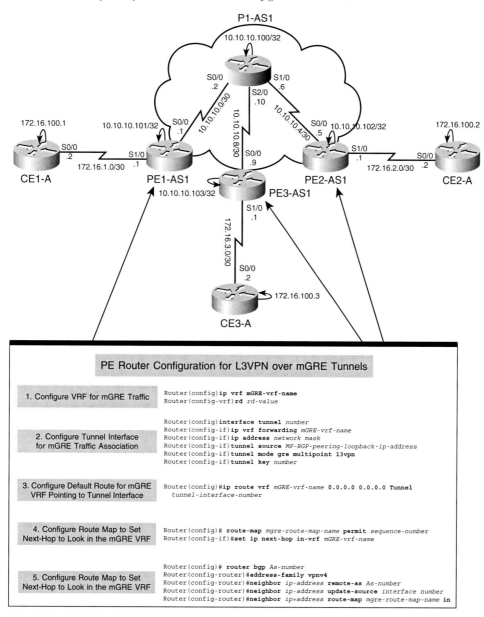

Figure 14-35 shows the Layer 3 VPN over mGRE tunnels configuration for the PE1-AS1, PE2-AS1, and PE3-AS1 routers. The highlighted portion depicts the important configuration steps for implementation of Layer 3 VPN over mGRE tunnels.

Figure 14-35 *Case Study 5: Layer 3 VPN over mGRE Configuration*

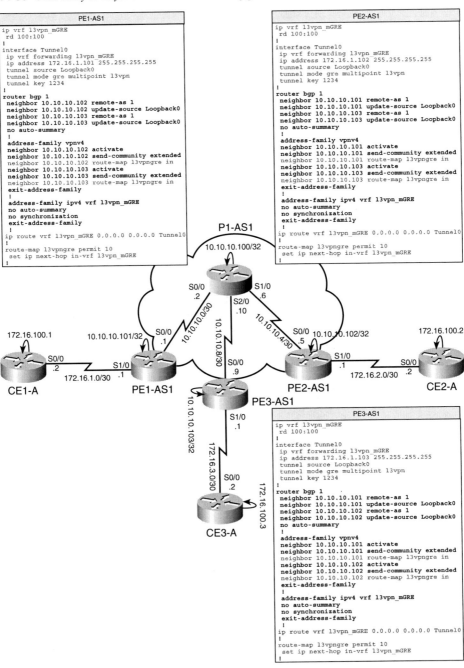

Verifications for Case Study 5

The verifications for Case Study 5 are shown in Figure 14-36.

Figure 14-36 *Case Study 5: Verifications*

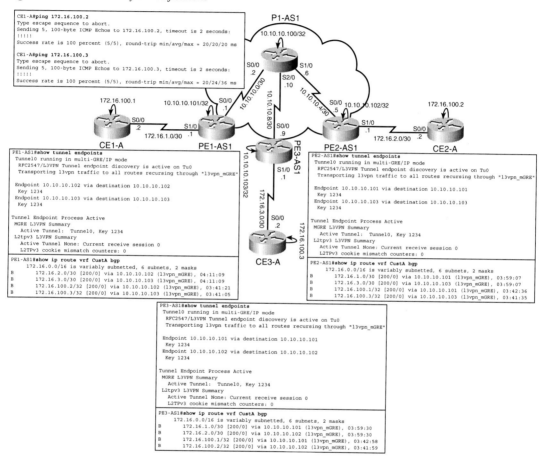

Final Configurations for Layer 3 VPN over mGRE Tunnels for PE Routers

Figure 14-37 shows the final configurations for PE Routers PE1-AS1, PE2-AS1, and PE3-AS1. Configurations for the P1-AS1 router and the CE routers remain the same as shown earlier in Figure 14-33.

Figure 14-37 *Case Study 5: Final Configurations for PE1-AS1, PE2-AS1, and PE3-AS1*

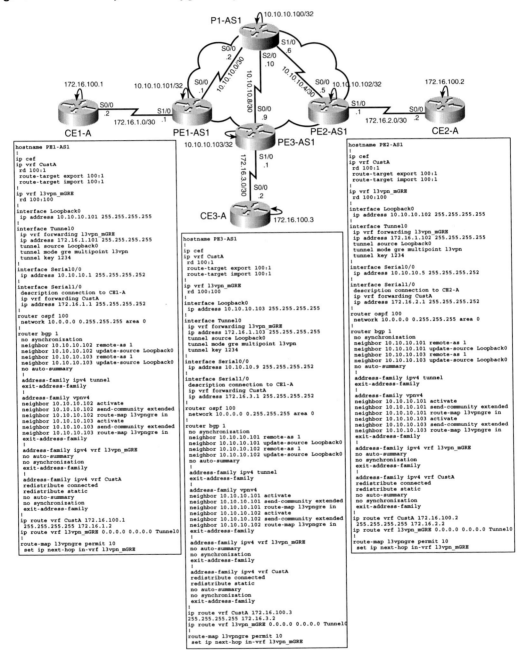

Case Study 6: Implementing Class-Based Tunnel Selection with MPLS Traffic Engineering

Figure 14-38 shows an SP network, consisting of PE Routers PE1-AS1 and PE2-AS1 and provider core Routers P1-AS1, P2-AS1, and P3-AS1, providing MPLS VPN services to Customer A Sites 1 and 2.

Figure 14-38 *Case Study 6: Topology*

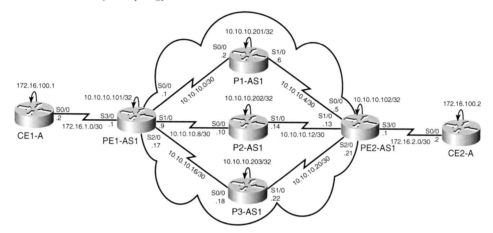

The SP wants to implement traffic engineering (TE) in conjunction with MPLS VPN matching the following paths:

- Higher priority traffic (real-time MPLS EXP=5) follows the path via P1-AS1.

- EXP=4 and EXP=3 follow the path via P2-AS1.

- All other EXP-based traffic will follow the path via P3-AS1.

Implementing Class-Based Tunnel Selection

MPLS TE Class-Based Tunnel Selection (CBTS) enables the SP to dynamically route and forward traffic of different classes of service (CoS) into different TE tunnels between the same tunnel headend and the same tailend where the tunnels can be DS-TE aware. The set of TE (or DS-TE) tunnels from same headend to same tailend that are configured to carry different CoS values is referred to as a "tunnel bundle." After configuration, CBTS dynamically routes and forwards packets into the tunnel that is configured to carry the CoS of the packets.

Figure 14-39 shows the base configurations for all devices in the network prior to the implementation of CBTS. The base configurations show the implementation of three static (explicit) tunnels on the PE1-AS1 router.

Figure 14-39 *Case Study 6: Base Configuration Prior to CBTS Implementation*

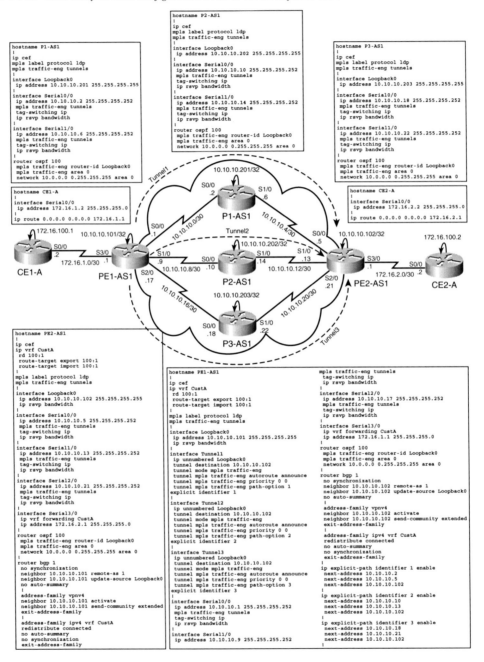

Configuring CBTS

Figure 14-40 outlines the configuration flowchart for the implementation of CBTS, as well as the configuration of the PE1-AS1 router to implement CBTS.

Figure 14-40 *Case Study 6: Configuration of CBTS*

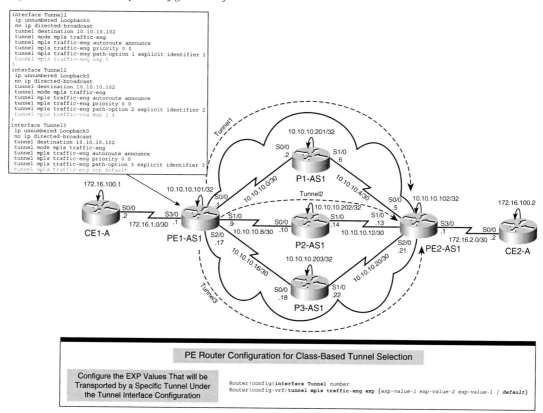

As shown in the highlighted section in Figure 14-40, the configuration of the PE1-AS1 router shows that Tunnel1 transports packets with MPLS EXP value of 5, Tunnel2 transports packets with MPLS EXP values of 3 and 4, and Tunnel3 is used to transport packets of all other MPLS EXP values.

CBTS supports tunnel selection based on the value of the EXP field that the headend router, taking into account the input Modular QoS CLI (MQC), imposes on the packet. If the input MQC modifies the EXP field value, MPLS TE CBTS uses the modified value for its tunnel selection. It is important to note that if the output MQC modifies the EXP field, CBTS ignores the change in the EXP value.

Verification of Class-Based Tunnel Selection

Verification of CBTS is shown in Figure 14-41. Verification of tunnel status by issuing a **show MPLS traffic-eng tunnels brief** on PE1-AS1 is shown along with verification of TE topology and next-hop pointing to all three tunnels and tunnel association into IGP.

Figure 14-41 *Case Study 6: Verification of CBTS*

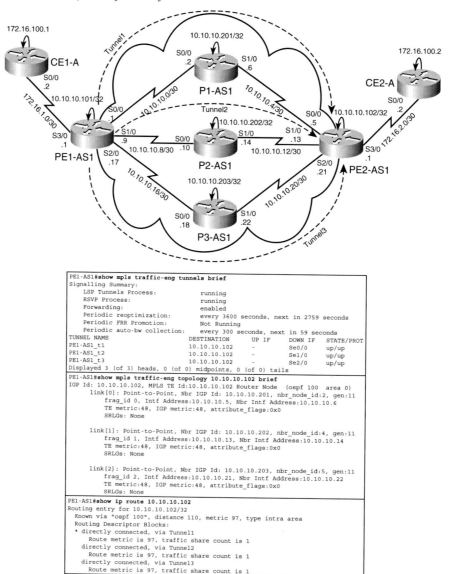

```
PE1-AS1#show mpls traffic-eng tunnels brief
Signalling Summary:
    LSP Tunnels Process:                running
    RSVP Process:                       running
    Forwarding:                         enabled
    Periodic reoptimization:            every 3600 seconds, next in 2759 seconds
    Periodic FRR Promotion:             Not Running
    Periodic auto-bw collection:        every 300 seconds, next in 59 seconds
TUNNEL NAME               DESTINATION    UP IF    DOWN IF    STATE/PROT
PE1-AS1_t1                10.10.10.102     -       Se0/0       up/up
PE1-AS1_t2                10.10.10.102     -       Se1/0       up/up
PE1-AS1_t3                10.10.10.102     -       Se2/0       up/up
Displayed 3 (of 3) heads, 0 (of 0) midpoints, 0 (of 0) tails
PE1-AS1#show mpls traffic-eng topology 10.10.10.102 brief
IGP Id: 10.10.10.102, MPLS TE Id:10.10.10.102 Router Node  (ospf 100  area 0)
      link[0]: Point-to-Point, Nbr IGP Id: 10.10.10.201, nbr_node_id:2, gen:11
               frag_id 0, Intf Address:10.10.10.5, Nbr Intf Address:10.10.10.6
               TE metric:48, IGP metric:48, attribute_flags:0x0
               SRLGs: None

      link[1]: Point-to-Point, Nbr IGP Id: 10.10.10.202, nbr_node_id:4, gen:11
               frag_id 1, Intf Address:10.10.10.13, Nbr Intf Address:10.10.10.14
               TE metric:48, IGP metric:48, attribute_flags:0x0
               SRLGs: None

      link[2]: Point-to-Point, Nbr IGP Id: 10.10.10.203, nbr_node_id:5, gen:11
               frag_id 2, Intf Address:10.10.10.21, Nbr Intf Address:10.10.10.22
               TE metric:48, IGP metric:48, attribute_flags:0x0
               SRLGs: None
PE1-AS1#show ip route 10.10.10.102
Routing entry for 10.10.10.102/32
  Known via "ospf 100", distance 110, metric 97, type intra area
  Routing Descriptor Blocks:
  * directly connected, via Tunnel1
      Route metric is 97, traffic share count is 1
    directly connected, via Tunnel2
      Route metric is 97, traffic share count is 1
    directly connected, via Tunnel3
      Route metric is 97, traffic share count is 1
```

Final Configurations for Case Study 6

The final configurations for Case Study 6 for the PE Routers PE1-AS1 and PE2-AS1 to implement CBTS are shown in Figure 14-42. For all other device configurations, refer Figure 14-39.

Figure 14-42 *Case Study 6: Final Configurations for PE Routers*

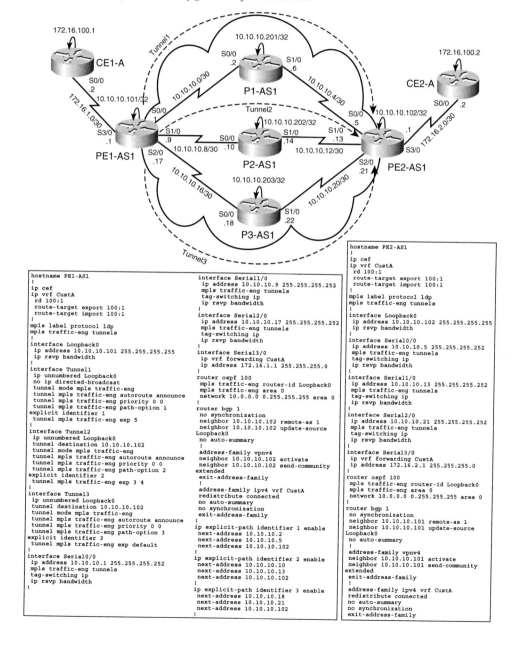

```
hostname PE1-AS1
!
ip cef
ip vrf CustA
 rd 100:1
 route-target export 100:1
 route-target import 100:1
!
mpls label protocol ldp
mpls traffic-eng tunnels
!
interface Loopback0
 ip address 10.10.10.101 255.255.255.255
 ip rsvp bandwidth
!
interface Tunnel1
 ip unnumbered Loopback0
 no ip directed-broadcast
 tunnel mode mpls traffic-eng
 tunnel mpls traffic-eng autoroute announce
 tunnel mpls traffic-eng priority 0 0
 tunnel mpls traffic-eng path-option 1
explicit identifier 1
 tunnel mpls traffic-eng exp 5
!
interface Tunnel2
 ip unnumbered Loopback0
 tunnel destination 10.10.10.102
 tunnel mode mpls traffic-eng
 tunnel mpls traffic-eng autoroute announce
 tunnel mpls traffic-eng priority 0 0
 tunnel mpls traffic-eng path-option 2
explicit identifier 2
 tunnel mpls traffic-eng exp 3 4
!
interface Tunnel3
 ip unnumbered Loopback0
 tunnel destination 10.10.10.102
 tunnel mode mpls traffic-eng
 tunnel mpls traffic-eng autoroute announce
 tunnel mpls traffic-eng priority 0 0
 tunnel mpls traffic-eng path-option 3
explicit identifier 3
 tunnel mpls traffic-eng exp default
!
interface Serial0/0
 ip address 10.10.10.1 255.255.255.252
 mpls traffic-eng tunnels
 tag-switching ip
 ip rsvp bandwidth
!
```

```
interface Serial1/0
 ip address 10.10.10.9 255.255.255.252
 mpls traffic-eng tunnels
 tag-switching ip
 ip rsvp bandwidth
!
interface Serial2/0
 ip address 10.10.10.17 255.255.255.252
 mpls traffic-eng tunnels
 tag-switching ip
 ip rsvp bandwidth
!
interface Serial3/0
 ip vrf forwarding CustA
 ip address 172.16.1.1 255.255.255.0
!
router ospf 100
 mpls traffic-eng router-id Loopback0
 mpls traffic-eng area 0
 network 10.0.0.0 0.255.255.255 area 0
!
router bgp 1
 no synchronization
 neighbor 10.10.10.102 remote-as 1
 neighbor 10.10.10.102 update-source
Loopback0
 no auto-summary
 !
 address-family vpnv4
 neighbor 10.10.10.102 activate
 neighbor 10.10.10.102 send-community
extended
 exit-address-family
 !
 address-family ipv4 vrf CustA
 redistribute connected
 no auto-summary
 no synchronization
 exit-address-family
!
ip explicit-path identifier 1 enable
 next-address 10.10.10.2
 next-address 10.10.10.5
 next-address 10.10.10.102
!
ip explicit-path identifier 2 enable
 next-address 10.10.10.10
 next-address 10.10.10.13
 next-address 10.10.10.102
!
ip explicit-path identifier 3 enable
 next-address 10.10.10.18
 next-address 10.10.10.21
 next-address 10.10.10.102
!
```

```
hostname PE2-AS1
!
ip cef
ip vrf CustA
 rd 100:1
 route-target export 100:1
 route-target import 100:1
!
mpls label protocol ldp
mpls traffic-eng tunnels
!
interface Loopback0
 ip address 10.10.10.102 255.255.255.255
 ip rsvp bandwidth
!
interface Serial0/0
 ip address 10.10.10.5 255.255.255.252
 mpls traffic-eng tunnels
 tag-switching ip
 ip rsvp bandwidth
!
interface Serial1/0
 ip address 10.10.10.13 255.255.255.252
 mpls traffic-eng tunnels
 tag-switching ip
 ip rsvp bandwidth
!
interface Serial2/0
 ip address 10.10.10.21 255.255.255.252
 mpls traffic-eng tunnels
 tag-switching ip
 ip rsvp bandwidth
!
interface Serial3/0
 ip vrf forwarding CustA
 ip address 172.16.2.1 255.255.255.0
!
router ospf 100
 mpls traffic-eng router-id Loopback0
 mpls traffic-eng area 0
 network 10.0.0.0 0.255.255.255 area 0
!
router bgp 1
 no synchronization
 neighbor 10.10.10.101 remote-as 1
 neighbor 10.10.10.101 update-source
Loopback0
 no auto-summary
 !
 address-family vpnv4
 neighbor 10.10.10.101 activate
 neighbor 10.10.10.101 send-community
extended
 exit-address-family
 !
 address-family ipv4 vrf CustA
 redistribute connected
 no auto-summary
 no synchronization
 exit-address-family
```

Case Study 7: Implementing Hub and Spoke Topologies with OSPF

When a hub and spoke design needs to be deployed using a MPLS VPN, a single CE router functions as the hub router with other CE routers connecting to the hub site over the SP MPLS infrastructure. Figure 14-43 shows a SP network implementing hub and spoke using OSPF for Customer A sites.

Figure 14-43 *Case Study 7: Hub and Spoke with OSPF Topology*

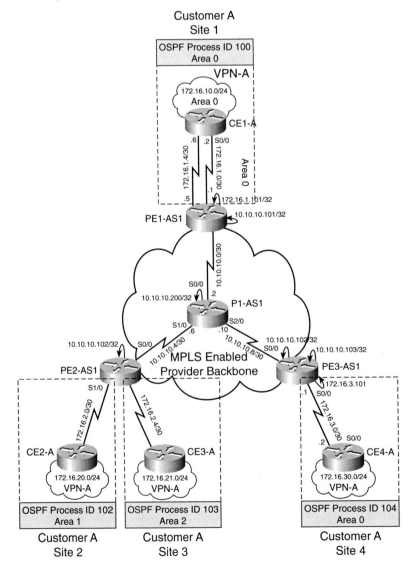

In the network illustrated in Figure 14-43, CE1-A is configured using OSPF PE-CE connectivity to PE1-AS1 and functions as the hub-site CE router for Customer A. CE Routers CE2-A, CE3-A, and CE4-A function as spoke CE routers. PE Router PE1-AS1 functions as the hub PE router, and PE2-AS1 and PE3-AS1 function as the spoke PE routers.

The flow of traffic from CE2-A to CE3-A will have to traverse CE1-A, which is the CE functioning as the hub for the MPLS VPN. In Figure 14-43, this does not occur if both the spoke CE routers on PE2-AS1 are configured in the same VRF. Therefore, individual VRFs or VPN instances need to be configured on the PE2-AS1 router mapping to each spoke router that has to be associated to the same hub and spoke MPLS VPN, because the PE2-AS1 router is connected to more than one spoke CE router.

If a VRF is configured on the hub PE router, PE1-AS1 mapping to Customer A traffic, this VRF can contain import RT values mapping to the export RT values of the individual VRFs on PE2-AS1. These routes will now have to be forwarded to the hub CE router CE1-A, which will then send them back to the PE Router PE1-AS1 for route propagation to the other spoke CE routers. To have the routes forwarded back from the CE1-AS1 to PE1-AS1, more than one interface is implemented between the hub PE and CE routers. In the absence of separate interfaces for traffic destined from hub PE to hub CE and from hub CE back to hub PE, all traffic will not traverse the hub CE router. Instead, all traffic will traverse through the hub PE router, which does not fulfill the hub and spoke design requirements.

Therefore, a single VRF is configured on the hub PE router, PE1-AS1, to import routes learned from remote CE Routers CE2-AS1 and CE3-AS1. By implementing OSPF PE-CE between PE1-AS1 and CE1-A, the hub CE Router CE1-A learns routes from the hub PE router.

During the redistribution of Routes from the MP-BGP superbackbone to the OSPF PE-CE process on the hub PE Router PE1-AS1, two processes can occur:

- An External Type 2 (E2) route, which is learned from a remote CE in a different area, is assigned a domain-tag value during translation from the BGP to the OSPF domain. The tag value is a 32-bit value entered in decimal format. The default value is calculated based on the BGP autonomous system (AS) number of the MPLS VPN backbone. The four highest bits are set to 1101, according to RFC 1745. The lowest 16 bits map the BGP AS number of the MPLS VPN backbone. If a user specifies the *tag*-value, the value does not have to follow any particular format. The tag-value can be changed under the VRF definition using the **domain-tag** *tag-value* command to a value not equal to the 32-bit definition for the AS propagating the route as previously mentioned. This enables repropagation of these routes into the MP-BGP backbone.

- An Inter-Area (IA) route, learned from a remote CE in the same area, is propagated with the down-bit set. Therefore, this route will not be repropagated into the MPLS VPN backbone. To disable the down-bit propagation, sham-links can be configured between the VRF processes on the PE routers to have all IA routes appear as O (intra-area) routes, thus enabling redistribution into the MP-BGP backbone.

The hub CE router needs two interfaces (either physical or logical) connecting to the hub PE router. The hub PE router will be configured with two VRFs mapping to each of these interfaces where one VRF will be used *to import routes* from the spoke CE routers and propagate the same to the hub CE router, and the other VRF will be used *to export routes* learned from the hub CE router back to the spoke CE routers.

The hub PE PE1-AS1 propagates information by exporting routes with an appropriate route-target back to the other PE routers, PE2-AS2 and PE3-AS1. On PE2-AS1 and PE3-AS1, the routes learned from PE1-AS1 are imported into the VRFs by configuring the appropriate import route-targets and thus connectivity is achieved.

Hub and Spoke with OSPFv2: Configuration of CE Routers and Spoke PE Routers

The hub CE router, CE1-A, and spoke CE routers, CE2-A, CE3-A, and CE4-A, are all configured for OSPFv2 PE-CE as per the network topology outlined in Figure 14-43. Regular OSPF configurations are the only requirement on the CE routers and have been outlined in Figure 14-44. IP addressing has been omitted for brevity.

As mentioned earlier, PE2-AS1 requires two individual VRFs for the CE connections to CE2-A and CE3-A to enable hub and spoke connectivity. On PE3-AS1, a single VRF is configured for route propagation to and from CE4-A. In addition, a loopback interface is configured on PE3-AS1 as part of the VRF mapping to Customer A to function as a sham-link endpoint on PE3-AS1 for the VRF routers. All other configurations are as explained earlier with OSPF PE-CE. Only the relevant configurations have been shown in Figure 14-44.

Configuration of Hub-PE Router and Verification of OSPF Hub and Spoke Operation

The hub PE Router PE1-AS1 is where all the important configurations are implemented for hub and spoke operation. Two VRFs, one for route propagation to CE1-A (VRF 2hub) and one for route reception from CE1-A (VRF 2spoke), are configured on the PE1-AS1 router. The nomenclature of VRFs is based on control plane propagation of routes. In addition, VRF 2hub is configured with a loopback interface to function as a sham-link endpoint. The sham-link configuration avoids routes propagating between CE4-A and CE1-A (both belonging to area 0) as IA routes. Instead, the routes from CE4-A will be seen as O (Intra-Area) routes at CE1-A. Therefore, the down bit is not set on these routes, and they can be propagated back into the MP-BGP superbackbone.

Figure 14-44 *Case Study 7: Hub and Spoke with OSPF Configuration for CE and Spoke PE Routers*

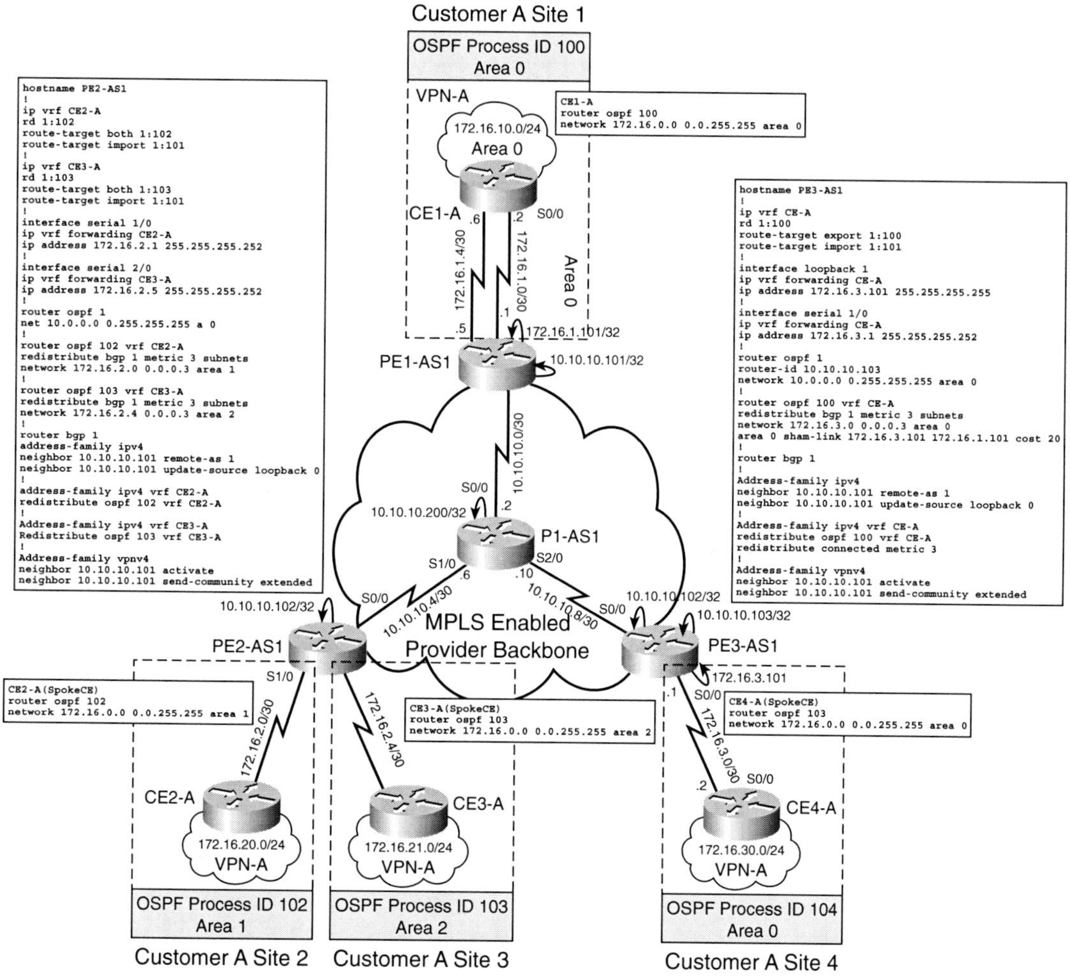

In addition, a domain-tag configuration is performed under the VRF 2hub (**domain-tag 100**) to enable E2 routes learned from CE2-A and CE3-A to be repropagated into the MP-BGP backbone by the CE1-A router.

The configuration of the hub PE, PE1-AS1, as well as the verification steps for OSPFv2 hub and spoke operation for Case Study 7 are shown in Figure 14-45.

Figure 14-45 *Configuration of PE1-AS1 and Verification of OSPFv2 Hub and Spoke Operation*

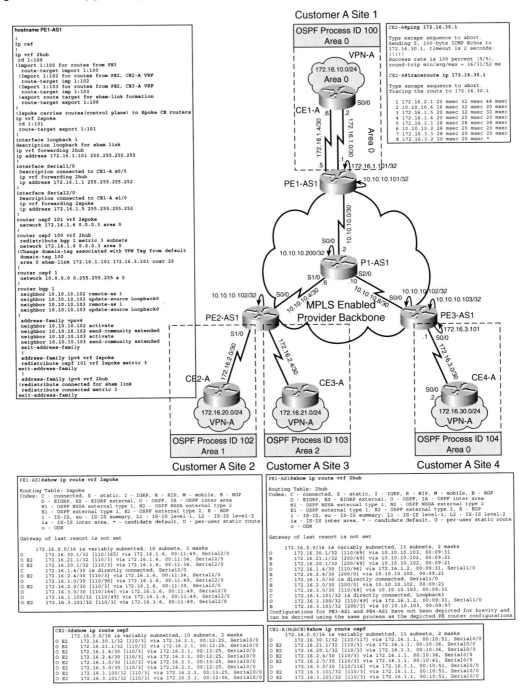

Case Study 8: Implementing Hub and Spoke Topologies with EIGRP

This case study provides configurations for the implementation of hub and spoke for Customer A sites by the SP, as shown in Figure 14-46.

Figure 14-46 *Case Study 8: Topology*

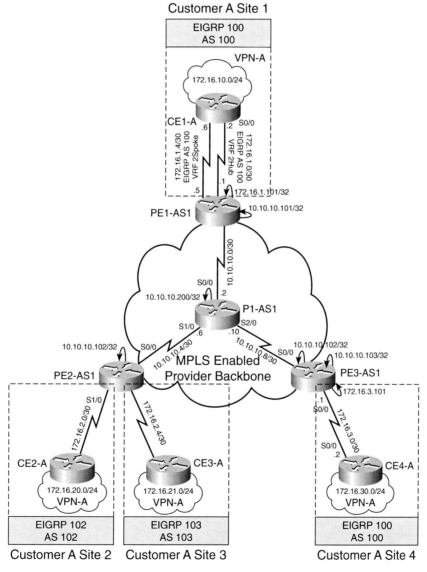

EIGRP is configured as the PE-CE routing protocol on the routers. The EIGRP AS number is configured as shown in Figure 14-46.

The configuration procedure to implement EIGRP PE-CE follows the same implementation as the other hub and spoke implementations in which two interfaces between the hub PE router and hub CE router in two separate VRFs are used. However, unlike the implementation of hub and spoke with BGP (discussed in Chapter 6, "Implementing BGP in MPLS VPNs") or OSPF (discussed in Case Study 7), no special configuration is required except the appropriate routing information configuration and exchange on all routers following regular EIGRP PE-CE configuration methodology.

Configurations for the CE and Spoke PE Routers

Figure 14-47 illustrates the configurations on the different CE and spoke PE routers to implement the hub and spoke implementation for Customer A in accordance with Figure 14-46. IP addressing has been omitted for brevity.

Figure 14-47 *Case Study 8: Configuration of CE and Spoke PE Routers*

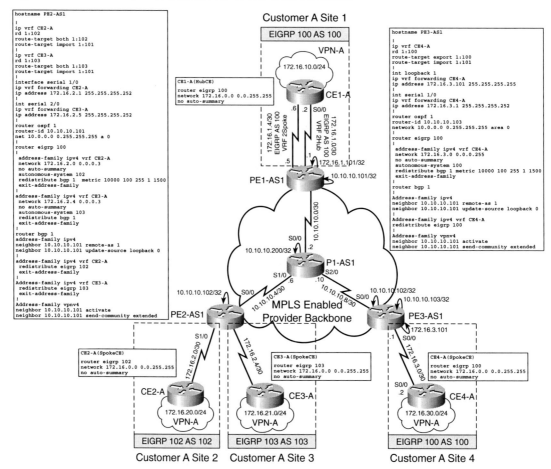

Configurations for the Hub PE Router and Verification of EIGRP Hub and Spoke Operation

Figure 14-48 shows the final configuration for the hub PE router to implement hub and spoke for Customer A in accordance with Figure 14-46. The verification steps are also shown in Figure 14-48.

Figure 14-48 *Case Study 8: Configuration of Hub PE Router and Verification*

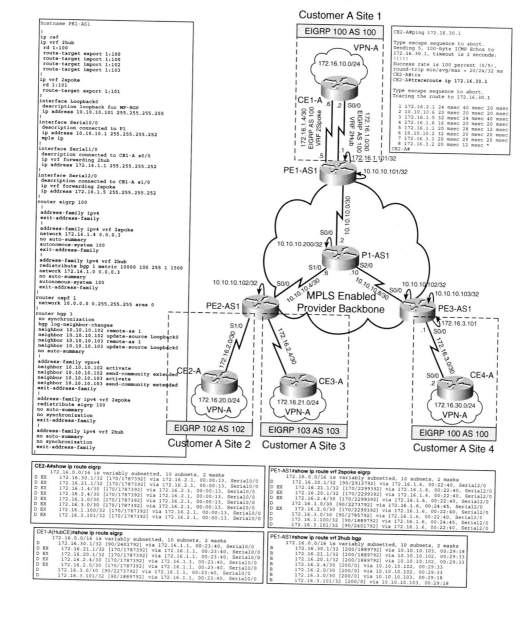

Case Study 9: Implementing VPLS Services with the GSR 12000 Series

VPLS services emulate an Ethernet bridge in an IP/MPLS network. It is an end-to-end architecture that allows IP/MPLS networks to provide multipoint Ethernet services. Operation is similar to an Ethernet bridge; that is, it forwards using the destination MAC address, learns source addresses, and floods broad-/multicast. Several IETF VPLS drafts exist that are based on LDP and BGP. This feature and its implementation on a GSR 12000 series router form the core of this case study.

Figure 14-49 depicts an MPLS-enabled GSR network that implements different VPLS services along with the base configurations prior to the implementation of VPLS services on the PE routers.

Figure 14-49 *Case Study 9: Topology and PE Router Configuration*

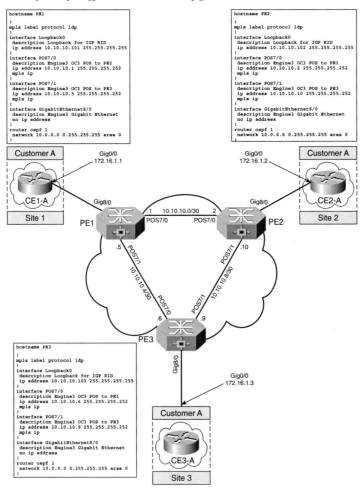

Theory and Operation of VPLS on a GSR 12000 Series

Figure 14-50 shows the various VPLS architectures that can be deployed in today's SP networks. VPLS is a service targeted for enterprise networks to connect geographically separate LAN segments together across a WAN. It enables these separate LAN segments to act as a single LAN. VPLS technology seamlessly enables transparent LAN services or TLS across WAN boundaries.

Figure 14-50 *VPLS Deployment Architectures*

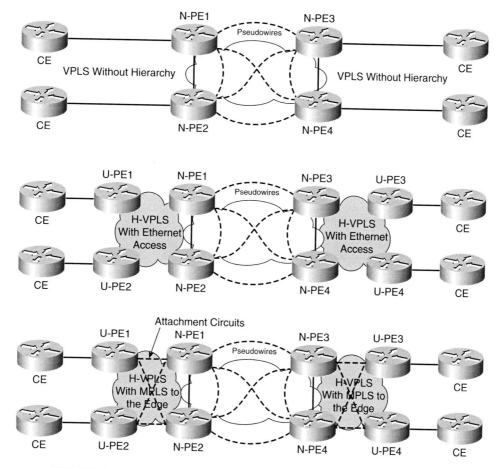

GSR VPLS can be used for the deployment of point-to-multipoint and multipoint-to-multipoint L2 VPN services on the ISE-based (Internet Services Engine or Engine 3) Ethernet LCs. With the introduction of ISE-based Ethernet LCs, GSR has the capability to do MAC address-based learning, forwarding/flooding, and aging. This enables GSR to extend the L2 VPN solution to include VPLS. At this juncture, VPLS implementation is targeted toward MPLS-based networks using LDP.

GSR supports the implementation of these VPLS services where the physical port can be of EtherType 0x8100 or 0x9100 categorized as the following services:

- **Ethernet VPLS service**—The attachment circuit is an Ethernet port.

- **VLAN VPLS service**—The attachment circuit is a dot1q VLAN subinterface.

- **QinQ VPLS service**—The attachment circuit is a sub-interface where the user specifies the inner and outer dot1q VLAN tags explicitly.

- **QinAny VPLS service**—The attachment circuit is a sub-interface where the user only specifics the outer dot1q VLAN tag explicitly, and the inner dot1q tag can be any VLAN value (i.e., 1-4095).

Table 14-1 summarizes the VPLS support details on the GSR routers in 12.0(32)S IOS release. For the latest information on platform and feature support and availability, visit http://cco.cisco.com.

Table 14-1   *VPLS Support on GSR Platforms*

Release	Route Processor	Edge Facing Cards	Core Facing Cards
IOS 12.0(32)S	PRP-1 PRP-2	Engine 3 ISE GE	Engine 3 ISE GE/POS Engine 5 SIP 600 Engine 5 SIP 401/501/601

GSR VPLS Packet Forwarding

Figure 14-51 shows the steps in the forwarding of a VPLS packet as it traverses the MPLS network illustrated earlier from CE1-A to CE2-A.

The steps highlighted in Figure 14-51 are as follows:

1. CE-1 sends unicast frames to CE-2 over the VLAN 2000 dot1q trunk.

2. VPLS instance VPLS_2000 on N-PE A **"learns"** CE-1 MAC address from VLAN 2000 dot1q trunk attachment circuit.

3. Because M2 is unknown, N-PE A **"floods"** (replicates) the frame to all the pseudo wires (pseudo wires go to N-PE B and N-PE C).

4. Both N-PE B and N-PE C **"learn"** CE-1 MAC address from pseudo wire. (Note: MAC is associated to the remote VC label.)

5. Because M2 is unknown, N-PE B and N-PE C **"flood"** the frame to all the local ports (and not the pseudo wires).

Figure 14-52 depicts the VPLS forwarding of a packet from CE2-A to CE1-A across the VPLS domain when CE2 replies to CE1.

Figure 14-51 *VPLS Packet Forwarding on GSR*

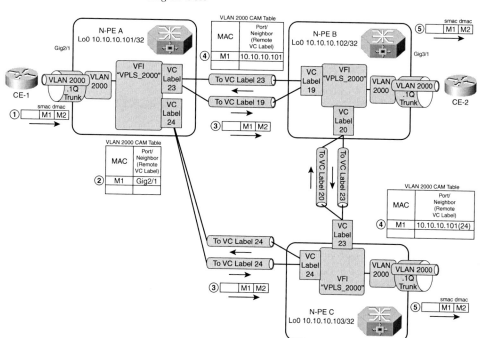

Figure 14-52 *VPLS Packet Forwarding on GSR from CE2-CE1*

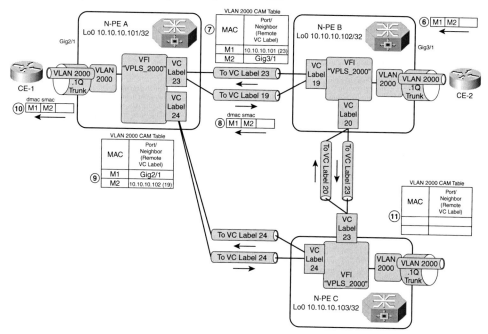

The steps outlined in Figure 14-52 are as follows:

6   CE-2 replies to CE-1 after finding the frame is destined for one of its hosts.

7   N-PE B **"learns"** CE-2 MAC address from VLAN 2000 dot1q trunk attachment circuit.

8   N-PE B inspects MAC table and forwards frame toward N-PE A (with remote label 23—frame is not sent to N-PE C).

9   N-PE A **"learns"** CE-2 MAC address from the pseudo wire.

10   N-PE A **"forwards"** frame to CE-1. N-PE A stops flooding frames to N-PE C and establishes a unicast forwarding data path.

11   N-PE C **"ages out"** MAC entry for CE-1 after the aging timer expires.

The full mesh of pseudo wires between all GSR PE routers guarantees frame delivery. To prevent packet forwarding loops in VPLS instance, split horizon functionality is enabled by default on attachment circuits and pseudo wires.

Each VPLS forwarding instance maintains one copy of a MAC table (qualified learning). The MAC table is a list of "known" MAC addresses and their forwarding information. The MAC table and its management are distributed—a copy of the MAC table is maintained on the route processor and on line cards. When a packet is received from an attachment circuit or pseudo wire, only the source MAC address is learned on the edge facing (imposition) line card. The destination address is not learned. Learning is performed by line card CPU. Two copies of a MAC table are created where the software copy is stored in the LC RP CPU memory, and the hardware copy is programmed into LC ASICs for hardware based forwarding.

For packets arriving on an attachment circuit, learning happens in the edge facing card (RX direction). For packets arriving on a pseudo wire, learning happens in the core facing card (TX direction). New entries learned are sent to the route processor, and it instructs all line cards participating in that VPLS instance to add the new address into their MAC table. The route processor maintains the master copy and periodically refreshes the copy on all line cards. Entries in the MAC table can age out, and the aging timer is configurable per VPLS instance. The MAC table size is configurable on a per forwarding instance basis.

GSR VPLS implementation also supports a rich feature set for association of QoS. On the ingress side, the VPLS feature can be used with

- VPLS traffic classification based on the destination address being known, unknown, or multicast
- Traffic classification based on VLAN P bits

- Setting MPLS EXP bits in the VC label
- Color aware and color blind 1 rate 2 color policer
- Color aware and color blind 2 rate 3 color policer
- Setting MPLS EXP bits as a result of policer action
- Per port/VLAN/QinQ/QinAny interface shaping

On the egress side, the VPLS feature can be used with

- Setting VLAN P bits
- Per port/VLAN/QinQ/QinAny interface shaping
- Per port/VLAN/QinQ/QinAny WRED and MDRR

One of the key features on the GSR is that, on the same physical port, the user can enable VPLS on a set of subinterfaces and, on the rest of the subinterfaces, enable any other Layer 2 or 3 features (i.e., L2 AToM, or IPv4 or IPv6 features) with full QoS. This is possible because each subinterface is allocated its own set of queues, and its properties are programmed in hardware ASICs.

GSR VPLS Requirements and Configuration

This list summarizes VPLS caveats in IOS 12.0(32)S. It applies to Engine 3 GE imposition line card only on 12.0(32)S:

- Edge facing engine 3 GE line card cannot have dissimilar attachment circuits associated with the same VPLS instance (i.e., cannot have Ethernet and VLAN attachment circuits on same line card). Only homogeneous attachment circuits are allowed.
- On Engine 3 GE imposition line card, one VLAN subinterface is supported per VPLS instance on a port.
- Engine 3 GE line card can be used as an edge or a core facing line card. The same line card cannot be used for edge and core facing links.

Refer to http://www.cisco.com for more information on other specific caveats by IOS release when implementing VPLS on the GSR.

Figure 14-53 shows the steps required for the configuration of different VPLS on the PE routers (GSR) when implementing Ethernet, VLAN, QinQ, and QinAny services.

Figure 14-53 *Configuration Flowchart for GSR VPLS Services*

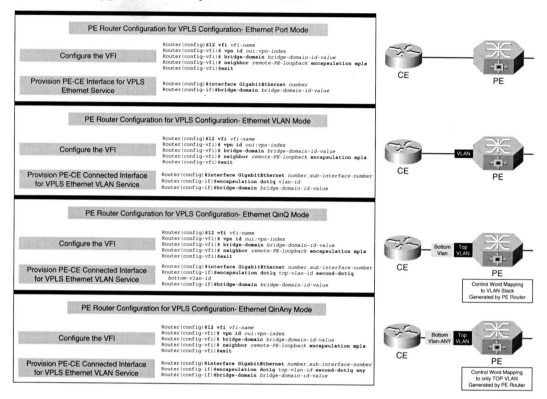

As shown in Figure 14-53, the only difference between the QinQ and QinAny modes is that a control word mapping to the top as well as bottom VLAN is generated on ingress in the QinQ mode whereas the control word mapping to only the top VLAN is generated on ingress in the QinAny mode.

Figure 14-54 shows the configuration of the PE routers when used to implement each of the VPLS services depicted in Figure 14-50.

Figure 14-54 *Configuration for GSR VPLS Services*

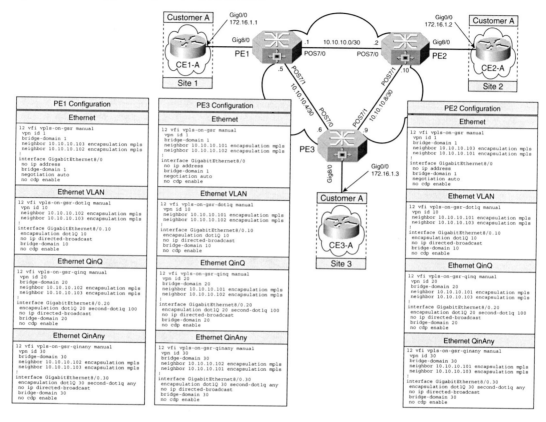

Verification of GSR VPLS service operation can be performed by issuing any one of the following commands on the PE routers. Visit cco.cisco.com for more information on the following commands:

- **show vfi name** *name-of-vpls-VFI-instance*
- **show xconnect interface** *interface*
- **show mpls l2transport vc** *vc-id* **detail**
- **show mac address-table bridge-domain** *bridge-domain-id*

Case Study 10: BGP Site of Origin

Site of Origin (SoO) is one of the attributes a PE router assigns to a prefix prior to redistributing any VPNv4 prefixes. SoO in BGP is configured at neighbor level and is used to manage MPLS VPN traffic and to prevent transient routing loops from occurring in complex and mixed network topologies. SoO uniquely identifies the site from which the PE router learned the prefix. All prefixes learned from a particular site must be assigned the same site of origin attribute, even if the site is multiply connected to a single PE, or is connected to multiple PEs. The objective of this case study is to demonstrate SoO configuration when BGP PE-CE routing protocol is used In this case study, CE1-A and CE2-A belong to the same site, and this site is connected to multiple PE routers PE1-AS1 and PE2-AS1. Figure 14-55 shows the topology where all Customer A sites belong to BGP AS 65001.

Figure 14-55 *SoO in BGP PE-CE Based MPLS VPN Network*

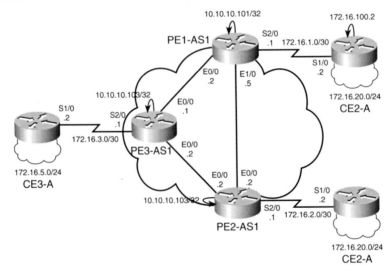

Figure 14-56 shows the relevant configuration to configure and verify SoO in BGP PE-CE based MPLS VPN network.

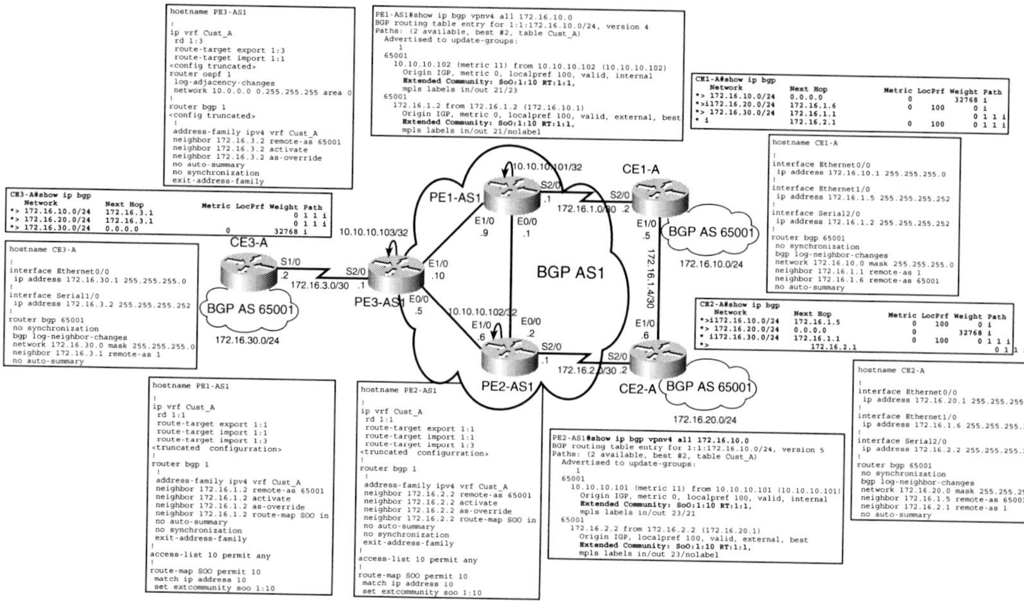

Figure 14-56 *Configure and Verify BGP SoO*

Command Reference

Command	Description
Router(config)#**ip multicast-routing vrf** *vrf_name*	Enables multicast routing functionality on a per-VRF basis.
Router(config-vrf)#**mdt default** *group-address*	Configures the default MDT group-address for the mVPN multicast multipoint tunnel.
Router(config-vrf)#**mdt data** *group-address* *wildcard-bits-defining-range* {**threshold** *threshold-in-kbps* [**list** *access-list-number*] | **list** *access-list-number*}	Defines the data MDT group-address range for the mVPN, as well as the threshold values defining the groups that will associate with the data MDT.
Router(config-if)#**ip pim** {**sparse-mode** | **dense-mode** | **sparse-dense-mode**}	Enables PIM on the interface.
Router(config)#**ip pim ssm default**	Enables SSM on the router.
Router(config-router)#**capability vrf-lite**	Configures the CE OSPF process as a OSPF multi-vrf CE capable process.

continues

(Continued)

Command	Description
Router(config)# **vrf selection source** *source-IP-address source-IP-mask* **vrf** *vrf_name*	Configures the IP addresses mapping to a specific VRF table when implementing VRF selection.
Router(config-if)#**ip vrf select source**	Enables the interface for VRF selection based on source IP address.
Router(config-if)#**ip vrf receive** *vrf-name*	Configures the interface for mapping to addresses that will associate with a specific VRF when implementing VRF selection.
Router(config)#**ip prefix-list** *prefix-list-name* [**seq** *seq-value*] {**deny** *network/length*	**permit** *network/length*} [**ge** *ge-value*] [**le** *le-value*]	Configures traffic to map to a specific VRF when implementing PBR VRF selection.
Router(config-if)# **standby** *hsrp-group-number* **IP** *virtual-IP-address-of-hsrp-group*	Enables HSRP on the VRF interface.
Router(config-if)#**standby** [*group-number*] **priority** *priority* [**preempt** [**delay** [*minimum*	*sync*] *delay*]]	Configures the HSRP standby group and priority, delay, and preemption.
Router(config-if)#**standby** [*group-number*] **timers** *hellotime holdtime*	Configures the HSRP timers on VRF interface.
Router(config-if)#**standby** [*group-number*] **track** *interface-type interface-number* [*interface-priority*]	Configures the interface to be tracked for HSRP on VRF interface to activate.
Router(config)# **interface** *interface-connected-to-services-ce-type number* Router(config)# **ip nat outside** router(config)# **interface** *interface-connected-to-MPLS-domain-type number* router(config-if)# **ip nat inside**	Configures the NAT inside and outside interfaces for NAT integration to MPLS VPN.
Router(config)# **ip nat pool** *nat-pool-name start-range-of-IP-addresses end-range-of-IP-addresses* **netmask** *netmask*	Configures NAT pool for IP addresses that will undergo NAT translation.
Router(config)#**ip nat inside source-list** [*access-list-name*	*access-list-number*] **pool** *nat-pool-name* **vrf** *vrf_name2*	Associates NAT pool with customer VRFs.
Router(config)#**pseudowire-class** *class_name* Router(config-pw-class)#**encapsulation mpls**	Configures the pseudo-wire class for L2 VPN pseudo-wire switching.

(Continued)

Command	Description
Router(config)#**l2 vfi** *name* **point-to-point**	Configures the virtual forwarding interface.
Router(config-vfi)#**neighbor** *ip-address* *vc-id* {**encapsulation mpls** | **pw-class** *pw-class-name*}	Configures the neighbor with which the ASBR will form an L2 VFI connection.
Router(config-if-xconn)#**backup peer** *peer-backup-router-id vc-id* {**encapsulation mpls** | **pw-class** *pw-class-name*}	Configures the backup peer for a primary L2 VPN VC.
Router(config-if-xconn)#**backup delay** {*enable-delay-in-seconds*} {*disable-delay-in-seconds* | **never**}	Configures a backup delay for L2 VPN backup VC.
Router#**xconnect backup force-switchover** {**interface** *interface-info* | **peer** *peer-ip-address vcid*}	Initiates switchover from primary to backup for L2 VPN redundancy enabled VCs.
Router(config-if)#**tunnel mode gre multipoint l3vpn**	Configures the tunnel as a multipoint GRE tunnel.
Router(config-if)#**tunnel key** *number*	Configures the tunnel key for the mGRE tunnel.
Router(config-if)#**set ip next-hop in-vrf** *mGRE-vrf-name*	Set the next hop for matching prefixes to map to the mGRE tunnel.
Router(config-vrf)#**tunnel mpls traffic-eng exp** {*exp-value-1 exp-value-2 exp-value-1* | **default**}	Associates an MPLS EXP value to be transported by a MPLS TE tunnel.
Router(config-vfi)# **bridge-domain** *bridge-domain-id-value*	Configures the bridge domain ID for a Layer 2 VFI instance on a GSR 12000 series.
Router(config-if)#**bridge-domain** *bridge-domain-id-value*	Associates interface with bridge domain on a GSR 12000 series.
Router(config-if)#**encapsulation dot1q** *vlan-id*	Enables VPLS Ethernet VLAN service on GE subinterface (GSR).
Router(config-if)#**encapsulation dot1q** *top-vlan-id* **second-dot1q** *bottom-vlan-id*	Enables VPLS Ethernet QinQ service on GE subinterface (GSR).
Router(config-if)#**encapsulation dot1q** *top-vlan-id* **second-dot1q any**	Enables VPLS Ethernet QinAny Service on GE subinterface (GSR).

INDEX

D

J–L

N

O

P

T

U

V